Communication Mosaics

FROM THE WADSWORTH SERIES IN COMMUNICATION STUDIES

FIFTH EDITION

Communication
Mosaics

AN INTRODUCTION TO
THE FIELD OF COMMUNICATION

Julia T Wood

LINEBERGER DISTINGUISHED PROFESSOR OF HUMANITIES
THE UNIVERSITY OF NORTH CAROLINA AT CHAPEL HILL

THOMSON

WADSWORTH

Australia · Brazil · Canada · Mexico · Singapore · Spain · Uniited Kingdom · United States

THOMSON

WADSWORTH

Communication Mosaics: An Introduction
to the Field of Communication, Fifth Edition
Julia T. Wood

Publisher: Lyn Uhl
Communication Editor: Jaime Perkins
Senior Development Editor: Renée Deljon
Assistant Editor: John Gahbauer
Editorial Assistant: Laura Localio
Associate Technology Project Manager: Lucinda Bingham
Marketing Manager: Erin Mitchell
Marketing Assistant: Teresa Jessen
Marketing Communications Manager: Jessica Perry
Project Manager, Editorial Production: Marti Paul
Creative Director: Rob Hugel
Art Director: Maria Epes
Print Buyer: Nora Massuda

Permissions Editor: Roberta Broyer
Production: Mary Douglas, Rogue Valley Publications
Text Designer: Gopa & Ted2, Inc.
Photo Researcher: Paul Forkner, Myrna Engler Photo
    Research
Copy Editor: April Wells-Hayes
Illustrator: Pam Brossia, Lachina Publishing Services
Cover Designer: Gopa & Ted2, Inc.
Cover Image: *Birth of a Planet*, 22″ x 24″ Glass Mosaic,
    © 2005 Carl and Sandra Bryant, www.forbeyart.com
Cover Printer: Quebecor World/Taunton
Compositor: G&S Book Services
Printer: Quebecor World/Taunton

Library of Congress Control Number: 2006932466

ISBN-13: 978-0-495-10057-7
ISBN-10: 0-495-10057-9

Thomson Higher Education
10 Davis Drive
Belmont, CA 94002-3098
USA

For more information about our products, contact us at:
Thomson Learning Academic Resource Center
1-800-423-0563

For permission to use material from this text or product, submit a request online at **http://www.thomsonrights.com**.
Any additional questions about permissions can be submitted by e-mail to **thomsonrights@thomson.com**.

For Daniel and Harrison and the fantastic fooly bear:
And what could she say?

Brief Contents

Contents

PART III: CONTEXTS OF COMMUNICATION

List of Boxes

FYI

FYI—Diversity

FYI—Technology

Preface

I wrote *Communication Mosaics* to support survey courses that introduce students to the broad and exciting field of communication. Unlike other forms of the introductory course, the survey approach usually doesn't include performance assignments such as giving speeches and participating in group discussions. Instead, the survey course aims to provide a comprehensive view of the communication field, giving attention to topics and contexts beyond those that are typically covered in performance oriented introductory classes—such as mass communication, organizational communication, and communication technologies—and focusing on conceptual understanding of the breadth and importance of communication in many spheres of our lives.

Responses to earlier editions of this book indicate that many faculty want a textbook specifically designed to support a survey approach to the introductory course. Student feedback to previous editions and ten years of class testing indicate that students, too, find it useful to take a course that gives them an expansive introduction to the communication discipline. In addition to welcoming the approach of this book, faculty and students have been generous in offering feedback, which I've used to improve this edition.

In the pages that follow, I explain my vision of this book and the features I've woven into it and then call attention to changes I made in preparing the current edition.

▶COMMUNICATION AS A MOSAIC

As the title of the book suggests, communication is an intricate mosaic composed of parts that are distinct yet interrelated. All of the parts work together to create the whole of communication. This book increases students' awareness of the importance of basic communication skills and processes and shows students how those common elements surface in specific settings where people communicate.

The book is divided into three parts. Part I introduces students to the discipline of communication, provides foundations for studying communication, and describes careers for people who have strong communication backgrounds and skills. Chapter 1 introduces the book, identifies values of studying communication, defines and models the communication processes, and describes careers for people who have strong academic training in communication. Chapter 2 surveys the discipline's evolution and methods of conducting research so that students understand the long and rich intellectual history of the field. This chapter also highlights the discipline's breadth by identifying its primary areas of study and teaching.

Part II consists of six chapters, each of which focuses on one of the basic processes and skills that are central to a range of communication situations and goals. These basic communication skills and processes are:

▶ Perceiving and understanding

▶ Engaging in verbal communication

▶ Engaging in nonverbal communication

▶ Listening and responding

▶ Creating communication climates

▶ Adapting communication to cultures and social communities

These basic skills and processes shape the character and effectiveness of communication in a wide range of settings, although how each functions varies from one context to another. For example, we may use different listening skills when trying to understand a close friend and attending to television news.

Part III shows how the basic communication processes and skills covered in Part II function in seven specific contexts:

▶ Communication and personal identity

▶ Communication in personal relationships

▶ Communication in groups and teams

▶ Communication in organizations

▶ Public speaking

▶ Mass communication

▶ Technologies of communication

I have also included an appendix that demonstrates how the processes and skills covered in Part II apply to interviewing.

▶FEATURES OF *COMMUNICATION MOSAICS*

Accenting this book are six features that enhance students' learning and ensure the scholarly integrity of content.

Accessible, Conversational Style

Students who have reviewed this book say that the personal writing style motivated them to read the chapters and made the book more accessible and applicable to their lives. For this reason, in the current edition I retain the conversational style that invites students to engage the ideas in this book. I refer to myself as "I" rather than "the author," and I address students as "you" rather than "the student." I also use informal language, such as contractions, just as people do in everyday conversations. In the opening chapter of the book, I introduce myself to students so they know something about my view of communication and my motivations for writing this book.

Another way in which I've personalized my writing style is by including examples and reflections from my own life. In addition, I enlarge the conversation beyond just the reader and me by including in all chapters reflective comments from students at my university and other campuses around the country. To protect privacy, I've changed the names of the students who wrote the commentaries.

Learning about communication should be enjoyable. I don't think textbooks have to be dry or burdened with unnecessary jargon. When it's necessary to use specialized terms, I define them so that students understand what they mean, but I've written this book in an accessible, personal style to make it more interesting to read.

Foundation in Research and Theory

A textbook is only as good as the research and theory on which it is built. *Communication Mosaics* draws on the impressive body of research and theory developed by scholars of communication. Although I include important work from scholars in other fields, I draw most heavily on the published research of communication scholars because it is most directly relevant.

Communication Mosaics reflects my conviction that theory and practice go together. Years ago, renowned scholar Kurt Lewin said, "There is nothing so practical as good theory." His words remain true today. In this book, I blend theory and practice so that each draws on and enriches the other. Effective practice is theoretically informed: It is based on knowledge of how and why the communication process works and what is likely to result from different kinds of communication. At the same time, effective theories have pragmatic value: They help us understand experiences in our everyday lives. Each chapter in this book is informed by the impressive theories and research generated by scholars of communication as well as scholars in other fields. The perspectives and skills recommended reflect current knowledge of effective communication practices.

Integrated Attention to Social Diversity

Social diversity is a defining aspect of the present era. The United States and the world include people of different ages, sexual orientations, races and ethnicities, sexes, abilities, spiritual commitments, and economic circumstances.

These differences directly affect communication. Thus, the idea of universal communication goals and principles must be replaced with understandings of how goals and principles are used differently by diverse people and how communication is adapted to contexts, especially cultural contexts. *Communication Mosaics* emphasizes social diversity in three specific ways. First, Chapter 8 offers in-depth coverage of the relationships between communication and culture: how cultural factors influence communication style, how communication shapes culture, and how we adapt our ways of communicating to particular people and contexts. Second, I weave research on social diversity into all chapters of the book. For example, Chapter 10 explains differences in how women and men typically communicate in personal relationships. Third, examples in the chapters, as well as photographs, feature a wide range of people.

Comprehensive Coverage of Technologies of Communication

Technology increasingly infuses our lives, and this phenomenon is reflected throughout this edition of *Communication Mosaics*. Every chapter includes examples and research related to technologies of communication. For example, Chapter 4 notes how language has changed in response to new technologies. We have coined new words (*hypertext, IM*) and developed new meanings for existing words (*mouse, hamster*). Chapter 10's coverage of personal relationships examines how communication technologies affect the ways in which we meet and get to know friends and romantic partners and the means we have for maintaining long-distance relationships. You will also find a full chapter, Chapter 15, on technologies of communication that have changed and are continuing to change how we think, relate, and act in personal, professional, and social contexts, as well as new FYI—Technology boxes integrated throughout the book to highlight related information about technology.

Finally, technology is also used to extend students' learning; *Communication Mosaics* is accompanied by numerous digital resources (see details following) integrated into every chapter. Additionally, a number of features and end-of-chapter questions include references to websites where students can learn more about particular forms and contexts of communication.

Student Commentaries

Woven into each chapter are commentaries from students' journals and papers. Although students at my university wrote many of these, students at other universities have also sent me commentaries, many of which are included in this edition. I include student commentaries because in more than 30 years of teaching I've learned that students have much to teach each other and me. The commentaries show how different people relate communication principles and research to their own lives. I encourage students who use this edition to send me their comments and reflections so the next edition can reflect their perspectives and experiences too.

Pedagogical Features

This book includes six features that are specifically designed to maximize learning.

Focus Questions Opening each chapter are focus questions that orient students to the chapter and help them organize how they read and study the material.

For Your Information (FYI) Featured in each chapter are "For Your Information" boxes that highlight communication research and the role of communication in everyday life. I use these boxes to call students' attention to particularly interesting and important aspects of communication in a variety of settings. In this edition, some of the FYI boxes specifically focus on technology (FYI—Technology) or diversity (FYI—Diversity), both of which are key themes of communication in our era.

Sharpen Your Skill Each chapter also includes selected "Sharpen Your Skill" exercises that invite students to apply skills and principles discussed in the text. Some of these exercises encourage students to practice a particular skill. Others invite students to observe how communication concepts and principles discussed in the text show up in everyday interactions. Still others ask students to reflect on the ways in which particular skills, theories, or concepts have shaped who they are and how they communicate.

End-of-Chapter Resources Following each chapter are study resources gathered under the heading Review, Reflect, Extend. These resources include questions that encourage students to reflect on what they have read and to extend and apply the material presented in the chapter, as well as a list of key concepts (with page references), and further recommended resources, including articles, books, films, and websites.

Highlighted Key Terms Within each chapter, I've boldfaced key concepts and terms that students should learn. All boldfaced terms are repeated in a list at the end of each chapter to encourage students to check their retention after they have read the chapter. By each term, I've noted the page on which the term first appears and is defined so that students can easily review concepts. Boldfaced terms are also defined in the glossary at the end of the book.

▶ ***Experience Communication Case Study*** At the end of each chapter, I present a short case study that illustrates how ideas covered in the chapter show up in actual communication. To make the cases engaging and realistic, ThomsonNOW also provides videos in which professional actors perform the scenarios presented in each case study. Please note that the transcripts at the end of Chapters 2 and 13, and the videos available for each online, however, are not case studies. Instead, the first shows Tim Muehlhoff, a professor of communication, being interviewed by a student about the relevance of ethics to communication, and the second presents a speech by Rebecca Ewing. Questions that encourage students to apply chapter theories and principles accompany the case studies, interview, and speech both at the end of their respective chapters and online.

▶CHANGES IN THIS EDITION

Because I teach at a public university, I am very sensitive to the cost of textbooks, and I am not willing to publish new editions of my books with only cosmetic changes. A new edition should offer substantive changes to justify the expense to students. I believe instructors who are familiar with previous editions of this book will notice significant changes in this edition that are responsive to generous feedback from instructors and students.

As I mentioned, to prepare this edition I read many reviews of the previous editions. Some reviews were written by instructors who teach a basic communication course. Instructors' feedback led me to make the following changes:

Increased Attention to Communication Technologies in Everyday Life

This edition further integrates technology into all chapters and highlights it in multiple ways. First, every chapter now includes examples of the ways communication technologies affect how we live, work, and interact. Second, I identify related online resources for students that can be accessed by clicking corresponding numbered WebLinks online and accessible through ThomsonNOW. Third, I've also included more FYI boxes (FYI—Technology) that focus on technologies of communication that are part of our everyday lives. Finally, I have also revised Chapter 15 for this edition to emphasize how technologies affect our thinking, feelings, and behavior in interpersonal, social, and professional contexts.

The Latest Knowledge About Human Communication

This edition includes more than 130 new references to studies published since the previous edition went to press.

Streamlined Presentation

I've worked to avoid the phenomenon of "page creep," which happens when an author adds new material without condensing or eliminating any of the material that existed in the previous edition Throughout the book, I've reduced the number of features, tightened prose, and eliminated dated research. This edition is no longer than the previous one, yet it includes new information and the most essential application of concepts and principles.

Increased Emphasis on Intercultural Communication

Chapter 8 provides information about intercultural communication, including differences between communication in individualistic and collectivist cultures and the relationship between culture and high-context and low-context communication styles. In addition to Chapter 8's detailed coverage of intercultural communication, I've woven issues of social and cultural diversity into all chapters, often highlighting them in new FYI – Diversity boxes.

Emphasis on Practical Skills

A final change in this edition is a stronger focus on developing practical communication skills. Every chapter in Parts II and III of this edition provides guidelines for communicating effectively (appearing in a shaded section under the heading "Guidelines for . . ."). Along with discussion in the section, I include at least one Sharpen Your Skill exercise to emphasize further the importance of developing practical skills.

I hope that this edition of *Communication Mosaics* retains the strengths that instructors and students found in previous editions while also benefiting from their generous suggestions for improvement.

►RESOURCES FOR STUDENTS AND INSTRUCTORS

Accompanying this book is an integrated suite of resources to support both students and instructors, many of which are available free of charge when you order them or access them for your students.

Instructor Resources

Instructors who adopt this book can request a number of resources to support their teaching.

- ▶ The **Instructor's Resource Manual** by Janie Crouch, PhD, Tidewater Community College, offers guidelines for setting up your course, sample syllabi, chapter-by-chapter outlines of content, suggested topics for lectures and discussion, and a wealth of class-tested exercises and assignments. It also includes a test bank with questions marked according to varying levels of difficulty.

- ▶ **Instructor's Website.** The password-protected instructor's website includes electronic access to the Instructor's Resource Manual, downloadable versions of the book's PowerPoint slides, and a link to the Opposing Viewpoints Resource Center. To gain access to the website, simply request a course key by opening the site's home page.

Instructor Resources CD-ROM with Multimedia Manager. This disc contains an electronic version of the Instructor's Resource Manual, Exam-View computerized testing, and ready-to-use Microsoft® PowerPoint® presentations, prepared by Catherine Wright, PhD, George Mason University, corresponding with the text. The PowerPoint slides contain text, images, and cued videos of the case studies, interview, and speech and can be used as is or customized to suit your course needs. This all-in-one lecture tool makes it easy for you to assemble, edit, publish, and present custom lectures for your course. More information about ExamView follows.

ExamView® Computerized Testing enables you to create, deliver, and customize tests and study guides (both print and online) in minutes using the test bank questions from the Instructor's Resource Manual. Exam-View® offers both a *Quick Test Wizard* and an *Online Test Wizard* that guide you step-by-step through the process of creating tests, while its "what you see is what you get" interface allows you to see the test you are creating on-screen exactly as it will print or display online. You can build tests of up to 250 questions, using up to 12 question types. Using the complete word processing capabilities of Exam-View®, you can even enter an unlimited number of new questions or edit existing ones.

JoinIn™ on TurningPoint®. Thomson Wadsworth is now pleased to offer you JoinIn™ content for Response Systems tailored to *Communication Mosaics*, Fifth Edition, by Stacey Macchi, Western Illinois University, allowing you to transform your classroom and assess your students' progress with instant in-class quizzes and polls. TurningPoint® software lets you pose book-specific questions and display students' answers seamlessly within the Microsoft® PowerPoint® slides of your own lecture, in conjunction with the "clicker" hardware of your choice. Enhance how your students interact with you, your lecture, and each other.

Turn-It-In. This proven online plagiarism-prevention software promotes fairness in the classroom by helping students learn to correctly cite sources and allowing instructors to check for originality before reading and grading papers. Turnitin quickly checks student papers against billions of pages of Internet content, millions of published works, as well as millions of student papers, and within seconds generates a comprehensive originality report.

▶ **ThomsonNOW™ on WebCT® and Blackboard®.** Now you and your students can access ThomsonNOW's powerful and fully integrated online teaching and learning system through your familiar WebCT® or Blackboard® interface, giving you all the course management and communication tools you know, paired with the flexibility and control of ThomsonNOW.

▶ **Thomson Wadsworth Communication Video and DVD Library.** Thomson Wadsworth's video and DVD series for Speech Communication includes Communication Scenarios for Critique and Analysis (Volumes I–IV), Student Speeches for Critique and Analysis (Volumes I–VIII), and CNN Today videos and DVDs for Human Communication, Public Speaking, Interpersonal Communication, and Mass Communication.

▶ **Election 2004: Speeches from the Campaign.** This CD-ROM allows students to see the power and importance of public speaking and its relevance in our society and includes both full and excerpted speeches from the 2004 United States presidential campaign. Students can view speeches from the Democratic and Republican conventions as well as a variety of other speeches delivered throughout the campaign. After students view these speeches, they have the option of evaluating them based on specific speech criteria.

▶ *The Teaching Assistant's Guide to the Basic Course* is available to instructors who adopt this textbook. Katherine G. Hendrix, who is on the faculty at the University of Memphis, prepared this resource specifically for new instructors.

Based on leading communication teacher training programs, this guide discusses some of the general issues that accompany a teaching role and offers specific strategies for managing the first week of classes, leading productive discussions, managing sensitive topics in the classroom, and grading students' written and oral work.

▶ **The Thomson Wadsworth Communication Resource Center.** This site, **http://communication.wadsworth.com,** offers a rich collection of web links, suggested class activities, Internet-based teaching tools, and product information for your course.

Student Resources

Students have the option of utilizing a rich array of resources to enhance and extend their learning while using *Communication Mosaics.* These resources (or access to them) are available for individual sale to students through **http://www.thomsonedu.com.**

▶ The **Student Companion** to this edition, which I wrote with Larry Edmonds of Arizona State University, provides students with interactive summaries of chapter content, vocabulary lists, self-tests, and practical activities that help them to develop skills in communicating and apply those skills in their everyday interactions.

Thomson **NOW!** is an online study system designed to help students put their time to the best use. After reading a chapter, students take the assignable NOW pre-test to identify concepts discussed in the chapter that they may not fully understand. Based on the results of this diagnostic test, the system creates a personalized study plan that directs each student to specific learning resources and activities. To see if they're ready for an exam, students may take the NOW post-test to check their understanding. ThomsonNow for *Communication Mosaics,* Fifth Edition, provides pages from the text in ebook format; the chapter's case study, interview, and speech videos; and the book's Key Concept flashcards, WebLinks, and other learning resources. For more information, visit **http://www.thomsonedu.com,** where you'll find a link to ThomsonNOW.

▶ **InfoTrac College Edition with InfoMarks™.** This online library provides access to more than 18 million reliable, full-length articles from over 5,000 academic and popular periodicals. Students also have access to InfoMarks—stable URLs that can be linked to articles, journals, and searches to save valuable time when doing research—*and* to the InfoWrite online resource center, where students can access grammar help, critical thinking guidelines, guides to writing research papers, and much more. For more information about InfoTrac College Edition and the InfoMarks linking tool, visit **http://www.infotrac-college.com** and click on "User Demo."

Speech Builder Express. This online program coaches students through the entire process of preparing speeches and provides the additional support of built-in video speech models, a tutor feature for concept review, and direct links to InfoTrac College Edition™ and an online Dictionary and Thesaurus. Equipped with their speech type or purpose, a general topic, and preliminary research, students respond to the program's customized prompts to complete interactive activities that require critical thinking about all aspects of creating an effective speech. Students are able to specify a specific speech purpose, identify an organizational pattern, write a thesis statement or central idea, establish main points, integrate support material, craft transitions, plan visual aids, compose their speech introduction and conclusion, and prepare their bibliography to complete formal speech outlines. Students are also able to stop and start work whenever they choose, and complete, save online, export to Microsoft® Word®, or e-mail up to five outlines.

vMentor gives your students access to virtual office hours—one-on-one, online tutoring help from a subject-area expert, at no additional cost. In vMentor's virtual classroom, students interact with the tutor and other students using two-way audio, an interactive whiteboard for illustrating the problem, and instant messaging. To ask a question, students simply click to raise a "hand." With vMentor your students can connect to experts who will assist them in understanding the concepts covered in your course when you're not available.

Thomson Audio Study Products for *Communication Mosaics,* **Fifth Edition.** Prepared by Shirley Oakley, Coastal Georgia Community College, this text's mobile contents provides short chapter summaries to give students the opportunity to review chapter content in audio format and offers periodic updates on media issues in the news. A passcode can be packaged with the text, or purchased individually, so that students can download these digital audio files to their computers or MP3 players.

▶ *The Art and Strategy of Service-Learning Presentations,* **Second Edition,** is available bundled with *Communication Mosaics.* Authored by Rick Isaacson and Jeff Saperstein of San Francisco State University, this handbook provides guidelines for connecting service-learning work with classroom concepts and advice for working effectively with agencies and organizations.

▶ *A Guide to the Basic Course for ESL Students* is available bundled with the book. Specifically for communicators whose first language is not English, it features FAQs, helpful URLs, and strategies for managing communication anxiety.

These resources are available to qualified adopters, and ordering options for student supplements are flexible. Please consult your local Thomson sales representative for more information, to evaluate examination copies of any of these instructor or student resources, or product demonstrations. You may also contact the Thomson Wadsworth Academic Resource Center at 800-423-0563, or visit us at **http://www .thomsonedu.com.** Additional information is also available at **http://www.thomson edu.com/communication/wood.**

►ACKNOWLEDGMENTS

Although my name is the only one that appears as the author of this book, I could not have written it without the help of many people. I want to take a moment to acknowledge the support and assistance of a number of people who have influenced how I think and write.

I am deeply indebted to the Thomson/Wadsworth team. Everyone on that team has been extraordinarily professional and helpful throughout the evolution of this book. Leading the group is Jaime Perkins, Communication Editor. In addition to Jaime, I am grateful to other key members of the team at and working with Thomson Wadsworth: Lyn Uhl, publisher; Renée Deljon, senior development editor; and Erin Mitchell, marketing manager. Also integral to the development of this edition were Marti Paul, content production manager; Mary Douglas, project manager, Rogue Valley Publications; April Wells-Hayes, copy editor; Paul Forkner, photo researcher, Myrna Engler Photo Research; John Gahbauer, assistant editor; Laura Localio, editorial assistant; Lucinda Bingham, associate technology product manager; Maria Epes, executive art director; and Gopa, who designed the text and cover. This book is truly a collaborative effort that involved and reflects the contributions of everyone on the team.

I am also indebted to scholars and teachers of communication who contributed helpful comments and suggestions that guided this revision, reviewers Cheryl Bailey, Western Illinois University; Janine Crouch, Tidewater Community College; Wesley Durham, University of Southern Indiana; Shirley Oakley, Coastal Georgia Community College; and Catherine Wright, George Mason University—as well as survey respondents Marcia Berry, Azusa Pacific University; Anita Chirco, Keuka College; Tresha Dutton, Whatcom Community College; Ann Bainbridge Frymier, Miami University; Jill Hall, Jefferson Community College; Christine Hirsch, State University of New York at Oswego; Ee Lin Lee, Western Washington University; Shannon McCraw, Southeastern Oklahoma State University; Darrin S. Murray, Loyola Marymount University; Mark Nelson, The University of Alabama; Shirley Oakley, Coastal Georgia Community College; Clark D. Olson, Arizona State University; Lynne Orr, William Paterson University; Doug Radke, Blue Mountain Community College; Cynthia A. Ridle, Western Illinois University;

I am also indebted to the reviewers of this book's previous editions: Jess K. Alberts, Arizona State University; Mary Allen, Valencia Community College; Bob Alexander, University of Louisiana at Monroe; Mary Carpenter, New York University; Diane O. Casagrande, West Chester University; Robert A. Cole, State University of New York Oswego; Stephanie J. Coopman, San Jose State University; Marcia Dixson, Indiana–Purdue at Fort Wayne; Carol Dostal, Indiana–Purdue at Fort Wayne; Belle A. Edson, Arizona State University; Darin Garard, Santa Barbara City College; Susan Cain Giusto, Augusta State University; Jonathan M. Gray, Southern Illinois University–Carbondale; Jonathan M. Gray, Southern Illinois University Carbondale; Joy L. Hart, University of Louisville; Javette Hayes, California State University, Fullerton; Patrick Herbert, Northeast Louisiana University; Patrick J. Herbert, University of Louisiana–Monroe; Jodee Hobbs, Northeast Louisiana University; Bobbie R. Klopp, Kirkwood Community College; Branislav Kovacic, University of Hartford; Krista Longtin, Indiana University–Purdue University Indianapolis; Matt McAllister, Virginia Tech; Sandra Metts, Illinois State University; Teresa A. Nance, Villanova University; Kim P. Niemczyk, Palm Beach Community College; Marjukka Ollilainen, Virginia Tech; Rebecca Parker, Western Illinois University; Nan Peck, Northern Virginia County College; Laura Wheeler Poms, George Mason University; Valerie Renegar, San Diego

State University; Mark A. Schlesinger, University of Massachusetts–Boston; Helen M. Sterk, Marquette University; Sharlene R. Thompson, The University of Oklahoma; Scott Vitz, Indiana–Purdue at Fort Wayne; Guy Warner, Augusta State University; John T. Warren, Bowling Green State University; Sue L. Wenzlaff, Austin Peay State University, David W. Worley, Indiana State University; and Joseph B. Zubrick, University of Maine–Presque Isle.

The ideas in this book were also influenced by students in my classes and by students at other colleges and universities around the country. They provided insightful feedback and suggestions for ways to improve *Communication Mosaics.* In class discussions, conferences, e-mail notes, and written comments, students push me to do more and tell me which communication issues are prominent in their lives. Invariably, students teach me at least as much as I teach them. Because students are so thoughtful, I include many of their thoughts as Student Voices in this book.

Finally, I thank those with whom I am closest. For more than 30 years, Robert (Robbie) Cox has been my partner in love, life, and work. Robbie is my greatest fan and my most rigorous critic, and both his support and his criticism shape all that I write. Special friends LindaBecker, Todd, and Nancy sharpen my thinking and writing by testing my ideas against their experiences communicating with others. My sister Carolyn remains one of the most positive, perceptive, and delightful presences in my life, as do my youngest friends: Cam, who is 23; Michelle, who is 16; Daniel, who is 13; and Harrison, who is 8. These young people continuously remind me of the magic and wonder in human relationships. And of course I must express my appreciation to the four-legged members of my family: Sadie, Ms. Wicca, and Cassidy. When my two-footed friends are asleep and I am writing at 2 AM or 3 AM, it's Sadie, Wicca, and Cassidy who keep me company.

Communication Mosaics

1 A First Look at Communication

▶ **FOCUS QUESTIONS**

1. What are the benefits of studying communication?

2. How is communication defined?

3. What communication processes and skills are relevant in all contexts?

4. How do different models represent the process of human communication?

5. What careers are open to people with strong backgrounds in communication?

▶ The leader of your team seems to be afraid of conflict. Whenever there is a hint of disagreement between team members, the leader jumps in and smoothes things over. What can you do to ensure that conflict is allowed and managed well so the team can be thorough and critical in its work?

▶ While browsing the Internet, you find a message that contains racist slurs. You think you should respond but aren't sure what to say.

▶ You sense that a co-worker feels on guard whenever you make a suggestion for working more efficiently, and you want to say something to reduce the defensiveness, but you don't know what to say.

▶ Whenever there is a positive story about the president, your newspaper carries it on the top half of the front page. However, whenever there is a negative story about the president or a positive article on his challenger, the story is on an inside page of the paper. You wonder if there is any significance to placement of stories.

▶ At the end of this term, the person you've been dating will graduate and take a job in a city a thousand miles away. You're concerned about sustaining intimacy when you have to communicate across the distance.

▶ At work, you're on a team that includes people from Mexico and Germany. You've noticed that in some ways they communicate differently from American-born workers. You aren't sure how to interpret their styles of communicating or how to interact effectively with them.

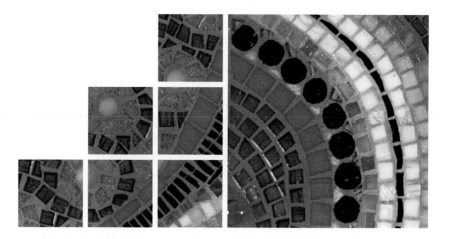

▶ You can't keep up with your e-mail and all the information you find on the web. You don't want to be out of touch with the world, but you sometimes feel overwhelmed by the sheer amount of information that comes in every day.

▶ A major political figure speaks at your campus, and you attend. You try to listen carefully, but you aren't sure how to evaluate what the speaker says.

From the moment we arise until we go to bed, our days are filled with communication challenges and opportunities. Unlike some subjects you study, communication is relevant to every aspect of your life. We communicate with ourselves when we psych ourselves up for big moments and talk ourselves into or out of various courses of action. We communicate with others to build and sustain personal relationships, perform our jobs, advance in our careers, and participate in social and civic activities. Even when we're not around other people, we are involved in communication as we interact with mass media and communication technologies. All facets of our lives involve communication.

Although we communicate continually, we aren't always effective. People who do not have strong communication knowledge and skills are limited in their efforts to achieve personal, professional, and social goals. On the other hand, people who communicate well have a strong advantage in personal, social, and professional life. Therefore, learning about communication and developing your skills as a communicator are keys to a successful and fulfilling life.

Communication Mosaics is designed to introduce you to basic communication processes and skills that can enhance your effectiveness in a range of communication situations. This book is written for anyone who is interested in human communication. If you are a communication major, this book and the course it accompanies will give you a firm foundation for more advanced study. If you are majoring in another discipline, you will gain a basic understanding of communication, and you will have opportunities to strengthen your skills as a communicator.

This book is divided into three sections. Part I, which includes this chapter and Chapter 2, introduces you to communication as a field of study and discusses a number of careers open to people with strong communication knowledge and skills. Part II highlights six processes and skills that are relevant to the many forms and settings of human communication. Part III traces the operation of those basic communication processes and skills in specific contexts ranging from communication with yourself to communication on the Internet.

This first chapter provides an overview of the book and the discipline of communication. To open the chapter, I first introduce myself and point out the perspective and features of the book. Second, we consider how communication affects us personally, socially, professionally, and culturally. Third, we define communication and discuss progressively sophisticated models of the communication process. Finally, we survey some of the careers that people with strong backgrounds in communication are qualified to pursue.

▶An Introduction to the Author

As an undergraduate, I enrolled in a course much like the one you're taking now. In that course, I became fascinated by the field of communication, and my interest has endured for more than 30 years. Today, I am still captivated by the field—more than ever, in fact. I see communication both as a science that involves skills and knowledge and as an art that reflects human imagination and wisdom in adapting basic processes and skills to diverse situations and people. Because communication is central to personal identity and cultural life, it is one of the most dynamic, fastest-growing areas of study in higher education. It is a field that offers insights, skills, and knowledge relevant to our personal and collective well-being.

When I was a student, I always wondered about the authors of my textbooks. Who were they? Why did they write the books I was told to read? Unfortunately, the authors never introduced themselves, so I didn't find answers to my questions about them. I want to start our relationship differently by telling you something about myself. I am a 55-year-old, middle-income, European American woman who has strong spiritual beliefs and a deep commitment to public education. For 30 years, I have been married to Robert (Robbie) Cox, a professor of communication at my university and a national leader of the Sierra Club.

As is true for all of us, who I am affects what I know and how I think, feel, and communicate. Therefore, many of the ideas and examples in these chapters reflect what I have learned in my research, teaching, and life. I grew up in a small rural town in the South. After completing my education, I joined the faculty at the University of North Carolina at Chapel Hill, where I now teach and conduct research on personal relationships, communication theory, and gender, communication, and culture. My experiences communicating with others are another source of the examples I use to illustrate the communication processes, concepts, and skills we will discuss in this book. Research by other scholars also informs my perspective. The hundreds of references at the end of this book have shaped both my understanding of human communication and the way I introduce you to the field.

Other facets of my identity also influence what I know and how I write. My thinking is influenced by my roles as a daughter, sister, romantic partner, friend, aunt, professional, and member of spiritual and civic groups. On a broader level, I am defined by categories the culture uses to classify people—for instance, race, gender, socioeconomic level, and sexual orientation. Belonging to these culturally created categories has given me certain kinds of insight and has limited other insights. As a woman, I understand discrimination based on sex because I've experienced it. Being middle class has shielded me from personal experience with hunger, poverty, and bias against the poor; and being heterosexual has spared me from being the direct target of homophobia. Because Western culture tends to treat Whites as the norm, not as a racial category, I was not socialized to think about my race and its meaning. However, critical race theorists have taught me to interrogate Whiteness as fully as any other racial category.

Although I can use cultural categories to describe myself, they aren't as clear or definitive as we sometimes think. For instance, the category "woman" isn't as homogeneous as it sounds. Women differ from one another because of their race–ethnicities, sexual orientations, socioeconomic status, abilities and disabilities, and a range of other factors. Likewise, "Whiteness" is not a homogenous category. Whites differ greatly as a result of factors such as gender, sexual orientation, socioeconomic status, abilities and disabilities, and so forth. The same is true of people we can place in any category—they are alike in the particular way that distinguishes the category, yet they are also different from one another in many ways.

Your identity also influences what you know and how you communicate. Think about the experiences that have shaped you—how they influence what you know, and how you interpret others and their styles of communicating. As you consider your identity, ask yourself how you are similar to and different from others who belong to the same culturally defined groups in which you place yourself. If you are a man, for instance, how is your identity as a man influenced by your racial and ethnic background, socioeconomic status, sexual orientation, spiritual commitments, and so forth? If you reflect on this, I suspect you will discover how profoundly your identity shapes your personal choices and your views of social life.

Although our identities limit what we personally know and experience, they don't completely prevent us from gaining insight into people and situations different from our own. From my relationships with a range of people and from reading, I've gained some understanding of communication styles that differ from my own, as well as awareness of kinds of discrimination and privilege that I haven't personally experienced. As I mentioned before, critical race theorists have taught me to think critically about Whiteness as a racial category. I've also learned from watching others communicate in situations at my workplace and in community groups. Media and technologies of communication have given me insight into diverse people and situations all over the world. All of these resources allow me—and will allow you, if you so choose—to move beyond the limits of personal identity and experiences to appreciate and participate in the larger world. Because humans and their situations are diverse, we need to learn about a variety of people, lifestyles, personal and social milieus, and cultures.

We need to understand and communicate effectively with people who differ from us. What we learn by studying and interacting with people from different cultures and social communities expands our appreciation of the richness and complexity of humanity. In addition, learning about and forming relationships with different people enlarges our repertoires of communication skills. Throughout *Communication Mosaics*, we discuss ways in which membership in different cultural and social groups affects communication goals and styles.

▶An Introduction to *Communication Mosaics*

To provide a context for your reading, let me share my vision of this book. The title reflects the idea that communication is an intricate mosaic made up of basic processes and skills that are relevant to the range of situations in which we interact. In any particular context, some aspects of communication stand out, and others are subdued. For instance, in a public speaking situation, presentation style stands out, and communication climate is less obvious. On the other hand, in team interaction, communication that nurtures a productive climate may be more pronounced than a commanding presentational style. Thus, we can think of communication as a mosaic made up of different, yet related, tiles. Like the varying tiles in a mosaic, the components of communication are distinct yet interrelated.

Communication Mosaics is divided into three parts. The first part of this book consists of two chapters that introduce you to the discipline of communication by explaining its history, research methods, contemporary breadth, and career options. Part II introduces you to six basic communication processes, concepts, and skills relevant to a range of goals and settings of interaction:

▶ Perceiving and understanding others

▶ Engaging in verbal communication

▶ Engaging in nonverbal communication

▶ Listening and responding to others

▶ Creating and sustaining communication climates

▶ Adapting communication to cultural contexts

Each of these skills is related to all the others. For example, how we perceive others is related to the ways we create and interpret verbal and nonverbal communication. How we interact with co-workers affects and is affected by our verbal and nonverbal styles of communication. The interaction climates we establish in personal and professional relationships are shaped by questions we ask, statements we make, our listening skills, and our nonverbal communication. For example, our skill in communicating with doctors is made up of our ability to listen critically, to ask questions, and to adapt our communication to the context of a medical conference. The basic communication processes you'll study in this book are present in all forms and contexts of communication.

Because communication is a continuous part of life, we need to understand how the basic processes and skills covered in Part II relate to a broad spectrum of communication encounters, so Part III explores seven communication contexts that are common in our lives:

▶ Communication with yourself

▶ Interaction with friends and romantic partners

▶ Communicating in groups and on teams

▶ Communication in organizations

▶ Public speaking

▶ Mass communication

▶ Communication technologies

An appendix shows how the skills discussed in Part II surface in interviews.

▶THE VALUES OF STUDYING COMMUNICATION

Why should we study communication? It's obvious that careers such as law, sales, and teaching require strong communication skills. However, even if you don't pursue a career in one of those fields, communication will be essential in your work. You may want to persuade your boss you deserve a raise, represent your neighborhood in a zoning hearing, speak out on environmental issues, or participate in civic groups. To advance in your career, you'll need to know how to build good climates and manage conflict constructively in work teams. You may need to deal with co-workers who tell racist jokes or harass you sexually. To have healthy, enduring relationships, you'll need to know how to listen sensitively, communicate support, deal with conflicts, and understand communication styles different from your own. To be an informed citizen, you'll need to understand how mass media work, and you'll need critical thinking skills to analyze their messages. In short, communication skills are vital to personal and professional well-being and to the health of our society.

Because you've been communicating all your life, you might ask why you need to study communication formally. One good reason is that formal study can improve skill. Some people have a natural talent for singing or athletics. Yet they can become even better singers or athletes if they take voice lessons or study theories of offensive and defensive play. Likewise, even if you communicate well now, learning about communication can make you more effective. Theories and principles of communication help us make sense of what happens in our everyday lives, and they help us to have the impact we desire. For instance, learning about gender-based differences might help you understand why many women enjoy talking about relationships more than most men do. Learning about cultural differences might allow you to grasp the meanings of culture-specific communication norms for touching others and for asserting oneself.

Communication is woven into all facets of our lives. We talk, listen, think, share confidences with intimates, ask and answer questions, participate on teams, attend public presentations, exchange information with co-workers, watch television programs, chat online with friends, and so forth. From birth to death, communication is central to our personal, professional, and civic lives.

Personal Life

George Herbert Mead (1934) said that humans are talked into humanity. He meant that we gain our personal identities by communicating with others. In our earliest years, our parents told us who we were: "You're smart," "You're so strong," "You're such a funny one." We first see ourselves through the eyes of others, so their messages form the foundations of our self-concepts. Later, we interact with mass communication and communication technologies as well as teachers, friends, romantic partners, and co-workers who communicate their views of us. Thus, how we see ourselves reflects the views of us that others communicate.

The profound connection between communication and identity is dramatically evident in children who are deprived of human contact. Case studies of children who have been isolated from others for a long time show that they have no concept of themselves as humans, and their mental and psychological development is severely hindered by lack of language. The FYI box on the following page presents a dramatic example of what can happen when human infants are deprived of interaction with other humans.

Communication also directly influences our physical well-being. The morning that I began this chapter, I read a newspaper story with the headline "Arguing hurts the heart in more ways than one" (Fackelmann, 2006). The story summarized a study showing that couples who exchange nasty comments during marital spats were more likely to have clogged arteries. This is consistent with a large body of research that shows that communicating with others promotes health, whereas social isolation is linked to stress, disease, and early death (Crowley, 1995). People who lack close friends are more anxious and depressed than people who are close to others (Jones & Moore,

GHADYA KA BACHA

Ghadya Ka Bacha, or the "wolf boy," was found in 1954 outside a hospital in Balrampur, India. He had calloused knees and hands, as if he moved on all fours, and he had scars on his neck, suggesting he had been dragged about by animals.

Ramu, which was the name the hospital staff gave the child, showed no interest in others but became very excited once when he saw wolves on a visit to the zoo. Ramu lapped his milk from a glass instead of drinking as we do, and he tore apart his food.

Most doctors who examined Ramu concluded that he had grown up with wolves and therefore acted like a wolf, not a person (Shattuck, 1980).

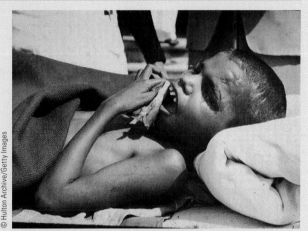

© Hulton Archive/Getty Images

In this photo, Ramu is eating raw meat. What do Ramu's behaviors suggest about how we develop self-concepts?

1989). Heart disease is also more common among people who lack strong interpersonal relationships (Ornish, 1998; Ruberman, 1992). In one study, women with metastatic breast cancer who belonged to support groups in which they talked with others survived twice as long, on average, as those who did not. Some survived 15 years or longer after the study of the connection between interpersonal contact and health was conducted (McClure, 1997). Clearly, healthy interaction with others is important to our physical and mental well-being.

Personal Relationships

Effective communication is the heart of personal relationships. We build connections with others by revealing our private identities, asking questions and listening to the answers, working out problems, remembering shared history, and making plans for the future. Marriage counselors have long emphasized the importance of communication for healthy, enduring relationships (Beck, 1988; Gottman & Carrère, 1994). A primary distinction between relationships that endure and those that collapse is the presence of effective communication. Couples who learn how to discuss their thoughts and feelings, adapt to each other, and manage conflict constructively tend to sustain intimacy over time. Friends also rely on good communication to keep in touch, provide support, and listen sensitively. The FYI box on page 7 demonstrates the centrality of good communication to enduring personal relationships.

Communication is important for more than solving problems or making personal disclosures. For most of us, everyday talk and nonverbal interaction are the essence of relationships (Barnes & Duck, 1994; Duck, 1994a, 1994b; Spencer, 1994; Wood & Duck, 2006). Although dramatic moments affect relationships, it is our unremarkable, everyday interaction that sustains the daily rhythms of our intimate connections (Wood & Duck, 2006). Partners weave their lives together through small talk about mutual friends, daily events, and other mundane topics. Couples involved in long-distance romances say they miss most not being able to share small talk (Gerstel & Gross, 1985).

In addition to studying how communication enhances relationships, interpersonal communication scholars investigate the role of communication in destructive relationship patterns such as abuse and violence. Teresa Sabourin and Glen Stamp (1995) have identified strong links between verbal behaviors and reciprocal violence between spouses. Other communication scholars (Lloyd & Emery, 2000; Meyers, 1997; West, 1995; Wood, 2001b, 2004b) have documented a range of social and interpersonal influences on violence between intimates.

▶ Sandy

When my boyfriend moved away, the hardest part wasn't missing the big moments. It was not talking about little stuff or just being together. It was like we weren't part of each other's life when we didn't talk about all the little things that happened or we felt or whatever.

Sandy's comment is the first of many student voices you'll encounter in this book. In my classes, students teach me and each other by sharing their insights, experiences, and questions. Because I believe students have much to teach us, I've included reflections written by students at my university and other campuses. As you read these, you will probably identify with some, disagree with others, and be puzzled by still others. Whether you agree, disagree, or are perplexed, I think you will find that the student voices expand the text and spark thought and discussion in your class and elsewhere. I also welcome your commentaries about issues that strike you as you read this book. You may send them to me in care of Thomson Wadsworth, 10 Davis Drive, Belmont CA 94002.

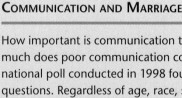

fyi

COMMUNICATION AND MARRIAGE

How important is communication to marriage? How much does poor communication contribute to divorce? A national poll conducted in 1998 found answers to these questions. Regardless of age, race, sex, or economic standing, Americans say communication problems are the number one cause of divorce. Fifty-three percent of those polled said lack of effective communication was the principal cause of divorce. Other causes lagged far behind. When asked the primary reason for divorce, 29% said money problems, 7% said interference from relatives, and 5% said sexual problems. To learn more about this poll, go to the book's online resources and click on WebLink 1.1.

Professional Life

Communication skills are critical for success in professional life. The value of communication is clearly apparent in professions such as teaching, law, sales, and counseling, where talking and listening are central to effectiveness. Many attorneys, counselors, and businesspeople major in communication before pursuing specialized training (Morreale & Vogl, 1998).

In other fields, the importance of communication is less obvious but nonetheless present. One survey found that 79% of corporate executives in New York City ranked the ability to express ideas verbally as the most important quality they looked for when interviewing potential employees (Silverstone, Greenbaum, & MacGregor, 1987). Health-care professionals rely on communication skills to talk with patients about

© Fisher/Thatcher/Stone/Getty Images

Communication skills are vital to professional success.

medical problems and courses of treatment and to gain cooperation from colleagues, patients, and families for continued care (Berko, Wolvin, & Wolvin, 1992). Doctors who do not listen well are less effective in treating patients, and they're more likely to be sued than doctors who do listen well (Beckman, 2003; Levine, 2004; Milia, 2003). According to a 1998 poll, people who feel they are effective communicators are more successful in a variety of careers (you can read the results of this poll in detail by going to the book's online resources and clicking on WebLink 1.2). And in a 2001 survey, 71% of 4,000 human resource professionals identified communication skills as critical to doing their jobs well (Morreale, 2001).

Even highly technical jobs require communication skills. Specialists have to be able to listen carefully to the needs of their clients and customers. They also need to be skilled in explaining technical ideas to people who lack their expertise. Ann Darling and Deanna Dannels (2003) asked engineers whether communication skills were important to their professional effectiveness. The engineers reported that their success on the job depended on listening well, presenting ideas clearly, and negotiating effectively with others. Fully 75% of the engineers said that communication skills had consequences for their career advancement.

When the National Association of Colleges and Employers asked 480 companies to identify the applicant qualities that were most important in their hiring decisions, communication skills were at the very top of the list (Schneider, 1999). Conversely, executives in large companies report that employees who are poor communicators are expensive: 14% of each work week is wasted because of poor communication (Thomas, 1999). Sean, an older, returning student, makes this observation about the relevance of communication skills to his professional success:

▶ Sean

I'm taking this course because I need communication skills to do my job. I didn't think I would when I majored in computer science and went into technology development. But after two years, another guy and I decided to launch our own technical support company. We had trouble getting investors to provide start-up capital, because neither of us knew how to give an effective presentation. We had the tech skills but not the communication ones. Finally, we got our company launched and discovered that we didn't know much about how to supervise and lead either. Neither of us had ever taken courses in how to motivate and support people who work for you. So I'm taking this course as a night student, and I think it will make a major difference in how I do my job and whether our company succeeds.

Civic Life

Communication skills are vital to the health of our society. From painting on the walls of caves to telling stories in village squares to interacting on the Internet, people have found ways to communicate with each other to organize and sustain a common social world. To be effective, citizens in a democracy must be able to express ideas and evaluate the ethical and logical strength of the claims and reasoning of public figures. To make informed judgments, voters need to listen critically to candidates' arguments and responses to questions. We also need to listen critically to proposals about goals for our communities, for the institutions at which we work, and for the organizations on which we depend for services.

Communication skills are especially important for effective interaction in our era, which is characterized by social diversity. In pluralistic cultures such as ours, we need to understand people who communicate differently from us. Healthy civic and social engagements depend on our ability to listen thoughtfully to a range of perspectives and styles of communicating and to adapt our communication to diverse people and contexts.

▶ Luanne

I used to feel it was hard to talk with people who weren't raised in the United States like I was. Sometimes it seems that they have a totally different way of talking than I do, and we don't understand each other naturally. But I've been trying to learn to understand people from other places, and it really is making me realize how many different ways of communicating people have. With so many cultures now part of this country, nobody can get by without learning how to relate to people from other cultures.

▶ David

As an African American male, I sometimes feel as though I am a dash of pepper on top of a mountain of salt. I have attended many classes where I was the only African American out of 50 or even 100 students. In these classes, the feeling of judgment is cast down upon me for being different. Usually what I learn about is not "people," like the course says, but White people. Until I took a communication course, the only classes that included research and information on African Americans were in the African American curriculum. This bothered me because White Americans are not the entire world.

Luanne was a student in one of my courses, and David wrote to me after taking a basic communication course at a college in the western United States. Luanne's reflection shows that she is aware of the importance of understanding the communication of people from cultures that differ from her own. David's comment illustrates both the importance of weaving diversity into the study of communication and the value of student commentaries. The FYI box on the following page further highlights the importance of understanding diverse people in order to communicate effectively.

Communication, then, is important for personal, relationship, professional, and civic life. Because communication is a cornerstone of human experience, your decision to study it will serve you well.

▶DEFINING COMMUNICATION

We've been using the word *communication* for many pages, but we haven't yet defined it clearly. **Communication** is a systemic process in which people interact with and through symbols to create and interpret meanings. Let's unpack this definition by explaining its four key terms.

The Features of Communication

Process Communication is a **process,** which means that it is ongoing and dynamic. It's hard to tell when communication starts and stops, because what happens before we talk with someone may influence our interaction, and what occurs in a particular encounter may affect the future. That communication is a process means it is always in motion, moving forward and changing continually. We cannot freeze communication.

Systems Communication takes place within **systems.** A system consists of interrelated parts that affect one another. In family communication, for instance, each family member is part of the system (Galvin, Dickson, & Marrow, 2006). The physical environment and the time of day also are elements of the system that affect interaction. People interact differently in a living room and on a beach, and we may be more alert at certain times of day than at others. The history of a system also affects communication. If a workplace team has a history of listening sensitively and working out problems constructively, then when someone says, "There's something we need to talk about," the others are unlikely to become defensive. On the other hand, if the team has a record of nasty conflicts and bickering, the same comment might arouse strong defensiveness.

Because the parts of a system are interdependent and continually interact, a change in any part of a system changes the entire system. When a new person joins a team, he or she brings new perspectives that, in turn, may alter how other team members work. The team develops new patterns of interaction, subgroups realign, and team performance changes. The interrelatedness of a system's parts is particularly evident in intercultural communication. A successful executive knows to be more assertive and competitive when talking with someone from Great Britain or Canada than when talking with someone from Pakistan or Costa Rica. When a corporation moves its opera-

---

DIVERSITY

fyi

U.S. DEMOGRAPHICS IN THE TWENTY-FIRST CENTURY

The United States is home to a wide range of people with diverse ethnic, racial, cultural, and geographic backgrounds. And the proportions of different groups are changing. Currently, one in three U.S. residents is a minority. The following shifts in the ethnic makeup of the United States are predicted to take place between 2005 and 2050 (One in Three, 2006; U.S. Bureau of the Census, 2004; Yankelovich, 2005):

	2005	2050
African Americans	12%	14%
Asians	4%	8%
Caucasians	71%	53%
Hispanics (of any race)	13%	25%

The Multicultural Pavilion provides an excellent bibliography for those who want to learn more about multiculturalism. To access this site, go to the book's online resources and click on WebLink 1.3.

tions to a new country, transformations affect everything from daily interaction on the factory floor to corporate culture.

Systems are not collections of random parts, but organized wholes. For this reason, a system operates as a totality of interacting elements. A family is a system, or totality, of interacting elements that include family members, their physical locations, their jobs and schools, and so forth. Before systems theory was developed, therapists who worked with disturbed members of families often tried to "fix" the person who supposedly was causing problems for the family. Thus, alcoholics might be separated from their families and given therapy to reduce the motivation to drink or to increase the desire not to drink. Often, however, the alcoholic resumed drinking shortly after rejoining the family because the behavior of the "problem person" was shaped by the behaviors of other family members and other elements of the family system.

In a similar manner, organizations sometimes send managers to leadership training programs but do not provide training for the manager's subordinates. When the manager returns to the office and uses the new leadership techniques, subordinates are distrustful and resistant. They were accustomed to the manager's former style, and they haven't been taught how to deal with the new style of leadership.

Because systems are organized wholes, they are more than simple combinations of parts. As families, groups, organizations, and societies evolve, they discard old patterns, generate new forms of interacting, lose some members, and gain new members. As parts of a system interact over time, new elements of the system emerge. Groups and teams develop norms that regulate communication, as well as histories of success and failure that influence members' confidence and team spirit. When new topics are introduced on electronic bulletin boards, new subscribers join, old ones leave, and lines of communication between people are reconfigured. Personal relationships grow beyond the two original parts (partners) to include trust or lack of trust, shared experiences, and private vocabularies. Systems include not only their original parts but also changes in those original elements and new elements that are created as a result of interaction.

Systems vary in how open they are. **Openness** is the extent to which a system affects and is affected by outside factors and processes. Some tribal communities are relatively closed systems that have little interaction with the world outside. Yet most cultures are fairly open to interaction with other cultures. This is increasingly true today as more and more people immigrate from one culture to another and as people travel more frequently and to more places. The more open the system, the more factors influence it. Mass media and communication technologies expand the openness of most societies and thus the influences on them and their ways of life.

A final point about systems is that they strive for but cannot sustain equilibrium. On one hand, systems seek a state of equilibrium, or **homeostasis.** That's why families create routines, organizations devise policies and procedures, individuals develop habits, groups generate norms, online communities develop conventions and abbreviations, and cultures generate rituals and traditions.

Yet no living system can sustain absolute balance or equilibrium. Change is inevitable and continuous. Sometimes, it's abrupt (a company moves all of its operations to a new country); at other times, it's gradual (a company begins to hire people from different cultures). Sometimes, influences outside a system prompt change (legislation affects importing and exporting in other countries). In other cases, the system generates change internally (an organization decides to alter its marketing targets). To function and survive, members of the system must continually adjust and change.

Communication is also affected by the larger systems within which it takes place. For example, different cultures have distinct understandings of appropriate verbal and nonverbal behaviors. Many Asian cultures place a high value on saving face, so Asians try not to cause personal embarrassment to others by disagreeing overtly. It is inappropriate to perceive people from Asian cultures as passive if they don't assert themselves in the ways that many Westerners do. Arab cultures consider it normal for people to be nearer to one another when talking than most Westerners find comfortable. And in Bulgaria, head nods mean "no" rather than "yes" (Munter, 1993). Different regions of the same country may also have different ways of communicating—Lori Anne makes this point in her commentary. Even within a single culture, there are differences based on region, ethnicity, religion, and other factors. Therefore, to interpret communication, we have to consider the systems in which it takes place. In Chapter 8, we'll discuss different communication practices in diverse cultural contexts.

▸ Lori Anne

I was born in Alabama, and all my life I've spoken to people whether I know them or not. I say hello or something to a person I pass on the street just to be friendly. When I went to a junior college in Pennsylvania, I got in trouble for being so friendly. When I spoke to guys I didn't know, they thought I was coming on to them or something. And other women would just look at me like I was odd. I'd never realized that friendliness could be misinterpreted.

Symbols Communication is symbolic. We don't have direct access to one another's thoughts and feelings. Instead, we rely on **symbols,** which are abstract, arbitrary, and ambiguous representations of other things. We might symbolize love by giving a ring, by saying "I love you," or by closely embracing someone. A promotion might be symbolized by a new title and a larger office (and a raise!). Later in this chapter and also in Chapter 4, we'll have more to say about symbols. For now, just remember that human communication involves interaction with and through symbols.

Meanings Finally, our definition focuses on **meanings,** which are at the heart of communication. Reflecting on the evolution of the communication discipline, distinguished scholar Bruce Gronbeck (1999) notes that the field has moved increasingly toward a meaning-centered view of human communication. Meanings are the significance we bestow on phenomena, or what they signify to us. We do not find meanings in experience itself. Instead, we use symbols to create meanings. We ask others to be sounding boards so we can clarify our thinking, figure out what things mean, enlarge our perspectives, check our perceptions, and label feelings to give them reality. In all these ways, we actively construct meaning by interacting with symbols.

Communication has two levels of meaning (Watzlawick, Beavin, & Jackson, 1967). The **content level of meaning** contains the literal message. If a person knocks on your door and asks, "May I come in?" the content-level meaning is that the person is asking your permission to enter. The **relationship level of meaning** expresses the relationship between communicators. In our example, if the person who asks, "May I come in?" is your friend and is smiling, you would probably conclude that the person is seeking friendly interaction. On the other hand, if the person is your supervisor and speaks in an angry tone, you might interpret the relationship-level meaning as a signal that your supervisor is not satisfied with your work and is going to call you on the carpet. The content-level meaning is the same in both examples, but the relationship-level meaning differs.

In many cases, the relationship level of meaning is more important than the content level. The relationship level of meaning often expresses a desire to connect with another person (Gottman & DeClaire, 2001). For example, this morning Robbie said to me, "I've got a late meeting today, so I won't be home until 6 or so." The content-level meaning is obvious—Robbie is informing me of his schedule. The relationship-level meaning, however, is the more important message that Robbie wants to stay connected with me and is aware that we usually have catch-up conversation around 5 P.M. each day. The content level of meaning of IMs is often mundane, even trivial: <waz up?> <not much here. U?> On the relationship level of meaning, however, this exchange express interest and a desire to stay in touch. The Sharpen Your Skill box on this page invites you to pay attention to both levels of communication in your interactions.

> ### *Noticing Levels of Meaning in Communication*
>
> The next time you talk with a close friend, notice both levels of meaning.
>
> What is the content-level meaning?
>
> To what extent are liking, responsiveness, and power expressed on the relationship level of meaning?
>
> **SHARPEN YOUR SKILL**

▶MODELS OF COMMUNICATION

To complement the definition of communication we have just discussed, we'll now consider models of the human communication process. Over the years, scholars in communication have developed a number of models that reflect increasingly sophisticated understandings of the communication process.

Linear Models

Harold Laswell (1948) advanced an early model that described communication as a linear, or one-way, process in which one person acts on another person. This is also called a *transmission model* because it assumes that communication is transmitted in a straightforward manner from a sender to a receiver. His was a verbal model consisting of five questions that described early views of how communication works:

Who?

Says what?

In what channel?

To whom?

With what effect?

Claude Shannon and Warren Weaver (1949) refined Laswell's model by adding the concept of **noise.** Noise is anything that interferes with the intended meaning of communication. Noises may distort understanding. Figure 1.1 shows Shannon's and Weaver's model. Although linear, or transmission, models such as these were useful starting points, they are too simplistic to capture the complexity of human communication.

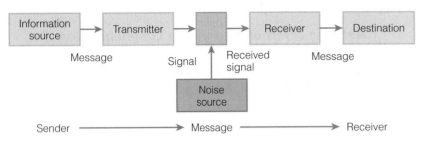

Figure 1.1   THE LINEAR MODEL OF COMMUNICATION
Source: Adapted from Shannon & Weaver, 1949.

Interactive Models

The major shortcoming of the early models was that they portrayed communication as flowing in only one direction, from a sender to a receiver. Commenting on this limitation, Bruce Gronbeck (1999) noted that linear views are inaccurate because communication processes "are bidirectional, not unidirectional; are dialogic, not monologic; and hence are processes best described not by bullets or arrows hitting their targets, but rather by congregations of voices together building the frameworks of shared meanings" (p. 13). The linear model suggests that a person is only a sender or a receiver and that receivers passively absorb senders' messages. Clearly, this isn't how communication occurs.

When communication theorists realized that listeners respond to senders, they added **feedback** to their models. Feedback is a response to a message. It may be verbal or nonverbal, and it may be intentional or unintentional. Wilbur Schramm (1955) depicted feedback as a second kind of message. In addition, Schramm pointed out that communicators create and interpret messages within personal fields of experience. The more communicators' fields of experience overlap, the better they can understand each other.

Adding fields of experience to models clarifies why misunderstandings sometimes occur. You jokingly put down a friend, and he takes it seriously and is hurt. You offer to help someone, and she feels patronized. Adding fields of experience and feedback allowed Schramm and other communication scholars to develop models that portray communication as an interactive process in which both senders and receivers participate actively (Figure 1.2).

Transactional Models

Although an interactive model was an improvement over the linear one, it still didn't capture the dynamism of human communication. The interactive model portrays communication as a sequential process in which one person communicates to another, who then sends feedback to the first person. Yet people may communicate simultaneously instead of taking turns. Also, the interactive model designates one person as a sender and another person as a receiver. In reality, communicators both send and receive messages. While handing out a press release, a public relations representative watches reporters to gauge their interest. The "speaker" is listening; the "listeners" are sending messages.

A final shortcoming of the interactive model is that it doesn't portray communication as changing over

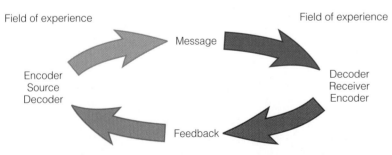

Figure 1.2   THE INTERACTIVE MODEL OF COMMUNICATION
Source: Adapted from Schramm, 1955.

time as a result of what happens between people. For example, new employees are more reserved in conversations with co-workers than they are after months on the job, getting to know others and organizational norms. What they talk about and how they interact change over time. To be accurate, a model should include the feature of time and should depict communication as varying, not constant. Figure 1.3 is a transactional model that highlights the features we have discussed.

Consistent with what we've covered in this chapter, our model includes noise that can distort communication. Noise includes sounds, such as a lawn mower or background chatter, as well as interferences within communicators, such as mental biases and preoccupation, that hinder effective listening. In addition, our model emphasizes that communication is a continually changing process. How people communicate varies over time and in response to their history of relating.

The outer lines on our model emphasize that communication occurs within systems that affect what and how people communicate and what meanings they create. Those systems, or contexts, include the shared systems of the communicators (campus, town, culture) and the personal systems of each communicator (family, religious associations, friends). Also note that our model, unlike previous ones, portrays each person's field of experience and his or her shared fields of experience as changing over time. As we encounter new people and grow personally, we alter how we interact with others.

Finally, our model doesn't label one person a sender and the other a receiver. Instead, both are defined as communicators who participate equally, and often simultaneously, in the communication process. This means that at a given moment in communication, you may be sending a message (speaking or wrinkling your brow), listening to a message, or doing both at the same time (interpreting what someone says while nodding to show you are interested). To understand communication as a transactional

"It's funny how two intelligent people can have such opposite interpretations of the tax code!"

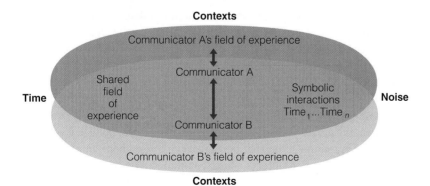

Figure 1.3 A TRANSACTIONAL MODEL OF COMMUNICATION
Source: Adapted from Wood, 1997, p. 21.

process is to recognize that self and others are involved in a shared process: Communication is *we*-oriented (How can we understand each other? How can we work through this conflict?) rather than *me*-oriented (This is what I mean. This is what I want.) (Lafasto & Larson, 2001).

In summary, the most accurate model of communication represents it as a transactional process in which people interact with and through symbols over time to create meaning.

▶Careers in Communication

Now that you clearly understand what communication is, you may be wondering what kinds of careers are open to people with strong backgrounds in the discipline. As we've seen, communication skills are essential to success in most fields. In addition, people who major in communication are particularly equipped for certain careers.

Research

Communication research is a vital and growing field of work. Many faculty members combine teaching and research. In this book, you'll encounter a good deal of academic research that helps us understand how communication works—or fails to work.

In addition to academic research, communication specialists help organizations by studying processes such as message production and marketing (Morreale & Vogl, 1998). Companies want to know how people respond to advertisements, logos, and product names. Communication researchers also assist counselors by investigating the ways in which communication helps and harms relationships.

Education

Teaching others about communication is another exciting career path for people with extensive backgrounds in the field. I find nothing more exciting than opening students' eyes to the power of communication and working with them to improve their skills. Across the nation, communication teachers at all levels are in demand. Secondary schools, junior colleges, colleges, universities, technical schools, and community colleges offer communication classes.

The level at which people are qualified to teach depends on how extensively they have pursued the study of communication. Generally, a bachelor's degree in communication education and a teaching certificate are required for teaching in elementary and secondary schools. A master's degree in communication qualifies a person to teach at community colleges, technical schools, and some junior colleges and colleges. The doctoral degree in communication generally is required for a career in university education, although some universities offer short-term positions to people with master's degrees (Morreale & Vogl, 1998).

Although generalists are preferred for many teaching jobs, college level faculty can focus on areas of communication that particularly interest them. For instance, my research and teaching focus on interpersonal communication and gender and communication. Other college faculty specialize in areas such as oral traditions, intercultural communication, family communication, health communication, organizational dynamics, and performance.

What do you infer about the person at the left based on the context and what he is doing?

Communication educators are not limited to communication departments. In recent years, more and more people with advanced degrees in communication have taken positions in medical and business schools. Doctors need training in listening sensitively to patients, explaining complex problems and procedures, and providing comfort, reassurance, and motivation. Similarly, good businesspeople know not only their businesses but also how to explain them to others, how to present themselves and their companies or products favorably, and so on.

Mass Communication: Journalism, Broadcasting, Public Relations, and Advertising

Careers in mass communication are attractive to many people with backgrounds in communication. Strong communication skills are necessary for careers in journalism, public relations, broadcasting, and advertising. Good journalists know how to listen carefully and critically when conducting interviews. They also know how to write clearly so that readers are drawn to their stories and understand what they are presenting.

Effective public relations depend on understanding actual and potential customers, clients, and consumers and adapting messages to their interests, desires, and concerns. For example, if you had been in charge of public relations for Tylenol at the time some bottles of the pain reliever were tampered with, what would you have done to restore the public's confidence in the product? The public relations team for Tylenol that actually confronted this problem immediately alerted the public to the danger, and then announced that the company would immediately develop tamper-resistant packaging (which it did). As an additional measure to restore public confidence in the product, the public relations team offered consumers free bottles of the newly packaged product. This was an effective public relations campaign because it addressed the public's fears, demonstrated the company's commitment to safety, and showed good will by offering free products.

Effective advertising professionals also depend on solid understandings of communication and skill in basic communication processes. They need to understand how actual and potential consumers of the product they are advertising will perceive visual images and language that represents their product. Advertisers need to brand products so that consumers associate the product with a particular key message or theme. McDonald's advertising team has been effective in branding McDonald's as family friendly; Porsche is branded as "the ultimate driving experience"; and Nike is identified with the "just do it" attitude.

Training and Consulting

Consulting is another career that welcomes people with backgrounds in communication. Businesses train employees in group communication skills, interview techniques, and interpersonal interaction. Some large corporations have entire departments devoted to training and development. People with communication backgrounds often join these departments and work with the corporation to design and teach courses or workshops that enhance employees' communication skills.

fyi

CAREERS IN COMMUNICATION

Learn more about careers open to people with strong training in communication.

The National Communication Association publishes *Pathways to Careers in Communication.* In addition to discussing careers, this booklet provides useful information on the National Communication Association and its many programs. To read an excerpt from *Pathways to Careers in Communication,* go to the book's online resources for this chapter and click on WebLink 1.4.

In addition, communication specialists may join or form consulting firms that provide communication training to government and businesses. One of my colleagues consults with nonprofit organizations to help them develop work teams that interact effectively. Other communication specialists work with politicians to improve their presentational styles and sometimes to write their speeches. I consult with attorneys as an expert witness and a trial strategist on cases involving charges of sexual harassment and sex discrimination. Other communication consultants work with attorneys on jury selections and advise lawyers about how dress and nonverbal behaviors might affect jurors' perceptions of clients.

Human Relations and Management

Because communication is the foundation of human relations, it's no surprise that many communication specialists build careers in human development or in the human relations departments of corporations. People with solid understandings of communication and good personal communication skills are effective in public relations, personnel, grievance management, negotiation, customer relations, and development and fund-raising (Morreale & Vogl, 1998).

Communication degrees also open doors to careers in management. The most important qualifications for management are not technical skills but the abilities to interact with others and to communicate effectively. Good managers know how to listen, express ideas, build consensus, create supportive climates, and balance tasks and interpersonal concerns in dealing with others. Developing skills such as these gives communication majors a firm foundation for effective management. The FYI box on page 18 shows you how to learn about careers in communication that might appeal to you.

▶SUMMARY

In this chapter, we've taken a first look at human communication. We noted its importance in our lives, defined communication, and discussed models, the most accurate of which is a transactional model that accurately represents the dynamism of communication.

In the final section of this chapter, we considered career opportunities open to people who specialize in communication. An array of exciting career paths is available for people who enjoy interacting with others and who want the opportunity to be part of a dynamic discipline that evolves constantly to meet changing needs and issues in our world.

Review, Reflect, Extend

The Key Concepts, For Further Reflection and Discussion questions, Recommended Resources, and Experience Communication Case Study that follow will help you review, reflect on, and extend the information and ideas presented in this chapter. A diverse selection of online resources is also available through ThomsonNOW. These resources include Speech Builder Express, InfoTrac College Edition, interactive videos, vMentor, and Thomson Audio Study Products.

Thomson™ NOW! is an online study system designed to help you put your time to the best use. After reading a chapter, take the NOW pre-test to identify concepts discussed in the chapter that you may not fully understand. Based on the results of this diagnostic test, the system will create a personalized study plan that directs you to specific learning resources and activities. To see if you're ready for an exam, take the NOW post-test to check your understanding.

For more information or to access this book's online resources, visit **http://www.thomsonedu.com**.

▶KEY CONCEPTS

The terms following are defined in the chapter on the page number indicated, and they appear in alphabetical order, with definitions, in the Glossary, which begins on page 369. The book's online resources also include flash cards and crossword puzzles to help you learn these terms and the concepts they represent.

communication, 10	meaning, 12	relationship level of meaning, 12
content level of meaning, 12	noise, 13	symbol, 12
feedback, 14	openness, 11	system, 10
homeostasis, 11	process, 10	

► FOR FURTHER REFLECTION AND DISCUSSION

The questions below can also be found among the book's online resources for this chapter, where you have the option of e-mailing your responses to your instructor, if required.

1. Using each of the models discussed in this chapter, describe communication in your class. What does each model highlight and obscure? Which model best describes and explains communication in your class?

2. Interview a professional in your field of choice. Identify communication skills that person thinks are most important for success. Which of those skills do you already have? Which skills do you need to develop or improve? How can you use this book and the course it accompanies to develop the skills you need to be effective in your career?

3. Go to the placement office on your campus, and examine descriptions of available positions. Record the number of job notices that call for communication skills.

► RECOMMENDED RESOURCES

1. Visit the website of the National Communication Organization, which can be accessed by going to the book's online resources and clicking on WebLink 1.5. Access one or more pages on the site that are particularly relevant to your interests in communication.

2. Watch the film *An Unfinished Life*. Analyze the communication among the four main characters, with a focus on the system within which they operate. What are the elements of the system? Identify two changes in the relationship system, and trace how those affect all parts of the system as the film evolves.

Experience Communication Case Study

THE NEW EMPLOYEE

The book's online resources include an interactive video of the communication situation featured in the case study scripted below. Apply what you've learned in this chapter by analyzing the case study, using the questions that follow the script as a guide. These questions are also available online with the video.

Your supervisor asks you to mentor a new employee, Toya, and help her learn the ropes of the job. After two weeks, you perceive that this person has many strengths. She is responsible and punctual, and she takes initiative on her own. At the same time, you note that Toya is careless about details: She doesn't proofread reports, so they contain errors in spelling and grammar, and she doesn't check back to make sure something she did worked. You've also noticed that Toya seems very insecure and wants a lot of affirmation and praise. You want to give her honest feedback so she can improve her job performance, yet you are afraid she will react defensively if you bring up her carelessness. You ask Toya to meet with you to discuss her first two weeks on the job. The meeting begins:

You: Well, you've been here for two weeks. How are you liking the job?

Toya: I like it a lot, and I'm trying to do my best every day. Nobody has said anything, so I guess I'm doing okay.

Jason Harris/© Wadsworth

You: Well, I've noticed how responsible you are and how great you are about being a self-starter. Those are real strengths in this job.

Toya: Thanks. So I guess I'm doing okay, right?

You: What would you say if someone suggested that there are ways you can improve your work?

Toya: What do you mean? Have I done something wrong? Nobody's said anything to me. Is someone saying something behind my back?

▼ ▼

1. What would you say next to Toya? How would you meet your ethical responsibilities as her mentor and also adapt to her need for reassurance?

2. What responsibilities do you have to Toya, to your supervisor, and to the company? How can you reflect thoughtfully about potential tensions between these responsibilities?

3. How would your communication differ if you acted according to a linear model of communication, as opposed to a transactional one?

2 The Field of Communication in Historical and Contemporary Perspective

▶ **FOCUS QUESTIONS**

1. In what context did the study and teaching of communication begin?

2. What methods do communication scholars use to conduct research?

3. What areas of study and teaching constitute the discipline of communication today?

4. What themes unify areas of study within the field of communication?

My father loved to tell me stories about my ancestors—his parents, grandparents, and great-grandparents. When I was 7 years old and bored with his stories, I asked my father what any of that "ancient history" had to do with me. He responded with a stern lecture—one of many he gave me—in which he told me that family members who had come before me had shaped our family. He went on to tell me that I couldn't understand him or myself without understanding the history of my family.

At the time, I wasn't fully convinced of my father's reasoning, but I did start listening with more attention. In the years that followed, I realized he was right. My father's parents and grandparents had been farmers. Although he became an attorney, my father retained a deep love of animals and the land, which he passed on to me and my siblings. I discovered that my impulsive personality was not new in the family; Charles Harrison Wood, my great grandfather, had been known for being more than a little rowdy and impetuous. I also learned that my father's brother Arch had frequently gotten in trouble for his pranks, another tendency I inherited. Later, when it became clear that I had a keen talent for organizing, I felt a kinship with my father's mother, whose organizational skills had been well known in our home county.

Just as you can't fully appreciate your present family without knowing about its history, you can't understand an academic discipline without learning about its development over time. This chapter introduces you to the communication discipline. We first discuss the long and rich intellectual history of the discipline. Second, we consider methods of conducting communication research. The third section of the chapter sur-

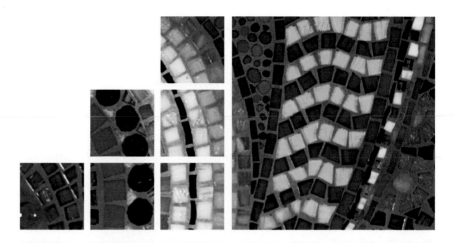

veys the major areas of the contemporary field and highlights themes that unify the different areas.

▶THE HISTORY OF THE COMMUNICATION FIELD

As the title of this book suggests, communication is a mosaic, each part of which contributes to the overall character of the field. The scholarly and teaching traditions that define communication have evolved since the discipline's birth more than 2,500 years ago.

Classical Roots: Rhetoric and Democratic Life

One theme in the mosaic is that communication plays a vital role in democratic societies. The art of rhetoric was born in the mid-400s B.C. in the port city of Syracuse on the island of Sicily, when Sicilians overthrew an oppressive political regime and established a democratic society. The first order of business under the new democratic constitution was to bring legal claims against the overthrown tyrannical government.

To do this, citizens needed to learn to speak effectively and persuasively. They needed to explain how they had been harmed by the overthrown government and argue for rights such as the return of land seized by leaders of the former regime. In this dramatic context, Corax and Tisias emerged as the first theorists and teachers of rhetoric, or persuasive speaking. They taught citizens in this newborn democracy how to present their claims forcefully and effectively.

Rhetoric continued to be central to democratic life in ancient Greece and Rome. Among the most influential philosophers and teachers of rhetoric in this era were such men as Socrates, Aristotle, Isocrates, and Plato. Plato, who was a student of Socrates, lived from 428 to 348 B.C.E. (Borchers, 2006). In Athens, he founded a school called the Academy. Plato believed that truth is absolute and can be known only in ideal forms and not concrete reality. Plato was suspicious of rhetoric because he recognized the possibility of misusing rhetoric to manipulate and deceive.

Aristotle, who lived from 384 to 322 B.C.E. (Borchers, 2006), was a student of Plato. Like many students and teachers today, Aristotle and Plato did not always see eye to eye. A major difference between them was that Aristotle believed truth could be discerned from careful observation of reality. Aristotle's view of truth was related to his belief that rhetoric is central to civic life in a democratic society. He understood that citizens could participate fully only if they were able to speak well and engage

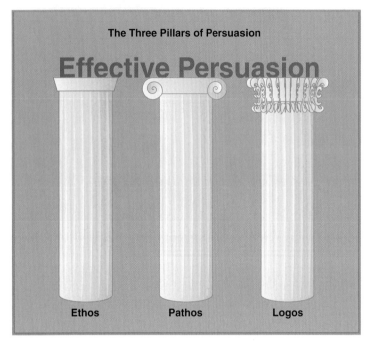

The Three Pillars of Persuasion

Effective Persuasion

Ethos Pathos Logos

Figure 2.1 THE THREE PILLARS OF PERSUASION

in discussion and debate about issues of the day. Aristotle taught citizens the five canons of rhetoric (see the FYI box on page 25). His students learned how to analyze audiences, discover ideas and proofs to support claims, organize messages effectively, speak with clarity and vigor, memorize the content of speeches, and deliver speeches effectively.

One of the enduring contributions to our knowledge of rhetoric was Aristotle's thinking about how persuasion occurs. He theorized that there are three ways to persuade, which he called *proofs* (Figure 2.1). **Ethos** is proof based on a speaker's credibility (trustworthiness, expertise, and good will). **Pathos** is proof that appeals to listeners' emotions. **Logos** is based on logic and reasoning. If you think about your experiences in listening to speakers, you're likely to discover that, like people in Aristotle's time, you respond to ethos, pathos, and logos.

Ancient Greece was also home to another group of teachers who took quite a different approach to rhetoric. These teachers viewed truth as relative, and they encouraged speakers to adjust their ideas to specific contexts and listeners. Known as *Sophists,* these teachers focused on building the best arguments to move audiences (Borchers, 2006). Today, specious or deceptive reasoning in argumentation is referred to as *sophistic.*

Liberal Education

A second theme in the mosaic is that effective communication is central to liberal education, which was the primary mission of American college education during the 1800s and most of the 1900s. For centuries after Aristotle taught in the *agora* (marketplace) in Athens, rhetoric held a premier spot in liberal education in Europe and the United States. Following Aristotle's view that rhetoric is a practical art, teachers of rhetoric provided pragmatic advice to students who wanted to be effective public speakers.

In the nineteenth century, many of the most prestigious universities in the United States established chairs of rhetoric, held by distinguished scholars and civic leaders. Among these was the future president John Quincy Adams, who held the first Boylston Professor of Rhetoric Chair at Harvard University (Foss, Foss, & Trapp, 1991). In the 1800s and early 1900s, rhetoric was taught as a practical art that prepared people for responsible participation in civic life. The emphasis on teach-

fyi

T E C H N O L O G Y

LEARNING FROM ANCIENT THEORISTS

You can study with great ancient rhetorical theorists online. Plato's most famous texts are *Gorgias* (the name of one of the most influential Sophists), which presents his view that rhetoric is dangerous, and *Phaedrus,* which offers a less critical view of rhetoric. To read *Gorgias,* go to the book's online resources for this chapter and click on WebLink 2.1. To read *Phaedrus,* click on WebLink 2.2. To learn about Aristotle's views of rhetoric, click on WebLink 2.3.

ing that marked this period explains why the first national professional organization, founded in 1914, was named the National Association of Teachers of Public Speaking.

In the 1900s, the communication discipline began to include more than public speaking. In the early twentieth century, philosopher John Dewey taught at the University of Chicago, which was the intellectual hub of the United States at that time. A pragmatic philosopher, Dewey championed progressive thinking in cultural life. For Dewey, this also meant championing communication in a broad sense. He realized that to have any impact on cultural life, progressive thinking must be communicated. In others words, people must be able to voice their ideas and to listen thoughtfully and critically to the ideas of others.

Dewey's interest in progressive thinking and citizen participation grew out of the political context of his time, and that context influenced the field as a whole. After the two world wars, communication professionals felt an urgent need to understand the connections between communication and Hitler's rise to power, the development of prejudice against social groups, willingness to follow authoritarian leaders, the effects of propaganda, and changes in attitudes and beliefs.

In the early 1900s, two major professional communication organizations were formed. The first was the Association for Education in Journalism and Mass Communication (AEJMC), which was founded in 1912. AEJMC promotes both academic and applied journalism, and it sponsors key research journals and conferences on journalistic practice, scholarship, and teaching. Today, AEJMC has more than 3,500 members worldwide.

The second organization, formed at roughly the same time, was founded in 1914. Its members were speech teachers, so it was called Speech Teachers of America (STA). However, that name did not endure. The organization changed its name three times, each change signaling evolution in the organization's scope and view of itself. In 1950, the name was changed to Speech Association of America (SAA) to reflect the organization's increasing interest in scholarship as well as teaching. In 1970, the name was changed again to the Speech Communication Association (SCA), a change that emphasized the growing interest in forms of communication other than speech—for instance, nonverbal communication. Finally, in 1997 members voted to change the name to the National Communication Association (NCA), which is its name today. With more than 7,000 members in 20 countries, NCA's mission is to advance research, teaching, and service relevant to human communication.

> ## fyi WISDOM FROM ANCIENT TEACHERS
>
> Ancient teachers of rhetoric taught students to master five specific canons, or arts, of public speaking that remain relevant today:
>
> ▶ Invention: The art of discovering ideas for speaking and arguments, or proofs to support claims and increase a speaker's credibility
>
> ▶ Organization: The art of arranging ideas clearly and effectively to enhance a speaker's credibility
>
> ▶ Style: The art of speaking well with grace, clarity, and vitality
>
> ▶ Memory: The art of familiarizing oneself with the content of one's speech so that one's energies can be devoted to delivery and interaction with listeners
>
> ▶ Delivery: The art of presenting a speech effectively and credibly

Broadening the Field

In the mid-twentieth century, another part of the mosaic of communication emerged: scientific, empirical research, which gained prominence in almost all of the social sciences. Marking the advent of scientific research in the communication field was the formation of the International Communication Association (ICA) in 1950. Today, the ICA has more than 3,000 members.

When the ICA was first formed, it contrasted with the NCA in two particular ways. First, the NCA, then called the SCA (Speech Association of America), was steeped in the humanities, which typically are built through qualitative research. Complementing the NCA's intellectual and methodological interests, the ICA allied itself primarily with the social scientific tradition, which tends to favor quantitative methods of research. Scholars who identified with the social scientific tradition conducted research to learn more about such issues as the factors that influence a speaker's credibility, the effects of following rational models of decision making, the responses of group members to different leadership styles, the impact of self-disclosure on romantic relationships, the impact of mass media on individuals, and the effects of various kinds of evidence on persuasive impact. Social scientific research continues today as one of several intellectual traditions that contribute to the ever-growing body of knowledge created by communication scholars.

A second difference between the two organizations, in the 1950s and for years after, was membership. As the names suggest, the NCA was a national organization that represented the interests of United States scholars of communication and primarily encouraged research in American communication. The ICA, on the other hand, explicitly sought to attract an international membership and to support research on communication beyond the borders of the United States. The ICA's international flavor explains why areas such as cultural studies, which have been keenly influenced by European scholars, are more prominent in the ICA than in the NCA.

Although the NCA and the ICA continue to reflect the intellectual and methodological inclinations present when they were formed, distinctions between the two organizations are a matter of degree. Today, the NCA includes many members whose research is primarily or entirely quantitative, and the ICA includes many members who generally favor qualitative research. Also, both organizations now have international memberships, and both promote research on communication in a range of cultures and geographic areas.

The 1960s and 1970s saw a new motif in the communication mosaic. In the United States, this was a time of unprecedented social and political upheaval. The civil rights movement and the second wave of the women's movement shook up long-standing patterns of personal and social relations. At the same time, youth culture ushered in new ideas about how people should interact and what was important in life. Many college students felt that personal relationships were central to life and that these should receive more time and attention than the traditional curriculum provided. Responding to these currents in social life, the communication discipline expanded to encompass interpersonal communication. Many colleges and universities began to offer classes in nonverbal behavior, family communication, and interaction in intimate relationships. Student interest in the expanded communication curriculum was very high and continues to be so today. The interpersonal emphasis also affected group communication courses, adding sensitivity training and human relations to the traditional coverage of group decision making.

The field continues to broaden to address a range of communication forms and contexts. In recent years, for instance, health communication has become a major subarea of the discipline. Scholars and teachers of health communication focus on issues such as doctor–patient interaction, organizational communication in health institutions, and media efforts to promote good health practices.

Communication, Power, and Empowerment

Beginning in the 1960s and continuing to the present day, another feature has become increasingly prominent in the communication mosaic: the relationship between communication and power in cultural life. The tumultuous 1960s and 1970s were marked by social and political movements that questioned established power hierarchies. Two of the most notable of these movements were the civil rights movement, which challenged racial discrimination in the United States, and the women's movement, which identified, challenged, and attempted to change conventional gender roles in both public and private realms of life. Many scholars and teachers of communication embraced a critical focus on social movements and began to investigate the communicative dynamics that social movements employ and the ways in which social movements affect individuals and society.

The expansion of the field's interests to questions of power reflects the influence of French philosopher Michel Foucault (1970, 1972a, 1972b, 1978), who was deeply concerned with who is and who is not allowed to speak in a society. More specifically, Foucault illuminated the ways in which culturally entrenched rules—often unwritten and unacknowledged—define who gets to speak, to whom we listen, and whose views are counted as important.

Building on Foucault's ideas, communication scholars study the ways in which some people's communication is allowed and other people's communication is disallowed or disrespected. Equally, communication scholars seek to empower people whose voices historically have been muted, so that they can participate fully in public and private interactions that shape the character of personal and collective life. Consider one example. Historically, decisions about environmental issues that affect the health and environment of communities have been made almost entirely by privileged citizens: scientists and middle- and upper-class citizens. Left out of these vital discussions have been many members of the working class and citizens without formal education (Cox, 2006a). These ordinary citizens often are made voiceless by institutional barriers and administrative practices that define their concerns and their ways of speaking as inappropriate. Phaedra Pezzullo (2001) documented how this happened—and how

it was changed—in one Southern community that was suffering the effects of a toxic landfill.

Interest in relationships between communication and power has reshaped many areas of the field. Rhetorical scholars have broadened their interests beyond individual speakers. Many of today's rhetorical scholars study the gay rights, pro-life and pro-choice, environmental, and other social movements. In their work, they examine coercive tactics, symbolic strategies for defining issues (think of the power of terms such as *pro-life* and *pro-choice* compared with *pro-abortion* and *anti-abortion*), and how social movements challenge and change broadly held cultural practices and values.

Effective public speaking is vital to social movements.

Scholars in other areas of the field share an interest in critical perspectives that focus on ways in which communication shapes and is shaped by the historical, social, and political contexts in which it occurs. Today, faculty in interpersonal and organizational communication conduct research and teach about how new technologies affect personal relationships and reshape societies, how events such as the Million Man March influence families and communities, how particular organizational cultures and practices affect employees' productivity and job satisfaction, and how national trends such as downsizing and outsourcing affect workers on the job and in their personal lives.

As this brief historical overview shows, the field of communication is responsive to the changing needs of individuals and society. Perhaps this is why the field has expanded, even during periods of downsizing in many colleges and universities. Just as the citizens of Athens found that Aristotle's teachings helped them prepare for effective participation in their society, today's students realize that the modern field of communication offers them remarkably effective skills for understanding and participating in the world in which they live.

►Conducting Research in Communication

Like other scholarly disciplines, communication is based on knowledge gained from rigorous research (Baxter & Bebee, 2004). Much of the research described in this book explores how and why communication works and why it sometimes doesn't work as we intend. So that you can understand how scholars acquire knowledge, we'll discuss three primary approaches to communication research. These three approaches are not incompatible. Many scholars rely on multiple approaches to study how communication works. Further, even scholars who do not use multiple methods in their own research rely on research that employs a range of methods.

Quantitative Research

As we noted earlier, communication scholars use **quantitative research methods** to gather information in numerical form. Descriptive statistics measure human behavior in terms of quantity, frequency, or amount. For example, in the 1998 survey mentioned in Chapter 1, we saw that 53% of Americans think ineffective communication is the principal cause of divorce. Kelly McCollum reports that in 1999, 93% of college students used the Internet for educational purposes.

A second method of quantitative research is gathering information through surveys, instruments, questionnaires, or interviews that measure how people feel, think, act, and so forth. Surveys are very valuable when a researcher wants to discover general trends among a particular group of people—members of an institution, for example, or Americans in general. Surveys often are used in organizations to gain information about employee morale, response to company policies, and relationships between job satisfaction and factors such as leadership style, participation on teams, and quality of communication between co-workers. Once survey data are gathered, they may be analyzed using a variety of statistical methods that help researchers detect patterns in communication and assess their strength and importance.

A third method of quantitative research is the experiment, a study in which researchers control the context and what happens in it to measure how one variable that can be manipulated (called the *independent variable*) affects other variables (called *dependent variables*). Linda Acitelli (1988) conducted an experiment to learn whether women and men differ in their desire to engage in relationship talk. She had half of the participants in her study read scenarios in which a husband and wife discussed a conflict or problem in their relationship. The other half of the respondents read scenarios in which a husband and wife engaged in general talk about their relationship when there was no specific problem or issue. Acitelli found that both women and men thought relationship talk was satisfying when there was a problem, but when there was no specific tension to be resolved, women thought relationship talk was significantly more satisfying than men did.

Qualitative Research

A second approach used by many scholars of communication is **qualitative research methods,** which provide non-numerical knowledge about communication. Qualitative methods are especially valuable when researchers want to study aspects of communication that cannot easily be quantified, such as the meanings of experience, the function of rituals in organizational life, and how we feel about and engage in online communication. Three methods of qualitative research are most prominent in the communication discipline.

Textual analysis is the interpretation of symbolic activities. Texts are not limited to formal written texts or orally presented speeches. Scholars who engage in textual analysis might interpret the meaning of the AIDS quilt, community-building rituals among refugees, tours of toxic waste sites, self-disclosures in chat rooms on the web, and stories told in families. In each case, communication practices are interpreted, rather than measured, to understand their significance.

Another qualitative method is *ethnography,* in which researchers try to discover what symbolic activities mean by immersing themselves in those activities and their contexts and gaining insight into the perspectives of those who are native to the context. At the center of ethnographic research is a commitment to understanding what communication means from the perspective of those involved rather than from that of an outside, uninvolved observer. Dwight Conquergood, a distinguished ethnographic scholar, provided insight into the meaning of communicative practices among Laotian refugees (1986) and Chicago street gangs (Conquergood, Friesema, Hunter, & Mansbridge, 1990). To achieve this, Conquergood lived in those communities and participated in their daily activities to learn how his subjects perceived their behavior and its meaning.

A third important method of qualitative scholarship is *historical research,* which provides knowledge about significant past events, people, and activities. Many rhetorical theorists and critics rely on historical research to achieve important insight into thinkers who shaped the field, such as Socrates, Plato, and St. Augustine (Conley, 1990). Historical research also studies pivotal rhetorical works, such as Elizabeth Cady Stanton's speech, "The Declaration of Sentiments," which was the keynote address at the first women's rights convention in 1848 (Campbell, 1989), Martin Luther King Jr.'s "I Have a Dream" speech in 1963 (Cox, 1989), and the power of television programming to shape perceptions of social movements (Dow, 2004). The data for historical scholarship include original documents, such as drafts of speeches and notes for revision, records that describe events and public reaction to them, and biographical studies of key figures.

Critical Research

A third approach to communication scholarship is **critical research methods,** in which scholars identify and challenge communication practices that oppress, marginalize, or otherwise harm individuals and social groups.

Critical scholars think that the traditional research goals of understanding, explanation, and prediction are insufficient if academics want the knowledge they generate to have practical consequences. Therefore, critical scholars are passionately committed to using their research to advance social awareness and progress. For this group, specific communication practices are seen as means of reflecting, upholding, and sometimes challenging cultural ideology. For example, the practice of punching a time clock, used in many organizations, upholds the notion that workers are responsible to those who have the means to own and run businesses. The meaning of punching a time clock is tied to an overall ideology that stipulates who does and who does not have power in society.

Some critical scholars (Grossberg, 1997) contribute through original theorizing that helps us understand how certain groups and practices become dominant and how dominant ideologies sometimes are challenged and changed in a society. Other critical scholars engage in empirical work to reveal how particular practices work and whom they benefit and harm. For example, Lana Rakow's (1992) critical analysis of television advertisements shows that they harm many women by advancing unrealistic and unachievable ideals of beauty. Other critical scholars have challenged racist and sexist practices in U.S. media (Wilson, Gutiérrez, & Chao, 2003) and have raised questions about how communication technologies shape individual thinking and social relationships (Anderson, 2003; Meyrowitz, 1985; Ong, 2002; Subrahmanyam, Kraut, Greenfield, & Gross, 2001).

Although the quantitative, qualitative, and critical approaches are distinct orientations to conducting research, they are not necessarily inconsistent or incompatible. In fact, scholars often rely on more than one research method in an effort to gain multifaceted understanding of what is being studied. Likewise, scholars often combine different kinds of data or theoretical perspectives to gain a fuller understanding of what is being studied than they would get from any single type of data or theoretical lens.

Studying phenomena in multiple ways is called **triangulation,** a term that shares the same root term as *trigonometry.* Just as trigonometry involves calculating the distance to a particular point by viewing that point in relation to two other points, triangulated research involves studying phenomena from multiple points of view. Communication researchers rely on different types of triangulation. Data triangulation relies on multiple sources of data. For example, to study gender bias in sports reporting, researchers (Eastman & Billings, 2000) used three sources of data: *The New York Times,* CNN's *Sports Tonight,* and ESPN's *SportsCenter.* Researcher triangulation occurs when two or more researchers gather and analyze data so that the data are interpreted through multiple perspectives. Methodological triangulation involves using two or more methodological approaches to study a phenomenon. To study the relationship between stereotypical media messages about race and ethnicity, and consumers' social judgments of races and ethnicities, Dana Mastro (2003) employed both quantitative and critical methods. Triangulated research allows scholars to study communication from multiple points of view and thus to gain robust understandings of that which is studied.

In summary, communication scholars rely on quantitative, qualitative, and critical approaches to research. Each approach is valuable, and each has contributed to the overall knowledge that makes up communication as a scholarly discipline. Often, researchers combine these approaches in triangulated studies. In this book, you'll encounter research reflecting all three of the primary approaches we've discussed, so that you can appreciate the range of methods that scholars use to generate knowledge about human communication. Much of this research is woven into the text of chapters, and selected findings from research are highlighted in FYI boxes.

▶THE BREADTH OF THE COMMUNICATION FIELD

As we have seen, the communication discipline originally focused almost exclusively on public communication. Although public speaking remains a vital skill, it is no longer the only focus of the communication field. The modern discipline can be classified into 10 primary areas.

Intrapersonal Communication

Intrapersonal communication is communication with ourselves, or self-talk. You might wonder whether *intrapersonal communication* is another term for *thinking*. In one sense, yes. Intrapersonal communication does involve thinking because it is a cognitive process that occurs inside us. Yet because thinking relies on language to name and reflect on ideas, it is also communication (Vocate, 1994). Chiquella makes this point in her commentary.

▶ Chiquella

I figure out a lot of things by thinking them through in my head. It's like having a trial run without risk. Usually, after I think through different ideas or ways of approaching someone, I can see which one would be best.

One school of counseling focuses on enhancing self-esteem by changing how we talk to ourselves (Ellis & Harper, 1977; Rusk & Rusk, 1988; Seligman, 1990, 2002). For instance, you might say to yourself, "I blew that test, so I'm really stupid. I'll never graduate, and, nobody will hire me." This kind of talk lowers self-esteem by convincing you that a single event (blowing one test) proves you are worthless. Therapists who realize that what we say to ourselves affects our feelings urge us to challenge negative self-talk by saying, "One test is hardly a measure of my intelligence. I did well on the other test in this course, and I have a decent overall college record. I shouldn't be so hard on myself." What we say to ourselves can enhance or diminish self-esteem. (See the Sharpen Your Skill box below.)

We engage in self-talk to plan our lives, to rehearse different ways of acting, and to prompt ourselves to do or not do particular things. Intrapersonal communication is how we remind ourselves to eat in healthy ways ("No saturated fats"), show respect to others ("I need to listen to Grandmother's story"), check impulses that might hurt others ("I'll wait until I'm calmer to say anything"), impress interviewers ("I'll research the company before my interview"), and prepare to speak effectively in public contexts ("I'll need a good visual aid so listeners can see the relationships I'm talking about").

Intrapersonal communication also helps us rehearse alternative scenarios

Analyze Your Self-Talk

Pay attention to the way you talk to yourself for the next day. When something goes wrong, what do you say to yourself? Do you put yourself down with negative messages? Do you generalize beyond the specific event to describe yourself as a loser or as inadequate? The first step in changing negative self-talk is to become aware of it. We'll have more to say about how to change negative self-talk in Chapter 9.

SHARPEN YOUR SKILL

and their possible outcomes. To control a disruptive group member, you might consider telling the person to shut up, suggesting that the group adopt a rule that everyone should participate equally, and taking the person out for coffee and privately asking him or her to be less domineering. You will think through the three options (and perhaps others), weigh the likely consequences of each, and then choose one to put into practice. We engage in internal dialogues continuously as we reflect on experiences, sort through ideas, and test alternative ways of acting.

Interpersonal Communication

A second major emphasis in the field of communication is interpersonal communication, which is communication between people. **Interpersonal communication** is not a single thing but rather a continuum that ranges from quite impersonal to highly interpersonal (Figure 2.2). The more we interact with a person as a distinct individual, the more interpersonal the communication is.

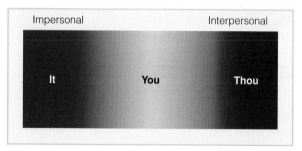

Figure 2.2 THE COMMUNICATION CONTINUUM

Scholars of interpersonal communication study how communication creates and sustains relationships and how partners communicate to deal with the normal and extraordinary challenges of maintaining intimacy over time (Canary & Stafford, 1994; Duck & Wood, 1995; Spencer, 1994; Wood & Duck, 2006). Research shows that intimates who listen sensitively and talk openly have the greatest chance of sustaining a close relationship over time. Research in this area has also shown that communication is a pivotal influence on how personal relationships develop over time. For example, researchers have shown that in healthy intimate relationships, partners not only feel empathy for each other, but they communicate empathy, including concern for each other's well-being (Hakansson & Montgomery, 2003; Kerem, Fishman, & Josselson, 2002).

Performance Studies

A third area of the field is performance studies. Scholars and teachers in this area focus on the ways in which we perform our personal, professional, and social identities and the ways in which performance allows us to understand experiences. Many performance scholars are particularly interested in the role of performances in everyday life. For example, how do we perform and thus create our gender identities by enacting femininity and masculinity in daily interactions? How do we perform and thus continuously re-create our ethnic identities? Performance scholars also investigate the personal and social significance of oral traditions: how storytelling reflects and reproduces cultural traditions, how witnessing affirms others in their struggles, and how personal narratives allow people to make sense of the experiences in their lives.

A third interest of performance scholars addresses issues of power, which we discussed previously. Recognizing the political potential of performance, scholars, teachers, and artists inquire into the ways in which performances sustain or challenge cultural values and practices. Some performance scholars are involved with community theater, which aims to address problems in particular communities. For example, two of my colleagues founded Generations at Play, which brings together residents of retirement homes and high school and college students. Working as a group, these people create performances that challenge intergenerational stereotypes and barriers.

Group and Team Communication

A fourth branch of the field is small-group communication, including communication in decision-making committees and work teams. Small-group research focuses on leadership, member roles, group features, agendas for achieving group goals, and managing conflict. Because groups involve more than one or two people, much teaching and research in this area focuses on how members coordinate their resources to arrive at collective decisions. In Chapter 11, we'll consider how we adapt basic communication processes to be effective when we participate in groups and teams.

Some scholars who focus on group communication (Barker, 1999; Sewell, 1998) study the dynamics of self-managing teams. Interestingly, although self-directed teams are often described as free from the usual hierarchy of power, many such teams become self-governing or self-policing. When this happens, the teams replace the standard power figure with their own enforcement of the hierarchy's values and policies (Ashcraft & Mumby, 2004). Some self-managing teams enforce organizational norms for participation by defining people who miss meetings as "deviant" and requiring anyone who misses a meeting to account for or apologize for the absence (Mumby & Stohl, 1992). Other scholars of group communication focus on topics such as managing conflict in groups (LaFasto & Larson, 2001) and improving group performance (Frey, 2003).

Public Communication

Public speaking remains an important branch of the communication field. Even though many people will not pursue careers that call for extensive formal speaking, most of us will have opportunities to speak publicly. In addition, we all will be in situations where speaking up is a responsibility. My editor makes presentations to his sales representatives to explain what his books are about and how to spotlight important features to professors who may want to use them in their courses. I recently coached my doctor, who was asked to address her colleagues on a development in treatment of renal disease. My plumber presents workshops to his staff to inform them of new developments in plumbing products and to teach them how to communicate effectively with customers. My brother-in-law relies on public speaking skills to try cases in court, and my sister gives public speeches to raise money for a center for abused children. My editor, doctor, plumber, brother-in-law, and sister don't consider themselves public speakers, but public speaking is a part of their lives.

Rhetorical critics study communication events such as Martin Luther King Jr.'s "I Have a Dream" speech and debates on public policies. Critics often take a role in civic life by evaluating how well public figures support their positions and respond to challenges from opponents. Scholars of public communication are also interested in discovering and teaching principles of effective and ethical persuasion (Dillard & Pfau, 2002; Simons, Morreale, & Gronbeck, 2001). Research has also enlightened us about the kinds of argument, methods of organizing ideas, and forms of proof that listeners find ethical and effective.

Within the area of public communication are sub-areas such as argumentation and political communication. Argumentation focuses on how to build effective arguments by using sound reasoning and strong evidence and by developing ideas in ways that respond to listeners' beliefs, concerns, and goals. Skill in argumentation is essential for attorneys and anyone else who aims to persuade others. Political communication has also emerged as a sub-area of public communication. Scholars of political communication are particularly interested in how politicians connect or fail to connect with voters, how political campaigns succeed or falter, how social movements build awareness of issues such as the environment (Cox, 2006a), and how rhetorical skills influence the process of policy making (Cox & McCloskey, 1996).

Organizational Communication

Communication in organizations is another growing area of interest. The work of communication scholars has identified communication skills that enhance professional success, and scholars have traced the effects of various kinds of communication on morale, productivity, and commitment to organizations. Scholars of organizational communication study interviewing, listening, leadership, new technologies of communication, and decision making.

In addition, scholars have begun to focus substantial attention on organizational culture and personal relationships in professional settings. **Organizational culture** is the general term for the understandings about an organization's identity and codes of thought and action that members of an organization share. Some organizations think of themselves as families. From this understanding emerge rules for how employees should interact and how fully they should commit to work. Studies of organizational culture also shed light on the continuing problem of sexual harassment. A number of communication scholars have analyzed how some institutions trivialize complaints of sexual harassment and sustain an organizational culture that implies that sexual harassment is acceptable (Bingham, 1994; Clair, 1993; Conrad, 1995; Conrad & Poole, 2002; Strine, 1992; Taylor & Conrad, 1992).

Another area of increasing interest is personal relationships between co-workers. As we increase the number of hours we spend on the job, and as the number of working

"I don't know how it started, either. All I know is that it's part of our corporate culture."

women increases, opportunities for romantic and sexual relationships in the workplace also increase. Obviously, this adds both interest and complication to life in organizations, as Melbourne notes in her commentary. Co-workers may also be close friends, a relationship that is complicated if one person has higher status than the other. Communication scholar Ted Zorn (1995) analyzed "bosses and buddies," relationships in which one friend is the boss of the other. Zorn discovered a number of ways people cope with the often-contradictory rules for communication between friends and between superiors and subordinates. He identified potential values and hazards of friendships on the job.

▶ Melbourne

It was a real hassle when my supervisor and I started going out. Before, he gave me orders like he did all the other servers, and none of us thought anything about it. But after we started dating, he would sort of ask me, instead of tell me, what to do, like saying, "Mel, would you help out in section seven?" Another thing was that if he gave me a good station where tips run high, the other servers would give me trouble because they thought he was favoring me because we go out. And when he gave me a bad station, I'd feel he was being nasty for personal reasons. It was a mess being his employee and his girlfriend at the same time.

Personal relations on the job also require that people from diverse cultures and social communities learn to understand each other's styles of communicating. For example, women tend to make more "listening noises," such as "um," "uh-huh," and "go on," than men do. If men don't make listening noises when listening to women colleagues, the women may mistakenly think the men aren't interested. Conversely, men may misinterpret women's listening noises as agreement rather than simply interest. Such misunderstandings can strain professional relations. Some scholars of organizational communication study and conduct workshops on effective communication between the sexes (Murphy & Zorn, 1996).

Mass Communication

Mass communication is an exciting area in the modern field of communication. From a substantial body of research, we have learned a great deal about how media represent and influence cultural values. For instance, the use of young female models in ads and glamorous young women as reporters and news anchors perpetuates the cultural feminine ideal, which centers on youth and beauty. Films that portray men as daring, brave, and violent perpetuate strength and boldness as masculine ideals.

Media sometimes reinforce cultural stereotypes about race and ethnicity. For example, television shows and movies most often cast African Americans in supporting roles, not principal roles. In addition, entertainment programming often portrays Black men as lazy and unlawful and casts them as athletes or entertainers (Entman & Rojecki, 2000; Evans, 1993; Merritt, 2000). Hispanic Americans and Asian Americans often are cast in the roles of villains or criminals (Holtzman, 2000; Merritt, 2000).

Researchers have shown that major network news programs are likely to show Black defendants in mug shots without names but offer multiple pictures and names of White defendants (Entman, 1994); research shows, too, that media continue to reflect sexism and racism (Wilson, et al., 2003). This differential treatment encourages viewers to perceive African Americans as an undifferentiated group. Dana Mastro (2003) reported that negative stereotypes of races in media have affected social judgments of races. Communication scholars heighten awareness of how media shape—and sometimes distort—our perceptions of ourselves and society. Franklin's commentary addresses this point.

▶ Franklin

I hate the way television shows African Americans. Most of the time they are criminals or welfare cases or drunks or Uncle Toms. When I watch TV, I understand why so many people think Blacks are dumb, uneducated, and criminal. We're not, but you'd never know it from watching television.

Technologies of Communication

We are in the midst of a technological revolution that provides us with the means to communicate in more ways at faster speeds with greater numbers of people throughout the world than ever before. How do new technologies and the accompanying acceleration of the pace of interaction influence how we think, work, and form relationships? Some scholars caution that new technologies may undermine human community (Assmann, 2006; Hyde, 1995), whereas others celebrate the social networks and productivity technology allows (Lea & Spears, 1995). Other scholars claim that new communication technologies will fundamentally transform how we think and process information (Chesebro, 1995; Subrahmanyam et. al., 2001; Turkle, 2004). And some technology scholars worry that the abundance of information we can now get on any topic is useless unless we learn how to evaluate it critically and transform raw information into knowledge (Gants, 1999; Lane & Shelton, 2001).

Clearly, the verdict on the effects of new technologies will not be in for some time. Meanwhile, we all struggle to keep up with our increasingly technological world. Today, students conduct much of their research on the web or through specialized information services on the Internet, and friends and romantic partners use cell phones and instant messaging to stay in touch throughout the day (Carl, 2006). Communication scholars will continue to study whether emerging technologies merely alter how we communicate or actually change the kinds of relationships we build.

Your Mediated World

How do new technologies of communication affect your interactions? If you use the Internet, how are your electronic exchanges different from face-to-face interactions? Have you made any acquaintances or friends through electronic communication? Did those relationships develop differently from ones formed through personal contact? Do you feel differently about people you have never seen and those you see face to face?

SHARPEN YOUR SKILL

Intercultural Communication

Although intercultural communication is not a new area of study, its importance has grown in recent years. The United States has always been made up of many peoples, and demographic shifts in the last decade have increased the pluralism of this country. Increasing numbers of Asians, Latinos and Latinas, Eastern Europeans, and people of other ethnic backgrounds immigrate to the United States and make their homes here. They bring with them cultural values and styles of communicating that differ from those of citizens whose ancestors were born in the United States.

Studying intercultural communication increases our insight into different cultures' communication styles and meanings. For example, a Taiwanese woman in one of my graduate classes seldom spoke up and wouldn't enter the heated debates that are typical of graduate classes. One day after class, I encouraged Mei-Ling to argue for her ideas when others challenged them. She replied that doing so would be impolite. Her culture considers it disrespectful to contradict others. In the context of her culture, Mei-Ling's deference did not mean that she lacked confidence.

A particularly important recent trend in the area of intercultural communication is research on different social communities within a single society. Cultural differences are obvious in communication between a Nepali and a Canadian. Less obvious are differences in communication between people who speak the same language. Within the United States are distinct social communities based on race, gender, sexual preference, and other factors. Members of social communities such as these participate both in the overall culture of the United States and in the more specialized norms and practices of their communities. Larry Samovar and Richard Porter (2001) have identified distinctive styles of communication used by women, men, African Americans, Caucasians, Native Americans, gays and lesbians, people with disabilities, and other groups in our country. Recognizing and respecting different communication cultures increases personal effectiveness in a pluralistic society. Meikko's commentary reminds us of how cultural values are reflected in language.

▶ Meikko

What I find most odd about Americans is their focus on themselves. Here, everyone wants to be an individual who is so strong and stands out from everyone else. In Japan, it is not like that. We see ourselves as parts of families and communities, not as individuals. Here, *I* and *my* are the most common words, but they are not often said in Japan.

Scholars and teachers of intercultural communication do not limit their work to minority or nondominant cultures and social communities. A good example of this is the growing interest in what is called Whiteness studies. This area of research and teaching explores what it means to be White. Members of dominant or majority groups often perceive their identities and communication as "standard" or "normal" and perceive the identities and communication of all other groups as different from those of majority groups. Whiteness studies help us realize that White (and other dominant groups) is just as much a race–ethnicity as Black or Native American, and that White communication practices are shaped by cultural influences as much as those of other groups are.

© Michael Keller/Corbis

Our communication reflects the social communities to which we belong.

Ethics and Communication

A final area of study and teaching in the field focuses on the relationship between ethics and communication. Because all forms of communication involve ethical issues, this area of interest is both a focus of scholarship in its own right and an integral part of all other areas in the discipline. For instance, an ethical aspect of intrapersonal communication is the influence of stereotypes on our judgments of others.

In the realm of interpersonal communication, honesty, compassion, and fairness in relationships are ethical concerns. Conformity pressures that sometimes operate in groups are an ethical issue. The area of organizational communication includes ethical questions about the right of institutions to regulate employees' personal lives. Do companies have a right to refuse insurance to employees who smoke, skydive, or race cars on their own time? Ethical issues also surface in public communication. For example, does speaking for oppressed groups misrepresent their experiences or even reinforce oppression by keeping others silent (Alcoff, 1991)?

From interpersonal to public situations, people confront such ethical issues as concealing evidence, misusing statistics, and misrepresenting information. Attitudes and actions that encourage or hinder freedom of speech are relevant to a range of communication contexts. Are all members of organizations equally empowered to speak? Is it right for audiences to shout down a speaker with unpopular views? How does the balance of power between partners affect each person's freedom to express himself or herself in a relationship? Because ethical issues infuse all forms of communication, I weave ethical themes into each chapter of this book.

Blurring the Lines

The 10 areas of the field that we've just discussed are not as discrete as they may seem. Just as technologies of communication have converged in significant ways, so, too, do areas of the communication discipline converge and interact. For example, you may have seen *The Blair Witch Project.* Clearly, it is mass communication. At the same time, it's also a rich study of interpersonal relationships, everyday performances, and group interaction. How the film was marketed offers a case study in organizational and public communication. Technologies of communication interact with interpersonal communication in increasingly complex ways. To stay in touch, I and my niece Michelle IM each other several times each day. Our IM's are both technological and interpersonal communication. Similarly, when we chat with friends via e-mail or in chat rooms, we're

D I V E R S I T Y

fyi

LEARNING ABOUT INTERCULTURAL COMMUNICATION

The web provides abundant resources for learning about communication between people from different cultures. One of the best sites offers many links to multicultural and intercultural sites of interest. To gain access to the website of the Society for Cross-Cultural Research, go to the book's online resources for this chapter and click on WebLink 2.4.

simultaneously engaging in interpersonal and technological communication. Mass communication technology such as television and satellites allow citizens to watch public speeches as they happen. These examples remind us that the areas of communication often overlap and interact.

▶Unifying Themes in the Communication Field

After reading about the many different areas in communication, you might think that the field is a collection of unrelated interests. That isn't accurate. Although there are distinct elements in the communication mosaic, common themes unify the diverse areas of the discipline, just as common colors and designs unify a tile mosaic. Three enduring concerns—symbolic activities, meaning, and ethics—unify the diverse areas of communication.

Symbolic Activities

Symbols are the basis of language, thinking, and nonverbal communication. Symbols are arbitrary, ambiguous, and abstract representations of other phenomena. For instance, a wedding band is a symbol of marriage in Western culture, *Julia* is a symbol for me (my name), and a smile is a symbol of friendliness. Symbols allow us to reflect on our experiences and ourselves. Symbols also allow us to share experiences with others, even if they have not had those experiences themselves. We will discuss symbols in greater depth in Chapters 4 and 5, which deal with verbal and nonverbal communication, respectively.

Meaning

Closely related to interest in symbols is the communication field's concern with meaning. The human world is a world of meaning. We don't simply exist, eat, drink, sleep, and behave. Instead, we imbue every aspect of our lives with significance, or meaning. When I feed my cat, Sadie, she eats her food and then returns to her feline adventures. However, we humans layer food and eating with meanings beyond the mere satisfaction of hunger. Food often symbolizes special events or commitments. For example, kosher products reflect commitment to Jewish heritage, turkey is commonly associated with commemorating the first Thanksgiving in the United States (although vegetarians symbolize their commitment by *not* eating turkey). Eggnog is a Christmas tradition, and mandel brot is a Hanukkah staple. Birthday cakes celebrate an individual, and we may fix special meals to express love to others.

Some families consider meals occasions to come together and share lives, whereas in other families meals are battlefields on which family tensions are played out. A meal can symbolize status (power lunches), romance (candles, wine), a personal struggle to stick to a diet, or an excuse to spend two hours talking with a friend. Humans imbue eating and other activities with meaning beyond their functional qualities. Our experiences gain significance as a result of the values and meanings we attach to them.

Because we are symbol users, we actively interpret events, situations, experiences, and relationships. We use symbols to name, evaluate, reflect on, and share experiences, ideas, and feelings. In fact, as Benita's commentary points out, when we give names to things, we change how we think about them. Through the process of communicating with others, we define our relationships. Do we have a friendship, or something else? How serious are we? Do we feel the same way about each other? Is this conflict irresolvable, or can we work it out and stay together?

▶ **Benita**

It's funny how important a word can be. Nick and I had been going out for a long time, and we really liked each other, but I didn't know if this was going to be long-term. Then we said we loved each other, and that changed how we saw each other and the relationship. Just using the word *love* transformed who we are.

To study communication, then, is to study how we use symbols to create meaning in our lives. As we interact with others, we build the meaning of friendship, team spirit, and organizational culture (Andersen, 1993; Wood, 1992a). Leslie Baxter says that "relationships can be regarded as webs of significance" spun as partners communicate (1987, p. 262). By extension, all human activities are webs of significance spun with symbols and meaning.

Ethics

A third theme that unifies the field of communication is concern with ethical dimensions of human interaction. As we have seen, ethics and communication is one area of study and teaching in the field. Yet interest in ethics is not confined to that single area. **Ethics** is a branch of philosophy that focuses on moral principles and codes of conduct. What is right? What is wrong? What makes something right or wrong? Communication inevitably involves ethical matters because people affect each other when they interact. Therefore, it's important to think seriously about what sort of moral guidelines we should follow in our communication and in our judgments of others' communication.

One ethical principle that is applicable to a broad range of situations is allowing others to make informed and willing choices. Adopting this principle discourages us from deceiving others by distorting evidence, withholding information, or coercing consent. Another important principle of ethical communication is respect for differences between people. Embracing this guideline deters us from imposing our ways and our values on others whose experiences and views of appropriate communication may differ from our own.

▶SUMMARY

Like most fields of study, communication includes many areas, which have evolved over a long and distinguished intellectual history. In this chapter we reviewed the more than 2,500-year history of the discipline of communication and noted how it has changed over time. We also discussed methods of conducting research that are used by scholars of communication.

The final section of the chapter described 10 areas that are part of the modern field of communication, and we noted that these areas are unified by abiding interests in symbolic activities, meanings, and ethics, as well as by a common interest in basic processes that form the foundations of personal, interpersonal, professional, and mediated communication. The foundations established in this chapter and in Chapter 1 prepare us for chapters that focus on basic processes and skills that pertain to a wide range of communication contexts.

Review, Reflect, Extend

The Key Concepts, For Further Reflection and Discussion questions, Recommended Resources, and Experience Communication Case Study that follow will help you review, reflect on, and extend the information and ideas presented in this chapter. A diverse selection of online resources is also available through ThomsonNOW. These resources include Speech Builder Express, InfoTrac College Edition, interactive videos, vMentor, and Thomson Audio Study Products.

Thomson NOW! is an online study system designed to help you put your time to the best use. After reading a chapter, take the NOW pre-test to identify concepts discussed in the chapter that you may not fully understand. Based on the results of this diagnostic test, the system will create a personalized study plan that directs you to specific learning resources and activities. To see if you're ready for an exam, take the NOW post-test to check your understanding.

For more information or to access this book's online resources, visit **http://www.thomsonedu.com**.

▶ KEY CONCEPTS

The terms below are defined in the chapter on the page number indicated, and they appear in alphabetical order, with definitions, in the Glossary, which begins on page 369. The book's online resources also include flash cards and crossword puzzles to help you learn these terms and the concepts they represent.

critical research methods, 29
ethics, 40
ethos, 24
interpersonal communication, 32

intrapersonal communication, 31
logos, 24
organizational culture, 34
pathos, 24

qualitative research methods, 29
quantitative research methods, 28
triangulation, 30

▶ FOR FURTHER REFLECTION AND DISCUSSION

The questions below can also be found among the book's online resources for this chapter, where you have the option of e-mailing your responses to your instructor, if required.

1. Review the areas of communication discussed in the section on the breadth of the communication field. In which areas do you feel most competent as a communicator? In which areas do you feel less competent? Identify one goal for improving your communication competence that you can keep in mind as you read the rest of this book.

2. This chapter provides an overview of the field of communication and notes how it has evolved in response to social changes and issues. What major changes do you anticipate in U.S. society in the next 50 years? What kinds of changes in the field of communication might be prompted by the social changes you anticipate?

▶ RECOMMENDED RESOURCES

1. Go to your library or an online database, such as InfoTrac College Edition, that provides full articles from academic journals. Read this article:

Elise Dallimore, Julie Hertenstein, and Marjorie Platt. (2004). Classroom participation and discussion effectiveness: Student-generated strategies. *Communication Education*, 53, 103–115.

After reading the article, answer the following questions:

a. What methods of research were used by the authors to conduct this study?

b. What teacher behaviors did students identify as most helpful in enhancing the quality of classroom discussion?

c. How might the findings of this study be applied to other contexts, such as communication in work groups and parent–child conversations?

2. Josina Makau and Ron Arnett's edited 1997 book, *Communication Ethics in an Age of Diversity* (Urbana: University of Illinois Press), provides very readable chapters that explore the roles of communication ethics in an era marked by social diversity.

Experience Communication Case Study

COMMUNICATION ETHICS

Jason Harris/© Wadsworth

The book's online resources include an interactive video of the communication situation featured in the case study scripted below. Apply what you've learned in this chapter by analyzing the case study, using the questions that follow the script as a guide. These questions are also available online with the video.

This case study differs from the others in this text because it is an actual interview, not an enacted fictional scenario. In an informal setting, Jenna Hiller asks Dr. Tim Muehlhoff some questions about communication and ethics, and Dr. Muehlhoff's responses elaborate on and clarify material covered in this chapter.

Student: In Chapter 2, Dr. Wood states that "ethical issues infuse all forms of communication." Can you explain what she means?

Professor: Well, in Chapter 2 she defines ethics as a branch of philosophy that's concerned with moral principles and conduct—what's right and what's wrong. But can you see how much personal choice is involved in that definition? Who gets to decide what is right and what is wrong? I was in Barnes & Noble a couple of months ago and saw a book called *What Would Machiavelli Do? The Ends Justify the Meanness.* Now, you may remember that Machiavelli was one of the most ruthless politicians, and he lived in the early 1500s. He believed that success was the goal, and you should get it however you wanted to. And in the book, this author says, "This book is for people with the courage to leave decency and kindness behind, and seize the future by the throat and have it cough up money, power, and superior office space." So if Machiavelli is your ethical guide, then, when giving a speech, make up statistics. Plagiarize part of it, and say that it's your speech. When it comes to interpersonal communication, win an argument at all costs. Manipulate a person's emotions. If they've confided information to you, go ahead and use their words against them. In small-group communication, ignore a particular person you don't agree with. Every time they start to talk, you just interrupt them. But you know, Machiavelli's not our only choice. What would our communication look like if we asked the question, "What would Gandhi do?" or "What would Martin Luther King Jr., do?" or "What would Jesus do?" How would that change how we communicate with people? We would choose what is right for everybody. We would choose to try to respect everybody. Machiavelli or Gandhi are some of the choices we have to make in all of our communication.

Student: I'm still not sure I understand what you mean. I don't see how listening and responding to others involves ethical choices.

Professor: Well, my favorite quote about listening comes from Reuel Howe's book, *The Miracle of Dialogue.* In it, he says, "I cannot hear you because of what I expect you to say." And it's true, isn't it? We often judge people prematurely. We form unethical stereotypes of people, and then we respond to the stereotype rather than the person. For instance, when I was teaching at UNC-Chapel Hill with Julia Wood, there was a colleague of ours who was heavily criticized for using gangsta rap lyrics in a commencement address. And I was one of the critics. Even though I had not heard the speech, I thought to myself, "How can you use lyrics that are filled with anger, racism, and sexism?"—until I actually sat in on his class and listened to his rationale. I found out that this professor did not condone violence or sexism. He did argue that there's a lot we can learn about individuals by listening to their music. And I remember him saying once, "Hear the violence in those songs and condemn it. Hear the sexism, and condemn it. But also hear the pain and the hopelessness, and respond to it." You see, I had formed a caricature of this man, a stereotype—and that's unethical. Ethical communication means I allow you to speak for yourself, and then I respond to what you say—but I don't put words in your mouth and conform you to the image I want you to have.

Student: Also in Chapter 2, Dr. Wood states that a principle for ethical communication is respecting differences between people. Am I supposed to just accept everyone and every value?

Professor: There's an old Jewish proverb that says, "It is folly and shame to speak before listening." The folly part I think we can understand. It's folly for me to respond to you if I don't know what you're saying. That's uninformed communication.

The second part deals with ethics. It is shameful for me to respond to you before I listen. In other words, I view you as an inferior. I don't even need to listen to your perspective before I respond to it. Ethical communication does not mean that I have to accept the views of every person. It does mean that all my communication needs to be informed, and I treat people as equals, not as people who are inferior to me. In Chapter 3, Julia talks about communication climates, which is the overall mood between two people when they communicate. Now imagine what that communication climate would be like if our communication was both informed and respectful.

▾ ▾

1. Dr. Tim Muehlhoff quoted the following statement from *The Miracle of Dialogue:* "I cannot hear you because of what I expect you to say." Recall some instances in your own life where you have been unable to hear what someone was saying because of your expectations and stereotypes of that person.

2. Dr. Muehlhoff also noted that he had seen a book entitled *What Would Machiavelli Do?* He then suggested there are many people we might pick as our ethical guides. Whom would you pick as your guide for ethical communication? Fill in the blank in this sentence: What would _____ do? What ethical principles for communication follow from your choice of an ethical guide?

3. What ethical choices did Dr. Muehlhoff make in his conversation with Jenna Hiller about the relevance of ethics to communication?

4. Review "The New Employee," the case study for Chapter 1. What ethical choices did the senior employee make in communicating with Toya?

3 Perceiving and Understanding

▶ **FOCUS QUESTIONS**

1. What processes are involved in perceiving?

2. What factors influence our perceptions?

3. How does the self-serving bias affect the accuracy of our perceptions?

4. Does mind reading help or hinder communication?

5. How can we use language to enhance skill in perceiving?

A year ago, Robbie and I adopted a young dog who had been abandoned by her former family. Our new puppy, whom we named Cassidy (which was quickly shortened to Cassie), seemed so small to us—she was fully grown and weighed just 35 pounds. Previously, we'd owned an Irish setter and a Lab mix who each weighed about 70 pounds, twice what Cassie weighed. A few weeks after Cassie joined our family, my 6-year-old nephew, Harrison, came to spend a week with us. I picked him up at the airport, and we drove home, chattering all the way. When I opened the door of our home and he stepped in, Cassie ran to meet the new person and shower him with kisses. "She's so big," Harrison shrieked as Cassie jumped on him, putting her paws on his shoulder so that her head was even with Harrison's. "She's a big, BIG dog," he announced. Because we were accustomed to dogs twice Cassie's size, and because Robbie and I are fully grown, Cassie seemed very small to us. But to a boy who weighed 45 pounds and was less than 4 feet tall, she seemed large! Our perceptions reflected our different experiences and even our physical sizes. Perceptions—and differences among people's perceptions—are major influences on human communication.

This chapter focuses on a basic communication process, perception, which is critical to our efforts to create meaning and thus to our communication. Perception is the process by which we notice and make sense of experience and stimuli around us. To explore the relationships between perception and communication, this chapter discusses three interrelated facets of perceiving and considers primary influences on how people perceive and why they sometimes differ in their perceptions. We'll conclude

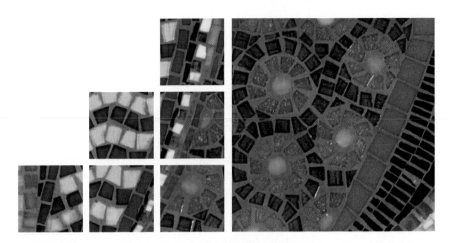

the chapter by identifying ways in which skillful perception can improve our effectiveness as communicators.

▶The Perception Process

Perception is the active process of selecting, organizing, and interpreting people, objects, events, situations, and activities. The first thing to notice in this definition is that perception is an active process. We are not passive receivers of what is "out there" in the external world. Instead, we select certain things to notice, and then we organize and interpret what we have selectively noticed. What anything means to us depends on which aspects of it we attend to and how we organize and interpret what we notice.

Perception and communication influence each other. Perception shapes our understanding of others' communication and the choices we make in our own communication. For example, if you perceive a co-worker as hostile, you are likely to communicate defensively or to minimize interaction. Communication also influences our perceptions of people and situations. The language and nonverbal behaviors that other people use affect our perceptions of their intelligence, friendliness, and so forth.

The second important aspect of the definition is that perception consists of three interrelated processes: selection, organization, and interpretation (Figure 3.1). These processes blend into one another. We organize perceptions even as we select what to perceive, and we interpret in an ongoing manner. Each process affects the other two. What we notice about people and situations influences how we interpret them. Also, our interpretation of a person or situation directs us to selectively notice certain, and not other, aspects of the person or setting.

Selection

Stop for a moment and notice what is going on around you right now. Is music playing in the background? Or do you perhaps hear several different kinds of music from different places? Is the room warm or cold, messy or clean, large or small, light or dark? Is laundry piled in the corner waiting to be washed?

Can you smell anything: food cooking, the odor of cigarette smoke, traces of cologne? Who else is in the room and nearby? Do you hear other

Figure 3.1 The Perception Process

conversations? Is a window open? Can you hear sounds of activities outside? Is it raining? Now, think about what's happening inside you. Are you tired or hungry? Do you have a headache or an itch anywhere? On what kind of paper is your book printed? Is the type large, small, easy to read?

Chances are that you weren't conscious of most of these phenomena when you began reading this chapter. Instead, you focused on reading and understanding the material in the chapter. You selectively attended to what you defined as important in this moment, and you were unaware of many other things going on around you. This is typical of how we live our lives. We can't attend to everything in our environment, because far too much is there, and most of it isn't relevant to us at any given time.

A number of factors influence which stimuli we notice. First, some qualities of external phenomena draw our attention. For instance, we notice things that **STAND OUT** because they are larger, more intense, or unusual. We're more likely to hear a loud voice than a soft one and to notice a bright shirt more than a drab one. We also pay attention to what matters to us, so out of a long list of messages that appear when you open your e-mail box, you're likely to first notice those from friends. Change also compels attention, which is why we become more attentive when a speaker shows a slide to enliven a speech or when a new person joins a dialogue on the Internet.

Sometimes, we deliberately influence what we notice by talking to ourselves. We tell ourselves to be alert when we have to drive while we're tired. We remind ourselves to speak loudly when we are addressing a large group without a microphone. We prompt ourselves not to interrupt during team discussions. We remind ourselves to stay in character when we have claimed an alternate identity in online chat rooms. These are examples of intrapersonal communication that helps us attend selectively to specific behaviors.

Education is a process of learning to name and pay attention to things we haven't previously noticed. Right now, you're learning to be more conscious of the selectiveness of your perceptions, so in the future you will notice your selectivity more. In English courses, you learn to recognize how authors craft characters and use words to create images. In on-the-job training, you learn what you are expected to notice and to do.

Our needs, interests, and motives influence what we choose to notice. If you're bored in your job, you're likely to notice ads for other jobs. If you are interested in politics, you're likely to pay attention to political stories in the news. If you've just broken up with a partner, you're more likely to notice attractive and available people than if you are in a satisfying relationship. Motives also explain the oasis phenomenon, in which thirsty people in a desert see an oasis although none is present. If we want something badly enough, we may perceive it when it doesn't exist.

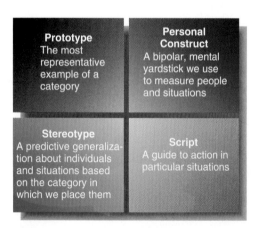

Figure 3.2 Cognitive Schemata

Organization

We don't perceive randomly; instead, we organize our perceptions in meaningful ways. **Constructivism** is a theory that holds that we organize and interpret experience by applying cognitive structures called **cognitive schemata,** or just **schemata** (the singular noun is *schema*). We rely on four schemata to make sense of phenomena: prototypes, personal constructs, stereotypes, and scripts (see Figure 3.2).

Prototypes **Prototypes** are knowledge structures that define the clearest or most representative examples of some category (Fehr, 1993). For example, you probably have a prototype of a great teacher, a true friend, and a superb team leader. You may also have prototypes of people in India or Afghanistan that are based on what you have witnessed in mass media. A prototype is an ideal, or best example, of a category. We use prototypes to define such exemplars: Jane represents confidence; Burt exemplifies a comfortable, casual friend; Ned is an ideal co-worker. The person who exemplifies a whole group, or category, is the category's prototype. We classify people by category by asking which of our prototypes they most closely resemble. We then consider how they measure up to the prototype, or ideal, of the category. Damion explains his prototype of a good friend.

▶ Damion

My ideal of a friend is my buddy Jackson. He stood by me when I got into a lot of trouble a couple of years ago. I got mixed up with some guys who used drugs, and I started using them. Pretty soon, the coach caught on to me, and he suspended me from the team. That made me feel like a total loser, and I got deeper into drugs. Jackson didn't give up on me, and he wouldn't let me give up either. He took me to a drug center and went with me every day for three weeks. He never turned away when I was sick or even when I cried most of one night when I was getting off the drugs. He just stood by me. Once I was straight, Jackson went with me to ask the coach about getting back on the team.

Prototypes are useful to us because they allow us to group people, events, and situations into broad categories. However, when our prototypes don't match those of others, we may run into problems. For example, if your prototype of an ideal team meeting is

What is your prototype of an effective leader?

© Amy Etra/PhotoEdit

joking around a lot with co-workers, and the team leader's prototype of an ideal meeting is getting down to business and staying on task, you may find your job on the line!

Personal Constructs A **personal construct** is a mental yardstick that allows us to measure a person or situation along a bipolar dimension of judgment (Kelly, 1955). Examples of personal constructs are *intelligent–not intelligent, kind–not kind,* and *trustworthy–not trustworthy.* How intelligent, kind, and trustworthy is a speaker, journalist, friend, or co-worker? Whereas prototypes help us decide into which broad category a person, situation, or event fits, personal constructs allow us to make more detailed assessments of particular qualities of phenomena we perceive. Nai Lee's commentary offers an example of a personal construct.

▶ Nai Lee

One of the ways I look at people is by whether they are individualistic or related to others. In Korea, we think of ourselves as members of families and communities. The emphasis on individuals was the first thing I noticed when I came to this country, and it is still an important way I look at people.

In any context, we rely on a limited set of personal constructs. If you are thinking about a person as a date, you're likely to rely on constructs such as *fun–not fun, intelligent–not intelligent,* and *attractive–not attractive.* When perceiving a co-worker, you're more likely to rely on constructs such as *reliable–not reliable, cooperative–not cooperative, experienced–not experienced,* and *motivated–not motivated.* Constructs such as *fair–not fair, knowledgeable–not knowledgeable,* and *interesting–not interesting* may guide your perceptions of teachers. We assess people according to the constructs we use, not according to all the constructs that *could* be used. Thus, we may not perceive qualities that are not highlighted by the constructs we apply. This reminds us that the processes of selecting and organizing interact to affect our perceptions.

Stereotypes A **stereotype** is a predictive generalization about a person or situation. Based on the category (established by prototypes) in which we place something and how it measures up against personal constructs we apply, we predict what it will do. For instance, if you define someone as a liberal, you might stereotype the person as likely to vote Democratic, to support social services, and to oppose the death penalty. You may have stereotypes of fraternity and sorority members, professors, athletes, and people from other cultures.

▶ Winowa

People have a stereotype of Native Americans. People who are not Native Americans think we are all alike—how we look, how we act, what we believe, what our traditions are. But that isn't true. The Crow and Cherokee are as different as people from Kenya and New York. Some tribes have a history of aggression and violence; others have traditions of peace and harmony. We worship different spirits and have different tribal customs. All these differences are lost when people stereotype us all as Native Americans.

Stereotypes don't necessarily reflect actual similarities among phenomena that you group into a single category, as Winowa's commentary illustrates. Our stereotypes may keep us from seeing differences between people we have grouped into a category, as the FYI box on this page demonstrates.

Stereotypes may be accurate or inaccurate. In some cases, we have incorrect understandings of a group, and in other cases some members of a group don't conform to the behaviors we think are typical of the group as a whole. Although we need stereotypes in order to predict what will happen, we should remember that they are selective, subjective, and not necessarily complete or accurate. In her commentary, Phyllis describes how a stereotype affects her.

▶ Phyllis

I'll tell you what stereotype really gets to me: the older student. I'm 38 and working on a B.A., and I'm tired of being treated like a housewife who's dabbling in courses. Some students treat me like their mother, not a peer. And some faculty are even worse. One professor told me that I shouldn't worry about grades because I didn't have to plan a career like the younger students. Well, I am planning a career, I am a student, and I am serious about my work.

Scripts The final cognitive schema we use to organize perceptions is the script, which is a guide to action. A **script** is a sequence of activities that spells out how we and others are expected to act in a specific situation. If you run into a friend who is with someone you don't know, and your friend says, "Hi, this is Ben," you don't have to think about what you are supposed to say; your meeting-new-person script tells you that you should say, "Hi, I'm (your name)" and perhaps smile or offer to shake hands. Although we're often unaware of them, scripts guide many of our daily activities. You have a script for greeting casual acquaintances as you walk around campus ("Hey, how ya doing?" "Fine." "See ya."). You have scripts for checking in with friends online (<hi. where r u?> <gotta take a call. brb.>) (Carl, 2006). You also have scripts for talking with professors, engaging in interviews, and communicating online. Scripts organize perceptions into lines of action.

Dianne Holmberg and Samantha MacKenzie (2002) studied scripts for dating relationships. They found that partners who see their relationship as consistent with their perceptions of normative scripts for dating have more positive evaluations of their relationships than do partners who perceive inconsistency between most people's perceptions of how dating relationships progress and

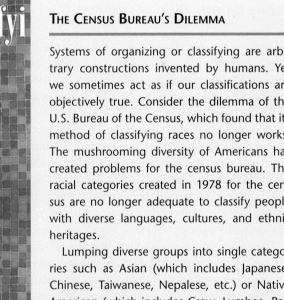

D I V E R S I T Y

THE CENSUS BUREAU'S DILEMMA

Systems of organizing or classifying are arbitrary constructions invented by humans. Yet we sometimes act as if our classifications are objectively true. Consider the dilemma of the U.S. Bureau of the Census, which found that its method of classifying races no longer works. The mushrooming diversity of Americans has created problems for the census bureau. The racial categories created in 1978 for the census are no longer adequate to classify people with diverse languages, cultures, and ethnic heritages.

Lumping diverse groups into single categories such as Asian (which includes Japanese, Chinese, Taiwanese, Nepalese, etc.) or Native American (which includes Crow, Lumbee, Paiute, etc.) is inappropriate. The traditional classifications count Middle Easterners as White, and Alaskans as Alaskan Natives rather than as people born in the United States. Another deficiency of the standard categories is that they don't acknowledge multiracial identities, which many citizens have.

What script do you have for a dating relationship?

Sizing Up Others

Pay attention to the cognitive schemata you use the next time you meet a new person. First, notice how you classify the person. Do you categorize her or him as a potential friend, date, co-worker, and so on? Identify your prototype of the category into which you place the person.

Next, identify the constructs you use to assess the person. Do you focus on physical constructs (*attractive–not attractive*), mental constructs (*intelligent–not intelligent*), psychological constructs (*secure–not secure*), or interpersonal constructs (*available–not available*)? Would different constructs be prominent if you used a different prototype to classify the person?

Third, note how you stereotype the person. According to the prototype and constructs you've applied, what do you expect him or her to do? Would your expectations differ if you had placed him or her in a different category?

Finally, identify your script, or how you expect interaction to unfold between you according to the prototype, personal constructs, stereotypes, and scripts that you applied.

SHARPEN YOUR SKILL

what is happening in their own relationship. Similarly, Sandra Metts (2006) has identified consistent scripts for heterosexual flirting.

Prototypes, personal constructs, stereotypes, and scripts are cognitive schemata that organize our thinking about people and situations. We use them to make sense of experience and to predict how we and others will act. The Sharpen Your Skill box on this page invites you to reflect on how your cognitive schemata affect your perceptions of others.

Interpretation

To interpret experiences, we ask why something happens or why someone says or does or doesn't do a particular thing. **Interpretation** is the subjective process of creating explanations for what we observe and experience. If you have ever been around a young child, then you know that "Why?" is an incessant question: Why is the sky blue? Why are you angry with me? Why do we have to go to the dentist? Why can't I have the toy I want? Children's interest in *why* is a search to figure out what causes things to happen and people to act as they do. Although adults are perhaps more sophisticated than children, we are no less interested in figuring out why things happen and why people behave as they do.

Attributions Our quest to figure out the why of things brings us to the concept of **attribution,** which is the act of explaining why something happens or why a person acts a particular way. (For the classic research in this area, see Heider, 1958; Kelley, 1967.) We *attribute* our own and others' behaviors to causes.

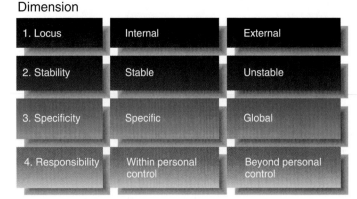

Dimension

Figure 3.3 THE DIMENSIONS OF ATTRIBUTION

Attributions have four dimensions. The first is the *internal–external locus:* the attribution of a person's behavior to internal factors ("He's short tempered") or external factors ("The traffic jam frustrated him"). The second dimension is *stability,* the explanation of actions as the result of stable, enduring factors that won't change over time ("She's a nervous person"; "This job is always stressful") or variable (unstable) temporary factors ("She's nervous right now because of a big deal she's closing"; "This is a stressful period at work"). The third dimension is *specificity,* the explanation of actions as the result of global factors ("She's intelligent") or specific factors ("She's gifted at math"). Finally, the dimension of *control* is the ascribing of responsibility for actions either to people themselves ("She doesn't try to control her temper") or to factors beyond their personal control ("She has a chemical imbalance"). Figure 3.3 illustrates the three dimensions of attribution.

The Self-Serving Bias Although we need explanations of our own and others' behaviors, the explanations, or attributions, we develop aren't necessarily accurate. Research shows that we tend to construct attributions that serve our personal interests (Hamachek, 1992; Sypher, 1984). This phenomenon is known as the **self-serving bias.** Thus, we are inclined to attribute our positive actions and our successes to internal and stable factors. We're also likely to claim that good results come about because of the personal control we exerted. In her commentary, Chandra reflects on a self-serving attribution.

▶ Chandra

I wait tables to make money for school. It used to be that when I didn't make good tips, I would say that the customers were cheap or in bad moods or my manager assigned me to a slow station. When I made good tips, I always thought that it was because I am such a considerate server. Then we got a new manager, who told me that I made better tips when I was feeling good. He pointed out that I was really friendly and attentive to customers when I was in a good mood but that I could be careless when I felt down.

You might attribute making an A on a test to being a smart person (internal, stable, global) who studies hard (personal control). On the other hand, we tend to avoid

IT'S NEVER OUR FAULT!

Have you ever had an argument with your boyfriend or girlfriend and thought later that your partner's behavior was inappropriate, inconsiderate, or mean? Have you also thought that your own behavior was justified and appropriate? If so, you're in good company.

In 1999, Astrid Schutz reported her study of married couples in southwest Germany. Relying on qualitative methods, Schutz independently interviewed each spouse about a particular marital conflict. Schutz then coded the interviews to learn how spouses perceived the conflict process. She interpreted the data to discover who was labeled as the person who did or said something that was objectionable or failed to do or say something that should have been done or said.

Schutz also coded interviews to reveal who each partner labeled as the person who objected to the behavior or lack of behavior. Finally, Schutz coded each person's account of the conflict, using 27 dimensions that described attributions, needs, and feelings. She then used chi-square tests (a statistical method that measures the significance of differences) to measure the differences in partners' descriptions of conflicts.

Schutz found that each person tended to describe the conflict in a manner that faulted his or her partner. Most accounts labeled the partner's behavior or lack of behavior as responsible for the conflict. She also found that most people described their own behaviors as reasonable, appropriate, well-intentioned, and justified in light of the other's behavior. On the other hand, most people described their partners' behaviors as unfair, irrational, inconsiderate, ill intentioned, and unjustified.

This study adds support to the well-documented tendency of people to engage in self-serving biases when they interpret their own and others' actions.

taking responsibility for negative actions and failures and instead attribute them to external and unstable events that are beyond personal control. To explain a failing grade on a test, you might say that you did poorly because the professor (external) put a lot of tricky questions on that particular test (unstable, specific) so that regardless of how hard you studied, you couldn't do well (outside personal control). The self-serving bias can distort our perceptions, leading us to take excessive credit for what we do well and to deny responsibility for our failings. It can also lead us to judge others less kindly than ourselves (Manusov, 2006; Schutz, 1999; Sedikides et al., 1998). The FYI box on this page shows how the self-serving bias may shape our perceptions of arguments.

In summary, perception involves three interrelated processes. The first, selection, involves noticing certain things and ignoring others within the total context. The second process is organization, wherein we use prototypes, personal constructs, stereotypes, and scripts to order what we have selectively perceived. Finally, we engage in interpretation to make sense of the perceptions we have gathered and organized. Attributions are a primary way we explain what we and others do. And although we've discussed each process separately, they interact continually. Thus, our interpretations shape the knowledge schemata we use to organize experiences, and how we organize perceptions affects what we notice and interpret. We're now ready to consider some factors that influence what and how we perceive.

▶INFLUENCES ON PERCEPTION

A few years ago, I went to a neighborhood picnic at which a neighbor who did not attend was discussed. The absent person had been behaving oddly ever since he moved into our neighborhood. He had thrown a rock at one person's dog, had been seen going into another neighbor's house when nobody was home, had been verbally abusive to several members of the community, and had shot squirrels and birds, which nobody else in the neighborhood did.

At the picnic, neighbors were sharing stories of what he had done and what it meant. A woman who is a psychologist ventured the opinion that he was suffering from depression and perhaps guilt, which had overcome his judgment. The legal aspects of his behavior were the focus of an attorney's comments, who observed that the man could be arrested for breaking and entering and verbal harassment. A third person, who had recently left an abusive partner, was afraid that our neighbor posed a threat to all of us. Those of us who have dogs and cats were concerned that the neighbor might shoot our pets. As this example illustrates, people don't always perceive in the same ways. How each of us perceived our neighbor was shaped by many factors in our backgrounds, our training, and our individual interests.

Physiological Factors

The most obvious reason perceptions vary among people is that we differ in our sensory abilities and physiologies. The five senses are not the same for all of us. Music that one person finds deafening is barely audible to another. Salsa that is painfully hot to one diner may seem mild to someone else. On a given day on my campus, students wear everything from shorts and sandals to jackets, a sign that they have different sensitivities to cold. Some people have better vision than others, and some are color blind. These differences in sensory abilities affect our perceptions.

Our physiological states also influence perception. If you are tired, stressed, or sick, you're likely to perceive things more negatively than when you are well and rested. For instance, a playful insult from a friend might anger you if you were feeling down but might not bother you if you felt good. Each of us has a biorhythm, which influences how alert we are at different times of day. I'm a morning person, so that's when I prefer to teach classes and write. I am less alert and less creative later in the day.

Other aspects of physiology affect perceptions. Recently, a friend came to my house to visit. We decided to brew a pot of coffee, and I asked her to get a bag of coffee beans from a shelf in my kitchen. She looked at the shelf and said, "I can't reach it." The shelf never seemed high to me, but I am 5' 8", and she is 5' 2". What seems high or tall to us differs because of our own heights. The cartoon on page 54 makes the same point humorously by showing that an adult and child have different perceptions of large icicles.

Expectations

Imagine that a friend tells you she wants you to meet a person whom she describes as "one of the coolest people I've ever met: He's funny and considerate and so interested in other people. You'll find him really easy to talk to and lots of fun." Chances are you would expect to like the new person and would in fact perceive the good qualities your friend led you to expect. If your friend had instead said, "This guy is a real drag. He's always cracking bad jokes, and he's self-centered," you might expect not to like the man, and you might see only his shortcomings.

Based on a series of studies, John Bargh (1997, 1999) reports that how we act may be affected by subliminal priming of expectations. In one study, participants were told that they would be taking two tests. The researcher told each participant to go into a room and take a test and then to come out of the room and find the researcher to progress to the second test. One-half of the participants then took a test that presented them with a group of terms related to politeness. The other half of the participants took a test that presented them with a group of terms related to rudeness.

When participants finished the test and went to look for the researcher, they found the researcher talking with another person. Of the participants who had worked with the terms related to rudeness, 63% interrupted the researcher's conversation, but only 17% of the participants who had worked with politeness terms interrupted the conversation. Apparently, their perceptions of appropriate behavior were affected by exposure to words that made rudeness or politeness salient to them.

Expectations affect our perceptions in a variety of communication situations. If we are told in advance that a new person on the job is "a real team player," we're likely to notice the new employee's cooperative behaviors and not likely to see competitive or self-serving behaviors that the new person may also present. If we're forewarned that a speaker tends to distort facts, we're likely to perceive misrepresentations in the speech. On the other hand, if we're told that the speaker is trustworthy, we may listen less critically and not perceive any slanting or distortions. Our sense of time has been radically reshaped by communication technologies that lead us to expect extremely quick exchanges. Just a decade ago, most people expected replies to business correspondence within a week to 10 days. Now, many people expect nearly instant responses, and we grumble if a friend isn't online when we IM her or him or if an e-mail message isn't answered for several hours.

The influence of expectations on communication is the basis of **positive visualization,** which is a technique used to enhance success in a variety of situations by teaching people to visualize themselves positively. According to psychologists, positive visualization works because we act as we see ourselves. Businesses coach managers to visualize successful negotiations and meetings (Lau, 1989). Athletes learn to imagine playing well, and those who engage in positive visualization improve their athletic performance (Porter & Foster, 1986).

Positive visualization is also used to reduce speaking anxiety by guiding apprehensive speakers through imagined positive speaking experiences. This technique allows people to form a mental picture of themselves as effective speakers and to then enact that mental picture in actual speaking situations (Hamilton, 1996). Researchers report that positive visualization is especially effective in reducing chronic communication apprehension (Ayres & Hopf, 1990; Bourhis & Allen, 1992). The goal of positive visualization is to create detailed positive images of yourself in communication situations. Such visualizations encourage positive expectations of your actual communication. The Sharpen Your Skill box on page 55 shows you how to use positive visualization to build positive expectations of yourself as a public speaker.

Our expectations box situations, events, and others so that we can make reasonable anticipations. What happens when our expectations are violated? That's the ques-

tion asked by **expectancy violation theory.** Research shows that when our expectations are violated, we become more cognitively alert as we struggle to understand and cope with unexpected behaviors or events (Afifi & Metts, 1998; Bevan, 2003; Burgoon, 1993).

Three aspects of a violation of expectations influence how we will interpret it (Afifi & Metts, 1998). First, our interpretations are affected by whether the violation is positive (someone gives you a gift that you had not anticipated) or negative (your supervisor, whom you thought was very supportive, yells at you). Second, our interpretations are influenced by the extent to which the behavior deviates from expected behavior. If your supervisor simply withheld positive feedback, that would be a lesser violation of your expectations than if the supervisor criticized you in front of your co-workers. Third, our interpretations are affected by the impact of the violation on a relationship. Think about the different impacts on a dating relationship if the person you are dating doesn't call when she or he promises and if she or he dates your best friend.

Visualizing Positive Communication

First, imagine yourself speaking to three friends about a topic that matters to you. Now, visualize your friends as nodding and asking questions that tell you they are interested in what you say. Notice that they are looking intently at you, and their postures are attentive.

Now, imagine that someone you don't know joins your friends, and you continue speaking. It's okay if you feel a little anxious, but visualize the stranger as becoming attentive to your communication. Notice how the new person looks at you with admiration.

Next, imagine that you are asked to speak on the same topic to a student group, and you agree. Visualize the room in which you speak: It is a small conference room in the campus student union. The room seems warm and comfortable. When you enter, 20 people are there to hear you. Notice that they smile when you walk to the front of the room. See how they look at you expectantly because they are interested in your topic.

Visualize yourself starting your talk. You begin by telling the listeners that, like them, you are a student. Notice that they nod and acknowledge the connection. Feel yourself relaxing and feeling confident. Then, you tell them what you will cover in your talk. Notice how your words flow easily and smoothly. See the nods and smiles of your listeners. As you speak, they act interested and seem impressed by your knowledge. When you are through, the listeners break into spontaneous applause.

SHARPEN YOUR SKILL

Cognitive Abilities

In addition to physiological, cultural, and social influences, perception is shaped by our cognitive abilities. How elaborately we think about situations and people, and the extent of our knowledge of others, affect how we select, organize, and interpret experiences.

Cognitive Complexity People differ in the number and type of knowledge schemata they use to organize and interpret people and situations. **Cognitive complexity** is the number of personal constructs used (remember, personal constructs are bipolar dimensions of judgment), how abstract they are, and how elaborately they interact to shape perceptions. Most children have fairly simple cognitive systems. They rely on few schemata, focus more on concrete constructs (*tall–not tall*) than abstract psychological ones (*secure–not secure*), and often don't perceive relationships between different perceptions (How is security related to extroversion?).

Many adults have greater cognitive complexity, which affects the accuracy of perceptions. The older we get, the richer is our perspective for perceiving situations and people. Thus, compared with a person of 20, someone who is 60 has a more complex fund of experiences on which to draw in perceiving. Throughout my 20s, I was easily

© Jeff Greenberg/PhotoEdit

One gift of growing older is enriched perspective. What might these people be able to share that two 20-year-olds cannot?

upset when my classes didn't go well or when a friend and I argued. Often, I became disheartened because I perceived these as significant problems. In my mid-30s, my father died. After his death, a less-than-perfect class or a minor argument with a friend didn't acutely distress me, because I had a very different perspective on what a serious problem was.

The extent of discrimination that is still experienced by women, minorities, and gays and lesbians understandably discourages many college students. I am more hopeful than some because I have seen significant changes in my lifetime. When I attended college, women and minorities were not admitted on an equal basis with Caucasian men, and almost all gays and lesbians concealed their sexual orientations. When I entered the job market, there were few laws to protect women, minorities, and gays and lesbians against discrimination in hiring, pay, and advancement. The substantial progress made during my life leads me to hold optimistic perceptions about society's ability to further alleviate the inequities that still exist.

Cognitive complexity influences our perceptions of others. If you can think of people only as good or bad, you have limited ways of perceiving others. Similarly, people who focus on concrete data tend to have less sophisticated understandings than people who also perceive psychological data. For example, you might notice that a person is attractive, tells jokes, and talks a lot. At a more abstract psychological level, you might infer that the behaviors you observe reflect a secure, self-confident personality. This is a more sophisticated explanation because it includes perceptions of why the person acts as she or he does.

What if you later find out that the person is quiet in classes? Someone with low cognitive complexity would have difficulty integrating the new information with earlier observations, would likely either dismiss the new information because it doesn't fit or replace the former perception with the more recent data and redefine the person as shy. A more cognitively complex person would integrate all the information into a coherent account. Perhaps a cognitively complex person would interpret the person as more confident in social situations than in academic ones. Research shows that cognitively complex people are flexible in interpreting complicated phenomena and are able to integrate new information into their thinking about people and situations. People who are less cognitively complex tend to ignore information that doesn't fit their impressions or to throw out old ideas and replace them with new impressions (Crockett, 1965; Delia, Clark, & Switzer, 1974). Either way, they screen out some of the nuances and inconsistencies that are part of human nature.

Person-Centeredness **Person-centeredness** is the ability to perceive another as a unique individual. When we perceive distinctions between people, we can adapt our communication to particular individuals. Person-centeredness is linked to cognitive complexity. People who are cognitively complex are able to perceive others and situations in more comprehensive and integrated ways than are less cognitively complex people. This allows them to adapt their communication to particular listeners (Zorn, 1991). Thus, an effective politician may adopt a different speaking style and emphasize different topics when talking with elderly citizens, elementary school children, members of unions, and business executives. Skillful group leaders recognize and adapt their communication to differences in members' abilities, needs, and so forth. When chatting online, we use common shorthand (for instance, *brb, lol*) with people we know understand it, as Emma points out.

▶ **Emma**

I talk differently when I'm e-mailing my parents and aunt than when I'm chatting online with friends. My parents and aunt don't know a lot of standard online lingo like *myob* [mind your own business], *OMG* [oh my gosh] or abbreviations like *r* for *are* and *u* for *you*. It takes more time to explain them to the family than it takes to just spell everything out.

To adapt communication to others, we must understand something about them. In relationships that aren't highly personal, communicators sometimes tailor messages to the general characteristics of groups. For example, more educated people tend to be more critical and better informed, so effective speakers include strong evidence and show respect for listeners' knowledge when addressing people with high levels of education. Because uncertainty and change foster anxiety, effective managers communicate reassurance and provide maximum information to subordinates during times of organizational change. To be effective in a job interview, an interviewee should research the history and image of the company to find out what the company looks for in new employees.

We have different degrees of insight into people with whom we interact. You need to know your intimates well to create satisfying relationships; you need to know professors and co-workers less well but well enough to work with them; you need to know clerks only well enough to transact business. As we get to know someone better, we gain insight into how he or she differs from others in their group ("Rob's not like other political activists"; "Ellen's more interested in people than most computer science majors are"). The more we interact with someone and the greater the variety of experiences we have together, the more knowledge we gain about their motives, feelings, and behaviors. As we come to understand others as individuals, we fine-tune our perceptions of them. Consequently, we rely less on stereotypes to perceive them.

Person-centeredness is not the same as empathy. **Empathy** is the ability to feel *with* another person—to feel what he or she feels in a situation. Feeling with another is an emotional response that some scholars believe is not really possible. Our feelings tend to be guided by our emotional tendencies and experiences, so it may be impossible to feel precisely what another person feels. However, it is possible to recognize others as unique persons, to identify connections between us and them, and to adapt our communication to their frames of reference (Muehlhoff, 2006). In his commentary, Steve explains how he developed person-centeredness with his girlfriend, Sherry.

▶ **Steve**

You really have to know somebody on an individual basis to know what they like and want. When I first started dating Sherry, I sent her red roses to let her know I thought she was special. That's the "lovers' flower," right? It turns out there were zillions of red roses at her father's funeral. Now, they make Sherry sad because they remind her he's dead. I also took her chocolates once, before I found out that she's allergic to chocolate. By now I know what she likes, but my experience shows that the general rules don't always apply to individuals.

When we take the perspective of another person, we try to grasp his or her perceptions and meanings. To do this, we have to suspend our own perspective long enough to enter the world of another person. This allows us to gain some insight into that person's point of view so we can communicate more effectively with him or her. At a later point in interaction, we may choose to express our perspective or disagree with the other person's views. This is appropriate and important in honest communication, but voicing our views is not a substitute for the equally important skill of attempting to understand another's perspective.

Social Roles

Our social roles also shape our perceptions and our communication. Both the training we receive to fulfill a role and the actual demands of the role affect what we notice and how we interpret, evaluate, and respond to it. Because I'm a teacher, my perceptions of classes focus on how interested students seem, whether they appear to have read assigned material, and whether what they're learning is useful in their lives. Students have told me that they think about classes in terms of number and difficulty of tests, whether papers are required, and whether the professor is interesting. We have different ways of perceiving classes. When I am consulting with attorneys, I am more careful to state evidence for the ideas and suggestions I offer than I am in casual conversations with friends.

People's professions influence what they notice and how they think and act. In the earlier example, members of my community perceived our odd

---

Noticing Individualism

How do the individualistic values of our culture influence our perceptions and activities? Check it out by observing the following:

▸ How is seating arranged in restaurants? Are there large communal eating areas or private tables and booths for individuals or small groups?

▸ How are living spaces arranged? How many people live in the average house? Do families share homes?

▸ How many people share a car in your family? How many cars are there in the United States?

The United States is a fiercely individualistic country that expects and rewards personal initiative and regards each person as unique and important. Other cultures, including Hispanic and Asian ones, are more collectivist and define identity in terms of membership in family and community rather than individuality. Because families are more valued in collectivist cultures, elders are given great respect and care. Rather than perceiving themselves as autonomous, as is typical in cultures that value **individualism,** people in communal cultures tend to think of themselves as members of and accountable to groups.

Differences between collectivist and individualistic cultures are also evident in child-care policies. More communal countries have policies that reflect the value they place on families. In every developed country except the United States, new parents, including adoptive parents, receive a period of paid parental leave, and some countries provide nearly a year's paid leave (Douglas, 2004; Wood, 2007).

SHARPEN YOUR SKILL

neighbor differently because of our distinct professional roles, as well as other factors. The attorney in the group focused on the legal—or illegal—nature of the neighbor's behavior, and the psychologist's training led her to perceive his behaviors as evidence of emotional problems.

Membership in Cultures and Social Communities

Membership in a culture influences perceptions. A **culture** consists of beliefs, values, understandings, practices, and ways of interpreting experience that a number of people share (Klopf, 1991). In addition to an overall culture, people may belong to social communities that shape their experiences, perspectives, and knowledge. A **social community** is a group of people who are part of an overall society (for example, America) but also distinct from the overall society in that they hold values, understandings, and practices that are not shared by people outside the group. Gender, race, religion, and sexual orientation are examples of criteria that may indicate the existence of a social community and may affect how members of the community act—including how they communicate.

The overall culture to which we belong also influences our perceptions. Western culture's emphasis on technology and its offspring, speed, lead us to expect things to happen fast—almost instantly. Whether it's instant coffee, instant messages, or instantly available digital photos, we live at an accelerated pace. We express-mail letters, fax memos, e-mail notes, jet across the country, and microwave meals. In countries such as Nepal, Belize, and Mexico, life proceeds at a more leisurely pace, and people spend more time talking, relaxing, and engaging in low-key activities. The Sharpen Your Skill box on page 58 invites you to trace how one American value, individualism, is reflected in cultural practices and everyday behaviors.

In summary, differences based on physiology, expectations, cognitive abilities, social roles, and membership in cultures and social communities affect how we perceive others and experiences. By extension, all these influences on perception affect how we communicate.

▶GUIDELINES FOR IMPROVING SKILL IN PERCEIVING

In the final pages of this chapter, we identify four guidelines for enhancing skills in perceiving people and situations in ways that enhance your understanding of them and facilitate effective communication.

Avoid Mind Reading

Because perception is subjective, people differ in what they notice and in the meaning they attribute to it. One of the most common problems in communication is **mind reading,** which in this sense means assuming we understand what another person thinks or feels. When we mind read, we act as if we know what's on someone else's mind, and this can get us into trouble. For example, we can misinterpret a co-worker's absence from meetings if we assume that it signals disinterest instead of competing commitments. Mind reading is also a common cause of tension between spouses (Dickson, 1995; Gottman, 1993).

Consider a few examples of the problems mind reading can cause. One person might assume a friend was angry because the friend hasn't responded to e-mail or instant messages for 24 hours. This guess could well be wrong—the friend might be preoccupied or might have a malfunctioning Internet connection. Mind reading also occurs when we say or think, "I know he's upset" (Has he said he is upset?) or "She doesn't care about me anymore" (maybe she is too preoccupied or worried to be attentive). In actuality, we seldom really know what others think, feel, or perceive. When we mind read, we impose our perspectives on others instead of allowing them to say what they think. This can cause misunderstandings and resentment because most of us prefer to speak for ourselves.

Check Perceptions with Others

The second guideline follows directly from our insight that mind reading is generally inadvisable. Because perceptions are subjective, checking our perceptions with others is a good idea. In the earlier example, we could ask, "Why didn't you respond?" Rather than assuming a friend is angry, it might be valuable to ask, "Are you angry with me?" It's especially important to check perceptions when communicating online, because we don't have access to many of the nonverbal cues that help us interpret face-to-face communication. Sarcasm, irony, and other forms of communication may not be obvious online. Checking perceptions enhances clarity between people and invites productive dialogue, not blame and defensiveness.

Perception checking is an important communication skill because it helps people arrive at mutual understandings of each other and their interaction. To check perceptions, first state what you have noticed. For example, you might say, "Lately, you've seemed less pleased with my work." Then, you check whether the other perceives the same thing: "Have you felt less satisfied with my work?" Finally, it's appropriate to invite the other person to help you understand her or his behavior. So in the example, if the other person agrees that he or she is less pleased with your work, you could say, "Can you give me some insight into what, specifically, is unsatisfactory?" If the other person doesn't agree that she or he is less pleased with your work, a useful question might be, "Is there some reason why you've given me less feedback and not offered me additional assignments?"

When checking perceptions, it's important to use a tentative tone rather than a dogmatic or accusatory one. This minimizes defensiveness and encourages good discussion. Just let the other person know that you are perceiving something and would like that person to clarify his or her perceptions of what is happening and what it means. The

---

Perception Checking

To gain skill in perception checking (and all communication behaviors), you need to practice. Try this:

1. Monitor your tendencies to mind read, especially in established relationships in which you feel you know your partners well.

2. The next time you catch yourself mind reading, stop. Instead, tell the other person what you are noticing and invite her or him to explain how she or he perceives what's happening. First, find out whether your partner agrees with you about what you noticed. Second, if you agree, find out how your partner interprets and evaluates what is happening.

3. Engage in perception checking for two or three days so that you have lots of chances to see what happens. When you've done that, reflect on the number of times your mind reading was inaccurate.

4. Think about how your perception checking affected interaction with your friends and romantic partners.

SHARPEN YOUR SKILL

Sharpen Your Skill feature on the preceeding page provides guidance for developing skill in checking perceptions.

Distinguish Facts from Inferences and Judgments

Effective communicators recognize the difference between factual statements and nonfactual statements such as inferences and judgments. A fact is based on observation or proof. For instance, "The student, Taylor, is late to class most days" is a factual statement. An **inference** is a deduction that goes beyond what you know or assume to be a fact. For instance, if Taylor's teacher has known other students who were late to class because they didn't care about the class, the teacher might generalize from them to infer, "Taylor doesn't care about this class." Note that the inference goes beyond facts that the teacher knows about Taylor as an individual.

A **judgment** is a belief or opinion that is based on observations, feelings, assumptions, or other phenomena that are not facts. In our example, the teacher might judge that "Taylor is an irresponsible student." But judging Taylor ,as irresponsible goes beyond the facts. Taylor's lateness to class may be due to a work shift that ends right before the class. The teacher might treat Taylor differently if a work shift, rather than irresponsibility, explained the tardiness. To communicate effectively, we need to avoid mistaking nonfactual statements for factual ones. The Sharpen Your Skill box above allows you to check your ability to distinguish facts from inferences and judgments.

It's easy to confuse inferences with facts when we use language that makes inferences and judgments appear to be factual. When we say, "This person is rude," we've made a statement that sounds factual, and we may then perceive it as factual when it really isn't. To avoid this tendency, substitute a more tentative word for *is*. For instance, "This person seems rude" and "This person may be rude" are more tentative statements that keep us from treating an inference or judgment as a fact. The Sharpen Your Skill box that appears to the right allows you to develop your skill in using tentative language.

Monitor the Self-Serving Bias

We discussed the self-serving bias earlier in this chapter. You'll recall that it involves attributing our successes and nice behaviors to internal, stable qualities

© Rob Lewine/Corbis

Effective teamwork requires members to check perceptions with each other.

that we control and attributing our failures and bad behaviors to external, unstable factors beyond our control. Because this bias can distort perceptions, we need to monitor it carefully. **Monitoring** is the process of calling behaviors or other phenomena to our attention so that we can observe and regulate them. Try to catch yourself in the act of explaining away your failures or adverse behaviors as not your fault and taking personal credit for accomplishments that were helped along by luck or situational factors.

Monitoring the self-serving bias also has implications for how we perceive others. Just as we tend to judge ourselves generously, we may judge others harshly. Monitor your perceptions to see whether you attribute others' successes and admirable actions to external factors beyond their control and their shortcomings and blunders to internal factors they can (should) control. If you do this, substitute more generous explanations for others' behaviors, and notice how that affects your perceptions of them. The FYI box on this page discusses research that links different attributional tendencies to different levels of satisfaction with personal relationships. Words crystallize perceptions. Until we label an experience, it remains nebulous and less than fully formed in our thinking. Only when we name our feelings and thoughts do we have a clear way to describe and think about them. But just as words crystallize experiences, they can freeze thought. Once we label our perceptions, we may respond to our labels rather than to the actual phenomena.

ATTRIBUTION PATTERNS AND RELATIONSHIP SATISFACTION

Investigations have shown that happy and unhappy couples have distinct attribution styles (Bradbury & Fincham, 1990; Fletcher & Fincham, 1991; Graham & Conoley, 2006; McNulty & Karney, 2001). Happy couples make relationship-enhancing attributions. Such people attribute nice things a partner does to internal, stable, and global reasons. "She got the film for us because she is a good person who always does sweet things for us." They attribute unpleasant actions by a partner to external, unstable, and specific factors. "He yelled at me because all the stress of the past few days made him short with everyone."

Unhappy couples use reverse attribution patterns. They explain nice actions as resulting from external, unstable, and specific factors. "She got the tape because she had some extra time today." They see negative actions as stemming from internal, stable, and global factors. "He yelled at me because he is a nasty person who never shows any consideration to anybody else." Negative attributions encourage pessimistic views and sap motivation to improve a relationship. Whether positive or negative, attributions may be self-fulfilling prophecies.

▶SUMMARY

In this chapter, we've discussed perception, which is a basic communication process. As we have learned, perceiving involves selecting, organizing, and interpreting experiences. These three facets of the perception process are not separate in practice; instead, they interact such that each affects the others.

What we selectively notice affects how we organize and interpret phenomena. At the same time, our interpretations influence what we notice in the world around us. Selection, organization, and interpretation interact continually in the process of perception. Our sensory capacities and physiological conditions affect what we perceive. In addition, expectations, cognitive abilities, social roles, and cultural context influence how we perceive experiences and how we communicate with ourselves and others.

Skillful perception enhances communication. We discussed four guidelines for enhancing skills in perceiving. First, because people perceive differently, we should avoid mind reading. Extending this, we discussed the importance of checking perceptions, which involves stating how we perceive something and asking how another person perceives it. A third guideline is to distinguish facts from inferences in our perceptions and the symbols we use to label them. Finally, monitoring self-serving bias helps us perceive ourselves more accurately. We need to know when we are making factual descriptions and when we are making inferences that we should check.

Review, Reflect, Extend

The Key Concepts, For Further Reflection and Discussion questions, Recommended Resources, and Experience Communication Case Study that follow will help you review, reflect on, and extend the information and ideas presented in this chapter. A diverse selection of online resources is also available through ThomsonNOW. These resources include Speech Builder Express, InfoTrac College Edition, interactive videos, vMentor, and Thomson Audio Study Products.

Thomson NOW! is an online study system designed to help you put your time to the best use. After reading a chapter, take the NOW pre-test to identify concepts discussed in the chapter that you may not fully understand. Based on the results of this diagnostic test, the system will create a personalized study plan that directs you to specific learning resources and activities. To see if you're ready for an exam, take the NOW post-test to check your understanding.

For more information or to access this book's online resources, visit **http://www.thomsonedu.com**.

▶KEY CONCEPTS

The terms below are defined in the chapter on the page number indicated, and they appear in alphabetical order, with definitions, in the Glossary, which begins on page 369. The book's online resources also include flash cards and crossword puzzles to help you learn these terms and the concepts they represent.

attribution, 51	empathy, 57	judgment, 61
cognitive complexity, 55	expectancy violation theory, 55	mind reading, 59
cognitive schemata, 46	individualism, 58	monitoring, 62
constructivism, 46	inference, 61	perception, 45
culture, 59	interpretation, 50	personal construct, 48

▶ FOR FURTHER REFLECTION AND DISCUSSION

The questions below can also be found among the book's online resources for this chapter, where you have the option of e-mailing your responses to your instructor, if required.

1. Pay attention to how you communicate with people both online and face to face. What differences can you identify in how you communicate in each medium? What differences can you identify in how others communicate with you online and in person?

2. How do physiological factors affect your perceptions? How do your biorhythms affect your daily schedules?

3. Read a local paper, and pay attention to how the language in stories shapes your perceptions of events and people. Identify examples of selective language in reporting.

4. Think of someone you know who is person centered. Describe the specific skills this person uses and how they affect his or her communication.

5. Go to a grocery store, and notice how products are placed on shelves (at eye level, lower, or higher) and the colors and designs on product packaging. Identify factors discussed in this chapter that are used to make products stand out and gain shoppers' attention.

▶ RECOMMENDED RESOURCES

1. Learn more about fact–inference confusion and other ways in which language and perception affect our thinking by visiting the website of the Institute of General Semantics. You can access it by going to the book's online resources for this chapter and clicking on WebLink 3.1.

2. Paul Watzlawick (1984). *The invented reality: How do we know what we believe we know?* Don't let the publication date of this book fool you. It is as useful today as when it was published in raising awareness of how our perceptions shape our sense of reality.

3. The accomplished golfer Tiger Woods refuses to be totalized as Black or Asian or Caucasian or Indian or Caucasian because he is all of those, not just one of them. He coined the term *Cablinasian* to define his ethnicity. Visit Tiger's official website by going to the book's online resources and clicking on WebLink 3.2.

Experience Communication Case Study

COLLEGE SUCCESS

The book's online resources include an interactive video of the communication situation featured in the case study scripted on the next page. Apply what you've learned in this chapter by analyzing the case study, using the questions that follow the script as a guide. These questions are also available online with the video.

Your friend Jim tells you about a problem he's having with his parents. According to Jim, his parents have unrealistic expectations of him. He tends to be an average student, usually making Cs, a few Bs, and an occasional D in his courses. His parents are angry that his

grades aren't better. Jim tells you that when he went home last month, his father said this:

Jim's father: I'm not paying for you to go to school so you can party with your friends. I paid my own way and still made Phi Beta Kappa. You have a free ride, and you're still just pulling Cs. You just have to study harder.

Jim [to you]: I mean, I like to hang out with my friends, but that's got nothing to do with my grades. My dad's this brilliant guy, I mean, he just cruised through college; he thinks it's easy. I don't know how it was back then, but all my classes are *hard*. I mean, no matter how much studying I do, I'm *not* gonna get all As. What should I do? I mean, how do I convince them that I'm doing everything I can?

Jason Harris/© Wadsworth

▾▾▾

1. Both Jim and his parents make attributions to explain his grades. Describe the dimensions of Jim's attributions and those of his parents.

2. How might you assess the accuracy of Jim's attributions? What questions could you ask him to help you decide whether his perceptions are well founded or biased?

3. What constructs, prototypes, and scripts seem to operate in how Jim and his parents think about college life and being a student?

4. What could you say to Jim to help him and his parents reach a shared perspective on his academic work?

4 *Engaging in Verbal Communication*

▶ **FOCUS QUESTIONS**

1. How are language and thought related?

2. What abilities are possible because humans use symbols?

3. What are the practical implications of recognizing that language is a process?

4. How do rules guide verbal communication?

5. How can you improve your verbal communication?

Many children in the United States grow up hearing the nursery rhyme, "Sticks and stones can break my bones, but words can never hurt me." By now, most of us have figured out that it isn't true. Words are very powerful. The nursery rhyme would be more accurate if we revised it to say, "Sticks and stones can break my bones, but words can *really* hurt me." Words can harm us, sometimes terribly. Children often bully each other with name calling (Nicholson, 2006). As children get older, the verbal bullying continues, with some of the cruelest verbal attacks occurring among adolescent girls (Greenfield, 2002; Simmons, 2002). If you've ever been called hurtful names, you know how deeply words can wound.

Words can also enchant, comfort, teach, amuse, and inspire us. Have you ever read a poem or heard a song that captivated you? Have you ever felt bad and talked to a friend who said just the right thing—healing words? Have you ever been inspired to change something about yourself because of a great speech you heard? In the weeks after the September 11, 2001, attacks on the United States, the national anthem was played on television and radio stations, and people who normally didn't express patriotism sang along. The words mattered to us; their meaning was revitalized by the threat to our country.

Language is our most powerful tool. It allows us to plan, dream, remember, evaluate, reflect on ourselves and the world around us, and define who we are and want to be. In short, our ability to use language gives us the power to create reality. Because

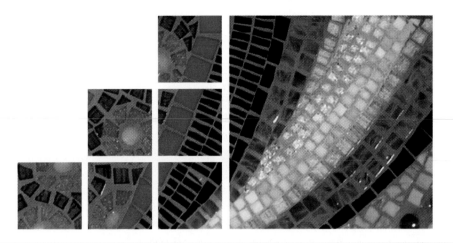

language is so powerful, we need to understand it and use it in responsible, ethical ways. This chapter will enhance your understanding of human language and your ability to use it effectively. The FYI box on page 68 shows how language creates reality.

In this chapter, we take a close look at verbal communication, and we explore the power of words in our lives. We begin by defining symbols and discussing principles of verbal communication. Next, we'll examine how language enables us to create meanings for ourselves, for others, and for our experiences. Finally, we'll identify guidelines for effective verbal communication. In Chapter 5, we'll explore the companion system, nonverbal communication.

▶Language and Meaning

Language consists of **symbols,** which are representations of people, events, and all that goes on around us and in us. All language is symbolic, yet not all symbols are linguistic. **Nonverbal communication** includes symbols that aren't words, such as facial expressions, dress, and tone of voice.

Features of Language

Verbal communication, or language, consists of symbols in the form of spoken or written words. For instance, your name is a symbol that represents you. *Dormitory* is a symbol for a particular kind of building. *Democracy* is a symbol for a particular political system. *Love* represents a particular intense feeling. In combination with nonverbal symbols, verbal symbols form the core of the human world of meaning. As a first step in understanding the power of language, we'll examine three characteristics of symbols: arbitrariness, ambiguity, and abstraction.

Arbitrariness Language is **arbitrary,** which means that verbal symbols are not intrinsically connected to what they represent. For instance, the term *chat room* has no natural relationship to spaces for interaction within particular online communities. Certain words and terms seem right because as a society we agree to use them in particular ways, but they have no inherent correspondence to their referents. Because meanings are arbitrary instead of necessary, they change over time. The word *apple* used to refer exclusively to a fruit, and *mouse* and *hamster* used to refer to rodents, whereas today all three words are likely to be used to refer to computers.

Language also changes as we invent new words or imbue existing words with new meanings. The English language now has 500 times the number of words that it had only 400 years ago (Wurman, 1989). Through mass communication, commentators have enlarged the political vocabulary with such terms as *Watergate* (which was followed by *Irangate* and *Monicagate*), *gender gap*, and *political correctness*. *Cyberspace, hyperlink, information superhighway, buddy list, instant messaging, hypertext,* and *World Wide Web* are terms we've invented to refer to communication technologies. To express feelings in online communication, people have invented *emoticons* (also a newly coined word) such as :) for "smile," :(for "frown," :D for "grin," :/ for "frustrated," and ;) for "wink."

Because language is a living process that reflects the lives of its users, it changes as the people who use it change. In America, language continually incorporates words from people of diverse cultures and social communities. For example, some terms from the hip-hop subculture have entered into mainstream English. Words such as *machismo* and *karma* come from other languages and have been incorporated into English relatively recently. The English language includes many older words that originated in other cultures (Carnes, 1994): *Chocolate* comes from the language of the Nahuatl Native American tribe, *cotton* comes from Arabic, *klutz* comes from Yiddish, *khaki* comes from Hindi, and *zombie* comes from language used by the Kongo group.

Language is so dynamic that publishers of *The Oxford English Dictionary* have a new word team whose job is to consider which new words should be added to formal dictionaries.

LANGUAGE CREATES REALITY

In naming things, language brings them into human consciousness. Here are a few examples of phenomena of which all of us are aware but which became social realities only when they were given names:

▶ *Blog* entered the language only in recent years. First there was the web, and then there were *weblogs,* soon shortened to *blogs.* You can read more about "net language" by going to the book's online resources for this chapter and clicking on WebLink 4.1.

▶ *Domestic partners* refers to gay and lesbian couples or cohabiting, unmarried heterosexuals.

▶ *Birth mother* designates a woman who gives birth but does not keep the child.

▶ *Date rape* is a term created to define as criminal an activity that for a long time took place without being named.

▶ *Environmental justice* refers to a movement to ensure that environmental dangers such as sites for storing toxic wastes are distributed fairly instead of being the burden of poor communities (Cox, 2006a; Pezzullo, 2001).

▶ *Blended family* refers to a family that includes children from one or both partners' previous relationships. Although such families have long existed, only in recent years were they named.

What terms can you add to illustrate how naming things gives them a social reality that they cannot otherwise have?

In the most recent edition of *The Oxford English Dictionary*, words added included *ego-surfing* (searching the Internet for references to your name), *irritainment* (programming that irritates viewers but that viewers feel compelled to watch), and *fashionista* (a devotee of cutting-edge fashions) (Smith, 1999).

Ambiguity Language is **ambiguous,** which means it doesn't have clear-cut, precise meanings. The term *good friend* means someone to hang out with to one person and someone to confide in to another. The words *Christmas, Kwanzaa,* and *Hanukkah* have distinct connotations for people with different religious and cultural backgrounds, and

Thanksgiving may mean different things to Native Americans and European Americans. The meanings of these words vary according to cultural contexts and individuals' experiences. The language is the same, but what it means varies in relation to personal experiences, interests, identities, and backgrounds.

Although language doesn't mean exactly the same thing to everyone, within a culture many words have an agreed-upon range of meanings. In learning to communicate, we learn not only words but also the meanings and values of our society. Thus, all of us know that the word *dogs* refers to four-footed creatures (and occasionally to hot dogs), but each of us also attributes personal meanings based on dogs we have known and how our families and cultures regard dogs. In some cultures, some people regard dogs as food—not a meaning of *dogs* in the United States! Conversely, many Westerners eat beef, whereas in Hindu cultures cows are sacred.

The ambiguity of language can lead to the misunderstandings that sometimes plague communication. A friend recently told me of misunderstandings that arose when he tried to negotiate a contract with a Japanese firm. My friend, Erik, said that when he made his initial proposal,

What are the personal, religious, legal, and social meanings of words used in marriage vows?

O-Young, who represented the Japanese company, nodded his head and said, "This is very good." Encouraged, Erik made additional suggestions, and O-Young smiled and responded, "This is a fine idea," and "I admire your work on the project." Yet O-Young consistently refused to sign the contract that contained Erik's proposals. Finally, another American businessperson explained to Erik that Japanese culture regards it as rude to refuse another person directly. To someone socialized in Japanese society, outright disagreement or rejection causes another person to lose face, and that is to be avoided at all costs. Once Erik understood that apparently favorable responses did not mean O-Young agreed with him, their negotiations became much more productive. The United States developed a training program in cultural sensitivity to prepare delegates to participate in the United Nations Conference on Women. The delegates were told that many Asian women would not sign agreements and contracts even if they gave what Americans perceive as verbal and nonverbal indications of agreement. Like O-Young, many women in Asian countries are reluctant to disagree overtly.

Problems arising from the ambiguity of language can cause misunderstandings between people. A supervisor criticizes a new employee for "inadequate quality of work." The employee assumes the supervisor wants more productivity; the supervisor means that the employee should be more careful in proofing material to catch errors. Spouses often have different meanings for "doing their share" of home chores. To many women, it means doing half the work, but to men it tends to mean doing more than their fathers did, which is still less than their wives do (Hochschild & Machung, 2003).

► Ron

A while ago, I told my girlfriend I needed more independence. She got all up-set because she thought I didn't love her anymore and was pulling away. All I meant was that I need some time with the guys and some for just myself. She said that the last time a guy said he wanted more independence, she found out he was dating out on her.

Ambiguous language is a common source of misunderstandings in relationships. For instance, Anya might ask her husband, Bryan, to be more loving, but she and he have different understandings of what "more loving" means. Consequently, Bryan may do more housework to express his love, whereas Anya wanted them to spend more time together. Suggesting that a co-worker should be more responsive doesn't specify what you want. To be clear, more specific language is advisable. For instance, you might say to your co-worker, "I'd like you to give me feedback on the ideas I present."

Abstraction Finally, language is **abstract,** which means that words are not the con-crete or tangible phenomena to which they refer. They stand for those phenomena—ideas, people, events, objects, feelings, and so forth, but they are not the things they represent. In using language, we engage in a process of abstraction in which we move farther and farther away from external or objective phenomena. Words vary in their degree of abstractness. *Reading matter* is an abstract term that includes everything from philosophy books to the list of ingredients on a cereal package. *Book* is a less ab-stract word. *Textbook* is even less abstract. And *Communication Mosaics* is the most concrete term because it refers to a specific textbook.

Our perceptions are one step away from the phenomena because perceptions are selective and subjective, as we learned in Chapter 3. We move a second step away from phenomena when we label a perception with language that is value laden. We abstract even further when we respond, not to behaviors or our perceptions of them, but to the labels we impose. This process can be illustrated as a ladder of abstraction (Figure 4.1), a concept developed by two early scholars of communication, Alfred Korzybski (1948) and S. I. Hayakawa (1962, 1964).

As language becomes increasingly abstract, the potential for confusion mushrooms. One way this happens is by overgeneralization. Mass communication often relies on highly general, abstract language to describe groups of people. Terms such as *inner-city youth, immigrant,* and *senior citizen* encourage us to notice distinctions between young people who live in the hearts of cities and young people who live elsewhere, between people who immigrate to the United States and those who were born here, between people who are elderly and people who are not. At the same time, highly gen-eral terms for social groups, such as Asian American, Hispanic American, or African American, incline us to see commonalities among people within the categories but not to recognize distinctions among them. The FYI box on page 72 shows how labels for racial and ethnic groups have changed and how, with these changes, our perceptions of groups have evolved.

Overly general language can distort how partners think about a relationship. They may make broad, negative statements, such as, "You never go along with my prefer-ences" or "You always interrupt me." In most cases, highly abstract communication involves overgeneralizations that are inaccurate. Yet by symbolizing experience this

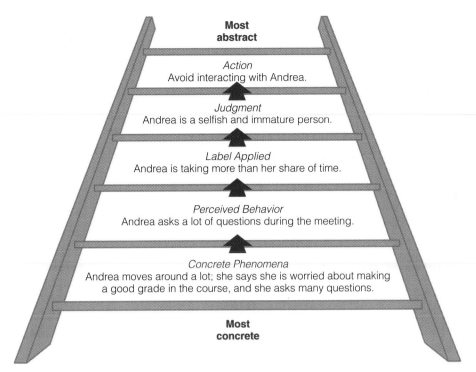

**Most
abstract**

Action
Avoid interacting with Andrea.

Judgment
Andrea is a selfish and immature person.

Label Applied
Andrea is taking more than her share of time.

Perceived Behavior
Andrea asks a lot of questions during the meeting.

Concrete Phenomena
Andrea moves around a lot; she says she is worried about making
a good grade in the course, and she asks many questions.

**Most
concrete**

Figure 4.1 THE LADDER OF ABSTRACTION

way, partners frame how they think about each other. Researchers have shown that
we are more likely to recall behaviors that are consistent with how we've labeled people than to recall behaviors that are inconsistent (Fincham & Bradbury, 1987). When
we say a friend is *insensitive,* we're likely to notice instances in which he is insensitive and to overlook times when he is sensitive. Similarly, if we label a co-worker *lazy,*
we predispose ourselves to notice lazy behaviors and not to perceive behaviors that
show conscientiousness.

We can minimize misunderstandings by using specific language instead of abstract
terms. Saying, "You interrupted me a moment ago" is clearer than saying, "You're so
dominating." It's clearer to say, "I would like you to look at me when I'm talking" than

Doonesbury

BY GARRY TRUDEAU

to say, "I wish you'd be more attentive." The Sharpen Your Skill box on the following page provides an opportunity for you to develop skill in reducing the confusion caused by ambiguous language.

THE LANGUAGES OF RACE AND ETHNICITY

Our labels for races and ethnicities have changed over time (Davis, 1997; Delgado, 1998; Johnson, 1999; Martin et al., 1996; Orbe & Harris, 2001; Tanno, 1997).

▸ In America's early years, Catholic Irish and Eastern European immigrants were not defined as White. Today they are.

▸ Historic and current labels for African Americans include *negroes, coloreds, African Americans, people of color, Blacks,* and *Afro-Americans.*

▸ Historic and current labels for indigenous people of Alaska include *Eskimo* and *Inuk.*

▸ Historic and current labels for Asians and Asian Americans include *Asians, Asian nationals,* and *Orientals,* as well as more specific ethnic labels such as *Japanese, Korean Americans,* and *Vietnamese Americans.*

▸ Native Americans may be called *Indians* or *Native Americans* or by labels that reference their specific nations, such as *Oneida* and *Sioux.*

▸ European Americans may be called *Whites, Caucasians, European Americans,* or just plain *Americans,* which reflects the naive presumption that, in America, Whiteness is the "normal" race.

▸ Labels for Hispanics include *Hispanics, Latinos* and *Latinas, Chicanos* and *Chicanas,* and more specific labels, such as *Cubanos.*

Principles of Communication

Now that we understand that language is arbitrary, ambiguous, and abstract, we're ready to consider three principles of communication. These principles help us understand how we create meaning for our interactions.

Interpretation Creates Meaning Because language is abstract, ambiguous, and arbitrary, we have to interpret it to determine what it means (Duck, 1994a, 1994b; Shotter, 1993). Interpretation is an active, creative process we use to make sense of experiences. Although we're usually not conscious of the effort we invest in interpreting words, we continually engage in the process of constructing meanings.

John Searle (1976, 1995) distinguishes between **brute facts** and **institutional facts.** Brute facts are objective, concrete phenomena and activities. Institutional facts are the meanings of brute facts based on human interpretation. The words we use represent institutional facts. Borrowing an example from Searle (1976), during a football game one brute fact is that periodically people gather into roughly circular clusters. We name that activity the *huddle,* or *huddling,* and the institutional fact is that the players are planning their next play. Searle's point is that we create our reality by naming things according to institutional facts, or the social meanings we attribute to them.

If someone says to you, "Get lost," you have to think about the context and the person who made it to decide whether it's an insult, friendly needling, or a colloquial way of saying you are out of line. People for whom English is a second language find idioms such as "get lost" even more difficult to interpret than native speakers of English do (Lee, 2000). Go to the book's online resources and click on WebLink 4.2 to learn more about idioms that can be confusing to people for whom English is a second language. What the words mean depends on the relationship between communicators as well as the self-esteem and previous experiences of the person who is told to get lost. Similarly, if you say "hello" to someone who makes no response, you have to decide how to interpret the silence. Is the person ignoring you, angry with you, or preoccupied? How you interpret others' communication has at least as much to do with you as with what other people communicate.

Communication Is Guided by Rules Although each of us draws on his or her individual experiences to interpret language, the process of interpretation is not entirely personal. Without realizing it, we learn rules in the process of being socialized into a particular culture, and these rules guide our communication and how we interpret the communication of others (Argyle & Henderson, 1985; Shimanoff, 1980). **Communication rules** are shared understandings among members of a particular culture or social group about what communication means and what behaviors are appropriate in various situations. Children often are taught that *please* and *thank you* are magic words that they should use. We learn that *sir* and *ma'am* are polite words to use when addressing our elders or people who have authority over us. In the course of interacting with our families and others, we unconsciously absorb rules that guide how we communicate and how we interpret others' communication. Research shows that children begin to understand and follow communication rules by the time they are 1 or 2 years old (Miller, 1993).

Communicating Clearly

To express yourself clearly, it's important to translate ambiguous words into concrete language. Practice translating with these examples:

Ambiguous Language	Concrete Language
You are rude.	I don't like it when you interrupt me.
We need more team spirit.	_____
I want more freedom.	_____
Let's watch a good program.	_____
Your work is sloppy.	_____
That speaker is unprofessional.	_____

SHARPEN YOUR SKILL

Two kinds of rules guide our communication (Cronen, Pearce, & Snavely, 1979; Pearce, Cronen, & Conklin, 1979). **Regulative rules** regulate interaction by specifying when, how, where, and with whom to communicate about certain things. For instance, European Americans generally don't interrupt when someone is making a formal presentation, but in more informal settings interruptions may be appropriate. Some African Americans follow a different rule; it specifies that audience members should participate in public speeches by calling out responses. Thus, for some African American audiences at speaking events, the call–response pattern is an appropriate form of communication. The rules of some cultures say that interrupting in any context is impolite.

Some families have a rule that people cannot argue at the dinner table, whereas other families regard arguments as a normal accompaniment to meals. Families also teach us rules about how to communicate in conflict situations (Honeycutt, Woods, & Fontenot, 1993; Jones & Gallois, 1989; Yerby, Buerkel-Rothfuss, & Bochner, 1990). Did you learn that it's appropriate or inappropriate to yell at others during conflict? Regulative rules also define when, where, and with whom it's appropriate to show affection and disclose private information. Regulative rules vary across cultures; what is considered appropriate in one society may be regarded as impolite or offensive elsewhere.

Constitutive rules define what a particular communication means or stands for. We learn that certain kinds of communication show (or are interpreted by cultural rules to show) respect (listening attentively, not correcting), professionalism (speaking effectively, taking a voice), and rudeness (talking over others). We also learn what communication is expected if we want to be perceived as a good friend (sharing confidences, defending our friends when others criticize them), a responsible employee (making good contributions in group meetings, creating supportive climates), and a desirable romantic partner (offering support, expressing affection). Like regulative rules, constitutive rules are shaped by cultures. The Sharpen Your Skill box on this page allows you to reflect on rules that you follow in your communication.

Rules guide our everyday interactions by telling us when to communicate, what to communicate, and how to interpret others' verbal and nonverbal communication. Casual social interactions tend to adhere to rules that are widely shared in a society. Interaction between intimates also follows rules, but these are private rules that reflect special meanings partners have created (Duck, 2006; Wood, 2006). Television networks follow rules for what can and cannot be said and shown during specific times and rules for how often they insert commercials. Chat rooms develop specific and often unique rules for how people express themselves and respond to one another. Every organization develops a distinctive culture, which includes rules about how members interact with one another.

Few rules are rigidly fixed. Like communication itself, most rules are subject to change. When we decide a rule is not functional, we negotiate changes in it. A company may find that its rule for making decisions by consensus no longer works once the company triples in size, so voting becomes a constitutive rule to define decision making. When we don't have a rule for a particular kind of interaction, we invent one and often negotiate and refine it until it provides the assistance we want in structuring communication. When couples have a child, they often find they don't have any guidelines for new communication situations, so they develop rules: "It is appropriate to tend to the baby while talking with each other," "We take turns eating so one of us is free to hold the baby," or "Interrupting our conversation when the baby cries does not count as rudeness."

It's important to understand that we don't have to be aware of communication rules in order to follow them. For the most part, we're really not conscious of the rules that

Communication Rules

Think about the regulative and constitutive rules you follow in your verbal communication. For each item listed here, identify two rules that guide your verbal behavior.

Regulative Rules

List rules that regulate your verbal communication when

1. Talking with elders
2. Interacting at dinnertime
3. Having first exchanges in morning
4. Greeting casual friends on campus
5. Talking with professors

Constitutive Rules

How do you use verbal communication to show

1. Trustworthiness
2. Ambition
3. Disrespect
4. Support
5. Anger

After you've identified your rules, talk with others about their rules. Are there commonalities among your rules that reflect broad cultural norms? What explains differences in individuals' rules?

SHARPEN YOUR SKILL

guide how, when, where, and with whom we communicate about various things. We may not realize we have rules until one is broken, and we become aware that we had an expectation. A study by DeFrancisco (1991) revealed that some spouses have a clear pattern in which husbands interrupt wives and are unresponsive to topics wives initiate. The couples were unaware of the rules, but their communication nonetheless sustained the pattern. Becoming aware of communication rules empowers you to change those that do not promote good interaction, as Emily's commentary illustrates.

▶ Emily

My boyfriend and I had this really frustrating pattern about planning what to do. He'd say, "What do you want to do this weekend?" And I'd say, "I don't know. What do you want to do?" Then he'd suggest two or three things and ask me which of them sounded good. I would say they were all fine with me, even if they weren't. And this would keep on forever. Both of us had a rule not to impose on the other, and it kept us from stating our preferences, so we just went in circles about any decision. Well, two weekends ago I talked to him about rules, and he agreed we had one that was frustrating. So we invented a new rule that says each of us has to state what we want to do, but the other has to say if that is not okay. It's a lot less frustrating to figure out what we want to do since we agreed on this rule.

Punctuation Affects Meaning We punctuate communication to interpret meaning. Like the punctuation you studied in grammar classes, **punctuation** of verbal communication is a way to mark a flow of activity into meaningful units. Punctuation is our perception of when interaction begins and ends (Watzlawick, Beavin, & Jackson, 1967).

Before we can attribute meaning to communication, we must establish its boundaries. Usually this involves deciding who initiated communication and when the interaction began. If a co-worker suggests going out to lunch together, you might regard the invitation as marking the start of the interaction. If you return another person's phone call, you might perceive the original call as the beginning of the episode. If someone insults you, you might regard the insult as the act that marks the start of a quarrel.

When we don't agree on punctuation, problems may arise. If you've ever heard children arguing about who started a fight, you understand the importance of punctuation. Communication on the Internet often is punctuated differently by participants who join the dialogue at different times. I once read a message that was a defense of flaming (dramatically disparaging others on the Internet). Because I view flaming as discouraging freedom of speech, I wrote a critical response to the message. The person to whom I wrote replied that the message that disturbed me was a sarcastic reply to an earlier message that I had not seen. Because people enter electronic dialogues at different times, it's difficult to know who launched a particular topic or which messages initiate ideas and which are responses to earlier messages. Similarly, new members of organizations may not understand relationships (allies and enemies) or policies.

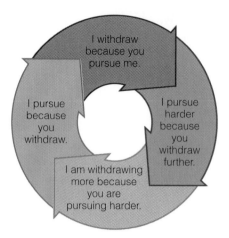

Figure 4.2 THE DEMAND–WITHDRAW PATTERN

In personal relationships, a common instance of conflicting punctuation is the demand–withdraw pattern (Figure 4.2; Bergner & Bergner, 1990; Caughlin & Vangelisti, 2000; Christensen & Heavey, 1990). In this pattern, one person tries to create closeness through personal talk, and the other strives to maintain autonomy by avoiding intimate discussion. The more the first person demands personal talk ("Tell me what's going on in your life"; "Let's talk about our future"), the more the second person withdraws ("There's nothing to tell"; "I don't know about the future"; silence). The people involved may be friends, romantic partners, or a parent and an adolescent child (Caughlin & Ramey, 2005). Each person punctuates the interaction as having started with the other: The demander thinks, "I pursue because you withdraw," and the withdrawer thinks, "I withdraw because you pursue." There is no objectively correct punctuation, because it depends on subjective perceptions.

When people don't agree on punctuation, they don't share meanings for what is happening between them. To break out of unconstructive cycles such as demand–withdraw, people need to realize that they may punctuate differently and should discuss how each of them experiences the pattern. The Sharpen Your Skill box on the next page encourages you to check perceptions to see if you and another person are punctuating congruently.

Interpretation, communication rules, and punctuation influence the meaning we assign to language. These three principles highlight the creativity involved in constructing meaning to make sense of communication. We're now ready to explore the power of symbols by discussing uniquely symbolic abilities.

►SYMBOLIC ABILITIES

The ability to use language allows humans to live in a world of ideas and meanings. Instead of reacting without reflection to our concrete environments and experiences, we think about them and sometimes transform what they mean. Philosophers of language have identified six ways in which symbolic capacities affect our lives (Cassirer, 1944; Langer, 1953, 1979). As we discuss each, we'll consider how to recognize the constructive power of language and minimize the problems it can cause (Figure 4.3).

Figure 4.3 SYMBOLIC ABILITIES

1. Symbols define phenomena.

2. Symbols evaluate phenomena.

3. Symbols allow us to organize experiences.

4. Symbols allow us to think hypothetically.

5. Symbols allow self-reflection.

6. Symbols define relationships and interactions.

Language Defines Phenomena

As we noted earlier in this chapter, the most basic symbolic ability is definition. We use words to define ourselves, others, experiences, relationships, feelings, and thoughts (Monastersky, 2002). A friend of mine puts his savings into separate accounts designated for travel, retirement, and emergencies. Last spring, he told me he couldn't afford a summer vacation because he'd used up his travel fund. I pointed out that he had extra money in his emergency fund that he could use for a vacation. "No," he replied, "that account isn't for vacations." He had defined the accounts in specific ways that shaped his view of the money available for various expenses. The symbols we use define what things mean to us.

The labels we use to define others affect how we perceive them. When we label someone, we focus attention on particular aspects of that person and her or his activities. At the same time, we necessarily obscure other aspects of that person's identity. A person might be a loving father, a conservative, a concerned citizen, and a demanding supervisor. Each label directs our attention to certain aspects of the person and away from others. We might talk with the conservative about editorials on government policies, discuss community issues with the concerned citizen, seek advice on child rearing from the father, and try to clarify the expectations of the supervisor. If we define someone as a Latina, that may be all we notice about the person, although there are many other aspects of her identity. This implies that we have an ethical responsibility to consider how our language shapes our perceptions of others. Orest's reflection makes this point clearly.

▶ Orest

A lot of people relate to me as Asian, like that's all I am. Sometimes in classes, teachers ask me to explain the "Asian point of view," but they do not ask me to explain my perspective as a pre-med major or a working student. I am an Asian, but that is not all that I am.

Totalizing is responding to a person as if one label totally represents that person. We fix on one symbol to define someone and fail to recognize many other aspects of the person. Some people totalize gay men and lesbians by noticing only their sexual orientation. Interestingly, we don't totalize heterosexuals on the basis of *their* sexual orientation. Totalizing also occurs when we dismiss people by saying, "She's old," "He's just a jock," or "She's an illegal alien." Totalizing is not the same as stereotyping. When we stereotype someone, we define the person in terms of the characteristics of a group. When we totalize another, we negate most of that person by spotlighting a single aspect of his or her identity. Reneé points out a form of totalizing that really bothers her.

SHARPEN YOUR SKILL

Punctuating Interaction

The next time you and another person enter an unproductive cycle, stop the conversation and discuss how each of you punctuates interaction.

1. What do you define as the start of interaction?
2. What does the other person define as the beginning?
3. What happens when you learn about each other's punctuation? How does this affect understanding between you?

► **Reneé**

Okay, here's my issue. I love fashion—I mean I really love great clothes, jewelry, shoes, make up—all of it! I'm always the first to wear a cool new style. So a lot of people brand me ditsy or silly. But I'm also Phi Beta Kappa and I've been accepted to law school. Why do people think that if you're into fashion, you can't also be smart and serious?

The symbols we use affect how we think and feel. If we describe our work in terms of frustrations, problems, and disappointments, we're likely to feel negative about it. On the other hand, if we describe rewards, challenges, and successes, we're likely to feel more positive about our work. The way we define experiences in relationships also affects how we feel about them. Several years ago, my colleagues and I asked romantically involved couples how they defined differences between them (Wood et al., 1994). We found that some people defined differences as positive forces that energize a relationship and keep it interesting. Others defined differences as problems or barriers to closeness. We noted a direct connection between how partners defined differences and how they acted. Partners who viewed differences as constructive approached their disagreements with curiosity, interest, and an expectation of growth through discussion. In contrast, partners who labeled differences as problems dreaded disagreements and tried to avoid talking about them.

People who consistently use negative labels to describe their relationships heighten their awareness of aspects of the relationships that they don't like and diminish their awareness of aspects that they do like (Cloven & Roloff, 1991). In contrast, partners who focus on good facets of relationships are more conscious of virtues in partners and relationships and are less bothered by flaws (Bradbury & Fincham, 1990; Fletcher & Fincham, 1991).

Mass communication also defines people and events in ways that can shape our perceptions. Conservative commentators sometimes refer to "knee-jerk liberals" and "tree huggers," whereas the same groups of people are called "progressives" and "environmentalists" by more liberal commentators. Depending on which commentators you listen to, you might have different perceptions of these groups.

Language Evaluates Phenomena

As we noted when we discussed the ladder of abstraction, language is not neutral; it is laden with values. We describe people we like with language that accents their good qualities and downplays their flaws ("My friend is self-confident"). Just the reverse is true of our language for people we don't like ("My enemy is arrogant"). We might describe people who speak their minds as honest, assertive, outspoken, courageous, or authoritarian. Each word has a distinct connotation. Restaurants choose language that enhances the attractiveness of menu entries. A dish described as "tender, milk-fed veal sautéed in natural juices and topped with succulent chunks of lobster" sounds more appetizing than one described as "meat from a baby calf that was kept anemic to make it tender, then slaughtered, cooked in blood, and topped with the flesh of a crustacean that was boiled to death."

The language we use also has ethical implications in terms of how it affects others. Most people with disabilities prefer not to be called "disabled," because that totalizes them in terms of a disability. The term *African American* emphasizes cultural heritage, whereas *Black* focuses on skin color. *Hispanic* defines people by the Spanish language spoken in countries of origin, whereas *Latina* and *Latino* highlight the geographic origin of women and men, respectively.

Loaded language is words that slant perceptions, and thus meanings, exceedingly. Loaded language encourages extreme perceptions. Terms such as *geezer* and *old fogy* incline us to regard older people with contempt or pity. Alternatives such as *senior citizen* and *elderly person* reflect more respectful attitudes.

An interesting communication phenomenon is the **reappropriation** of language. This happens when a group reclaims a term used by others to degrade its members, and treats that terms as a positive self-description. Reappropriation aims to remove the stigma from term that others use pejoratively. For instance, some women and feminist musicians have reappropriated the term *girl* to *resist* the connotations of childishness. One collective of punk rock female bands calls itself Riot Grrrls. Some gay men and lesbians have reappropriated the term *queer* and use it as a positive statement about their identity. Southern writer Reynolds Price developed cancer of the spine that left him paraplegic. He scoffs at terms such as *differently abled* and *physically challenged;* he refers to himself as a *cripple* and to others who do not have disabilities as *temporarily able-bodied.* Perhaps the most controversial example of reappropriation is some African Americans' use of a word that was a racial epithet for years. In his book *Nigger: The Strange Career of a Troublesome Word* (2002), Harvard law professor Randall Kennedy traces the word's history and found that the word *nigger* is derived from *niger,* which is the Latin word for the color black. By the eighteenth century in America, it had become a particularly offensive racial slur. Today, Kennedy notes, the word is still a vile slur when used by non-Blacks, but some Blacks have reappropriated the term and use it as a positive term among themselves.

▶ Maynard

I'm as sensitive as the next guy, but I just can't keep up with what language offends what people anymore. When I was young, *negro* was an accepted term, then it was *Black,* and now it's *African American.* Sometimes I forget and say *Black* or even *negro,* and I get accused of being racist. It used to be polite to say *girls,* but now that offends a lot of the women I work with. Just this year, I heard that we aren't supposed to say *blind* anymore, and we're supposed to say *visually impaired.* I just can't keep up.

Probably many of us sympathize with Maynard, who was 54 when he took a course with me. Keeping up with changes in language is difficult, and occasionally we may offend someone unintentionally. Nonetheless, we should try to learn what terms hurt or insult others and avoid using them. We also should tell others when they've referred to us in ways we dislike. As long as you speak assertively but not confrontationally, others are likely to respect your ideas.

Language Organizes Experiences

Words organize our perceptions of events and experiences in our lives. As we learned in Chapter 3, the categories into which we place people influence how we interpret them and their communication. A criticism may be viewed as constructive if made by someone we categorize as a friend but insulting if made by someone we classify as an enemy. The words don't change, but their meaning varies depending on the category into which we place the person speaking them. Because symbols organize our perceptions, they allow us to think about abstract concepts such as justice, integrity, and good family life. We use broad concepts to transcend specific concrete activities and enter the world of conceptual thought and ideals. Because we think abstractly, we don't have to consider each object and experience individually. Instead, we can think in general terms.

Our capacity to abstract can also distort thinking. A primary way this occurs is by stereotyping, which is thinking in broad generalizations about a whole class of people or experiences. Examples of stereotypes are "Management doesn't care about labor," "Teachers are smart," "Jocks are dumb," "Feminists hate men," "Religious people are good," and "Conflict is bad." Notice that stereotypes can be positive or negative generalizations.

Common to all stereotypes is the classification of an experience or person according to a category based on general knowledge of that category. When we use terms such as *Native American, lesbian, White male,* and *working class,* we may see only what members of each group have in common and not perceive differences among individuals in the group. Clearly, we have to generalize; we simply cannot think about each and every thing in our lives as a specific instance. However, stereotypes can blind us to important differences among phenomena we lump together. Therefore, we have an ethical responsibility to monitor stereotypes and to stay alert to differences between things we place in any category.

Language Allows Hypothetical Thought

Where do you hope to be 5 years from now? What is your fondest childhood memory? What would you do if you won the lottery next week? To answer these questions, you must engage in **hypothetical thought,** which is thinking about experiences and ideas that are not part of your concrete, daily reality. Because we can think hypothetically, we can plan, dream, remember, set goals, consider alternative courses of action, and imagine possibilities.

Language allows us to name and imagine possibilities beyond what currently exists. Technology experts have conceived of many possibilities, such as implantable memory chips that will allow us to speak another language without having learned it. This kind of memory chip is still on the drawing boards of technology innovators, but we can think about it now because we have the term *implantable memory chip.* Not too many years ago, technology innovators imagined worldwide networks that connected people through computers; today that dream is a reality.

Hypothetical thought is possible because we are symbol users. Words give form to ideas so that we can hold them in our minds and reflect on them. We can contemplate things that have no real existence, and we can remember ourselves in the past and project ourselves into the future. Our ability to inhabit past, present, and future explains why we can set goals and work toward them, even though we do not realize the goal immediately (Dixson & Duck, 1993). For example, you've invested many hours in attending classes, studying, and writing papers because you have the idea of yourself as someone with a college degree. The degree is not real now, nor is the self that you will become once you have the degree. Yet the idea is sufficiently real to motivate you to work hard for many years. You can imagine yourself wearing academic regalia at your graduation, think of yourself as having a degree, and visualize yourself working in the career you plan to enter.

Hypothetical thought can enrich personal relationships by allowing intimates to remember shared moments. One of the strongest glues for intimacy is the ability to remember a history of shared experiences (Bruess & Hoefs, 2006; Cockburn-Wootten & Zorn, 2006; Wood, 2006). Because they can remember rough times they have weathered, intimates can often get through trials in the present. Language that symbolizes a shared future ("When we're rocking on the porch at 80") also fuels intimacy. We interact differently with people we don't expect to see again and with those who are ongoing parts of our lives. Talking about future plans and dreams, another use of hypothetical thought, knits intimates together because it makes real the idea that more is yet to come (Acitelli, 1993; Wood, 2006).

Hypothetical thought also allows us to imagine being in places we have never visited. Television programs and websites show us faraway countries and expose us to people with different values, traditions, and ways of living. When we listen to or see programs or visit sites to learn about other cultures, we can think about these cultures and imagine visiting them.

Thinking hypothetically helps us improve who we are. We notice progress we have made when we can remember earlier versions of ourselves, and we motivate further self-growth when we envision additional improvements in ourselves. Your ability to think hypothetically enables you to chart a path of continuous growth. As Duk-Kyong points out, remembering ourselves at earlier times also allows us to notice progress we make toward achieving our goals.

Couples communicate about past experiences and family events. How does this affect intimacy?

▶ **Duk-Kyong**

Sometimes I get very discouraged that I do not yet know English perfectly and that there is much I still do not understand about customs in this country. It helps me to remember that when I came here 2 years ago I did not speak English at all, and I knew nothing about how people act here. Seeing how much progress I have made helps me to not be discouraged with what I do not yet know.

Language Allows Self-Reflection

Just as we use language to think about times in the past and future and to shape our perceptions of others, we use it to reflect on ourselves. We think about our existence and reflect on our actions. In his classic work in this area, George Herbert Mead

© Carolyn C. Wood

When my niece Michelle told me she had learned to read, she was bursting with pride. How might reflecting on this accomplishment affect how Michelle thinks about herself?

(1934) noted that self-reflection is the foundation of human identity. Since Mead's original work, other scholars have developed his ideas and reaffirmed their importance (Atkinson & Housley, 2003; Leeds-Hurwitz, 2006; Sandstrom, Martin, & Fine, 2001).

He believed that our capacity to use symbols to think about ourselves was responsible for civilized society. According to Mead, the self has two aspects: the *I* and the *me.* The *I* is the spontaneous, creative self. The *I* acts impulsively in response to inner needs and desires, regardless of social norms. The *I* is the part of you that wants to send a really nasty e-mail message to a chat room visitor whom you find offensive.

The *me* is the socially conscious part of self that monitors and moderates the *I*'s impulses. The *me* reflects on the *I* from the social perspectives of others. The *me* is the part of you that says, "Hey, don't send that message, or you'll get flamed." The *I* is impervious to social conventions, but the *me* is keenly aware of them. If your supervisor criticizes your work, your *I* may want to tell that boss off, but your *me* censors that impulse and reminds you that subordinates are not supposed to criticize their bosses.

Because we have both spontaneous and reflective parts of ourselves, we can think about who we want to be and set goals for becoming the self we desire. We can feel shame, pride, and regret for our actions—emotions that are possible because we self-reflect. We can control what we do now by casting ourselves forward to consider how we might feel about our actions later—a point that Tiffany makes in her commentary.

▶ Tiffany

My mother-in-law thinks it's wrong that I go to school instead of being a full-time homemaker and mother. She constantly criticizes me for neglecting my children and home. So many times I have wanted to tell her to butt out of my family, but I stop myself by reminding myself that in the long term it's important to me and my husband and the kids to maintain decent relations.

As Tiffany's commentary points out, self-reflection also empowers us to monitor ourselves. When we monitor ourselves, the *me* notices and evaluates the *I*'s impulses and may modify them based on the *me*'s awareness of social norms. For instance, during a discussion with a co-worker you might say to yourself, "I'm just sitting here like a lump on a log. I need to show that I'm interested in what he's saying." Based on your monitoring, you might listen more carefully, give feedback, and ask questions to show interest. Effective public speakers monitor audiences. If members of the audience start looking bored, speakers adapt by changing speaking pace or volume or by introducing a visual aid to add interest. When interacting with people from different cultures, we monitor by reminding ourselves that they may not operate by the same values and communication rules that we do. Self-reflection allows us to monitor our communication and adjust it to be effective and ethical.

Self-reflection also allows us to manage the image we present to others. When talking with teachers and supervisors, you may consciously use language that represents you as respectful, attentive, and responsible. When interacting with parents, you may repress some language that surfaces in discussions with your friends. When communicating with someone you'd like to date, you may use language that is personal and conveys friendliness. We continually use language to manage the images we project in particular situations and with specific people.

Language Defines Relationships and Interaction

A sixth way in which language creates meaning in our lives is by defining relationships and interaction. Our verbal communication conveys messages about how we perceive ourselves and others. "Mr. Buster" symbolizes a more formal relationship than "Phil." We also use language to regulate interaction. We signal that we want to speak by saying, "Excuse me" or "Let me jump in here." We invite others to speak by saying, "Do you have an opinion about this?" or "I'd like to hear what you think about the issue." You'll recall that in Chapter 1 we discussed two levels of meaning: the content level and the relationship level. Verbal communication, as well as nonverbal communication, conveys three dimensions of relationship-level meanings (Mehrabian, 1981).

Responsiveness One facet of relationship-level meaning is *responsiveness*. Through questions and statements of agreement or disagreement, we show our interest in others' communication. When we give thoughtful feedback to a colleague, we show responsiveness. When we ask an interviewee to elaborate ideas, we demonstrate interest in him or her. Different social and cultural groups learn distinct rules for showing responsiveness. For instance, women generally display greater verbal responsiveness than men do (Montgomery, 1988; Ueland, 1992), and Koreans tend to limit verbal responses more than Americans typically do.

Liking A second dimension of relationship-level meaning is *liking*. We express liking verbally when we say, "I really enjoy being with you," "I'm glad we're working on the same team," and so forth. Conversely, we verbally communicate dislike by saying, "I don't have time for you right now," or "I don't want to work with you on the team." In addition to these general rules shared in Western society, particular social groups instill more specific rules. Masculine socialization emphasizes emotional control and independence, so men are less likely than women to verbalize their feelings of affection for most other people. Feminine socialization encourages many women to verbalize inner feelings.

Power The third aspect of relationship-level meaning is *power*. We use verbal communication to define dominance and to negotiate status and influence. Men typically exceed women in efforts to establish control over others. Research has shown that men are more likely than women to exert control verbally by controlling conversations, having the last word, interrupting, and correcting others (DeFrancisco, 1991). People in positions of power in organizations often express control with authoritative statements such as, "That's how it's going to be" and "I've heard all I want to hear." Like many aspects of communication, the power dimension of relationship meaning is influenced by culture. Western cultures tend to favor competitiveness and overt displays of power more than many other cultures. For example, in negotiations Japanese tend to understate their initial position, stress areas of agreement with other negotiators, and work to avoid failure, or loss of face, for any of the negotiators. This is quite different from American negotiating tendencies, such as overstating initial positions to appear strong, being adversarial, and trying to make sure they win and other negotiators lose (Weiss, 1987).

Summing up, we use language to define and evaluate phenomena, organize experiences, think hypothetically, self-reflect, and define relationships and interaction. Each of these abilities helps us create meaning in our personal, professional, and social relationships.

►Guidelines for Effective Verbal Communication

Because language is arbitrary, abstract, and ambiguous, the potential for misunderstanding always exists. In addition, individual and cultural differences foster varying interpretations of language. Although we can't completely eliminate misunderstandings, we can minimize them by following four guidelines for using verbal communication effectively.

Engage in Person-Centered Communication

The single most important guideline for using language effectively is to be person centered in your communication. Recall from Chapters 1 and 3 that person-centered communication is adapted to specific, unique individuals with whom we interact. Effective communicators are aware of other people and their perspectives, and this awareness is reflected in the talk of effective communicators (Muehlhoff, 2006). When I talk with colleagues about communication theories, I use language that is specialized and incomprehensible to people who aren't specialists. When I talk with undergraduate students about the same theories, I adapt my language to students' experiences and knowledge. Medical doctors need highly specialized vocabularies to discuss medical problems with other doctors, but they should translate that vocabulary into ordinary language when talking with patients. In public presentations, speakers adapt their language to the knowledge and attitudes of listeners. If listeners already favor what a speaker advocates, the speaker can use more impassioned language than if listeners are opposed to what he or she advocates. Person-centered communicators try to understand and adapt to the perspectives of listeners.

Be Conscious of Levels of Abstraction

We can reduce the likelihood of misunderstandings by being conscious of levels of abstraction. Much confusion results from language that is excessively abstract. For instance, a professor says, "Your papers should demonstrate a sophisticated conceptual grasp of material and its pragmatic implications." Would you know how to write a paper to satisfy the professor? Probably not, because the language is so abstract that it is hard to figure out what the professor wants. Here's a more concrete description: "Your papers should include definitions of the concepts and specific examples that show how they apply to your personal life." This second statement offers a clearer explanation of what the professor expects.

Abstract language is not always inadvisable. The goal is to use a level of abstraction that suits particular communication objectives and situations. Abstract words are appropriate when speakers and listeners have similar concrete knowledge about what is being discussed. For example, long-term friends can say, "Let's just hang out" and understand the activities implied by the abstract term *hang out*. More concrete language is useful when communicators don't have shared experiences and interpretations. For example, early in a friendship the suggestion to hang out would be more effective if it included specifics: "Let's hang out today—maybe watch the game and go out for pizza." Abstract language may also be useful when a communicator wants to create *strategic ambiguity,* in which meaning is *not* crystal clear. Politicians routinely use abstract language because it allows them to claim later that what they are saying is consistent with the strategically ambiguous statements made earlier.

Although abstract language is appropriate in some situations, it often contributes to misunderstandings. For example, online communication is easily misunderstood because it lacks many of the nonverbal cues that clarify meaning, and it is often condensed into phrases and incomplete thoughts. Abstract language may also promote misunderstandings when people talk about changes they want in one another. For example, "I want you to show more initiative in your work" could mean that the person who is speaking wants the other person to work more hours, take on new projects, or seek less direction from supervisors. Vague abstractions promote misunderstanding when people don't share concrete referents for the abstract terms they use.

Qualify Language

Another strategy for increasing the clarity of communication is to qualify language. Two types of language require qualification. First, we should qualify generalizations so that we don't mislead ourselves or others into mistaking a general statement for an absolute one. "Politicians are crooked" is a false statement because it is overly general. A more accurate statement would be, "A number of politicians have been shown to be dishonest." Qualifying reminds us that our perceptions are tied to specific times, places, and circumstances.

We should also qualify language when describing and evaluating people. A **static evaluation** is an assessment that suggests that something is unchanging. Static evaluations are particularly troublesome when applied to people: "Ann is selfish," "Don is irresponsible," "Vy is rude." Whenever we use the word *is*, we suggest that something is fixed. In reality, we aren't static but continually changing. A person who is selfish at one time may be generous at other times. A person who is irresponsible on one occasion may be responsible in different situations. Ken's commentary illustrates that static evaluations can be both inaccurate and irritating.

► Ken

Parents are the worst for static evaluations. When I first got my license 7 years ago, I had a fender bender and then got a speeding ticket. Since then, I've had a perfect record, but you'd never know it from what they say. Dad's always calling me "hot rodder," and Mom goes through this safety spiel every time I get ready to drive somewhere. You'd think I was the same now as when I was 16.

One technique for qualifying language is to index words. **Indexing** is a technique to remind us that our evaluations apply only to specific times and circumstances (Korzybski, 1948). To index, we would say "Ann $_{\text{June 6, 1997}}$ acted selfishly," "Don $_{\text{on the task committee}}$ was irresponsible," and "Vy$_{\text{in college}}$ was rude." See how indexing ties description to a specific time and circumstance? Mental indexing reminds us that we and others are able to change in remarkable ways.

Own Your Feelings and Thoughts

We often use verbal language in ways that obscure our responsibility for how we feel, think, and act. For instance, people say, "You made me mad," "You hurt me," or "You made me do that," as if what they felt or did were caused by someone else. When a person says, "You're so demanding," the person really means that she or he feels pressured by what someone else wants or expects. Feeling pressured is that person's response. Although others can influence us, they seldom actually determine how we feel. Our feelings and thoughts result from how we interpret others' communication. Although how we interpret what others say may lead us to feel certain ways, it is *our* interpretations, not others' communication, that guide our responses.

In certain contexts, such as abusive relationships, others may powerfully shape how we think and feel. Yet even in these extreme situations, we need to remember that we, not others, are responsible for our feelings. We can disapprove of what others do without surrendering control of our thoughts, feelings, and actions. Telling others they make you feel some way is also likely to arouse defensiveness, which doesn't facilitate healthy personal or professional relationships. Effective

Figure 4.4   *I-* and *You*-Language

You-Language	I-Language
You hurt me.	I feel hurt when you ignore what I say.
You make me feel small.	I feel small when you tell me that I'm selfish.
You're really domineering.	When you shout, I feel dominated.
You humiliated me.	I felt humiliated when you mentioned my problems in front of your friends.

communicators take responsibility for themselves by using language that owns their thoughts and feelings. They claim their feelings and do not blame others for what happens within themselves.

To take responsibility for your feelings, rely on **I-language**, not **you-language.** I-language identifies the speaker's or perceiver's thoughts and feelings whereas you-language attributes intentions, motives onto another person. Figure 4.4 gives examples of *I-* and *you*-language. There are two differences between *I*-language and *you*-language. First, *I*-statements own responsibility, whereas *you*-statements project it onto another person. Second, *I*-statements are more descriptive than *you*-statements. *You*-statements tend to be accusations that are abstract and unspecific. This is one reason that *you*-language is ineffective in promoting change. *I*-statements, on the other hand, provide concrete descriptions of behaviors without holding the other person responsible for how we feel.

Some people feel awkward when they first start using *I*-language. This is natural because most of us have learned to rely on *you*-language. With commitment and practice, however, you can learn to communicate using *I*-language. Once you feel comfortable using it, you will find *I*-language has many advantages. First, it is less likely than *you*-language to make others defensive, so *I*-language opens the doors for dialogue. Second, *I*-language is more honest. We deceive ourselves when we say, "You make me feel . . ." because others don't control how we feel. Finally, *I*-language is more empowering than *you*-language. When we say, "You did this" or "You made me feel that," we give control of our emotions, thoughts, and actions to others. This reduces our personal power and our motivation to change what is happening. Using *I*-language allows you to own your feelings while also explaining to others how you interpret their behaviors.

Learning to Use I-Language

For the next 24 hours, pay attention to instances in which you use *you*-language. Catch yourself saying, "You made me angry," "You're being pushy," or engaging in other uses of *you*-language. Whenever you do so, change your language to *I*-language: "I feel angry when you . . . ," "I feel pressured when you . . .".

Do your thoughts and feelings about what is happening change when you substitute *I*-language for *you*-language?

SHARPEN YOUR SKILL

▶SUMMARY

In this chapter, we've explored the nature and power of verbal communication. Verbal symbols shape who we are, what we do, and what our experiences mean. Because they are arbitrary, ambiguous, and abstract, words do not have objective concrete meanings. Instead, their significance reflects our life experiences and the views of the culture and the social groups to which we belong.

To create meaning with language and to interact with others, we follow rules of communication, and we punctuate interaction. As we have seen, regulative rules specify when, where, with whom, and how we communicate verbally. In addition, we follow constitutive rules, which define the meanings of specific forms of verbal communication within particular social groups. A final aspect of creating the meaning of communication is punctuation of the beginnings and endings of interactions.

The ability to use language allows us to create meaning. By defining, evaluating, and classifying phenomena, language allows us to order our experiences and feelings. In addition, we use language to think hypothetically, to self-reflect, and to define relationships and interactions. Our ability to use symbols is a key part of the foundation of communication and human life. We increase the effectiveness of our verbal communication when we are person-centered and conscious of levels of abstraction, as well as own our thoughts and feelings, and when we qualify language appropriately. In Chapter 5, we'll see how nonverbal communication complements and extends verbal communication by allowing us to create meaning.

Review, Reflect, Extend

The Key Concepts, For Further Reflection and Discussion questions, Recommended Resources, and Experience Communication Case Study that follow will help you review, reflect on, and extend the information and ideas presented in this chapter. A diverse selection of online resources is also available through ThomsonNOW. These resources include Speech Builder Express, InfoTrac College Edition, interactive videos, vMentor, and Thomson Audio Study Products.

Thomson NOW! is an online study system designed to help you put your time to the best use. After reading a chapter, take the NOW pre-test to identify concepts discussed in the chapter that you may not fully understand. Based on the results of this diagnostic test, the system will create a personalized study plan that directs you to specific learning resources and activities. To see if you're ready for an exam, take the NOW post-test to check your understanding.

For more information or to access this book's online resources, visit **http://www.thomsonedu.com**.

▶KEY CONCEPTS

The terms below are defined in the chapter on the page number indicated, and they appear in alphabetical order, with definitions, in the Glossary, which begins on page 369. The book's online resources also include flash cards and crossword puzzles to help you learn these terms and the concepts they represent.

abstract, 70
ambiguous, 68
arbitrary, 67
brute facts, 72
communication rules, 73
constitutive rules, 73
hypothetical thought, 80
I, 82

I-language, 87
indexing, 86
institutional facts, 72
loaded language, 79
me, 82
nonverbal communication, 67
punctuation, 75
reappropriation, 79

regulative rules, 73
static evaluation, 85
symbol, 67
totalizing, 77
verbal communication, 67
you-language, 87

▶ FOR FURTHER REFLECTION AND DISCUSSION

The questions below can also be found among the book's online resources for this chapter, where you have the option of e-mailing your responses to your instructor, if required.

1. To appreciate the importance of symbolic capacities, imagine the following: living only in the present without memories or hopes and plans; thinking only in terms of literal reality, not what might be; and having no broad classifications to organize experience. With others in the class, discuss how your life would be different without the symbolic abilities discussed in this chapter.

2. In the chapter, we learned that language names experiences and that language is continuously evolving. Can you think of experiences, feelings, or other phenomena for which we don't yet have names? What is a good term to describe someone with whom you have a serious romance? *Boyfriend* and *girlfriend* no longer work for many people. Do you prefer *significant other, romantic partner, special friend,* or another term?

3. Visit chat rooms and online discussion forums and notice the screen names that people use. How do the names people create for themselves shape perceptions of their identities? What screen names do you use? Why did you choose them?

▶ RECOMMENDED RESOURCES

1. Visit the Institute of General Semantics website by going to the online resources for this chapter and clicking on WebLink 4.3.

2. Pinker, S. (1994). *The language instinct: How mind creates language.* New York: HarperPerennial. This book provides a very accessible discussion of how language works. Unlike some books on the subject of language, this one is written with clarity and a sharp sense of humor.

Experience Communication Case Study

THE ROOMMATES

The book's online resources include an interactive video of the communication situation featured in the case study scripted on the next page. Apply what you've learned in this chapter by analyzing the case study, using the questions that follow the script as a guide. These questions are also available online with the video.

Bernadette and Celia were assigned to be roommates a month ago when the school year began. Both were initially pleased with the match because they discovered commonalities in their interests and backgrounds. They are both sophomores from small towns, they have similar tastes in music and television programs, and they both like to stay up late and sleep in. Lately, however, Bernadette has been irritated by Celia's housekeeping—or lack of it!

Celia leaves her clothes lying all over the room. When they cook, Celia often leaves the pans and dishes for hours, and then it's usually Bernadette who cleans them. Bernadette

Jason Harris/© Wadsworth

feels she has to talk to Celia about this problem, but she hasn't figured out how or when to talk. When Celia gets in from classes, Bernadette is sitting on her bed, reading a textbook.

Celia: Hey, Bernie, how's it going?

Celia drops her book bag in the middle of the floor, flops on the bed, and kicks her shoes off onto the floor. As Bernadette watches, she feels her frustration peaking and decides now is the time to talk to Celia about the problem.

Bernadette: You shouldn't do that. You make me nuts the way you just throw your stuff all over the room.

Celia: I don't "throw my stuff all over the room." I just took off my shoes and put my books down, like I do every day.

Bernadette: No, you didn't. You dropped your bag right in the middle of the room, and you kicked your shoes where they happen to fall without ever noticing how messy they look. And you're right—that *is* what you do every day.

Celia: There's nothing wrong with wanting to be comfortable in my own room. Are we suddenly going for the Good Housekeeping seal of approval?

Bernadette: Comfortable is one thing. But you're so messy. Your mess makes me really miserable.

Celia: Since when? This is the first I've heard about it.

Bernadette: Since we started rooming together, but I didn't want to say anything about how angry you make me. I just can't stand it anymore. You shouldn't be so messy.

Celia: Sounds to me like you've got a problem—you, not me.

Bernadette: Well it's you and your mess that are my problem. Do you have to be such a slob?

1. Identify examples of *you*-language in this conversation. How would you change it to *I*-language?

2. Identify examples of loaded language and ambiguous language.

3. Do you agree with Celia that the problem is Bernadette's, not hers? Explain your answer.

4. To what extent do Celia and Bernadette engage in dual perspective to understand each other?

5 Engaging in Nonverbal Communication

> **FOCUS QUESTIONS**

1. What is nonverbal communication?

2. What types or forms of nonverbal behavior have scholars identified?

3. How does nonverbal communication express cultural values?

4. How can you improve your effectiveness in using and interpreting nonverbal communication?

> Ben Thompson has traveled to Japan to negotiate a joint business venture with Haru Watanabe. They both seem to see the mutual benefit of the project, yet Thompson feels something is wrong in their negotiations. Every time they talk, Watanabe seems uneasy and refuses to hold eye contact. Thompson wonders whether Watanabe is trying to hide something. Meanwhile, Watanabe wonders why Thompson is behaving so rudely if he wants to work together.

> In the library, Maria notices a nice-looking guy two tables away. When he looks up at her, she lowers her eyes. After a moment, she looks back at him just for a second. A few minutes later, he comes over, sits down beside her, and introduces himself.

> Liz Fitzgerald gives a final glance to be sure the dining room table is just right for dinner: The placemats and blue linen napkins are out, and the silver and glasses sparkle; the bowl of flowers in the middle of the table adds color, and the serving dishes are warmed and ready to be filled with roast beef, buttered new potatoes, and fresh rolls. Liz whisks balsamic vinegar and olive oil together, adds a trace of fresh basil, and sprinkles it on the spinach salad just before calling the family to dinner.

> Across town, Benita Bradsher is also preparing dinner for her family. She puts a big spoon in the pot of mashed potatoes and transfers it from the stove to the kitchen table. Next, she piles plates, paper napkins, knives, spoons, and forks in the middle

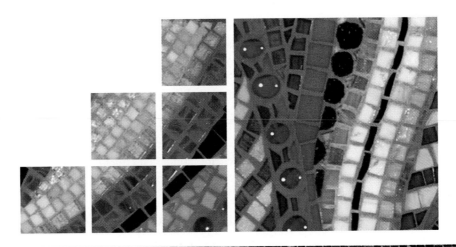

of the table. She takes the ground beef casserole from the oven, puts it on a pot-holder on the table, and calls her family to dinner.

Many of us grew up hearing that actions speak louder than words. The wisdom of this axiom is that nonverbal communication can be as powerful as or more powerful than words. Facial expressions can express love, suspicion, competitiveness, sorrow, interest, anger, and hatred. Body postures can convey relaxation, nervousness, boredom, and power. Physical objects can symbolize professional identity (stethoscope, briefcase), personal commitments (wedding band, school sweatshirt), and lifestyle (comfortable furniture casually arranged, stiff furniture in formal rooms).

In this chapter, we explore the fascinating realm of nonverbal interaction. We will identify principles of nonverbal communication and then discuss types of nonverbal behavior and guidelines for effectiveness.

The examples that opened this chapter illustrate the power of nonverbal communication. In the first case, Thompson and Watanabe have difficulty because of different nonverbal communication norms in Japan and the United States. Ben Thompson has learned that eye contact is a sign of honesty and respect, so he looks directly at Haru Watanabe when they talk. In Watanabe's culture, however, direct eye contact is considered rude and intrusive, so he doesn't meet Thompson's gaze and feels uncomfortable when Thompson looks directly at him.

In the library, we see a clear example of gendered patterns of nonverbal communication. Maria follows feminine communication norms by indirectly signaling her interest and waiting for the man to initiate contact. He in turn enacts the rules of masculine communication culture by gazing directly at her and moving to her table.

In the final example, nonverbal communication reflects differences in socioeconomic level. Whereas Liz Fitzgerald sets her table with cloth napkins, placemats, silver, crystal, and a vase of flowers, Benita Bradsher sets her table with pans off the stove and a casual pile of utensils and paper napkins that people can take. What each woman serves and how she sets her table reflect the teachings of social groups to which she belongs and the time she has in which to prepare a meal.

Gender, ethnicity, sexual orientation, socioeconomic level (or status), and membership in social groups are aspects of our identities that we communicate day in and day out. Recognizing this, Candice West and Don Zimmerman (1987) and Judith Butler (1990, 1993) observe that we "do gender" or "perform gender" continually by behaving in ways that symbolize femininity or masculinity according to our culture's views. We also "do" race, class, and sexual orientation by nonverbally symbolizing those facets of identity. Nonverbal communication, like its verbal cousin, allows us to establish identity, express thoughts and feelings, reflect on ourselves, define and regulate relationships, and create interaction climates. Like words, nonverbal communication powerfully shapes meaning in our lives.

►Principles of Nonverbal Communication

Nonverbal communication is a major dimension of human life. It includes all aspects of communication other than words. In addition to gestures and body language, nonverbal communication includes *how* we utter words (inflection, volume), features of environments that affect meaning (temperature, lighting), and objects that affect personal images and interaction patterns (dress, jewelry, furniture). According to classic research by Ray Birdwhistell (1970) and Albert Mehrabian (1981), nonverbal communication accounts for 65% to 93% of the total meaning of communication. This suggests that nonverbal behaviors make up more of our overall communication than verbal ones. Five principles of nonverbal communication clarify its importance in human interaction.

Nonverbal Communication Is Ambiguous

Like verbal communication, nonverbal behavior can be ambiguous. We can never be sure that others understand the meanings we intend to express with our nonverbal behavior. Conversely, we can't know whether they read meanings into our behaviors that we do not intend. The ambiguity of nonverbal communication also arises because meanings change over time. Spreading apart the first two fingers meant victory during the world wars and came to stand for peace during the 1960s. Both victory and peace are arbitrary meanings of this particular nonverbal behavior.

Nonverbal behaviors also reflect and perpetuate distinct organizational identities: Bankers, attorneys, and many other professionals are expected to wear business suits or dresses to work, whereas many high-tech companies encourage employees to wear jeans and other informal attire. Each way of dressing reflects a particular organizational ethos. In formal organizations, employees often work behind closed doors in private offices and do not go into another person's office unless they have business to conduct. In more informal organizations, employees may work in common spaces or in offices with open doors, and casual visiting is a normal part of daily interaction.

Like verbal communication, nonverbal communication is learned and guided by rules. The rules that guide it reduce the ambiguity of nonverbal communication by telling us what certain behaviors are understood to count as (constitutive rules) and when and where certain behaviors are appropriate and inappropriate (regulative rules). For example, most of us understand that people take turns speaking, and that we should whisper in libraries but it's appropriate to yell at ball games. We know that we are supposed to raise our hands if we want to ask a question during a lecture but don't need to raise our hands to speak when interacting with friends. We dress differently for religious services, classes, dates, and job interviews. Insignia that nonverbally communicate rank define people in the military, and salutes are the standard way to acknowledge other military people. These agreed-upon rules reduce but don't completely eliminate the ambiguity of nonverbal communication.

Nonverbal Behaviors Interact with Verbal Communication

Communication researchers have identified five ways in which nonverbal behaviors interact with verbal communication (Andersen, 1999). First, nonverbal behaviors may repeat verbal messages. For example, you might say "yes" while nodding your head. In making a public presentation, a speaker might hold up one, two, and three fingers when saying "first," "second," and "third," to let listeners know she or he is moving from the first to the second to the third point of a speech.

Second, nonverbal behaviors may highlight verbal communication, as when you use inflection to emphasize certain words: "This is the *most* serious consequence of the policy I'm arguing against." Third, nonverbal communication may also complement, or add to, words. When you see a friend, you might say, "I'm glad to see you" and underline the verbal message with a smile. When joking in an e-mail message, you might add the emoticon :). Speakers often emphasize verbal statements with forceful gestures and increases in volume and inflection; capital or boldfaced letters are used to symbolize the same emphasis in online communication.

Fourth, nonverbal behaviors may contradict verbal messages (Knapp & Hall, 2006). For instance, a group member says, "Nothing's wrong" in a hostile tone of voice. Fifth, we sometimes substitute nonverbal behaviors for verbal ones. You might roll your eyes to show that you disapprove of something or shrug your shoulders instead of saying "I don't know." In all these ways, nonverbal behaviors augment or replace verbal communication.

Nonverbal Communication Regulates Interaction

Nonverbal communication can organize interaction between people. You generally know when someone else has finished speaking, when a professor welcomes discussion from students, and when a co-worker expects you to speak. Nonverbal cues, more than verbal ones, tell us when to speak and keep silent. By averting our eyes or by increasing our speaking volume and rate, we signal that we don't want to be interrupted. When we're finished talking, we look at others to signal, "Okay, now someone else can speak." Most Westerners invite specific people to speak by looking directly at them (Drummond & Hopper, 1993; Knapp & Hall, 2006), yet eye contact is used less to regulate interaction in many Asian cultures. Speakers often step aside from a podium to signal that they are finished. Although we're usually unaware of how nonverbal actions regulate interaction, we rely on them to know when to speak and when to remain silent.

Nonverbal Communication Establishes Relationship-Level Meanings

You'll recall that the relationship level of meaning defines individuals' identities and relationships between people. Nonverbal communication can be powerful in expressing relationship-level meanings (Keeley & Hart, 1994). In fact, some communication scholars call nonverbal communication "the relationship language" because it so often expresses how people feel about one another (Richmond & McCroskey, 1995; Sallinen-Kuparinen, 1992). We use nonverbal communication to convey the three dimensions of relationship-level meaning we discussed in Chapter 4: responsiveness, liking, and power. Yet how people communicate responsiveness, liking and disliking, and power depends on the rules of their cultures.

Responsiveness We use eye contact, inflections, facial expressions, and body posture to show interest in others, as Maria did in one of the examples that opened this chapter. In formal presentations and casual conversations, we signal interest by holding eye contact and assuming an attentive posture. As the example with Haru Watanabe and Ben Thompson reveals, however, all cultures do not have the same rules for eye contact. To express lack of interest, Westerners tend to avoid or decrease visual contact and adopt a passive body position or turn away from the other person. Members of Asian cultures are less likely to overtly express lack of interest.

Harmony in people's postures and facial expressions may reflect how comfortable they are with each other (Berg, 1987; Guerrero & Floyd, 2006; Capella, 1991) and how much they support each other (Trees, 2000). In a cohesive team, many nonverbal behaviors typically signal that members are responsive to one another. In less cohesive groups, nonverbal behavior shows less responsiveness. Happy couples sit closer to one another and engage in more eye contact than unhappy couples do (Noller, 1986, 1987). Similarly, in work settings people who like one another often sit together and exchange eye contact.

▶ Maryam

Americans do more than one thing at a time. In Nepal, when we talk with someone, we are with that person. We do not also write on paper or have television on. We talk with the person. It is hard for me to accept the custom of giving only some attention to each other in conversation.

Liking Nonverbal behaviors are keen indicators of whether we feel positive or negative about others. Smiles and friendly touching among Westerners usually are signs of positive feelings, whereas frowns and belligerent postures express antagonism (Keeley & Hart, 1994). Political candidates shake hands, slap backs, and otherwise touch people whose votes they want. These are general rules of Western society; particular social groups instill more specific rules. For example, women generally sit closer together and engage in more eye contact and more friendly touching than men do (Atsuko, 2003; Knapp & Hall, 2006).

▶ Ellen

Secretaries are the best decoders. They can read their bosses' moods in a heartbeat. I am a secretary, part-time now that I'm taking courses, and I can tell exactly what my boss is thinking. Sometimes, I know what he feels or will do before he does. I have to know when he can be interrupted, when he feels generous, and when not to cross his path.

Power We use nonverbal behaviors to assert dominance and to negotiate status (Andersen, 1999; Remland, 2000). Compared with women, men generally assume more space and use greater volume and more forceful gestures to assert their ideas (Hall, 1987; Major, Schmidlin, & Williams, 1990). Men are also more likely to move into others' spaces, as the man in the library moved to Maria's table in one of the examples that opened this chapter.

Space also expresses power relations. The connection between power and space is evident in the fact that CEOs usually have large, spacious offices, entry-level and midlevel professionals have smaller offices, and secretaries often have minuscule workstations, even though secretaries often store and manage more material than executives. A widely understood regulative communication rule is that people with status or power have the right to enter the space of people with less power, but the converse is not true. Similarly, more powerful people are more likely to touch others, interrupt, and approach more closely than less powerful people (Hall, Coats, & Smith-LeBeau, 2004). Space may reflect power differences between family members. Adults usually have more space than children, and men are more likely than women to have their own rooms and to sit at heads of tables. The Sharpen Your Skill exercise on this page will help you become more attentive to nonverbal modes of expressing power.

Silence, a powerful form of nonverbal communication, can also be a means of exerting control. We sometimes use silence to stifle others' conversation in meetings. Silence accompanied by a glare is doubly powerful in conveying disapproval. Interviewers sometimes use silence to let interviewees know that they are not satisfied with answers given and to prompt interviewees to elaborate. In a number of Native American cultures and some Asian cultures, silence signals mindful attentiveness.

Nonverbal Communication Reflects Cultural Values

Like verbal communication, nonverbal patterns reflect rules of specific cultures. This implies that most nonverbal communication isn't instinctual but is learned in the process of socialization. For instance, dress considered appropriate for women varies across cultures; some women in some

---

Noticing Spatial Clues to Power Relations

Observe a business setting—an office or other work context. To sharpen your insight into spatial indicators of power, answer the following questions:

1. Who has more space? Who has less?

2. Who enters the space of others? Who does not?

3. Who touches others?

4. Who uses commanding gestures? Who does not?

SHARPEN YOUR SKILL

© Goodshoot/Jupiter Images

What does this person's office space communicate about his status?

countries wear miniskirts, whereas some women in other countries wear veils. Most European Americans consider it inappropriate to touch or hold hands with same-sex friends, but this is an acceptable way of showing closeness among many Asians and Asian Americans (Orbe & Harris, 2001).

Have you ever seen the bumper sticker that says, "If you can read this, you're too close"? That slogan proclaims Americans' territoriality. We want our private spaces, and we resent and sometimes fight anyone who trespasses on what we consider our territory. We want private homes, and many people want large lots to increase the distance between them and others. In more collectivist cultures, people tend to be less territorial. For instance, Brazilians routinely stand close to one another in shops, buses, and elevators, and when they bump into each other, they don't apologize or draw back, as U.S. citizens do. In other countries, such as Hong Kong, people are used to living and working in very close quarters, so feelings of territoriality are less pronounced (Chan, 1999).

Western culture prizes time, and that is evident in the presence of clocks in most or all rooms of homes and public spaces and in the nearly universal use of wristwatches, which are not worn by people in many other cultures. Westerners' time consciousness is also reflected in the technological devices that are now part of many people's daily attire. We carry pagers and iPods, have cell phones in our cars, and carry laptop computers and palm pilots that allow us to maintain nearly instant contact with others. Orientations toward time are less rigid among other cultural groups, such as Hispanics. Norms for touching also reflect cultural values (Axtell, 1998).

► Yumiko

I try to teach my daughter to follow the customs of my native Japan, but she is learning to be American. I scold her for talking loud and speaking when she has not been addressed, but she tells me all the other kids talk loud and talk when they wish. I tell her it is not polite to look directly at others, but she says everyone looks at others here. She communicates as an American, not a Japanese.

Patterns of eye contact also reflect cultural values. U.S. society values frankness and assertion, so meeting another's eyes is considered appropriate and a demonstration of personal honesty. Yet in many Asian and northern European countries, direct eye contact is considered abrasive and disrespectful (Hall, 1969). Many Latinos and Latinas express attentiveness and respect by avoiding direct eye contact, whereas European Americans express attentiveness and respect by maintaining it (Orbe & Harris, 2001). In Brazil, eye contact often is so intense that many Northern Europeans consider it staring, which they find rude.

The five principles of nonverbal communication we have discussed provide a foundation for a closer look at specific kinds of nonverbal communication.

►TYPES OF NONVERBAL BEHAVIORS

Because so much of our interaction is nonverbal, this symbol system includes many kinds of communication. In this section, we will consider ten forms of nonverbal behavior, noticing how we use each to create and interpret meanings:

▶ Kinesics (face and body motion)

▶ Haptics (touch)

▶ Physical appearance

▶ Olfactics (smell)

▶ Artifacts (personal objects)

▶ Proxemics (personal space)

▶ Environmental factors

▶ Chronemics (perception and use of time)

▶ Paralanguage (vocal qualities)

▶ Silence

Kinesics

Kinesics is a technical term that refers to body position and body motions, including those of the face. Our bodies communicate a great deal about how we see ourselves. A speaker who stands erect and appears confident announces self-assurance, whereas someone who slouches and shuffles may seem to say, "I'm not very sure of myself." We also communicate moods with body posture and motion. For example, someone who walks quickly with a resolute facial expression appears more determined than someone who saunters along with an unfocused gaze. Similarly, researchers (Gunns, Johnston, & Hudson, 2002) found that people whose nonverbal behaviors indicate they have sufficient vigor to take care of themselves and move quickly are less likely to be attacked than people whose posture and movements indicate less vitality. We sit rigidly when we are nervous and adopt a relaxed posture when we feel at ease. Audiences show interest by alert body posture.

Body postures and gestures may signal whether we are open to interaction. Speakers who stay behind podiums and read notes often are perceived as less open than speakers who interact more actively with audiences. Someone who sits with arms crossed and looks downward may be perceived as saying, "Don't bother me." That's also a nonverbal strategy students sometimes use to dissuade teachers from calling on them in class. To signal that we'd like to interact, we look at others and sometimes smile. We use gestures to express how we feel about others and situations. We use one hand gesture to say "okay" and a different hand gesture to communicate contempt.

© AP/World-Wide Photos

How do Barack Obama's gestures and facial expression influence your perceptions of his effectiveness?

Our faces are intricate messengers. Our eyes can shoot daggers of anger, issue challenges, express skepticism, or radiate love. The face is particularly powerful in conveying liking and responsiveness (Keeley & Hart, 1994; Patterson, 1992). Many speakers smile to suggest that they are open and friendly. Smiles and warm gazes signal that we like others and are happy being around them (Gueguen & De Gail, 2003; Walker & Trimboli, 1989). Americans often cross their legs while seated, but this is highly offensive according to cultural rules in Ghana and Turkey (Samovar & Porter, 2001).

Poets call the eyes the "windows of the soul" for good reason. Our eyes communicate important and complex messages about how we feel, and we often look at others' eyes to judge their emotions, honesty, interest, and self-confidence. This explains why strong eye contact tends to heighten the credibility of public speakers in Western societies. It may also be why customers leave larger tips to servers who maintain eye contact while serving them (Davis & Kieffer, 1998). Yet eye contact is not universally regarded as positive. Among traditional Hasidic Jews, for example, boys are taught not to look into women's eyes.

Haptics

Haptics is a term for nonverbal communication involving physical touch. Many communication scholars believe that touching and being touched are essential to healthy life (Ackerman, 1990; Whitman, White, O'Mara, & Goeke-Morey 1999). In disturbed families, parents sometimes push children away and handle them harshly, nonverbally signaling rejection. Conversely, researchers have learned that babies who are massaged thrive more than babies who are touched less (Mwakalye & DeAngelis, 1995).

Research suggests some general sex differences in touching behavior. Compared to men, women are more likely to engage in touch to show liking and intimacy (Andersen, 1999), whereas men are more likely than women to use touch to assert power and control (Jhally & Katz, 2001).

Physical Appearance

Western culture places an extremely high value on **physical appearance** and on specific aspects of appearance. We first notice obvious physical qualities such as sex, skin color, and size. Based on physical qualities, we may make inferences about others' personalities. Although these associations may have no factual basis, they can affect personal and social relationships as well as decisions about hiring, placement, and promotion.

Kangaroo Care

Kangaroo Care is the title of Susan Ludington-Hoe's 1993 book. In it, she tells the story of an accidental discovery about the importance of touch to human survival. Until recently, it was typical for Western hospital workers to take newborn babies to nurseries where sophisticated monitoring devices could be used to ensure the babies' health. Babies born prematurely were almost certainly entrusted to medical technology.

The wisdom of separating newborns from mothers was challenged by an accidental finding from a hospital in Bogotá, Colombia. In the 1980s, the hospital experienced a serious lack of resources, including blankets used to wrap newborns. To keep the babies warm, hospital workers placed the naked babies on their mothers' naked chests. The babies thrived—more than they had when wrapped in blankets (Miller, 2006). Because the skin-to-skin contact between mothers and babies is similar to that of kangaroo moms and babies, the technique was dubbed "kangaroo care." Since the accidental discovery in Bogotá, hospitals in the United States have reported that premature babies who experience skin-to-skin contact with their moms are less fussy and calmer than babies who do not (Miller, 2006).

SHARPEN YOUR SKILL

Cultures prescribe ideals for physical form, and these vary across cultures. Western cultural ideals today emphasize thinness in women and muscularity and height in men (Bordo, 1999; Davison & Birch, 2001; Kilbourne, 2004; Mirzoeff, 1998). The cultural ideal of slimness in women leads many women to become preoccupied with dieting and other means of weight control (Buss, 2001). If you'd like to learn more about eating disorders and help for people who have them, go to the book's online resources and click on WebLink 4.1. In her commentary, Cass makes a point that will be familiar to many women.

▸ Cass

I've been dieting since I was in grammar school. I'm 5' 5" and weigh 102 pounds, but I want to weigh less. I look at the models in magazines and the women in films, and they are so much slimmer than I am. I have to watch everything I eat and exercise all the time, and I'm still too fat.

This general cultural standard for attractiveness is modified by ethnicity and socio-economic class. Traditional African societies perceive full-figured bodies as symbols of health, prosperity, and wealth, all of which are desirable (Bocella, 2001). African Americans who embrace this value accept or prefer women who weigh more than the ideal for European American women (Root, 1990; Thomas, 1989). But ethnicity doesn't operate in isolation. Class membership modifies ethnic views about weight. Research shows that African American women who identify strongly with their ethnic cultures tend to resist Caucasian preoccupations with thinness. On the other hand, middle-income African American women who are upwardly mobile may deemphasize their ethnic identities, and they are more susceptible to anxiety about weight and to eating disorders (Bocella, 2001).

Physical appearance includes physiological characteristics, such as eye color and height, as well as ways in which we manage, or even alter, our physical appearance. For instance, many people control their physical appearance by dieting, using steroids and other drugs, coloring their hair, having plastic surgery, wearing colored contact lenses, and using makeup. We can manage many facets of the physical impression we create, and Westerners seem increasingly interested in doing so: Plastic surgeries of many types are on the rise for both men and women (Gilman, 1999a, 1999b).

Olfactics (Smell)

Olfactics (from the word *olfactory*, which refers to the sense of smell) is a term for odors and scents—or, more precisely, our perception of them. Mark Knapp and Judith Hall (2006), who study nonverbal behavior, note that the "scientific study of the human olfactory system is in its infancy" (p 196). Even so, we know that smell is a form of communication. Dogs can track people or other animals by smell, and animals in the wild track prey by smell. The smell of freshly baked bread or cookies often makes us feel comfortable and warm (and hungry!). Also, as Andy notes, scents we choose to wear can be personal signatures.

▶ **Andy**

I dated this one girl for two years, and then we broke up last year. By now, I pretty much don't think about her unless I pass somebody who is wearing the cologne she wore. One sniff of that transports me back when she and I were together.

Body odors produced by pheromones, the sex-specific chemicals our bodies produce, may affect sexual attraction. Male sweat contains a pheromone derived from progesterone, whereas female sweat contains a pheromone linked to estrogen (Bakalar, 2006). Although most smells trigger olfactory responses, heterosexual men and women respond to the pheromones of the opposite sex with increased activity in the hypothalamus, which is linked to sexual behavior. Interestingly, a recent study reported that lesbians respond with elevated hypothalamic activity to the estrogen-like pheromone of other women (Bakalar, 2006).

Artifacts

Artifacts are personal objects we use to announce our identities and to personalize our environments. Clothing is one of the most common forms of artifactual communication. Although clothing for students has become more unisex in recent years, once you venture beyond the campus context, gendered styles are evident and expected (Abdullah, 1999). More women than men wear makeup and jewelry. Women are also more likely than men to wear clothes that have lace or other softening touches, high-heeled shoes, and hose. Typically, men wear less jewelry, clothes with less adornment, and functional shoes (Klein, 2001; Johnson, Roberts, & Warell, 2002). Men's clothing is looser and less binding, and it includes pockets for wallets, change, keys, and so forth. In contrast, women's clothing often doesn't include pockets, so women need purses to hold personal items.

We also use artifacts to express our cultural and ethnic identities. Indians may wear saris, Native Americans may wear jewelry with tribal symbols, and African Ameri-

1-5 ©1994 by King Features Syndicate, Inc. World rights reserved.

cans may wear clothes and jewelry of traditional African design. In recent years, many stores have begun to carry a greater range of styles in clothing and jewelry, so people can acquire artifacts that express their cultural heritage. Further, as any college student knows, school symbols adorn everything from T-shirts and sweatshirts to car bumpers and notebooks. Wearing something with a symbol of your school on it expresses your membership in or loyalty to that campus community.

Artifacts may also be used to announce professional identity. Nurses and doctors wear white and often drape stethoscopes around their necks; executives carry briefcases, whereas students more often tote backpacks. White-collar professionals tend to wear tailored outfits and dress shoes, whereas blue-collar workers often dress in jeans or uniforms and boots. The military requires uniforms that define individuals as members of the group. In addition, stripes, medals, and insignia signify rank and accomplishments.

We also use artifacts to define settings and personal territories (Bateson, 1990; Wood, 2006). When the president of the United States speaks, the setting usually is decked with symbols of national identity and pride, such as the flag. At annual meetings of companies, the chair usually speaks from a podium that bears the company logo. In much the same manner, we claim our private spaces by filling them with objects that matter to us and that reflect our experiences and values. Lovers of art adorn their homes and offices with paintings and sculptures that reflect their interests. Religious families often express their commitments by displaying pictures of holy scenes and the Bible, the Koran, or another sacred text. Professionals may decorate their offices with expensive furniture and framed awards to announce their status or with pictures of family to remind them of people they cherish. Websites, too, are defined by artifacts such as photos, animations, and colors that express the creators' personalities and interests. Like other kinds of nonverbal communication, artifacts' meanings vary across cultures, as the FYI on this page illustrates.

> **D I V E R S I T Y**
>
> **fyi**
>
> ### CULTURAL RULES FOR GIFT GIVING
>
> Giving gifts can lead to misunderstandings when giver and recipient are from different cultures (Axtell, 1990a, 1990b).
>
> ▶ A Chinese person might not appreciate the gift of a clock, because clocks symbolize death in China.
>
> ▶ Giving a gift to an Arab person on first meeting would be interpreted as a bribe.
>
> ▶ Bringing flowers to a dinner hosted by a person from Kenya would cause confusion because in Kenya flowers express sympathy for a loss.
>
> ▶ In Switzerland, giving red roses is interpreted as a signal of romantic interest. Also, the Swiss consider even numbers of flowers bad luck, so never give a dozen.

Proxemics and Personal Space

Proxemics refers to space and how we use it. The classic research on proxemics was done by Edward Hall 40 years ago (Hall, 1968). At the time, Hall reported that every culture has norms for using space and for how close people should be to one another. In the United States, we interact with social acquaintances from a distance of 4 to 12 feet but are comfortable with 18 inches or less between us and friends or romantic partners (Hall, 1968). Most people who were born and raised in the United States consider it normal for individuals to have separate spaces or rooms. As Sucheng points out, however, what is considered a normal amount of individual space varies from culture to culture.

► **Sucheng**

In United States, each person has so much room. Every individual has a separate room to sleep and sometimes another separate room to work. Also, I see that each family here lives in a separate house. People have much less space in China. Families live together, with sons bringing their families into their parents' home and all sharing the same space. At first, when I came here, it felt strange to have so much space, but now I sometimes feel very crowded when I go home.

Space also announces status, with greater space and more desirable space assumed by those with higher status in a culture. Research shows that women and minorities generally have less space than European American men in the United States (Andersen, 1999). It's no coincidence that industries expose our most vulnerable communities to pollutants and carcinogens that they seldom foist on middle- and upper-class people. The meaning of this pattern is very clear: "The space of minorities and poor people is often invaded and contaminated, but the territory of more affluent citizens is respected" (Cox, 2006b).

How people arrange space may reflect closeness and desire, or lack of desire, for interaction. Rigidly organized businesses often have private offices with doors that are usually closed and little common space. Couples who are highly interdependent tend to have more common space and less individual space in their homes than do couples who are more independent (Fitzpatrick, 1988; Werner, Altman, & Oxley, 1985). Similarly, families that enjoy interaction arrange furniture to invite conversation and eye contact. In families that seek less interaction, chairs may be far apart and may face televisions instead of each other (Burgoon, Buller, & Woodhall, 1989; Keeley & Hart, 1994).

The ways that offices are arranged may invite or discourage interaction and may foster equal or unequal power relationships between people. Some professors and executives have desks that face their office doors and a chair beside the desk to promote open communication with people who come to their offices. Other professors and executives turn their desks away from the door and place chairs opposite their desks, which configures the space hierarchically. Whether office doors are open or shut may also indicate willingness to interact.

Environmental Factors

Environmental factors are elements of settings that affect how we feel, think, and act. We feel more relaxed in rooms with comfortable chairs than in rooms with stiff, formal furniture. Candlelit dining tables may promote romantic feelings; and churches, synagogues, and temples use candles to foster respect.

Restaurants use environmental features to control how long people spend eating. For example, low lights, comfortable chairs or booths, and soft music often are part of the environment in upscale restaurants. On the other hand, fast-food eateries have hard plastic booths and bright lights, which encourage diners to eat and move on. To maximize profit, restaurants want to get people in and out as quickly as possible. Studies show that fast music in restaurants speeds up the pace of eating; on average, people

© Charles Jean Marc/Corbis

© Warren Morgan/Corbis

How does each of the restaurants pictured here use environmental features to shape customers' behavior?

eat 3.2 mouthfuls a minute when the background music is slow and 5.1 mouthfuls a minute when rock music is played ("Did You Know?" 1998). Restaurants use a variety of environmental cues to create the atmosphere they want—to encourage customers to linger, or to encourage them to eat and run. You can identify some of the environmental features that affect a restaurant's atmosphere by completing the Sharpen Your Skill feature on this page.

In the same way that restaurants and other public places use environmental factors to influence mood and behavior, we choose colors, furniture arrangements, and other things to create the atmosphere we desire in our home. The FYI on the following page describes feng shui, a very elaborate system of managing environments to affect moods and happiness.

Chronemics

Chronemics refers to how we perceive and use time to define identities and interaction. We use time to negotiate and convey status (Levine & Norenzayan, 1999). There seems to be an unwritten but widely understood cultural rule stipulating that people with high status can keep people with less status waiting. Conversely, people with low status are expected to be punctual in Western society. It is standard practice to have to wait, sometimes a good while, to see a doctor even when you have an appointment. This carries the message that the doc-

Increasing Awareness of Environmental Influences

Observe a restaurant in which you feel rushed and another restaurant in which you feel like taking your time. Describe the following for each restaurant:

1. How much space is there between tables?

2. What kind of lighting is used?

3. What sort of music and sound are in the place?

4. How comfortable are the chairs?

5. What colors and art do you see?

Can you make any generalizations about environmental features that promote relaxation and those that do not?

SHARPEN YOUR SKILL

D I V E R S I T Y

fyi

FENG SHUI

Does your home encourage a free flow of energy? Does it foster prosperity, health, and happiness? If not, the problem could be bad *feng shui* (pronounced "fung shway"). Feng shui is a 3,000-year-old Asian art that focuses on relationships between external environments and the inner self (Kaufman, 1996; Spear, 1996). Feng shui aims to arrange furniture and walls and objects in a space to be in harmony with the earth. When an environment is in harmony with the earth, it is assumed that those in that environment will be similarly in harmony with the natural world and its positive energies (Wydra, 1998).

Feng shui has recently found its way westward. For $200 to $500 an hour, a feng shui consultant will come to your home or office and help you arrange the space to promote blessings, fortune, and the life force (*chi*). He or she will advise you to get plants with rounded leaves to promote upward and outward energy, to get the red out of your bedroom if you suffer from lack of sleep or put more red in the bedroom if your problem is lack of passion, and to use mirrors and lights to enhance, diminish, or redirect energy. Feng shui is based on a complex grid called a *bagua* that charts nine specific elements that affect the flow of energy. Many principles of feng shui are consistent with research findings on nonverbal communication. Some feng shui advisers even claim that principles of this ancient Asian system can give you insights into potential mates. For instance, Nancilee Wydra (1998) says you should be wary of someone whose space is filled with childhood photos (which indicates a focus on the past) or who has no pets or plants (which indicates low interest in nurturing).

The Feng Shui Institute was founded by Nancilee Wydra, who has degrees in psychiatric social work and interior design. Her goal is to translate the ancient art of feng shui into a practice that is viable in contemporary Western societies. In addition to writing books on feng shui, Wydra writes a national column and appears on national television. To learn more about her and the Feng Shui Institute, go to the book's online resources and click on WebLink 5.2.

tor's time is more valuable than yours. Subordinates are expected to report punctually to meetings, but bosses are allowed to be tardy.

Chronemics expresses cultural attitudes toward time. Western societies value time and its cousin, speed (Bertman, 1998; Keyes, 1992; Schwartz, 1989). We want computers, not typewriters, and many of us replace our computers and software as soon as faster versions become available. We often try to do several things at once to get more done, rely on the microwave to cook faster, and take for granted speed systems such as instant copying and photos (McGee-Cooper, Trammel, & Lau, 1992). Many other cultures have far more relaxed attitudes toward time and punctuality. In many South American countries, it's normal to come to meetings or classes after the announced time of starting, and it's not assumed that people will leave when the scheduled time for ending arrives. Whether time is savored and treated casually or counted and hoarded reflects broad cultural attitudes.

The length of time we spend with different people reflects the extent of our interest in them and affection for them. A manager spends more time with a new employee who seems to have executive potential than with one who seems less impressive. A speaker gives a fuller answer to a question from a high-status member of the audience than to one from a person with less status. We spend more time with people we like than with those we don't like or who bore us. Researchers report that increased contact among college students is a clear sign that a relationship is intensifying, and reduced time together signals decreasing interest (Baxter, 1985; Dindia, 1994; Tolhuizen, 1989).

Chronemics also involves expectations of time, which are influenced by social norms. For example, you expect a class to last 50 or 75 minutes. Several minutes before the end of a class period, students often close their notebooks and start gathering their belongings, signaling the teacher that time is up. A similar pattern often is evident in business meetings. We expect religious services to last approximately an hour, and we might be upset if a rabbi or minister talked for two hours.

In a classic study of time, Lakoff and Johnson (1980) found that westerners' view of time as a precious commodity to be hoarded and saved is reflected in many everyday expressions: "You're *wasting* my time," "This new software program will *save* time," "That mistake *cost* me three hours," "I've *invested* a lot of time in this class," "I can't *afford* to go out tonight," "I can make up for *lost* time by using a shortcut," and "I'm *running out* of time."

Paralanguage

Paralanguage is communication that is vocal but not actual words. Paralanguage includes sounds, such as murmurs and gasps, and vocal qualities, such as volume, rhythm, pitch, and inflection. Our voices are versatile instruments that tell others how to interpret us and what we say. Vocal cues signal others to interpret what we say as a joke, a threat, a statement of fact, a question, and so forth. Effective public speakers modulate inflection, volume, and rhythm to enhance their presentations.

We use vocal cues to communicate feelings to friends and romantic partners. Whispering, for instance, signals confidentiality or intimacy, whereas shouting conveys anger or excitement. Depending on the context, sighing may communicate empathy, boredom, or contentment. Research shows that tone of voice is a powerful clue to feelings between marital partners. Negative vocal tones often reveal marital dissatisfaction (Noller, 1987). Negative intonation may also signal dissatisfaction or disapproval in work settings. A derisive or sarcastic tone can communicate scorn clearly. On the other hand, a warm voice conveys liking, and a playful lilt suggests friendliness.

Our voices affect how others perceive us. To some extent, we control vocal cues that influence image. For instance, we can deliberately sound confident in job interviews or when asking for a raise. The president adopts a solemn voice when announcing military actions. Most of us know how to make ourselves sound apologetic, seductive, or angry when those images suit our purposes. In addition to the ways we intentionally use our voices, natural and habitual vocal qualities affect how others perceive us. For instance, people who speak at slow to moderate rates are perceived as having greater control over interaction than people who speak more rapidly (Tusing & Dillard, 2000).

▶ Leah

Everyone in my family knew that when Mother raised her voice we were in trouble, but when our father lowered his, we were in trouble. His voice would drop to this low volume and get very slow and deep. It was a signal to take cover FAST!

Our ethnic heritage and identification influence how we use our voices. In general, African American speech has more vocal range, inflection, and tonal quality than European American speech (Garner, 1994). In general, African Americans are also more likely than European Americans to signal interest in what another person is saying by making listening sounds ("um hmm," "yeah, yeah") (Brilhart & Galanes, 1995). Paralanguage also reflects gender. Men's voices tend to have louder volume, lower pitch, and less inflection, features that conform to cultural views of men as assertive and emotionally controlled. Women's voices typically have higher pitch, softer volume, and more inflection, features consistent with cultural views of women as emotional and deferential. Socioeconomic level influences pronunciation, rate of speech, and accent.

Silence

A final type of nonverbal behavior is **silence,** which is a lack of communicated sound. Although silence is quiet, it can communicate powerful messages. "I'm not speaking to you" speaks volumes. Silence can convey contentment when intimates are so comfortable they don't need to talk. Silence can also communicate awkwardness, as you know if you've ever had trouble making conversation on a first date. Yet the awkwardness that many westerners feel when silence falls is not felt by people from some other cultures, as Jin Lee explains.

► Jin Lee

In the United States, people feel it is necessary to talk all of the time, to fill in any silence with words and more words. I was not brought up that way. In my country, it is good to be silent some of the time. It shows you are listening to another, you are thinking about what the other says, you are respectful and do not need to put in your words.

Some parents discipline children by ignoring them. No matter what the child says or does, the parents refuse to acknowledge the child's existence. The silencing strategy may also surface later in life. We sometimes deliberately freeze out others when we're angry with them (Williams, 2001). In some military academies, such as West Point, silence is a method of stripping a cadet of personhood if the cadet is perceived as having broken the academy's honor code. On the job, silence may signal disapproval, as peers often ostracize whistle-blowers and union-busters. People who violate the rules of chat rooms may be silenced by getting no responses to their messages.

Audiences sometimes shout down speakers they dislike; when angry, romantic partners may refuse to speak; and the Catholic Church excommunicates people who violate its canons. Like other forms of communication, silence—and what it means—is linked to culture. European Americans tend to be talkative; they are inclined to fill in silence with words. Among Native Americans, however, historically silence conveys respect, active listening, and thought about what others are saying (Braithwaite, 1990; Carbaugh, 1998).

We've seen that nonverbal communication includes kinesics, haptics, physical appearance, olfactics, artifacts, proxemics, environmental factors, chronemics, paralanguage, and silence. The final section of this chapter gives guidelines for improving nonverbal communication.

▶Guidelines for Effective Nonverbal Communication

Nonverbal communication, like verbal communication, can be misinterpreted. Following these two guidelines should reduce nonverbal misunderstandings in your interactions.

Monitor Your Nonverbal Communication

Think about the preceding discussion of ways we use nonverbal behaviors to announce our identities. Are you projecting the image you desire? Do others interpret your facial and body movements in ways consistent with the image you want to project? Do friends ever tell you that you seem uninterested when really you *are* interested? If so, you can monitor your nonverbal actions to more clearly communicate your involvement and interest in conversations. To reduce the chance that work associates will think you're uninterested in meetings, use what you've learned in this chapter to engage in nonverbal behaviors that others associate with responsiveness and attention.

Think also about how you arrange your personal spaces. Have you set up your room, office, apartment, or home to invite the kind of interaction you prefer, or are they arranged in ways that undercut your goals as a communicator? Paying attention to the nonverbal dimensions of your world can empower you to use them more effectively to achieve your interpersonal goals.

Interpret Others' Nonverbal Communication Tentatively

Although popular advice books promise to show you how to read nonverbal communications, no sure-fire formula exists. It's naive to think we can decode something so complex and ambiguous.

In this chapter, we've discussed findings about the meanings people attach to nonverbal behaviors. We can never be sure what a particular behavior means to specific people in a particular context (Manusov, 2004). For instance, we've said that sitting close together indicates liking. As a general rule, this is true. However, sometimes contented friends and couples like to have physical distance between them. Partners may also avoid physical closeness when one has a cold or flu.

People socialized in non-Western cultures learned distinct rules for proxemics. Because nonverbal communication is ambiguous and personal, we should not assume we can interpret it with precision. An ethical principle of communication is to qualify interpretations of nonverbal behavior with awareness of personal and contextual considerations.

Personal Qualifications Generalizations about nonverbal behavior state what is generally the case. They don't tell us about the exceptions to the rule. For instance, although eye contact generally is a sign of responsiveness, some people close their eyes to concentrate when listening. Sometimes people who cross their arms and condense into a tight posture are expressing hostility or lack of interest in interaction. However, the same behaviors might mean that a person is cold and trying to conserve body heat. Most people use less inflection and adopt a slack posture when they're not really interested in what they're talking about. However, the same behaviors may mean merely that we're tired.

Because nonverbal behaviors are ambiguous and vary between people, we need to be cautious about how we interpret these behaviors. A key principle is that we construct the meanings we attach to nonverbal communication. A good way to keep this in mind is to rely on *I*-language, not *you*-language, which we discussed earlier. *You*-language might lead us to inaccurately say of someone who doesn't look at us, "You're communicating lack of interest." A more responsible statement would use *I*-language to say, "When you don't look at me, I feel you're not interested in what I'm saying." Using *I*-language reminds us to take responsibility for our judgments and feelings. In addition, we become less likely to make others defensive by inaccurately interpreting their nonverbal behavior.

Contextual Qualifications   Like the meaning of verbal communication, the significance of nonverbal behaviors depends on the contexts in which they occur. Our nonverbal communication reflects the various settings we inhabit. We are more or less formal, relaxed, and open depending on context. Most people are more at ease and confident in their own territories than in someone else's, so we tend to be more relaxed in our homes and offices than in business places; teams often win games when they have the "home turf" advantage. We also dress according to context—a suit for a job interview, jeans or casual slacks and a shirt for a game.

Immediate physical settings are not the only factor that affects nonverbal communication. As we have seen, all communication reflects the values and understandings of particular cultures. We are likely to misinterpret people from other

---

Using I-Language about Nonverbal Behaviors

This exercise extends principles of *I*-language we discussed in Chapter 4 to the context of nonverbal communication. Practice translating *you*-language into *I*-language to describe nonverbal behaviors.

| **Example** | *You*-language | You're staring at me. |
| | *I*-language | When you look at me so intensely, I feel uncomfortable. |

You-Language	**I-Language**
You're lying—I can tell because you won't look me in the eye.	_____
Your perfume stinks.	_____
Don't you smirk when I'm talking.	_____
You look lazy when you slouch.	_____

SHARPEN YOUR SKILL

cultures when we impose the norms and rules of our culture on them (Emmons, 1998). A Tibetan woman who makes little eye contact is showing respect according to the norms of her country, although a North American might view her as evasive. This suggests that we have an ethical responsibility not to assume that our rules and norms apply to the behaviors of others.

Even within the United States, we have diverse communication cultures, and each has its rules for nonverbal behavior. Ethical communicators try to adopt dual perspective when interpreting others, especially when they and we belong to different cultures. To enhance your awareness of cultural influences on communication, Chapter 8 deals with that topic in detail.

▶SUMMARY

In this chapter, we've explored the fascinating world of nonverbal communication. We learned that nonverbal communication is symbolic and functions to supplement or replace verbal messages, regulate interaction, reflect and establish relationship-level meanings, and express cultural membership. These five principles of nonverbal behavior help us understand the complex ways in which nonverbal communication operates and what it may mean.

We discussed ten types of nonverbal communication, each of which reflects cultural rules and expresses our personal identities and feelings toward others. We use nonverbal behaviors to announce and perform our identities, relying on actions, artifacts, and contextual features to embody what our culture has taught us is appropriate for our gender, race, class, sexuality, and ethnicity. Because nonverbal communication is ambiguous, we construct its meaning as we notice, organize, and interpret nonverbal behaviors that we and others enact. Effectiveness requires that we learn to monitor our nonverbal communication and to exercise caution in interpreting that of others.

Review, Reflect, Extend

The Key Concepts, For Further Reflection and Discussion questions, Recommended Resources, and Experience Communication Case Study that follow will help you review, reflect on, and extend the information and ideas presented in this chapter. A diverse selection of online resources is also available through ThomsonNOW. These resources include Speech Builder Express, InfoTrac College Edition, interactive videos, vMentor, and Thomson Audio Study Products.

Thomson NOW! is an online study system designed to help you put your time to the best use. After reading a chapter, take the NOW pre-test to identify concepts discussed in the chapter that you may not fully understand. Based on the results of this diagnostic test, the system will create a personalized study plan that directs you to specific learning resources and activities. To see if you're ready for an exam, take the NOW post-test to check your understanding.

For more information or to access this book's online resources, visit **http://www.thomsonedu.com**.

▶ KEY CONCEPTS

The terms below are defined in the chapter on the page number indicated, and they appear in alphabetical order with definitions in the Glossary, which begins on page 369. The book's online resources also include flash cards and crossword puzzles to help you learn these terms and the concepts they represent.

artifacts, 102
chronemics, 105
environmental factors, 104
haptics, 100

kinesics, 99
nonverbal communication, 94
olfactics, 101
paralanguage, 107

physical appearance, 100
proxemics, 103
silence, 108

▶ FOR FURTHER REFLECTION AND DISCUSSION

The questions below can also be found among the book's online resources for this chapter, where you have the option of e-mailing your responses to your instructor, if required.

1. Attend a gathering of people from a culture different from yours. It might be a meeting at a Jewish temple if you're Christian, an African American church if you are White, or a meeting of Asian students if you are Western. Observe nonverbal behaviors of the people there: How do they greet one another? How much eye contact accompanies interaction? How close to one another do people sit?

2. Describe the spatial arrangements in the home of your family of origin. Was there a room in which family members interacted a good deal? How was furniture arranged in that room? Who had separate space and personal chairs in your family? What do the nonverbal patterns reflect about your family's communication style?

3. Think about current gender prescriptions in the United States. How are men and women "supposed" to look? How are these cultural expectations communicated? How might you resist and alter unhealthy cultural gender prescriptions?

4. What ethical considerations should affect how you interpret the nonverbal communication of people from cultures other than your own?

▶ RECOMMENDED RESOURCES

1. Use your InfoTrac College Edition to compare advertisements in magazines targeted primarily to White readers (for example, *Better Homes & Gardens*) and to Black readers (*Ebony*). Identify differences in the physical shapes of models and in the number of ads for weight loss.

2. R. E. Axtell. (1998). *Gestures: The do's and taboos of body language around the world*. New York: John Wiley. This is a very readable book that provides fascinating examples of how different cultures interpret gestures.

3. *Tootsie* remains one of the best films ever made depicting gendered nonverbal communication. View the film, and notice how lead actor Dustin Hoffman changes his nonverbal behaviors when he is portraying Michael Dorsey, a male, and Dorothy Michaels, a female.

Jason Harris/© Wadsworth

Experience Communication Case Study

TEAMWORK

The book's online resources include an interactive video of the communication situation featured in the case study scripted below. Apply what you've learned in this chapter by analyzing the case study, using the questions that follow the script as a guide. These questions are also available online with the video.

A project team is meeting to discuss the most effective way to present its recommendations for implementing a flextime policy on a trial basis. Members of the team are Jason (the team leader), Erika, Victoria, Bill, and Jensen. They are seated around a rectangular table with Jason at the head.

Jason: So we've decided to recommend trying flextime for a two-month period and with a number of procedures to make sure that people's new schedules don't interfere with productivity. There's a lot of information to communicate to employees, so how can we do that best?

Victoria: I think it would be good to use PowerPoint to highlight the key aspects of the new procedures. People always seem to remember better if they see something.

Bill: Oh, come on. PowerPoint is so overused. Everyone is tired of it by now. Can't we do something more creative?

Victoria: Well I like it. It's a good teaching tool.

Bill: I didn't know we were teaching. I thought our job was to report recommendations.

Victoria: So what do you suggest, Bill? [She nervously pulls on her bracelet as she speaks.]

Bill: I don't have a suggestion. I'm just against PowerPoint. [He doesn't look up as he speaks.]

Jason: Okay, let's not bicker among ourselves. [He pauses, gazes directly at Bill, then continues.] Lots of people like PowerPoint, lots don't. Instead of arguing about its value, let's ask what it is we want to communicate to the employees here. Maybe talking about our goal first will help us decide on the best means of achieving it.

Erika: Good idea. I'd like for us to focus first on getting everyone excited about the benefits of flextime. If they understand those, they'll be motivated to learn the procedures, even if there are a lot of them.

Jensen: Erika is right. That's a good way to start. Maybe we could create a handout or PowerPoint slide—either would work—to summarize the benefits of flextime that we've identified in our research.

Jason: Good, okay now we're cooking. Victoria, will you make notes on the ideas as we discuss them?

Victoria opens a notebook and begins writing notes.

Noticing that Bill is typing into his personal digital assistant (PDA), Jason looks directly at Bill and says, "Are you with us on how we lead off in our presentation?"

Bill: Sure, fine with me. [He puts the PDA aside but keeps his eyes on it.]

Erika: So maybe then we should say that the only way flextime can work is if we make sure that everyone agrees on procedures so that no division is ever missing more than one person during key production hours.

Jensen: Very good. That would add to people's motivation to learn and follow the procedures we've found are effective in other companies like ours. I think it would be great if Erika could present that topic because she did most of the research on it.

He smiles at Erika, and she pantomimes tipping her hat to him.

Jason: [He looks at Erika with a raised brow, and she nods.] Good. Okay, Erika's in charge of that. What's next?

Victoria: Then it's time to spell out the procedures and . . .

Bill: You can't just spell them out. You have to explain each one—give people a rationale for them or they won't follow them.

Victoria glares at Bill, then looks across the table at Erika, who shrugs as if to say, "I don't know what's bothering Bill today."

Jason: Bill, why don't you lead off, then, and tell us the first procedure we should mention and the rationale we should provide for it.

Bill looks up from his PDA, which he's been using again. He shrugs and says harshly, "Just spell out the rules, that's all."

Victoria: Would it be too much trouble for you to cut off your gadget and join us in this meeting, Bill?

Bill: Would it be too much trouble for you to quit hassling me?

Jason: [He turns his chair to face Bill squarely.] Look, I don't know what's eating you, but you're really being a jerk. If you've got a problem with this meeting or someone here, put it on the table. Otherwise, be a team player.

1. Identify nonverbal behaviors that regulate turn taking within the team.

2. Identify nonverbal behaviors that express relationship-level meanings of communication. What aspects of team members' nonverbal communication express liking or disliking, responsiveness or lack of responsiveness, and power?

3. How do artifacts affect interaction between members of the team?

4. If you were the sixth member of this team, what kinds of communication might you enact to help relieve tension in the group?

6 Listening and Responding to Others

► **FOCUS QUESTIONS**

1. What does the listening process include?

2. How do listening and hearing differ?

3. What obstacles interfere with effective listening?

4. How is effective listening for information different from effective listening to support others?

5. How we can improve our listening skills?

Got a minute?" Stan asks as he enters Suzanne's office.

"Sure," Suzanne agrees, without looking up from the report she is reading for a meeting later today. Lately, her supervisor has criticized her for being unprepared for meetings, and she wants to be on top of information today.

"I'm concerned about Frank. He's missed several days lately, and he's late half the time when he gets in to work," Stan begins. "He hasn't given me any explanation for his absences and tardiness, and I can't keep overlooking it."

"Yeah, I know that routine," Suzanne says with irritation. "Last month, Barton missed two days in a row and left early several other days."

"That's exactly what I'm talking about," Stan agrees. "I can't let Frank disregard rules that everyone else follows, but I don't want to come down too hard on him, especially when I don't know why he's missing so much time."

"I told Barton that I'd had it, and from now on he could either be at work when he should be or give me a darned good reason for why he wasn't," Suzanne says forcefully. Her mind wanders back to relive the confrontation with Barton.

"I wonder if the two situations are really similar," Stan says.

Suzanne realizes she was lost in her own thoughts. "Sorry, I didn't catch what you said," she says.

"I was wondering if you're saying that I should handle Frank like you handled Barton," Stan says.

"You have to enforce the rules, or he'll walk all over you." Suzanne's eyes drift back to the report she was reading when Stan dropped by.

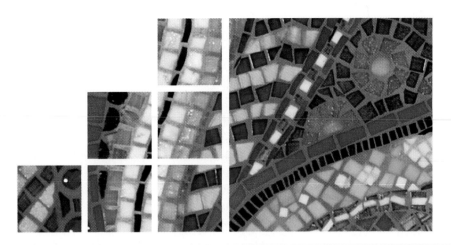

"I hate to be so hard on Frank," Stan says.

"Remember last year when Cheryl kept missing work? Well, I tried to be subtle and hint that she couldn't skip work. In one ear and out the other. You have to be firm."

"But Frank's not like Barton or Cheryl," Stan says. "He's never tried to run over me or shirk his work. I have a hunch something is going on that's interfering with his work. Cheryl and Barton both had patterns of irresponsibility."

"I don't think my staff is any less responsible than yours. I'm a good supervisor, you know," Suzanne snaps.

"That's not what I meant. I just meant that I don't think I need to hit Frank over the head with a two-by-four," Stan says.

"And I suppose you think that's what I did?"

"I don't know. I wasn't there. I'm just thinking that maybe our situations are different," says Stan.

How would you describe the conversation between Stan and Suzanne? Is Suzanne a good communicator? Is she sensitive to Stan's concerns? Does she respond helpfully to him?

When we think about communication, we usually focus on talking. Yet, in the communication process, **listening** is at least as important as talking. As obvious as this seems, few of us devote as much energy to listening as we do to talking.

In the conversation between Stan and Suzanne, poor listening is evident in several ways. First, Suzanne is preoccupied with a report she is reading. Reading it diverts her attention from Stan and limits her ability to maintain eye contact and give Stan nonverbal responses to his comments. If she really wants to listen to Stan, she should put the report aside. A second problem is Suzanne's tendency to monopolize the conversation, turning it into an occasion to discuss *her* supervisory problems instead of Stan's concerns about Frank's behavior. Third, Suzanne listens defensively, interpreting Stan as criticizing her when he suggests that he might act differently. Like Suzanne, most of us don't listen as well as we could much of the time. When we listen poorly, we are not communicating well.

Studies of people ranging from college students to professionals show that the average person spends 45% to 53% of waking time listening to others; that's more time than we spend in any other communication activity (Buckley, 1992; Nichols, 1996; Weaver, 1972). We listen in classes, at public lectures, to television and radio, in conversations, during interviews, on the job, and when participating in teamwork. If we add the time we listen while doing other things, the total listening time is even greater. Ineffective listening can be costly.

When people don't listen well on the job, they may miss information that can affect their professional effectiveness and advancement (Deal & Kennedy, 1999). In a survey, 1,000 human resource professionals ranked listening as the number one quality of effective managers (Windsor, Curtis, & Stephens, 1997). Skill in listening is also linked to resolving workplace conflicts (Van Styke, 1999). Ineffective listening in the classroom diminishes learning and performance on tests. In personal relationships, poor listening can hinder understanding of others, and we may be less than ideally sensitive. Not listening well to public communication leaves us unfamiliar with important issues and uninformed when we cast our votes. Learning to listen well enhances personal, academic, social, and professional effectiveness.

fyi

WHO LISTENS?

We might do well to heed wisdom offered by Mother Teresa shortly before her death in 1997. Here's an excerpt from Dan Rather's interview with Mother Teresa (Bailey, 1998).

Rather: What do you say to God when you pray?

Mother Teresa: I listen.

Rather: Well, what does God say?

Mother Teresa: He listens.

This chapter explores listening, which is the fourth of the six basic communication processes. First, we'll consider what's involved in listening and discuss obstacles to effective listening. Next, we'll examine common forms of ineffective listening. In the third section of the chapter, we'll look at skills needed for good listening in various situations. Finally, we'll identify ways to improve listening effectiveness.

▶ THE LISTENING PROCESS

Although we often use the words *listening* and *hearing* as if they were synonyms, actually they're not. **Hearing** is a physiological activity that occurs when sound waves hit functioning eardrums. Hearing is not the only way we receive messages. We also receive them through sight, as when we notice nonverbal behaviors, read lips, or interpret American Sign Language (ASL). In addition to hearing, or physically receiving messages, listening involves being mindful, selecting and organizing information, interpreting communication, responding, physically receiving messages and remembering (Figure 6.1).

Being Mindful

Mindfulness is focusing on what is happening in the moment (Wood, 1997, 2004a). When you are mindful, you don't think about what you did yesterday or the paper you need to write or a problem in your relationship or your response to what someone is saying. Instead, mindful listeners focus on the people with whom they are interacting. One advantage of e-mail is that we can choose to go online only when we are ready to be mindful. We demonstrate mindfulness with verbal and nonverbal signals that we are paying attention and interested in what others say (Deal & Kennedy, 1999). Simone's commentary highlights the impact of mindfulness on communication.

Figure 6.1 THE LISTENING PROCESS
Source: Adapted from Wood, 1997, p. 21.

▶ Simone

The best listener I've ever met was Nate, a guy I worked with on the campus newspaper. He wrote the best stories on special speakers who came to campus. At first, I thought he just got more interesting personalities to interview than I did. But then he and I had a couple of joint interviews, and I saw how he listened. When an interviewee was talking, Nate gave the person his undivided attention—like there was nobody else and nothing else around. People really open up when you treat them like the most interesting person in the world.

Mindfulness isn't a talent that comes naturally to some people and not others. It's an ethical commitment to attend fully to others in particular moments. No techniques will make you a good listener if you don't choose to be mindful. Thus, your choice of whether to be mindful is the foundation of how you listen—or fail to. Obviously, mindfulness is important in personal relationships. It is equally if less obviously important in professional life. Pamela Kruger (1999) talked with business executives and concluded that "leaders must know how to listen. . . . But first, and just as important, leaders must *want* to listen" (p. 134). The Sharpen Your Skill activity on this page provides guidelines for developing mindfulness.

Mindfulness enhances communication in two ways. First, attending mindfully to others increases our understanding of their thoughts and feelings. When we concentrate on another's communication, we gain insight into his or her thoughts and feelings. Second, mindfulness promotes more complete communication by others. When we really listen to others, they tend to elaborate their ideas and express their feelings in greater depth. Mindfulness is a continuous part of effective listening; as such, it affects all other aspects of the listening process.

Developing Mindfulness

Mindfulness develops with commitment and practice. Four guidelines will help you develop mindfulness.

1. Empty your mind of thoughts, ideas, and plans so that you are open to listening to another.

2. Concentrate on the person with whom you are communicating. Say to yourself, "I want to focus on this person and what she or he is saying and feeling."

3. Don't be surprised if distracting thoughts come up or you find yourself thinking about your responses instead of what the other person is saying. This is natural. Just push away diverting thoughts and refocus on the person with whom you are talking.

4. Evaluate how well you listened when you were focusing on being mindful. If you aren't as fully engaged as you want to be, remind yourself that mindfulness is a habit of mind and a way of living. Developing your ability to be mindful is a process that requires time and practice.

SHARPEN YOUR SKILL

Physically Receiving Communication

In addition to mindfulness, listening involves physically receiving communication. We might receive it by hearing sounds, interpreting nonverbal behaviors, reading lips or ASL. Sometimes, we physically receive a message, and this causes us to become mindful; in other instances, choosing to be mindful allows us to receive communication we might otherwise miss.

Most of us take hearing for granted. However, people who do not hear well may have difficulty receiving oral messages (Carl, 1998). When we speak with someone who has a hearing impairment, we should face the person and verify that we are coming across clearly. Our ability to receive messages also declines if we are tired or stressed. You may have noticed that it's hard to sustain attention in long classes. Physical reception of messages is also hampered if others are talking around us, if TVs, stereos, or radios are on, and if there are competing visual cues.

Other physiological factors—ones inside of us—influence how and how well we listen. Women and men seem to differ in how they listen. As a rule, women are more attuned than men to all that is going on around them. Men tend to focus, shape, and direct their hearing in specific ways, whereas women are more likely to notice contexts, details, and tangents, as well as major themes in interaction ("Men Use," 2000; Weaver, 1972). The discrepancy between rates of speaking and hearing also influences listening. The average person can understand approximately 300 words a minute, yet the average person speaks at a rate of approximately 100 words a minute. This leaves a lot of free time for listeners to sort and interpret speech.

T E C H N O L O G Y

iyi

VIDEOCONFERENCING FOR DEAF EDUCATION

At the Delaware School for the Deaf, high school students have regular tutoring sessions with students in deaf education at Valdosta State University in Georgia. To bridge the distance between students and tutors, both schools have computer labs equipped with webcams. It's a win-win situation: the students at Valdosta get valuable hands-on experience to refine their skills, and the students at Delaware get individual attention and help (Kiernan, 2006).

Selecting and Organizing Communication

The third element of listening is selecting and organizing material. As we noted in Chapter 3, we don't perceive everything around us. Instead, we selectively attend to some aspects of communication and disregard others. What we attend to depends on many factors, including physiological influences, expectations, cognitive structures, social roles, and membership in cultures and social communities. If we are preoccupied, we may not notice, select, and organize material effectively. In the example that opened this chapter, Suzanne's involvement with her report impeded her ability to listen to Stan. If you want to communicate effectively, you should take responsibility for controlling thoughts and concerns that can interfere with listening. Once again, mindfulness comes into play. Choosing to be mindful doesn't guarantee that our minds won't stray, but it does mean that we will bring ourselves back to the moment.

We can monitor our tendencies to attend selectively by remembering that we are more likely to notice stimuli that are intense, loud, or unusual. Therefore, we may overlook communicators who don't call attention to themselves with volume and bold gestures. If we're aware of this tendency, we can guard against it so we don't miss out on people and messages that may be important.

As you'll recall from Chapter 3, we use cognitive schemata to organize our perceptions. As you listen to other people, you decide how to categorize them by deciding which of your prototypes they most closely resemble: friend with a problem, professional rival, supervisor, and so forth. You then apply personal constructs to assess whether they are smart or not smart, honest or dishonest, reasonable or unreasonable, open to advice or not open, and so on. Next, you apply stereotypes to predict what they will do. Finally, you choose a script that seems appropriate to follow in interacting.

When you perceive a friend as distraught, you can reasonably predict that he needs to vent and may not want advice until he has first had a chance to express his feelings. On the other hand, when a co-worker comes to you with a problem that must be solved quickly, you assume she might welcome concrete advice or collaboration. Your script for responding to the distraught friend might be to say, "You sound really upset; let's talk." With a colleague who is facing a deadline, you might adopt a more directive script and say, "Here's what I suggest to fix the problem and stay on schedule."

Listeners actively define the listening situation and construct its meaning. When we define someone as emotionally upset, we're likely to rely on a script that tells us to back off and let her air her feelings. On the other hand, if we perceive someone as confused, we might follow a script that tells us to help him clarify his feelings. It's important to realize that *we construct others and their communication* by the schemata we use to organize our perceptions of them. Because our perceptions can be wrong, we should be ready to revise them in the course of interacting.

Interpreting Communication

The fourth aspect of listening is **interpretation.** When we interpret, we put together all that we have selected and organized to make sense of communication. Effective interpretation depends on your ability to understand others on their terms. Certainly, you won't always agree with other people's feelings and thoughts. Recognizing others' viewpoints doesn't mean you agree with them, but it does mean you make an earnest effort to grasp what they think and feel. This is an ethical responsibility of listening.

▶ Maggie

Don and I didn't understand each other's perspective, and we didn't even understand that we didn't understand. Once, I told him I was really upset about a friend of mine who needed money for an emergency. Don told me she had no right to expect me to bail her out, but that had nothing to do with what I was feeling. He would have seen the situation in terms of rights, but I didn't, and he didn't grasp my take. Only after we got counseling did we learn to listen to each other instead of listening through ourselves.

As Maggie notes in her commentary, to respect another person's perspective is to give a special gift. What we give is regard for the other person and a willingness to open ourselves to that person's way of looking at the world. Too often, we impose our meanings on others, we try to correct or argue with them about what they feel, or we crowd out their words with ours. As listening expert Robert Bolton has observed, good listeners "stay out of the other's way" so they can learn how the speaker views the situation (1986, p. 167).

Responding

Effective listening involves **responding,** which includes expressing interest, asking questions, voicing our own ideas on a topic, and otherwise communicating attentiveness. As we noted in Chapter 1, communication is a transactional process in which we simultaneously receive and send messages. Skillful listeners give signs that they are involved in interaction, even though they are not speaking at the moment (Barker & Watson, 2000; Purdy & Borisoff, 1997). We respond not only when others finish speaking but throughout interaction. At public presentations, audience members show interest by looking at speakers, nodding their heads, and adopting attentive postures. Nonverbal behaviors, such as looking out a window and slouching, signal that you aren't involved. We also show lack of involvement or interest by yawning, looking bored, or staring blankly (Deal & Kennedy, 1999).

Good listeners show that they're engaged. The only way that others know we are listening is through our feedback. Indicators of engagement include attentive posture, head nods, eye contact, and vocal responses such as "Mmhmm" and "Go on." When we demonstrate involvement, we communicate that we care about the other person and what she or he says.

Remembering

Many listening experts regard **remembering** as the final aspect of the listening process. We forget a lot of what we hear. Eight hours after receiving a message, we recall only about 35% of our interpretations of the message. Because we forget about two-thirds of the meanings we construct from others' communication, it's important to make sure we hang on to the most important third (Cooper, Seibold, & Suchner, 1997; Fisher, 1987). Selectively focusing our attention is particularly important when we listen to presentations that contain a great deal of information. Later in this chapter, we'll discuss strategies for improving retention.

Listening is a complex process that involves being mindful, physically receiving messages, selecting and organizing information, interpreting communication, responding, and remembering. We're now ready to consider hindrances to the listening process so we can recognize and manage them.

© image 100/Albany

Effective listening requires active, mindful engagement throughout interaction.

▶Obstacles to Effective Listening

There are two broad types of obstacles to listening well: situational obstacles that are in communication contexts, and internal obstacles that are within communicators.

Situational Obstacles

Learning about situational hindrances to listening can help us guard against them or compensate for the interference they create.

Message Overload The sheer amount of communication in our lives makes it difficult to listen fully to all of it. **Message overload** occurs when we receive more messages than we can effectively process. For good reason, our era has been dubbed "the information age." Each day, we are inundated by messages from media (newspapers, magazines, television, radio), electronic systems (e-mail, telephone, the Internet, bulletin boards, faxes), and other people (parents, friends, children, teachers, supervisors, subordinates). We simply can't be mindful of and totally involved in all the messages that come our way. Instead, we have to make choices about which communication gets our attention.

Message overload often occurs in educational contexts. Students who take four or five classes each term must deal with four or five sets of readings, class lectures, and discussions—a load that can overwhelm even the most conscientious student. Message overload may also occur when communication occurs simultaneously in multiple channels. For instance, you might suffer information overload if a speaker is presenting information orally while showing a slide with complex statistical data. In such a situation, it's difficult to decide whether to focus your listening energy on the visual message or the oral one.

Message Complexity Listening may also be impeded by **message complexity,** which exists when a message we are trying to understand is highly complex, is packed with detailed information, or involves intricate reasoning. The more detailed and complicated the ideas, the more difficult they are to follow and retain. Many jobs today are so specialized that communication between co-workers involves highly complex messages (Cooper, 1999; Hacker, Gross, & Townley, 1998). Effective communicators make an effort to reduce the complexity of their messages and to avoid unnecessary jargon. When speakers don't translate complex ideas into understandable language, effective listeners have to invest more effort. When you listen to messages that are dense with information, taking notes can improve your retention.

Environmental Distractions **Environmental distractions** constitute a third impediment to effective listening. These are occurrences in the communication setting that interfere with effective listening. Distractions exist in all communication

THE POWER OF RESPONSIVE LISTENING

To test the effect of responsive listening, researchers taught students in a college psychology course to give different responses to their professor. The professor was a boring lecturer who read his notes in a monotone, seldom gestured, and did little to engage students. After the first few minutes of class, the students changed their postures, kept greater eye contact, nodded, and so forth. Shortly after the students began responding, the lecturer started using gestures, increased his speaking rate and inflection, and began to interact with students visually and verbally. Then, at a prearranged signal, the students stopped showing interest. Within a few minutes, the lecturer returned to his old lecture style. The students' responses affected the professor's communication (Bolton, 1986).

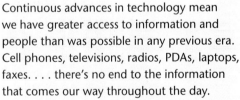

T E C H N O L O G Y
SUPERSATURATION

Continuous advances in technology mean we have greater access to information and people than was possible in any previous era. Cell phones, televisions, radios, PDAs, laptops, faxes. . . . there's no end to the information that comes our way throughout the day.

Media scholar Todd Gitlin (2005) refers to the never-ending flow of information as a "media torrent" that leads to supersaturation, or being constantly in touch, constantly informed, and constantly overloaded with information, whether we want it or not. Two other media scholars, Jane Brown and Joanne Cantor (2000), use the term *perpetual linkage* to refer to always being connected to others.

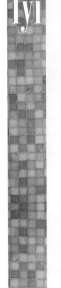

situations. It might be a television in the background, side comments during a conference, or muffled traffic sounds from outside. Increasingly, we have to deal with the buzzes of pagers and the ring tones of cell phones when we are talking with others in public places. Jimmy's description of the distractions in his environment may be familiar to many students.

► Jimmy

It's impossible to listen well in my apartment. Four of us live there, and at least two different stereos are on all the time. Usually, there's also a TV going, and there may be conversations or phone calls too. We're always asking each other to repeat something or skipping over whatever we don't hear. If we go out to a bar or something, the noise is just as bad. Sometimes, I think we don't really want to listen, and all the distractions protect us from having to.

Effective listeners reduce environmental distractions. It's considerate to turn off a television or turn down music if someone wants to talk with you. Closing a door eliminates hallway noises. Closing your laptop allows you to attend more fully to a conversation. Private conversations can be deferred until after a group meeting so that they don't interfere with listening. Professionals often hold their phone calls when they are talking with clients or business associates. Even when we can't eliminate distractions, we can usually reduce them or change our location to one that is more conducive to good listening.

Internal Obstacles

In addition to situational impediments to effective listening, four internal obstacles hinder our efforts to listen well.

Preoccupation One of the most common hindrances to listening is **preoccupation.** When we are absorbed in our thoughts and concerns, we can't focus on what someone else is saying. Perhaps you've attended a class right before taking a test in another class and later realized you got almost nothing out of the first class. That's because you were preoccupied with the upcoming test. If you open your e-mail box and find 20 messages, you may be preoccupied by a sense of obligation to read and respond to all of them, so you are not fully, mindfully focused on reading and responding to each one as you open it. In the example that opened this chapter, Suzanne's preoccupation with a report impeded her ability to listen to her colleague. When we are preoccupied with our thoughts, we aren't mindful.

Prejudgments A second internal obstacle to good listening is **prejudgment**—the tendency to judge others or their ideas before we've heard them. Sometimes we think we already know what someone will say, so we don't listen carefully. In other cases, we decide in advance that others have nothing to offer us, so we tune them out. A study of doctor–patient communication found that, on average, doctors interrupted patients 23 seconds into patients' explanations of medical problems (Levine, 2004). Doctors who assume they already know what a patient has to say are likely to miss key information that is needed to understand a patient's medical concerns. Keeping an open mind when listening to speakers with whom you disagree is also advisable. Keith's commentary provides an example of the negative impact of prejudgments on listening.

▶ **Keith**

My parents are so quick to tell me what I think and feel or should think and feel that they never listen to what I do feel or think. Last year, I told them I was thinking about taking a year off from school. Before I could explain why I wanted to do this, Dad was all over me about the need to get ahead in a career. Mom said I was looking for an easy out from my studies. What I wanted to do was work as an intern to get some hands-on experience in media production, which is my major. I wasn't after an easy out, and I do want to get ahead, but they couldn't even hear me through their own ideas about what I felt.

When we prejudge, we mind read. As we noted in Chapter 3, mind reading is assuming we know what others feel, think, and are going to say, and we may then fit their messages into our preconceptions. This can lead us to misunderstand what they mean because we haven't really listened to them on their terms. When we impose our prejudgments on others' words, at the relationship level of meaning we express a disregard for them and what they say. Prejudgments also affect the content level of meaning because we may not grasp important content when we decide in advance that someone has nothing of value to say. This can be costly on the job, where we are expected to pay attention and understand information even if we don't like it or the person expressing it.

Lack of Effort   Listening is hard work: We have to be mindful, focus on what others say, interpret and organize messages, remember, and respond. We also have to control distractions inside ourselves and in situations. Sometimes we aren't willing to invest the effort to listen well. In other instances, we want to listen, but we're tired, ill, hungry, or distracted by other physiological factors (Isaacs, 1999). When this happens, it's effective to postpone interaction until you have the energy to listen mindfully. If you explain that you want to listen well, the other person is likely to appreciate your honesty and your commitment to listening.

Not Recognizing Diverse Listening Styles   A final hindrance to effective listening is not recognizing and adjusting to different listening styles that reflect diverse cultures and social communities (Brownell, 2002). For example, Nepalese people typically give little vocal feedback during conversation, because they consider it disrespectful to make sounds while someone else is talking. Other cultures exhibit differences in listening rules based on age, ethnicity, gender, and other aspects of identity.

There are also differences between social groups in the United States. In general, women are more active than men in giving verbal and nonverbal feedback, using head nods, facial expressions, and responsive questions to show interest. If you realize that people differ in how they listen and express interest, you are unlikely to misinterpret others (Wood, 2007). For instance, some African Americans call out responses to a speaker or preacher as a way to show interest in what the speaker is saying. A speaker who doesn't understand this pattern is likely to misinterpret the responses as interruptions. Conversely, some African Americans may perceive European American listeners as uninterested because they don't participate by calling out during a speech or sermon. Nancy's reflections on her perceptions as a White person at a Black church illustrate the importance of recognizing and respecting diverse listening styles.

▶ Nancy

I was amazed the first time I went to a Black church. Members of the congregation kept speaking back to the minister and exclaiming over what they liked. At first, I was alienated, but after a while I got into the spirit, and I felt a whole lot more involved in the service than I ever had in my own church.

Forms of Ineffective Listening

Now that we've discussed obstacles to effective listening, let's identify six common forms of ineffective listening. Some may seem familiar because you and people you know probably engage in them at times.

Pseudolistening **Pseudolistening** is pretending to listen. When we pseudolisten, we appear attentive, but our minds are really elsewhere. Sometimes we pseudolisten because we don't want to hurt a friend who is sharing experiences. We also pseudolisten when communication bores us but we feel it is important to appear attentive. Superficial social interaction and boring lectures are communication situations in which we may consciously choose to pseudolisten so that we seem polite even though we really aren't involved. On the job, we may need to appear interested in what others say because of their positions. Pseudolistening is inadvisable, however, when we really want to understand another's communication.

Monopolizing **Monopolizing** is hogging the stage by continually focusing communication on ourselves instead of on the person who is talking. Two tactics are typical of monopolizing. One is *conversational rerouting*, in which a person shifts the topic of talk to himself or herself. For example, if Ellen tells her friend Marla that she's having trouble with her roommate, Marla might reroute the conversation by saying, "I know what you mean. My roommate is a real slob." And then Marla launches into an extended description of her roommate problems. In the workplace, people with higher status may shift conversations to themselves and their accomplishments; as a result, they don't listen to others. In both personal and work relationships, rerouting takes the conversation away from the person who is talking and focuses it on oneself.

A second monopolizing tactic, *interrupting*, can occur in combination with rerouting: A person interrupts and then introduces a new topic. In other cases, diversionary interrupting involves questions and challenges that disrupt or challenge the person who is speaking. Monopolizers may fire questions that express doubt about what a speaker says ("What makes you think that?" "How can you be sure?" "Did anyone else see what you did?") or prematurely offer advice to establish their command of the situation and perhaps to put down the other person ("What you should do is . . ."; "You really blew that. What I would have done is . . ."). Both rerouting and diversionary interrupting monopolize conversations. They are the antithesis of good listening.

It's important to realize that not all interruptions are attempts to monopolize communication (Goldsmith & Fulfs, 1999). In some situations, we interrupt the flow of others' talk to show interest, to voice support, and to ask for elaboration. Interrupting

for these reasons doesn't divert attention from the person speaking; instead, it affirms that person and keeps the focus on her or him.

Selective Listening   A third form of ineffective listening is **selective listening,** which involves focusing only on particular parts of communication. We listen selectively when we screen out parts of a message that we dislike or find boring. We also listen selectively when we attend only to communication that interests us or with which we agree.

One form of selective listening is focusing only on aspects of communication that interest us or correspond to our opinions and feelings. We screen out message content that doesn't interest us or that is irrelevant to our needs. If you are worried about a storm, you may listen selectively to weather reports and disregard news and music on the radio. Students often become highly attentive in classes when teachers say, "This will be on the test." In the workplace, we may become more attentive when communication addresses topics such as raises, layoffs, and other matters that may affect us directly.

Selective listening also occurs when we reject communication that bores us or is inconsistent with our values, opinions, or choices. We may selectively filter out a co-worker's criticisms of our work. We may also screen out communication that makes us uncomfortable. A smoker may choose not to listen to messages about the dangers of smoking. We all have subjects that bore us or make us uncomfortable, and we may be tempted not to listen to communication about them.

Defensive Listening   **Defensive listening** involves perceiving a personal attack, criticism, or hostile undertone in communication when none is intended. When we listen defensively, we assume others don't like, trust, or respect us, and we read these motives into whatever they say, regardless of how innocent their communication actually is. Some people are generally defensive, expecting insults and criticism from all quarters. They hear threats and negative judgments in almost anything said to them. Thus, an innocent remark such as, "Have you finished the report yet?" may be perceived as criticism that the report hasn't been turned in yet.

In other instances, defensive listening is confined to areas where we judge ourselves inadequate or to times when we feel negative about ourselves. A woman who fears she is not valued in her job may interpret committee assignments as signs that she is not well regarded. A person who perceives herself or himself as unattractive may perceive genuine compliments as false. Someone who has been laid off may perceive work-related comments as personal criticism of his or her unemployment.

Ambushing **Ambushing** is listening carefully for the purpose of gathering ammunition to use in attacking a speaker. Ambushing often relies on an extreme form of monopolizing in which interruptions are constant and intentionally disruptive. Political candidates routinely listen carefully to their opponents in order to undercut them.

Ambushing may also plague work life, especially in organizations that encourage employees to compete with one another in order to stand out. These employees display no openness, make no effort to understand the other's meaning, take no interest in recognizing value in what another says, and do not want genuine dialogue. Eric provides another example of ambushing.

▶ Eric

One brother at my [fraternity] house is a real ambusher. He's a pre-law major, and he loves to debate and win arguments. No matter what somebody talks about, this guy just listens long enough to mount a counterattack. He doesn't care about understanding anybody else, just about beating them. I've quit talking when he's around.

Literal Listening **Literal listening** involves listening only to the content level of meaning and ignoring the relationship level of meaning. When we listen literally, we do not listen to what's being communicated about the other person or about our relationship with that person. For example, one member of a work team might avoid eye contact, shrug his shoulders, and say in a flat voice, "I guess I can go along with this decision." If other group members listen only to his literal message, they will assume the group has reached a decision. However, the relational level of meaning, conveyed through the lack of eye contact, the resigned shrug, and the monotone voice, suggests the member is not happy with the decision. It's likely that this member will not be fully committed to the decision and will not be enthusiastic in implementing it. Literal listening neglects others' feelings and our connections with them.

▶GUIDELINES FOR EFFECTIVE LISTENING

Our discussion of listening and the obstacles to it provides a foundation for improving our effectiveness as listeners. The key guideline is to adapt listening to specific communication goals and situations. Two major kinds of listening, **informational and critical listening** and **relationship listening,** require different skills and attitudes. We'll discuss how to be effective in these two kinds of listening and briefly discuss other types of listening.

Develop Skills for Informational and Critical Listening

Much of our listening is to gain and evaluate information. We listen for information in classes and professional meetings, when we are learning a new job, during important news stories, when we need to understand a medical treatment, and when we are getting directions. In all these cases, the primary purpose of listening is to gain and understand information.

Closely related to informational listening is critical listening: We listen to make judgments about people and ideas. Like informational listening, critical listening requires attending closely to the content of communication. Yet critical listening goes beyond gaining information to analyze and evaluate it and the people who express it. We decide whether a speaker is credible and ethical by judging the thoroughness of a presentation, the accuracy of evidence, the carefulness of reasoning, and personal confidence and trustworthiness. Informational and critical listening call for skills that help us gain and retain information. Critical listening also calls for skill in evaluating information.

Be Mindful The first step in listening to information critically is to make a decision to attend carefully, even if the material is complex and difficult. This may mean that you time your conversations, whether phone, online, or face to face, so that you have the mental energy to be mindful. Don't let your mind wander if information gets complicated or confusing. Avoid daydreaming, and stay focused on learning as much as you can. Later, you may want to ask questions if material isn't clear or if you have reservations about evidence or logic.

Control Obstacles You can also minimize distractions. You might shut a window to block out traffic noises or adjust a thermostat so that the room's temperature is comfortable. In addition, you should minimize psychological distractions by emptying your mind of the many concerns, ideas, and prejudgments that can interfere with attending to the communication at hand.

Ask Questions Asking speakers to clarify their messages or to elaborate allows you to understand information you didn't grasp at first and to deepen your insight into content you did comprehend. Recently, I listened to a talk on national economic issues. After a fairly technical speech, audience members asked these questions: "Could you explain what you meant by the M2 money supply?" "How does inflation affect wages?" and "Can you clarify the distinction between the national debt and the deficit?" These questions showed that the listeners had paid attention and were interested in further information. Questions compliment a speaker because they show that you are interested and want to know more.

Critical listening often calls for asking more probing questions. "What is the source of your statistics on the rate of unemployment?" "Is a seven-year-old statistic on welfare current enough to tell us anything about welfare issues today?" "Have you met with any policy makers who hold a point of view contrary to yours? What is their response to your proposals?" "All the sources you quoted in your presentation are fiscal conservatives. Does this mean your presentation and your conclusions are biased?" "Do you stand to benefit personally if we vote for what you are advocating?"

T E C H N O L O G Y

LAPTOP VERSUS LECTURE

Many colleges and universities that require students to have laptops are having second thoughts. The problem? It seems that instead of using laptops to enhance what they learn from lectures, some students are using them to find alternatives to lectures—net surfing, IMing and e-mailing friends, online shopping, or working on assignments (Young, 2006). Students claim that they are skilled at multitasking and therefore can attend to lectures while doing other tasks. Professors aren't so sure.

© Tom Bean/Corbis

This park official is teaching visitors how to protect themselves from Lyme disease. Are the visitors using good listening skills?

Use Aids to Recall To remember important information, we can apply principles of perception we discussed in Chapter 3. For instance, we learned that we tend to notice and recall stimuli that are repeated. To use this principle to increase your retention, repeat important ideas to yourself immediately after hearing them. This moves new information from short-term to long-term memory (Estes, 1989). Repeating the names of people when you meet them can save you the embarrassment of having to ask them to repeat their names.

Another way to increase retention is to use mnemonic (pronounced "*knee monic*") devices, which are memory aids that create patterns that help you remember what you've heard. For instance, the mnemonic device MPSIRR is made up of one letter representing each of the six parts of listening (mindfulness, physical reception, selecting and organizing, interpreting, responding, remembering). You can also invent mnemonics to help you recall personal information. For example, ROB is a mnemonic for remembering that Robert from Ohio is studying Business.

Organize Information A third technique for increasing your retention is to organize what you hear. When communicating informally, most people don't order their ideas carefully. The result is a flow of information that isn't coherently organized and so is hard to retain. We can impose order by regrouping what we hear. For example, suppose a friend tells you that he's confused about long-range goals, doesn't know what he can do with a math major, wants to locate in the Midwest, wonders whether graduate school is necessary, likes small towns, needs some internships to try out different options, and wants a family eventually. You could organize this stream of concerns into two categories: academic issues (careers for math majors, graduate school, internship opportunities) and lifestyle preferences (Midwest, small town, family). Remembering these two categories allows you to retain the essence of your friend's concerns, even if you forget many of the specifics.

D I V E R S I T Y

fyi

LISTENING TO A SECOND LANGUAGE

Asking questions is especially important and appropriate for non-native speakers of the speaker's language. People who have learned English as a second language may not understand idioms such as *in a heartbeat* (fast), *not on your life* (very unlikely), or *off the wall* (wacky) (Lee, 1994, 2000). Another listening difficulty for non-native speakers of a language is the ability to distinguish between sounds. Recent research shows that this ability is learned, not innate. By the age of one, if not sooner, babies can hear and distinguish between sounds of languages they hear spoken (Monastersky, 2001). Non-Chinese people have difficulty distinguishing between two distinct sounds in Mandarin Chinese: *qi,* which is approximately like the English *ch* sound, and *xi,* which is approximately like the English *sh* sound. People who are native to Japan have a hard time distinguishing between the English sounds *ra* and *la.* To read more about learning English as a second language, go to the book's online resources and click on WebLink 6.1.

Develop Skills for Relationship Listening

Listening for information focuses on the content level of meaning in communication. Yet, often we are as concerned or even more concerned with the relationship level of meaning, which has to do with feelings and relationships between communicators. We engage in relationship listening when we listen to a friend's worries, let a romantic partner tell us about problems, counsel a co-worker, or talk with a parent about health concerns. Specific listening attitudes and skills enhance our ability to listen supportively (Nichols, 1996).

Be Mindful The first requirement for effective relationship listening is mindfulness, which is also the first step in informational listening. When we're listening to give support, however, we focus on feelings that may not be communicated explicitly. Thus, mindful relationship listening involves looking for feelings and perceptions that are "between the words." As listening scholar Gerald Egan notes, "Total listening is more than attending to another person's words. It is also listening to the meanings that are buried in the words and between the words and in the silences in communication" (1973, p. 228).

Suspend Judgment When listening to provide support, it's important to avoid judgmental responses. When we judge, we add our evaluations to other people's experiences, and this moves us away from them and their feelings. Our judgments may also lead others to become defensive and unwilling to talk further with us. To curb judgment, we can ask whether we really need to evaluate right now. Even positive evaluations ("That's a good way to approach the problem") can make others uneasy and less willing to communicate openly with us. The other person may reason that if we make positive judgments, we could also make negative ones. José's commentary illustrates the values of suspending judgment when listening relationally.

Improving Recall

Apply the principles we've discussed to enhance memory.

1. The next time you meet someone, repeat his or her name to yourself three times after you are introduced. Do you find that the name sticks better?

2. After your next communication class, take 15 minutes to review your notes in a quiet place. Read them aloud so you hear as well as see the main ideas. Does this increase your retention of the material?

3. Invent mnemonics that help you remember basic information in communication.

4. Organize complex ideas by grouping them into categories. To remember the main ideas of this chapter, you might use major subheadings to form categories: listening process, obstacles to listening, and listening goals. Creating the mnemonic POG (process, obstacles, goals) could help you remember those topics.

If you want to take a test to measure your listening skills, go to the book's online resources and click on WebLink 6.2.

SHARPEN YOUR SKILL

▶ **José**

My best friend makes it so easy for me to tell whatever is on my mind. She never puts me down or makes me feel stupid or weird. Sometimes, I ask her what she thinks, and she has this way of telling me without making me feel wrong if I think differently. What it boils down to is respect. She

respects me and herself, and so she doesn't have to prove anything by acting better than me.

Only if someone asks for our evaluation should we offer it when we are listening
to offer support. Even if our opinion is sought, we should express it in a way that
doesn't devalue others. Sometimes people excuse strongly judgmental comments
by saying, "You asked me to be honest" or "I mean this as constructive criticism."
Too often, however, the judgments are not constructive and are harsher than can-
dor requires. Good relationship listening includes responses that communicate
respect and support.

Strive to Understand the Other's Perspective One of the most important
principles for effective relationship listening is to concentrate on grasping the
other person's perspective by being person centered (Nichols, 1996). This means
we have to step outside of our point of view at least long enough to understand
another's perceptions. We can't respond sensitively to others until we understand
their perspective and meanings. To do this, we must put aside our views and focus
on their words and nonverbal behaviors for clues to others feelings and thoughts.

One communication skill that helps us gain insight into others is the use of
minimal encouragers. These are responses that gently invite another person to
elaborate. Examples of minimal encouragers are "Tell me more," "Really?" "Go
on," "I'm with you," "Then what happened?" "Yeah?" and "I see." We can also
use nonverbal minimal encouragers, such as a raised eyebrow to show that we're
involved, a nod to signal that we understand, or widened eyes to demonstrate that
we're fascinated. Minimal encouragers say we are listening and interested. They
encourage others to keep talking so we can grasp what they mean. Keep in mind
that these are *minimal* encouragers; they shouldn't take the focus away from the
other person. Effective minimal encouragers are brief interjections that prompt,
rather than interfere with, the flow of another's talk.

Paraphrasing is a second way to gain insight into others' perspectives. To
paraphrase, we reflect our interpretations of others' communication back to them.
For example, a friend might confide, "With all the news on teenagers and drugs,
I wonder if my kid brother is messing around with drugs." You could paraphrase
this way: "It sounds as if you may suspect your brother may be taking drugs."
This paraphrase allows us to clarify whether the friend has any evidence of the
brother's drug involvement. The response might be, "No, I don't have any reason
to suspect him, but I just worry because drugs are so pervasive in high schools
now." This tells us that the friend's worry is about general trends, not about evidence that her brother is using drugs. Paraphrasing can also be a way to check
perceptions to see whether we understand another person's meaning: "Let me see
if I followed you. What you're saying is that . . . ."

A third way to enhance understanding of others is to ask questions. For instance, we might ask, "How do you feel about that?" or "What do you plan to
do?" Another reason we ask questions is to find out what a person wants from us.
Sometimes it isn't clear whether someone wants advice, a shoulder to cry on, or
a safe place to vent feelings. If we can't figure out what's wanted, it's appropriate
to ask, "Are you looking for advice or a sounding board?" Asking directly signals that we really want to help and allows others to tell us how we can best do

that. The Sharpen Your Skill feature on this page will help you develop your skill in paraphrasing.

Express Support Once you have understood another's meanings and perspective, relationship listening should focus on communicating support. This doesn't necessarily require us to agree with another's perspective or ideas. It does call upon us to communicate support for the person. To illustrate how we can support someone even if we don't agree with his or her position, consider the following exchange between a son and his father:

Son: Dad, I'm changing my major to acting.

Father: Oh.

Son: Yeah, I've wanted to do it for some time, but I hesitated because acting isn't as safe as accounting.

Father: That's certainly true.

Son: Yeah, but I've decided to do it anyway. I'd like to know what you think about the idea.

Father: The idea worries me. Starving actors are a dime a dozen. It just won't provide you with any economic future or security.

Son: I understand acting isn't as secure as business, but it is what I really want to do.

Father: Tell me what you feel about acting—why it matters so much to you.

Son: It's the most creative, totally fulfilling thing I do. I've tried to get interested in business, but I just don't love that like I do acting. I feel like I have to give this a try, or I'll always wonder if I could have made it. If I don't get somewhere in 5 or 6 years, I'll rethink career options.

Father: Couldn't you finish your business degree and get a job and act on the side?

Son: No. I've got to give acting a full shot—give it everything I have to see if I can make it.

Father: Well, I still have reservations, but I guess I can understand having to try something that matters this much to you. I'm just concerned that you'll lose years of your life to something that doesn't work out.

Son: Well, I'm kinda concerned about that too, but I'm more worried about wasting years of my life in a career that doesn't turn me on than about trying to make a go of the one that does.

Father: That makes sense. I wouldn't make the choice you're making, but I respect your decision and your guts for taking a big gamble.

Practice Paraphrasing

Learning to paraphrase enhances communication. You can develop skill in paraphrasing by creating paraphrases of the following comments:

▶ "I don't know how they expect me to get my work done when they don't give me any training on how to use this new software program."

▶ "I've got three midterms and a paper due next week, and I'm behind in my reading."

▶ "My parents don't understand why I need to go to summer school, and they won't pay my expenses."

▶ "My son wants to go to summer school and expects us to come up with the money. Doesn't he understand what we're already paying for the regular school year?"

SHARPEN YOUR SKILL

This dialogue illustrates several principles of effective relationship listening. First, note that the father's first two comments are minimal encouragers that invite his son to elaborate on his thoughts and feelings. The father also encourages his son to explain how he feels. Later, the father suggests a compromise solution, but his son rejects that, and the father respects the son's position. It is important that the father makes his position clear, but he separates his personal stance from his respect for his son's right to make his own choices. Sometimes it's difficult to suspend judgment, particularly if we don't agree with the person speaking, as in this example. However, if your goal is to support someone, the ideal listening style is sensitive, responsive involvement without evaluation.

Develop Skills for Other Listening Goals

In addition to listening for information, to make critical evaluations, and to provide support, we listen for pleasure and to discriminate.

Listening for Pleasure Sometimes we listen for pleasure, as when we attend concerts or play CDs. Listening for enjoyment is also a primary purpose when we go to comedy shows or when an acquaintance tells a joke. When listening for pleasure, we don't need to concentrate on organizing and remembering as much as we do when we listen for information, although retention is important if you want to tell the joke to someone else later. Yet listening for pleasure does require mindfulness, hearing, and interpretation.

Listening to Discriminate In some situations, we listen to make fine discriminations in sounds in order to draw accurate conclusions and act appropriately in response. For example, doctors listen to discriminate when they use stethoscopes to assess heart function or chest congestion. Parents listen to discriminate a baby's cries for attention, food, reassurance, or a diaper change. Skilled mechanics can distinguish engine sounds far more keenly than most other people. Mindfulness and keen hearing abilities are skills that assist listening to discriminate.

Mindfulness is a prerequisite for effective listening of all types. With the exception of mindfulness, each listening purpose tends to emphasize particular aspects of the listening process and to put less weight on others. Whereas evaluating content is especially important in listening critically, it is less crucial when listening for pleasure. Hearing acoustic nuances is important when listening to discriminate but not vital to listening for information. Selecting, organizing, and retaining information matter more when we are listening for information than when we are listening for pleasure. Deciding on your purpose for listening allows you to use the most pertinent communication skills.

▶ SUMMARY

Listening is a major and vital part of communication, yet too often we don't consider it as important as talking. In this chapter, we've explored the complex and demanding process of listening. We began by distinguishing between hearing and listening. The former is a straightforward physiological process that doesn't take effort on our part. Listening, in contrast, is a complicated process involving being mindful, hearing, selecting and organizing, interpreting, responding, and remembering. Listening well takes commitment and skill.

Obstacles in ourselves as well as in situations and messages jeopardize effective listening. Message overload, complexity of material, and noise are external obstacles to listening. In addition, our preoccupations and prejudgments, lack of effort, and not recognizing differences in listening styles can hamper listening. The obstacles to listening often lead to various forms of ineffective listening, including pseudolistening, monopolizing, selective listening, defensive listening, ambushing, and literal listening. Each form of ineffective listening prevents us from being fully engaged in communication.

We also discussed different purposes for listening and identified the skills and attitudes that advance each purpose. Informational and critical listening require us to adopt a mindful attitude and to think critically, to organize and evaluate information, to clarify understanding by asking questions, and to develop aids to retention of complex material. Relationship listening also requires mindfulness, but it calls for other distinct listening skills. Suspending judgment, paraphrasing, giving minimal encouragers, and expressing support enhance the effectiveness of relationship listening.

Review, Reflect, Extend

The Key Concepts, For Further Reflection and Discussion questions, Recommended Resources, and Experience Communication Case Study that follow will help you review, reflect on, and extend the information and ideas presented in this chapter. A diverse selection of online resources is also available through ThomsonNOW. These resources include Speech Builder Express, InfoTrac College Edition, interactive videos, vMentor, and Thomson Audio Study Products.

Thomson NOW! is an online study system designed to help you put your time to the best use. After reading a chapter, take the NOW pre-test to identify concepts discussed in the chapter that you may not fully understand. Based on the results of this diagnostic test, the system will create a personalized study plan that directs you to specific learning resources and activities. To see if you're ready for an exam, take the NOW post-test to check your understanding.

For more information or to access this book's online resources, visit **http://www.thomsonedu.com**.

▶ KEY CONCEPTS

The terms below are defined in the chapter on the page number indicated, and they appear in alphabetical order, with definitions, in the Glossary, which begins on page 369. The book's online resources also include flash cards and crossword puzzles to help you learn these terms and the concepts they represent.

▶FOR FURTHER REFLECTION AND DISCUSSION

The questions below can also be found among the book's online resources for this chapter, where you have the option of e-mailing your responses to your instructor, if required.

1. Review the types of ineffective listening discussed in this chapter. Do any describe ways in which you attend (or don't attend) to others? Select one type of ineffective listening in which you engage and work to minimize it in your interactions.

2. What do you see as the ethical principles that guide different listening purposes? What different moral goals and responsibilities accompany informational and critical listening and relationship listening?

3. Keep a record of your listening for two days. How much of your listening is informational, critical, relational, for pleasure, and to discriminate? Describe differences in how you listen to meet each goal.

▶RECOMMENDED RESOURCES

1. Use your InfoTrac College Edition to find and read articles that focus on listening in the workplace. What conclusions are drawn about the importance of listening in professional life?

2. The film *Erin Brockovich* dramatically illustrates the power of listening. Watch the film, and pay attention to how Julia Roberts, in the role of Erin Brockovich, shows she is listening carefully to people who have been harmed by toxic chemicals.

Experience Communication Case Study

FAMILY HOUR

The book's online resources include an interactive video of the communication situation featured in the case study scripted below. Apply what you've learned in this chapter by analyzing the case study, using the questions that follow the script as a guide. These questions are also available online with the video.

Jason Harris,/© Wadsworth

Over spring break, 20-year-old Josh visits his father. He wants to convince his family to support him in joining a fraternity that has given him a bid. On his second day home, after dinner Josh decides to broach the topic. His dad is watching the evening news on television when Josh walks into the living room. Josh sits down and opens the conversation.

Josh: Well, something pretty interesting has happened at school this semester.

Dad: I'll bet you found a girlfriend, right? I was about your age when your mother and I started dating, and that was the best part of college. I still remember how she looked on our first date. She was young then, and she was very slender and pretty. I saw her and thought she was the loveliest thing I'd ever seen. Before long, we were a regular item. Yep, it was about when I was 20, like you are now.

Josh: Well, I haven't found a girlfriend, but I did get a bid from Sigma Chi.

Dad: Sigma Chi. What is that—a fraternity?

Josh: Yeah, it's probably the coolest fraternity on campus. I attended some rush parties this semester—mainly out of curiosity, just to see what they were like.

Dad: Why'd you do that? Before you ever went to college, I told you to steer clear of fraternities. They cost a lot of money, and they distract you from your studies.

Josh: Well, I know you told me to steer clear of fraternities, but I did check a few out. I'd be willing to take a job to help pay the membership fee and monthly dues. Besides, it's not that much more expensive when you figure I'd be eating at the house.

Dad: Do you realize how much it costs just for you to go to that school? I'm paying $14,000 a year! When I went to school, I had to go to state college because my parents couldn't afford to send me to the school of my choice. You have no idea how lucky you are to be going to the school you wanted to go to and have me footing all of the bills.

Josh: But we could work it out so that a fraternity wouldn't cost you anything. Like I said, I . . .

Dad: If you want to take a job, fine. I could use some help paying your tuition and fees. But you're not taking a job just so you can belong to a party house.

Josh: I thought they were just party houses too, until I attended rush. Now, I went to several houses that were that way, but Sigma Chi isn't. I really liked the brothers at Sigma Chi. They're interesting and friendly and fun, so I was thrilled when . . .

Dad: I don't want to hear about it. You're not joining a fraternity. I told you what happened when I was in college. I joined one, and pretty soon my Dean's List grades dropped to Cs and Ds. When you live in a fraternity house, you can't study like you can in your dorm room or the library. I should know. I tried it and found out the hard way. There's no need for you to repeat my mistake.

Josh: But, Dad, I'm not you. Joining a fraternity wouldn't necessarily mean that my grades . . .

Dad: What do you mean, you're not me? You think I wasn't a good student before I joined the fraternity? You think you're so smart that you can party all the time and still make good grades? Let me tell you something, I thought that too, and, boy! Was I ever wrong. As soon as I joined the house, it was party time all the time. There was always music blaring and girls in the house and poker games—anything but studying. I wasn't stupid. It's just not an atmosphere that encourages academic work.

Josh: I'd like to give it a try. I really like these guys, and I think I can handle being in Sigma Chi and still . . .

Dad: Well, you think wrong!

▼ ▼

1. What examples of ineffective listening are evident in this dialogue?

2. If you could advise Josh's father on listening effectively, what would you tell him to do differently?

3. What advice would you offer Josh on listening more effectively to his father?

7 Creating Communication Climates

▶ **FOCUS QUESTIONS**

1. What kinds of communication foster defensive and supportive communication climates?

2. In what ways can conflict enrich relationships?

3. How can we confirm both ourselves and others?

4. When is it appropriate to show grace toward others?

▶ You have scheduled a performance review with Simon, who began working for you 6 months ago. You need to call his attention to some problems in his work while also showing that you value him and believe he can improve his performance.

▶ You know your friend Steve is worried about not having gotten any offers after interviewing with 16 companies. You want to let him know it's okay for him to talk with you about his concerns.

▶ You have agreed to talk to a group of parents who are concerned about drugs at the school where you work. You know the parents are worried and may regard you as just a spokesperson for the school. To be effective, you'll have to show that you share their concerns and that they can trust you.

In each of these situations, achieving your goals depends on your ability to create an effective **communication climate,** which is the emotional tone of a relationship between people. Perhaps you feel foggy-headed when the sky is overcast and feel upbeat when it's sunny. Do you respond differently to the various seasons? In much the same way that physical climates influence moods, communication climates affect how people feel and interact with one another. We feel on guard when a supervisor blames us, when a co-worker acts superior, when someone flames us on the Internet, or when a friend judges us. In each case, the communication climate is overcast.

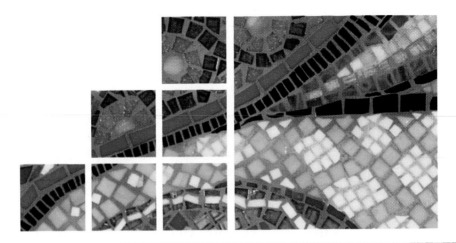

Creating constructive climates is a basic skill that influences the effectiveness of communication in all contexts. Work teams with supportive, productive climates foster good professional relationships and productivity. In social relationships, healthy climates allow people to feel at ease. In personal relationships, we want trusting, affirming climates that let us disclose private feelings and thoughts without fear of criticism or ridicule. Effective climates for public speaking situations foster trust and respect between speakers and listeners. Thus, communication climates are basic to all settings and forms of interaction.

This chapter focuses on communication climate. We'll begin by discussing *interpersonal confirmation* as a keystone of positive communication climates. Next, we'll identify specific kinds of communication that foster defensive and supportive communication climates. In the third section of the chapter, we'll consider the role of conflict in relationships, and we'll see that creating healthy communication climates helps us manage conflict constructively in personal and professional relationships. Finally, we'll discuss guidelines for creating and sustaining healthy communication climates.

▶LEVELS OF CONFIRMATION AND DISCONFIRMATION

Philosopher Martin Buber (1957, 1970) believed that each of us needs interpersonal *confirmation* to be healthy and to grow. Communication scholars (Anderson, Baxter, & Cissna, 2004; Arnett, 2004; Stewart, Zediker, & Black, 2004) have drawn on Buber's work to develop philosophies of communication that emphasize interpersonal confirmation as a basis of meaningful dialogue. The essence of **interpersonal confirmation** is the expressed valuing of another person. We all want to feel we are valued by co-workers on the job, by audiences in public speaking settings, and by intimates in personal relationships. When others confirm us, we feel appreciated and respected. When they disconfirm us, we feel discounted and devalued.

Few climates are purely confirming or purely disconfirming. Most relationships include both confirming and disconfirming communication, so the relationship climate is a mix of the two types or, over time, the relationship cycles between feeling confirming and feeling disconfirming (Figure 7.1). Extending Buber's philosophical work, communication scholars (Cissna & Sieburg, 1986) have identified three levels of confirmation that affect communication climates: recognition, acknowledgment, and endorsement.

Recognition

The most basic form of interpersonal confirmation is **recognition,** the expression of awareness of another person's existence. We recognize others by nonverbal behaviors (a smile, a handshake, looking up when someone enters your room) and by verbal com-

munication ("Hello," "Good to meet you," "Welcome home"). We disconfirm others at a fundamental level when we don't recognize their existence. For example, you might not speak to a person when you enter a room, or you might not look at a teammate who comes late to a meeting. Not responding to another's comments is also

Figure 7.1   THE CONTINUUM OF COMMUNICATION CLIMATES

a failure to give recognition. As we noted in Chapter 5, silence is sometimes used to disconfirm another's existence.

Acknowledgment

A second, more powerful level of interpersonal confirmation is **acknowledgment**: attentiveness to what a person feels, thinks, or says. Nonverbally, we acknowledge others by nodding our heads or by making strong eye contact to show we are listening. Verbal acknowledgments are direct responses to others' communication. If a friend says, "I'm really worried that I blew the LSAT exam," you could acknowledge that by responding, "So the exam made you anxious, huh?" This paraphrasing response acknowledges the thoughts and feelings of the other person. If a co-worker tells you, "I'm not sure I have the experience to handle this assignment," you could acknowledge that comment by saying, "Sounds as if you're feeling more challenged than you'd like." We disconfirm others when we don't acknowledge their feelings, thoughts, or words. For instance, if you responded to your friend's statement about the LSAT by saying, "Want to go out and catch a film tonight?" your response would be an irrelevancy that ignored what your friend said. We also fail to acknowledge others if we deny the feelings they communicate: "You did fine on the LSAT," "There's no need to worry about handling this assignment." Lack of acknowledgment may also take the form of nonresponse to a friend's comment or nonresponse to ideas expressed in meetings or memos (Conrad & Poole, 2002). Lisa explains how she feels when others refuse to acknowledge her statements about her needs.

▶ Lisa

I'm amazed by how often people won't acknowledge what I tell them. A hundred times, I've been walking across campus, and someone's come up and offered to guide me. I tell them I don't need help, but they put an arm under my elbow to guide me. I am blind, but I can think just fine. I know if I need help. Why can't they acknowledge that?

Endorsement

The highest level of interpersonal confirmation is **endorsement**—accepting a person's feelings or thoughts as valid. This doesn't necessarily mean agreeing with the person's thoughts or feelings, but it does mean accepting them as real for that person. You could endorse the friend who is worried about the LSAT by saying, "It's natural to be worried about the LSAT when you have so much riding on it." You could endorse your colleague at work by saying, "Anyone would be uneasy about taking on such a big new responsibility." We fail to endorse others when we reject their thoughts and feelings. For example, it would be disconfirming to say, "How can you complain about a new responsibility when so many people are being laid off? You should be glad to have a job." This response rejects the validity of the other person's expressed feelings and may close the lines of communication between the two of you. In her commentary, Jennie provides an example of how hurtful it can be not to feel endorsed by friends.

Interpersonal confirmation is a key to building supportive, trusting communication climates.

▶ **Jennie**

My father died two years ago. We were very close, so I was upset and sad for a long time. After a couple of months, some of my friends said things like, "You need to move on," or "It's time to quit mourning for your father." Those comments made me feel like I was crazy to still be grieving. I felt like they were saying what I was feeling wasn't right or something.

In sum, there are three levels of interpersonal confirmation. When we confirm someone, we say, "You matter to me; I care what you feel or think; I accept your feelings and thoughts." When we disconfirm another, we say, "You don't exist; your ideas don't matter; I deny what you think and feel." Disconfirmation is not mere disagreement. After all, disagreements can be productive and healthy. What is disconfirming is to be told that we don't exist or matter or that our feelings and thoughts are crazy, wrong, stupid, or deviant. The Sharpen Your Skill feature on page 142 encourages you to notice confirming and disconfirming communication in online conversations.

If you think about what we've discussed, you'll probably find that the relationships in which you feel most valued and comfortable are those with high degrees of recognition, acknowledgment, and endorsement. Confirming and disconfirming messages are

Figure 7.2 LEVELS OF CONFIRMATION AND DISCONFIRMATION

	Confirming Messages	*Disconfirming Messages*
Recognition	You exist.	You don't exist.
	Hello.	Silence
Acknowledgment	Listening	Not listening
	I'm sorry you're hurt.	You'll get over it.
	I know you're worried.	Let's drop the subject.
Endorsement	What you think is true.	You are wrong.
	What you feel is okay.	You shouldn't feel what you do.
	I feel the same way.	Your feeling doesn't make sense.
	What you feel is normal.	It's stupid to feel that way.

a primary means by which we create communication climates (Figure 7.2). We'll now consider other forms of communication that affect climates.

▶DEFENSIVE AND SUPPORTIVE CLIMATES

Communication researcher Jack Gibb (1961, 1964, 1970) studied the relationship between communication and climate. He began by noting that in some climates we feel defensive whereas in others we feel supported. Gibb identified six types of communication that promote defensive climates and six contrasting types of communication that foster supportive climates.

Evaluation versus Description

As we noted in Chapter 4's discussion of the evaluative nature of language, we tend to feel defensive when others evaluate us, particularly when they evaluate us negatively (Stone, Patton, & Heen, 1999). Few of us are comfortable when we are the targets of judgments (Conrad & Poole, 2002). Negative evaluations are most likely to arouse defensiveness. Examples of evaluative statements are "You have no discipline," "It's dumb to feel that way," and "That's a stupid idea."

Descriptive communication doesn't evaluate others or what they think and feel. Instead, it describes behaviors without passing judgment. In Chapter 4, we discussed *I*-language, in which a speaker takes responsibility for what she or he feels and avoids judging others. For example, "I feel upset when you scream" describes what the person

Confirmation and Disconfirmation in Online Communication

Confirming and disconfirming communication is not limited to face-to-face interactions. It also establishes climates in online communication.

To gain insight into the particular forms of communication that create confirming and disconfirming climates, visit a chat room of your choosing. Take notes on communication that expresses or denies recognition, acknowledgment, and endorsement of others. What differences can you identify between confirming and disconfirming communication in chat rooms?

SHARPEN YOUR SKILL

speaking feels or thinks, but it doesn't evaluate another. On the other hand, "You upset me" evaluates the other person and holds her or him responsible for what you feel. "I felt hurt when you said that" describes your feelings, whereas "You hurt me" blames another for your feelings.

Descriptive language may refer to others, but it does so by describing, not evaluating, their behavior (for example, "You seem to be less involved in team meetings lately" versus "You're not involved enough in our team"; "You've shouted three times today" versus "Quit flying off the handle"). Nonverbal communication can also convey evaluation—a raised eyebrow expresses skepticism, a frown communicates disapproval. Therefore, it's important to keep facial cues and other nonverbal messages as nonevaluative as the words themselves. The Sharpen Your Skill feature on page 144 gives you an opportunity to practice using descriptive language.

Certainty versus Provisionalism

The language of certainty is absolute and often dogmatic. It suggests there is only one valid answer, point of view, or course of action. Because certainty proclaims an absolutely correct position, it slams the door on further discussion. Leaders can stifle creativity if they dogmatically state what the team should produce (Fisher, 1998). There's no point in talking with people who demean any point of view but their own. Certainty is also communicated when we repeat our positions instead of considering others' ideas. Monika provides an example of certainty and its impact on her relationship with her father.

▶ Monika

My father is totally closed-minded. He has his ideas, and everything else is crazy. I told him I was majoring in communication studies, and he said I'd never get a job as a speechwriter. He never asked what communication studies is, or I would have told him it's a lot more than speechwriting. He always assumes that he knows everything about whatever is being discussed. He has no interest in information or other points of view. I've learned to keep my ideas to myself around him—there's no communication.

One form of certainty communication is **ethnocentrism.** Ethnocentrism is a perspective based on the assumption that our culture and its norms are the only right ones. For instance, someone who says, "It's always disrespectful to be late" reveals insensitivity to societies that are less time conscious than the United States. Certainty is also evident when we say, "My mind can't be changed," "Only a fool would think that," or "There's no point in further discussion."

An alternative to certainty is *provisionalism,* which relies on tentative language to signal openness to other points of view. Provisional language indicates that we are willing to consider alternative positions, and this encourages others to voice their ideas. Provisional language lessens the chance that others will feel they have lost face in the interaction. Provisional communication includes such statements as "The way I tend to see the issue is . . . ," "One way to look at this is . . . ," and "It's possible that . . .". Note that each comment shows that the speaker realizes that other positions also could be

Using Descriptive Language

To develop skill in supportive communication, translate the following evaluative statements into descriptive ones:

Evaluative	Descriptive
This report is poorly done.	This report doesn't include background information.

You're lazy.

I hate the way you dominate conversations with me.

Stop obsessing about the problem.

You're too involved.

You're excluding me from the team.

SHARPEN YOUR SKILL

reasonable. Tentative communication reflects an open mind, which is why it invites continued conversation.

Strategy versus Spontaneity

Defensiveness is a natural response when we think others are using strategies to manipulate us. Effective communication takes thought, planning, and effort to adapt to others so that we can share meaning, but that doesn't necessarily mean that communication must be manipulative. Strategic communication, in contrast, aims to manipulate one person by keeping motives or intentions hidden. An example of strategic communication is this: "Would you do something for me if I told you it really mattered?" If the speaker doesn't tell us what we're expected to do, it feels like a setup. In work situations, employees may become defensive if they feel management is trying to trick them into thinking their jobs are more important than they are (Conrad & Poole, 2002).

We may also feel that someone is trying to manipulate us with a comment such as "Remember how I helped you with that project you were behind on last month?" After a preamble like that, we suspect a trap of some sort. Nonverbal behaviors may also convey strategy, as when a speaker pauses a long time before answering a question or refuses to look at listeners. A sense of deception pollutes the communication climate.

Spontaneity stands in contrast to strategy. Spontaneous communication may well be thought out, yet it is also open, honest, and not manipulative. "I really need your help with my computer" is more spontaneous than "Would you do something for me if I told you it really mattered?" Likewise, it is more spontaneous to ask for a favor in a straightforward way ("Would you help me?") than to preface a request by reciting everything you've done for someone else. Many people say that they enjoy online communication because it is spontaneous, especially in chat rooms and IM exchanges.

Control versus Problem Orientation

Like strategy, controlling communication attempts to dominate others. In response, others often feel defensive, and they may respond with resentment or even rebellion (Stone et al., 1999). For instance, it is controlling for someone to insist that his or her preference should prevail over others' preferences. Whether the issue is trivial (which movie to see) or serious (which policy a group will recommend), controllers try to impose their points of view on others. Winning an argument or having the last word is more important than finding the best solution. Controlling communication prompts defensiveness because the relationship-level meaning is that the person exerting control thinks she or he has greater power, rights, or intelligence than others. It's disconfirming to be told that our opinions are wrong, that our preferences don't matter, that we have to obey, or that our ideas are faulty.

Controlling communication is particularly objectionable when it is combined with strategies. For example, a wife who earns a higher salary than her husband might say to him, "Well, I like the Honda more than the Ford you want, and it's my money that's going to pay for it." The speaker not only pushes her preference but also implies that her salary gives her greater power.

Rather than imposing a preference, problem-oriented communication focuses on resolving tensions and problems. The goal is to work collaboratively to come up with something that everyone finds acceptable. Here's an example of problem-oriented communication: "It seems that we have really different ideas about how to get started on this task. Let's talk through what each of us wants and see if we can find a way for all of us to achieve what we need." Note how this statement invites collaboration and confirms the other people and the team's relationship by expressing a desire to meet all members' needs.

Problem-oriented communication tends to reduce conflict and foster an open interaction climate (McKinney, Kelly, & Duran, 1997; McNutt, 1997). The relationship level of meaning in problem-oriented interaction emphasizes that the communicators care about and respect each other. In contrast, controlling behaviors aim for one person to triumph over others, an outcome that undercuts harmony.

Neutrality versus Empathy

We tend to become defensive when others act in a neutral manner, especially if we are talking about topics about which we have strong feelings. Neutral communication implies indifference to others and what they say. Consequently, it may create defensiveness.

In contrast to neutrality, expressed empathy confirms the worth of others and shows concern for their thoughts and feelings. We communicate empathy when we say, "I can understand why you feel that way," "It sounds like you feel uncomfortable with your job," or "I don't blame you for being worried about the situation." Gibb stressed that empathy doesn't necessarily mean agreement; instead, it conveys respect for others and what they think and feel. Especially when we don't agree with others, it's important to show that we respect them as people. Doing so fosters a supportive climate and keeps lines of communication open, even if differences continue to exist.

© Jon Feingersh/Corbis

How is the woman on the right communicating support and empathy to her friend?

Superiority versus Equality

Most of us feel on guard with people who act as if they are better than we are. Consider several messages that convey superiority: "I know a lot more about this than you"; "You don't have my experience"; "Is this the best you could do?"; "You really should go to my hairdresser." Each of these messages says loudly and clearly, "You aren't as good (smart, competent, attractive) as I am." Predictably, the frequent result is that we try to save face by shutting out the people and messages that belittle us. Carl's experience in his job provides an example of the impact of communication that conveys superiority.

▶ Carl

I am really uncomfortable with one of the guys on my team at work. He always acts like he knows best and that nobody else is as smart or experienced. The other day, I suggested a way we might improve our team's productivity, and he said, "I remember when I used to think that." What a put-down! You can bet I won't go to him with another idea.

We feel more relaxed and comfortable communicating with people who treat us as equals. At the relationship level of meaning, expressed equality communicates respect and equivalent status between people. This promotes an open, unguarded climate in which interaction flows freely. We can have special expertise in certain areas and still show regard for others and what they think, feel, and say. Creating a climate of equality allows everyone to be involved without fear of being judged inadequate.

We've seen that confirmation, which may include recognizing, acknowledging, and endorsing others, is the basis of healthy communication climates. Our discussion of defensive and supportive communication enlightens us about specific kinds of communication that express confirmation or disconfirmation. The Sharpen Your Skill activity on this page invites you to apply what you've learned about communication that fosters defensiveness and supportiveness. Our discussion of communication climates is a good foundation for considering the role of conflict in human relationships and how building and sustaining affirmative communication climates allows us to manage conflict productively.

Assessing Communication Climates

Use the behaviors we've discussed as a checklist for assessing communication climates. The next time you feel defensive, ask yourself whether others are communicating superiority, control, strategy, certainty, neutrality, or evaluation.

In a communication climate that you find supportive and open, ask whether the following behaviors are present: spontaneity, equality, provisionalism, problem orientation, empathy, and description.

To improve defensive climates, be a model of supportive communication. Resist the tendency to respond defensively. Instead, be empathic, descriptive, and spontaneous, show equality and tentativeness, and be problem oriented.

SHARPEN YOUR SKILL

▶CONFLICT AND COMMUNICATION

Conflict exists when people who depend on each other have different views, interests, values, responsibilities, or objectives and perceive their differences as incompatible. The presence of conflict doesn't mean a relationship is in trouble, although how people manage conflict does affect relationship health. Typically, conflict is a sign that people are involved with each other. If they weren't, differences wouldn't matter and wouldn't need to be resolved. Co-workers argue because they care about issues that affect all of them; romantic partners engage in conflict when they face tensions and disagreements that jeopardize their relationship. When tensions arise, it's good to remember that we have conflict only with people who matter to us. In other words, a strong connection and the desire to preserve it usually underlie the conflict.

Conflict Can Be Overt or Covert

Conflict can be overt or covert. **Overt conflict** exists when people express differences in a straightforward manner. They might discuss a disagreement, honestly express different points of view, or argue heatedly about ideas. In each case, differences are out in the open.

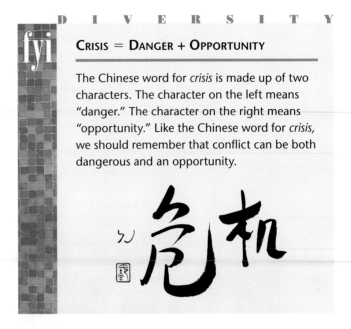

D I V E R S I T Y

fyi

CRISIS = DANGER + OPPORTUNITY

The Chinese word for *crisis* is made up of two characters. The character on the left means "danger." The character on the right means "opportunity." Like the Chinese word for *crisis,* we should remember that conflict can be both dangerous and an opportunity.

危机

▶ Carlotta

My roommate doesn't tell me when she's mad or hurt or whatever. Instead, she plays these games that drive me crazy. Sometimes, she refuses to talk to me and denies that anything is wrong. Other times, she "forgets" some of my stuff when she gets our groceries. I have to guess what is wrong because she won't tell me. It strains our friendship.

Yet, as Carla points out, not all conflict is overt. **Covert conflict** exists when people express disagreement or difference only indirectly. For instance, if you're annoyed that your roommate left the kitchen a mess, you might play the stereo when she or he is sleeping. It's almost impossible to resolve conflicts when we don't communicate openly about our differences.

Conflict Can Be Managed Well or Poorly

Because conflict is inevitable and can be productive, we need to understand how to manage conflict so that it is healthy for us, for our relationships, and for decision making. Clyde Feldman and Carl Ridley (2000) identify four key components of the conflict process. Their four-component model breaks down the complex process of conflict so that we can think about it and our options for managing it:

▶ Conflicts of interest: Goals, interests, or opinions that seem incompatible

▶ Conflict orientations: Individuals' attitudes toward conflict

▶ Conflict responses: Overt behavioral responses to conflict

▶ Conflict outcomes: How conflict is managed and how the process of conflict affects relationships between people

Conflicts of Interest The first component of conflict is goals, interests, or views that are perceived as incompatible. You want to set up a time each day when you and a friend will both be online for instant messages, but your friend doesn't want to do that. You believe money should be enjoyed, and your partner believes in saving for a rainy day. You want your team to meet twice weekly, and another member of the team wants to meet only monthly. When we find ourselves at odds with people who matter to us, we need to resolve conflict, preferably in a way that doesn't harm the relationship.

Conflict Orientations The second component is how we perceive conflict. Do you view conflict as negative? Do you assume that everyone is bound to lose in conflict situations? Your answers to these questions shape your orientation toward conflict and thus how you approach it. One of the greatest influences on orientations toward conflict is cultural background. Societies such as the United States accept conflict and assertive competition. Other societies teach people to avoid conflict and to seek harmony with others.

How people respond to conflict reflects one of three distinct orientations: *lose–lose, win–lose,* and *win–win.* Each of these is appropriate in some situations; the challenge is to know when each view is constructive.

The **lose–lose** approach to conflict assumes that conflict results in losses for everyone. One of my colleagues avoids conflict whenever possible because he feels that everyone loses when there is disagreement. The lose–lose view presumes that conflict cannot produce positive outcomes. Although the lose–lose perspective usually is not beneficial, it has merit in specific circumstances. Some issues aren't worth the effort of conflict. For instance, my father-in-law and I disagree strongly about political matters. I no longer talk with him about politics, because inevitably we both lose in such conversations. Similarly, in order to maintain a positive working relationship, co-workers may avoid discussing issues on which they disagree strongly, as long as resolving their differences is not relevant to job performance.

The **win–lose** orientation to conflict assumes that one person wins at the expense of the other. A person who perceives conflict as a win–lose matter thinks that whatever one person gains is at the other's expense and that what one person loses benefits the other. Partners who disagree about whether to move to a new location that provides better job prospects for only one of them might lock into a yes–no mode in which they can see only two alternatives: move or don't move. They are unlikely to make an effort to find a mutually acceptable solution, such as moving to a third place that meets both partners' needs adequately, or temporarily having a long-distance relationship so each

Conflict is inevitable in relationships. Do these two co-workers seem to be managing their difference of opinion constructively?

© Steve Chenn/Corbis

person can maximize professional opportunities. The more person A argues for moving, the more B argues for not moving. Eventually, one of them "wins," but at the cost of the other and the relationship.

A win–lose orientation toward conflict tends to undermine relationships because someone has to lose. There is no possibility that both can win, much less that the relationship can. For this reason, win–lose orientations should really be called win–lose–lose because when one person wins, both the other person and the relationship can lose.

Before you dismiss win–lose as a totally unconstructive orientation to conflict, let's consider when it might be effective. Win–lose can be an appropriate orientation when we have low commitment to a relationship and little desire to take care of the person with whom we disagree. When you're buying a car, for instance, you want the best deal you can get, and you have little concern for the dealer's profit. I adopted a win–lose approach to conflict with doctors when my father was dying. The doctors weren't doing all they could to help him, because they saw little value in investing time in a dying patient, but I wanted everything possible done to comfort my father. We had opposing views, and I cared less about whether the doctors were happy and liked me than about "winning" the best medical care for my father.

Bizarro

The **win–win** view of conflict assumes that there are usually ways to resolve differences so that everyone gains. For people who view conflict as interactions in which all parties can win, the goal is to come up with a resolution that is acceptable to everyone. A person is willing to make some accommodations in order to build a solution that lets others win, too. When partners adopt win–win views of conflict, they often find solutions that neither had thought of previously. This happens because they are committed to their own and the other's satisfaction. Sometimes win–win attitudes result in compromises that satisfy enough of each person's needs to provide confirmation and to protect the health of the relationship. Tess describes a situation in which she and her partner worked to find a way for both of them (and their relationship) to win.

▶ Tess

One of the roughest issues for Jerry and me was when he started working most nights. The time after dinner had always been "our time." When Jerry took the new job, he had to stay in constant contact with the California office. Because of the time difference, at 6 P.M., when Jerry and I used to do something together, it's only 3 P.M. on the West Coast, and the business day is still going. I was hurt that he no longer had time for us, and he was angry that I wanted time he needed for business. We kept talking and came up with the idea of spending a day together each weekend, which we'd never done. Although my ideal would still be to share evenings, this solution keeps us in touch with each other.

What we learned about perception in Chapter 3 reminds us that how we perceive and label conflict powerfully affects what it means to us and how we craft resolutions. We're unlikely to find a win–win solution when we conceive conflict as win–lose or lose–lose.

Conflict Responses The third component of conflict is how we respond to it. A series of studies identified four responses to conflict (Rusbult, 1987; Rusbult, Johnson, & Morrow, 1986; Rusbult & Zembrodt, 1983; Rusbult, Zembrodt, & Iwaniszek, 1986). Figure 7.3 summarizes these responses to conflict, which are active or passive, depending on whether they address problems. Responses are also constructive or destructive in their effect on relationships.

The *exit response* involves leaving a relationship, either by walking out or by psychologically withdrawing. "I don't want to talk about it" is a vocal exit response. Because exit is forceful, it is active; because it fails to resolve tension, it can be destructive. However, there are situations in which exit can be a positive response, especially if it is only temporary. For instance, if you know that you will say or do something you will regret if you don't walk away from an argument, exiting is a valuable short-term response.

The *neglect response* occurs when a person denies or minimizes problems. "You're making a mountain out of a molehill" is a neglect response that denies that a serious issue exists. The neglect response is also disconfirming because it fails to acknowledge and respect how another feels. Neglect can be destructive because it evades difficulties, and it is passive because it doesn't actively promote discussion.

The *loyalty response* is staying committed to a relationship despite differences. Loyalty involves hoping that things will get better on their own. Loyalty is silent allegiance, so it is passive. Because loyalty doesn't end a relationship and preserves the option of addressing tension later, loyalty can be constructive. However, if people never get around to addressing the tension or problem, loyalty can harm a relationship.

Finally, *voice* is an active, constructive response to conflict because it focuses on dealing directly with problems and trying to help the relationship by managing differences. A person who says to a co-worker, "I want to talk about the tension between us" exemplifies the voice response to conflict.

Figure 7.3 RESPONSES TO CONFLICT
Source: Adapted from Wood, 1997, p. 21.

Although most people have one or two habitual responses to conflict, we can develop skill in other styles of responding. Constructive strategies (voice and loyalty) are advisable for relationships that you want to maintain. Of those two, voice is generally stronger because it actively addresses conflict. Loyalty can be useful as an interim strategy when people need time to reflect or cool off before dealing with tension. Once you understand your current ways of responding to conflict, you can consider whether you want to develop skill in alternative styles.

Conflict Outcomes The final component of conflict is the outcome. When most people think of conflict outcomes, they think of the decision that has resulted and whose preferences have prevailed. Although these are indeed outcomes of conflict, they are neither the only ones nor the most important.

A conflict's impact on a relationship may be a more significant and enduring outcome than the actual decision. Relationship outcomes are influenced more by how we manage conflict than by the resolution itself. Conflicts can actually strengthen relationships when people build a supportive interpersonal climate and work to sustain that climate as a part of managing conflict. Harm to relationships is most likely when people disconfirm each other and cultivate defensive communication climates. Because our choices of how to manage conflict have impact on relationships, we need to be especially careful to communicate in respectful and affirming ways, even if we differ, when conflicts arise.

Although many people have negative views of conflict, it can benefit both our relationships and ourselves. Managed constructively, conflict can help us grow personally and professionally, and it can strengthen our connections with others. Conflict prompts us to consider different points of view. Based on what we learn, we may change our opinions, behaviors, or goals. Conflict can also increase our insight into relationships, situations, and ourselves.

▶Guidelines for Creating and Sustaining Healthy Communication Climates

To translate what we've covered in this chapter into practical information, we'll discuss five guidelines for building and sustaining healthy climates.

Communicate in Ways That Confirm Others

Throughout this chapter, we've seen that interpersonal confirmation is a cornerstone of healthy communication climates. Although interpersonal confirmation is important, it isn't always easy to give. When we disagree with what others think or do, it may be difficult to confirm them. However, we've emphasized that interpersonal confirmation is not the same as agreement. You can confirm someone as a person even if you don't admire the person's ideas or actions. Interpersonal confirmation occurs when we recognize others, acknowledge or attend to them, and endorse what they feel, think, say, and do as understandable. We can communicate interpersonal confirmation even if we do not agree with others' feelings, beliefs, or actions.

▶ Dean

My supervisor did an excellent job of letting me know I was valued when I got passed over for a promotion last year. He came to my office to talk to me before the promotion was announced. He told me both I and the other guy were qualified but that he had seniority and also field experience I didn't have. Then he assigned me to a field position for six months so I could get the experience I needed to get promoted. His talk made all the difference in how I felt about staying with the company.

Communication can express both confirmation of another person and disagreement with that person. In fact, research tells us that people expect real friends to give honest feedback, even if it isn't always pleasant to hear (Rawlins, 1994). Similarly, in the workplace, managers who give honest feedback, including criticism, are more likely to build strong working relationships with subordinates than are managers who avoid criticism and conflict (Fisher, 1998). This implies that we have an ethical responsibility to be honest in our communication. It is false friends who tell us only what we want to hear. We can offer honest feedback within a context that assures others we value and respect them, as Dan's commentary illustrates.

▶ Dan

When I first came to school here, I got in with a crowd that drank a lot. At first, I drank only on weekends, but pretty soon I was drinking every night and drinking more and more. My grades were suffering, but I didn't stop. Then my friend Betsy told me she wanted to help me stop drinking. The way she talked to me, I knew that she was being honest because she cared. She was a better friend than all my drinking buddies because she cared enough not to let me hurt myself. All my buddies just stood by and said nothing.

Communicate in Ways That Confirm Yourself

It is just as important to confirm yourself as others. You are no less valuable than others, your needs are no less important, and your preferences are no less valid. It is a misunderstanding to think that the interpersonal communication principles we've discussed concern only how we behave toward others. They pertain equally to how we should treat ourselves. Thus, it is ethical to confirm others and ourselves equally.

You confirm yourself when you express your thoughts and feelings honestly. By doing that, you show that you respect yourself. You also give others a chance to understand who you are. You communicate ethically when you assert your feelings, ideas, and preferences while honoring those of others. If you don't assert yourself in the workplace, you give up the possibility of influencing the quality of work produced and how it is organized. If you don't assert yourself in personal relationships, you undercut your own and your partner's respect for your ideas, feelings, and needs, as Maria points out in her commentary.

▶ Maria

Ever since I was a kid, I have muffled my own needs and tried to please others. I thought I was taking care of relationships, but actually I was hurting them, because I felt neglected. My resentment poisoned relationships in subtle but potent ways. Now, I'm learning to tell others what I want and need, and that's improving my relationships.

Figure 7.4 Aggression, Assertion, and Deference

Aggressive	Assertive	Deferential
I demand that we spend time together.	I'd like to create more time for us.	If you don't want us to spend time with each other, that's okay with me.
Get this report done today. I need it.	I need to have this report today. Can you manage that?	I need this report today, but if you can't get it done, that's all right.
Tell me what you're feeling; I insist.	I would like to understand more how you feel.	If you don't want to talk about how you feel, okay.
I don't care what you want; I'm not going to a movie.	I'm really not up for a movie tonight.	It's fine with me to go to a movie if you want to.

Assertive communication is not aggressive. Aggressive communication occurs when one person puts herself or himself ahead of others or derides others' thoughts, feelings, goals, or actions. In contrast, assertive communication simply expresses the speaker's thoughts, feelings, preferences, and goals without disparaging anyone else. You communicate assertively when you express yourself firmly and unapologetically.

Assertive communication is also not deferential. Unlike deference, assertion doesn't subordinate your needs to those of others. Assertion also differs from passive aggression, in which a person blocks or resists while denying that she or he is doing so. Assertion is a matter of clearly stating what you feel, think, or want. This should be done without disparaging others and what they feel, think, or want. You should simply state your feelings in an open, descriptive manner. Figure 7.4 illustrates how aggression, assertion, and deference differ. Even when people disagree or have conflicting needs, each person can state her or his feelings and confirm the other's perspective. Usually, there are ways to acknowledge both viewpoints, as Dean's comments illustrate.

Respect Diversity among People

Just as individuals differ, so do relationships in personal and professional life. There is tremendous variety in what people find comfortable, affirming, and satisfying. For this reason, it's counterproductive to try to force all people and relationships to fit into a single mode. For example, you might know one co-worker who enjoys a lot of verbal banter and another who is offended by it. There's no need to try to persuade the second co-worker to engage in verbal teasing or the first one to stop doing so. You may be comfortable disclosing in online communication,

Communicating Assertively

The following statements are deferential or aggressive. Revise each one so that it is assertive.

1. I'm going to the party regardless of what you want.
2. I'll lend you the money, even though I may have to work an extra shift to get it.
3. We're getting the car that I like, and that's it!
4. They don't have vegetarian entrees at the restaurant you want to go to, but I can just eat a salad.

SHARPEN YOUR SKILL

but some of the people you meet online don't share that preference. You may not always face most people when you talk with them, but you should face people with visual limitations (see the FYI feature on the following page). To build and sustain supportive, confirming climates, we need to adapt our communication to people's differences.

Because people and relationships are diverse, we should strive to respect a range of communication choices and relationship patterns. In addition, we should be cautious about imposing our meaning on others' communication. People from different social groups, including distinct groups in the United States, have learned different communication styles. What westerners consider to be open, healthy self-disclosure may feel offensively intrusive to people from some Asian societies. European Americans can misinterpret as abrasive the dramatic, assertive speaking style of some African Americans. Especially in the workplace, it's important to understand that people vary widely in communication styles. To communicate effectively, we need to respect diversity among people. Valaya makes this point in her commentary.

▶ Valaya

One of the most hard adjustments for me has been how Americans assert themselves. I was very surprised that students argue with their teachers. We would never do that in Taiwan. It would be extremely disrespectful. I also see friends argue, sometimes very much. I understand this is a cultural difference, but I have trouble accepting it. I learned that disagreements very much hurt relationships.

It's also appropriate to ask others to explain behaviors that are not familiar to you. For instance, Valaya might ask other students what it means to them when they argue with teachers, and other students might ask Valaya what it means to her not to argue with teachers. Asking others what their communication means lets them know that they matter to you, and it allows us to gain insight into perspectives other than our own.

Time Conflict Effectively

A fourth guideline for creating effective communication climates is to time them so that each person can be mindful and so that the context and available time allow for constructive discussion. Most of us are irritable when we are sick, tired, or stressed, so conflict is unlikely to be managed well. It's also generally more productive to discuss problems in private rather than in public settings. It takes time to manage conflict constructively, so it's wise not to engage in conflict when we have limited time. It's impossible to express ourselves clearly, to listen well, to be confirming, and to respond sensitively when a stopwatch is ticking in our minds.

Be flexible about when you engage in conflict. Some people prefer to tackle problems as soon as they come up, whereas other people need time to reflect

D   I   V   E   R   S   I   T   Y

fyi

GUIDELINES FOR COMMUNICATING WITH PEOPLE WITH DISABILITIES

Effective communication can help create supportive climates when we interact with people who have disabilities. The following guidelines are provided by the AXIS Center for Public Awareness of People with Disabilities. You can visit AXIS's website by going to the book's online resources and clicking on WebLink 7.1.

▶ When talking with someone who has a disability, speak directly to the person, not to a companion or interpreter.

▶ When introduced to a person with a disability, offer to shake hands. People who have limited hand use or who have artificial limbs can usually shake hands.

▶ When meeting a person with a visual impairment, identify yourself and anyone who is with you. If a person with a visual impairment is part of a group, preface your comments to that person with his or her name.

▶ You may offer assistance, but don't provide it unless your offer is accepted. Then, ask the person how you can best assist (ask for instructions).

▶ Treat adults as adults. Don't patronize people in wheelchairs by patting them on the shoulder or head; don't use childish language when speaking to people who have no mental disability.

▶ Respect the personal space of people with disabilities. It is rude to lean on a wheelchair; that is part of a person's personal territory.

▶ Listen mindfully when talking with someone who has difficulty speaking. Don't interrupt or supply words. Just be patient, and let the person finish. Don't pretend to understand if you don't. Instead, explain what you understood and ask the person if you understood correctly.

▶ When you talk with people who use wheelchairs or crutches, try to position yourself at their eye level and in front of them to allow good eye contact.

▶ It is appropriate to wave your hand or tap the shoulder of people with hearing impairments as a way to get their attention. Look directly at the person and speak slowly, clearly, and expressively. When talking to people who lip read, face a good light source, and keep your hands, cigarettes, and gum away from your mouth.

▶ Relax. Don't be afraid to use common expressions such as "See you later" to someone with a visual impairment or "Did you hear the news?" to someone with hearing difficulty. They're unlikely to be offended and may turn the irony into a joke.

before interacting. If one person feels ready to talk about a problem but the other doesn't, it's wise to delay discussion if possible. Of course, this works only if the person who is ready agrees to talk about the issue at a later time. In his book *Anger at Work* (1996), Dr. Hendrie Weisinger recommends taking a "time out" if emotions are raw or tempers are flaring. For instance, suppose someone says something to you that makes you very angry. What would you do? Dr. Weisinger suggests you tell the other person that you want to discuss the issue but you need 10 minutes. You might say you have to make a phone call first or explain that you'd prefer to cool down.

A third way to use timing to promote positive conflict is **bracketing,** which marks off (or brackets) peripheral issues for later discussion. In the course of conflict, multiple issues often surface. If we try to deal with each one as it arises, we get sidetracked from the immediate or main issue. Bracketing other concerns for later discussion lets us keep conflict focused productively. Keep in mind, however, that bracketing works only if people actually do return to the issues they set aside.

Show Grace When Appropriate

Finally, an important principle to keep in mind during conflict is that **grace** is sometimes appropriate. Although the idea of grace has not traditionally been discussed in communication texts, it is an important part of spiritual and philosophical thinking about ethical communication. You don't have to be religious or know philosophy to show grace. All that's needed is a willingness to sometimes excuse someone who has no right to expect your compassion or forgiveness. Showing grace when appropriate is equally important in personal and professional relationships.

Grace is granting forgiveness, putting aside our needs, or helping another save face when no standard says we should or must do so. Rather than being prompted by rules or expectations, grace springs from a generosity of spirit. Grace isn't forgiving when we *should* do so (for instance, excusing people who aren't responsible for their actions). Nor is grace allowing others to have their way when we have no choice (deferring when our supervisor insists, for example). Instead, grace is kindness that is neither earned nor required. For instance, two roommates agree to split chores, and one doesn't do her share during a week when she has three tests. Her roommate might do all the chores even though there is no expectation of this generosity. It's also an act of grace to defer to another person's preference when you could impose yours. Similarly, when someone hurts you and has no right to expect forgiveness, you may choose to forgive anyway. We do so not because we have to, but because we want to. Grace is a matter of choice.

Grace is given without strings. We show kindness, defer our needs, or forgive a wrong *without any expectation of reward or reciprocity.* Grace isn't doing something nice to make a co-worker feel grateful or indebted to us. Nor is it grace when we do something with the expectation of a payback. For an act to be one of grace, it must be done without conditions or expectation of return.

Grace is not always appropriate. Generosity of spirit can be exploited by people who take advantage of kindness. Some people repeatedly abuse and hurt others, confident that pardons will be granted. When grace is extended and then exploited, extending it again may be unwise. However, if you show grace in good faith and another takes advantage, you should not fault yourself. Kindness and a willingness to forgive are worthy moral precepts. Those who abuse grace, not those who offer it, are blameworthy.

Because Western culture emphasizes the assertion and protection of self-interest, grace is not widely practiced or esteemed. We are told to stand up for ourselves, to not let others walk on us, and to refuse to tolerate transgressions. It is important to honor and assert ourselves, as we've emphasized throughout this book. Yet self-assertion can work in tandem with generosity toward others.

None of us is perfect. We all make mistakes, hurt others with thoughtless acts, fail to meet responsibilities, and occasionally do things we know are wrong. Sometimes there is no reason others should forgive us when we wrong them; we have no right to expect exoneration. Yet human relations must have some room for redemption, for the extension of grace when it is not required or earned.

The guidelines we've discussed combine respect for self, others, relationships, and communication. Using these guidelines should enhance your ability to foster healthy, affirming climates in your relationships with others.

▶SUMMARY

In this chapter, we've explored communication climate as a foundation of interaction with others. A basic requirement for healthy communication climates is interpersonal confirmation. Each of us wants to feel valued, especially by those for whom we care most deeply. When communicators recognize, acknowledge, and endorse each other, they give the important gift of interpersonal confirmation. They say, "You matter to me." We discussed particular kinds of communication that foster supportive and defensive climates in relationships.

Communication that fosters supportive climates also helps us manage conflict constructively. We discussed lose–lose, win–lose, and win–win approaches to conflict and explored how each affects interaction. In addition, conflict patterns are influenced by whether people respond by exiting, neglecting, being loyal, or giving voice to tensions. In most cases, voice is the preferred response because it is the only response that allows people to deal with conflict actively and constructively.

To close the chapter, we considered five guidelines for building healthy communication climates. The first one is to accept and affirm others, communicating that we respect them even though we may not always agree with them or share their feelings. A companion guideline is to accept and assert ourselves. Each of us is entitled to voice our thoughts, feelings, and needs. Doing so honors ourselves and helps others understand us. A third guideline is to respect diversity. Humans vary widely, as do their preferred styles of communicating. When we respect differences between people, we gain insight into the fascinating array of ways humans interact.

The fourth and fifth guidelines concern communicating when conflicts arise. We learned that we can make choices about timing that increase the likelihood of constructive climate. In addition, we discussed the value of showing grace—unearned, unrequired compassion—when that is appropriate.

Review, Reflect, Extend

The Key Concepts, For Further Reflection and Discussion questions, Recommended Resources, and Experience Communication Case Study that follow will help you review, reflect on, and extend the information and ideas presented in this chapter. A diverse selection of online resources is also available through ThomsonNOW. These resources include Speech Builder Express, InfoTrac College Edition, interactive videos, vMentor, and Thomson Audio Study Products.

Thomson NOW! is an online study system designed to help you put your time to the best use. After reading a chapter, take the NOW pre-test to identify concepts discussed in the chapter that you may not fully understand. Based on the results of this diagnostic test, the system will create a personalized study plan that directs you to specific learning resources and activities. To see if you're ready for an exam, take the NOW post-test to check your understanding.

For more information or to access this book's online resources, visit **http://www.thomsonedu.com**.

▶ KEY CONCEPTS

The terms following are defined in the chapter on the page number indicated, and they appear in alphabetical order, with definitions, in the Glossary, which begins on page 369. The book's online resources also include flash cards and crossword puzzles to help you learn these terms and the concepts they represent.

acknowledgment, 140	endorsement, 141	overt conflict, 147
bracketing, 156	ethnocentrism, 143	recognition, 140
communication climate, 138	grace, 156	win–lose, 148
conflict, 146	interpersonal confirmation, 139	win–win, 149
covert conflict, 147	lose–lose, 148	

▶ FOR FURTHER REFLECTION AND DISCUSSION

The questions below can also be found among the book's online resources for this chapter, where you have the option of e-mailing your responses to your instructor, if required.

1. Think about the most effective work climate you've ever experienced. Describe the communication in that climate. How does the communication in that situation reflect the skills and principles discussed in this chapter?

2. Consider the ethical principles reflected in the communication behaviors discussed in this chapter. What ethical principles underlie confirming communication and disconfirming communication?

3. Interview a professional in the field you plan to enter or return to after completing college. Ask your interviewee to describe the kind of climate that is most effective in his or her work situation. Ask what specific kinds of communication foster and impede a good working climate. How do your interviewee's perceptions relate to the material covered in this chapter?

4. How often do you use exit, voice, loyalty, and neglect responses to conflict? What are the effects?

5. When do you find it most difficult to confirm others? Is it hard for you to be confirming when you disagree with another person? After reading this chapter, can you distinguish disagreement from disconfirmation?

▶RECOMMENDED RESOURCES

1. Use your InfoTrac College Edition to find and read research on conflict and communication.

2. Redford Williams, M.D., and Virginia Williams, Ph.D. (1993). *Anger kills: Seventeen strategies for controlling the hostility that can harm your health.* New York: HarperPerennial. This is a very readable book, which details the harm that anger and hostil-ity cause us and provides practical advice on ways to own and manage your anger to interact more effectively with others.

3. To learn how gender and other facets of identity affect communication, including listening, go to the book's online resources and click on WebLink 7.2.

Experience Communication Case Study

CLOUDY CLIMATE

The book's online resources include an interactive video of the communication situation featured in the case study scripted below. Apply what you've learned in this chapter by analyzing the case study, using the questions that follow the script as a guide. These questions are also available online with the video.

Andy and Martha married 5 years ago when they completed graduate school. Last week, Andy got the job offer of his dreams—with one problem: He would have to move 1,500 miles away. Martha loves her current job and has no interest in moving or in living apart. Andy sees this job as one that could really advance his career. For the past week, they have talked and argued continually about the job offer. Tonight, while they are preparing dinner in their kitchen, they have returned to the topic once again. We join them midway in their discussion, just as it is heating up.

Jason Harris/© Wadsworth

Andy: So, today I was checking on the costs for flights from here to Seattle. If we plan ahead for visits, we can get round-trip flights for around $300. That's not too bad.

Martha: While you're thinking about finances, you might consider the cost of renting a second apartment out there. We agreed last night that it would be too expensive to live apart.

Andy: I never agreed to that. Martha, can't you understand how important this job is to my career?

Martha: And what about our marriage? I suppose that's not important?

Andy: [He grabs a knife and begins cutting an onion.] I never said that! If you'd pull with me on this, our marriage would be fine. You're just not . . .

Martha: [She slams a pot on the stove.] Not what? Not willing to be the traditional supportive wife, I assume.

Andy: [He grimaces, puts down the knife, and turns to face Martha.] That isn't what I was going to say. I never asked you to be a traditional wife or to be anything other than who you are, but I want you to let me be myself too.

Martha: If you want to be yourself, then why did you get married? Marriage is about more than just yourself—it's about both of us and what's good for the two of us. You're not thinking of us at all.

Andy: And I suppose you are? You're only thinking about what you want. You don't seem to give a darn what I want. You're being incredibly selfish.

Martha: [She slams her hand against the counter and shouts.] Selfish?! I'm selfish to care about our marriage?

Andy: You're using that to manipulate me, as if I don't care about the marriage and you do. If you really cared about it, maybe you'd consider moving to Seattle so we could be together.

Martha: [She raises her eyebrows and speaks in a sarcastic tone.] And just a minute ago, you said you weren't asking me to be a traditional wife. Now you want me to be the trailing spouse so you can do what you please. Dandy!

Andy: I didn't say that. You're putting words in my mouth. What I said was . . .

Martha: What you said was I should move to Seattle and support whatever it is you want to do.

Andy: [He slams the knife into the cutting board.] I did not say that. Quit telling me what I said!

He takes a deep breath, lowers his voice, then continues.: Look, Martha, can we just step back from this argument and try to look at the options with a fresh eye?

Martha: I've looked all I want to look. I've heard all I want to hear. You know where I stand on this, and you know I'm right even if you don't want to admit it.

1. Identify examples of mind reading, and describe their impact on Martha's and Andy's discussion.

2. Identify communication that fosters a defensive interpersonal climate.

3. To what extent do you think Andy and Martha feel listened to by the other?

4. Do you perceive any relationship-level meanings that aren't being addressed in this conversation?

8 Adapting Communication to Cultures and Social Communities

▶ **FOCUS QUESTIONS**

1. How do cultures and social communities shape communication?

2. How does communication shape cultures and social communities?

3. What is ethnocentric bias?

4. How do people respond to cultural differences in communication?

I s it more important for society to be well ordered or to provide personal freedom to its members? How you answer that question is influenced by the culture to which you belong. If you identify with a culture that emphasizes individualism, you probably rank personal freedom as more important than social order. However, if you identify with a culture that emphasizes collective well-being, you probably think an orderly society is more important than personal freedom (Hofstede, 1991; Simons & Zielenziger, 1996). The value people assign to individualism and collectivism influences how they communicate. For instance, in cultures that emphasize collective goals and harmony, people generally do not state their positions directly or strongly and do not promote themselves. This is only one of many ways in which communication and culture are linked.

To participate effectively in today's world, we must recognize that communication is profoundly related to culture. Effectiveness in social and professional life demands that you adapt your communication to people of varied cultural backgrounds. The competitive style of negotiation customary among Americans may offend Taiwanese businesspeople. Friendly touches that are comfortable to most Americans may be perceived as rude and intrusive by Germans. Americans typically form lines to enter buildings and rooms, but in India people don't form lines; instead they push and shove to get a place, and that's not perceived as rude (Spano, 2003). In some cultures, direct eye contact is interpreted as honesty and openness. In other cultures, however, it is interpreted as disrespect. These examples highlight the importance of adapting communication to various cultures and social communities, which is the focus of this chapter.

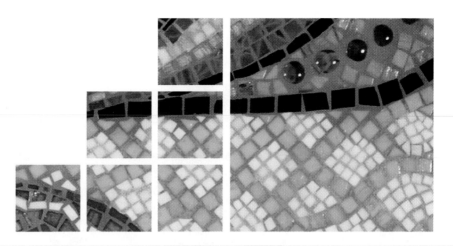

In this chapter, we discuss the sixth basic communication process: adapting communication to cultures and social communities. The first half of the chapter explores relationships between communication and the cultural systems in which it is embedded. In this section, we also consider ways in which distinct social communities within cultures shape distinctive styles of communication. The second half of the chapter discusses guidelines for adapting communication effectively to diverse cultures and social groups.

▶RELATIONSHIPS BETWEEN CULTURE AND COMMUNICATION

Communication is closely linked to culture because communication expresses, sustains, and alters culture (Healey & O'Brien, 2004; Schaller & Crandall, 2004). Your culture directly shapes how you communicate, teaching you whether interrupting is appropriate, how much eye contact is polite, and whether conflict is desirable. We are not born knowing how, when, and to whom to speak, just as we are not born with attitudes about cooperating or competing. We acquire attitudes as we interact with others, and we then reflect cultural teachings in the way we communicate.

Although the word *culture* is part of our everyday vocabulary, it's difficult to define. Culture is part of everything we think, do, feel, and believe, yet we can't point to a thing that is culture. Most simply defined, **culture** is a way of life—a system of ideas, values, beliefs, customs, and language that is passed from one generation to the next and that sustains a particular way of life (Spencer, 1982, p. 562).

© Taxi/Getty Images

What would be different in this photo if the two people were both Americans or if one was a woman?

In Chapter 1, we discussed systems, which are made up of interacting, interrelated parts. Because cultures are systems, the interconnected parts of any culture affect one another and the whole. For example, the technological revolution has had multiple and far-reaching implications for cultural life. Communication technologies allow us to interact with people who are not geographically close. Today many people form and sustain friendships and romantic relationships over the Internet (Lea & Spears, 1995; Nua, 2002). Telecommuting allows people who previously worked in offices to do their jobs in their homes. Multinational organizations can hold virtual conferences that allow employees around the world to communicate in real time and with full audio and visual contact. The one factor

This family from Yurt communicates differently from Westerners. What can you infer about Yurtish culture from the dress, artifacts, and proxemics?

© Liu Liqun/Corbis

of technology affects other factors, such as how, where, and with whom we communicate, as well as the boundaries of work and personal life. Because cultures are holistic, no change is isolated from the overall system.

To gain a deeper understanding of how culture and communication influence each other, we will discuss five central relationships between culture and communication.

D I V E R S I T Y

fyi

CODE TALKERS

During World War II, a special group of soldiers serving on Iwo Jima developed a private code that enemy intelligence never broke. Because all the soldiers in this group were Navajo, the code they devised was based on the Navajo language, which is not written down and not understood by non-Navajos. Dubbed "code talkers," this group of soldiers invented a 400-word code that was extremely secure. Drawing on the strong nature theme in Navajo life and language, the code included the Navajo words for *owl* (observer), *hawk* (dive bomber), and *egg* (bomb).

We Learn Culture in the Process of Communicating

We learn a culture's views and rules in the process of communicating. By observing and interacting with others and being exposed to mass communication, we learn language (the word *dog*) and what it means (a pet to love, a working animal, or food to eat). In other words, in learning language we learn the values of our culture. Children aren't born knowing that they should respect their elders or worship youth; they aren't born thinking that people should wear dresses and suits or saris; at birth, they don't perceive piercing or tattoos as attractive or ugly; they don't enter the world thinking of themselves as individuals or members of groups. We learn cultural values and norms in the process of communicating with others.

From the moment of birth, we begin to learn the beliefs, values, and norms of our society (Schaller & Crandall, 2004). You learn to respect your elders or to devalue them by how you see others communicate with older people, how you hear others refer to older people, and how the media portray older citizens. We learn what ideal bodies are from media and from others' talk about people of various physical proportions. As Intan points out, we also learn nonverbal communication from the culture into which we are socialized.

▶ **Intan**

Eye contact is the hardest part of learning American culture. In my home, it would be very rude to do that. We look away or down when talking so as not to give insult. In America, if I look down, it is thought I am hiding something or am dishonest. So I am learning to look at others when we talk, but it feels very disrespectful still to me.

Both conscious and unconscious learning are continuous processes through which we learn language and internalize culture so that it is seamlessly part of who we are and how we see the world. As we learn language, we learn cultural values that are encoded in language. The FYI feature on page 164 provides an interesting example of values reflected in language and how they were used in one case.

Communication Is a Primary Indicator of Culture

One of the best indicators that a culture or social community exists is communication (Hecht, Collier, & Ribeau, 1993). Because we learn to communicate in the process of interacting with others, people from different cultures use communication in different ways and attach different meanings to communicative acts.

Research by intercultural communication scholars shows one way to distinguish cultures is by the extent to which they value individualism or collectivism (Gudykunst, 1991; Hofstede, 1991; Samovar & Porter, 2001; Triandis, 1995; Zormeier & Samovar, 2000).

Individualistic cultures regard each person as distinct from other people, groups, and organizations. Individualistic cultures value personal freedom, individual rights, and independence. Communication in individualistic cultures tends to be assertive and often competitive. Rituals and roles celebrate successful individuals—Most Valuable Player, Salesperson of the Month, Chief Executive Officer, Team Leader. Self-reliance is highly valued, as are personal initiative, accomplishment, and growth.

Collectivist cultures regard people as deeply connected to one another and to their families, groups, and communities. Collectivist cultures value intergroup order and harmony, group welfare, and interdependence (Abe, 2004; Samovar & Porter, 2001; Zormeier & Samovar, 2000). Within collectivist cultures, communication tends to be other-oriented and cooperative, and collective accomplishments are more valued than personal ones. Cultural rituals and roles tend to celebrate communal achievements more than individual ones.

Communication reflects and expresses the individualistic or collectivist values of cultures. For example, many Asian languages include numerous words to describe particular relationships: my grandmother's brother, my father's uncle, my youngest son, my oldest daughter. This linguistic focus reflects the cultural emphasis on collective life (see the FYI feature on this page) and family relationships (Ferrante, 1995; Triandis, 1990). Reflecting the American and English cultural emphasis on individualism, the English language has fewer words to describe the range of kinship bonds. As Maria points out in her commentary, people from individualistic cultures often misunderstand the values and choices of people from collectivist cultures.

▶ Maria

I get hassled by a lot of girls on campus about being dependent on my family. They say I'm too close to my folks and my grandparents and aunts and uncles and cousins. But what they mean by "too close" is I'm closer with my family than most Whites are. It's a White standard they're using, and it doesn't fit me. Strong ties with family and the community are important, good values we learn in Mexico.

Individualistic and collectivist cultures tend to have distinct communication styles (Hall, 1981). Individualistic cultures generally rely on a **low-context communication style,** which is very explicit, detailed, and precise. Because people are regarded as distinct individuals, communicators do not assume that others will share their meanings or values. Instead, everything must be spelled out carefully and clearly. Because self-expression and personal initiative are valued in individualistic cultures, argument and persuasion are perceived as appropriate (Chen & Starosta, 1998).

Collectivist cultures typically rely on a **high-context communication style,** which is indirect and undetailed and which conveys meanings more implicitly than explicitly. Because people are regarded as interconnected, it is assumed they are much alike in terms of their values and understandings. Thus, there is no need to spell everything out. Instead, communicators assume that others will understand what isn't stated and will be able to use shared knowledge of situations and relationships to interpret vague statements.

DIVERSITY

fyi

LEARNING TOGETHERNESS

Traditional Korean schools teach children to identify with a group. Bathroom breaks are a collective enterprise: All children in a class go to a large room and use the bathroom together (Ferrante, 1995). In the United States, that would be considered at least immodest and perhaps vulgar. The Asian view of personal identity as rooted in larger groups also explains why Asians who lose face feel they have humiliated their entire families and communities.

Consider a concrete example of the difference between high-context and low-context communication styles. A man using low-context communication style might invite friends to dinner this way: "Come to our home at 7 P.M. tomorrow, and we'll eat around 8:30. Feel free to bring your baby with you. When he gets tired, you can put him to bed in the guest room." A woman using a high-context communication style might invite the same friends to dinner this way: "Please come to our home tomorrow evening." The speaker using low-context spelled out everything—when to arrive, when to expect a meal, that the baby is invited, that there is a place for the baby to sleep, even that the invitation is for dinner. By contrast, the high-context speaker said only, "Please come to our home tomorrow evening." This speaker assumed that the guests would share her understandings—being invited into a home in the evening implies that dinner will be served, that 7 P.M. is an appropriate time to arrive, that 8:30 is a typical time to eat dinner, that the baby is welcome, and that there will be a place for the baby to sleep. For people who have learned a high-context communication style, the low-context style seems overly literal and seems to belabor the obvious (Who wouldn't serve dinner to guests in the evening? Guests' families are always included in invitations.).

Multiple Social Communities May Coexist in a Single Culture

Groups with distinct ways of life can coexist in a single society or geographic territory. In fact, each of us belongs to multiple social groups as well as at least one culture (Kanno, 2003). We may identify with a national culture, a religious tradition, a gender, an ethnic–racial group, and perhaps other groups. Each of our cultural identifications affects who we are and how we communicate.

Most societies have a dominant, or mainstream, way of life. Although many groups may exist within a single society, not all identify equally with the dominant culture. European, heterosexual, landowning, able-bodied men who were Christian (at least in heritage, if not always in actual practice) created mainstream Western culture. Yet Western society includes many groups outside the cultural mainstream. Gay men, lesbians, bisexuals, and transgendered people experience difficulty in a society that communicates that they are not normal and

Communicating Culture

Locate a standard calendar and an academic calendar for your campus. Which of the following holidays of different cultural groups are recognized and treated as holidays by suspension of normal campus and community operations?

Christmas	Passover	Saka
Yom Kippur	Kwanzaa	Hegira
Elderly Day	Seleicodae	Martin Luther King Day
Hanukkah	Easter	

What do calendars communicate about the place of different groups in a culture?

SHARPEN YOUR SKILL

refuses to grant them social standing or legal rights (Howey, 2002; Sheridan, 2001). Mainstream customs in America often ignore or marginalize American citizens who are Jewish, Buddhist, or Hindu. The Sharpen Your Skill feature on this page encourages you to notice that many American calendars recognize Christian holidays but not holidays important to non-Christians.

We are affected not only by the culture as a whole but also by our membership in social communities or groups within the culture (Harding, 2004; Healey & O'Brien, 2004; Winters & DeBose, 2004). A culture includes a number of **social communities,** groups of people who live within a dominant culture yet also belong to another social group or groups. For many years, social groups that were distinct from mainstream culture were called *subcultures.* However, the prefix *sub* connotes inferiority, as if subcultures were somehow less than "real cultures" (Samovar & Porter, 2001). The term *social community* is a less judgmental way to refer to groups of people who belong to both a dominant culture and one or more particular groups within that culture.

Standpoint theory illuminates the importance of social communities. **Standpoint theory** claims that social groups within a culture distinctively shape the perceptions, identities, and opportunities of members. From membership in a particular social community, people may learn a **standpoint** that reflects the social, symbolic, and material circumstances of a particular social group that shape members' perspectives on themselves, others, communication, and social life. Race, gender, class, and sexual preference are primary ways in which Western culture groups people.

In an early discussion of standpoint, philosopher Georg Wilhelm Friedrich Hegel (1807) pointed out that standpoints reflect power positions in society. To illustrate, he noted that masters and slaves perceive slavery very differently. Extending Hegel's point, we can see that those in positions of power have a vested interest in preserving the system that gives them privileges. Therefore, they are unlikely to perceive its flaws and inequities. On the other hand, those who are disadvantaged by a system are able to see inequities and discrimination (Wood, 1993a, 1993d).

A culture's conventional, nonverbal communication often reflects the perspective of dominant groups. For example, the dominance of people without disabilities is reflected in the number of buildings that do not have ramps or bathroom facilities for people who use wheelchairs, and public presentations that do not include signers for people with hearing limitations. Many campus and business buildings feature portraits of White men but few of women or people of color. Mostafa's commentary illustrates how his standpoint affects his perceptions of his school.

▶ Mostafa

I went to a Black college for two years before transferring here, and it's like two different worlds. There, I saw a lot of brothers and sisters all the time, and I had Black teachers. There were portraits of Black leaders in buildings and Black magazines in the bookstore. Here, I've had only one Black teacher, and I see fifty Whites for every one Black on campus. I've yet to see a Black person's portrait hung in any campus building, and I have to go to specialty stores to buy Black magazines. The whole atmosphere on this campus communicates, "White is right."

Of the many social communities, gendered communities have been most extensively studied. Because we know more about gender than about other social communities, we'll explore gender as an example of a social community. However, the principles and patterns that characterize the gendered social communities that we'll discuss also apply to other social communities.

Scholars have investigated the communication of people socialized in different gender communities. One of the earliest studies reported that children's play is sex segregated, that boys and girls tend to play different kinds of games (Maltz & Borker, 1982). Games that girls favor, such as house and school, involve few players, require talk to negotiate how to play because there aren't clear-cut guidelines, and depend on cooperation and sensitivity among players. Baseball, soccer, and war, which are typical boys' games, require more players and have clear goals and rules, so less talk is needed to play. Most boys' games are highly competitive, both between teams and for individual status within teams. Interaction in games teaches boys and girls distinct understandings of why, when, and how to use talk.

Research on women's and men's communication reveals that the rules we learn through play remain with many of us as we grow older. For instance, women's talk generally is more expressive and focused on feelings and relationships, whereas men's talk tends to be more instrumental, assertive, and competitive (Clark, 1998; Johnson, 1996; Martin et al., 2000; Wood, 1998, 2001b, 2001c, 2007). Men tend to prefer jokes that include aggression and sexual references, whereas women tend to prefer jokes that involve wordplay (Wiseman, 2003). These gender preferences are not constant; they vary across cultures. For instance, Germans tend to view jokes or other forms of humor as inappropriate during business meetings, whereas joking is a common part of American business interaction (Lewis, 1996). In professional contexts, women generally engage in more personal communication with subordinates and peers than men do (Helgeson, 1990; Natalle, 1996). Many women favor management styles that are more collaborative than those typical of men. In personal relationships, women tend to be more interested in talking about relationship issues than men are.

▶ Larry

Finally, I see what happens between my girlfriend and me. She always wants to talk about us, which I think is stupid unless we have a problem. I like to go to a concert or do something together, but then she says that I don't want to be with her. We speak totally different languages.

Larry's commentary illustrates another general gender difference—what each gender tends to perceive as the center of a relationship. For many men who were socialized in masculine communities, activities tend to be a key foundation of friendships and romantic relationships (Inman, 1996; Swain, 1989; Wood & Inman, 1993). Thus, men who are socialized in masculine communities typically build and sustain friendships by doing things together (playing soccer, watching sports) and doing things for one another. For many women who are socialized in feminine communities, communication is the crux of relationships. Communication is not only a means to other ends but also an end in itself (Acitelli, 1993; Duck & Wood, 2006; Riessman, 1990). The Sharpen Your Skill feature on page 170 invites you to apply our discussion of gendered speech communities to yourself.

Although we have focused on gender to show how social communities shape communication, gender isn't the only social community that affects how people communicate. Research finds that communication patterns vary between social classes. For example, working-class people tend to live closer to and rely more on extended families than middle- and upper-class people do (Acker, 2005; Cancian, 1989). Different racial and ethnic groups also teach group members distinctive ways of interacting. Communication scholar Mark Orbe (1994) describes the United States as separate societies divided by race. Research also suggests that African Americans generally communicate more assertively than European Americans (Johnson, 2000; Orbe & Harris, 2001; Ribeau, Baldwin, & Hecht, 1994). What some African Americans perceive as authentic, powerful exchanges may be viewed as confrontational by people from different social groups because the latter learned different rules for what counts as wit and what counts as antagonism. Notice, however, that these are generalizations; they do not describe the communication of all Blacks or all Whites.

As social communities, African Americans and Hispanics have stronger commitments to collective interests such as family or race, whereas European Americans tend to be more individualistic (Gaines, 1995; Nelson, 1998). As a rule, African Americans also communicate more interactively than European Americans (Hecht et al., 1993; Weber, 1994).

▶ **Michelle**

I'm offended when I read that Blacks communicate differently from Whites. I don't, and neither do a lot of my Black friends. Both of my parents were professionals, and I attended good schools, including a private one for two years. I speak the same way Whites do. When the author of our book says Blacks engage in call and response or talk differently from Whites, it makes it sound like Blacks are different from Whites—like we don't know how to communicate like they do. If the author isn't Black, how does she know how we communicate?

Your Gendered Standpoint

To what extent are your own communication behaviors, listed here, consistent with those identified by research as typical of your gender?

▶ What you see as the purpose of talking

▶ What you regard as the center of relationships (talking or doing or both)

▶ Your listening style

SHARPEN YOUR SKILL

Michelle wrote her comment after reading a previous edition of this book. She's correct that not all Blacks communicate the same way and not all Blacks communicate differently from Whites, who also don't communicate homogeneously. What you've read about the communication patterns of African Americans, Hispanic Americans, or other social groups is based on research, much of which was conducted by scholars who are members of the groups described. I include this research because many minority students have complained to me about textbooks that present only middle-class White communication patterns and present those as standard or correct. They have told me that this makes them feel erased. This point of view is reflected in Jason's comment, which he wrote after reading the same book Michelle criticized.

▶ **Jason**

This is the first time since being at this school that I've seen Blacks really included in a textbook or a class, other than my Af-Am classes. I think that's good, like it affirms my identity as a Black. If I have to study how Whites communicate, why shouldn't they learn how I communicate and why I communicate that way? I think we're all broadened if we know more about more kinds of people and how they think and act and talk.

In this book, I include credible research on a variety of social groups so that we understand a range of ways in which people communicate. Yet it's critical to remember that statements about any group's communication are generalizations, not universal truths. Each of us communicates in some ways that are consistent with the patterns of particular social communities to which we belong, and in other ways our communication departs from norms for those communities. In part, that is because we belong to many groups. Michelle is not only Black (a racial–ethnic group) but also upper middle class (a socioeconomic group). Jason is Black, and he is from a working-class family. This may shed light on why Jason identifies with what African American scholars report as traditional Black communication patterns and why Michelle does not. Similarly, descriptions of European American communication are not equally true of European Americans who belong to the upper class and the working class.

Even within a single culture or social community, there is variation. Furthermore, not everyone who technically belongs to a particular culture adopts the communication practices typical of that culture. For instance, many middle-class and upper-class Blacks do not communicate in ways that research has shown are common in traditional Black communities. Likewise, not all women communicate in ways consistent with the patterns typical of feminine social communities, and not all men communicate in ways that scholars have identified as common in masculine communities. Although membership in cultures and social communities influences how we communicate, it is not the only influence, and it does not affect all members of groups in the same way.

Communication Expresses and Sustains Cultures

Communication simultaneously reflects and sustains cultural values. Each time we express cultural values, we also perpetuate them. When some Asian Amer-

Passing tradition from one generation to the next is how cultures sustain themselves. In this photo, a Jewish elder instructs a young boy in Jewish traditions.

© Bill Aron/PhotoEdit

D   I   V   E   R   S   I   T   Y

PROVERBS EXPRESS CULTURAL VALUES

Every culture has proverbs that express its values and pass them from one generation to the next. Following are some proverbs that reflect values in particular cultures (Samovar & Porter, 2001).

▶ "A zebra does not despise its stripes." Among the Masai of Africa, this saying encourages acceptance of things and oneself as they are.

▶ "Know the family and you will know the child." This Chinese proverb reflects the belief that individuals are less important than families.

▶ "The child has no owner." "It takes a whole village to raise a child." These African adages express the idea that children belong to whole communities, not just to biological parents.

▶ "Better to be a fool with the crowd than wise by oneself." "A solitary soul neither sings nor cries." These Mexican proverbs reflect a strong commitment to collectivism.

To learn about proverbs in other cultures, including Turkey and Palestine, access the book's online resources and click on WebLinks 8.1 and 8.2.

icans avoid displaying emotions, they fortify and express the value of self-restraint and the priority of reason over emotion. When some Westerners argue, speak up for their ideas, and compete in conversations, they uphold the values of individuality and assertiveness. Communication, then, is a mirror of a culture's values and a primary means of keeping them woven into the fabric of everyday life.

The Western preoccupation with time and efficiency is evident in the abundance of words that refer to time (*hours, minutes, seconds, days, weeks*) and in common phrases such as "Let's not waste time." Among Buddhists, the saying "Something cannot become nothing" expresses the belief that life continues in new forms after what Westerners call death. In the United States, "The early bird gets the worm" implies that initiative is valuable, and "Nice guys finish last" suggests that winning is important and that it's more important to be aggressive than nice. The FYI feature on page 171 offers further examples of the cultural values expressed in proverbs.

Communication Is a Source of Cultural Change

In addition to reflecting culture, communication is a source of cultural change. Social communities in the United States have used communication to resist the mainstream's efforts to define their identity. Whenever a group says, "No, the way you describe Americans doesn't fit me," that group initiates change in the cultural understandings.

A primary way in which communication propels change is by naming things in ways that shape how we understand them. For instance, the terms *environmental racism* and *environmental justice* were coined to name the practice of locating toxic waste dumps and other environmental hazards in communities where people tend to be poor and non-White. The term *Google* (and variations such as *Googling*) is based on a particular online search engine, Google. The term *sexual harassment* names a practice that certainly is not new but only lately has been labeled and given social reality. Mary's commentary explains how important the label is.

▶ Mary

It was 15 years ago, when I was just starting college, that a professor sexually harassed me, only I didn't know to call it that then. I felt guilty, like maybe I'd done something to encourage him, or I felt maybe I was overreacting to his kissing me and touching me. But after the Clarence Thomas–Anita Hill hearings in 1991, I had a name for what happened—a name that said he was wrong, not me. It was only then that I could let go of that whole business.

As a primary tool of social movements, communication prompts changes in cultural life. The civil rights and Black power movements motivated Black Americans to assert the value and beauty of Black culture. Simultaneously, African Americans used communication to persuade non-Black citizens to rethink their attitudes and practices. Marches for gay pride and AIDS awareness challenge social attitudes about gay men and lesbians just as marches for immigrants' rights challenge attitudes toward immigrants.

In addition to instigating change directly, communication accompanies other kinds of cultural change. Antibiotics had to be explained to medical practitioners and to a general public that believed infections were caused by fate, not by viruses and bacteria. Ideas and practices borrowed from one culture must be translated into other cultures; for example, the Japanese system of management has been adapted to fit the culture of many U.S. companies. Calamities also must be defined and explained: Did the volcano erupt because of pressure in the earth or because of the anger of the gods? Did we lose the war because we had a weak military or because our cause was wrong? Do technologies enrich cultural life or diminish it? Cultures use communication to define what change means and implies for social life.

Both an overall culture and particular social communities shape our perceptions and ways of communicating. Yet we can learn to appreciate different cultural systems and the diverse forms of communication they foster, as well as the ways in which multiple social identities shape our communication. Doing so enables us to adapt our communication effectively in response to the diverse people with whom we interact.

TECHNOLOGY

fyi

THE DIGITAL DIVIDE

The technological revolution isn't affecting all cultures and social communities the same way. Some scholars use the term **digital divide** to refer to the gap between communities with full access to technologies and communities with less access or no access (Assmann, 2006; Rantanen, 2004; Warschauer, 2003). Consider these facts:

▶ More than one-third of all online users live in English-language zones.

▶ People in rural areas are less likely to have broadband access.

▶ In the United States, Caucasians are more likely to have access to technologies such as the Internet than are African Americans or Hispanics.

These and other facts about the digital divide can be found by going to the book's online resources and clicking on WebLink 8.3. Clicking on WebLink 8.4 will take you to the Digital Divide Network, a large online community for educators, activists, policy makers, and concerned citizens who want to bridge the digital divide.

▶GUIDELINES FOR ADAPTING COMMUNICATION TO DIVERSE CULTURES AND SOCIAL COMMUNITIES

To participate effectively in a culturally diverse world, we must adapt our communication to different contexts and people. Effective adaptation occurs when we tailor our verbal and nonverbal symbols and our ways of perceiving, creating climates, listening, and responding. We'll consider four guidelines for adapting communication in ways that are sensitive to different cultures and communities.

Engage in Person-Centered Communication

The single most important guideline for adapting communication effectively is to engage in person-centered communication. From our discussion in Chapter 3, you'll recall that person-centeredness involves recognizing another person's perspective and taking that into account as you communicate. For instance, it's advisable to refrain from using a lot of idioms when talking with someone for whom English is a second language. Similarly, a man who has dual perspective might realize that a woman may appreciate empathy and supportive listening more than advice. The point is that competent communicators adapt to the perspectives of those with whom they interact.

We don't need to abandon our perspectives to accommodate those of others. In fact, it would be as unethical to stifle your views as to ignore those of others. Person-centeredness requires us to understand both our own and another's points of view and to respect both when we communicate. Most of us can accept and grow from differences, but we feel disconfirmed if others don't recognize or acknowledge our perspectives.

Person-centeredness requires us to negotiate between awareness of group tendencies and equal awareness of individual differences. For example, we should realize that Asian Americans generally are less assertive than European Americans, yet we shouldn't assume that every Asian American will be deferential or that every European American will be assertive. What describes a group accurately may not apply equally to every member of the group. A good guideline is to assume that each person with whom you communicate fits some, but not other, generalizations about his or her social communities.

Respect Others' Feelings and Ideas

Has anyone ever said to you, "You shouldn't feel that way"? If so, you know how infuriating it can be to be told that your feelings aren't valid, appropriate, or acceptable. Equally destructive is to be told our thoughts are wrong. When someone says, "How can you think something so stupid?" we feel disconfirmed.

One of the most disconfirming forms of communication is speaking for others when they are able to speak for themselves (Alcoff, 1991; Wood, 1998). Marsha Houston (2004, p. 124), an accomplished communication scholar, explains how claiming understanding can diminish a person. She writes that White women should never tell African American women that they understand their experiences as Black women. Here's Houston's explanation:

> I have heard this sentence completed in numerous, sometimes bizarre, ways, from "because sexism is just as bad as racism," to "because I watch The Cosby Show," to "because I'm also a member of a minority group. I'm Jewish . . . Italian . . . overweight. . . ." Similar experiences should not be confused with the same experience; my experience of prejudice is erased when you identify it as "the same" as yours.

Generally, it's rude and disempowering to speak for others. Just as we should not speak for others, we should not assume we understand how they feel or think. As we have seen, distinct experiences and cultural backgrounds make each of us unique. We seldom completely grasp what another person feels or thinks. Although it is supportive to engage in dual perspective, it isn't supportive to presume that we understand experiences we haven't had, as Susan's commentary points out.

▶ Susan

I hate it when people tell me they understand what it's like to have a learning disability. For one thing, there are a lot of learning disabilities, and I resent being lumped in a broad category. For another thing, if someone doesn't have dyslexia, which is my problem, they don't know what it means. They have no idea what it's like to see letters scrambled or wonder if you are seeing words right. People shouldn't say "I understand" what they haven't experienced.

In a class I taught, a Latina student commented on discrimination she faces, and a White male student said, "I know what you mean. Prejudice really hurts." Although he meant to be supportive, his response angered the woman, who retorted, "You don't know what I mean. You have no right to pretend you do until you've been female and non-White." When we claim to share what we haven't experienced, we take away from others' lives and identities.

Respecting what others say about their thoughts and feelings is a cornerstone of effective communication. Ethical communicators do not attempt to speak for others and do not assume they understand people whose standpoints are not their own. If you don't understand what others say or do, ask them to explain. This

shows that you are interested and respect their experience. It also paves the way for greater understanding between people of different backgrounds. We grow when we open ourselves to perspectives that differ from ours.

Resist Ethnocentric Bias

Most of us unreflectingly use our home culture and social communities as the standards for judging others. Some Japanese regard Americans as rude for maintaining direct eye contact, whereas some Americans perceive Japanese as evasive for averting their eyes. European Americans' self-references may appear egocentric to Koreans, and Koreans' tendency to play down individual achievements may seem passive to Westerners. People who were raised in Mexico may regard native-born Americans as obsessed with time and schedules, whereas native born Americans may perceive Mexican Americans as unpunctual. How we judge others depends more on the perspective we use to judge than on what others say and do (Wood, 1997, 1998).

Using our culture as the standard for judging other cultures can interfere with good communication. **Ethnocentrism** is the tendency to regard ourselves and our way of life as normal and superior to other people and other ways of life. Literally, ethnocentrism means to put our ethnicity (*ethno*) at the center (*centrism*) of the universe.

Ethnocentrism encourages negative judgments of anything that differs from our ways. In extreme form, ethnocentrism can lead one group of people to feel it has the right to dominate other groups and suppress other cultures. The most abhorrent example of ethnocentrism was Nazi Germany's declaration that Aryans were the "master race," followed by the systematic genocide of Jewish people. Yet we need not look to such dramatic examples as Nazi Germany to find ethnocentrism. It occurs whenever we judge someone from a different culture as less sensitive, honest, ambitious, good, or civilized than people from our culture.

To reduce ethnocentrism, we should remember that what is considered normal and right varies between cultures. **Cultural relativism** recognizes that cultures vary in how they think and behave as well as in what they believe and value. Cultural relativism is not the same as moral relativism. We can acknowledge that a particular practice makes sense in its cultural context without approving of it. Cultural relativism reminds us that something that appears odd or even wrong to

---

Becoming Self-Reflective about Your Culture

We can't resist ethnocentric bias unless we understand our own culture and the values that it tries to instill in us. Earlier in this chapter, we identified proverbs that express values in non-Western culture. Now, we'll do the reverse by looking at common sayings and proverbs in the United States. Read the adages below, and identify what they reflect about cultural values.

▹ "You can't be too rich or too thin."

▹ "A stitch in time saves later nine."

▹ "A watched pot never boils."

▹ "It's the squeaky wheel that gets the oil."

▹ "You've made your bed, now lie in it."

What other sayings can you think of that express key Western values?

SHARPEN YOUR SKILL

us may seem natural and right from the point of view of a different culture. This facilitates respect, even when differences exist.

Recognize That Adapting to Cultural Diversity Is a Process

Developing skill in intercultural communication takes time. We don't move suddenly from being unaware of how people in other cultures interact to being totally comfortable and competent in communication with them. Adapting to cultural diversity is a gradual process that takes time, experience with a variety of people, and a genuine desire to know and appreciate cultural differences.

Responses to diversity range from total rejection to full participation in a different culture's communication styles. At particular times in our lives, we may find ourselves adopting different responses to diversity or to specific forms of diversity. We may also find that our responses to people with different cultural backgrounds evolve over the course of our relationships with them. That's natural in the overall process of recognizing and responding to diversity in life.

Resistance A common response to diversity is **resistance,** which occurs when we reject the beliefs of particular cultures or social communities. Resistance denies the value and validity of particular cultural styles (Berger, 1969). Without education or reflection, many people evaluate others based on the standards of their own culture. Some people, including Maggie (see her commentary), think their judgments reflect universal truths. They aren't aware that they are imposing the arbitrary yardstick of their particular culture and ignoring the yardsticks of other cultures. Devaluing whatever differs from our ways limits human experience and diminishes cultural life.

▶ Maggie

I'm tired of being told I should "appreciate" difference. In most cases, I don't. If people from other countries want to live in America, they should act and talk like Americans. They should adapt, not me.

Resistance may be expressed in many ways. Hate crimes pollute campuses and the broader society. Denial of other cultures leads to racial slurs, anti-Semitic messages, and homophobic attacks. Resistance may also motivate members of a culture or social community to associate only with each other and to remain unaware of commonalities among people with diverse backgrounds. Insulation within a single culture occurs in both majority and minority groups.

Members of social groups may also resist and deny their group identities to fit into the mainstream. **Assimilation** occurs when people give up their ways and adopt the ways of the dominant culture. Philosopher Peter Berger (1969) calls this *surrendering* because it involves giving up an original cultural identity for a new one. For many years, assimilation was the dominant response of immigrants to the United States. The idea of America as a "melting pot" encouraged newcomers to melt into the mainstream by surrendering any ways that made them different from native-born citizens.

More recently, the melting pot metaphor has been criticized as undesirable because it robs individuals of their unique heritages. Jesse Jackson proposed the alternative metaphor of the family quilt. This metaphor portrays the United States as a country in which diverse groups' values and customs are visible, as are the individual squares in a quilt, and at the same time each group contributes to a larger whole, just as each square contributes to a quilt's overall beauty.

Some people use another form of resistance to provoke change in cultural practices and viewpoints. For example, heterosexuals who refuse to refer to their partners as "spouses" are resisting mainstream culture's refusal to grant legal status to gay and lesbian commitments. When culturally advantaged people resist and challenge the devaluation of disadvantaged groups, they can be powerful agents of change.

Tolerance A second response to diversity is **tolerance,** which is an acceptance of differences whether or not one approves of or even understands them. Tolerance involves respecting others' rights to their ways even though we may think their ways are wrong, bad, or offensive. Judgment still exists, but it's not actively imposed on others. Tolerance is open-mindedness in accepting the existence of differences, yet it is less open-minded in perceiving the value of alternative lifestyles and values. Although tolerance is not as divisive as resistance, it does not actively foster a community in which people appreciate diversity and learn to grow from encountering differences.

Understanding A third response to diversity is **understanding** that differences are rooted in cultural teachings and that no customs, traditions, or behaviors are intrinsically better than any others. This response builds on the idea of cultural relativism, which we discussed earlier. Rather than assuming that whatever differs from our ways is a deviation from a universal standard (ours), a person who understands realizes that diverse values, beliefs, norms, and communication styles are rooted in distinct cultural perspectives.

People who respond to diversity with understanding might notice that a Japanese person doesn't hold eye contact but would not assume that the Japanese person was devious. Instead, an understanding person would try to learn what eye contact means in Japanese society in order to understand the behavior in its native cultural context. Curiosity, rather than judgment, dominates in this stage, as we make active efforts to understand others in terms of the values and traditions of their cultures.

Respect Once we move beyond judgment and begin to understand the cultural basis for ways that differ from ours, we may come to **respect** differences. We can appreciate the distinct validity and value of placing family above self, of arranged marriage, and of feminine and masculine communication styles. We don't have to adopt others' ways in order to respect them on their terms.

Respect allows us to acknowledge genuine differences between groups yet remain anchored in the values and customs of our culture (Simons, Vázquez, & Harris, 1993). Learning about people who differ from us increases our understanding of them and thus our ability to communicate effectively with them. What is needed to respect others is the ability to see them and what they do on their terms, not ours. In other words, respect avoids ethnocentrism.

Participation A final response to diversity is **participation,** in which we incorporate some practices and values of other groups into our own lives. More than other responses, participation encourages us to develop skills for participating in a multicultural world in which all of us can take part in some of each other's customs. Harvard professor Henry Louis Gates (1992) believes that the ideal society is one in which we build a common civic culture that celebrates both differences and commonalities.

People who respond to diversity by participating learn to be **multilingual,** which means they are able to speak and understand more than one language or more than one group's ways of using language. Many people are already at least bilingual (also termed *code switching*). Many African Americans know how to operate in mainstream Caucasian society and in their distinct ethnic communities (Orbe, 1994). Bilingualism, or code switching, is also practiced by many Asian Americans, Mexican Americans, lesbians, gay men, and members of other groups that are simultaneously part of a dominant and a minority culture (Gaines, 1995).

I and my partner, Robbie, have learned how to communicate in both feminine and masculine styles. He was socialized to be assertive, competitive, instrumental, and analytical in conversation, whereas I learned to be more deferential, cooperative, relationship oriented, and creative. When we were first married, we were often frustrated by differences in our communication styles. I perceived him as insensitive to feelings and overly linear in his conversational style. He perceived me as being too focused on relationship issues and inefficient in moving from problems to solutions. Gradually, each of us learned to understand and then respect the other's ways of communicating. Still later, we came to participate in each other's styles, and now both of us are fluent in both languages. Not only has this improved communication between us, but it has made us more competent communicators in general.

People reach different stages in their abilities to respond to particular cultures and social communities. The different responses to cultural diversity that we've discussed represent parts of a process of learning to understand and adapt to diverse cultural groups. In the courses of our lives, many of us will move in and out of various responses as we interact with people from multiple cultures. At specific times, we may find we are tolerant of one cultural group, respectful of another, and able to participate in yet others.

▶ SUMMARY

In Chapter 1, we learned that communication is systemic. Because it is systemic, it must be understood as existing within and influenced by multiple contexts. In this chapter, we've focused on cultures and social communities as particularly important systems that shape and are shaped by communication.

Five principles summarize the relationships between culture and communication. First, we learn a culture in the process of communicating with others. Second, language is a primary indicator that a culture exists. Third, multiple social communities may coexist within a single culture, and people may belong to multiple cultures and social communities. Fourth, communication both reflects and sustains cultures. The final principle is that communication is a potent force for changing cultural life.

The final section of this chapter identified four guidelines for communicating effectively in a socially diverse world. The most fundamental is to engage in person-centered communication, which enables us to adapt to the perspectives and communication styles of others. Extending this, the second guideline is to respect what others present as their feelings and ideas. In most situations, speaking for others is presumptuous, and disregarding what they express is rude. The third guideline for adapting communication is to resist ethnocentrism, which is the greatest threat to effective cross-cultural communication. Finally, we learned that adapting to diversity is a process. We may find that our response to diversity changes as we grow personally and as we develop relationships with people who differ from us. Moving beyond the belief that our ways are the only right ways allows us to understand, respect, and sometimes participate in a diverse world and to enlarge ourselves in the process.

Although this chapter has focused on differences between people, it would be a mistake to be so aware of differences that we overlook our commonalities. No matter what culture we belong to, we all have feelings, dreams, ideas, hopes, fears, and values. Our common humanity transcends many of our differences, an idea beautifully expressed in a 1990 poem by Maya Angelou.

Human Family

I note the obvious differences
between each sort and type, but we are more alike, my friends
than we are unalike.
We are more alike, my friends
than we are unalike.

from *I Shall Not Be Moved* by Maya Angelou. Copyright © 1990 by Maya Angelou. Used by permission of Random House, Inc.

Review, Reflect, Extend

The Key Concepts, For Further Reflection and Discussion questions, Recommended Resources, and Experience Communication Case Study that follow will help you review, reflect on, and extend the information and ideas presented in this chapter. A diverse selection of online resources is also available through ThomsonNOW. These resources include Speech Builder Express, InfoTrac College Edition, interactive videos, vMentor, and Thomson Audio Study Products.

Thomson NOW! is an online study system designed to help you put your time to the best use. After reading a chapter, take the NOW pre-test to identify concepts discussed in the chapter that you may not fully understand. Based on the results of this diagnostic test, the system will create a personalized study plan that directs you to specific learning resources and activities. To see if you're ready for an exam, take the NOW post-test to check your understanding.

For more information or to access this book's online resources, visit **http://www.thomsonedu.com**.

▶KEY CONCEPTS

The terms following are defined in the chapter on the page number indicated, and they appear in alphabetical order, with definitions, in the Glossary, which be- gins on page 369. The book's online resources also include flash cards and crossword puzzles to help you learn these terms and the concepts they represent.

assimilation, 177
collectivst culture, 165
cultural relativism, 176
culture, 163
digital divide, 173
ethnocentrism, 176

high-context communication style, 166
individualistic culture, 165
low-context communication style, 166
multilingual, 179
participation, 179
resistance, 177

respect, 178
social community, 167
standpoint, 168
standpoint theory, 167
tolerance, 178
understanding, 178

▶FOR FURTHER REFLECTION AND DISCUSSION

The questions below can also be found among the book's online resources for this chapter, where you have the option of e-mailing your responses to your instructor, if required.

1 To understand how your standpoint influences perceptions, enter a culture different from the one you are used to. If you are Caucasian, you might attend services at a Black church or a meeting of an African American community group. Do you notice your Whiteness more in this context? If you are not Caucasian, reflect on the differences in how you perceive situations in which Caucasians are the majority and your race is the minority. With others in your class, discuss the effect of standpoint on perceptions and communication.

2. Continue the exercise started on page 176 by listing common sayings or adages in your culture. Decide what each saying reflects about the beliefs, values, and concerns of your culture.

3. Consider metaphors for U.S. society. For many years, it was described as a melting pot, a metaphor that suggested that all the differences between people from various cultures would melt down and merge into a uniform culture. In recent years, Jesse Jackson has referred to the United States as a family quilt, whereas Flora Davis (1991) calls the United States a salad bowl. What do you think she means by the salad bowl metaphor? What metaphor do you prefer?

4. As a class, discuss the tension between recognizing individuality and noting patterns common in specific social groups. Is it possible to recognize both that people have standpoints in social groups and that members of any group vary? You might recall the concept of totalizing from Chapter 4 to assist your consideration of this issue.

▶RECOMMENDED RESOURCES

1. Fern Johnson. (2000). *Speaking culturally: Language diversity in the United States.* Thousand Oaks, CA: Sage. This book provides excellent historical information about different groups in the United States and the different ways in which they understand and use language.

2. Lena Williams. (2002). *It's the little things: Everyday interactions that anger, annoy, and divide the* *races.* New York: Harvest/Harcourt. This book offers clear examples of communication misunderstandings between Blacks and Whites.

3. The 2002 film *Windtalkers* tells the story of the Najavo soldiers who developed a code that enemy intelligence couldn't break. This was discussed in the FYI box on page 166.

Experience Communication Case Study

THE JOB INTERVIEW

The book's online resources include an interactive video of the communication situation featured in the case study scripted below. Apply what you've learned in this chapter by analyzing the case study, using the questions that follow the script as a guide. These questions are also available online with the video.

Mei-ying Yung is a senior who has majored in computer programming. Mei-ying's aptitude for computer programming has earned her much attention at her college. She has developed and installed complex new programs to make advising more efficient and to reduce the frustration and errors in registration for courses. Although she has been in the United States for 6 years, in many ways Mei-ying reflects the Chinese culture where she was born and where she spent the first 15 years of her life. Today, Mei-ying is interviewing for a position at New Thinking, a fast-growing tech company that specializes in developing programs tailored to the needs of individual companies. The interviewer, Barton Hingham, is 32 years old and a native of California, where New Thinking is based. As the scenario opens, Ms. Yung walks into the small room in which Mr. Hingham is seated behind a desk. He rises to greet her and walks over with his hand outstretched to shake hers.

Hingham: Good morning, Ms. Yung. I've been looking forward to meeting you. Your résumé is most impressive.

Ms. Yung looks downward, smiles, and limply shakes Mr. Hingham's hand. He gestures to a chair, and she sits down in it.

Hingham: I hope this interview will allow us to get to know each other a bit and decide whether there is a good fit between you and New Thinking. I'll be asking you some questions about your background and interests. And you should feel free to ask me any questions that you have. Okay?

Yung: Yes.

Hingham: I see from your transcript that you majored in computer programming and did very well. I certainly didn't have this many As on *my* college transcript!

Yung: Thank you. I am very fortunate to have good teachers.

Hingham: Tell me a little about your experience in writing original programs for business applications.

Yung: I do not have great experience, but I have been grateful to help the college with some of its work.

Hingham: Tell me about how you've helped the college. I see you designed a program for advising. Can you explain to me what you did to develop that program?

Jason Harris/© Wadsworth

Yung: Not really so much. I could see that much of advising is based on rules, so I only need to write the rules into a program so advisers could do their jobs more better.

Hingham: Perhaps you're being too modest. I've done enough programming myself to know how difficult it is to develop a program for something with as many details as advising. There are so many majors, each with different requirements and regulations. How did you program all of that variation?

Yung: I read the handbook on advising and the regulations on each major, and then programmed decision trees into an advising template. Not so hard.

Hingham: Well, that's exactly the kind of project we do at New Thinking. People come to us with problems in their jobs, and we write programs to solve them. Does that sound like the kind of thing you would enjoy doing?

Yung: Yes. I very much like to solve problems to help others.

Hingham: What was your favorite course during college?

Yung: They are all very valuable. I enjoy all.

Hingham: Did you have one course in which you did especially well?

Yung: [blushing, looking down] I would not say that. I try to do well in all my courses, to learn from them.

Later Barton Hingham and Molly Cannett, another interviewer for New Thinking, are discussing the day's interviews over dinner.

Cannett: Did you find any good prospects today?

Hingham: Not really. I thought I was going to be bowled over by this one woman—name's Mei-ying Yung—who has done some incredibly intricate programming on her own while in college.

Cannett: Sounds like just the kind of person we're looking for.

Hingham: I thought so, too, until the interview. She just didn't seem to have the gusto we want. She showed no confidence or initiative in the interview. It was like the transcript and the person were totally different.

Cannett: Hmmm, that's odd. Usually when we see someone who looks that good on paper, the interview is just a formality.

Hingham: Yeah, but I guess the formality is more important than we realized: Yung was a real dud in the interview. I still don't know what to make of it.

▼▼

1. How does Mei-ying Yung's communication reflect her socialization in Chinese culture?

2. How could Mei-ying be more effective without abandoning the values of her native culture?

3. What could enhance Barton Hingham's ability to communicate effectively with people who were raised in non-Western cultures?

9 Communication and Self-Concept

▶ **FOCUS QUESTIONS**

1. What role does communication play in developing personal identity?

2. What is the *generalized other,* and how does it shape personal identity?

3. What are the values and risks of self-disclosing communication?

4. How can you create a supportive context for your personal growth?

When I was 8 years old, I thought I would grow up to be a novelist. By age 12, my parents had taught me to cook and bake, and it become clear to me that I would be a pastry chef. When I was 20 and in love with my college sweetheart, I realized I would be a stay-at-home wife and mother. When I was 22 years old and had left my college sweetheart, I was sure that I would be single and a teacher. Then I began graduate school and met Robbie, and I started to define myself as a scholar and teacher and a partner to Robbie. Today, I am not single, not a novelist, not a stay-at-home wife and mother, and not a pastry chef, although I do bake bread every week. My sense of who I am has changed as a result of experiences and people that have affected how I see myself.

How did you define yourself when you were 8, 12, and 20 years old? It's likely that your definition of yourself today is different from your definition of yourself at earlier times in your life. Our sense of ourselves changes as we experience new relationships, situations, and people. How you see yourself today is shaped by others' interactions with you throughout your life. Similarly, the self you become in the future will reflect people and experiences that have happened as well as those to come.

In this chapter, we will explore how the self is formed and how it changes in the process of communicating with others and with ourselves. First, we will define the self and explore the central role of communication in creating the self. In the second section of the chapter, we'll discuss guidelines for enhancing your self-identity.

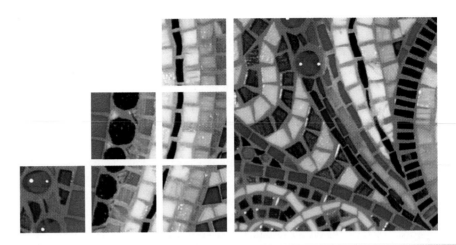

▶ COMMUNICATION AND PERSONAL IDENTITY

The **self** is an ever-changing system of perspectives that is formed and sustained in communication with others and ourselves. This definition emphasizes that the self is a process. Each of us continually evolves and changes in response to experiences throughout our lives. The definition also calls attention to the idea that the self consists of perspectives: views about ourselves, others, and social life that arise out of our experiences and interactions with others. Finally, the definition highlights communication as a critically important influence on who we are and how we see ourselves.

The Self Arises in Communication with Others

The distinguished scholar, George Herbert Mead, spent most of his career studying how humans develop selves. His conclusion was that the self is not innate but is acquired in the process of communicating with others. We weren't born with clear understandings of who we are and what our value is. Instead, we develop these understandings in the process of communicating with others who tell us who we are, what we should and should not do, how valuable we are, and what is expected of us. As we take others' perspectives into ourselves, we come to perceive ourselves through their eyes.

One particularly powerful way in which communication shapes the self is through **self-fulfilling prophecies**—expectations or judgments of ourselves that we bring about through our own actions. If you have done poorly in classes where teachers didn't seem to respect you and have done well with teachers who thought you were smart, you know what a self-fulfilling prophecy is. Because we internalize others' perspectives, we may label ourselves as they do and then act to fulfill the labels we have internalized. We may try to live up or down to the ways we and others define us.

When I was 7 years old, I took a swimming class. No matter how hard I tried to follow the teacher's directions, I sank in the pool. I couldn't swim and couldn't even float. After 3 weeks, the teacher told me that I would never learn to swim and I should stay away from water. For the next 43 years, I accepted the teacher's label of *nonswimmer* and didn't try to swim. When I was 50, Robbie challenged my statement that I couldn't swim. He said I could learn to swim if I wanted to, and he volunteered to coach me. After just a few days of one-on-one coaching, I was swimming and floating. Now, I feel safe going in pools or the ocean because I am not trapped by an outdated,

fyi

A POSITIVE PROPHECY

For years, Georgia Tech ran a program called Challenge, a course designed to help disadvantaged students succeed academically. Yet when administrators reviewed the records, they found that students enrolled in Challenge did no better than disadvantaged students who did not attend.

Norman Johnson, a special assistant to the president of Georgia Tech, explained the reason for the dismal results of Challenge. He said, "We were starting off with the idea the kids were dumb. We didn't say that, of course, but the program was set up on a deficit model." Then Johnson suggested a new strategy: "Suppose we started with the idea that these youngsters were unusually bright, that we had very high expectations of them?" (Raspberry, 1994, p. 9A).

Challenge teachers were then trained to expect success from their students and to communicate their expectations through how they treated students. The results were impressive: In 1992, 10% of the first-year Challenge students had perfect 4.0 grade point averages for the academic year. That 10% was more than all the minority students who had achieved 4.0 averages in the entire decade of 1980–1990. By comparison, only 5% of the students who didn't participate in Challenge had perfect averages. When teachers expected Challenge students to do well and communicated those expectations, the students in fact did do well—a case of a positive self-fulfilling prophecy.

inaccurate label. I no longer accept and act to fulfill that prophecy. Like me, many of us believe inaccurate things about ourselves. In some cases, the labels were once true but aren't any longer, yet we continue to apply them to ourselves (remember indexing, which we discussed in Chapter 4). In other cases, the labels were never valid, but we believed them anyway. Sometimes, children are mislabeled as slow when the real problem is that they have physiological difficulties such as impaired vision or they are struggling with a second language.

Even when the true source of difficulty is discovered, the children already may have adopted a destructive self-fulfilling prophecy. If we accept others' judgments, we may fulfill their prophecies. The FYI feature on this page illustrates the power of positive (and negative) prophecies. To explain the impact of others on ourselves, Mead identified two kinds of others whose communication influences how we see ourselves and what we believe is possible and desirable for us.

Particular Others The first perspectives that affect us are those of **particular others.** As the term implies, these are specific people who are especially significant to us and who shape how we see ourselves. Mothers, fathers, siblings, peers, and, often, day-care providers are others who are significant to us in our early years. For some of us, particular others also include aunts, uncles, grandparents, and friends. In general, Hispanics, Latinas and Latinos, Asians and Asian Americans, and African Americans often have closer and larger extended families than European Americans. As Eugenio points out in his commentary, people other than parents can affect how children come to see themselves, others, and the social world (Gaines, 1995).

▶ Eugenio

My father was not at home much when I was growing up. He worked in Merida, where the tourists go and spend money. My grandfather lived with us, and he raised me. He taught me to read and to count, and he showed me how to care for our livestock and repair the roof on our house after the rains each year. He is the one who talked to me about life and what matters. He is the one who taught me how to be a man.

The process of seeing ourselves through the eyes of others is called **reflected appraisal,** or the "looking-glass self" (Cooley, 1912). As infants interact with others, they learn how others see them—they see themselves in the looking glass, or mirror, of others' eyes. This is the beginning of a self-concept. Note that the self starts outside of us with others' views of who we are. In other words, we first see ourselves from the perspectives of others. If parents communicate to children that they are special and cherished, the children will come to see themselves as worthy of love. On the other hand, children whose parents communicate that they are not wanted or loved may come to think of themselves as unlovable.

Who are the people who are your looking glass? For whom are you a looking glass?

Reflected appraisals are not confined to childhood but continue throughout our lives. Sometimes, a teacher is the first to see potential in a student that the student has not recognized in herself or himself. When the teacher communicates that the student is talented in a particular area, the student may come to see himself or herself that way. Later, in professional life we encounter co-workers and bosses who reflect their appraisals of us (we're on the fast track, average, or not suited to our positions). The friends and romantic partners we choose throughout life become primary looking glasses for us.

The Generalized Other The second perspective that influences how we see ourselves is the perspective of the **generalized other.** The generalized other is the collection of rules, roles, and attitudes endorsed by the overall society and social communities to which we belong (Mead, 1934). In other words, the generalized other is made up of the views of society and social communities to which we belong.

Broadly shared social perspectives are communicated by other people who have internalized those views and also by social institutions such as schools and media. For example, when we read popular magazines and go to movies, we are inundated with messages about how we are supposed to look and act. We learn how our culture defines success, and we are likely to internalize this view. Communication from media infuses our lives, repeatedly telling us how we are supposed to be, think, act, and feel. Access to the web and the Internet expands the perspectives we encounter, which may become part of how we view the world and our place in it.

Institutions that organize our society communicate values that further convey the perspective of the generalized other. For example, our judicial system asserts that, as a society, we value laws and punish those who break them. The number of prisons and ceaseless media attention to crime further tell us that Western society values lawful behavior and punishes unlawful behavior. The Western institution of marriage communicates society's view that when people marry they become a single unit, which is why the law assumes that married couples have joint ownership of property. In other societies, parents arrange marriages, and newlyweds become part of the husband's family. The number of schools, as well as the extent of graduate and professional education, inform us that Western society values learning.

Institutions also reflect and express prevailing social prejudices. For instance, we may be a lawful society, but many wealthy defendants can afford better legal counsel than poor ones can. Similarly, although we claim to offer equal educational opportunities to all, many students whose families have money and influence can get into better schools than students whose families have limited financial resources (Cose, 2004). These and other values are woven into the fabric of our culture, and we learn them with little effort or awareness. Only by making a conscious and sustained effort can we become more aware of what society communicates about different groups. We have an ethical responsibility to reflect carefully on social values so that we can make conscious choices about which ones we will accept for ourselves.

From the moment we enter the world, we interact with others. As we do, we learn how they see us, and we take their perspectives inside ourselves. Once we have internalized the views of particular others and the generalized other, we engage in internal dialogues with those social perspectives. Through the process of internal dialogues, or conversations with ourselves, we reinforce the social values we have learned and the views of us and the world that others have communicated.

Communication with Family Members

For most of us, family members are the first and most important influence on how we see ourselves. Because family interaction dominates our early years, it usually sculpts the foundations of our self-concepts. Parents and other family members communicate who we are and what we are worth through direct definitions, identity scripts, and attachment styles.

Direct Definition As the term implies, **direct definition** is communication that explicitly tells us who we are by labeling us and our behaviors. Parents and other family members define us by the symbols they use to describe us. For instance, parents might say, "You're my sweet little girl" or "You're a big, strong boy" and thus communicate to the child what sex it is and what the sexual assignment means (girls are sweet, boys are big and strong). Children who hear such messages may internalize their parents' views of the sexes and use those as models for themselves.

Family members provide direct communication about many aspects of who we are. Positive labels enhance our self-esteem (Brooks & Goldstein, 2001): "You're so smart," "You're sweet," "You're great at soccer." Negative labels can damage children's self-esteem (Vachss, 1994): "You're a troublemaker," "You're stupid," and "You're impossible" are messages that can demolish a child's sense of self-worth. Direct defi-

© Steve Chenn/Corbis

Parents' communication is a key influence on self-concept.

nition also takes place as family members respond to children's behaviors. If children clown around and parents respond by saying, "What a cut-up; you really are funny," the children learn to see themselves as funny. If a child receives praise for dusting furniture ("You're great to help me clean the house"), helping others is reinforced as part of the child's self-concept. From direct definition, children learn what parents value and expect of them, and this shapes how they regard themselves and what they expect of themselves.

Identity Scripts Family members also shape our self-concepts by communicating **identity scripts,** which are rules for living and identity (Berne, 1964; Harris, 1969). Like scripts for plays, identity scripts define our roles, how we are to play them, and the basic elements of what our families see as the right plot for our lives. Think back to your childhood to recall some of the identity scripts that your family communicated to you. Were you told, "Our family doesn't do that kind of thing," "Save your money for a rainy day," "Always help others," "Look out for yourself," or "Live by God's word"? These are examples of identity scripts people learn in families.

Our basic identity scripts are formed early, probably by age 5. This means that fundamental understandings of who we are and how we are supposed to live are forged when we have almost no control. We aren't allowed to coauthor or even edit our initial identity scripts, because adults have power. As children, we aren't even conscious of learning scripts. It is largely an unconscious process by which we internalize scripts that others write and assign to us, and we absorb them with little if any awareness. As adults, however, we are no longer passive recipients of others' scripts. We have the capacity to review the identity scripts that were given to us and to challenge and change those that do not fit the selves we now choose to be. The Sharpen Your Skill feature on this page invites you to review your identity scripts and challenge those that no longer work for you.

Attachment Styles Finally, parents communicate who we are through their **attachment styles,** patterns of parenting that teach us how to view ourselves and personal relationships. From his studies of interaction between parents and children, John Bowlby (1973, 1988) concluded that we learn attachment styles in our earliest relationships. These early relationships are especially important because they form expectations for later relationships (Bartholomew & Horowitz, 1991; Miller, 1993; Trees, 2006). Four distinct attachment styles have been identified (see Figure 9.1).

Reflecting on Your Identity Scripts

To take control of our lives, we must first understand influences that shape it currently. Identify the identity scripts your parents taught you.

1. First, recall explicit messages your parents gave you about "who we are" and "who you are." Can you hear their voices telling you codes you were expected to follow?

2. Next, write down the scripts. Try to capture the language your parents used in teaching the scripts.

3. Now review each script. Which ones make sense to you today? Are you still following any that have become irrelevant or nonfunctional for you? Do you disagree with any of them?

4. Commit to changing scripts that aren't productive for you or that conflict with values you now hold.

In some cases, we can rewrite scripts. To do so, we must become aware of the scripts we were taught and take responsibility for scripting our lives.

SHARPEN YOUR SKILL

Views of self

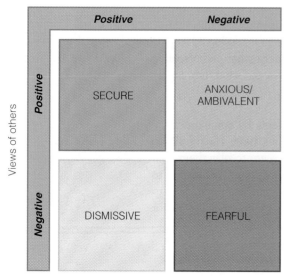

Figure 9.1 ATTACHMENT STYLES

A **secure attachment style** develops when a child's primary caregiver responds in a consistently attentive and loving way to a child. In response, the child develops a positive sense of self-worth ("I am lovable") and a positive view of others ("People are loving and can be trusted"). People with secure attachment styles tend to be outgoing, affectionate, and able to handle the challenges and disappointments of close relationships without losing self-esteem. A majority of middle-class children in the United States are securely attached, but fewer children in lower economic classes are (Greenberg, 1997).

A **fearful attachment style** is cultivated when the caregiver communicates in negative, rejecting, or even abusive ways to a child. Children who are treated this way often infer that they are unworthy of love and that others are not loving. Thus, they learn to see themselves as unlovable and others as rejecting. Not surprisingly, people with fearful attachment styles are apprehensive about relationships. Although they often want close bonds with others, they fear others will not love them and that they are not lovable. Thus, as adults they may avoid others or feel insecure in relationships. In some societies, members of certain groups learn early that they are less valuable than members of other groups. Zondi makes this point in her commentary.

▶ Zondi

In South Africa, where I was born, I learned that I was not important. Most daughters learn this. My name is Zondomini, which means between happiness and sadness. The happiness is because a child was born. The sadness is because I am a girl, not a boy. I am struggling now to see myself as worthy as a woman.

A **dismissive attachment style** is also promoted by caregivers who are uninterested in, rejecting of, or abusive toward children. People who develop this style do not accept the caregiver's view of them as unlovable. Instead, they dismiss others as unworthy. Consequently, children develop a positive view of themselves and a low regard for others and relationships. This prompts a defensive tendency to view relationships as unnecessary and undesirable.

The final pattern is the **anxious/ambivalent attachment style,** which is the most complex of the four. Each of the other three styles results from some consistent pattern of treatment by a caregiver. The anxious/ambivalent style, however, is fostered by inconsistent treatment from the caregiver. Sometimes the adult is loving and attentive, yet at other times she or he is indifferent or rejecting. The caregiver's communication is not only inconsistent but also unpredictable. He or she may respond positively to something a child does on Monday and react negatively to the same behavior on Tuesday. Naturally, this unpredictability creates great anxiety in a child (Miller, 1993). Because children tend to assume that adults are right, children often assume that they themselves are the source of any problem. In her commentary, Noreen explains how inconsistent behaviors from her father confused and harmed her as a child.

▶ Noreen

When I was little, my father was an alcoholic, but I didn't know that then. All I knew was that sometimes he was nice to me, and sometimes he was really nasty. Once, he told me I was his sunshine, but later that same day he said he wished I'd never been born. Even though now I know the alcohol made him mean, it's still hard to feel I'm okay.

In adult life, people who have anxious/ambivalent attachment styles tend to be preoccupied with relationships. On one hand, they know that others can be loving, so they're drawn to relationships. On the other hand, they realize that others can hurt them and be unloving, so they are uneasy with closeness. Reproducing what the caregiver did, people with anxious/ambivalent attachment styles may act inconsistently. One day they invite affection, the next day they rebuff it and deny needing closeness.

The attachment style learned in a child's first close relationship tends to persist (Bartholomew & Horowitz, 1991; Belsky & Pensky, 1988; Bowlby, 1988; Guerrero, 1996). However, this is not inevitable. We can modify our attachment styles by challenging the unconstructive views of us that were communicated in our early years and by forming relationships, particularly romantic ones, that foster secure connections today (Banse, 2004; Neyer, 2002).

Communication with Peers

Peers are the second group of people whose communication influences our self-concept. From childhood playmates to work associates, friends, and romantic partners, we interact with peers throughout our lives. As we do, we learn how others see us, and this affects how we see ourselves.

Reflected Appraisals Just as we reflect the appraisals of us that were communicated by family members (looking glasses), we also reflect the appraisals of us that peers communicate. If our peers communicate that they think we are smart, we are likely to see ourselves as smart. If others communicate that they see us as dumb or unlikable, we may reflect their appraisals by thinking of ourselves in those ways. Reflected appraisals of peers join with those we saw in the eyes of family members and shape our self-images. Peers' appraisals of us have impact throughout our lives. We're affected by our co-workers' judgments of our professional competence, our neighbors' views of our home and family, and the appraisals of friends.

Social Comparisons A second way in which communication with peers affects self-concept is through **social comparison,** our rating of ourselves relative to others with respect to our talents, abilities, qualities, and so forth. Whereas reflected appraisals are based on how we think others view us, in social comparisons we use others to evaluate ourselves.

fyi

VIRTUAL IDENTITY DEVELOPMENT

Having make-believe friends is common among children. With technology, today's children are creating their own make-believe friends and even their own identities. One popular game, The Sims, allows players to create families and living spaces and then to direct interactions among family members. Marjorie Taylor (1999), a psychologist who has studied imaginary playmates, says that children create Sims characters that are just like themselves or characters that allow them to experiment with different identities. Researchers who study both children and technology think such games are great resources that help children learn to think about relationships and ways of interacting with others (Schiesel, 2006).

© Dennis MacDonald/PhotoEdit

Who are your sources for social comparisons today? How do you assess yourself relative to them?

We gauge ourselves in relation to others in two ways. First, we compare ourselves with others to decide whether we are like them or different from them. Are we the same age, color, or religion? Do we have similar backgrounds, interests, political beliefs, and social commitments? Assessing similarity and difference allows us to decide with whom we fit. Research has shown that people generally are most comfortable with others who are like them, so we tend to gravitate toward those we regard as similar (Whitbeck & Hoyt, 1994). However, this can deprive us of diverse perspectives of people whose experiences and beliefs differ from ours. When we limit ourselves only to people like us, we impoverish the social perspectives that form our understandings of the world.

Second, we engage in social comparisons to assess specific aspects of ourselves. Because there are no absolute standards of beauty, intelligence, musical talent, athletic ability, and so forth, we measure ourselves in relation to others. Am I as good a goalie as Hendrick? Am I as smart as Maya? Through comparing ourselves to others, we decide how we measure up on various criteria. This is normal and necessary if we are to develop realistic self-concepts. However, we should be wary of using inappropriate standards of comparison. It isn't realistic to judge our attractiveness in relation to stars and models, or our athletic ability in relation to professional players.

Self-Disclosure Our self-concepts are also affected—challenged, changed, reinforced, enlarged—by our self-disclosures and others' responses to them. **Self-disclosure** is the revelation of personal information about ourselves that others are unlikely to learn on their own. We self-disclose when we express private hopes and fears, intimate feelings, and personal experiences, perceptions, and goals.

Self-disclosures vary in how personal they are. To a co-worker who is upset about not receiving a promotion, you might disclose your experience in not getting a promotion some years ago. To your best friend, you might disclose more intimate feelings and experiences. Although we don't reveal our private selves to everyone and don't do it a great deal of the time even with intimates, self-disclosure is an important kind of communication. How others respond to our self-disclosures can profoundly affect how we see and accept ourselves, as Tim's commentary shows. Self-disclosure is most likely to take place when the communication climate is affirming, accepting, and supportive.

▶ **Tim**

Two years ago, I had a crisis with my faith. I was afraid to tell any of my friends because they are all Christians. I thought they would think less of me because I was doubting. Finally, I had to tell someone, so I told Steven, who had pledged his life to Christ at the same time I did. He was incredible about accepting what I said—about accepting me when I was doubting. He let me talk, and he helped me work through my doubts without judging me. I think his acceptance is a big reason I could accept my own doubts and get beyond them.

A number of years ago, Joseph Luft and Harry Ingham created a model that describes different kinds of knowledge and perceptions that are related to self-concept and personal growth (Luft, 1969). They called the model the Johari Window, which is a combination of their first names, Joe and Harry (Figure 9.2). The panes, or areas, in the Johari Window refer to four types of information and perceptions that are relevant to the self:

▶ The open, or free, area contains information that is known both to ourselves and to others. Your name, your major, and your tastes in music are probably information that you share easily with others. Our co-workers and casual acquaintances often know information about us that is in our open area.

▶ The blind area contains perceptions of us that others have but we don't. For example, others may perceive us as leaders, even though we don't see ourselves that way. Co-workers and supervisors may recognize strengths, weaknesses, and potentials of which we are unaware. Friends may see us as more or less generous than we perceive ourselves.

▶ The hidden area contains information and perceptions that we have about ourselves but choose not to reveal to others. You might not tell most people about your vulnerabilities or about traumas you've experienced. You might conceal self-doubts when interviewing for a job. Even with our closest intimates, we may choose to preserve some areas of privacy.

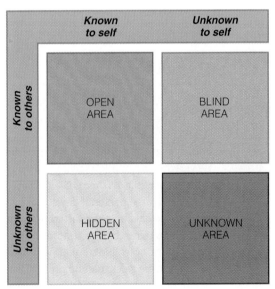

Figure 9.2 THE JOHARI WINDOW

▶ The unknown area is made up of information about ourselves that neither we nor others know. The unknown area is the most difficult to understand because, as the area's name implies, it contains information and perceptions that are not known. We cannot know how we will handle a job layoff, a family crisis, or a serious medical problem until we experience these things. The unknown area includes your untapped resources, untried talents, and unknown reactions to experiences you've never had. David, who started college after serving in the Army, provides an example of what had been an unknown to him.

▶ David

I was shipped out to Iraq shortly after American troops were assigned there. Talk about scared—I was terrified. I was also really unsure of how I would do. Could I stand up to the physical challenges? Would I freeze up in battle? Could I kill someone if I had to? Being a soldier in Iraq taught me some things about myself I don't think I could have learned any other way.

Because a healthy self-concept requires knowledge of yourself, it's important to gain access to information in our blind and unknown areas. To reduce your unknown area, you might enter unfamiliar situations. You might also try novel activities, interact with people whose cultural backgrounds differ from yours, and experiment with new ways of communicating. To decrease your blind area, you could ask others how they perceive you, or you could pay attention to how they act toward you. To diminish your hidden area, in carefully chosen relationships you might disclose information that you do not share with most people.

Uncertainty reduction theory asserts that people find uncertainty uncomfortable and so are motivated to use communication to reduce uncertainty. Uncertainty is very high during initial encounters. Because we find uncertainty uncomfortable, we use both indirect and direct strategies to reduce it (Berger, 1977, 1988; Gudykunst, 1995; Kim, 1995). We gain information indirectly by observing the person: How does Chris react to various people and situations? Does Chris like spicy foods? Does Chris listen to the same kinds of music that I do? Is Chris easily irritated? How flexible is Chris in adapting when there is a change in plans? We also use direct communication to gain information and reduce our uncertainty about a new acquaintance: Where are you from? What's your major? Do you follow politics? What's your family like?

Self-disclosure is another form of communication that we may use to reduce uncertainty early in relationships. We want to share our private selves and see how others respond to our disclosures. We may also hope that if we disclose something personal, others will reciprocate by disclosing to us, which would reduce our uncertainty. Because there are risks in self-disclosing, it's wise not to disclose too much too quickly. Initial self-disclosures should involve limited risk to the discloser: I am afraid of heights; I hope I get accepted to law school. If low-level disclosures are met with respect and affirmation, higher-level disclosures may follow: I have a difficult relationship with my father; I went into a serious depression a few years ago.

TECHNOLOGY

fyi

ONLINE IDENTITY

Some people invent online personalities that don't match them—different races, sexes, sexual orientations, physical appearances, and so forth. Experimenting with identity can be very helpful to adolescents as they try out different versions of themselves, a process that is critical to personal development. A shy teen may create an extroverted online identity that allows her or him to test how it feels to be more sociable. Experimenting with identity online may be safer than doing it in real life, where drugs, crime, HIV-AIDS, rape, and other dangers can turn an experiment into a tragedy (Turkle, 2004).

According to researchers, careful self-disclosure not only fosters personal growth but also tends to increase closeness, at least among Westerners (Derlega & Berg, 1987; Hansen & Schuldt, 1984). Yet people vary in their perceptions of the link between disclosure and intimacy. For some people, talk is a primary way to develop intimacy, whereas other people regard sharing experiences and being together as more conducive to closeness than talking intimately.

Although self-disclosure is important in the early stages of a relationship, it is not a primary communication dynamic in most enduring relationships (Dindia, 2000; Wood & Duck, 2006b). When we're first getting to know colleagues, friends, or intimate partners, we have to reveal parts of ourselves and learn about them, so disclosures are necessary and desirable. However, in relationships that endure over time, disclosures make up little of the total communication. Once co-workers and friends have established relationships, the bulk of their communication focuses on task issues, not further personal disclosures. In intimate relationships, frequency of disclosure also tends to decline over time, yet partners continue to reap the benefits of the trust and depth of personal knowledge created by early disclosures. Also, partners do continue to disclose new experiences and insights to one another; it's just that mature relationships usually see less disclosure than embryonic ones.

Although infrequent self-disclosures do not necessarily indicate a lack of closeness, a noticeable decline in the level of disclosure that has become standard in a relationship may be a sign that intimacy is declining. When a friendship, a romance, or a close working relationship wanes, typically the depth of disclosure decreases (Baxter, 1987; Duck & Wood, 2006). For good reason, we are reluctant to trust others with our secrets and personal emotions when we no longer want closeness or when we sense the other is pulling away.

Communication with Society

As we noted earlier, particular others are not the only influence on how we view ourselves. We now consider in more detail how communication with the generalized other shapes self-concept. As we interact with the generalized other, we learn which aspects of identity society considers important, how society views various social groups, and, by extension, how it views us as members of particular groups. Modern Western culture emphasizes race, gender, sexual orientation, and socioeconomic level as key aspects of personal identity and value (Andersen & Collins, 1998; Healey & O'Brien, 2004).

Race In North America, race is considered a primary aspect of personal identity (Collins, 1998; González, Houston, & Chen, 2004). The race that has been favored historically in the United States is Caucasian. In the early years of this country's life, some people considered it normal and right for White men to own Black women, men, and children and to require them to work for no wages and in poor conditions. Later, some people considered it natural that White men could vote but Black men could not. White men had the rights to be educated, to pursue professional careers, and to own property, as well as other basic freedoms that were denied Blacks.

As a result of the civil rights movement, discrimination against people of color has steadily declined. Even so, Caucasian privilege continues today. White children often have access to better schools with more resources than do children of African American or Latin heritage (Cose, 2004). The upper levels of government, education, and business are dominated by European American men, whereas people of color continue to fight for equal rights in admission, hiring, and advancement. Ellis Cose (2004) reports that Blacks, and especially Black men, recognize and sometimes internalize the generalized other's perspective that Blacks are less admirable than Whites. Derrick's reflection illustrates this point.

▶ Derrick

If my mama told me once, she told me a million times: "You got to work twice as hard to get half as far because you're Black." I knew that my skin was a strike against me in this society since I can remember knowing anything. When I asked why Blacks had to work harder, Mama said, "Because that's just how it is." I guess she was telling me that's how this society looks on African Americans.

Gender Gender is another category that is important in Western culture. Historically, Western society has valued men more than women and considered men more rational, competent, and entitled to various social advantages and opportunities. In the 1800s, women were not allowed to own property, gain professional training, or vote.

Society's gender prescriptions are less rigid today than they were in the past. Many men wear jewelry, tweeze their eyebrows, and use gels and spray to style their hair; many women wear slacks and don't use make-up. Recently, the term *metrosexual* was coined to describe people, particularly men, who fit some of society's expectations for both sexes. Despite relaxation in the generalized other's views of gender, social gender prescriptions persist (Pollock, 2000; Vannoy, 2001). In most cultures, girls and women are expected to be caring, deferential, and cooperative, whereas boys and men are supposed to be independent, assertive, and competitive. Women who violate social expectations of gender by asserting themselves or refusing to defer are likely to receive social disapproval, to be called bitches, and otherwise to be reprimanded for violating prescriptions for their gender. Beth's commentary indicates how others respond to her lack of conformity to the generalized other's perspective on femininity. Men who refuse to conform to social views of masculinity and who are gentle and caring risk being called wimps.

▶ Beth

I get along with kids, but I don't want to have any of my own. I don't really like kids. Everyone—my parents, my friends, my boyfriend—thinks that is so weird. But I know a lot of guys who don't like kids, and nobody thinks they're weird or anything.

Sexual Orientation A third aspect of identity that is salient to the generalized other in Western culture is sexual orientation. Historically and today, heterosexuals are viewed as normal, and people who have other sexual orientations are often regarded as abnormal. Society communicates this viewpoint not only directly but also through privileges given to heterosexuals but denied to gay men, lesbians, and bisexuals. For example, a woman and a man can be married in any state or culture. Marriage confers social and legal recognition of their commitment (Wood, 2006b). For years, United States law has refused to allow marriage between two men or two women who want to be life partners. In recent years, we have witnessed challenges to this law. Many gay men and lesbians reject and resist negative social views of their identity, and they form communities that support positive self-images. These communities can serve as a generalized other that is different from the mainstream culture.

Recently, Massachusetts passed a law allowing gays and lesbians to marry. At the same time, religious and secular groups are challenging same-sex marriage. Regardless of whether same-sex marriage is able to sustain legal standing, the very fact that some Americans support it and some areas choose to perform same-sex marriage shows that social disapproval of gays and lesbians is diminishing. Society is also becoming more aware of other sexual orientations and sexualities, including transsexuals and transgendered and intergendered people (Glenn, 2002). As with race and gender, the generalized other's perspective on sexuality and sexual orientation is not fixed but evolving. A transgendered woman whom I know wrote the following reflection on what it felt like growing up biologically male when she felt female and how she feels now that she lives as a woman.

▶ Christine

Being accepted as the girl I am has been my dream from age 4 or 5. Becoming a woman among women has been my dream for over 30 years. I was brought up in the Roman Catholic church. From a very early age I disliked the church. I'm sure a large part of my rejection was also due to "god" never answering my prayers to have me wake up as a girl. I cried so many nights as a child.

Never did I appreciate how so quickly life-changing living as an integrated, authentic self would be. Never in my wildest dreams did I believe that "genetic" women ("gg's" as the community calls them—genetic girls) would so quickly embrace me, invite me into their private world, and want to help me find my place among them.

Socioeconomic Level Socioeconomic level is a fourth facet of identity that the generalized other considers important. Because North America is an income-conscious society, the income level to which we belong affects everything from how much money we make to the kinds of schools, jobs, friends, and lifestyle choices we see as possibilities for ourselves. Socioeconomic level is difficult to pinpoint because, unlike sex and race, it is not necessarily physically visible. Even though we can't see or point to socioeconomic level, it—and the generalized other's views of different socioeconomic levels—profoundly shapes our lives.

Socioeconomic level isn't just the amount of money a person has. It's a basic part of how we understand the world and how we think, feel, and act (Acker, 2005). Socioeconomic level affects which stores we shop in, the restaurants we patronize, and the schools we attend. It influences how we dress, including our views of what it means to be well dressed. It also influences who our friends are, what forms of recreation we enjoy, where we live and work, the schools we attend, and what kind of vehicles we drive (Bornstein & Bradley, 2003; Langston, 1998; Lareau, 2003).

▶ Geneva

I don't fit in at this college. That hits me in the face every day. I walk across campus and see girls wearing shoes that cost more than all four pairs I own. I hear students talking about restaurants and trips that I can't afford. Last week, I heard a guy complaining about being too broke to get a CD player for his car. I don't own a car. I don't know how to relate to these people who have so much money. Without my scholarship, I could never have come here. I know students here see the world differently than I do, and they see themselves as entitled to a lot more than I think I'm entitled to.

As Geneva's commentary indicates, socioeconomic level affects our ideas about what we need and what we are entitled to. For example, people with economic security have the resources and leisure time to seek fulfillment of abstract needs such as self-actualization. They can afford therapy, yoga, retreats for spiritual development, and elite spas to condition their bodies. These are not feasible for people who are a step away from poverty. Members of the middle and upper income levels assume they will attend college and enter good professions, yet these often are not realistic options for people who have lower incomes (Langston, 1998). Guidance counselors may encourage academically gifted lower-income students to go to work or pursue vocational education after high school, whereas they routinely steer middle-income students of average ability toward good colleges and high-status careers. In such patterns, we see how the perspective of the generalized other shapes not just our sense of who we are but also the concrete realities of our lives.

Race, gender, sexual preference, and socioeconomic level are primary in our society's views of individuals and their worth. It's important to realize that these views of identity intersect. Race interacts with gender, so women of color experience double oppression and devaluation in our culture (Anzaldúa, 1999; Hernández & Rheman, 2002; Higginbotham, 1992; Lorde, 1992; Zinn & Dill, 1996). Socioeconomic level and gender are also interlinked, with women far more likely than men to live at the poverty level. Gender and race intersect, so Hispanic and Black men face barriers not faced by White men.

In addition to race, gender, sexual preference, and socioeconomic level, the generalized other communicates other views that we may internalize. For instance, Western societies clearly value intelligence, competitiveness, individualism, and ambition. People, especially men, who conform to these social values, receive more respect than those who don't. Mainstream Western society also values slimness, particularly in Caucasian women. Because society places such emphasis on slenderness in women, eating disorders are epidemic; as many as 80 out of 100 fourth-grade girls diet, and most of them are well within normal weight limits (Gottlieb, 2000; Kilbourne, 2004; Nichter, 2000). The generalized other expresses physical ideals for men as well. Strength and sexual prowess are two expectations of "real men," which may explain why increasing numbers of men are having pectoral implants and penis enlargement surgery (Bordo, 1999). Leah's commentary illustrates another change in social views—from thinking online relationships are poor substitutes for "real relationships" to recognizing that very important, close relationships can form and grow online.

▶ **Leah**

I was a bridesmaid in one of my closest friends' wedding last year. I'd never met Katrina until the dress rehearsal, because we had met and become friends online. For three years, we chatted daily, sometimes many times in a day. We helped each other get through bad boyfriends and other challenges. My parents thought it was crazy that I would fly across the country to be in the wedding of someone I'd never met (at least not met in person), but I felt closer to Katrina than most of my friends on campus.

As we interact with particular others and participate in social life (the generalized other), we learn what and whom our society values. We also learn how our society sees us in terms of our race, gender, sexual orientation, socioeconomic level, and other factors. If we do not reflect on the ethical and pragmatic implications of these values, we may internalize them and come to share the views generally endorsed in our society.

The human self originates in communication. From interaction with family members, peers, and society as a whole, we learn the prevailing values of our culture and of particular people who are significant to us. What we learn guides how we perceive and communicate with others and ourselves. We're now ready to discuss three challenges related to personal growth.

▶GUIDELINES FOR COMMUNICATING WITH OURSELVES

Throughout this chapter, we've drawn on the basic communication processes covered in Part I of this book. For example, we've noted that others are an especially important influence on the process of perceiving ourselves. Our sense of identity evolves as we listen to others and observe their actions toward us. We've also learned that the symbols others use to define us shape how we perceive ourselves and that we can edit our self-talk to change our self-concepts. To demonstrate further how basic communication processes apply to interaction with ourselves, we will discuss three guidelines for communicating with ourselves in ways that foster personal growth and a healthy society.

Reflect Critically on Social Perspectives

We've seen that people tend to internalize the perspectives of the generalized other. In many ways this is useful, even essential, for collective life. If we all made up our own rules about when to stop and go at traffic intersections, wrecks would proliferate. If each of us operated by our own inclinations, we would have no shared standards regarding tax payment, robbery, and so forth. Life would be chaotic.

Yet not all social views are as constructive as traffic rules and criminal law. The generalized other's unequal valuing of different social groups fuels discrimination against people whose only fault is not being what society currently defines as normal or good. Each of us has an ethical responsibility to exercise critical judgment about which social views we personally accept and which ones we will allow to guide our behaviors, attitudes, and values. In addition, we have an ethical obligation to use our communication to contribute to constructive change in our society.

The generalized other's perspective is not fixed, nor is it based on objective, absolute truths. Instead, the values and views endorsed by a society at any given time are arbitrary and subject to change. The fluidity of social values becomes especially obvious when we consider how widely values differ between cultures. For example, the Agta people in the Philippines and the Tini Aborigines in Australia view hunting skill as a feminine ideal (Estioko-Griffin & Griffin, 1997). A group in French Polynesia recognizes three sexes (Glenn, 2002), and some groups in India have a category of identity for female men (Nanda, 2004).

Social views also change over time in a single society. For instance, in the early twentieth century many people with disabilities were kept in their homes or put in institutions. Today, many schools place students who have physical or mental disabilities in regular classes. Also, as we have seen, the Western generalized other's perspectives on race, gender, and sexual orientation are not what they were 50 or even 5 years ago.

Social perspectives change in response to individual and collective efforts to revise social meanings. Each of us has an ethical responsibility to speak out against social perspectives that we perceive as wrong or harmful. By doing so, we participate in the ongoing process of refining who we are as a society and the views of the generalized other that affect how we see ourselves and each another.

Identifying Social Values in Media

Select four popular magazines, and read the articles and advertisements in the magazines.

▶ What do the articles and ads convey about what and who is valued in the United States?

▶ What do articles convey about how women or men are regarded and what they are expected to be and do?

▶ How many ads aimed at women focus on beauty, looking young, losing weight, taking care of others, and attracting men?

▶ How many ads aimed at men emphasize strength, virility, success, and independence?

To extend this exercise, note the cultural values conveyed by television, films, billboards, and news stories. Pay attention to who is highlighted and how different genders, races, and professions are represented.

SHARPEN YOUR SKILL

Commit to Personal Growth

Most of us perceive ways we could improve as communicators. Maybe we want to be more assertive, more mindful when listening, or more confident as public speakers. Following three suggestions will help you nurture your own personal growth.

Set Realistic Goals Although willpower can do marvelous things, it has limits. We need to recognize that trying to change how we see ourselves works only if our goals are realistic. It's not realistic and usually not effective to expect dramatic growth immediately. If you are shy and want to be more extroverted, it's realistic to decide that you will speak up more often and attend more social functions. On the other hand, setting the goal of being the life of the party may not be reasonable.

Realistic goals require realistic standards. Dissatisfaction with ourselves often stems from unrealistic expectations. In a culture that emphasizes perfectionism, it's easy to be trapped into expecting more than is humanly possible. If you set a goal of being a totally perfect communicator in all situations, you set yourself up for failure. More reasonable and more constructive is to establish a series of small goals that you can meet. You might focus on improving one communication skill. When you are satisfied with your ability at that skill, you can focus on a second one.

Assess Yourself Fairly Being realistic also involves making fair assessments of ourselves. This requires us to make reasonable social comparisons, place judgments of ourselves in context, realize that we are always in process, and assess ourselves in the perspective of time. Remembering our discussion of social comparison, we know that selecting reasonable yardsticks for ourselves is important. Comparing your academic work with that of a certified genius is not appropriate. It is reasonable to measure your academic performance against others who have intellectual abilities and life situations similar to yours. Setting realistic goals and selecting appropriate standards of comparison are important guidelines when you want to bring about change in yourself. Fenton's commentary illustrates this point.

To assess ourselves effectively, we also should appreciate how our individual qualities and abilities fit together to form the whole self. Recall systems theory, which we discussed in Chapter 1. It reminds us that we treat ourselves unfairly if we judge specific aspects of our communication outside their overall context. Most often, we do this by highlighting our shortcomings and overlooking what we do well. This leads to a distorted self-perception.

It's more realistic to judge yourself from an overall perspective. Babe Ruth hit 714 home runs, and he also struck out 1,330 times. If he had defined himself only in terms of his strikeouts, he probably would never have become a world-

Sally Forth

renowned baseball player. One of my colleagues faults himself for being slow to grade and return students' papers. He compares himself with others in my department who return students' work more quickly. However, this man has twice as many office hours as any of his colleagues, which should temper his self-criticism about the length of time he takes to return papers. His judgment that he is slow in returning papers is based on comparing himself with colleagues who spend less time talking with their students than he does. However, he doesn't compare himself with them when thinking about his office hours. In our efforts to improve self-concept, then, we should acknowledge our strengths and virtues as well as parts of ourselves we want to change.

To create and sustain a healthy self-concept, we also need to be attentive to unrealistic assessments of us that others may make. Bosses sometimes have unreasonable expectations. If we measure our abilities by the unreasonable standards of our bosses, we may underestimate our effectiveness. Parents also can have expectations that are unrealistic or inconsistent with our goals and values. We should consider others' views of us, but we should not accept them uncritically.

A key foundation for improving self-concept is to accept yourself as someone in process. The human self is continuously in process, always changing, always becoming. This implies several things. First, it means that it's healthy to accept who you are now as a starting point. You don't have to like or admire everything about yourself, but accepting who you are today allows you to move forward. The person you are today has been shaped by all the experiences, interactions, reflected appraisals, and social comparisons during your life. You cannot change your past, but you do not have to be bound by it forever. Only by realizing and accepting who you are now can you grow in new ways.

Accepting yourself as in process also implies that you realize you can change. Who you are today is not who you will be in 5 or 10 years. Because you are in process, you are always changing and growing. Don't let yourself be hindered by negative self-fulfilling prophecies or by the belief that you cannot change (Rusk & Rusk, 1988). You can change if you set realistic goals, make a genuine commitment, and work for the changes you want. Just remember that you are not fixed as you are but always in the process of becoming.

Self-Disclose Appropriately   Appropriate self-disclosure can foster personal awareness, which is a foundation of growth and change. For self-disclosure to be safe and to foster growth, it should take place gradually and with appropriate caution. It's unwise to tell anyone too much about ourselves too quickly, especially if revelations could be used against us. We begin by disclosing superficial information ("I haven't had experience in this kind of assignment," "I'm afraid of heights"). If a person responds to early disclosures with acceptance, we're likely to reveal progressively more intimate information ("My father served time in prison," "I'm not very skillful at reprimanding people for poor work"). If the person accepts these disclosures, communication may continue to deepen.

In the early stages of relationship development, reciprocity of disclosure seems important. If you mention a personal weakness to a new acquaintance, you'll be more comfortable if the other person shares a weakness, too. Most of us are willing to keep disclosing to a person we don't know well only as long as the other person is also revealing personal information (Cunningham, Strassberg, & Haan,

1986). This principle also applies to contexts other than personal relationships: For example, when we self-disclose to a co-worker, we are likely to feel a bit nervous if no reciprocal disclosure is forthcoming. The need to reciprocate disclosures immediately recedes in importance once a stable relationship is established.

Along with potential advantages, self-disclosure also entails risks (Derlega et al., 1993). The risks of self-disclosure found by communication researchers include that others might reject you or think less of you, that private information you share could be used against you, that being too honest could hurt others, and that you might lose power by exposing weaknesses. These are important risks. Being careful to self-disclose gradually and appropriately lessens these risks.

Create a Supportive Context for the Change You Seek

Just as it is easier to swim with the tide than against it, it is easier to promote changes in ourselves in contexts that support our efforts. You can do a lot to create a climate that supports your growth by choosing contexts and people who help you realize your goals.

First, think about settings. If you want to improve your physical condition, it makes more sense to participate in intramural sports than to hang out in bars. If you want to lose weight, it's better to go to restaurants that serve healthful foods and offer light choices than to go to cholesterol castles. If you want to become more outgoing, you need to put yourself in social situations rather than in libraries. But libraries are a better context than parties if your goal is to improve academic performance. Bob's commentary illustrates the influence of setting on personal behavior.

© Jeffry W. Myers/Corbis

Halloween costumes allow children to experiment with different identities. What was your favorite costume when you were a child?

▶ **Bob**

I never drank much until I got into this one group at school. All of them drank all the time. It was easy to join them. In fact, it was pretty hard not to drink and still be one of the guys. A while ago, I decided I was drinking too much. It was hard enough not to drink, because the guys were always doing it, but what really made it hard was the ways the guys got on me for abstaining. They let me know I was being uncool and made me feel like a jerk. Finally, I had to get a different apartment to stop drinking.

Second, the people we are with have a great deal to do with how we see ourselves and how worthy we feel we are. This means you can create a supportive

fyi   ## UPPERS, DOWNERS, AND VULTURES

Uppers are people who communicate positively about us and who reflect positive appraisals of our self-worth. They notice our strengths, see our progress, and accept our weaknesses and problems without discounting us. When we're around uppers, we feel more upbeat and positive about ourselves. Uppers aren't necessarily unconditionally positive in their communication. A true friend can be an upper by recognizing our weaknesses and helping us work on them.

Instead of putting us down, an upper believes in us and helps us believe in our capacity to change.

Downers are people who communicate negatively about us and our worth. They call attention to our flaws, emphasize our problems, and put down our dreams and goals. When we're around downers, we tend to feel down about ourselves. Reflecting their perspectives, we're more aware of our weaknesses and less confident of what we can accomplish. Downers discourage belief in ourselves.

Vultures are extreme downers. They attack our self-concepts, just as actual vultures prey on their victims. Sometimes vultures initiate harsh criticism of us. In other cases vultures discover our weak spots and exploit them, picking us apart by focusing on sensitive areas in our self-concept. By telling us we are inadequate, vultures demolish our self-esteem.

context by consciously choosing to be around people who believe in you and encourage your personal growth. It's equally important to steer clear of people who pull you down or say you can't change. In other words, people who reflect positive appraisals of us enhance our ability to improve. One way to think about how others' communication affects how we feel about ourselves is to recognize that people can be uppers, downers, or vultures (Simon, 1977). The FYI feature on this page explains uppers, downers, and vultures.

Other people are not the only ones who can be uppers, downers, and vultures whose communication affects our self-concepts. We also communicate with ourselves, and our messages influence our self-esteem. One of the most crippling kinds of self-talk in which we can engage is **self-sabotage.** This involves telling ourselves we are no good, we can't do something, there's no point in trying to change, and so forth. We may be repeating judgments others made of us or inventing negative self-fulfilling prophecies. Either way, self-sabotage defeats us because it undermines our belief in ourselves. Self-sabotage is poisonous; it destroys our motivation to grow.

We can be downers or even vultures to ourselves, just as others can be. In fact, we can probably do more damage to our self-concept than others can because we are most aware of our vulnerabilities and fears. This may explain why vultures were originally described as people who put themselves down (Simon, 1977). We can also be uppers for ourselves. We can affirm our worth, encourage our growth, and fortify our sense of self-worth. Positive self-talk is a useful way to interrupt and challenge negative messages from yourself and others. The next time you hear yourself saying, "I can't do this," or someone else says, "You'll never change," challenge the self-defeating message by saying out loud to yourself, "I can do it. I will change." Use positive self-talk to resist counterproductive communication about yourself.

Before leaving this discussion, we should make it clear that improving your self-concept is not facilitated by uncritical positive communication. None of us grows and improves when we listen only to praise, particularly if it is less than honest. The true uppers in our lives offer constructive criticism to encourage us to reach for better versions of ourselves.

▶SUMMARY

In this chapter, we explored the self as a process that evolves over the course of our lives. We saw that the self is not present at birth but develops as we interact with others. Through communication, we learn the perspectives of particular others and the generalized other, or the broad social community. Reflected appraisals, direct definitions, and social comparisons further shape how we see ourselves and how we change over time. The perspective of the generalized other includes social views of aspects of identity, including race, gender, sexual preference, and income level. However, these are arbitrary social constructions that we can challenge. When we resist counterproductive social views, we promote change in society.

The second half of the chapter focused on concrete ways we can apply basic communication processes to facilitate our personal growth and our participation in society. As members of a culture, we have an ethical obligation to use our communication to speak out against social values that we consider wrong or harmful. In doing so, we participate in the continuous evolution of our collective world.

In addition, you can foster your personal growth by setting realistic goals and assessing yourself fairly. Creating contexts that support the changes you seek makes it easier to promote those changes. Transforming how we see ourselves is not easy, but it is possible. We can make amazing changes in who we are and who we will become when we embrace our human capacity to make choices.

Review, Reflect, Extend

The Key Concepts, For Further Reflection and Discussion questions, Recommended Resources, and Experience Communication Case Study that follow will help you review, reflect on, and extend the information and ideas presented in this chapter. A diverse selection of online resources is also available through ThomsonNOW. These resources include Speech Builder Express, InfoTrac College Edition, interactive videos, vMentor, and Thomson Audio Study Products.

Thomson NOW! is an online study system designed to help you put your time to the best use. After reading a chapter, take the NOW pre-test to identify concepts discussed in the chapter that you may not fully understand. Based on the results of this diagnostic test, the system will create a personalized study plan that directs you to specific learning resources and activities. To see if you're ready for an exam, take the NOW post-test to check your understanding.

For more information or to access this book's online resources, visit **http://www.thomsonedu.com**.

►KEY CONCEPTS

The terms following are defined in the chapter on the page number indicated, and they appear in alphabetical order, with definitions, in the Glossary, which begins on page 369. The book's online resources also include flash cards and crossword puzzles to help you learn these terms and the concepts they represent.

anxious/ambivalent attachment style, 190	identity script, 189	self-sabotage, 204
attachment style, 189	particular others, 186	social comparison, 191
direct definition, 188	reflected appraisal, 187	uncertainty reduction theory, 194
dismissive attachment style, 190	secure attachment style, 190	upper, 204
downer, 204	self, 185	vulture, 204
fearful attachment style, 190	self-disclosure, 192	
generalized other, 187	self-fulfilling prophecy, 185	

►FOR FURTHER REFLECTION AND DISCUSSION

The questions below can also be found among the book's online resources for this chapter, where you have the option of e-mailing your responses to your instructor, if required.

1. Set one specific goal for personal growth as a communicator. Goals you could establish are to listen better, to be more assertive, or to learn about communication cultures that differ from yours. Apply what you learn during the semester to your personal goal.

2. Discuss society's views (the generalized other) of women and men. What are current social expectations for each sex? What behaviors, appearances, and attitudes violate social prescriptions for gender? Do you agree or disagree with these social expectations?

3. To what extent do you feel you have an ethical responsibility to improve yourself and contribute to enhancing others? How does your standpoint as a member of specific social groups influence your views on this question?

►RECOMMENDED RESOURCES

1. If you would like to learn more about how the attachment styles discussed in this chapter affect children, go to the book's online resources and click on WebLink 9.1.

2. T. Rusk and N. Rusk. (1988). *Mindtraps: Change your mind, change your life.* Los Angeles: Price Stern Sloan. This book offers practical advice on how to change yourself by challenging self-defeating intrapersonal communication.

3. The film *Nell* dramatizes the impact of communication with others on self-concept. View the film, and notice how Nell's world changes as she begins to communicate with others.

4. Some societies have more rigid lines for class membership than the United States does. One of the most rigid systems is the caste system in India. To learn about how a person's caste affects his or her opportunities in life, go to the book's online resources and click on WebLink 9.2.

Experience Communication Case Study

PARENTAL TEACHINGS

The book's online resources include an interactive video of the communication situation featured in the case study scripted following. Apply what you've learned in this chapter by analyzing the case study, using the questions that follow the script as a guide. These questions are also available online with the video.

Kate McDonald is in the neighborhood park with her two children, 7-year-old Emma and 5-year-old Jeremy. The three of them walk into the park and approach the swing set.

Kate: Jeremy, why don't you push Emma so she can swing? Emma, you hang on tight.

Jeremy begins pushing his sister, who squeals with delight. Jeremy gives an extra-hard push that lands him in the dirt in front of the swing set. Laughing, Emma jumps off, falling in the dirt beside her brother.

Kate: Come here, sweetie. You've got dirt all over your knees and your pretty new dress.

Kate brushes the dirt off Emma, who then runs over to the jungle gym set that Jeremy is now climbing. Kate smiles as she watches Jeremy climb fearlessly on the bars.

Kate: You're a brave little man, aren't you? How high can you go?

Jason Harris/© Wadsworth

Encouraged by his mother, Jeremy climbs to the top bars and holds up a fist, screaming, "Look at me, Mom! I'm king of the hill. I climbed to the very top!"

Kate laughs and claps her hands to applaud him. Jealous of the attention Jeremy is getting, Emma runs over to the jungle gym and starts climbing. Kate calls out, "Careful, honey. Don't go any higher. You could fall and hurt yourself." When Emma ignores her mother and reaches for a higher bar, Kate walks over and pulls her off, saying, "Emma, I told you that is dangerous. Time to get down. Why don't you play on the swings some more?"

Once Kate puts Emma on the ground, the girl walks over to the swings and begins swaying.

▼▼

1. Identify examples of direct definition in this scenario. How does Kate define Emma and Jeremy?

2. Identify examples of reflected appraisal in this scenario. What appraisals of her son and daughter does Kate reflect to them?

3. What do Emma's and Jeremy's responses to Kate suggest about their acceptance of her views of them?

4. To what extent does Kate's communication with her children reflect normative gender expectations in Western culture?

10 Communication in Personal Relationships

▶ **FOCUS QUESTIONS**

1. What is the typical process of friendship development?

2. How do romantic relationships typically escalate and deteriorate?

3. What kinds of communication help sustain long-distance romances?

4. To what extent are long-term romantic relationships equitable for women and men?

5. What is the cycle of intimate partner abuse?

When my mother could no longer live alone, Robbie (my partner) and I invited her to live with us in our home. She lived in our home for the final 14 months of her life. As you might imagine, during this period I felt much sadness. What you might not realize is that I also experienced a great deal of joy and personal growth as important relationships in my life gained depth. Mother and I grew close in new ways, and my ties with Robbie, my sister Carolyn, and close friends were deepened as I shared with them the fears and feelings that accompany losing a parent.

My experience is not unusual. All of us count on family, close friends, and romantic partners in good times as well as bad. Our intimates help us get through rough and unhappy moments, and they celebrate our joys and victories. Try to imagine that suddenly you have no close friends and no romantic partner. How would your life be different? What would be missing? If you're like most people, a great deal would be missing. Close relationships are important sources of growth, pleasure, comfort, and fulfillment. We need people who care about us and who let us care about them.

Healthy, effective communication is the heartbeat of strong personal relationships. In previous chapters, we've discussed self-disclosure, communication climate, supportive communication styles, listening, and conflict management cornerstones of communication. In this chapter, we focus on how those and other communication processes apply to the specific context of relationships with family, friends, and romantic partners. The first section of the chapter defines personal relationships and identifies their

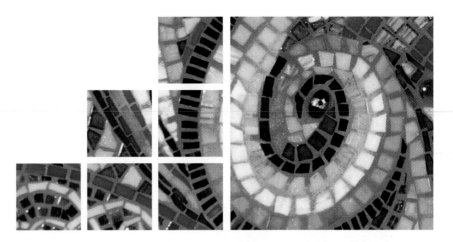

special features. In the second section of the chapter, we'll examine four guidelines for sustaining healthy personal relationships in our era.

▶Understanding Personal Relationships

A **personal relationship** is a voluntary commitment between irreplaceable individuals who are influenced by rules, relationship dialectics, and surrounding contexts. This definition highlights important qualities that distinguish personal relationships from other kinds of human connections.

Features of Personal Relationships

Personal relationships are unique: Each one is distinctive as a result of commitment, rules, surrounding contexts, and relationship dialectics. We'll discuss each of these features and then explore typical evolutionary paths of friendships and romantic relationships.

Uniqueness Most of our relationships are social, not personal. A **social relationship** is one in which participants interact according to general social roles rather than unique individual identities. For instance, you might exchange lecture notes with a classmate and talk about politics with a co-worker. In each case, the person could be replaced by someone else who took the same role. You could find other people with whom to swap class notes and discuss politics. In social relationships, the individual people are less important than the roles they fulfill. The value of social relationships lies more in what participants do than in who they are personally, because a variety of people could fulfill the same functions.

In personal relationships, however, the particular people and what they create between them define the connection. Many people are committed not so much to marriage in the abstract as to living their lives with a particular person. Friendships also involve unique bonds with specific people. Others cannot replace intimate partners, best friends, or parents. When one person in a personal relationship leaves or dies, that relationship ends, although it may remain strong in memory. We may later have other intimates, but a new spouse or best friend will not be a duplicate of the former one. Unlike social relationships, personal ones are unique, and partners are irreplaceable.

Commitment The sparks and the emotional high of being in love or discovering a new friend stem from **passion,** an intense feeling based on the rewards of involvement with another person. Passion is why we have the sensations of butterflies in the stomach and giddiness. As exciting as passion is, it isn't the basis of enduring relationships.

© Royalty-Free/Corbis

Shared time and experiences are important investments that fuel commitment.

Commitment is the decision to remain with a relationship. The hallmark of commitment is the intention to share the future (Beck, 1988; Ragan, 2003). Committed friends and romantic partners assume they will stay together. Because commitment assumes a shared future, partners are unlikely to bail out if the going gets rough. Instead, they weather bad times (Le & Agnew, 2003; Lund, 1985). Unlike passion, commitment is a decision to stay together despite trouble, disappointments, sporadic restlessness, and lulls in emotional depth.

Commitment grows out of **investment:** what we put into a relationship that we could not retrieve if the relationship were to end (Rusbult, Drigotas, & Verette, 1994). When we care about another person, we invest time, energy, thought, and feelings in interaction. In doing this, we invest *ourselves* in others. We also make material investments that can't be recovered if a relationship ends. Gifts, money spent on dates, and so forth cannot be recovered fully if the relationship ends. Investments are powerful because they are personal choices to give things that can't be recovered. We can't get back the feelings and energy we invest in a relationship. We can't recover history shared with another. The more we invest in a relationship, the more difficult it is to end it (Brehm, Miller, Perlman, & Campbell, 2001; Dainton, 2006). Sarah points out that investing heavily in a relationship can trap a person.

▶ Sarah

When Sean and I were first married, I was so happy I didn't care about anything else. My friends tried to talk me out of quitting school, but I wanted to work to put Sean through medical school. Then, we had one baby and another and a third, and I was a stay-at-home mom who was totally involved in family. Then things started unraveling between Sean and me. I thought about a divorce. But then I thought, "Where could I go? How could I support myself and the kids?" I hadn't finished college, so I couldn't earn a decent income. My job skills were rusty because I'd been out of the job market for 10 years. It was like I was trapped because I'd put too much in the marriage to leave.

Relationship Rules All relationships have **rules** that guide how partners communicate and interpret each other's communication. As in other communication contexts, rules in relationships define what is expected in certain kinds of relationships (friends should be loyal), the meaning of particular kinds of communication (hugs count as affection, silence as anger), and when, how, and in what circumstances various kinds of communication are appropriate. Typically, relationship rules are unspoken understandings between partners. Although friends and romantic partners may never explicitly discuss rules, they learn how important rules are if they violate one, as Miguel's commentary illustrates.

▶ Miguel

Sherry and I had been dating for about six months when some of my friends from another school came to visit on their spring break. We decided to go out on Saturday night to hear a local band. It never occurred to me to check with Sherry, because we hadn't made plans for that night. But she was so mad at me. She said, "We always go out on Fridays and Saturdays"—like it was written in stone or something.

As we noted in Chapter 4, two kinds of rules guide our communication. *Constitutive rules* define how to interpret communication. For instance, some people count listening to problems as caring, whereas others count engaging in activities to divert attention from problems as caring (Tavris, 1992; Wood, 2001c). Families often have constitutive rules that define what kinds of communication symbolize love and commitment (visiting at least three times a year, remembering birthdays). Romantic partners work out constitutive rules that define the kinds of communication that express loyalty, support, rudeness, love, joking, acceptance, and so forth. Constitutive rules are worked out over time as people in personal relationships learn what things mean to each other and what each of them needs and wants.

Regulative rules govern interaction by specifying when and with whom to engage in various kinds of communication. For example, friends and family members often operate according to a regulative rule that says it's okay to criticize each other in private but to do so in front of others is not acceptable. Many children are taught that it's impolite to interrupt others, particularly elders. Some romantic partners limit physical displays of affection to private settings.

Friends, families, and romantic partners generate rules that define what they want and expect in terms of emotional support, time, and practical help. Equally important are "shalt not" rules that define what each won't tolerate. For example, most Westerners would consider it a betrayal if a friend became sexually involved with their romantic partner. Some families have strong "shalt not" rules that members cannot marry outside their race, religion, or ethnic group. Rules regulate both trivial and important aspects of interaction. Not interrupting may be a rule, but breaking it probably won't wreck a good friendship. On the other hand, deceitful communication or abuse may sound the death knell of a friendship. The Sharpen Your Skill box on page 212 highlights some common rules in Western friendships and invites you to see if they apply to your friendships.

Affected by Contexts Personal relationships are not isolated from the social world. Instead, the surroundings of relationships influence interaction between people (Allan, 1993; Baxter, 1993; Dainton, 2006; Felmlee, 2001; Klein & Milardo, 2000). Neighborhoods, social circles, family units, and society as a whole affect friendships and

T E C H N O L O G Y

STAYING IN TOUCH

Today's college students tend to stay in touch with their parents. On average, college students call, e-mail or send text messages to their parents 10.4 times a week. Not surprisingly, the main topic of communication is finances (30.6% of students), but that's not the only topic. College students also talk with parents about career planning (19.9%), academics (12.6%), health and safety (7.7%), and personal relationships (7.2%) (Setoodeh, 2006).

romances. For instance, Western culture values heterosexual marriage, which means that men and women who marry generally receive more social support than do singles, cohabiting heterosexuals, or gay and lesbian couples (Strasser, 1997).

Our families of origin influence what we look for in people with whom we want close relationships. Our families pass on their views of the importance of social status, income, appearance, race, religion, intelligence, and so on (Monsour, 2002). Our social circles establish norms for such activities as religious involvement, drinking, political activism, participation in community groups, studying, and partying. Circumstances in the larger society may also influence interaction between intimates. For instance, during deep recessions people who are laid off may experience a diminished sense of self-worth. Because personal relationships are systems (see Chapter 8), shifts in financial security and self-worth reverberate throughout relationships, causing ripples of change throughout the systems. The many social contexts of our lives affect what we expect of relationships and how we communicate in them.

Particular others as well as the generalized other, which we discussed in Chapter 9, affect activities and expectations in personal relationships. Families may voice approval or disapproval of our choices of intimates or the way we organize our private relationships. Our society's technological advances and mobility make long-distance relationships more possible than ever (Carl, 2006; Sahlstein, 2006a, b), perhaps even inevitable. The growing number of dual-career couples is revising traditional expectations about how much each partner participates in earning income, homemaking, and child care (Galvin, 2006). As our society becomes more culturally diverse, interracial, interreligious, and interethnic personal relationships become more common and more socially accepted. The number of interracial marriages tripled between 1970 and 2002, and interracial dating grew at an even higher rate (Troy & Laurenceau, 2006). Thus, our social circles and the larger society as well are contexts that influence the relationships we form and the ways we communicate within them.

Rules of Friendship

Researchers (Argyle & Henderson, 1984) asked Westerners what it takes to maintain a good friendship. Below are 11 rules that people identified in 1984. Which of these rules apply to your friendships today?

1. Stand up for a friend who isn't around.
2. Share your successes and how you feel about them.
3. Give emotional support.
4. Trust and confide in each other.
5. Help a friend when she or he needs it.
6. Respect a friend's privacy.
7. Try to make friends feel good.
8. Tolerate your friend's friends.
9. Don't criticize a friend in front of others.
10. Don't tell a friend's confidences to other people.
11. Don't nag or focus on a friend's faults.

SHARPEN YOUR SKILL

Relationship Dialectics A final quality of personal relationships is the presence of **relationship dialectics.** These are opposing and continuous tensions that are normal in all close relationships. Leslie Baxter, a scholar of interpersonal communication, and her colleagues identified three relationship dialectics (Anderson, Baxter, & Cissna, 2004; Baxter, 1990, 1993; Baxter & Montgomery, 1996).

The **autonomy/connection** dialectic involves the desires to be separate, on the one hand, and to be connected, on the other, the opposition of which creates tension. Because we want to be deeply linked to others, we cherish spending time with our intimates, sharing experiences, and feeling connected. At the same time, each of us needs an independent identity. We don't want relationships to swallow our individuality, so we seek distance, even from our intimates.

Most people in personal relationships experience a continuous friction as a result of the contradictory desires for autonomy and connection (Beck, 1988; Erbert, 2000). Friends and romantic partners may vacation together and be with each other constantly for a week or more. They're often surprised when they return home and crave time apart. Intense immersion in togetherness prompts us to reestablish independent identity. When we get together with our families during holidays, we're often excited about catching up and talking intensely. Yet we often feel glad when the visit is over and we can part from families for a time. Both autonomy and closeness are natural human needs. The challenge is to nurture both individuality and intimacy.

The dialectic of **novelty/predictability** is the opposition of the desire for familiar routines and the desire for novelty. We like a certain amount of routine to provide security and predictability in our lives. Friends often have standard times to get together, families develop rituals for holidays and birthdays, and romantic couples settle on preferred times and places for going out (Bruess & Hoefs, 2006; Duck, 2006; Wood, 2006a). Yet too much routine is boring, so we seek novel experiences. Friends may take up a new sport together, families may plan unusual vacations, and romantic partners might explore a new restaurant or do something spontaneous and different to introduce variety into their customary routine.

The third dialectic, **openness/closedness,** involves the desire for openness in tension with the desire for privacy. Although intimate relationships sometimes are idealized as totally open and honest, complete openness would be intolerable (Baxter, 1993, 2006; Petronio, 1991; Petronio & Caughlin, 2006). Most of us want to share our inner selves with our intimates, yet sometimes we may not feel like disclosing, and we may not care to discuss some topics with anyone. All of us need some privacy, and intimates need to respect that in each other. Families often share deep feelings and thoughts but don't discuss sexual activities and attitudes. Friends and romantic partners, on the other hand, may talk about sex and other personal topics but may not share family secrets. Wanting some privacy doesn't mean that people don't enjoy togetherness, nor does it signal that a relationship is in trouble. It means only that we need both openness and closedness in our lives.

Researchers have identified four ways in which friends and romantic partners deal with dialectical tensions (Baxter, 1990; Baxter & Simon, 1993). One response, called **neutralization,** negotiates a balance between the opposing dialectical forces. This involves striking a compromise in which both needs are met to an extent, but neither is fully satisfied. A couple might agree to be generally open but not highly disclosive.

Separation addresses one need in a dialectic and ignores the other. For example, friends might agree to make novelty a priority and suppress their needs for routine. Separation also occurs when partners cycle between dialectical poles to favor each pole alternately. Couples involved in long-distance relationships often spend weekends in close contact and don't see each other during the week.

A third way to manage dialectics is **segmentation,** in which partners assign each pole to certain spheres, issues, activities, or times. For instance, friends might be open about many topics but respect each other's privacy and refrain from prying in one or two areas. Family members often are connected about family matters but operate independently in other ways. Romantic partners might be autonomous in their professional activities yet connected in their interaction in the home and in their involvement with children. Some couples symbolize autonomy in careers and connectedness in personal life by using a joint name in social circumstances (Smith-Jones) and individual names in professional circles (Ellen Smith, Frank Jones). Jessica's commentary explains how segmentation surfaces in her relationship with her father.

▶ Jessica

I can talk about anything with my mom. She's like my best friend. She knows all about every part of my life. With my dad, it's a different story. We can talk about my classes and my job and cars and stuff like that. What we never, never talk about is dating and my boyfriends. Mom says he doesn't like to think about his "little girl" being romantically involved. Maybe that's it. All I know is that we don't ever talk about boys in my life.

The final method of managing dialectics is **reframing.** This is a complex strategy that redefines apparently contradictory needs as not really in opposition. My colleagues and I found clear examples of reframing in a study of intimate partners (Wood et al., 1994). Some couples said that their autonomy enhances closeness because knowing they are separate in some ways allows them to feel safer when they are connected. Instead of viewing autonomy and closeness as opposing, these partners transcended the apparent tension between the two to define the needs as mutually enhancing.

Research suggests that separation, which fulfills one need and squelches the contradictory one, is generally the least satisfying response (Baxter, 1990). Repressing any natural human impulse diminishes us. The challenge is to satisfy the variety of needs that we experience and that nurture our personal development. Understanding that dialectics are natural and constructive allows us to accept and grow from the tensions they generate.

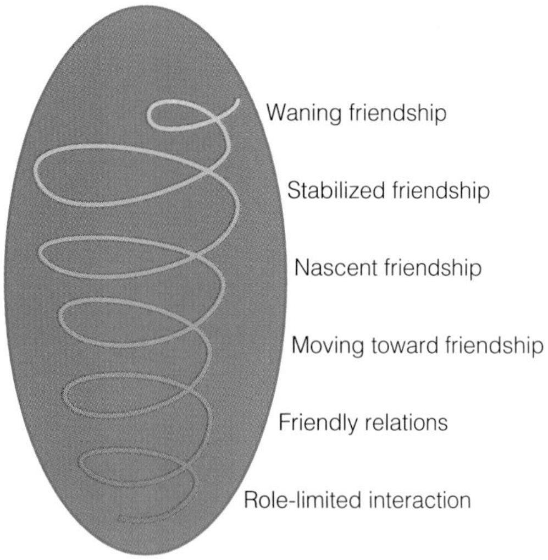

The Evolutionary Course of Personal Relationships

Every personal relationship develops at its own pace and in unique ways. Yet a majority of friendships and romances have some commonalities in their evolution.

Friendships Although friendships sometimes jump to life quickly, usually they unfold through a series of fairly predictable stages. Interpersonal communication researcher Bill Rawlins (1981, 1994) developed a six-stage model of how friendships develop (see Figure 10.1).

Waning friendship

Stabilized friendship

Nascent friendship

Moving toward friendship

Friendly relations

Role-limited interaction

Figure 10.1 THE STAGES OF FRIENDSHIP

Most friendships begin with *role-limited interactions*. We might meet a new person at work, through membership in teams or clubs, or by chance in an airport, store, or class. We might also meet a new person in a chat room or discussion forum and decide to move to private e-mail conversations with him or her (Parks & Floyd, 1996). During initial encounters, we tend to rely on standard social rules and roles. Generally, we stick with safe topics and exercise care in making disclosures, although disclosures sometimes are made more quickly online than in person (Lea & Spears, 1995; Parks & Roberts, 1998; Turkle, 1997). Willingness to take some risks early in a relationship may be greater when people aren't interacting face to face.

The second stage of friendship is *friendly relations*, in which each person checks the other out to see whether they have sufficient common ground and interests to develop a good friendship (Weinstock & Bond, 2000). According to communication scholar Michael Monsour (2002, 2006), most people seek friends who are like them in many ways, including age, background, interests, and status. Riddick tells Jason that he really likes adventure movies. If Jason says he does too, they've found a common interest and perhaps an activity they will share. A businessperson engages in small talk to see whether an associate wants to get more personal. People who have formed friendly relations over the Internet often talk about experiences, books, films, and ideas. Although friendly exchanges are not dramatic, they allow us to explore the potential for a deeper relationship with another person.

The third stage, *moving toward friendship*, involves stepping beyond social roles. To signal that we'd like to personalize a relationship, we could introduce a more personal topic than those we have discussed so far. We also move toward friendship when we schedule meetings and activities. People who have gotten to know each other over the Internet or on the web sometimes develop enough interest to meet in person. As people interact more personally, they begin to talk about feelings, values, goals, and attitudes (Yost, 2004). This personal knowledge forms the initial foundation of friendship. As Sylvia points out, the promise of an important new friendship can be very exciting.

> ### T E C H N O L O G Y
>
> **fyi**
>
> ### MEETING NEW PEOPLE THROUGH FACEBOOK
>
> Facebook is a wildly popular social networking service on college campuses, but it's also used by high schoolers and businesspeople. With 1½ million photos uploaded daily, Facebook is the number one site for photos and is the seventh most trafficked site in the United States (http://en.wikipedia.org/wiki/Facebook). Users create personal profiles, typically containing photos and lists of interests, exchange private or public messages, and join groups of friends. The viewing of detailed profile data is restricted to users from the same school or confirmed friends.
>
> Facebook began as a local effort at Harvard. Within a few weeks of its launch by Mark Zuckerberg in February 2004, more than half the undergraduate population at Harvard had registered. Just two months later, Facebook expanded to the rest of the Ivy League. By December 2004, Facebook had become a network phenomenon across the country. September 2005 saw the launch of a high school version of Facebook, which was originally kept totally separate from the college version. By October 2005, Facebook had expanded to universities outside the United States. To learn more about the history and usage of Facebook, go to the book's online resources and click on WebLink 10.1.

▶ **Sylvia**

One of the greatest feelings is being on the brink of a new friendship. It's that moment when you realize this person is going to be really special to you. It's like knowing something wonderful is going to happen and make your life richer. In a lot of ways, it's like infatuation early in a romantic relationship—anticipation and desire for more closeness.

The stage of *nascent friendship* is marked by increased involvement and caring. If initial interaction has been satisfying, people may begin to think of themselves as friends or as becoming friends. At this point, social norms and roles become less important in regulating interaction, and friends begin to work out their private ways of relating. When my friend Sue and I were in graduate school, we developed the ritual of calling each day between 5 and 6 P.M. to catch up. Some friends settle into patterns of getting together for specific things (watching games, shopping, racquetball, Saturday brunch, going to movies). Other friends share a wider range of times and activities. In this stage, people start thinking of themselves as friends, and they begin to work out private roles and rules for interaction. Thus, interaction between nascent friends establishes the basic patterns and climate of the friendship.

When friends are established in each other's lives, their relationship has stabilized. The benchmark of *the stabilized friendship* stage is the assumption of continuity. Whereas in earlier stages people didn't count on getting together unless they made a specific plan, stabilized friends assume they'll keep seeing each other. They no longer have to ask whether they'll get together, because they are committed to the relationship as continuous in their lives. Stabilized friends' communication reflects the assumption that they will keep seeing each other. For example, Luke might say, "What do you want to do this weekend?" rather than asking, "Do you want to get together this weekend?" The former question assumes that they will see each other.

Another criterion of this stage is trust. Through disclosing private information and responding with acceptance, friends earn each other's trust. In turn, they feel safe sharing even more intimate information and revealing vulnerabilities that they usually conceal (Monsour, 2002; Taylor, 2002). Stabilized friendships may continue indefinitely, in some cases for a lifetime.

Waning friendship exists when one or both people cease to be committed to their relationship. Sometimes friends drift apart because each is pulled in a different direction by career demands or personal circumstances. This reminds us of the influence of surrounding contexts on relationships. The common interests and experiences that once fueled the friendship begin to dissolve. Jean's commentary illustrates how changes can cause friendships to wither.

► Jean

Clark and I had been friends with Ted and Cori ever since we were undergraduates, all the way through our graduate programs, and for several years after we were all working. Then, Cori and Ted had a baby. At first, I didn't think it would affect our friendship, but gradually it did. Cori and Ted were always talking about their baby, and they wanted to bring the baby with them if we went out to dinner or had them to our house. And they were interested in issues like cloth versus disposable diapers and things that were just irrelevant to Clark and me. After a while it seemed there was nothing we really shared anymore.

Friendships may also deteriorate because they've run their natural course and become boring or are no longer enriching. The fact that some friendships don't last a lifetime doesn't mean that they aren't special and important for a period in our lives. The FYI box on this page points out that friends at a particular time and place in our lives are important to us, even though they aren't "forever friends." A third reason friendships end is the violation of rules. Telling a friend's secrets to a third person is a violation if you and your friend had an agreement to keep confidences. Being unsupportive in conversations may also violate rules of friendship. When friendships deteriorate, communication changes in predictable ways. Defensiveness and uncertainty rise, causing people to be more guarded and less open. Communication may also become more strategic as people try to protect themselves from further exposure and hurt.

Deterioration doesn't always lead to the end of the friendship. Even when serious violations occur between friends, relationships can sometimes be repaired. For this to happen, both friends must be committed to rebuilding trust and talking openly about their feelings and needs.

FRIENDS OF THE HEART AND FRIENDS OF THE ROAD

Lillian Rubin (1985) has made a career of studying close relationships, particularly friendships.

One of her more interesting findings is that there are two basic kinds of friends: friends of the heart and friends of the road.

Friends of the heart are people we meet who become part of us in enduring ways. They are soul mates with whom we feel deeply and permanently connected. If friends of the heart move far away from each other, they often stay in touch and visit. Even if they don't maintain regular contact, they feel deeply woven into each other's lives.

Friends of the road are friends we make and from whom we part as we travel the road of life. We make friends wherever we are, and we provide support, companionship, fun, and so forth. When they or we move, we make no effort to stay in touch or maintain any continuing sense of connection. Friends of the road are people we enjoy for a time, then leave behind.

Romantic Relationships Like friendships, many romantic relationships follow a similar evolutionary path. We perceive romantic relationships as escalating, navigating, or deteriorating. Within these three broad phases of romance are more specific stages (Figure 10.2).

Escalating romantic involvements typically involve six stages. The first stage is *no interaction*. We are aware of ourselves as individuals with particular needs, goals, and qualities that affect what we look for in romantic relationships. Before forming romantic relationships, we also have learned a number of constitutive and regulative communication rules that affect how we interact with others and how we interpret their communication.

The second stage is *invitational communication,* in which people verbally and nonverbally express interest in interacting (Metts, 2007). This stage involves both taking the initiative with others and responding to invitations they make

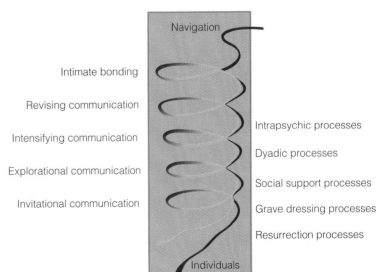

Intimate bonding
Revising communication
Intensifying communication
Explorational communication
Invitational communication

Navigation

Intrapsychic processes
Dyadic processes
Social support processes
Grave dressing processes
Resurrection processes

Individuals

Figure 10.2 THE EVOLUTION OF ROMANTIC RELATIONSHIPS

to us. "Want to dance?" "Where are you from?" and "Did you just move here?" are examples of invitations to interact. Invitational communication usually follows a conventional script for social conversation. The meaning of invitational communication is found on the relationship level, not the content level. "I love this kind of music" literally means that a person loves the music. On the relationship level of meaning, however, the message is "I'm available and interested. Are you?" Of all the people we meet, we are romantically attracted to only a few.

The two greatest influences on initial attraction are proximity and similarity. Proximity, or physical nearness, influences initial attraction. We can interact only with people we meet, whether in person or in cyberspace. Consequently, where we live, work, and socialize and the electronic networks in which we participate constrain the possibilities for relationships. This reminds us that communication is systemic. From our discussion in Chapter 1, recall that the systemic character of communication means that context affects what happens when people transact. Some contexts, such as college campuses, promote meeting potential romantic partners, whereas other contexts are less conducive to meeting and dating. Specialized electronic networks and home pages are set up for people who want to talk about particular topics, develop friendships, or meet potential romantic partners. Yet not all people have easy access to technology. People in lower economic strata are less likely to use the Internet, so they are less likely to meet people virtually and to develop relationships online (Flanigin, Farinola, & Metzger, 2000).

Similarity is also important in romantic relationships. In the realm of romance, "birds of a feather flock together" seems truer than "opposites attract." The **matching hypothesis** predicts that people will seek relationships with others who closely match their own values, attitudes, social background, and physical attractiveness. In general, we are attracted to people whose values, attitudes, and lifestyles are similar to ours. We tend to seek others who are similar to us in sexual orientation and values. Also important is similarity of social background because most people pair with others of their social background. In fact, social prestige influences dating patterns now more than it did in the 1950s (Whitbeck & Hoyt, 1994).

Similarity of personality is also linked to long-term marital happiness (Caspi & Harbener, 1990). In general, people tend to match themselves with people who are about as physically attractive as they are. We may fantasize about relationships with stunning people, but in reality we're likely to pass them by for someone at our level of attractiveness. In order for similarities between people to enhance attractive-

TECHNOLOGY

fyi

LOVE ONLINE

Worldwide, nearly 700 million people use the Internet (Global Reach, 2003). The average user spends most—70%—of her or his Internet time starting and building personal relationships (Nua Internet Surveys, 2002). One study of 852 undergraduates found that 46% of them had been involved in an online romantic relationship or knew someone who had been or currently was involved in an online romance (Wildemuth, 2001).

Although online romantic relationships and face-to-face romantic relationships are alike in some respects, they differ in notable ways. Compared to face-to-face relationships, online ones tend to form more rapidly, and they tend to involve more deliberate and sometimes deceptive attempts to control self-presentation (McQuillen, 2003; Walther, 1997). Also, online relationships foster idealized perceptions, so people involved in them are more likely than partners in face-to-face relationships to see each other in terms of what they want or need (McQuillen, 2003). Third, because physical presence is not part of online relationships, partners cannot experience the kind of closeness that is fueled by touch, shared silence, and nonverbal communication such as smiles and eye gaze (Cohen, 2001). Finally, online relationships tend to involve a lower level of commitment than offline relationships (Cornwell & Lundgren, 2001).

ness, the pair must recognize and communicate the similarities (Duck, 1994a, 1994b). In other words, attraction grows when people discuss common feelings, experiences, values, beliefs, backgrounds, and goals.

Explorational communication is the stage in which people explore the possibilities for a relationship. We communicate to announce our identities and learn about others'. As in early stages of friendship, potential romantic partners fish for common interests: "Do you like jazz?" "What's your family like?" "Do you follow politics?" As

we continue to interact with others, both breadth and depth of disclosure increase. People may talk about difficulties in their lives, reasons for divorces, health problems, and so forth. Because most of us perceive self-disclosure as a sign of trust, it tends to escalate intimacy. At this early stage of interaction, both people expect reciprocity of disclosure so that neither is more vulnerable than the other (Duck, 1992).

If explorational communication increases attraction, the relationship may escalate. *Intensifying communication* is the stage in which a relationship gains depth as a result of the increasing amount and intimacy of interaction. My students nicknamed this stage "euphoria" to emphasize the intensity and happiness it typi-

© Steve Prezant/Corbis

Euphoria!

cally embodies. During this phase, partners spend more and more time together, and they rely less on external structures such as movies or parties. During this phase, some couples are almost inseparable, a point made humorously in the cartoon below. They immerse themselves in the budding relationship and may feel they can't be together enough. They make further disclosures, fill in their biographies, and increasingly learn how the other feels and thinks. A study conducted by Brenda Meeks, Susan Hendrick, and Clyde Hendrick (1998) showed that satisfaction with romantic relationships is linked to making and receiving disclosures and being able to understand the partner's perspective.

The stage of *intensifying communication* often involves idealizing and personalized communication. Idealizing occurs when we see a relationship and partner as more

Zits

fyi

STYLES OF LOVING

Just as people differ in their tastes in food and dress, so do we differ in how we love. Researchers have identified six different styles of loving, each of which is valid, although not all styles are compatible with one another (Hendrick & Hendrick, 1996; Hendrick et al., 1984; Lee, 1973, 1988). Although these researchers refer to styles of "love," you will notice that both love and commitment characterize the styles. See whether you can identify your style of loving in the descriptions that follow:

Eros is a style of loving that is passionate, intense, and fast moving. Not confined to sexual passion, eros may be expressed in spiritual, intellectual, or emotional ways.

Storge (pronounced "store-gay") is a comfortable, "best friends" kind of love that grows gradually to create a stable, even-keeled companionship.

Ludus is a playful, sometimes manipulative style of loving. For ludic lovers, love is a challenge, a puzzle, a game to be relished but not to lead to commitment.

Mania is an unsettling style of loving marked by emotional extremes. Manic lovers often are insecure about their value and their partners' commitment.

Agape is a selfless kind of love in which a beloved's happiness is more important than one's own. Agapic lovers are generous, unselfish, and devoted.

Pragma is a pragmatic and goal-oriented style of loving. Pragmas rely on reason and practical considerations when initially selecting people to love.

wonderful, exciting, and perfect than they really are (Hendrick & Hendrick, 1988, 1996). During euphoria, partners often exaggerate each other's virtues, downplay or fail to notice vices, and overlook problems in the relationship. However, people experience intensifying in a variety of ways. A person who is calm and prefers to get to know someone gradually and as a friend first will not experience intensifying in the same way as a person who is impulsive and likes to move quickly in relationships. The FYI box on this page elaborates different styles of loving and committing.

It is also during euphoria that many couples begin to develop relationship vocabularies that include nicknames and private codes. Sometimes, Robbie and I greet each other by saying, *"Namaste."* This is a Nepali greeting that expresses goodwill. Saying it reminds us of our trek in the mountains of Nepal. Private language heightens partners' sense of being a special couple. Partners invent words and nicknames for each other, and they develop ways to send private messages in public settings. Private language both reflects and enhances intimacy ("Public Pillow Talk," 1987; Wood, 2006a).

Revising communication, although not part of escalation in all romantic relationships, occurs often enough to merit our consideration. During this stage, partners come down out of the clouds to talk about their relationship's strengths, problems, and potential for the future. With the rush of euphoria over, partners consider whether they want the relationship to last. In other words, they may assess whether they want to transform love into commitment. If so, they work through problems and obstacles to long-term viability. Some gay and lesbian partners have to resolve differences in openness about their sexual orientations. Couples may need to work out differences in religions and conflicts of location and career goals.

As you might expect, during this phase of romance, communication often involves negotiation and even conflict. This is natural because revising communication requires partners to talk about negative features of a relationship and ways to improve them. These topics seldom arise in earlier stages of romance because difficulties are not a serious problem until the couple contemplates a long-term future. Many couples are able to revise their relationships in ways that make them stronger and more able to endure. Other couples cannot resolve problems. Thus, people often fall in love and move through the intensifying stage yet choose not to stay together. As the FYI box on the next page points out, some couples have additional issues to work through in forming a long-term relationship.

Intimate bonding is the stage that occurs when partners decide to stay with a relationship permanently. This decision transforms a relationship from one based on past and present experiences and feelings into one with a future. Before they make a commitment, partners don't view the relationship as continuing forever. With commitment, the relationship becomes a given around which they arrange other aspects of their lives. This stage is analogous to stabilized friendship because the basis of both is assumed continuity.

Navigating is the ongoing process of communicating to sustain intimacy over time and in the face of changes in partners, the relationship, and surrounding contexts. Although navigating can be an extended stage in romantic intimacy, it is not stable. In fact, it may be quite dynamic. Couples continuously work through new problems, revisit old ones, and accommodate changes in their individual and joint lives. To use an automotive analogy, navigating involves both preventive maintenance and periodic repairs (Canary & Stafford, 1994). Navigating communication aims to keep intimacy satisfying and healthy and to deal with problems and tensions.

The nucleus of an established intimate relationship is its **relationship culture,** which is the private world of rules, understandings, meanings, and patterns of interacting that partners create for their relationship (Wood, 1982). A relationship culture is developed over time. By the time a couple commits to an intimate relationship, there is a well-established relationship culture, but it is not static. Instead, it will continue to evolve throughout the life of the relationship.

The concept of the relationship culture includes how a couple manages relationship dialectics. Chris and Jimmie may do a great many things together, whereas Lana and Kaya emphasize autonomy. Brent and Carmella may be open and expressive, whereas Marion and Paige prefer more privacy in their marriage. There aren't right and wrong ways to manage dialectics, because individuals and couples differ in their needs and in their preferences for managing tensions between autonomy and connection, openness and privacy, and novelty and routine.

A relationship culture includes communication rules that partners work out. Couples develop agreements, usually unspoken, about how to signal anger, love, sexual interest, and so forth. They also develop routines for contact. Some couples catch up while they fix dinner each day (Wood, 2006a), whereas other couples reserve weekends or a specific night for catching up (Duck, 2006). Especially important in navigating is small talk, through which partners weave the fabric of their history and their current lives, experiences, and dreams.

DIVERSITY

fyi

STAGES IN THE ESCALATION OF INTERRACIAL RELATIONSHIPS

Interracial romantic relationships are increasing in the United States. In addition to the stages generally followed in developing intimacy, partners in interracial relationships often deal simultaneously with relationship stages prompted by external pressures, such as biases against interracial dating and disapproval by friends and family members.

The following model (Foeman & Nance, 1999) describes four stages experienced by many interracial romantic partners.

1. Racial awareness: Each partner becomes conscious of his or her racial identity and views of the partner's racial identity. In addition, partners heighten awareness of broad social perspectives on their own and the other's racial groups.

2. Coping: The couple struggles with external pressures, including families' and friends' disapproval, and develops strategies to protect their relationship from external damage.

3. Identity emergence: Partners reject external definitions of who they are and declare their couple identity to others. Partners also develop a definition of the relationship for themselves.

4. Relationship maintenance: The couple works to preserve the relationship as it incorporates new challenges, such as having children, moving to new areas, and entering new social circles.

Not all intimately bonded relationships endure. Despite the popular belief that love is forever, often it isn't forever and may not even be for very long. Tensions within a relationship as well as pressures and problems in surrounding contexts may contribute to the ending of the intimate bond. Steve Duck (1982) proposed a five-phase model of relationship deterioration. Working together, Duck and I (Duck & Wood, 2006) recently revised his original model to emphasize the processual nature of relationship decline. Instead of representing relationship deterioration as a sequence of stages, Duck and his colleagues emphasize that relationships decline through a series of processes, each of which is complex and dynamic.

Intrapsychic processes launch relational deterioration. During these processes, one or both partners individually think about and sometimes brood about problems in the relationship and dissatisfactions with the other partner. It's easy for intrapsychic processes to become self-fulfilling prophecies: As gloomy thoughts snowball and awareness of positive features of the relationship ebbs, partners may actually bring about the failure of their relationship. There are some general sex and gender differences in what partners brood about during intrapsychic processes (Duck & Wood, 2006; Wood, 1993c, 1993d, 2007. For women, unhappiness with a relationship most often arises when communication declines in quality or quantity.

One of the first signs that a relationship may dissolve is brooding about problems and dissatisfaction.

Men are more likely to be dissatisfied by specific behaviors or the lack of valued behaviors. For instance, some men report being dissatisfied when their partners don't greet them at the door and make special meals (Riessman, 1990). For many men, dissatisfaction also arises if they have domestic responsibilities that they feel aren't a man's job (Gottman & Carrère, 1994). Existing research suggests that many women feel a relationship is breaking down if "we don't really communicate with each other anymore," whereas men are more likely to feel dissatisfied if "we don't do fun things together anymore."

Dyadic processes usually—but not always—come next. These processes first may involve the breakdown of established patterns, understandings, and rules that have been part of the relationship. Partners may stop talking after dinner, no longer bother to call when they are running late, and in other ways depart from rules and patterns that have defined their relational culture. As the fabric of intimacy weakens, dissatisfaction mounts. Partners may want to talk about their problems and dissatisfactions. Because many women are socialized to be sensitive to interpersonal nuances, they are generally more likely than men to notice tensions and early symptoms of relationship distress (Wood, 2007).

Dyadic process may involve conflict. Communication scholars report that many people avoid talking about problems, refuse to return calls from partners, and in other ways evade confronting difficulties (Baxter, 1984; Metts, Cupach, & Bejlovec, 1989). We have an ethical responsibility to consider whether we should avoid problems and conceal our thoughts and feelings from a partner. Although it is painful to talk about problems, avoiding discussion does nothing to resolve them and may make them worse. What happens during dyadic processes depends on how committed partners are, whether they perceive attractive alternatives to the relationship, and whether they have the communication skills to work through problems constructively.

A recent study (Battaglia et al., 1998) found that many college undergraduates follow a cyclical pattern when breaking up. They pull apart and get back together several times before actually ending the relationship. If partners lack commitment or the communication skills they need to restore intimacy, they enter into **social support processes,** which signal an increase in the likelihood of breaking up. At first, social support processes tend to center on telling others about problems in the relationship. Once relationship troubles are aired to people outside the relationship, it is harder to ignore them or their seriousness.

Another facet of social support processes is seeking comfort and assistance in dealing with a possible or probable breakup. Friends and family members can provide support by being available and by listening. Partners may give self-serving accounts of the breakup to save face and secure sympathy from others. Thus, Vera may tell her friends all the ways in which Frank was at fault and portray herself as the innocent party. Each partner may criticize the other and expect friends to take sides (Duck & Wood, 2006). Although self-serving explanations of breakups are common, they aren't necessarily constructive. We have an ethical responsibility to monitor communication during this period so that we don't say things we'll later regret.

If partners decide they will definitely part ways, they move into **grave dressing processes.** One important part of grave dressing is that partners decide, either separately or in collaboration, how to explain their problems to friends, co-workers, children, in-laws, and social acquaintances. When partners don't craft a joint explanation for breaking up, friends may take sides, gossip, and disparage one or the other partner (La Gaipa, 1982).

During grave dressing, each person also works individually to make sense of the relationship: what it meant, why it failed, and how it affected us. Typically, we mourn a relationship that has died. Even the person who initiates a breakup often is sad about the failure to realize what seemed possible at one time. Yet mourning and sadness may be accompanied by other, more positive outcomes from breakups. Ty Tashiro and Patricia Frazier (2003) surveyed undergraduates who had recently broken up with a romantic partner. They found that breakups generate not only distress but also personal growth. People reported that breaking up gave them new insights into themselves, improved family relationships, and clarified their ideas about future partners. Grave dressing processes allow partners to put the relationship to rest so that they can get on with their individual lives.

The final part of relationship deterioration is **resurrection processes,** which involve each ex-partner's moving ahead to a future without the other. The processes we've discussed describe how many people experience the evolution of friendship and romance. However, not everyone follows the pattern presented here. Some people skip one or more of the processes, and many of us cycle more than once through certain processes. For example, a couple might soar through euphoria, work out some tough issues in revising, then go through euphoria a second time. It's also normal for long-term

T E C H N O L O G Y

fyi

TRACKING BREAKUPS

Ever wish you had an easy way to know if someone you have a crush on breaks up with his or her current partner? Thanks to Single-Stat.us, now you do! Pay a small fee, and this service will notify you when someone who has a Myface profile breaks up. Mention SingleStat.us on your own Myface profile, and SingleStat.us will waive the fee.

Your Romance

Think about a romantic relationship that you have had. If the phases listed here were part of your relationship's evolution, how closely did what happened in each one match the discussion in this chapter?

Escalating

Intimate bonding

Navigating

Deterioration

SHARPEN YOUR SKILL

partners to move out of navigation periodically as they experience both euphoric seasons and intervals of dyadic breakdown. Similarly, couples may lapse into intrapsychic processes and then invest more in the relationship to revive their intimacy. What remains constant as long as intimacy exists is partners' commitment to a future and their investment in the relationship. The Sharpen Your Skill box on this page invites you to see if the process of relational evolution we've discussed describes a romantic relationship in your life.

▶GUIDELINES FOR COMMUNICATING IN PERSONAL RELATIONSHIPS

To sustain fulfilling personal relationships, partners rely on communication to deal with internal tensions and external pressures. How skillfully we manage these challenges is a major influence on the endurance and quality of personal relationships. We'll consider four specific guidelines to help friends and romantic partners sustain satisfying relationships.

Adapt Communication to Manage Distance

Geographic separation can be difficult for friends and romantic couples. Many of us will be involved in long-distance romantic relationships, because they are increasingly common. Fully 70% of college students are or have been in long-distance romances (Guldner, 2003), and even more have been or are involved in long-distance friendships and family relationships (Salhstein, 2006a, 2006b).

The number of long-distance relationships is likely to increase in the years ahead. Perhaps the two greatest problems for long-distance commitments are the lack of daily communication about small events and issues, and unrealistic expectations about interaction when partners are geographically together (Stafford, 2005). Greg's commentary offers an example of both of these problems.

▶ Greg

When Annie and I first moved to different cities, I don't know whether it was harder being apart or together. I missed her so much when we were apart for weeks at a time, and I really missed just being together in a laid-back kind of way. But whenever we were together, we both felt really pressured to be together every minute and not to have any disagreements or bad times. That's just not possible, and expecting it really caused us a lot of grief. Now, we are careful to call and stay in touch with e-mail so that we feel part of each other's regular lives. And we've learned that it's okay to have some private time even when we're together for only a few days.

The first problem—not being able to share small talk and daily routines—is a major loss, especially for people who don't have access to cell phones and e-mail. As we have seen, communication about ordinary topics weaves partners' lives together. Mundane conversations between friends and romantic partners are the foundation of relationships.

A second common problem is unrealistic expectations for time together. Because partners have so little time when they are physically together, they often believe that every moment must be perfect. They feel there should be no conflict and that they should spend every minute together. Yet this is an unrealistic expectation. The need for some autonomy may even be higher for long-distance couples because partners are used to living alone and have established independent rhythms that may not mesh well.

The good news is that these problems don't necessarily sabotage long-distance romance. Many couples maintain satisfying commitments despite geographic separation (Rohlfing, 1995; Stafford, 2006). To overcome the difficulties of long-distance love, partners engage in creative communication to sustain intimacy. Developments in communication technologies have increased the ways in which people can stay in touch. In addition to visiting each other several times each

COPING WITH GEOGRAPHIC SEPARATION

Following are some strategies that people report are helpful in sustaining long-distance love (Franklin & Ramage, 1999; Justice, 1999; Stafford, 2006):

1. Recognize that long-distance relationships are common; you're not alone.

2. Create more social support systems (friends) while separated from a romantic partner.

3. Communicate creatively; send video- and audiotapes.

4. Before separating, work out ground rules for going out with friends, phoning, visiting, and writing.

5. Use time together wisely: Be affectionate and have fun. Being serious all the time isn't smart.

6. Maintain honesty. Especially when partners live apart, they need to be straight with each other.

7. Build an open, supportive communication climate so you can talk about issues and feelings.

8. Maintain trust by abiding by ground rules that were agreed on, phoning when you say you will, and keeping lines of communication open.

9. Focus on the positive aspects of separation, such as career advancement or ability to concentrate on work.

10. Set a time limit for how long you'll be apart.

To discover additional ways of managing long-distance relationships, go to the book's online resources and click on WebLink 10.2.

year, my sister and I send each other videocassettes of important moments in our families' lives. My newspaper reported that a soldier serving in Iraq watched his daughter graduate from college in a live Internet broadcast (Hall, 2006).

Ensure Equity in Family Relationships

Today, most adults work outside the home. Therefore, partners in a relationship must balance the demands and pressures of two careers with investment in the relationship itself. Research shows that the greatest problem dual-career couples face is not geographic distance or trade-offs in career opportunities. Instead, it is the equity—or the lack of the equity—of the two partners' contributions toward joint responsibilities. According to **equity theory,** people are happier and more satisfied with equitable relationships than with inequitable ones. In equitable relationships, partners perceive that the benefits and costs of being in the relationship are about equal for each of them. Perceived inequity lowers relationship satisfaction. Researchers report that the happiest dating and married couples feel that partners invest equally (Buunk & Mutsaers, 1999; Hecht, Marston, & Larkey, 1994). When we think we are investing more than our partner is, we tend to be resentful. When it seems our partner is investing more than we are, we may feel guilty. Imbalance of either sort erodes satisfaction.

Although few partners demand moment-to-moment equality, most of us want our relationships to be equitable over time (Dainton & Zelley, 2006). Equity has multiple dimensions. We may evaluate the fairness of financial, emotional, physical, and other contributions to a relationship. One area that strongly affects satisfaction of spouses and cohabiting partners is equity in housework and child care. Inequitable division of domestic obligations fuels dissatisfaction and resentment, both of which harm intimacy (Anderson & Guerrero, 1998; Gottman & Carrère, 1994; Wood, 1998). Marital stability is more closely linked to equitable divisions of child care and housework than to income or sex life.

Traditionally, women were assigned care of the home and family because men were more likely to be the primary or only wage earners. That is no longer true. Today, most adults of both sexes work outside the home. Unfortunately, divisions of family and home responsibilities have not changed much in response to changing employment patterns. Even when both partners in heterosexual relationships work outside the home, in most dual-career families women do most of the child care and homemaking (Gerson, 2004; Guldner, 2003; Hochschild with Machung, 2003; Risman & Godwin, 2001; Steil, 2000; Taylor, 2002). In her commentary, Molly gives us insight into the resentment that can grow when both partners work outside the home but only one does a significant amount of work in and for the home.

Connect with Others in Long-Distance Relationships

If you are in a long-distance relationship, you can learn a lot from others who are or have been in one. There are websites and online communities devoted to long-distance relationships. Most of them offer advice, and some feature stories in which people who are in or have been in long-distance relationships share experiences and ideas about what worked and didn't work. Clicking on WebLinks 10.3, 10.4, and 10.5 within the book's online resources will take you to three sites that focus on managing long-distance relationships.

SHARPEN YOUR SKILL

▶ Molly

It really isn't fair when both spouses work outside the home but only one of them takes care of the home and kids. For years, that was how Jake's and my marriage worked, no matter how much I tried to talk with him about a fairer arrangement. Finally, I had just had it, so I quit doing everything. Groceries didn't get bought, laundry piled up, and he didn't have clean shirts, he didn't remember his mother's birthday (and for the first time ever, I didn't remind him), bills didn't get paid. After a while, he suggested we talk about a system we could both live with.

How do gay and lesbian partners manage domestic responsibilities? According to existing research, lesbian couples generally create more egalitarian relationships than either heterosexuals or gay men do. More than any other type of couple, lesbians are likely to communicate collaboratively to make decisions about domestic work and parenting (Huston & Schwartz, 1995). Consequently, lesbians are least likely to have negative feelings involving inequity (Kurdek, 1993). Gay men, like heterosexual men, tend to use the power derived from income to authorize inequitable contributions to domestic life. In gay couples, the man who makes more money has and uses more power, both in making decisions that affect the relationship and in avoiding housework (Huston & Schwartz, 1995). This suggests that power is the basis of gendered divisions of labor and that men, more than women, seek the privileges of power, including evasion of domestic work.

Not only do women usually do more of the actual labor of maintaining a home and caring for children, but also, as a rule, they assume a greater portion of **psychological responsibility,** which involves remembering, planning, and coordinating domestic activities (Wood, 2006b). Parents may alternate taking children to the doctor, but it is usually the mother who remembers when the kids need checkups, makes the appointments, and reminds the father to take the children. Both partners sign cards and give gifts, but in many families it is women who assume responsibility for remembering the birthdays and buying the cards and gifts (Steil, 2000). Successful long-term relationships in our era require partners to communicate collaboratively to design equitable divisions of responsibility.

Avoid Intimate Partner Violence

I was writing this chapter on May 19, 2006. That morning, my daily newspaper carried this headline: "Teens say dates often are violent." The article reported a study by the Centers for Disease Control and Prevention that found 1 in 11 teens are bruised by dates, and 8.9% of students in grades 9 through 12 reported experiencing physical violence from a date in the past year (Bowman, 2006).

Although we like to think of romantic relationships as loving, many are not. Violence and abuse are unfortunately common between romantic partners, and they cut across lines of socioeconomic status, race, and ethnicity (Goode, 2001; West, 1995). Violence is high not only in heterosexual marriages but also in dating and cohabiting relationships (Feldman & Ridley, 2000; Goode, 2001; Johnson &

Ferraro, 2000). It also appears that cohabiting couples have the highest incidence of violence of all couples: In addition to physical abuse, verbal and emotional brutality poison altogether too many relationships.

Although both sexes can engage in intimate partner violence, the majority of detected violence in intimacy is committed by men against women (Johnson, 2006; Johnson & Ferraro, 2000; Wood, 2004b). In the United States, each year 4 million incidents of violence against women by intimate partners are reported (National Coalition Against Domestic Violence, 1999) and 1,000 women are known to be murdered by boyfriends or husbands (http://www.fbi.gov/ucr/cius_00/contents.pdf). These are conservative figures that summarize only *reported* cases of intimate partner violence; many incidents go unreported. Although women are more often the victims of intimate partner violence, men, too, can be victims, as Travis notes in his commentary.

▶ **Travis**

A couple of years ago, I was in an abusive relationship, and I put a restraining order on my ex-girlfriend. She came to my house and attacked me anyway, and at first the police officer I called didn't believe me. After he'd investigated and talked to witnesses, he arrested her, but it was really upsetting to me that he just assumed I was at fault because I'm the male.

Violence seldom stops without intervention. Instead, in most cases it follows a predictable cycle: Tension mounts in the abuser; the abuser explodes, becoming violent; the abuser then is remorseful and loving; the victim feels loved and reassured that the relationship is working; then tension mounts anew, and the cycle begins again (Figure 10.3).

Communication and violence are related in two ways. Most obviously, patterns of communication between couples and abusers' patterns of intrapersonal communication can fuel tendencies toward violence. Some partners deliberately annoy and taunt each other, a pattern that can lead to extreme violence. Also, the language that abusers use to describe physical assaults on partners includes denial, trivializing the harm done, and blaming the partner or circumstances for "making me do it" (Johnson, 2006; Stamp & Sabourin, 1995; Wood, 2004b). These intrapersonal communication patterns allow abusers to deny their offenses, justify unjustifiable actions, and cast responsibility outside themselves.

Cultural communication practices that normalize violence also promote violence between intimates. Rape and other physical violations of

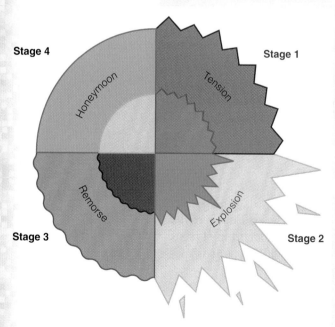

Figure 10.3 THE CYCLE OF ABUSE

women saturate the media. From magazines to films to television, violence is pervasive. News accounts camouflage the brutality of violence when they refer to "loving her too much" and "love that gets out of hand" (Meyers, 1994, 1997).

Violent relationships are *not* the fault of victims. Other than self-defense, there is no justification for physical violence against an intimate. A person cannot earn battering, nor do victims encourage it. If you know or suspect that someone you care about is a victim of abuse, don't ignore the situation, and don't assume it's none of your business. It is an act of friendship to notice and offer to help. Victims of violence must make the ultimate decision about what to do, but the support and concern of friends can help them.

Insist on Safer Sex

In this era of HIV and AIDS, sexual activities pose serious, even deadly threats (Greene, Frey, & Derlega, 2002). Despite vigorous public education campaigns, a great many people still don't practice safer sex, which includes abstinence, restricting sexual activity to a single partner who has been tested and found to be free of HIV and other sexually transmitted diseases, and using latex condoms (Reel & Thompson, 1994). In the United States alone, the number of people infected with HIV is approximately 800,000, and more than 430,000 people have died of AIDS (CDC, 1998). Just four years later, in 2002, the Centers for Disease Control reported that nearly 1 million people in the United States have HIV (Maugh, 2002).

Sexual attraction and sexual activity are not necessarily limited to romantic relationships. Friendships between heterosexual men and women, gay men, or lesbians sometimes include sexual tensions. Because Western culture so strongly emphasizes gender and sex, it's difficult not to perceive people in sexual terms (Johnson, Stockdale, & Saal, 1991; Schneider & Kenny, 2000). Even if sexual activity doesn't occur, sexual undertones may ripple beneath the surface of friendships. Sexual attraction, tension, or invitations can be problems between friends when one party does not want to have a sexual relationship. Trust may be damaged if someone you consider a friend makes a pass at you (Reeder, 2000). Once a friend transgresses the agreed-upon boundaries of a friendship, it's hard to know how to act with each other and what to expect. If friends decide that sexual activity is appropriate for them, they should communicate about ways to make sexual activities safer.

Although most college students know about sexually transmitted diseases, they don't consistently follow safer sex techniques. Communication scholars have found two primary reasons. First, ironically, many people find it more embarrassing to talk about sex than to engage in it. They find it awkward to ask direct questions of partners ("Have you been tested for HIV?" "Are you having sex with anyone else?") or to make direct requests of partners ("I want you to wear a condom," "I would like you to be tested for HIV before we have sex."). Because about 25% of people who are HIV positive are not aware of their medical infection, tests are imperative before having sexual relationships (Maugh, 2002). Naturally, it's difficult to talk explicitly about sex and the dangers of STDs. However, it is far more difficult to live with HIV or another disease or the knowledge that you infected another person.

A second reason people sometimes fail to negotiate safer sex is that alcohol or other drugs have diminished their rational thought and control. In a series of studies of college students' sexual activities, communication researchers Sheryl Bowen and Paula Michal-Johnson (1995, 1996) report that when people drink heavily, they are especially likely to neglect safer sex precautions. Alcohol and

Test Your Knowledge about Sexually Transmitted Diseases

Many people hold dangerous misunderstandings about sexually transmitted diseases (STDs). Here's a chance for you to test your knowledge against the facts (American Social Health Association, 2005; Cates, Herndon, Schulz,& Darroch, 2004; Weinstock, Berman, & Cates, 2004).

Misconception: If I'm tested for HIV and make sure any sexual partner is, I'm safe.

Get the Facts: HIV is not the only STD, and it's not the most common. Other STDs are genital warts, genital herpes, hepatitis B, chlamydia, gonorrhea, human papillomavirus (HPV), syphilis, and trichomoniasis. One in 20 people will get hepatitis B in his or her lifetime, and 15–25% of those who do will die from liver disease.

Misconception: I'm not taking much of a chance because few people have STDs.

Get the Facts: By age 25, 1 of 2 sexually active youths will contract an STD. More than 65 million Americans are currently living with an STD, and 15 million new cases are diagnosed each year.

Misconception: STDs affect older people.

Get the Facts: Half of all new STDs occur in people 15 to 24 years old. Each year, 1 in 4 teens contracts an STD.

Misconception: The incidence of STDs is declining.

Get the Facts: Some STDs, such as genital warts, are actually increasing.

Misconception: I can't catch an STD if I have only oral sex.

Get the Facts: Think again. You can catch STDs from oral, anal, or vaginal sexual activity. People who think oral sex is safe are mistaken.

Misconception: I could tell if someone had an STD because there are symptoms.

Get the Facts: Many STDs have no symptoms or no early ones. For instance, HPV, which 50% of sexually active people will contract at some point, often has no symptoms.

Misconception: STDs can be treated, so there aren't serious consequences even if I do get one.

Get the Facts: Some can be treated. Some are resistant to treatment. And because some have no symptoms, people may not seek treatment until it's too late.

Misconception: I see a doctor regularly, so I am tested for STDs.

Get the Facts: Most doctors do not routinely test for STDs.

Misconception: Other than HIV, STDs don't have major consequences.

Get the Facts: Because STDs often have no symptoms, they may go untreated for some time. Effects of STDs include infertility, blindness, liver cancer, increased vulnerability to HIV, and death.

Learn more about STDs by going to the book's online resources and clicking on WebLink 10.6.

SHARPEN YOUR SKILL

other drugs loosen inhibitions, including appropriate concerns about personal safety.

Good communication skills help ease the discomfort of negotiating safer sex. It is more constructive to say, "I feel unsafe having unprotected sex" than "Without a condom, you could give me an STD" (note that the first statement uses *I*-language, whereas the second one uses *you*-language). Relationship language fosters a positive communication climate; for example, talk about *our safety* and *our relationship* when negotiating sexual activity (Reel & Thompson, 1994). People who care about themselves and their partners are honest about their sexual histories and assertive about safer sex practices.

▶SUMMARY

In this chapter, we've explored communication in personal relationships, which are defined by commitment, uniqueness, relationship dialectics, relationship rules, and interaction with surrounding contexts. We traced the typical evolutionary paths of friendships and romances by noting how partners communicate during escalating, stabilizing, and declining trajectories of personal relationships. As we saw, communication is a primary dynamic in intimacy, influencing how we meet and get to know others, the patterns of interaction between friends and romantic partners, and the creation of relationship cultures that, ideally, are healthy and affirming.

In the final section of the chapter, we considered four important guidelines for friends and romantic partners. The communication principles and skills we have discussed in this and previous chapters can help us meet the challenges of sustaining intimacy across geographic distance, creating equitable relationships, resisting violence, and negotiating safer sex. Good communication skills are essential to managing these challenges so that we, our intimates, and the relationships we create survive and thrive over time.

Review, Reflect, Extend

The Key Concepts, For Further Reflection and Discussion questions, Recommended Resources, and Experience Communication Case Study that follow will help you review, reflect on, and extend the information and ideas presented in this chapter. A diverse selection of online resources is also available through ThomsonNOW. These resources include Speech Builder Express, InfoTrac College Edition, interactive videos, vMentor, and Thomson Audio Study Products.

Thomson NOW! is an online study system designed to help you put your time to the best use. After reading a chapter, take the NOW pre-test to identify concepts discussed in the chapter that you may not fully understand. Based on the results of this diagnostic test, the system will create a personalized study plan that directs you to specific learning resources and activities. To see if you're ready for an exam, take the NOW post-test to check your understanding.

For more information or to access this book's online resources, visit **http://www.thomsonedu.com**.

►Key Concepts

The terms following are defined in the chapter on the page number indicated, and they appear in alphabetical order, with definitions, in the Glossary, which be-gins on page 369. The book's online resources also include flash cards and crossword puzzles to help you learn these terms and the concepts they represent.

agape, 220
autonomy/connection, 213
commitment, 210
dyadic processes, 222
equity theory, 226
eros, 220
grave dressing processes, 223
intrapsychic processes, 222
investment, 210
ludus, 220

mania, 220
matching hypothesis, 218
neutralization, 213
novelty/predictability, 213
openness/closedness, 213
passion, 210
personal relationship, 209
pragma, 220
psychological responsibility, 227
reframing, 214

relationship culture, 221
relationship dialectics, 212
resurrection processes, 223
rules, 210
segmentation, 214
separation, 213
social relationship, 209
social support processes, 223
storge, 220

►For Further Reflection and Discussion

The questions below can also be found among the book's online resources for this chapter, where you have the option of e-mailing your responses to your instructor, if required.

1. Think about the distinction between love and commitment and the role each plays in personal relationships. Describe relationships in which commitment is present but love is not. Describe relationships in which love exists, but not commitment. What can you conclude about the impact of each?

2. Review the rules of friendship that researchers have identified (see the Sharpen Your Skill box on page 212). Do these match your experiences in friendships? Do you have additional rules that are unique to your close friendships?

3. Think about differences in the goals and rules for friendships and romantic relationships. Does com-paring the two kinds of relationships give you any insight into the difficulties that commonly arise when two people who have been friends become romantically involved? What are the difficulties of trying to be friends with someone with whom you've been romantically involved?

4. Are you now or have you been involved in a long-distance personal relationship, either friendship or romance? How did you communicate to bridge the distance? Do your experiences parallel the chapter's discussion of challenges in long-distance relationships?

►Recommended Resources

1. C. Hendrick & S. Hendrick (Eds.). 2000. *Close relationships: A sourcebook.* Thousand Oaks, CA: Sage. You probably won't want to read this entire book, but it's a great resource on research about a range of topics relevant to close relationships across the lifespan. If you want to know more about a particular issue or relationship dynamic (e.g., attachment styles, maintaining relationships, multiracial relationships), this reference is an excellent starting place.

2. Visit an online dating service. Identify qualities men and women claim they have and qualities men and women are looking for in romantic partners. What similarities and differences can you identify?

3. Many men as well as women are committed to ending violence against women. To learn more about men who are committed to stopping violence, go to the book's online resources and click on WebLink 10.7.

4. View the film, *About a Boy* (2002), directed by Paul and Chris Weitz. The story is about a surprising and unusual friendship between a selfish single man and a lonely boy. The central themes are friendship and support.

Experience Communication Case Study

ABUSE

The book's online resources include an interactive video of the communication situation featured in the case study scripted below. Apply what you've learned in this chapter by analyzing the case study, using the questions that follow the script as a guide. These questions are also available online with the video.

Amy met Hailley at the beginning of the school year. Amy was drawn to Hailley because she seemed confident and positive. Over several months, the two of them became good friends, sharing high and low points about school, family, and dates.

Two months ago, Hailley started dating Dan, a man who dropped out of college after two years and who now works as a waiter. At first, Hailley seemed happy with Dan, but then she started changing. She's become less extroverted and a lot less positive.

Often, when Amy suggests doing something together, Hailley says she can't because Dan might come over or call, and he doesn't like her not to be available to him. When Amy sees them together, she notices that he doesn't treat her with respect and often criticizes her harshly. For example, when Hailley said something to Dan when he was on his cell phone, he shouted, "Don't talk to me. I'm on the phone." Later, when Hailey dropped some papers, Dan said harshly, "You are so clumsy!"

Amy is concerned that Hailley may be in a relationship that is verbally and physically abusive. Amy thinks that Dan is damaging her self-concept, and she wants to help.

Amy: I'm just worried about you. I don't like the way he treats you.

Hailley: Because he called me clumsy? I am clumsy, and besides, if I do something stupid, I can't expect him not to notice.

Amy: But he doesn't show any respect for you at all.

Hailley: Well, he's a guy. He says what he's thinking. I know a lot of people's boyfriends like that. Besides, I don't think there's anything wrong with Dan. I think I just have to stop doing things that make him mad.

Jason Harris/© Wadsworth

▼ ▼

1. If you were Hailley's friend, what responsibilities would you have, if any, for helping her?

2. If you were Dan's friend, what might you say to alter his behaviors?

3. How does the concept of reflected appraisal, discussed in Chapter 9, apply to this case?

11 Communication in Groups and Teams

▶ **FOCUS QUESTIONS**

1. What are the differences between groups and teams?

2. Why are groups and teams becoming increasingly popular?

3. What are the potential strengths of group discussion?

4. What are the potential limitations of group discussion?

5. To what extent should leadership be assigned to a single group member?

Duke University basketball coach Mike Krzyzewski—"Coach K"—is known for developing winning teams. In 2001, Coach K's star center, Carlos Boozer, broke his foot in the second half of Duke's final regular season ACC game. Until that happened, Duke had been favored to win the ACC and NCAA tournaments. With the star player out of the game, Duke's chances looked slim. It was expected that Coach K would put in senior guard Nate James as a replacement, but instead the coach decided to start first-year player Chris Duhon, who was more likely to increase Duke's speed. Before announcing this decision, however, Coach K talked with James, an accomplished senior, and with Duhon, a far less experienced first-year player. Because Coach K spent time talking with both players, he avoided a situation that could have disrupted the team.

Coach K also decided to use a rotating trio of bench players: Reggie Love, Matt Christensen, and Casey Sanders. Initially, all three men felt that they couldn't contribute enough, but Coach K convinced them that they could. In an account of this time, Coach K said that the most important thing he did was to talk a lot with Love, Christensen, and Sanders to motivate them to hold the center and also to make it clear to them that Boozer would be the center again as soon as his injury healed. Together, Love, Christensen, and Sanders held down the center position until Boozer was able to rejoin the team.

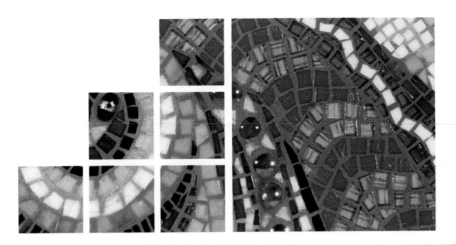

Sanders, who got the most minutes, was an unknown and unproven player, but under Coach K's encouragement, Sanders played with skill and spirit that maintained the team's rankings. Before the season ended, Boozer's injury healed, and Coach K faced the issue of replacing Sanders with Boozer. How could he do this without hurting the team's morale and motivation?

Coach K talked first with Sanders and asked him what he thought would be right. Sanders said it was up to the coach, but he wouldn't mind giving up his spot to Boozer. Coach K then asked Boozer what he thought was the best decision. Boozer, too, deferred to the coach but said he would be okay if Sanders stayed in play.

Why do you think Coach K approached the decision as he did? Why do you think Boozer and Sanders responded as they did? It's clear that all three men understood key principles of effective teamwork. Both players put the good of the team ahead of personal recognition. And Coach K knew that for the team to stay cohesive and maintain confidence in the decision and the lead player, both Boozer and Sanders must feel they had a voice in the decision, and both needed to be committed to the choice of players in the final games of the season (Krzyzewski & Phillips, 2001).

Have you had experiences in groups and teams where everyone participated and had a strong sense of commitment? Have you had other experiences with groups and teams that were neither cohesive nor productive? Based on all your experiences, do you enjoy working on groups and teams? If so, you have lots of company. If not, you also have lots of company. For every person who is enthusiastic about group work, there is another person who dreads or merely tolerates it. Research shows sound reasons for both points of view. Groups generally take more time to reach decisions than individuals do, yet group decisions often are superior to those made by a single person. Although group interaction can heighten creativity and commitment, it may also suppress individuals and their ideas.

Whether your experiences in groups have been positive, negative, or a mix of the two, you have probably belonged to a number of groups during your life. Pick up any newspaper, and you will see announcements for social groups, volunteer service committees, personal support groups, health teams, focus groups run by companies trying out new products, and political action coalitions. If you go online, you'll encounter a range of virtual groups that you can join to give and get personal support, exchange information, and share interests. It is a rare person who doesn't participate in many groups.

In this chapter, we'll build on what you've learned about communication to explore interaction in groups and teams. We begin by defining groups and teams and tracing their rising popularity. Next, we identify potential strengths and weaknesses of groups and teams. Then, we consider aspects of groups that affect communication. Finally, we discuss guidelines for effective participation in groups.

►UNDERSTANDING COMMUNICATION IN GROUPS AND TEAMS

There are many kinds of groups, each with distinctive goals and communication patterns. Social groups provide us with conversation and recreation with people we enjoy. Communication in social groups tends to be relaxed, informal, and more focused on the interpersonal climate than on a task. Personal growth groups enable people to deal with significant issues and problems in a supportive context. In personal growth groups, communication aims to help members clarify and address issues in their lives. Task groups exist to solve problems, develop policies, or achieve other substantive goals. The communication of task groups concentrates on evidence, reasoning, and ideas, as well as on organizing, discussing, and maintaining a healthy climate for interaction.

© AFP-Getty Images

Successful athletic teams are highly cohesive.

Although different types of groups have distinct primary purposes, most groups include three kinds of communication: *climate communication, procedural communication,* and *task communication.* For example, social groups devote the bulk of their talk to climate communication, yet they often move into task discussion, as when one friend asks another for advice in solving a problem. Task groups typically include some climate communication and a good deal of procedural communication, whereas personal growth groups include task communication to deal with members' issues, climate communication to create and sustain support and trust, and procedural communication to manage time and move conversation along.

For all types of groups, communication is a primary influence on productivity and the climate of interaction. Communication in groups and teams involves the basic processes we discussed in earlier chapters. For example, constructive group communication requires that members use effective verbal and nonverbal communication, check perceptions with one another, listen mindfully, build good climates, and adapt communication to each other and various group goals and situations.

Defining Groups and Teams

What is a group? Are six people standing in line to buy tickets a group? Are four businesspeople in an airport lounge a group? Unless people are interacting and involved in collective endeavors, a group does not exist. The foregoing examples describe collections of individuals but not groups.

For a group to exist, the people must interact, must be interdependent, must have a common goal, and must share some rules of conduct. Thus, we can define a **group** as three or more people who interact over time, depend on one another, and follow shared rules of conduct to reach a common goal. Individual members' goals may differ from or be in tension with the collective goal, but a common goal still exists (Frey, 2003; Rothwell, 2007). Group members perceive themselves as interdependent—as needing one another to achieve something, such as developing a policy for the workplace, fostering social ties between people, or promoting personal growth.

A **team** is a special kind of group characterized by different, complementary resources of members and by a strong sense of collective identity (Rothwell, 2007). Like all groups, teams involve interaction, interdependence, shared rules, and common goals. Yet teams are distinct from groups in two respects. First, teams consist of people who bring different and specialized resources to a common project. Second, teams develop greater interdependence and a stronger sense of identity than is standard for most groups. Team members have a stronger sense of team identity than members of most groups (Hoover, 2002; Lumsden & Lumsden, 2004). In other words, all teams are groups, but not all groups are teams.

Groups and teams develop rules that members understand and follow. You will recall from Chapter 4 that constitutive rules state what counts as what. For example, in some groups disagreement counts as a positive sign of involvement and critical thinking, whereas other groups regard disagreement as negative. Regulative rules regulate how, when, and with whom we interact. For instance, a group might have the regulative rules that members do not interrupt each other and that tensions between members are not discussed with outsiders. Groups generate rules in the process of interacting and figuring out what works for them.

Shared goals also characterize groups. Citizens form groups to accomplish political goals, to establish community programs, to influence zoning decisions, and to provide neighborhood security. Workers form groups to safeguard benefits and job security, and they work in teams to evaluate, make, and implement organizational policies and to improve productivity. Other groups form to promote personal growth (therapy and support groups), to nourish shared interests (backpacking groups, gardening clubs), to share their lives (families, shared housing groups), to socialize (fraternities and sororities), to engage in service work (Lions Club, Kiwanis Club), and to participate in sports and games (intramural teams, bridge clubs). Online groups form around members' shared interest in some activity, issue, or hobby. As Mieko's account shows, when a common goal dissolves, the group disbands or redefines its purpose.

TECHNOLOGY

fyi

VIRTUAL TEAMS

Increasingly, teams do their work virtually. Communication researchers Erik Timmerman and Craig Scott (2006) point out that the degree of virtualness varies. Some teams work face-to-face part of the time and online part of the time. Some teams rely entirely on videoconferencing, whereas other teams never even see each other but communicate via e-mail and groupware. Across teams with different degrees of virtualness, those that communicate effectively, especially in terms of members' responsiveness to one another, have the highest cohesiveness and greatest member satisfaction.

► **Mieko**

When I first came here to go to school, I felt very alone. I met some other students from Japan, and we formed a group to help us feel at home in America. For the first year, that group was most important to us because we felt uprooted. The second year, it was not so important, because we'd all started finding ways to fit in here, and we felt more at home. The third year, we decided not to be a group anymore. The reason we wanted a group no longer existed.

The Rise of Groups and Teams

Today, groups and teams are more than ever a part of work life (Godar & Ferris, 2004; Hoover, 2002; LaFasto & Larson, 2001). Whether you are an attorney working with a litigation team, a health-care professional on a medical team, or a factory worker on a team assigned to reduce production time, working with others probably will be part of your career. Your raises and advancement are likely to depend significantly on how effectively you communicate in groups. Because task groups and teams are especially common, we'll concentrate on them in this chapter. Of course, much of the information we'll discuss pertains to other types of groups as well. We'll identify six kinds of task groups that are prevalent in business and civic life (Sher & Gottlieb, 1989).

Project Teams Many businesses and professions rely on project teams, which consist of people who have expertise related to different facets of a project and who combine their knowledge and skills to accomplish a common goal. For example, to launch a new product, pharmaceutical companies often put together product teams that include scientists and doctors who understand the technical character of the new drug, along with other personnel who have expertise in marketing, product design, advertising, and customer relations. Working together, team members develop a coherent, coordinated plan for testing, packaging, advertising, and marketing the new product.

Focus Groups Focus groups are used to find out what people think about a specific idea, product, issue, or person. Focus groups are a mainstay of advertisers who want to understand attitudes, preferences, and responses of people whom they want to buy their product, vote for their candidate, and so forth. How do 21-to-25-year-olds respond to a name that might be given to a microbrew? How do retirees respond to a planned advertising campaign for cruises? Focus groups are also popular in political life: What do middle-income women and men think of a mayoral candidate's environmental record? How do young

fyi

TEAMWORK LACKING IN THE OR

Reports of errors in surgery are not uncommon. Have you ever wondered how a sponge could be left inside a patient or the wrong limb operated on? A recent research report (Nagourney, 2006) found that one contributor to surgical errors is poor teamwork among those working in the OR. A survey of more than 2,100 surgeons, anesthesiologists, and nurses at 60 hospitals showed that many teams suffer from weak teamwork. Doctors' disregard for nurses' expertise was one of the most commonly cited dynamics that undermined effective teamwork.

voters feel about economic issues? Do African Americans regard the candidate as trustworthy?

A focus group is guided by a leader or facilitator who encourages members to express ideas, beliefs, feelings, and perceptions relevant to the topic. The contributions of group members serve as the foundation for later decisions, such as how to refine the name of a product, improve perceptions of a political candidate's trustworthiness, and tailor advertising for cruises. The facilitator seldom offers substantive comments but encourages group members to express themselves, respond to each other, and elaborate their thoughts and feelings. Usually, the facilitator develops a list of questions in advance and uses these to encourage participants to talk (Lederman, 1990).

Brainstorming Groups When idea generation is the goal, brainstorming groups or brainstorming phases in group discussion are appropriate. The goal of **brainstorming** is to come up with as many ideas as possible. Because criticism tends to stifle creativity, brainstorming groups bar criticism and encourage imaginative, even wild, thinking. (Rules for brainstorming appear in Figure 11.1.)

Perhaps you are concerned that brainstorming might produce unrealistic ideas. That's not really a problem, because evaluative discussion follows brainstorming. During evaluation, members work together to appraise the ideas generated through brainstorming. During this stage, the group discards impractical ideas, refines weak or undeveloped contributions, consolidates related suggestions, and further discusses promising ones.

To set a tone for creative communication, leaders or facilitators of brainstorming groups express energy, stoke members' imaginations, and respond enthusiastically to ideas. If the group runs out of ideas, the leader may prompt members by saying, "Let's try to combine some of the ideas we already have," or "We're being too restrained—how about some wild proposals?"

Advisory Groups Advisory groups develop and submit recommendations to others, who make the final decisions. Advisory groups provide expert briefing to an individual or another group that is empowered to make a decision. For example, in my department I chaired the teaching committee, an advisory group that makes recommendations to the faculty. Our committee has recommended policies for peer evaluation of faculty teaching and for greater emphasis on teaching in tenure and promotion decisions.

Figure 11.1   RULES FOR BRAINSTORMING

▶ Do not evaluate ideas in any way. Both verbal and nonverbal criticism are inappropriate.

▶ Record all ideas on a board or easel so that all members of the group can see them.

▶ Go for quantity: The more ideas, the better.

▶ Build on ideas. An idea presented by one member of the group may stimulate an extension by another member. This is desirable.

▶ Encourage creativity. Welcome wild and even preposterous ideas. An idea that seems wacky may lead to other ideas that are more workable.

The faculty made the final decision to accept, reject, or modify my advisory group's recommendations.

Advisory groups may also consist of peers who advise each other. In a *Wall Street Journal* column addressed to small business owners, management consultant Howard Upton (1995) described a system of peer advisory groups developed by chief executives of the Petroleum Equipment Institute. The executives created groups of 10 to 12 presidents of the 700 distributorships in the United States and Canada. By conferring regularly, these presidents were able to advise each other on common problems, practices, and goals. The members found that by pooling experience and reports on methods of problem solving, they were able to enhance everyone's effectiveness.

High-ranking authorities in government and business are seldom experts on the range of issues relevant to decisions they must make. Those who track business trends say that "it is impossible for the head of any company, large or small, to succeed without benefit of outside advice" (Upton, 1995, p. A14). The solitary manager, president, or CEO who relies only on his or her own ideas is not functional in modern life. Advisory groups allow decision makers to benefit from other experts' information and advice pertinent to developing effective policies and making informed decisions.

Quality Improvement Teams   Originally called *quality circles*, today's **quality improvement teams** (also called *continuous quality improvement teams*) include three or more people who have distinct skills or knowledge and who work together to improve quality in an organization (Lumsden & Lumsden, 2004). These teams mix not only people with differing areas of expertise but also people at different levels in an organization's hierarchy. Thus, a secretary may contribute as much as a midlevel manager to a discussion of ways to improve office productivity.

The first few meetings of a quality improvement team typically focus on complaining about problems ("Quality Circles," 1991). This doesn't necessarily foster a negative climate, because complaining about shared frustrations allows members to become comfortable with one another and to establish some common ground. In addition, griping allows members to learn what issues are most recurrent and serious. After the initial venting of frustrations, quality improvement teams focus on identifying needs or problems, ways in which organizational functioning could be improved, and areas of stress or discontent for employees.

For quality improvement teams to be effective, management must support their work and recommendations. Nothing is more frustrating than to be asked to work on a problem but then to have recommendations ignored. When given support, quality improvement teams often generate impressive and creative solutions to organizational problems such as high costs, on-the-job accidents, and low worker morale. Quality improvement teams usually make reports on a regular basis (weekly or monthly) to keep management informed of their ideas and suggestions.

Decision-Making Groups   A sixth kind of task group exists to make decisions. In some cases, decision-making groups form to make a specific decision: What should be the company's policy on medical leave? What benefits and personnel should be cut to achieve a 15% decrease in annual expenses? Other decision-making groups are ongoing; they meet on a regular basis to make decisions about training and development, public relations, budgets, and other matters. (Figure 11.2 on page 241 summarizes one of the most popular methods of decision making.)

Figure 11.2 A STANDARD AGENDA FOR PROBLEM SOLVING

Task groups generally aim to solve problems ranging from how to improve morale to what policy to implement. A time-tested method for effective problem solving is the standard agenda, based on philosopher John Dewey's (1910) model of reflective thinking:

Phase 1: Define the problem.

Phase 2: Analyze information relevant to the problem.

Phase 3: Generate criteria to assess solutions.

Phase 4: Identify potential solutions.

Phase 5: Select the best solution.

Phase 6: Implement the solution (or recommend implementation of it).

Phase 7: Develop an action plan to monitor the effectiveness of the solution.

Sources: Dewey, 1910; Wood, 2001a.

▶POTENTIAL LIMITATIONS AND STRENGTHS OF GROUPS

A great deal of research has compared individual and group decision making. As you might expect, the research identifies potential weaknesses and potential strengths of groups.

Potential Limitations of Groups

The two most significant disadvantages of group discussion are the time needed for the group process and the potential of conformity pressures to interfere with high-quality decision making. Operating solo, an individual can think through ideas efficiently. In group discussion, however, all members have an opportunity to voice their ideas and to respond to the ideas others put forward. It takes substantial time for each person to express ideas, clarify misunderstandings, and respond to questions or criticisms. In addition, groups take time to deliberate about alternative courses of action. Therefore, group discussion probably is not a wise choice for routine policy making and emergency tasks. When creativity and thoroughness are important, however, the values of groups may be more important than the time they take.

Groups also have the potential to suppress individuals and encourage conformity. This can happen in two ways. First, conformity pressures may exist when a majority has an opinion different from that of a minority or a single member. Holding out for

Non Sequitur

your point of view is difficult when most or all of your peers have a different one. In effective groups, however, all members understand and resist conformity pressures. They realize that the majority is sometimes wrong and the minority, even just one person, is sometimes right. Members have an ethical responsibility to encourage expression of diverse ideas and open debate about different views.

Conformity pressures may also arise when one member is extremely charismatic or has more power or prestige than other members. Even if that person is all alone in a point of view, other members may conform to it. Sometimes a high-status member doesn't intend to influence others and may not overtly exert pressure. However, the other members still perceive the status, and it may affect their judgments. For example, President Kennedy's advisers regarded him so highly that in some cases they suspended their individual critical thinking and agreed with whatever he said (Janis, 1977). As this example illustrates, often neither the high-status person nor others are consciously aware of pressures to conform. This implies that members should be on guard against the potential to conform uncritically. Lance's commentary illustrates how a member who is perceived to have special status can suppress others' individual thought and creativity.

► Lance

I used to belong to a creative writing group where all of us helped each other improve our writing. At first, all of us were equally vocal, and we had a lot of good discussions and even disagreements that helped us grow as writers. But then one member of the group got a story accepted by a big magazine, and all of a sudden we thought of her as a better writer than any of us. She didn't act any different, but we saw her as more accomplished, so when she said something, everybody listened and nobody disagreed. It was like a wet blanket on our creativity because her opinion just carried too much weight once she got published.

Potential Strengths of Groups

The primary potential strengths of groups in comparison to individuals are greater resources, more thorough thought, heightened creativity, and enhanced commitment to decisions. A group obviously exceeds any individual in the ideas, perspectives, experiences, and expertise it can bring to bear on solving a problem. Especially in teams, the diverse resources of members enhance effectiveness. One member knows the technical aspects of a product, another understands market psychology, a third is talented in advertising, and so forth. Health-care teams consist of specialists who combine their knowledge to care for a patient.

Groups also tend to be more thorough than individuals. Aspects of an issue that one member doesn't understand, another person can explain; the details of a plan that bore one person interest another; the holes in a proposal that some members overlook are caught by others. Greater thoroughness by groups isn't simply the result of more people. It reflects interaction among members. When conformity pressures are controlled, discussion can promote critical and careful analysis because members propel each other's thinking. **Synergy** is a special kind of collaborative vitality that enhances

pret. As group size increases, the contributions of each member tend to decrease. You may have experienced frustration when participating in large online chat rooms and discussion forums. It can be hard to get your ideas in, and the sheer number of people contributing ideas can mean that no idea receives much feedback.

Because participation is linked to commitment, larger groups may generate less commitment to group outcomes than smaller groups do. Because participation also affects cohesion and satisfaction, larger groups may also be less cohesive and less satisfying than smaller ones (Benenson, Gordon, & Roy, 2000; DeCremer & Leonardelli, 2003).

▶ Yolanda

The worst group I was ever on had three members. We were supposed to have five, but two dropped out after the first meeting, so there were three of us to come up with proposals for artistic programs for the campus. Nobody would say anything against anybody else's ideas, even if we thought they were bad. For myself, I know I held back from criticizing a lot of times because I didn't want to offend either of the other two. We came up with some really bad ideas because we were so small we couldn't risk arguing.

As Yolanda's commentary shows, groups can be too small as well as too large. With too few members, a group has limited resources, which diminishes a primary value of group decision making. Also, members of small groups may be unwilling to criticize each other's ideas, because alienating one member would dramatically weaken the group. Most researchers agree that five to seven members is the optimal size for a group (Hamilton & Parker, 2001; Lumsden & Lumsden, 2004).

Power Structure

Power structure is a third feature that influences participation in small groups. **Power** is the ability to influence others in the achievement of goals (Rothwell, 2007). There are two distinct kinds of power.

Power over is the ability to help or harm others. This form of power usually is expressed in ways that emphasize and build the status of the person wielding influence. A team leader might exert positive power over a member by providing mentoring, giving strong performance reviews, and assigning the member high-status roles on the team. A leader could also exert negative power by withholding these benefits, assigning unpleasant tasks, and responding negatively to a member's contributions to meetings.

Power to is the ability to empower others to reach their goals (Boulding, 1990; Conrad & Poole, 2002). People who empower others do not emphasize their status. Instead, they act behind the scenes to enlarge others' influence and visibility and help others succeed. This kind of power creates opportunities for others, recognizes achievements, and helps others accomplish their goals. It builds team spirit so that group members are productive and satisfied (Boulding, 1990). This style of influence fosters a win–win group climate in which each member's success is perceived to advance the collective work. Go to the book's online resources and click on

WebLink 11.3 to visit a site that provides information on mediation as an example of *power to* instead of *power over.*

Within groups, power may be earned and distributed in distinct ways. Power may result from position (CEO, president, professor, best friend of the boss), or it may be earned (demonstrated competence or expertise). If all members of a group have roughly equal power, the group has a *distributed power structure.* On the other hand, if one or more members have greater power than others, the group has a *hierarchical power structure.* Hierarchy may take the form of one person who is more powerful than all the others, who are equal in power to one another. Alternatively, hierarchy may involve multiple levels of power. A leader might have the greatest power, three others might have power equal to each other's but less than the leader's, and four other members might have little power. The FYI box on page 247 summarizes the primary sources of power.

How are individual power and group power structure related to participation? First, members with high power tend to be the centers of group communication; they talk more, and others talk more to them. **Social climbing** is the attempt to increase personal status in a group by winning the approval of high-status members. If social climbing doesn't increase the status of those doing it, they often become marginal participants in groups. In addition, members with a great deal of power often have greater influence on group decisions. Members with more power tend to find discussion more satisfying than members with less power (Young et al., 2001). This makes sense because those with power get to participate more and get their way more often.

Power influences communication and is influenced by it (Barge & Keyton, 1994). In other words, how members communicate affects how much power they acquire. People who make good substantive comments, cultivate a healthy climate, and organize deliberations tend to earn power quickly. These are examples of earned power that is conferred because a member provides skills valued by the group. Members who demonstrate that they have done their homework and respond thoughtfully likewise gain power.

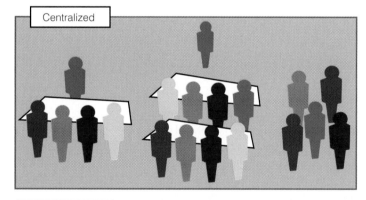

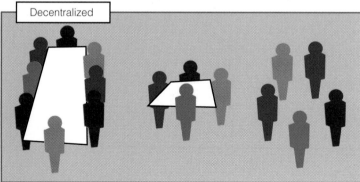

Figure 11.3 PATTERNS OF INTERACTION IN GROUPS

Interaction Patterns

Another important influence on communication in groups is interaction patterns (Figure 11.3). In centralized patterns, one or two people hold central positions, and most or all communication goes directly to them or is funneled through them.

Decentralized patterns promote more balanced communication. As you might suspect, the power of individual members often affects interaction patterns. If one or two members have greater power, a centralized pattern of interaction is likely to emerge. Decentralized patterns are more typical when members have roughly equal power.

fyi

FIVE BASES OF POWER

What is power? How does a person get it? There is more than one answer to each of these questions because there are different sources of power (Arnold & Feldman, 1986).

Reward Power	The ability to give people things they value, such as attention, approval, public praise, promotions, and raises
Coercive Power	The ability to punish others through demotions, firing, and undesirable assignments
Legitimate Power	The organizational role, such as manager, supervisor, or CEO, that results in others' compliance
Expert Power	Influence derived from expert knowledge or experience
Referent Power	Influence based on personal charisma and personality

Group Norms

A final feature of small groups is the presence of **norms**—guidelines that regulate how members act as well as how they interact with each other. Group norms control everything from the most trivial to the most critical aspects of a group's life. Relatively inconsequential norms may regulate meeting time and whether eating is allowed during meetings. More substantive norms govern how members express and analyze ideas, listen to one another, and manage conflict.

Norms grow directly out of interaction. For example, at an initial meeting some members might not pay attention when others are speaking. If this continues, a norm of disrespect will develop, and members will form the habit of listening poorly. On the other hand, one member might say, "I think we need to be more attentive to each other." If other members heed this suggestion, a norm of respectful communication may develop.

▶ Baxter

When our team first formed, everyone was pretty casual. There was a lot of kidding around before we got down to work at each meeting, and members often drifted in late. I didn't want to crack down at the beginning, because I thought that might dampen group spirit. With 20–20 hindsight, I now see I should have imposed some rules at the outset. I've tried to get members to get to meetings on time and buckle down to work, but I'm fighting against a history of being laid back.

As Baxter's commentary demonstrates, norms often become entrenched early in a group's life, so it's important to pay attention to them from the outset. By noticing

© Mark Richards/PhotoEdit

What can you tell about this group from the photo? Look for nonverbal clues regarding leadership, formality, and climate.

patterns and tendencies, you can exert influence over the norms that govern conduct in a group. Cohesion, size, power structure, interaction patterns, and norms are features of groups that affect participation, productivity, and satisfaction.

▶GUIDELINES FOR COMMUNICATING IN GROUPS AND TEAMS

To realize the strengths of group work and avoid its potential weaknesses, members must participate constructively, provide leadership, and manage conflict so that it benefits the group and its outcomes.

Participate Constructively

Because interaction is the heart of groups and teams, communication skills are vital to effectiveness. There are four kinds of communication in groups (Figure 11.4). The first three—task communication, procedural communication, and climate communication—are constructive because they foster good group climate and outcomes. The fourth kind of communication is egocentric, or dysfunctional, communication. It tends to detract from a healthy group climate and effective decision making.

Task Communication **Task communication** focuses on the problems, issues, or information before the group. It provides ideas and information, clarifies members' understanding, and critically evaluates ideas. Task contributions may initiate ideas, respond to others' ideas, or provide critical evaluation of information. Task comments also include asking for ideas and criticism from others.

Figure 11.4   TYPES OF COMMUNICATION IN GROUPS

Task Communication	Initiates ideas
	Seeks information
	Gives information
	Elaborates on ideas
	Evaluates, offers critical analysis
Procedural Communication	Establishes agenda
	Provides orientation
	Curbs digressions
	Guides participation
	Coordinates ideas
	Summarizes others' contributions
	Records group progress
Climate Communication	Establishes and maintains healthy climate
	Energizes group process
	Harmonizes ideas
	Recognizes others
	Reconciles conflicts
	Builds enthusiasm for the group
Egocentric Communication	Is aggressive toward others
	Blocks ideas
	Seeks personal recognition (brags)
	Dominates interaction
	Pleads for special interests
	Confesses, self-discloses, seeks personal help
	Disrupts task
	Devalues others
	Trivializes the group and its work

Procedural Communication If you've ever participated in a disorganized group, you understand the importance of **procedural communication.** It helps a group get organized and stay on track. Procedural contributions establish agendas, coordinate members' comments, and record group progress. In addition, procedural contributions may curb digressions and tangents, summarize progress, and regulate participation so that everyone has opportunities to speak and nobody dominates.

Climate Communication A group is more than a task unit. It is also people involved in a relationship that can be more or less pleasant and open. **Climate communication** focuses on creating and maintaining a constructive climate that encourages members to contribute freely and to evaluate ideas critically. Climate comments emphasize a group's strengths and progress, recognize members' contributions, reconcile conflicts, add humor, and build enthusiasm for the group and its work.

Egocentric Communication I was once on a committee that had one member who was continuously negative. If one person suggested an idea for our task, this member would say, "We've already tried that" or "It won't work." The member's negativity undermined the committee. Perhaps you've been in groups where one person was always negative, argumentative, or domineering. **Egocentric communication,** or dysfunctional communication, is used to block others or to call attention to oneself. It detracts from group progress because it is self-centered rather than group centered. Examples of egocentric talk are devaluing a member's ideas, trivializing group efforts, being aggressive toward others, bragging about personal accomplishments, dominating, disrupting group work, and pleading for special causes that aren't in the group's interests.

Task, procedural, and climate communication work together to foster productive, organized, and comfortable group discussion. Most of us are already skilled in one or two kinds of communication. For instance, some people have developed skill in reconciling conflicts and using humor to break tension. Other people have keen organizational talents that allow them to offer procedural leadership. Still others are especially skillful in analyzing information. The kinds of communication that you associate with yourself reflect your self-concept, which we discussed in Chapter 9. Egocentric communication, on the other hand, does not contribute to enjoyable group interaction or high-quality outcomes. Egocentric comments can sabotage a group's climate and hinder its progress in achieving its goals. If it occurs, others in the group should intervene to discourage it. Communicating clearly that egocentric behavior will not be tolerated in your group fosters norms for effective interaction.

Figure 11.5 provides a transcript of a group discussion that includes the four kinds of communication we've discussed. Notice how skillfully Ann communicates to defuse tension between Bob and Jan before it disrupts the group. You might also notice that Ed provides the primary procedural leadership for the group, and Bob is effective in interjecting humor to enhance the climate. Several members recognize contributions to the discussion. You can further improve your ability to recognize different kinds of group communication by completing the Sharpen Your Skill exercise on this page.

Noticing Communication in Groups

Observe a group meeting—either a group you belong to or one you visit. For 10 minutes of group discussion, keep track of the communication, noting whether each comment is task, procedural, climate, egocentric, or a combination of two or more. Do the patterns of communication give you insight into why the group is effective or ineffective?

SHARPEN YOUR SKILL

Provide Leadership

All groups need leadership. For decades, people thought that leaders were born, not developed. To identify the traits of leaders, researchers studied a range of personal qualities from intelligence to physical characteristics. This line of study failed to reveal any consistent traits of leaders. The lack of identifiable leader traits led researchers to realize that leadership is not based on inherent qualities in individuals. Instead, leadership is a set of behaviors that helps a group maintain a good climate and accomplish tasks in an organized way.

Figure 11.5   CODING GROUP COMMUNICATION

Ed:	Let's start by talking about our goals. [procedural]
Jan:	That's a good idea. [climate]
Bob:	I think our goal is to come up with a better meal plan for students on campus. [task]
Ed:	What do you mean by "better"? Do you mean cheaper or more variety or more tasteful? [task]
Ann:	I think it's all three. [task]
Ed:	Well, we probably do care about all three, but maybe we should talk about one at a time so we can keep our discussion focused. [procedural]
Bob:	Okay, I vote we focus first on taste—like it would be good if there were some taste to the food on campus! [task and climate (humor)]
Jan:	Do you mean taste itself or quality of food, which might also include nutrition? [task]
Bob:	Pure taste! When I'm hungry, I don't think about what's good for me, just what tastes good. [task and possibly climate (humor)]
Jan:	Well, maybe we want the food service to think about nutrition because we don't. [task]
Bob:	If you're a health food nut, that's your problem. I don't think nutrition is something that's important in the food service on campus. [task; may also be egocentric if his tone toward Jan is snide]
Ed:	Let's do this: Let's talk first about what we would like in terms of taste itself. [procedural] Before we meet next time, it might be a good idea for one of us to talk with the manager of the cafeteria to see whether they have to meet any nutritional guidelines in what they serve. [task]
Ann:	I'll volunteer to do that. [task]
Ed:	Great. Thanks, Ann. [climate]
Bob:	I'll volunteer to do taste testing! [climate (humor)]
Jan:	With your weight, you'd better not. [egocentric]
Bob:	Yeah, like you have a right to criticize me. [egocentric]
Ann:	Look, none of us is here to criticize anyone else. We're here because we want to improve the food service on campus. [climate] We've decided we want to focus first on taste, [procedural] so who has an idea of how we go about studying that? [task]

Leadership may be provided by one member or by several members who contribute to guiding group process and ensuring effective outcomes. Leadership exists when one or more members establish and maintain a good working climate, organize group processes, and ensure that discussion is substantive. Effective leadership also controls disruptive members who engage in egocentric communication. **Leadership,** then, is effective participation. Whether a group has one leader or shared leadership, the primary responsibilities of leaders are to organize discussion, to ensure sound research and reasoning, to promote norms for mindful listening and clear verbal and nonverbal communication, to create a productive climate, to build group morale, and to discourage egocentric communication that detracts from group efforts. Krystal's commentary provides an example of effective shared leadership.

▶ Krystal

The most effective group I've ever been in had three leaders. I was the person who understood our task best, so I contributed the most to critical thinking about the issues. But Belinda was the one who kept us organized. She could get us off tangents, and she knew when it was time to move on from one stage of work to the next. She also pulled ideas together to co-ordinate our thinking. Kevin was the climate leader. He could always tell a joke if things got tense, and he was the best person I ever saw for recognizing others' contributions. I couldn't point to any one leader in that group, but we sure did have good leadership.

When we realize that leadership is a set of communication behaviors that moves groups along, we understand that more than one person may engage in leadership in a specific group or team. Sometimes one member provides guidance on task and procedures, and another member focuses on building a healthy group climate by recognizing and responding to members' ideas and feelings (Goleman, McKee, & Boyatzis, 2002) as well as by encouraging cohesion.

Also, different people may provide leadership at different times. The person who guides the group at the outset may not be the one who advances the group's work in later phases. Depending on what a group needs at a specific time, different leadership functions are appropriate and may come from different members. Even when an official leader exists, other members may contribute much of the communication that provides the overall leadership of a group.

Manage Conflict Constructively

In Chapter 7, we learned that conflict is natural and can be productive. In groups and teams, conflict stimulates thinking, helps members consider diverse perspectives, and enlarges members' understanding of issues involved in making decisions and generating ideas (McClure, 2005). To achieve these goals, however, conflict must be managed skillfully. The goal is to manage conflict so that it enriches group processes and helps a group achieve collective goals. Although many of us may not enjoy conflict, we can nonetheless recognize its value—even its necessity—for effective group work. Trey's experience illustrates what can happen when a group puts conflict avoidance ahead of high-quality work.

▶ Trey

I used to think conflict was terrible and hurt groups, but last year I was a member of a group that had no—I mean, zero—conflict. A couple of times, I tried to bring up an idea different from what had been suggested, but my idea wouldn't even get a hearing. The whole goal was not to disagree. As a result, we didn't do a very thorough job of analyzing the issues, and we didn't subject the solution we developed to critical scrutiny. When our recommendation was put into practice, it bombed. We could have foreseen and avoided the failure if we had been willing to argue and disagree in order to test our idea before we put it forward.

Disruptive Conflict Effective members promote conflict that is constructive for the group's tasks and climate and discourage conflict that disrupts healthy discussion. Conflict is disruptive when it interferes with effective work and a healthy communication climate. Typically, **disruptive conflict** is marked by communication that is competitive as members vie with each other to wield influence and get their way. Accompanying the competitive tone of communication is a self-interested focus in which members talk about only their own ideas, solutions, and points of view. The competitive and self-centered communication in disruptive conflict fosters diminished cohesion and a win–lose orientation to conflict.

Group climate deteriorates during disruptive conflict. Members may feel unsafe volunteering ideas because others might harshly evaluate or scorn them. Personal attacks may occur as members criticize one another's motives or attack one another personally. Recall the discussion in Chapter 7 about communication that fosters defensiveness; we saw that defensive climates are promoted by communication that expresses evaluation, superiority, control orientation, neutrality, certainty, and closed-mindedness. Just as these forms of communication undermine healthy climates in personal relationships, they also interfere with group climate and productivity.

Constructive Conflict **Constructive conflict** occurs when members understand that disagreements are natural and can help them achieve their shared goals. Communication that expresses respect for diverse opinions reflects this attitude. Members also emphasize shared interests and goals. The cooperative focus of communication encourages a win–win orientation. Discussion is open and supportive of differences, and disagreements focus on issues, not personalities.

To encourage constructive conflict, communication should demonstrate openness to different ideas, willingness to alter opinions when good reasons exist, and respect for the integrity of other members and the views they express. Also, keep in mind that conflict grows out of the entire system of group communication. Thus, constructive conflict is most likely to occur when members have established a supportive, open climate of communication. Group climate is built throughout the life of a group, beginning with the first meeting. It is important to communicate in ways that build a strong climate from the start so that it is already established when conflict arises.

▶SUMMARY

In this chapter, we've considered small groups and how they operate. We defined groups as three or more people who meet over time, share understandings of how to interact, and have a common goal. Group members must recognize and manage the potential weaknesses of group discussion, notably conformity pressures and time, to realize the important advantages of group decision making.

Task teams are increasingly popular in modern professional life because they are often more effective than individuals in producing creative, high-quality decisions and securing members' commitment. Many factors, including cohesion, size, power, norms, and interaction patterns, influence communication in task groups and teams. Each of these features shapes the small group system within which communication transpires. Understanding and managing these influences should enable you to enhance the climate of groups, the quality of outcomes, and the efficiency of group processes.

In the final part of this chapter, we discussed three guidelines for effective communication in groups and teams. The first one, participating effectively, requires task, climate, and procedural contributions that foster good group climate and outcomes. Developing skill in constructive types of communication and avoiding egocentric comments will make you a valuable member of any group. The second guideline for effective communication in groups and teams is to ensure leadership, which may be provided by a single person or several members. Good leadership exists when one or more members communicate to organize discussion, to ensure careful work on the task, and to build cohesion, morale, and an effective climate for collective work. A third guideline is to manage conflict so that it enhances, rather than detracts from, group processes. In our discussion, we identified communication that fosters constructive conflict, which improves the quality of group decision making. Constructive conflict in groups, as we have seen, grows out of a supportive communication climate that is built over the course of a group's life.

Review, Reflect, Extend

The Key Concepts, For Further Reflection and Discussion questions, Recommended Resources, and Experience Communication Case Study that follow will help you review, reflect on, and extend the information and ideas presented in this chapter. A diverse selection of online resources is also available through ThomsonNOW. These resources include Speech Builder Express, InfoTrac College Edition, interactive videos, vMentor, and Thomson Audio Study Products.

Thomson™ NOW! is an online study system designed to help you put your time to the best use. After reading a chapter, take the NOW pre-test to identify concepts discussed in the chapter that you may not fully understand. Based on the results of this diagnostic test, the system will create a personalized study plan that directs you to specific learning resources and activities. To see if you're ready for an exam, take the NOW post-test to check your understanding.

For more information or to access this book's online resources, visit **http://www.thomsonedu.com**.

▶ KEY CONCEPTS

The terms following are defined in the chapter on the page number indicated, and they appear in alphabetical order, with definitions, in the Glossary, which begins on page 369. The book's online resources also include flash cards and crossword puzzles to help you learn these terms and the concepts they represent.

▶For Further Reflection and Discussion

The questions below can also be found among the book's online resources for this chapter, where you have the option of e-mailing your responses to your instructor, if required.

1. Interview a professional in the field you hope to enter after college. Ask her or him to identify how various groups and teams discussed in this chapter are used on the job. If you are already employed in a career, reflect on your experiences with groups on the job.

2. Recall the last group in which you participated. Did you find it effective in achieving its task goals? Was the climate comfortable? Now, describe your group according to key features discussed in this chapter: cohesion, size, interaction patterns, power, norms, leadership, and conflict. Do these features explain the climate and task effectiveness of your group?

3. Ask several people who have lived in non-Western cultures whether the cultural values that affect group communication in the United States are present in the countries where they lived. In your conversation, explore how differences in cultural values affect group interaction.

4. Observe a group discussion on your campus or in your town. Record the contributions made by members by classifying them as task, climate, procedural, or egocentric. Do the communication patterns you observe explain the effectiveness or ineffectiveness of the group?

▶Recommended Resources

1. Although *Twelve Angry Men* was produced many years ago, it remains an excellent film about group dynamics in a decision-making group, in this case a jury.

2. Ken Blanchard, John Carlos, and Alan Randolph wrote *Empowerment Takes More Than a Minute* (1998) to give working tools to people who want to be empowering leaders. The book is organized in story form, relying on an extended case study to provide hands-on advice, tools, and exercises for increasing employees' sense of empowerment. They emphasize the importance of personal contact, encouragement, and feedback between leaders and employees.

Experience Communication Case Study

Group Communication

The book's online resources include an interactive video of the communication situation featured in the case study scripted on the next page. Apply what you've learned in this chapter by analyzing the case study, using the questions that follow the script as a guide. These questions are also available online with the video.

Jason Harris/© Wadsworth

As members of the Student Government Financial Committee, Davinia, Joyce, Thomas, and Pat make decisions on how much funding, if any, to give various student groups that request support from the funds collected from student fees. They are meeting for the first time in a campus cafeteria.

Thomas: Well, we've got 23 applications for funding and a total of $19,000 that we can distribute.

Davinia: Maybe we should start by listing how much each of the 23 groups wants.

Joyce: It might be better to start by determining the criteria that we'll use to decide if groups get any funding from student fees.

Davinia: Yeah, right. We should set up our criteria before we look at applications.

Thomas: Sounds good to me. Pat, what do you think?

Pat: I'm on board. Let's set up criteria first and then review the applications against those.

Joyce: Okay, we might start by looking at the criteria used last year by the Financial Committee. Does anyone have a copy of those?

Thomas: I do. [He passes out copies to the other three people.] They had three criteria: service to a significant number of students, compliance with the college's nondiscrimination policies, and educational benefit.

Davinia: What counts as "educational benefit"? Did last year's committee specify that?

Joyce: Good question. Thomas, you were on the committee last year. Do you remember what they counted as educational benefit?

Thomas: The main thing I remember is that it was distinguished from artistic benefit—like a concert or art exhibit or something like that.

Pat: But can't art be educational?

Davinia: Yeah, I think so. Thomas, Joyce, do you?

Thomas: I guess, but it's like art's primary purpose isn't to educate.

Joyce: I agree. It's kind of hard to put into words, but I think educational benefit has more to do with information and the mind, and art has more to do with the soul. Does that sound too hokey? [Laughter.]

Pat: Okay, so we want to say that we don't distribute funds to any hokey groups, right? [More laughter.]

Davinia: It's not like we're against art or anything. It's just that the funding we can distribute is for educational benefit, right? [Everyone nods.]

Joyce: Okay, let's move onto another criterion. What is a significant number of students?

Thomas: Last year, we said that the proposals for using money had to be of potential interest to at least 20% of students to get funding. How does that sound to you?

Pat: Sounds okay, as long as we remember that something can be of potential interest to students who aren't members of specific groups. Like, for instance, I might want to attend a program on Native American customs even though I'm not a Native American. See what I mean?

Davinia: Good point; we don't want to define student interest as student identity or anything like that. [Nods of agreement.]

▼ ▽ ▼

Thomas: Okay, so are we agreed that 20% is about right, with the understanding that the 20% can include students who aren't in a group applying for funding? [Nods.] Okay, then do we need to discuss the criterion of compliance with the college's policies on nondiscrimination?

1. Classify each statement in this scenario as one of the forms of group communication (task, procedural, climate, egocentric). Is the balance among forms appropriate for a decision-making group?

2. Based on this discussion, does this group seem to have a single leader, or do different members provide leadership to the group?

3. How do you perceive the interaction pattern between members? Does everyone seem to be involved and participating?

4. Are any of the potential values of group versus individual decision making evident in this discussion?

12 *Communication in Organizations*

► **FOCUS QUESTIONS**

1. What is organizational culture?

2. How do rituals and routines express organizational values?

3. How do today's organizations today differ from those of earlier eras?

4. What are the advantages and disadvantages of personal relationships on the job?

Josh is a senior systems analyst at MicroLife, an innovative technology firm in Silicon Valley. Although he typically works more than 40 hours a week, his schedule varies according to his moods and his responsibilities for caring for his daughter, Marie. Some days, Josh is at his desk by 8 A.M., and on other days he gets to the office around noon. Life on the job is casual, as is dress. Sneakers, T-shirts, and jeans are standard attire for all employees at MicroLife. People drop by each other's offices without appointments and sometimes even without specific business to conduct.

When Josh first joined MicroLife, drop-by chats with longer-term employees gave him insight into the company. He can still remember hearing stories about Wayne Murray—fondly called "Wild Man Wayne"—who launched the company from a makeshift workstation in his garage. He also heard tale after tale of oddball ideas the company backed that became highly profitable. Josh really enjoys the creative freedom at MicroLife: Everyone is encouraged to think innovatively, to try new ways of doing things. Weekly softball games provide friendly competition between the Nerds (the team of systems analysts) and the Words (the team of software writers).

Jacqueline slips her shoes off under her desk, hoping nobody will see, because Bankers United has a strict dress code requiring suits, heels (for women), and clean-shaven faces (for men). On her first day at work, a manager took her out to lunch and mentioned two recent hires who "just didn't work out" because they didn't dress professionally. Jacqueline got the message. From other employees, she heard about people

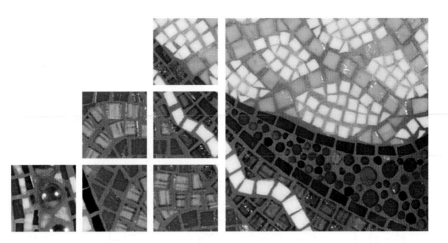

who had been given bad performance reviews for being late more than once in a six-month period. When Jacqueline suggested a way to streamline mortgage applications, she was told, "That isn't how we do things here." She quickly figured out that at Bankers United the operating mode was rigid rules rigidly enforced. Although she sometimes feels constrained by the authoritarian atmosphere of Bankers United, Jacqueline also likes having clear-cut rules to follow. For her, rules provide a kind of security.

Would you rather work for MicroLife or Bankers United? If you're a relaxed person who enjoys informality and does well in unstructured environments, MicroLife may appeal to you. On the other hand, if you like clear rules and a traditional working environment, Bankers United may be more attractive to you. Neither company is better in an absolute sense. Some businesses and professions can be flexible about dress and hours. As long as the work gets done—programs debugged, products developed—it doesn't matter how people dress and when they work. Other organizations must accommodate a time clock and must follow inflexible procedures to meet their objectives. For instance, hospitals must schedule operating rooms, and doctors, nurses, and anesthesiologists must be on time for surgery. Although organizations differ in many ways, common to them is the centrality of communication.

Communication in organizations is the topic of this chapter. In the first section, we'll identify key features of organizational communication. Next, we'll discuss the overall culture of the organization, which is what creates the interpersonal and task climate for its members. As we will see, organizational culture is created and expressed in communication. Every organization has a distinct culture that consists of traditions, structures, and practices that reflect and reproduce a particular form of work life and on-the-job relationships. In the third section of the chapter, we'll discuss three guidelines for communicating in organizations in our era.

▶KEY FEATURES OF ORGANIZATIONAL COMMUNICATION

Much of what you've learned in previous chapters applies to communication in organizations. For instance, successful communication on the job requires listening skills, verbal and nonverbal competence, and the abilities to build supportive climates and manage conflict. In addition, organizational communication has three distinct features: structure, communication networks, and links to external environments.

Structure

Organizations are structured. As Charles Conrad and Marshall Scott Poole (2004) point out, the very word *organization* means "structure." In organizations, structure provides predictability for members so that they understand roles, procedures, and expectations.

Most modern organizations rely on a hierarchical structure, which assigns different levels of power and status to different members and specifies the chain of command that says who is to communicate with whom about what. Although hierarchies may be more or less rigid, a loose chain of command doesn't mean there isn't one. My department, like many academic units, has a fairly loose structure in which members generally interact as equals. However, faculty are ultimately responsible to the chair of the department. He can reprimand or assign tasks to any faculty member, but we can't do the same to him.

"I've never actually seen a corporate ladder before."

From *The Wall Street Journal*; permission, Cartoon Features Syndicate.

Communication Networks

A second characteristic of organizational communication is that it occurs in **communication networks,** which are formal and informal links between members of organizations. In most organizations, people belong to multiple networks (Conrad & Poole, 2004). For example, in my department I belong to a social network that includes colleagues, students, and staff with whom I have personal relationships; task networks consisting of people with whom I can discuss teaching, research, and departmental life; and ad hoc networks that arise irregularly in response to specific crises or issues. I also belong to networks outside my department yet within the university. Overlaps between networks to which we belong ensure that we will communicate in various ways with many people in any organization.

In addition to networks in physical places of work, an increasing number of workers are part of virtual networks. The growth in telecommuting is striking. In 1991, only 1.4% of U.S. workers were telecommuters. In 1999, 5% were, and by 2020 it's expected that 40% of workers will telecommute (Stroup, 2001). Made possible by new technologies, telecommuting allows millions of people to work from their homes or mobile offices. Using computers, e-mail, and faxes, telecommuters do their work and maintain contact with colleagues without going to the physical job site. Results so far show that telecommuting raises the productivity and morale of employees while also saving organizations the expense of providing office space.

Electronic brainstorming groups are increasingly effective because members can remain anonymous and so are more willing to risk venturing creative ideas (Harris, 2002; Pinsonneault & Barki, 1999). And electronic brainstorming, also called virtual conferencing, isn't necessarily a one-time event. Virtual teams are becoming more and more common in the workplace (Godar & Ferris, 2004; Rothwell, 2007).

Links to External Environments

In Chapter 1, we discussed systems as interdependent, interacting wholes. Like other communication systems, organizations are embedded in multiple contexts that affect how they work and whether they succeed or fail. In other words, an organization's operation cannot be understood simply by looking within the organization. We must also look outside it to grasp how the organization is related to and affected by its contexts.

Consider the impact on a few U.S. organizations of the sharp rise in gas prices that began in the summer of 2005:

▶ Tourist attractions saw drops in attendance because people were driving less.

▶ Sales of hybrid cars and conventional cars with high miles-per-gallon ratings rose, while sales of low-mpg vehicles slumped.

▶ People who did travel by car spent less on hotels and meals on the road, to compensate (they said) for the high cost of gas.

▶ Transportation companies raised prices to offset the higher costs of gas for transporting merchandise.

T E C H N O L O G Y

fyi

BLOGGING TO IMPROVE COMMUNICATION WITH THE COMMUNITY

In May 2006, the Los Angeles Police Department became the first police force in the United States to have a blog. Chief William J. Bratton thought a blog would improve communication between police and community. Well . . . it at least increased communication. One response to Chief Bratton's initial message inviting dialogue with the public was this: "Good luck with your cesspool of crime, disease and victimhood" (Glazer, 2006). Despite that and a few other less-than-friendly posts, the majority of posts have been positive. And it has definitely become a communication hub—more than 24,000 visitors in the first week of its existence! To visit the LAPD blog, go to the book's online resources and click on WebLink 12.1.

Although internal factors may have contributed to the sales losses and gains of these businesses, clearly many organizations suffered because of factors outside their organizational boundaries. When economic times are good, when war is not a threat, and when inflation is in check, even mediocre companies survive and sometimes thrive. When external conditions are bad, even good companies can be hurt or driven out of business. All organizations are linked to and influenced by the contexts in which they are embedded.

Systems in which organizations exist influence communication in organizations. Directors, CEOs, and other leaders who feel pressured by economic problems may tighten controls, demand greater efficiency and productivity, and become less willing to spend money on bonuses and social events for employees. Organizations may also feel forced to change and adapt to emerging social, political, and economic conditions. As more people over 40 years of age want to return to school or take classes for personal growth, colleges have developed substantial continuing education programs to meet the demand. The current public concern about obesity has led to changes in food service organizations—even many fast-food restaurants now offer low-carb and low-fat menu items.

▶ORGANIZATIONAL CULTURE

In Chapter 8, we noted that cultures are characterized by shared values, behaviors, practices, and communication forms. Extending the idea of culture to organizations, communication scholars focus on **organizational culture,** which consists of ways of

Based on these photos, what can you infer about the culture in each of these two organizations?

thinking, acting, and understanding work that are shared by members of an organization and that reflect an organization's distinct identity.

Just as ethnic cultures consist of meanings shared by members of the ethnic groups, organizational cultures consist of meanings shared by members of organizations. Just as new members of ethnic cultures are socialized into preexisting meanings and traditions, new members of organizations are socialized into preexisting meanings and traditions (Mumby, 2006). Just as a culture's way of life continues even though particular people leave or die, an organization's culture persists despite the comings and goings of particular workers.

Scholars have gained insight into the ways in which communication creates, sustains, and expresses the culture of organizations (Pacanowsky, 1989; Pacanowsky & O'Donnell-Trujillo, 1982, 1983; Riley, 1983; Scott & Myers, 2005; Smircich, 1983). The relationship between communication and organizational culture is reciprocal: Communication between members of organizations creates, sustains, and sometimes alters the culture. At the same time, organizational culture influences patterns of communication between members.

As employees interact, they create, sustain, and sometimes change their organization's culture (Pacanowsky, 1989; Van Maanen & Barley, 1985). Four kinds of communication that are particularly important in developing and conveying organizational culture are vocabularies, stories, rites and rituals, and structures.

Vocabulary

The most obvious communication dimension of organizational culture is vocabulary. Just as the language of an ethnic culture reflects and expresses its history, norms, values, and identity, the language of an organization reflects and expresses its history, norms, values, and identity.

Hierarchical Language Many organizations and professions have vocabularies that distinguish levels of status among members. The military, for example, relies on language that continually acknowledges rank ("Yes, sir," "chain of command"), which reflects the close ties among rank, respect, and privilege. Salutes, as well as stripes and medals on uniforms, are part of the nonverbal vocabulary that emphasizes rank and status. In a study of police, researchers noted the pervasiveness of derogatory descriptions of suspects and informants. Officers routinely referred to *creeps, dirt-bags,* and *maggots* to emphasize the undesirable element with which police often deal (Pacanowsky & O'Donnell-Trujillo, 1983).

Unequal terms of address also communicate rank. For instance, the CEO may use first names ("Good morning, Jan") when speaking to employees. Unless given permission to use the CEO's first name, however, lower-status members of an organization typically use Mr., Ms., Sir, or Ma'am in addressing the CEO. Colleges and universities use titles to designate faculty members' rank and status: instructor, assistant professor, associate professor, full professor, and distinguished (or chaired) professor. Faculty generally use students' first names, whereas students tend to use titles to address their teachers: Dr. Armstrong or Professor Armstrong.

Masculine Language Because organizations historically have been run by men, and men have been the primary or exclusive members of them, it's not surprising that many organizations have developed and continue to use language more related to men's traditional interests and experiences than to women's (Ashcraft & Mumby, 2004; Mumby, 2007). Consider the number of phrases in the working world that are taken from sports (*home run, ballpark estimate, touchdown, develop a game plan, be a team player, take a time out, the starting lineup*), from military life (*battle plan, mount a campaign, plan of attack, under fire, get the big guns, defensive move, offensive strike*), and from male sexual parts and activities (a troublesome person is a "prick"; you can "hit on" a person, "screw" someone, or "stick it" *to* them; bold professionals have "balls").

Less prevalent in most organizations is language that reflects traditionally feminine interests and experiences (*put something on the back burner, percolate an idea, stir the pot, give birth to a plan*). Whether intentional or not, language that reflects traditionally masculine experiences and interests can bind men together in a community in which many women may feel unwelcome or uncomfortable (Murphy & Zorn, 1996).

Language in the workplace may also normalize sexist practices, including sexual harassment. Practices such as calling women "hon" and "sweetheart" and commenting on women's appearances spotlights women's sexuality and obscures their professional abilities and status. In 1992, Mary Strine analyzed the ways in which academic institutions define and describe sexual harassment so as to make it seem normal and acceptable. Shereen Bingham (1994, 1996) and others (Blair, Brown, & Baxter, 1994; Taylor & Conrad, 1992; Wood, 1992b, 1994c) have documented additional ways in which sexual harassment is normalized or resisted in the workplace.

Stories

Scholars of organizational culture recognize that humans are storytellers by nature. We tell stories to weave coherent narratives out of experience and to create meaning in our lives. Furthermore, the stories we tell do some real work in establishing and sustaining organizational cultures. In a classic study, Michael Pacanowsky and Nick O'Donnell-Trujillo (1983) identified three kinds of stories within the organizational context.

Corporate Stories Corporate stories convey the values, style, and history of an organization. Just as families have favorite stories about their histories and identities that they retell often, organizations have favorite stories that reflect their collective visions of themselves (Conrad & Poole, 2004; Mumby, 1993, 2006).

One important function of corporate stories is to socialize new members into the culture of an organization. Newcomers learn about the history and identity of an organization by listening to stories of its leaders as well as its trials and triumphs. For example, both Levi Strauss and Microsoft are known for an informal style of operation. Veteran employees regale new employees with tales about the laid-back character of the companies: casual dress, relaxed meetings, fluid timetables, and nonbureaucratic ways of getting things done. These stories socialize new employees into the cultures of the companies.

When retold among members of an organization, stories foster feelings of connection and vitalize organizational ideology. You've heard the term *war stories*, which refers to frequently retold stories about key moments such as crises, successes, and takeovers. When long-term members of organizations rehash pivotal events in their shared history, they cement the bonds between them and their involvement with the organization. Jed's commentary provides a good example of how stories express and reinforce organizational culture.

► Jed

I sing with the Gospel Choir, and we have a good following in the Southeast. When I first joined the group, the other members talked to me. In our conversations, what I heard again and again was the idea that we exist to make music for God and about God, not to glorify ourselves. One of the choir members told me about a singer who had gotten on a personal ego trip because of all the bookings we were getting, and he started thinking he was more important than the music. That guy didn't last long with the group.

Personal Stories Members of organizations also tell stories about themselves. Personal stories are accounts that announce how people see themselves and how they want to be seen by others (Cockburn-Wootten & Zorn, 2006). For example, if Sabra perceives herself as a supportive team player, she could simply tell new employees this by saying, "I am a supportive person who believes in teamwork." On the other hand, she could define her image by telling a story: "When I first came here, most folks were operating in isolation, and I thought a lot more could be accomplished if we learned to collaborate. Let me tell you something I did to make that happen. After I'd been on staff for three months, I was assigned to work up a plan for downsizing our manufacturing department. Instead of just developing a plan on my own, I talked with several other managers, and then I met with people who worked in manufacturing to get their ideas. The plan we came

How would this photograph of professionals be different if it had been taken 20 years ago?

up with reflected all of our input." This narrative gives a concrete, coherent account of how Sabra sees herself and wants others to see her.

Collegial Stories The third type of organizational story offers accounts of other members of the organization. When I first became a faculty member, a senior colleague took me out to lunch and told me anecdotes about people in the department and university. At the time, I thought he was simply sharing some interesting stories. As time went on, however, I realized he had told me who the players were so that I could navigate my new context.

Collegial stories told by co-workers forewarn us what to expect from whom. "If you need help getting around the CEO, Jane's the one to see. A year ago, I couldn't finish a report by deadline, so Jane rearranged his calendar so he thought the report wasn't due for another week." "Roberts is a real stickler for rules. Once when I took an extra 20 minutes on my lunch break, he reamed me out." "Pat trades on politics, not performance. Pat took several of the higher-ups out for lunch and golfed with them for the month before bonuses were decided." Whether positive or negative, collegial stories assert identities for others in an organization. They are part of the informal network that teaches new members of an organization how to get along with various other members of the culture. The Sharpen Your Skill box on this page invites you to notice how stories operate in an organization to which you belong.

Rites and Rituals

Rites and rituals are verbal and nonverbal practices that express and reproduce organizational cultures. They do so by providing standardized ways of expressing organizational values and identity.

Rites **Rites** are dramatic, planned sets of activities that bring together aspects of cultural ideology in a single event. Harrison Trice and Janice Beyer (1984) identified six kinds of organizational rites. *Rites of passage* are used to mark membership in different levels or

Noticing Stories and the Work They Do

Think about an organization to which you belong, perhaps one in which you have worked or one that you have had many opportunities to observe. Identify corporate, personal, and collegial stories you were told when you first entered the organization. How did these stories shape your understandings of the organization?

Extend the concept of organizational stories to your family's culture. What family stories taught you your family's history and values? What personal stories did your parents tell you to define who they are and what they stand for? Did family members talk about others? If so, what collegial stories did you hear about other relatives? Do the stories told in your family form a coherent account of its identity?

SHARPEN YOUR SKILL

© Flying Colours Ltd/Digital Vision/Getty Images

Recognizing employees who exemplify organizational values strengthens the organization's culture.

parts of organizations. For example, a nonverbal symbol of change may be the moving of an employee's office from the second to the fourth floor after a promotion. Special handshakes are nonverbal rites that symbolize communality among members of clubs and other groups. A desk plaque with a new employee's name and title is a rite that acknowledges a change in identity. *Rites of integration* affirm and enhance the sense of community in an organization. Examples are holiday parties, annual picnics, and graduation ceremonies.

Organizational cultures also include rites that blame or praise people. Firings, demotions, and reprimands are common *blaming rites*—the counterpart of which is *enhancement rites,* which praise individuals and teams that embody the organization's goals and self-image. Campuses bestow awards on faculty who are especially gifted teachers, and chaired professorships on outstanding scholars. Many sales companies give awards for productivity (most sales of the month, quarter, or year). Many organizations use listservs or organizational newsletters to congratulate employees on accomplishments. In my department, faculty meetings always open with announcements about honors and achievements of faculty members. This recognition rite gives each of us moments in the limelight. Audrey describes an enhancement rite in her sorority.

▶ Audry

In my sorority, we recognize sisters who make the dean's list each semester by putting a rose on their dinner plates. That way everyone realizes who has done well academically, and we can also remind ourselves that scholarship is one of the qualities we all aspire to.

Organizations also develop rites for managing change. *Renewal rites* aim to revitalize and update organizations. Training workshops serve this purpose, as do periodic retreats at which organizational members discuss their goals and the institution's health. Organizations also develop rituals for managing conflicts between members of the organization. *Conflict resolution rites* are standard methods of dealing with differences and discord. Examples are arbitration, collective bargaining, mediation, executive fiat, voting, and ignoring or denying problems. The conflict resolution rite that typifies an organization reflects the values of its overall culture.

Rituals **Rituals** are forms of communication that occur regularly and that members of an organization perceive as familiar and routine parts of organizational life. Rituals differ from rites in that rituals don't necessarily bring together a number of aspects of organizational ideology into a single event. Rather, rituals are repeated communication performances that communicate a particular value or role definition.

Organizations have personal, task, and social rituals. *Personal rituals* are routine behaviors that individuals use to express their organizational identities. In their study of organizational cultures, Pacanowsky and O'Donnell-Trujillo (1983) noted that Lou Polito, the owner of a car company, opened all the company's mail every day. Whenever possible, Polito hand-delivered mail to the divisions of his company to communicate his openness and his involvement with the day-to-day business.

Social rituals are standardized performances that affirm relationships between members of organizations (Mokros, 2006; Mumby, 2006). Some organizations have a company dining room to encourage socializing among employees. In the United Kingdom and Japan, many businesses have afternoon tea breaks. E-mail chatting and forwarding jokes are additional examples of socializing rituals in the workplace. Tamar Katriel (1990) identified a social ritual of griping among Israelis. *Kiturim*, the name Israelis give to their griping, most often occurs during Friday night social events called *mesibot kiturim*, which translates as "gripe sessions." Unlike griping about personal concerns, *kiturim* typically focuses on national issues, concerns, and problems. Some Jewish families engage in ritualized *kvetching*, which is personal griping that aims to air frustrations but not necessarily to resolve them. The point of the ritual is to complain, not to solve a problem. Sharon provides an example of an office griping ritual.

▶ Sharon

Where I work, we have this ritual of spending the first half-hour or so at work every Monday complaining about what we have to get done that week. Even if we don't have a rough week ahead, we go through the motions of moaning and groaning. It's kind of like a bonding ceremony for us.

Task rituals are repeated activities that help members of an organization perform their jobs. Perhaps a special conference room is used for particular tasks, such as giving marketing presentations, holding performance reviews, or making sales proposals. Task rituals are also evident in forms and procedures that members of organizations are expected to use to do various things. These forms and procedures standardize task performance in a manner consistent with the organization's view of itself and how it operates. In their study of a police unit, Pacanowsky and O'Donnell-Trujillo (1983) identified the routine that officers are trained to follow when they stop drivers for violations. The questions officers are taught to ask ("May I see your license, please?" "Do you know why I stopped you?" "Do you know how fast you were going?") allow them to size up traffic violators and decide whether to give them a break or a closer look. The Sharpen Your Skill exercise on this page allows you to notice rituals in an organization to which you belong.

Noticing Rituals in Your Organization

Think of an organization to which you belong. It could be your school or a more specific group such as a sports team, club, or workplace. Describe one ritual (personal, social, or task) and explain what it does for the organization and members. What would be missing if this ritual were abandoned?

SHARPEN YOUR SKILL

Structures

Organizational cultures are also represented through structural aspects of organizational life. As the name implies, **structures** organize relationships and interaction between members of an organization. We'll consider four structures that express and uphold organizational culture: roles, rules, policies, and communication networks.

Roles **Roles** are responsibilities and behaviors expected of people because of their specific positions in an organization. Most organizations formally define roles in job descriptions:

Training coordinator: Responsible for assessing needs and providing training to Northwest branches of the firm; supervises staff of 25 professional trainers, coordinates with director of human relations.

Instructor: Duties include teaching three classes per term, supervising graduate student theses, serving on departmental and university committees, and conducting research. Ph.D. and experience required.

A role is not tied to any particular person. Rather, it is a set of functions and responsibilities that could be performed by any number of people who have particular talents, experiences, and other relevant qualifications. If one person quits or is fired, another can be found as a replacement. Regardless of who is in the role, the organization will continue with its structure intact. The different roles in an organization are a system, which means they are interrelated and interacting. Each role is connected to other roles within the system. Organizational charts portray who is responsible to whom and clarify the hierarchy of power among roles in the organization.

Rules Rules, which we discussed in Chapters 1, 4, and 10, are patterned ways of interacting. Rules are present in organizational contexts just as they are in other settings of interaction. As in other contexts, organizational rules may be formal (in the contract or organizational chart) or informal (norms for interaction).

Within organizations, constitutive rules specify what various kinds of communication symbolize. Some firms count working late as evidence of commitment. Socializing with colleagues after work may count as showing team spirit. Taking on extra assignments, attending training sessions, and dressing like upper management may communicate ambition. The FYI box on page 270 discusses systemic and deliberate corporate operations that were illegal or immoral and suggests that, in some of these organizations, going along with unethical practices and not blowing the whistle counted as company loyalty. Lyle's commentary points out what counted as violating chain of command in his company.

▶ **Lyle**

I found out the hard way that a company I worked for was dead serious about the organizational chart. I had a problem with a co-worker, so I talked with a guy in another department I was friends with. Somehow my supervisor found out, and he blew a gasket. He was furious that I had "gone outside of the chain of command" instead of coming straight to him.

Regulative rules specify when, where, and with whom communication should occur. Organizational charts formalize regulative rules by showing who reports to whom. Other regulative rules may specify that problems should not be discussed with people outside the organization and that social conversations are (or are not) permitted during working hours. Some organizations have found that employees spend so much time online that productivity suffers, so rules regulating online time are instituted.

Policies **Policies** are formal statements of practices that reflect and uphold the overall culture of an organization. For example, my university's mission statement emphasizes the importance of teaching. Consistent with the organizational identity reflected in that mission statement, we have policies that require teaching evaluations and policies that tie good teaching performance to tenure, promotion, and raises. Most organizations codify policies governing such aspects of work life as hiring, promotion, benefits, grievances, and medical leave. The content of policies in these areas differs among organizations in ways that reflect the distinct cultures of diverse work environments.

Organizational policies also reflect the larger society within which organizations are embedded. For example, as public awareness of sexual harassment has increased, most organizations have developed formal policies that define sexual harassment, state the organization's attitude toward it, and detail the procedure for making complaints. Because of the prevalence of dual-career couples, many organizations have created departments to help place the spouses of people they want to hire.

Communication Networks As we noted earlier in this chapter, communication networks link members of an organization together through formal and informal forms of interaction and relationships. These networks play key roles in expressing and reinforcing the culture of an organization.

Job descriptions and organizational charts, which specify who is supposed to communicate with whom about what, are formal networks. Formal networks provide the order necessary for organizations to operate. They define lines of upward communication (subordinates to superiors; providing feedback, reporting results), downward communication (superiors to subordinates; giving orders, establishing policies), and horizontal communication (peer to peer; coordinating between departments).

TECHNOLOGY

KEEPING TRACK OF EMPLOYEES

More and more companies are instituting systems to monitor employees' online communication. One popular system, Worktrack, is used by employers to track workers who make home calls (for instance, technicians who repair heating and air conditioning). In addition to verifying that workers are actually at job sites, Worktrack monitors driving speed (Levy, 2004a). During a random check of employees' online activities, a chapter of the American Heart Association discovered that an employee had repeatedly visited a pornographic website. He was dismissed (Jones, 1999).

A number of employers also routinely screen employees' e-mail to filter out profanity, pornography, and sexist and racist jokes and language (Jones, 1999). Employees who protest that this is an invasion of privacy are learning that the courts regard e-mail and web access as company resources that employees are allowed to use. Court rulings do not support any expectation of privacy in e-mail and web communication on the job (Monmonier, 2002).

On the other hand, in a recent court case Judge John Spooner ruled that surfing the web at work is no different than reading a newspaper or talking with friends. Judge Spooner said, "The Internet has become the modern equivalent of a telephone or daily newspaper" (Surfing Web, 2006, p. 3A).

The informal communication network is more difficult to describe because it is neither formally defined nor based on fixed organizational roles. Friendships, alliances, carpools, and nearby offices can be informal networks through which a great deal of information flows. Most professionals have others within their organization with whom they regularly check perceptions and past whom they run certain ideas.

Communication outside the formal channels of an organization is sometimes called the *grapevine,* a term that suggests its free-flowing quality. Grapevine communication, although continual in organizational life, is especially active during periods of change (Davis, 1977, 1980). This makes sense because we engage in communication to reduce our uncertainty and discomfort with change. New information (a fresh rumor) activates the grapevine. Although details often are lost or distorted as messages travel along a grapevine, the information conveyed informally has a surprisingly high rate of accuracy: 75% to 90% (Hellweg, 1992). If details are important, however, the grapevine may be a poor source of information.

ORGANIZATIONS AND ETHICS—OR LACK THEREOF

In 2002, the Enron scandal was a huge news story. According to news reports, the accounting firm Arthur Andersen had knowingly misrepresented Enron's financial condition in ways that misled investors, many of whom lost substantial funds they had invested in Enron. Investigations revealed that knowledge of the misrepresentation was widespread, although not universal, among both Enron and Andersen employees. Shortly after the Enron story broke, companies such as Adelphia Communications and WorldComm were charged with illegal practices. Americans expressed shock and disbelief at the scandals.

Two years later, in 2004, news broke of U.S. soldiers' abuse of prisoners at Abu Ghraib prison in Iraq. Initially, the United States administration claimed the problem was a "few bad apples," who didn't represent what the U.S. military was about. As the story grew, however, it became clear that higher-ranking military personnel and members of the administration were aware of the abuses and did not intervene to stop them. Once again, Americans expressed shock that such a thing could happen.

Shock and outrage are legitimate responses to unethical behavior. However, perhaps Americans shouldn't have been shocked, because illegal activities are hardly new. Scandals in government are not unfamiliar to us—Watergate is a prime example of egregiously unlawful behavior at the highest levels of U.S. government. Between 1975 and 1990, fully two-thirds of the *Fortune 500* companies were convicted (not just accused) of crimes including price fixing, illegal dumping of toxic waste matter, and accounting violations (Conrad & Poole, 2002).

What should we conclude from these reports? Are organizations unethical, or is it simply that certain individuals (a few "rotten apples") in some organizations act illegally and unethically (Lefkowitz, 2003)? Although individuals are responsible for their ethical choices, it would be naive to assume that organizations aren't also blameworthy. Two organizational communication scholars, Charley Conrad and Marshall Scott Poole (2004), assert that the power structures, norms, and cultures in many organizations allow or even encourage unethical activities and punish those who resist or blow the whistle. One example of the systemic nature of unethical behavior is that, in 1996, 29 of 30 Harvard MBAs contacted for this study reported they had been ordered by superiors at their places of work to violate their personal ethics at least once (Barlow, 1996).

►GUIDELINES FOR COMMUNICATING IN ORGANIZATIONS

We'll discuss three guidelines that are particularly relevant to organizational communication in our era.

Adapt to Diverse Needs, Situations, and People

Consider the following descriptions of people who work in one company in my community:

▶ Eileen is 28, single, Jewish, fluent in English and Spanish, and the primary caregiver for her disabled mother.

▶ Frank is 37, a father of two, and a European American married to a full-time homemaker. He is especially skilled in collaborative team building.

▶ Denise is 30, single, European American, an excellent public speaker, and mother of a 4-year-old girl.

▶ Sam is 59, African American, father of two grown children, and married to an accountant. He is widely regarded as supportive and empathic.

▶ Ned is 42, divorced, European American, and recovering from a triple by-pass operation.

▶ Javier is 23, a Latino, and married to a woman who works full time. They are expecting their first child in a few months.

These six people have different life situations, abilities, and goals that affect what they need and want in order to be effective on the job. Eileen and Denise need flexible working hours so that they can take care of family members. Eileen may also expect her employer to respect Rosh Hashanah, Yom Kippur, Hanukkah, and other holidays of her religion. Ned may need extended disability leave and a period of part-time work while he recuperates from his heart surgery. Javier may want to take family leave when his child is born, a benefit that wouldn't be valued by Frank or Sam. These six people are typical of the workforce today. They illustrate the diversity of people, life situations, and needs that characterize the modern workplace (Earley & Gibson, 2002; Farr, 2003; Padavic & Reskin, 2002). The variety of workers is a major change, one that requires organizations to adapt.

The Industrial Revolution of the mid-1800s transformed a largely agrarian economy into one dominated by factories and centralized workplaces. The assembly line is not just how factories produced products; it is also a metaphor for how factories treated workers. All employees were expected to fit the same mold: identical work hours and benefits and identical dedication to their jobs, without complications from personal or family life. Many workers were men who, like Frank, had a wife who took care of home and family life. Other workers—men with wives who worked outside the home, single parents—had to devise child-care arrangements through kinship networks, babysitters, or a combination of the two. The workplace was not expected to accommodate employees' personal situations and needs.

In our era, quite a different workplace is emerging. Workers increasingly expect organizations to tailor conditions and benefits to their individual needs and circumstances. Many organizations have a cafeteria-style benefits package that allows employees to select benefits from a range of options that includes family leave, flexible working hours, employer-paid education, telecommuting, onsite day care, dental insurance, and personal days. Someone with primary caregiving responsibilities might sacrifice vacation time for additional family leave. A person nearing retirement might want maximum insurance and medical coverage but little family leave time. Flextime, which allows people to adjust working hours to their lifestyles, would be a valuable benefit for many workers. Employer-sponsored classes would be sought by workers who want to learn new skills that might accelerate their advancement. Still another increasingly cherished option is telecommuting, which allows workers to work in their homes or other locations removed from a central office.

The organizations that survive and thrive in an era of diversity will be those that adapt effectively to meet the expectations and needs of different workers and the present era (see the FYI box on page 272). Flexible rules and policies, rather than one-size-fits-all formulas, will mark the successful workplaces of the future.

fyi

TOMORROW'S ORGANIZATIONS

Work groups and teams will increasingly work virtually, with people connecting from different places and even different countries (Rothwell, 2007). Technologies such as text messaging, audio- and videoconferencing, and webcasts allow groups to work across time and distance. In future years, we're sure to see additional technologies that further facilitate virtual group work.

One of the best ways to learn about social and organizational trends that are reshaping the world of work is to read online magazines. *Entrepreneurial Edge* (WebLink 12.2 in the book's online resources) discusses emerging trends and resources for entrepreneurs. Another savvy site is an idea café created by business owners (WebLink 12.3 in the book's online resources), where you'll find advice on starting and running a business, using technologies, and networking. To create a virtual conference, go to the book's online resources and click on Weblink 12.4. It's free for as many as five members.

By extension, the most competent, most effective professionals will be those who are comfortable with a stream of changes in people and ways of working. You might work closely with a colleague for several years and then see little of that person if he or she modifies working hours to accommodate changes in family life. If you choose to telecommute, you will need to develop new ways of staying involved in the informal network (which may operate largely on the Internet) and having the amount of social contact you enjoy. Managers will need to find ways to lead employees who work in different locations and at different hours. Project teams may interact through e-mail bulletin boards as often as or more often than they interact face to face.

The workforce of today is different from that of yesterday, and today's workforce is not what we will see in the years ahead. Because rapid change is typical in modern work life, an adaptive orientation is one of the most important qualifications for success (Earley & Gibson, 2002). Openness to change and willingness to experiment are challenges for effective participation in organizations.

Expect to Move In and Out of Teams

Effective communication in today's and tomorrow's organizations requires interacting intensely with members of teams that may form and dissolve quickly. Whereas autonomous workers—single leaders, mavericks, and independent professionals—were prized in the 1940s, the team player is most highly sought today (Rothwell, 2007). John, who returned to school in his mid-forties, describes the changes in his job over the past 13 years.

▶ John

My job is entirely different today than when I started it 13 years ago. When I came aboard, each of us had his own responsibilities, and management pretty much left us alone to do our work. I found authors and helped them develop their ideas, Andy took care of all art for the books, someone else was in charge of marketing, and so forth. Each of us did our job on a book and passed the book on to the next person. Now the big buzzword is *team*. Everything is done in teams. From the start of a new book project, the author and I are part of a team that includes the art editor, marketing director, manuscript designer, and so forth. Each of us has to coordinate with the others continually; nobody works as a lone operator. Although I had reservations about teams at first, by now I'm convinced that they are superior to individuals working independently. The books we're producing are more internally coherent, and they are developed far more efficiently when we collaborate.

The skills we discussed in Part II of this book will help you perceive carefully, listen well, use verbal and nonverbal communication effectively, promote constructive climates, and adapt your style of interacting to the diverse people on your teams. The challenge is to be able to adjust your style of communicating to the expectations and interaction styles of a variety of people and to the constraints of a range of situations. The greater your repertoire of communication skills, the more effectively you will be able to move in and out of teams on the job.

Manage Personal Relationships on the Job

A third challenge of organizational life involves relationships that are simultaneously personal and professional. You probably will be involved in a number of such relationships during your life. In a 1995 study titled "Bosses and Buddies," Ted Zorn described his long friendship with a colleague who became his supervisor. Zorn described tensions that arose because of conflicts between the role of friend and those of supervisor and subordinate. Although management has traditionally discouraged personal relationships between employees, the relationships have developed anyway. The goal, then, is to understand these relationships and manage them effectively.

Friendships between co-workers or supervisors and subordinates often enhance job commitment and satisfaction (Allen, 2006; Mokros, 2006; Mumby, 2006; Zorn, 1995). This is not surprising, because we're more likely to enjoy work when we work with people we like. Yet workplace friendships also have

DIVERSITY

Employee Mistreatment in Culturally Diverse Organizations

We hear a lot about the increasing diversity of the workforce in the United States and elsewhere.

What we hear less about is emerging as a serious problem that seems more prevalent in culturally diverse workplaces than in culturally homogeneous ones. The problem is employee mistreatment. A recent study (Namie, 2000) reported that 23% of mistreated employees were from minority groups, and 77% of mistreated employees were women. Other research confirms that the majority of on-the-job discrimination and conflict involves minorities and women (Clair, 1998; Oetzel, 1998).

Mistreatment ranges from unlawful activities, such as harassment and inequitable benefits, to more subtle activities, such as stereotyping, ridicule, and intergroup conflict (Allen, 2006; Harlos & Pinder, 1999; Mumby, 2006; Vardi & Weitz, 2004). A majority of male employees (61%) and European Americans (56%) report that they are treated fairly in their work life, but a minority of female (30%) and members of minority groups (33%) report being treated equitably (Meares, Oetzel, Torres, Derkacs, & Ginossar, 2004).

Individuals who are treated unfairly in the workplace tend to withdraw, leave, become resentful, or experience anger, which may be expressed in a variety of ways. Clearly, these consequences are not limited to individual employees—they affect organizations' health and productivity. If employees are not contributing constructively on the job, then the entire organization suffers.

Get Informed about On-the-Job Relationships

Workplace relationships—whether romances or friendships—can enhance professional life and jeopardize careers. Before you get involved in a workplace romantic relationship or friendship, take the time to get informed so you can make informed choices.

Check out three online resources, all available as WebLinks within the book's online resources. Click WebLink 12.5 to visit About.com's human resources page, which provides information and advice on workplace dating, sex, and romance. WebLink 12.6 takes you to SelfGrowth.com, where Dr. Janet Yager discusses her research and offers some sound advice about both friendships and romances in the workplace. WebLink 12.7 will give you access to AppleOne.com's summary of the upside and downside of workplace romance.

SHARPEN YOUR SKILL

drawbacks. As Zorn's story illustrates, on-the-job friendships may involve tension between the role expectations for friends and for colleagues. A supervisor may have difficulty rendering a fair evaluation of a subordinate who is also a friend. The supervisor might err by overrating the subordinate–friend's strengths or might try to compensate for personal affection by being especially harsh in judging the friend–subordinate. Friendship may also constrain negative feedback, which is essential to effective performance on the job (Larson, 1984). Also, workplace friendships that deteriorate may create stress and job dissatisfaction (Sias, Heath, Perry, Silva, & Fix, 2004).

▶ **Anna**

It's hard for me now that my best friend has been promoted over me. Part of it is envy, because I wanted the promotion too. But the hardest part is that I resent her power over me. When Billie gives me an assignment, I feel like as my friend she shouldn't dump extra work on me. But I also know that as the boss she has to give extra work to all of us sometimes. It just doesn't feel right for my best friend to tell me what to do and evaluate my work.

Romantic relationships between people who work together are also increasing. Most women and men work outside the home, sometimes spending more hours on the job than in the home. In Chapter 10, we learned that proximity is a key influence on the formation of romantic relationships. It's no surprise, then, that people who see each other almost every day sometimes find themselves attracted to each other. Yet on-the-job romances pose challenges (Fox, 1998). They are likely to involve many of the same tensions that operate in friendships between supervisors and subordinates. In addition, romantic relationships are especially likely to arouse co-workers' resentment and discomfort. Romantic breakups also tend to be more dramatic than breakups between friends. As Eugene points out, when a workplace romance dies, tension and discomfort may arise.

▶ **Eugene**

Once I got involved with a woman where I was working. We were assigned to the same team and really hit it off, and one thing led to another, and we were dating. I guess it affected our work some, since we spent a lot of time talking and stuff in the office. But the real problem came when we broke up. It's impossible to avoid seeing your "ex" when you work together in a small office, and everyone else acted like they were walking on eggshells around us. She finally quit, and you could just feel tension drain out of everyone else in our office.

It's probably unrealistic to assume we can avoid personal relationships with people on the job. The challenge is to manage those relationships so that the workplace doesn't interfere with the personal bond and the intimacy doesn't jeopardize professionalism. Friends and romantic partners may need to adjust their expectations and styles of interacting so that personal and work roles do not conflict. It's also advisable to make sure that on-the-job communication doesn't reflect favoritism and privileges that could cause resentment in co-workers. It's important to invest extra effort to maintain an open communication climate with other co-workers.

▶SUMMARY

In this chapter, we've seen the importance of daily performances, such as rituals and storytelling, in upholding an organization's identity and a shared set of meanings for members of the organization. The culture of an organization is created, sustained, and altered in the process of communication between members of an organization. As they talk, interact, develop policies, and participate in the formal and informal networks, they continuously weave the fabric of their individual roles and collective life.

Organizations, like other contexts of communication, involve a number of challenges. To meet those challenges, we discussed three guidelines. One is to develop a large repertoire of communication skills so you can adapt effectively to diverse people, situations, and needs in the workplace. A second guideline is to be prepared to move in and out of teams rapidly, which is required in many modern organizations. Finally, we discussed ways to manage personal relationships in the workplace. It's likely that you and others will form friendships and perhaps romantic relationships with people in the workplace. The communication skills we've discussed throughout this book will help you navigate the tensions and challenges of close relationships on the job.

Review, Reflect, Extend

The Key Concepts, For Further Reflection and Discussion questions, Recommended Resources, and Experience Communication Case Study that follow will help you review, reflect on, and extend the information and ideas presented in this chapter. A diverse selection of online resources is also available through ThomsonNOW. These resources include Speech Builder Express, InfoTrac College Edition, interactive videos, vMentor, and Thomson Audio Study Products.

Thomson NOW! is an online study system designed to help you put your time to the best use. After reading a chapter, take the NOW pre-test to identify concepts discussed in the chapter that you may not fully understand. Based on the results of this diagnostic test, the system will create a personalized study plan that directs you to specific learning resources and activities. To see if you're ready for an exam, take the NOW post-test to check your understanding.

For more information or to access this book's online resources, visit **http://www.thomsonedu.com**.

▶ KEY CONCEPTS

The terms following are defined in the chapter on the page number indicated, and they appear in alphabetical order, with definitions, in the Glossary, which begins on page 369. The book's online resources also include flash cards and crossword puzzles to help you learn these terms and the concepts they represent.

communication network, 260
organizational culture, 261
policy, 268

rite, 265
ritual, 266
role, 267

structure, 267

▶ FOR FURTHER REFLECTION AND DISCUSSION

The questions below can also be found among the book's online resources for this chapter, where you have the option of e-mailing your responses to your instructor, if required.

1. Locate a copy of your college's policies governing students. From its policies concerning class attendance, drug use, and dishonorable conduct, what can you infer about the culture the college wants to promote? (Note how dishonorable conduct is defined; this differs among schools.)

2. Reflect on the corporate, personal, and collegial stories you heard during your first few weeks on a new job. What did these stories say about the organizational culture?

3. Think about a group to which you belong. It may be a work group or a social group such as a fraternity or interest club. Describe some common rites and rituals in your group. What do these rites and rituals communicate about the group's culture?

4. Interview a person over 45 who has a career that interests you. Ask the person to describe changes she or he has seen in her or his profession, such as the prominence of teams and changes in benefit packages, work schedules, and other features of professional life.

▶ RECOMMENDED RESOURCES

1. Visit the website of an organization you think you might like to join. Explore different links on the site to learn about the organization's policies and the image it presents. From the material on its site, what can you infer about the organization's culture?

2. The film *Remember the Titans* provides a dramatic account of a man who was assigned to coach a group of athletes in a recently integrated school. The players didn't work together well, largely because of ethnic differences and ethnocentric attitudes. This film provides rich insights into leadership and the development of a cohesive organizational culture for the team.

3. Robin Clair's book *Organizing Silence* (1998; Albany: State University of New York Press) offers an excellent analysis of ways organizations and their members silence employees who object to unfair treatment.

Experience Communication Case Study

ED MISSES THE BANQUET

Jason Harris/© Wadsworth

The book's online resources include an interactive video of the communication situation featured in the case study scripted below. Apply what you've learned in this chapter by analyzing the case study, using the questions that follow the script as a guide. These questions are also available online with the video.

Ed recently began working at a new job. Although he's been in his new job only five weeks, he likes it a lot, and he's told you that he sees a real future for himself with this company. But last week, a problem arose. Along with all other employees, Ed was invited to the annual company banquet, at which everyone socializes and awards are given for outstanding performance. Ed's daughter was in a play the night of the banquet, so Ed chose to attend his daughter's play rather than the company event. The invitation to the banquet had stated only, "Hope to see you there" and had not been RSVP, so Ed didn't mention to anyone that he couldn't attend. When he arrived at work the next Monday morning, however, he discovered the case was otherwise and had the exchange that follows with his manager. Later, when Ed talked with several co-workers who had been around a few years, he discovered that top management sees the annual banquet as a "command performance" that signifies company unity and loyalty.

Ed's manager: You skipped the banquet last Saturday. I had really thought you were committed to our company.

Ed: My daughter was in a play that night.

Ed's manager: I don't care *why* you didn't come. We notice who is really with us and who isn't.

1. How does the concept of constitutive rules, which we first discussed in Chapter 4, help explain the misunderstanding between Ed and his manager?

2. How might Ed use the informal network in his organization to learn the normative practices of the company and the meanings they have to others in the company?

3. How do the ambiguity and abstraction inherent in language explain the misunderstanding between Ed and his manager?

4. How would you suggest that Ed repair the damage done by his absence from the company banquet? What might he say to his manager? How could he use *I*-language, indexing, and dual perspective to guide his communication?

5. Do you think the banquet is a ritual? Why or why not?

13 *Public Communication*

▶ **FOCUS QUESTIONS**

1. To what extent is public speaking similar to conversation?

2. How can speakers enhance their credibility?

3. How do speakers construct effective thesis statements?

4. How do speakers support their claims?

5. How do speakers organize ideas effectively?

6. What are the advantages and disadvantages of different styles of delivery?

7. How can speakers manage speaking anxiety?

8. How can you be a listen critically to others' public speeches?

▶ Your school is considering raising tuition, and you want to speak out against the idea.

▶ Your supervisor asks you to speak to a group of college seniors about career opportunities in your company.

▶ A developer has announced plans to build a shopping center in your neighborhood, and you oppose the idea. The town council has announced that it will hear public statements on the developer's proposal at its next meeting.

▶ You are responsible for reporting your project team's findings to the CEO of your firm.

▶ You attend a public presentation in which the speaker misuses statistics to support the claim that industrial pollution will not harm your community. You want to challenge the speaker and give accurate information to other listeners.

These are just a few examples of people who speak in public situations. Public speaking is not limited to politicians or people in public life. Most members of organizations, from CEOs to entry-level and midlevel employees, are expected to speak within organizations and to various publics. Skill in public speaking

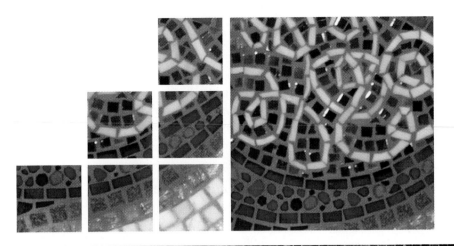

is important for parents who are concerned about a high school's reading list, for law enforcement officers who need to calm crowds or educate groups on self-defense, for public relations professionals who give press conferences, and for employees who want to persuade their employers to adopt or modify policies.

Speaking in public allows you to be an active citizen, an effective professional, and a responsible member of your community and the groups to which you belong. It allows you to affect what others believe, think, and do. Therefore, skill in public speaking is important both for individuals and for society. Equally important is skill in listening critically to the public communication of others. People who present their ideas effectively and listen critically to the ideas of others are capable of informed, vigorous participation in all spheres of life. The importance of free speech to democratic life is recognized by the First Amendment (see the FYI box on the right).

fyi

THE FIRST AMENDMENT

"Congress shall make no law respecting an establishment of religion, or prohibiting the free exercise thereof; or abridging the freedom of speech, or of the press; or the right of people peaceably to assemble, and to petition the Government for a redress of grievances."

This chapter focuses on public speaking. In the first part of the chapter, we will discuss the different purposes of public speaking and its distinctive features. The second section of the chapter provides an overview of planning and presenting public speeches. In the third section, we identify three guidelines for effective public communication: reducing speaking anxiety, adapting to audiences, and listening critically to public discourse. The complex process of public speaking cannot be taught in a single chapter. The *Student Companion* that accompanies this book provides detailed guidelines for crafting speeches. This chapter's goal is to give you a conceptual understanding of what is involved in public communication. The information we will cover will be especially useful in helping you become a more critical listener when you attend to others' public communication.

▶PUBLIC SPEAKING AS ENLARGED CONVERSATION

Many years ago, James Winans (1938), a distinguished professor of communication, remarked that effective public speaking is enlarged conversation. What Winans meant was that in many ways public speaking is quite similar to everyday talk. As Michael

Motley and Jennifer Molloy more recently stated, "Except for preparation time and turn-taking delay, public speaking has fundamental parallels to everyday conversation" (1994, p. 52). Whether we are talking with a couple of friends or speaking to an audience of 1,000 people, we must adapt to others' perspectives, create a good climate for interaction, use effective verbal and nonverbal communication, organize what we say so others can follow our ideas, support our claims, present our ideas in an engaging and convincing manner, and listen and respond to questions and comments about what we have said.

Thinking of public speaking as enlarged conversation reminds us that most public speaking is neither stiff nor exceedingly formal. In fact, some of the most effective public speakers use an informal, personal style that invites listeners to feel that they are interacting with someone, not being lectured. This means that effective public communication requires and builds on skills and principles that apply to communication in all contexts, as we discussed in Part II.

I learned that effective public speaking is much like conversation when I first taught a large course. Previously, I had taught small classes, and I relied on discussion. In the large class, I lectured in a fairly formal style because I thought that was appropriate for a class of 150 students. One day, a student asked a question, and I responded with another question. He replied, then another student added her ideas, and an open discussion was launched. Both the students and I were more engaged with one another and the course material than we had been when I lectured formally. That's when I realized that even in large classes effective teaching is enlarged conversation.

Noticing Conversational Speaking Style

Think about the professors who were most effective, and those who were least effective, in communicating course content. For each group of professors, answer these questions:

1. Did the professors use a formal or informal speaking style?
2. Did the professors state clearly what was important?
3. Did the professors give reasons for ideas and opinions they expressed?
4. Could you follow the professors' trains of thought?
5. Did the professors adapt their ideas to your knowledge and interests?
6. Did you feel involved in the classroom communication?

SHARPEN YOUR SKILL

Distinctive Features of Public Communication

Although public speaking is enlarged conversation, it differs from casual interaction in two ways. First, public speeches tend to involve more planning and preparation than informal conversations do. Second, in public speaking situations the audiences' contributions are less obvious and less immediate than the speakers'.

Greater Responsibility to Plan and Prepare When a friend asks your opinion on gun control, you respond without conducting research, carefully organizing your ideas, or practicing your delivery. Before speaking to a group of 50 people about gun control, however, you would be likely to do some research, to organize your ideas, and to practice delivering your speech. In public speaking situations, you have a responsibility to provide evidence and reasoning to support your beliefs, to structure your ideas clearly, and to practice your presentation so your delivery is engaging.

Listeners' expectations affect the planning and preparation needed for effective public speaking. We expect more evidence, clearer organization, and more polished delivery in public speeches than in casual conversations. Therefore, public speakers who do not prepare well are likely to disappoint listeners and to be judged inadequate. When you are giving a public speech, your responsibility is to analyze listeners, to do research, to organize ideas, and to practice and polish delivery.

Less Direct Interaction Public speaking also tends to be less directly interactive than many forms of communication, such as personal conversations, interviews, and team deliberations. In many contexts, communicators take turns talking, but speakers tend to dominate in public presentations. It would be a mistake, however, to think that listeners don't participate actively in public presentations. They are sending messages even as they listen: head nods, frowns, perplexed expressions, applause, smiles. Listeners communicate throughout a speech, primarily in nonverbal ways. As Cheryl Hamilton notes, effective public speakers "realize that successful communication is a two-way street" (1996, p. 29). In other words, good public speakers pay attention to what listeners are "saying" throughout their speeches.

Even though listeners participate actively, public speaking places special responsibility on speakers. To be effective, they must anticipate listeners' attitudes and knowledge and must adapt their presentation to the views of listeners. One of the first steps in planning a good public speech is to ask what audience members are likely to know about a topic and how they are likely to feel about it. Based on what you know or learn about listeners, you can make informed choices about what information to include and how to support and organize your ideas.

While actually giving a speech, you should also adapt to listeners' feedback. If some listeners look confused, you might add an example or elaborate on an idea. If listeners' nonverbal behaviors suggest that they are bored, you might alter your volume, incorporate gestures, change your speaking position, or offer a personal example to enliven your talk. Later in this chapter, we'll return to the topic of adapting to listeners. For now, you should realize that because public speaking gives the speaker primary control, the speaker has a special responsibility to be sensitive to listeners' ideas, values, interests, and experiences. With this background, we're ready to consider the purposes of public speaking.

The Purposes of Public Speeches

Traditionally, three speaking purposes have been recognized: to entertain, to inform, and to persuade. You probably realize that these purposes often overlap. For example, informative speeches routinely include humor or interesting comments to entertain listeners. Some of your favorite professors probably include stories and interesting examples to enliven informational lectures (see the Sharpen Your Skill exercise on page 280). Speeches to inform may also teach listeners something entirely new.

Sasha, a student in one of my classes, gave a speech on arranged marriages, which are still common in her native country. Her goal was to inform her classmates about the history of arranged marriages and why they work for many people. Although her primary goal was to inform, her speech had a persuasive aspect because she encouraged listeners not to impose their values on the practices of other cultures. This reinforces our earlier discussion of overlapping purposes in public speaking. Persuasive speeches often contain information about issues as well as content that is entertaining. Speeches intended to entertain may also inform and persuade, perhaps through the use of humor or dramatic narratives. Although purposes of speaking overlap, most speeches have one primary purpose.

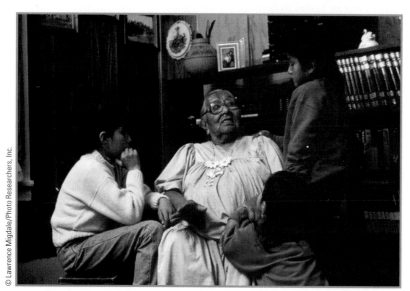

© Lawrence Migdale/Photo Researchers, Inc.

Narrative speaking is a vital part of many cultures. In these communities, storytelling weaves the past into the present.

Speaking to Entertain In a **speech to entertain,** the primary objective is to engage, interest, amuse, or please listeners. You might think that only accomplished comics and performers present speeches to entertain. Actually, many of us will be involved in speaking to entertain during our lives. You might be asked to give an after-dinner speech, to present a toast at a friend's wedding, or to make remarks at a retirement party for a colleague.

Humor, although often part of speeches to entertain, is not the only way we engage others. We also entertain when we tell stories. We share stories to share experiences, build community, pass on history, or teach a lesson. Parents share with children stories of their courtship; they discuss friends and relatives and keep family memories alive. Stories and the art of storytelling are especially important in cultures that emphasize oral communication (Einhorn, 2000; Fitch, 2000).

Speaking to Inform A **speech to inform** has the primary goal of increasing listeners' understanding, awareness, or knowledge of some topic. For example, a speaker might want listeners to understand what behaviors do and do not spread HIV or to make listeners aware of recycling programs. In both cases, the primary purpose is to enrich listeners' knowledge, although clearly the two topics have persuasive implications. A speeche to inform may also take the form of a demonstration, in which the speaker shows how to do something while giving a verbal explanation. For instance, a demonstration speech might show listeners how to use a new computer program or how to distinguish between poisonous and nonpoisonous species of mushrooms. As Gladys points out, however, speaking to inform may be more successful when speakers also entertain or otherwise capture listeners' interest.

▶ Gladys

I've taught second grade for eight years, and there's one thing I've learned: If you don't get the students' interest, you can't teach them anything. My education classes taught me to focus on content when planning lessons. But working in real classrooms with real children taught me that before a teacher can get content or information across to students, she has to first capture their interest.

Speaking to Persuade A **speech to persuade** aims to change listeners' attitudes, beliefs, or behaviors or to motivate them to take some action. Persuasive goals are to influence attitudes, to change practices, and to alter beliefs. Rather than primarily an entertainer or teacher, the persuasive speaker is an advocate who argues for a cause, issue, policy, attitude, or action. In one of my classes, a student named Chris gave a speech designed to persuade other students to contribute to the Red Cross blood drive. He began by telling us that he was a hemophiliac, whose life depended on blood donations. He then explained the procedures for donating blood (a subordinate informational purpose) so that listeners would not be deterred by fear of the unknown. Next, he described several cases of people who had died or had become critically ill because adequate supplies of blood weren't available. In the two weeks after his speech, more than one-third of the students who had heard his speech donated blood.

Persuasive speeches aim to influence—to change what people believe, think, or do. As communication scholar Cindy Griffin (2006) points out, many of the values and principles of the United States were carved out in key public speeches that changed what people believed and did. Consider a few examples of speeches that contributed to changing America:

MOVED TO SPEAK

Candace Lightner had never thought of herself as a public speaker. She had never sought the limelight and had seldom been required to speak out to others. Then, in 1980, her 13-year-old daughter was killed by a teenage drunk driver. Once she recovered from the immediate grief of her daughter's untimely death, Lightner began a crusade for stricter laws against drunk driving (Lightner, 1990; Sellinger, 1994).

She founded Mothers Against Drunk Driving (MADD), which now has thousands of members. In addition, Lightner persuaded state and federal legislators to approve stiffer laws and penalties for drunk driving and to raise the age for drinking to 21. Although not an outstanding speaker when she began her crusade, Lightner became a skillful speaker in order to get her message across.

▶ In 1841, Frederick Douglass spoke against slavery.

▶ In 1848, Elizabeth Cady Stanton advocated women's enfranchisement.

▶ In 1963, Martin Luther King Jr. gave his famous "I Have a Dream" speech.

▶ In 1964, President Lyndon Johnson explained affirmative action.

▶ In 2001, President Bush announced the War on Terror.

But speeches that change a country's laws and actions are not the only important forms of public speaking. I've seen citizens' votes affected by persuasive speeches that championed or criticized particular candidates. Likewise, I've seen students' attitudes and behaviors changed by classroom speeches that advocated wearing seat belts, giving blood, spaying and neutering pets, and community service. The FYI box on this page provides an example of how one average citizen became a persuasive advocate for stronger laws against drunk driving.

▶PLANNING AND PRESENTING PUBLIC SPEECHES

Effective public speaking is a process, not a static event. The process begins with understanding credibility and ways to earn it. The next steps are to define the purpose of speaking, develop a strong thesis statement, and decide how to organize the speech.

After her daughter was killed by a drunk driver, Candace Lightner began speaking in public to urge the passage of laws that crack down on drunk drivers.

Next speakers conduct research to identify evidence that can be used to support their ideas. Finally, speakers select delivery styles and practice the presentation. We will discuss each step. For more detailed guidance, refer to the *Student Companion* to this book.

Earning Credibility

Effective public speaking (and, indeed, communication in all contexts) requires credibility. **Credibility** exists when listeners believe in a speaker and trust what the speaker says. Credibility is based on listeners' perceptions of a speaker's position, authority, knowledge (also called expertise), dynamism, and trustworthiness (also called character). Therefore, to earn credibility, speakers should demonstrate that they are informed about their topics, that they are dynamic communicators, and that they are ethical in using evidence and reasoning.

A speaker's credibility is not necessarily static. Some speakers have high **initial credibility,** which is the expertise, dynamism, and character that listeners attribute to them before they begin to speak. Initial credibility is based on titles, experiences, and achievements that are known to listeners before they hear the speech. For example, Ralph Nader has high initial credibility in the area of consumer protection.

▶ Ricardo

Last month, I went to a lecture about getting started in financial planning. I figured the speaker just wanted to sell me something, so I didn't have too high a regard for him. But during his talk, he quoted lots of information from unbiased sources, so I saw that he really knew his stuff. He also didn't try to sell us anything, so I began to trust what he said. And he made the ideas really easy to follow with charts and handouts. By the time he was through, I thought he was excellent.

As Ricardo points out, a speaker with low initial credibility may gain strong credibility in the process of presenting a speech. Speakers may gain **derived credibility,** which listeners grant as a result of how speakers communicate during presentations. Speakers may earn derived credibility by providing clear, well-organized information and convincing evidence, and by an engaging delivery style. Speakers may also increase credibility during a presentation if listeners regard them as likable and as having goodwill toward the listeners (McCroskey & Teven, 1999).

Terminal credibility is a cumulative combination of initial and derived credibility. Terminal credibility may be greater or less than initial credibility, depending on how effectively a speaker has communicated.

Planning Public Speeches

A well-crafted speech begins with careful planning. Speakers should select a limited topic, define a clear purpose, and develop a concise thesis statement.

Select a Topic Speakers should select topics that they know and care about. When you choose a topic that matters to you, you have a head start in both knowledge and enthusiasm. Therefore, listeners are more likely to perceive you as knowledgeable and dynamic.

Speakers should also choose topics that are appropriate to listeners. It's important to consider listeners' values, backgrounds, attitudes, knowledge, and interests so that you can select topics and adapt how you address them in ways that respect the perspectives and interests of listeners.

Topics for speeches should be appropriate to the situation. If you are asked to speak at a professional meeting, your speech should address concerns and issues relevant to that profession. If you are speaking about someone who has won an award or who is retiring, the situation probably calls for a speech that praises the person.

Finally, effective topics are limited in scope. You may be concerned about education, but that topic is too broad for a single speech. You might narrow it to a speech on funding for education or training of teachers or some other specific aspect of your general area of interest.

Define the Speaking Purpose The second step in planning a speech is to define your general and specific purposes. The general purpose is to entertain, inform, or persuade. The **specific purpose** is exactly what you hope to accomplish. For example, specific purposes could be to get 25% of the audience to sign up to donate blood, to have listeners give correct answers to a quiz about the spread of HIV, to get 50% of the audience to sign a petition against gun control that you will send to Congress, or to get listeners to laugh at your jokes and enjoy the talk. The specific purpose of a speech states the behavioral response the speaker seeks: "I want listeners to agree to donate blood"; "I want listeners to sign a petition in support of the War on Terror."

Develop the Thesis The thesis statement is the single most important sentence in a speech. A clear **thesis statement,** which is the main idea of the entire speech, guides an effective speech: "Driving at 50 miles an hour saves lives, saves gas, and saves you from speeding tickets" or "The electoral college should be abolished because it does not represent the popular vote and does not fit the current times." Each of these thesis statements succinctly summarizes the focus of a speech (driving at 50 mph; abolishing the electoral college) and the main points of the speech (saving lives, saving gas, avoiding speeding tickets; unrepresentative, not fitted to current time). Once a speaker has a well-formed thesis statement, he or she is ready to consider how to organize the speech.

Organizing Speeches

Organization increases speaking effectiveness in several ways (Griffin, 2006). First, organization also affects comprehension of ideas. Listeners can understand, follow, and remember a speech that is well planned and well ordered. Listeners are less likely to retain the key ideas in a poorly organized speech. Second, experimental evidence shows that listeners are better persuaded by an organized speech than by a disorganized one. Finally, organization enhances speakers' credibility, probably because a carefully structured speech reflects well on a speaker's preparation and respect for listeners. When someone gives a disorganized speech, listeners may regard the person as incompetent or unprepared, which reduces derived and terminal credibility.

Organizing an effective speech is not the same as organizing a paper. Oral communication requires more explicit organization, greater redundancy, and simpler sentence structure. Unlike readers, listeners cannot refer to an earlier passage if they become confused or forget a point already made. Providing signposts to highlight organization and repeating key ideas increase listeners' retention of a message (Woolfolk, 1987).

Consistent with the need for redundancy in oral communication, good speeches tell listeners what the speaker is going to tell them, present the message, and then remind listeners of the main points. This means preparing an introduction, a body, and a conclusion. In addition, speakers should include transitions to move listeners from point to point in the speech.

The Introduction The introduction is the first thing an audience hears, and a good introduction does a lot of work. It should gain listeners' attention, give them a reason to listen, establish the credibility of the speaker, and state the thesis (the focus and the main points of the speech) (Miller, 1974).

The first objective of an introduction is to gain listeners' attention, which may also provide them with a motivation to listen. You might open with a dramatic piece of evidence, say, a startling statistic: "In the United States, four women per day are battered to death by intimates. Would you know what to do if you or a friend of yours was being abused?" This opening gives a dramatic example and a reason to listen to the speech. Other ways to gain attention are to present a striking visual aid (a photo of a victim of battering) or a dramatic example (the detailed story of a battered woman).

You could pose a question that invites listeners to think actively about the topic: "Have you ever feared for your life and had no way to escape?" Speakers may also gain listeners' attention by referring to personal experience with the topic: "For the past year, I have worked as a volunteer in the local battered women's shelter." Notice that this introductory statement establishes some initial credibility for the speaker.

The introduction should also include a thesis statement, which we discussed earlier. Your thesis should be a clear, short sentence that captures the main idea of your talk and the key points supporting that idea. A good thesis statement states the principal claim of a speech and the main points by which it will be developed: "In my talk, I will show you that vegetarianism is healthful, and I will demonstrate that a vegetarian diet is also delicious," or "To inform you about your legal rights in an interview, I will discuss laws that prohibit discrimination and protect privacy, tell you what questions are illegal, and inform you what you can do if an interviewer asks an illegal question." Crafting a strong introduction helps speakers earn credibility. In summary, a good introduction:

▶ Captures listeners' attention

▶ Motivates listeners to listen

▶ Informs listeners of the main idea (thesis) of the speech and the key points supporting that idea

▶ Enhances the speaker's credibility

The Body The body of a speech develops the thesis by organizing content into points that are distinct yet related. In short speeches of 5 to 10 minutes, two or three points usually are all that a speaker can develop well. Longer speeches may include more points. You can organize speeches in many ways, and each organizational pattern has distinct effects on the overall meaning (see Figure 13.1).

Figure 13.1 ORGANIZING SPEECHES

Topic: The Arctic National Wildlife Refuge

Speech 1: Temporal Organization

Thesis:	The history of the Arctic National Wildlife Refuge should guide our vision of its future.
Claim 1:	The Arctic National Wildlife Refuge has provided sanctuary to many endangered animal species.
Claim 2:	Today, mining and tourism industries are seeking to open up the Arctic National Wildlife Refuge to development.
Claim 3:	A better future is one in which the sanctuary is preserved for wildlife.

Speech 2: Spatial Organization

Thesis:	We must preserve the Arctic National Wildlife Refuge as one of the few remaining wild spaces in our nation.
Claim 1:	Most of the land in the United States has been developed for human use and profit.
Claim 2:	All that remains of truly wild lands are a few national parks, a few acres in Utah, and the Arctic National Wildlife Refuge.
Claim 3:	If we allow the Arctic National Wildlife Refuge to be opened to development, we will lose one of the last wild spaces we have.

Speech 3: Cause–Effects

Thesis:	Opening the Arctic National Wildlife Refuge to development would result in losses for fragile animals, biodiversity, and humans.
Claim 1:	If the refuge is opened to mining and industrial development, ten species of endangered animals will perish forever.
Claim 2:	Allowing development of the refuge would make unique biological forms extinct.
Claim 3:	If the refuge is opened to mining and industrial development, humans will lose a rare and precious national treasure.

Chronological patterns or *time patterns* organize ideas chronologically. They emphasize progression, sequences, or development. *Spatial patterns* organize ideas according to physical relationships. They are useful in explaining layouts, geographic relationships, or connections between parts of a system.

Topical patterns (also called *classification patterns*) order speech content into categories or areas. This pattern is useful for speeches in which topics break down into two or three areas that aren't related temporally, spatially, or otherwise. The *star structure*, which is a variation on the topical pattern, has several main points (as a star has five or six) that are related and work together to develop the main idea of a speech (Jaffe, 2007).

Wave patterns feature repetitions; each "wave" repeats the main theme with variations or extensions. *Comparative patterns* compare two or more phenomena (people, machines, planets, situations). This pattern demonstrates similarities between phenomena ("In many ways, public speaking is like everyday conversation") or differences between phenomena ("Public speaking requires more planning than everyday conversation").

Persuasive speeches typically rely on organizational patterns that encourage listeners to change attitudes or behaviors. *Problem–solution patterns* allow speakers to describe a problem and propose a solution. *Cause–effect* and *effect–cause patterns* order speech content into two main points: cause and effect. This structure is useful for persuasive speeches that aim to convince listeners that certain consequences will follow from particular actions.

A final way to organize a persuasive speech is the *motivated sequence pattern* (Gronbeck et al., 1994; Jaffe, 2007; Monroe, 1935). This pattern is effective in diverse communication situations, probably because it follows a natural order of human thought. The motivated sequence pattern includes five sequential steps. The *attention step* focuses listeners' attention on the topic with a strong opening ("Imagine this campus with no trees whatsoever"). The *need step* shows that a real and serious problem exists ("Acid rain is slowly but surely destroying the trees on our planet"). Next is the *satisfaction step*, in which a speaker recommends a solution to the problem described ("Stronger environmental regulations and individual efforts to use environmentally safe products can protect trees and thus the oxygen we need to live"). The *visualization step* intensifies listeners' commitment to the solution by helping them imagine the results that the recommended solution would achieve ("You will have air to breathe, and so will your children and grandchildren. Moreover, we'll have trees to add beauty to our lives"). Finally, in the *action step* the speaker appeals to listeners to take concrete action to realize the recommended solution ("Refuse to buy or use any aerosol products. Sign this petition to our representatives on Capitol Hill").

The Conclusion A good speech ends on a strong note. The conclusion is a speaker's last chance to emphasize ideas, increase credibility, and gain listeners' support or approval. An effective conclusion accomplishes two goals. First, it summarizes the main ideas of the speech. Second, it leaves listeners with a memorable final idea (a dramatic quote or example, a challenge, an unforgettable computer graphic, and so forth). These two functions of the conclusion echo the attention and thesis presented in the introduction.

Transitions The final aspect of organizing a speech is developing **transitions,** which are words, phrases, and sentences that connect ideas in a speech. Transitions signal listeners that you have finished talking about one idea and are ready to move to the next one. Within the development of a single point, speakers usually rely on such transitional words and phrases as *therefore, and so, for this reason,* and *as the evidence suggests.* To make transitions from one point to another, the speaker may use phrases: "My second point is . . ."; "Now that we have seen how many people immigrate to the United States, let's ask what they bring to our country." Speakers typically use one or more sentences to create transitions between the major parts of a speech (introduction, body, conclusion). A student in one of my classes moved from the body to the conclusion of his speech with this transition: "I have discussed in some detail why we need protection for wetlands. Before I leave you, let me summarize the key ideas."

Researching and Supporting Public Speeches

Evidence is material used to support claims, such as those made in a public speech. In addition, evidence may enhance listeners' interest and emotional response to ideas.

Evidence serves a number of important functions in speeches. First, it can be used to make ideas clearer, more compelling, and more dramatic. Second, evidence fortifies a speaker's opinions, which are seldom sufficient to persuade intelligent listeners. Finally, evidence heightens a speaker's credibility. A speaker who supports ideas well comes across as informed and prepared. Therefore, including strong evidence allows speakers to gain derived credibility during a presentation.

The effectiveness of evidence depends directly on whether listeners understand and accept it. This reinforces the importance of adapting to listeners, which we have emphasized throughout this book and which we will discuss again later in this chapter. Even if you quote the world's leading authority, the evidence won't be effective if your listeners don't find the authority credible (Olson & Cal, 1984). No matter how valid evidence is, it is effective only if listeners believe it. Consequently, your choices of evidence for your speech should take listeners' perspectives into account. You want to include support that they find credible, while also making sure your evidence is valid.

Four forms of support are widely respected, and each tends to be effective in specific situations and for particular goals. The kinds of evidence are **statistics, examples, comparisons,** and **quotations.** In addition, we will discuss *visual aids*, which are not a form of evidence but rather a means of presenting and enhancing other forms of evidence. For instance, a graph (visual aid) of statistics (evidence) enhances the impact of a speaker's point. Figure 13.2 summarizes the types of evidence and their uses.

Before including any form of evidence, speakers have an ethical responsibility to check the accuracy of material and the credibility of sources. It is advisable to ask questions such as these:

▶ Are the statistics still valid? Population demographics, social trends, and other matters become quickly outdated, so it's important to have current statistics.

▶ Does the person quoted have any personal interest in endorsing a certain point of view? For example, tobacco companies' statements about the harmlessness of tobacco may reflect personal and financial interests.

▶ Is the person an expert on the topic? It is inappropriate to rely on the **halo effect,** in which people who are well known in one area (such as sports stars) are quoted in an area outside their expertise (such as the nutritional value of cereal).

▶ Is an example representative of the point it is used to support? Is it typical of the general case?

▶ Are comparisons fair? For instance, it might be appropriate to compare Christianity and Buddhism as spiritual paths, but it would not be appropriate to compare them as religions that believe in a single god.

When presenting evidence to listeners, speakers have an ethical obligation to identify each source, including titles and qualifications, and to tell listeners its date, if the date matters. You can use an **oral footnote,** which acknowledges a source of evidence and sometimes explains the source's qualifications. For instance, a speaker might say, "Doctor Bingham, who won the 1988 Nobel Prize in physics, published a study in 1996 in which she reported that . . ." or "As Senator Bollinger remarked in 1997, . . ." Oral footnotes give appropriate acknowledgment to the source that initially generated the evidence, and they enable listeners to evaluate the speaker's evidence. Here's another example of an oral footnote, which was presented in a persuasive speech advocating stronger gun control laws: "In the June 2006 issue of *Marie Claire*, investigator

Figure 13.2 TYPES OF EVIDENCE AND THEIR USES

Examples provide concrete descriptions of situations, individuals, problems, or other phenomena.

Types:	Short (instance)
	Detailed
	Hypothetical
	Anecdotal
Uses:	To personalize information and ideas
	To add interest to a presentation
	To enhance dramatic effect

Comparisons (analogies) compare two ideas, processes, people, situations, or other phenomena.

Types:	Literal analogy (A heart is a pump.)
	Figurative analogy (Life is a journey.)
	Metaphor
	Simile
Uses:	To show connections between phenomena
	To relate a new idea to one that is familiar to listeners
	To provide interest

Statistics summarize quantitative information.

Types:	Percentages and ratios
	Demographic data
	Frequency counts
	Correlations
	Trends
Uses:	To summarize many instances of some phenomenon
	To show relationships between two or more phenomena (cause or correlation)
	To demonstrate trends or patterns

Quotations (testimony) restate or paraphrase the words of others, giving appropriate credit to the sources of the words.

Types:	Short quotation
	Extended quotation
	Paraphrase
Uses:	To add variety and interest
	To support a speaker's claims
	To draw on the credibility of people whom listeners know
	To include particularly arresting phrasings of ideas

Visual aids reinforce verbal communication and provide visual information and appeals.

Types:	Hand-made charts and graphs
	Overheads/transparencies
	Computer-created charts and graphs
	PowerPoint slides
	Objects, pictures, handouts, film clips
Uses:	To strengthen and underscore verbal messages
	To translate statistics into pictures that are understandable
	To add variety and interest
	To give listeners a vivid appreciation of a topic, issue, or point

Jennifer Friedlin reported that it took her only 30 minutes to buy a gun but 4 weeks to obtain a restraining order."

Developing Effective Delivery

As we have seen, dynamism is one dimension of a speaker's credibility. Therefore, an engaging delivery is important. **Oral style** should be more personal than written style (Wilson & Arnold, 1974). Speakers may include personal stories and personal pronouns, referring to themselves as *I* rather than *the speaker*. Also, speakers may use phrases instead of complete sentences, and contractions (*can't*) are appropriate. Speakers should also sustain eye contact with listeners and show that they are approachable. If you reflect on speakers you have found effective, you will probably realize that they seemed engaging, personal, and open to you.

Effective oral style is also more immediate and active than written style tends to be (Wilson & Arnold, 1974). This is important because listeners must understand ideas immediately, as they are spoken, whereas readers can take time to comprehend ideas. Speakers foster immediacy by using short sentences instead of complex sentences. Immediacy also involves following general ideas with clear, specific evidence or elaboration. Rhetorical questions ("Would you like to know that a good job is waiting for you when you graduate?"), interjections ("Good grief!"; "Look!"), and redundancy (Thompson & Grundgenett, 1999) also enhance the immediacy of a speech. The Sharpen Your Skill box on this page invites you to notice oral style in a speech.

Garfield

Throughout this book, we've seen that we should adapt our communication to its context. This basic communication principle guides a speaker's choice of a presentation style. The style of speaking that is effective at a political rally is different from the style that is appropriate for an attorney's closing speech in a trial; delivering a toast at a wedding requires a different style from that required for testifying before Congress. Each speaking situation suggests guidelines for presentation, so speakers must consider the context when selecting a speaking style.

Four styles of delivery are generally recognized, and each is appropriate in certain contexts. **Impromptu delivery** involves little or no preparation. It can be effective for speakers who know their material thoroughly. Many politicians speak impromptu when talking about their experience in public service and policies they advocate. Impromptu speaking generally is not advisable for novice speakers or for anyone who is not thoroughly familiar with a topic.

Probably the most commonly used presentational style is **extemporaneous delivery.** Extemporaneous speaking involves substantial preparation and practice, but it stops short of memorizing the exact words of a speech and relies on notes. Speakers conduct research, organize materials, and practice delivering their speeches, but they do not rehearse so much that the speeches sound canned. Attorneys, teachers, politicians, and others who engage in public speaking most often use an extemporaneous style of presentation because it allows them to prepare thoroughly and yet engage listeners when speaking.

Manuscript delivery, as the name implies, involves presenting a speech from a complete, written manuscript. In addition to the preparation typical of extemporaneous delivery, manuscript style requires the speaker to write out the entire content of a speech and to rely on the written document or a teleprompter projection when making the presentation. Few people can present manuscript speeches in an engaging, dynamic manner. However, manuscript delivery is appropriate, even advisable, in situations that call for precision. For instance, U.S. presidents generally use manuscripts for official presentations. In these circumstances, speakers cannot run the risk of using imprecise language.

An extension of the manuscript style of speaking is **memorized delivery,** in which a speaker commits an entire speech to memory and presents it without relying on a written text or notes. This style shares the primary disadvantage of manuscript speaking: the risk of a canned delivery that lacks dynamism and immediacy. In addition, the memorized style of delivery entails a second serious danger: forgetting. If a speaker is nervous, or if something happens to disrupt a presentation, the speaker may become rattled and forget all or part of the speech. Without the written text, he or she may be unable to get back on track.

© Chuck Savage/Corbis

Extemporaneous speaking allows speakers to be engaged with listeners.

When choosing a style of delivery, speakers should consider the advantages and disadvantages of each speaking style and the constraints of particular communication situations. No single style suits all occasions. Instead, the most effective style is one that suits the particular speaker and the situation. Regardless of which delivery style they use, effective speakers devote thought and practice to their verbal and nonverbal communication. It is important to select words that convey your intended meanings and that create strong images for listeners. Equally important are effective gestures, paralanguage, and movement. Because public speaking is *enlarged* conversation, nonverbal behaviors generally should be more vigorous and commanding than in personal communication.

▶Guidelines for Public Speaking

In this section, we discuss three guidelines for public speaking. The first two pertain to occasions when you might present a speech. The third focuses on effective, critical listening to speeches given by others.

Understand and Manage Speaking Anxiety

One of the most common challenges for public speakers is anxiety. The communication situations that prompt apprehension vary among people, as the commentaries by Tomoko and Trish illustrate.

> ▶ **Tomoko**
>
> Talking to a big group of people is no problem for me. I like being able to prepare what I want to say in advance and to control what happens. But I get very nervous about one-on-one talking. It's too personal and spontaneous for me to feel secure about what will happen.

> ▶ **Trish**
>
> I can talk all day with one friend or a few of them and be totally at ease, but put me in front of a group of people, and I just freeze. I feel I'm on display or something and everything I say has to be perfect and it all depends on me. It's just a huge pressure.

Both Trish and Tomoko are normal in feeling some anxiety about specific communication situations. Almost all of us sometimes feel apprehensive about talking with others (Behnke & Sawyer, 1999; Bippus & Daly, 1999; Richmond & Mc-Croskey, 1992). What many people don't realize is that a degree of anxiety is natural and may actually improve communication. When we are anxious, we become more alert and energetic, largely because our bodies produce adrenaline and extra blood sugar, which enhance our vigilance. The burst of adrenaline increases vitality, which can make speakers more dynamic and compelling. You can channel the extra energy that accompanies public speaking into gestures and movements that enhance your presentation.

You should also realize that anxiety is common for seasoned speakers. Many politicians feel nervous before and during a speech, even though they may have made hundreds or even thousands of speeches. Likewise, teachers who have taught for years usually feel tension before meeting a class, and such a seasoned journalist as Mike Wallace claims to get butterflies when conducting interviews. The energy fostered by communication anxiety allows speakers to be more dynamic and more interesting.

Although a degree of anxiety about speaking is natural, too much can interfere with effectiveness. When anxiety is great enough to hinder our ability to interact with others, communication apprehension exists. **Communication apprehension** is a detrimental level of anxiety associated with real or anticipated communication encounters (McCroskey, 1977; Richmond & McCroskey, 1992). Communication apprehension exists in degrees and may occur at times other than when we're actually speaking. Many people feel anxious primarily in advance of communication situations; they worry, imagine difficulties, and dread the occasion long before the communication occurs.

Causes of Communication Apprehension Communication apprehension may be situational or chronic (Motley & Molloy, 1994). Situational anxiety is limited to specific situations that cause apprehension: performance reviews on the job, first dates, or major social occasions. A common cause of situational apprehension is a past failure or failures in specific speaking situations. For example, my doctor called me one day to ask me to coach her for a speech she had to give to a medical society. When I asked why she thought she needed coaching, Eleanor told me that the last speech she had given was eight years earlier, in medical school. She was an intern, and it was her turn to present a case to the other interns and in front of the resident who supervised her. Just before the speech, she lost her first patient to a heart attack and was badly shaken. All her work preparing the case and rehearsing her presentation was eclipsed by the shock of losing the patient. As a result, she was disorganized, flustered, and generally ineffective. That single incident, which followed a history of successful speaking, was so traumatic that Eleanor developed acute situational speaking anxiety.

Chronic anxiety exists when we are anxious about most or all situations in which we are expected to speak. Chronic anxiety appears to be learned. In other words, we can learn to fear communication, just as some of us learn to fear dogs, heights, or lightning. One cause of learned communication apprehension is observation of other people who are anxious about communicating. If we see family members or friends perspiring heavily and feeling stressed about making presentations, we may internalize their anxiety as an appropriate response to speaking situations.

Reducing Communication Apprehension Because communication apprehension is learned, it can also be unlearned or reduced. Communication scholars have developed several methods of reducing speaking apprehension, four of which we'll discuss.

Systematic desensitization focuses on reducing the tension that surrounds the feared event by relaxing and thereby reducing the physiological features of anxiety, such as shallow breathing and increased heart rate (Beatty & Behnke, 1991). Once people learn to control their breathing and muscle tension, counselors ask them to think about progressively more difficult speaking situations.

A second method of reducing communication apprehension is **cognitive restructuring,** a process of revising how people think about speaking situations. According to this method, speaking is not the problem; rather, the problem is irrational beliefs about speaking. A key part of cognitive restructuring is learning to identify and challenge negative self-statements. Users of this method would criticize the statement "My topic won't interest everyone" for assuming that others will not be interested and that any speaker can hold the attention of everyone. Michael Motley and Jennifer Molloy (1994) report that apprehension decreases when people read a short booklet that encourages them to develop new, rational views of communication.

A third technique for reducing communication apprehension is **positive visualization,** which aims to reduce speaking anxiety by guiding apprehensive speakers through imagined positive speaking experiences. This technique allows people to form mental pictures of themselves as effective speakers and to then enact those mental pictures in actual speaking situations (Hamilton, 1996). Researchers report that positive visualization is especially effective in reducing chronic communication apprehension (Ayres & Hopf, 1990; Bourhis & Allen, 1992).

Skills training assumes that lack of speaking skills causes us to be apprehensive. This method focuses on teaching people such skills as starting conversations, organizing ideas, and responding effectively to others (Phillips, 1991).

After reading about these methods of reducing communication apprehension, you may think that each seems useful. If so, your thinking coincides with research that finds that a combination of methods is more likely to relieve speaking anxiety than any single method (Allen, Hunter, & Donahue, 1989). The major conclusion is that communication apprehension is not necessarily permanent. Ways to reduce it exist. Eliminating all communication anxiety is not desirable, however, because some vigilance can enhance a speaker's dynamism and alertness. If you experience communication apprehension that interferes with your ability to express your ideas, ask your instructor to direct you to professionals who can work with you.

Adapt Speeches to Audiences

A second guideline for effective public speaking is to adapt to audiences, a topic we discussed earlier in this chapter. Listeners are the whole reason for speaking; without them, communication does not occur. Therefore, speakers should be sensitive to listeners and should adapt to listeners' perspectives and expectations. You should take into account the perspectives of listeners if you want them to consider your views. We consider the views of our friends when we talk with them. We think about others' perspectives when we engage in business negotiations. We use dual perspective when communicating with children, dates, and neighbors. Thus, audience analysis is important to effectiveness in all communication encounters.

In one of my classes, a student named Odell gave a persuasive speech designed to convince listeners to support affirmative action. He was personally compelling, his delivery was dynamic, and his ideas were well organized. The only problems were that his audience had little knowledge about affirmative action, and he didn't explain exactly what the policy involves. He assumed listeners understood how affirmative action works, and he focused on its positive effects. His listeners were not persuaded, because Odell failed to give them the information necessary for their support. Odell's speech also illustrates our earlier point that speeches often combine more than one speaking purpose; in this case, giving information was essential to Odell's larger goal of persuading listeners.

The mistake that Odell made was failing to learn about his audience's knowledge of his topic. It is impossible to entertain, inform, or persuade people if we do not consider their perspectives on our topics. Speakers need to understand what listeners already know and believe and what reservations they might have about what we say (McGuire, 1989). To paraphrase the advice of an ancient Greek rhetorician, "The fool persuades me with his or her reasons, the wise person with my own." This advice—that effective speakers understand and work with listeners' reasons, values, knowledge, and concerns—is as wise today as it was more than 2,000 years ago.

Although politicians and corporations can afford to conduct sophisticated polls to find out what people know, want, think, and believe, most of us don't have the resources to do that. So how do ordinary people engage in goal-focused analysis? One answer is to be observant. Usually, a speaker has some experience in interacting with his or her listeners or people like them. Drawing on past interactions, a speaker may be able to discern a great deal about the knowledge, attitudes, and beliefs of listeners.

Gathering information about listeners through conversations or surveys is also appropriate. For example, I once was asked to speak on women leaders at a governor's leadership conference. To prepare my presentation, I asked the conference planners to send me information about the occupations and ages of people attending the conference. In addition, I asked the planners to survey the conferees about their experience as leaders and working with women leaders. The material I received informed me about the level of experience and the attitudes and biases of my listeners. Then I could adapt my speech to what they knew and believed.

By taking listeners into consideration, you build a presentation that is interactive and respectful. As we learned earlier in this chapter, listeners tend to confer credibility on speakers who show that they understand listeners and who adapt presentations to listeners' perspectives, knowledge, and expectations.

Listen Critically

A final guideline is to listen critically to speeches you hear. Because we often find ourselves in the role of listener, we should know how to listen well and critically to ideas that others present. As you will recall from Chapter 6, critical listening involves attending mindfully to communication in order to evaluate its merit. Critical listeners assess whether a speaker is informed and ethical and whether a speech is soundly reasoned and supported.

The first step in critical listening is to take in and understand what a speaker says. You cannot evaluate an argument or idea until you have grasped it and the information that supports it. Thus, effective listening requires you to concentrate on what a speaker says. You can focus your listening by asking questions such as these:

▶ What does the speaker announce as the purpose of the talk?

▶ What evidence does the speaker provide to support claims?

▶ Does the speaker have experience that qualifies him or her to speak on this topic?

▶ Does the speaker have any vested interest in what she or he advocates?

You probably noticed that these questions parallel those we identified in our earlier discussion of ways to improve your credibility when you are making speeches. The questions help you zero in on what others say so that you can make informed judgments of their credibility and the credibility of their ideas.

To listen critically, you should suspend your preconceptions about topics and speakers. You need not abandon your ideas, but you should set them aside long enough to listen openly to a speech, especially if you are predisposed to disagree with it. By granting a full and fair hearing to ideas that differ from yours, you increase the likelihood that your perspective and ideas will be well informed and carefully reasoned.

Critical listeners recognize fallacies in reasoning and do not succumb to them. To accept a speaker's ideas, critical listeners demand that the ideas be well supported with evidence and sound reasoning. The FYI box on this page summarizes some of the more common fallacies in reasoning in public communication.

fyi   COMMON FALLACIES IN REASONING

Ad hominem attack	You can't believe what Jane Smith says about voting, because she doesn't vote.
After this, therefore because of this (*Post hoc, ergo propter hoc*)	The new flextime policy is ineffective because more people have been getting to work late since it went into effect.
Bandwagon appeal	You should be for the new campus meal plan because most students are.
Slippery slope	If we allow students to play a role in decisions about hiring and tenure of faculty, pretty soon students will be running the whole school.
Hasty generalization	People should not be allowed to own pit bulls, because there have been instances of pit bulls attacking children.
Either–or	Tenure should be either abolished or kept as it is.
Red herring argument	People who own pit bulls should switch to cats. Let me tell you why cats are the ideal pet. . . .
Reliance on the halo effect	World-famous actor Richard Connery says that we should not restrict people's right to own firearms.

►SUMMARY

In this chapter, we discussed the role of public speaking in everyday life. We began by dispelling the widely held misperception that only a few, highly visible people engage in public speaking. As we saw, most of us will communicate publicly in the normal course of professional, civic, and personal life.

In the first part of the chapter, we noted that although public speaking is similar in many ways to other kinds of communication, it is distinct in the greater planning and practice it involves and the less obvious contributions of listeners. We also identified entertaining, informing, and persuading as general purposes of public speaking, and we noted that these goals often overlap.

The second section of this chapter described how to plan, organize, research, support, and deliver public speeches. Throughout our discussion, we highlighted how each aspect of speech development influences the credibility that listeners confer on speakers. To earn credibility, speakers should demonstrate that they are knowledgeable (mentioning personal experience with the topic and including good evidence), trustworthy (making ethical choices that show respect for listeners and for the integrity of evidence), and dynamic (engaging delivery).

The third section of the chapter focused on three guidelines related to public speaking. The first guideline is to understand and manage communication apprehension, which is normal and can be helpful in energizing speakers. If speaking anxiety is strong enough to hinder effective communication, ways to reduce it exist, and we reviewed four of these. A second guideline, to adapt speeches to listeners, is critical to effective public speaking. In our discussion, we emphasized that speakers have an ethical responsibility to consider listeners' perspectives, knowledge, and expectations as they plan, prepare, and present speeches. A final guideline is to listen critically to public speeches by others. Good listeners suspend their views long enough to give a full and fair hearing to what others say. As they listen, they identify and evaluate the quality of speakers' experience, evidence, and reasoning, which allows them to make informed critical assessments of the ideas presented.

Public communication is vital to personal and professional success and to the health of our society. Not reserved for people who have high status or who are in the public limelight, public speaking is a basic skill for us all. In this chapter, we have seen what is involved in presenting and listening to public presentations, and we have identified ways to enhance our effectiveness in this vital realm of social life.

Review, Reflect, Extend

The Key Concepts, For Further Reflection and Discussion questions, Recommended Resources, and Experience Communication Case Study that follow will help you review, reflect on, and extend the information and ideas presented in this chapter. A diverse selection of online resources is also available through ThomsonNOW. These resources include Speech Builder Express, InfoTrac College Edition, interactive videos, vMentor, and Thomson Audio Study Products.

Thomson NOW! is an online study system designed to help you put your time to the best use. After reading a chapter, take the NOW pre-test to identify concepts discussed in the chapter that you may not fully understand. Based on the results of this diagnostic test, the system will cre-

ate a personalized study plan that directs you to specific learning resources and activities. To see if you're ready for an exam, take the NOW post-test to check your understanding.

For more information or to access this book's online resources, visit **http://www.thomsonedu.com**.

▶ KEY CONCEPTS

The terms following are defined in the chapter on the page number indicated, and they appear in alphabetical order, with definitions, in the Glossary, which be-

gins on page 369. The book's online resources also include flash cards and crossword puzzles to help you learn these terms and the concepts they represent.

cognitive restructuring, 295
communication apprehension, 294
comparison (analogy), 289
credibility, 284
derived credibility, 284
evidence, 288
example, 289
extemporaneous delivery, 292
halo effect, 289
impromptu delivery, 292

initial credibility, 284
manuscript delivery, 292
memorized delivery, 292
oral footnote, 289
oral style, 291
positive visualization, 295
quotation, 289
skills training, 295
specific purpose, 285
speech to entertain, 282

speech to inform, 282
speech to persuade, 283
statistics, 289
systematic desensitization, 295
terminal credibility, 284
thesis statement, 285
transition, 288
visual aid, 289

▶ FOR FURTHER REFLECTION AND DISCUSSION

The questions below can also be found among the book's online resources for this chapter, where you

have the option of e-mailing your responses to your instructor, if required.

1. Think about presentations you hear (lectures by professors, talks on campus). How much do these speakers seem to take the audience into consideration in what they say? Does this affect the speakers' effectiveness?

2. During the next week, pay attention to evidence cited by others in public presentations. You might note what evidence is used on news programs, by professors in classes, and by special speakers on your campus. Evaluate the effectiveness of evidence pre-

sented. Are visuals clear and uncluttered? Do speakers explain the qualifications of sources they cite, and are those sources unbiased? What examples and analogies are presented, and how effective are they?

3. Note the use of stories to add interest and effect to public presentations. Describe a speaker who uses a story effectively and one who uses a story ineffectively. What are the differences between them? What conclusions can you draw about the effective use of stories in public presentations?

▶ RECOMMENDED RESOURCES

1. Webcorp, Inc. has created Historic Audio Archives that allow you to listen to significant speeches by famous people, including John Fitzgerald Kennedy,

Malcolm X, Richard Nixon, Adolf Hitler, and Winston Churchill. Listen to famous public speeches in Webcorp's audio archives by going to the book's online resources and clicking on WebLink 13.1. You can listen to Martin Luther King Jr.'s "I Have a Dream" speech by clicking on WebLink 13.2.

2. Use InfoTrac College Edition or another online periodicals database to access the journal *Vital*

Speeches, and read President George W. Bush's October 7, 2001, speech, "We Are at War Against Terrorism: The Attack on the Taliban." How did President Bush recognize American values in opening his speech? What evidence did he provide for declaring war?

Experience Communication Sample Speech

GRADUATED LICENSING

Jason Harris/© Wadsworth

The book's online resources include an interactive video of the communication situation featured in the case study scripted below. Apply what you've learned in this chapter by analyzing the speech, using the questions that follow the transcript as a guide. These questions are also available online with the video.

Rebecca Ewing was a junior at the University of North Carolina at Chapel Hill when she presented this persuasive speech for a course in public speaking. The assignment was to present a 4-to-6-minute speech that had two main points and at least two references. Rebecca graciously gave me her permission to reprint her speech here so that other students could learn to analyze public speaking and could study how a persuasive speech is crafted.

The text of the speech is printed in its entirety. As you read Rebecca's speech, you should critically assess the choices she made in planning, researching, developing, organizing, and presenting her ideas.

Although Rebecca's speech is strong, it is not perfect. As you read it, consider how it could be made even more effective. Also, think about different ways you might accomplish the speaker's objectives; can you identify alternative organizational structures, kinds of evidence, transitions, and so forth? Following the speech are five questions to guide your thinking about what Rebecca did and might have done.

The Case for Graduated Licensing

BY REBECCA EWING

It was a typical Friday night in a small town in Florida just two short years ago. Two 13-year-old girls, Margaux and Crystal, were planning a night out at the mall. At around 7:30 P.M., Crystal and Margaux met up with seven other friends. The group decided to head to another friend's apartment.

One of the teenagers, Nick, who had just turned 16, agreed to drive the eight of them to the friend's apartment. Soon, two in the group were up front, and the other seven were sardined in the back of Nick's Honda. None of the teens in the back seat could wear seatbelts.

Once on the highway, Nick quickly picked up speed. Then the girls became frightened and told Nick to slow down. Instead of slowing, Nick accelerated to 85 miles per hour and began to tailgate other cars. Eventually, Nick lost control of his car and jumped the median into oncoming traffic, resulting in a head-on collision. What happened next is every parent's nightmare. Nick and the front-seat passenger survived due to airbags. However, of the seven teens crammed into the back seat, only two survived, and both were severely injured. Regretfully, Margaux and Crystal did not make it (Barr, 1998, p. 79).

Sixteen-year-olds are faced with an incredible responsibility when it comes time to get their driver's licenses. But are they equipped to handle difficult driving situations? Is a 16-year-old mature enough to handle such an awesome responsibility? Every year, so many teenagers have their lives cut short in tragic car accidents due to lack of proper training and too much freedom at too young an age.

Sixteen is just too young for people to be driving without adult supervision. I think that the evidence I will present to you today will convince you to agree with me that 16 is too young for unsupervised driving. After I've established the dangers of giving licenses to 16-year-olds, I will propose a solution that has already proven its effectiveness in eight states.

I know that many of you are shaking your heads in disagreement. You are probably thinking that getting your driver's license was a rite of passage. That's the way it's always been. Why change the law now? What I believe is that we need to change the law to save lives like Margaux's and Crystal's and maybe yours and mine. Statistics show that 16- and 17-year-olds are responsible for 11% of car crashes, but they make up only 2% of the driving population (Cohen, 1997; Sharpe et al., 2001). This is a problem.

Why are teen drivers responsible for so many car crashes? A study conducted by the University of North Carolina's Highway Safety Research Center concludes—and I quote—"A major reason so many young people are involved in auto accidents is that they are poorly trained" (Henry, 1996, p. 128). Teenagers are poorly trained by both drivers' education and parents.

Parents need to take their children's passage into adulthood and driving more seriously. Parents don't spend enough quality time teaching their sons and daughters to drive defensively and to master good driving techniques.

Another reason for the high rate of teenage driving accidents is attitudes. For instance, most teenagers believe that driving is a ticket to new freedoms. They get caught up in the excitement of driving, and they make tragic mistakes. Take the story about Nick. If he had been more experienced and mature, he probably would not have piled seven people into the back of his small car. He probably wouldn't have sped excessively. He probably wouldn't have tailgated, especially at high speed. The *Reader's Digest* conducted an interview asking 400 teenagers between the ages of 15 and 19 about their experiences with other teen drivers who had not been drinking and were not under the influence of drugs. The results are shocking (Barr, 1998, p. 79).

Have You Ever Been with a Teen Driver Who . . .	**Yes**
Put so many a passengers in the car that there weren't enough seatbelts?	57%
Drove 20 mph or more over the speed limit?	53%
Tailgated, cut off, or tried to bump another vehicle?	14%
Did at least one of these activities?	82%

These findings make it clear that teenagers do not have the maturity of judgment required to handle the responsibility of driving without supervision. So what should we do about this? One approach to this problem would be to raise the age at which teens can get a driver's license.

According to an article in *U.S. News and World Report*, drivers who are over age 21 have fewer crashes and other problems than do younger drivers (Cohen, 1997, p. 80). Many countries don't even license drivers under 18.

However, in America, where mass transportation is less available, teenagers often need to drive to work and school, and parents want to stop chauffeuring. So raising the age for getting a driver's license to 18 or older is unlikely to gain support here.

So, what can we do? The National Highway Traffic Safety Administration urges states to adopt graduated licensing programs that extend the time required to qualify for the right to drive without supervision. The graduated licensing program is also known as the three-tiered system, and it has been adopted in eight states.

Let me explain how the system works. In the first stage, a person under the age of 16 can obtain a learner's permit that allows him or her to drive only when accompanied by a licensed adult (Cohen, 1997, p. 80). During this stage, the teenager becomes familiar with traffic rules and regulations. During this first stage, the novice driver also encounters unexpected situations and difficult driving conditions with the guidance of a licensed adult.

Stage two begins when a teenager has driven safely for one year. Then, the driver is issued a provisional license that allows him or her to drive without supervision during daylight hours. Drivers with provisional licenses must still be accompanied by a licensed adult for nighttime driving (Henry, 1996, p. 128).

Stage three occurs if someone with a provisional license has driven for six months without having any accidents and without getting any tickets. Then, the person can obtain an unrestricted driver's license. This completes the three-tiered system.

There is evidence that the three-tiered system works. Studies in California, Oregon, and Maryland have found crashes involving teenage drivers drop 5% to 16% when the three-tiered system is in effect (Cohen, 1997, p. 80). Now, that's a dramatic difference and a promise of lives that can be saved.

The drop in teen accidents has impressed legislators in other states to work for passage of the graduated licensing program in their states. The more quickly more states adopt the graduated licensing program, the more lives will be saved.

I've shown you that 16 is too young to drive without supervision, and I've demonstrated that the three-tiered licensing system, or a graduated licensing program, reduces the number of accidents involving young drivers.

So I urge each of you to contact your state legislators and politicians and ask them to support a graduated licensing program. It just might save the life of a sister, brother, or friend. It might save your life.

The graduated licensing program allows teenagers to accept the responsibilities that should go along with the privilege of driving. It encourages them not to make the mistakes that Nick made. Had he gone through a graduated licensing program, Crystal and Margaux might not be dead today.

References

Barr, S. (1998, June). Thrilled to death. *Readers' Digest,* pp. 74–81.

Cohen, W. (1997, December). Graduated licenses: How to reduce teens' road accidents. *U.S. News and World Report,* p. 80.

Henry, E. (1996, February). Why teen drivers crash. *Kiplinger's Personal Finance Magazine,* p. 128.

National Center for Policy Analysis. (2001). *Graduated Licensing Improves Safety.* Washington, DC: Author.

Sharpe, I., Molnar, L., Elliott, M., & Walker, P. (2001, Oct. 3). Graduated licensing in Michigan. *Journal of the American Medical Association, 286,* 8–12.

1. Did Rebecca provide a strong introduction with an attention device, a clear thesis, and a clear preview?

2. Are the sources of evidence credible? Why or why not? Is there any reason to suspect that the sources are biased?

3. What other kinds of evidence might the speaker have used to strengthen the persuasive impact of her message?

4. How did Rebecca adapt the message to listeners who were 19-to-24-year-old college students? Can you think of additional ways she might have adapted this message to these particular listeners?

14 *Mass Communication*

▶ **FOCUS QUESTIONS**

1. How do media shape our thinking?

2. To what extent is news constructed or created?

3. What is the *mean world syndrome?*

4. To what extent is the content of media controlled by powerful corporations?

5. How can you develop media literacy?

Where were you when the 9/11 terrorist attack on the United States occurred? Did you see live and replayed coverage of the attack and the death and damage it produced? What sounds and images come to mind when you think about the attack? If you are like most Americans, you spent much of September 11, 2001, and the days afterward watching television, listening to radio broadcasts, scanning the web, and reading newspaper accounts of the terrorist attack. I still have vivid images of the twin towers crumbling and collapsing, of courageous firefighters working to free victims trapped in the rubble, and of family members grieving for lost loved ones. I wasn't in New York or D.C. when the attacks happened, but I almost feel as if I had been, because television coverage placed me in those locations, gave me close-up, real-time coverage of what was happening, and introduced me to people who had escaped the twin towers and surviving family members of those who did not. When my parents were the age I am now, they didn't have such immediate access to real-time coverage of events happening all over the world. I do, and so do you, because we live in a world of mass communication.

Mass communication powerfully affects our lives. It influences our sense of who we are and want to be, our understandings of our own and other cultures, our attitudes and beliefs about a range of issues, and our general perspectives on social life. Today, **mass communication** is a major source of information and entertainment. Yet mass communication does more than report information and entertain us. It also presents us with views of human beings, events, issues, and cultural life. Mass com-

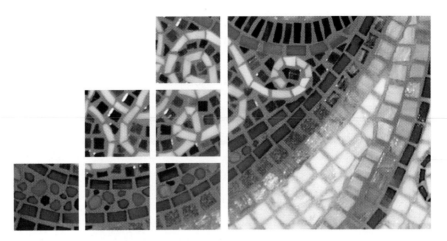

munication also grants a hearing and visibility to some people and some points of views, whereas it mutes other voices and viewpoints. Thus, mass communication is a powerful influence on our perceptions of issues, events, and people.

This chapter focuses on mass communication, particularly media such as television programming and advertising. Some technologies of communication are, in fact, aimed at mass audiences. However, because communication technologies are a major topic in themselves, we will cover them in Chapter 15. The first section of this chapter describes how mass communication has evolved historically. The second section of the chapter examines five theories that provide insight into how mass communication affects individuals and societies. We'll explore relationships between media, our views of the world, and how we think, feel, and act. In the third section of this chapter, we'll consider two guidelines for interacting with mass communication.

Mass communication makes it possible for us to see and hear what is happening almost anywhere in the world.

▶THE EVOLUTION OF MASS COMMUNICATION

Mass communication consists of all media that address mass audiences: books, film, television, radio, newspapers, magazines, and other forms of visual and print communication that reach masses of people, as well as some Internet-based communication (for example, blogs), which we will discuss in Chapter 15. Mass communication also includes computer technologies, such as the web and WebTV, that reach a great number of people; but it does not include one-on-one electronic communication, such as e-mail messages exchanged by friends.

Mass communication today is very different from mass communication in previous eras. Over the course of human history, humans have continually invented new ways of connecting, which indicate the power of our desire to communicate. As we have developed different media of mass communication, we have shaped not only what we know but, more fundamentally, how we think. More than 30 years ago, Marshall McLuhan was hailed as a prophet of the media. He claimed that the dominant media at any given time strongly shape both individual and collective life. The FYI box on this page offers insight into one of McLuhan's main ideas about the relationship between media and human consciousness.

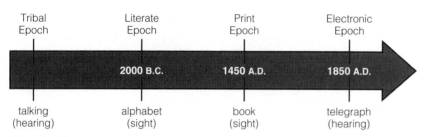

Figure 14.1   MEDIA EPOCHS IN HUMAN HISTORY

To explain how media shape our lives, McLuhan traced changes in Western society by identifying the media that emerged and dominated in four distinct eras (Figure 14.1; McLuhan, 1962, 1964; McLuhan & Fiore, 1967).

The Tribal Epoch

During the **tribal epoch,** the oral tradition reigned. People communicated face to face, giving and getting immediate feedback. Oral cultures were knitted together by stories and rituals that passed along the history and traditions of a culture, as well as by oral transmission of information and forms of entertainment. Reliance on the spoken word for information and recreation fostered cohesive communities and made hearing a dominant sense (McLuhan, 1969). As Derek points out in his commentary,

THE MEDIUM IS THE MESSAGE/MASSAGE

Marshall McLuhan probably is best known for his statement, "The medium is the message." For him, this statement had multiple meanings (McLuhan & Fiore, 1967). It implied, first, that the medium of communication determines the substance of communication. In other words, although the content of communication is not irrelevant, it is less important than the form or medium of communication. For example, McLuhan argued that the act of watching television shapes how we think, regardless of what we watch on television. He wrote that the dominant media of an age are more influential in our lives than any specific content conveyed by those media.

"The medium is the message" had other meanings for McLuhan. By changing only one letter, the statement becomes "The medium is the massage." This implies that media massage our consciousness and transform our perceptions. Finally, McLuhan sometimes made a play on words by saying, "The medium is the mass age," by which he meant that the dominant medium of the age had become mass communication.

tribal communities and the oral tradition they foster have not disappeared altogether. Although they no longer prevail in the United States, oral cultures continue among insulated communities in regions such as Appalachia and in groups that deliberately isolate themselves from mainstream culture (such as the Amish). Oral cultures also prevail in many undeveloped countries.

▶ Derek

I spent two years as a Peace Corps volunteer in some of the smaller and poorer countries in Africa. It was an incredible experience to live in societies that had no mass communication. Information was passed along by visitors who traveled into villages or by villagers who traveled to one of the larger cities and returned with news. What I noticed most about these societies is that people interact with each other more and more intensely than in the United States. Talking is living, talking is information, talking is entertainment, talking is history in oral cultures.

The Literate Epoch

Invention of the phonetic alphabet ushered in the **literate epoch** in many societies. Writing was based on symbol systems that allowed people to communicate without face-to-face interaction. With written communication came changes in human life. The emergence of written communication gave people individual access to mass messages. They could read when not in the presence of others in their communities. Because we can reread printed materials, reading requires less memory than oral communication. The alphabet also fostered the ascendance of sight as a primary sense. For those who could read and write, sight supplanted hearing as a dominant sense.

Writing also established a linear form for communication. In writing, letter follows letter, word follows word, sentence follows sentence. According to McLuhan, the continuous sequential order of print cultivated linear thinking and hence the development of disciplines based on linear logic, such as mathematics.

Although the invention of the alphabet made written communication possible, print did not immediately gain prominence as the dominant medium of communication. After the alphabet was developed, monks and scribes laboriously copied individual books and other written materials. Because there was as yet no way to mass-produce the written word, access to written media was limited to the elite classes of society and was not immediately available to the majority of people.

The Print Epoch

The **print epoch** began when Gutenberg invented the printing press in the fifteenth century, and literacy ascended in human history. The printing press made possible the printing of thousands of copies of a single book at moderate cost. Thus, access to the printed word was no longer limited to people with status and money but was increasingly accessible to members of all socioeconomic groups, making print a mainstream medium. Also, as Glenn Sparks (2006) points out, print made it possible "to detach oneself from the tribe and still have access to the important information of human culture" (p. 228). McLuhan asserted that the printing press was the first mechanism of mass production, which is why he credited it with inaugurating the Industrial Revolution of the 1800s (McLuhan, 1962).

Like other developments in media, the printing press changed human life. Reliance on the visual sense was no longer limited to an elite with access to individually copied books and print matter. In addition, mass-produced writing cultivated homogeneity because the same message could be delivered to many people. Ironically, widely available printed material further fragmented communities because each person could read a book, newspaper, or magazine in isolation from others. No longer was face-to-face contact necessary for communication (McLuhan & Fiore, 1967).

The Electronic Epoch

The dominance of print as a medium and the eye as a primary sense organ diminished with the invention of the telegraph, which was the forerunner of the **electronic epoch** in human history. According to McLuhan (1969), electronic media revived the oral tradition and made hearing and touch preeminent.

The telegraph was only the first of a long line of electronic media with the potential to revitalize a sense of community among people. The first television debuted in 1926. Today, assisted by satellite and cable transmissions, television allows us to see and hear what is happening almost anywhere in the world. We tune into television news programs to understand what is happening in Iraq or Afghanistan. We watch a live broadcast of a presidential speech and know what our president said and how he looked when he spoke. The increased access to information made possible by electronic communication led McLuhan to claim that electronic media created a **global village** (McLuhan & Fiore, 1967). In McLuhan's thinking, the instant communication that links people all over the world creates a modern world-wide community that resembles the tribal village (Sparks, 2006).

To understand McLuhan's ideas, reflect on the changes brought about by the emergence of new media in each of the epochs we have just discussed. Humans adapt to their environments by developing sensory abilities that enhance their ability to survive and function. When listening and speaking were the only ways to convey information, we developed keen oral and aural senses and memories. Once people could rely on printed forms of communication, sight supplanted hearing and speaking as the dominant sense, and memory became less important.

McLuhan died in 1980, almost four decades after electronic computers were invented (Cairncross, 2002). He left a partial manuscript that described the computer as a new medium that would change human beings and culture once again. Media scholar Paul Levinson (1999) maintains that much of McLuhan's thinking correctly anticipated the impact of digital communication. For example, use of computers seems

© Rick Gomez/Masterfile

Does mass communication discourage face-to-face interaction? How many families share a table without talking?

to improve our capacity to engage in multiple tasks simultaneously while also jeopardizing our ability to maintain focused attention on any single task (Healy, 1990; Urgo, 2000). In Chapter 15, we'll explore how communication technologies affect and perhaps change us.

Now that we've discussed how mass communication has evolved during human history, we're ready to explore theories that give insight into mass communication and its impact.

▶ THEORIES OF MASS COMMUNICATION

In this section, we'll discuss five theories of mass communication and its impact on us. As you read about these different theories, compare their claims to your own experiences with mass communication.

The Hypodermic Needle Model

An early theory of mass communication was the **hypodermic needle model,** which was also called the *magic bullet theory* and the *direct effects model.* According to this theory, media are powerful forces that directly affect vulnerable, passive audiences (Sparks, 2006). Today, it seems extreme to think that media are so powerful and humans are so powerless. However, the hypodermic needle theory makes sense in its historical context. The theory gained prominence in the 1930s after Hitler used mass communication (radio, film, and print material) to rise to power. Realizing that mass communication had been instrumental in Hitler's ascent, social scientists in America, some of whom had fled Nazi Germany, were concerned that mass communication was inherently a tool of propaganda (Campbell, Martin, & Fabos, 2004) and would be used for immoral purposes in America.

Although interest in the hypodermic needle theory makes sense when we consider its historical context, the theory was soon discredited. It fell out of favor for many of the same reasons that eroded confidence in the linear transmission models of communication we covered in Chapter 1: Scholars quickly realized that people (audiences of mass media) were not totally powerless but instead thought about mass-communicated messages and sometimes did not accept them. In addition, scholars rejected the simplicity of the hypodermic needle theory and claimed that human behavior is shaped by many factors, of which mass communication is just one. Rejection of the hypodermic needle theory fueled efforts to develop more sophisticated models of mass communication and its relationship to audiences.

Uses and Gratification Theory

Think about the last time you went to a movie. Did you attend because the story mattered to you? Did you go to escape from problems and worries? Did you attend because it featured stars you like? Did you only pay attention to the parts you liked? According to **uses and gratification theory,** which was first advanced in the 1940s, we choose to attend to mass communication to gratify ourselves (Communication Research, 1979; Sparks, 2006).

Uses and gratification theory assumes that in our quest for gratification we select media that we think will give us something we value or want. For example, if you are interested in national affairs, you might listen to National Public Radio. If you are concerned about whether a game will be rained out, you might watch the Weather Channel. If you invest in the stock market, you may subscribe to *The Wall Street Journal* to get daily news of business and the economy.

We use media for reasons other than to gain information. We also use media for pleasure. If you are bored and want excitement, you might choose to watch an action film. Similarly, you may read action stories because you derive pleasure from identifying with a hero or heroine whose life is more daring than your own. On my computer, I have saved a video clip of cats doing amusing things—one fighting with its own image in a mirror, one swinging from a chandelier, one trying to catch ping-pong balls while two people are playing the game. When I am bored with my work or when I encounter a writing block, I often take a break and click on the video to elevate my mood.

Music also powerfully affects our moods. According to Larry Grossberg, Ellen Wartella, and Charles Whitney (1998), "music fans are highly sophisticated in their ability to choose different music in order to manipulate their moods" (p. 253). We might choose soft music to enhance romantic feelings, rock to generate excitement, spirituals to arouse our spiritual awareness, and ritualistic chants and folk music to foster a sense of unity among protesters at a rally.

Whereas the hypodermic needle theory asked, "How do media affect us?" uses and gratification theory asks a quite different question: "What are the reasons people use media?" The latter question allowed researchers to begin figuring out how individuals' motivations shaped their choices of mass communication. For example, a classic study in the uses and gratification tradition asked people who regularly listened to radio soap operas what they gained from listening. Among the uses people cited were to escape real life, to find solutions to their troubles, and to get emotional release from their own worries (Herzog, 1944).

If people use media to gratify themselves, then we might expect that people will also create media if existing media do not satisfy them and others in their communities. That's exactly what happens. Most national and regional newspapers in the United States largely reflect the interests, concerns, and biases of middle-class Caucasian heterosexuals. Typically, they don't offer many stories that speak to the particular concerns of Hispanics, gays, Asian Americans, or other groups (Shim, 1997). More than 200 Spanish-language newspapers and 350 Native American newspapers have been created (Campbell, et al., 2004). These newspapers serve the interests of specific groups that are neglected by mainstream media. Likewise, the exploding number of satellite and cable channels expands our options for choosing media that gratify us.

Uses and gratification theory assumes that people are active agents who make deliberate choices among media to gratify themselves. We use media to gain information, to alleviate loneliness, to divert us from problems, and so forth. Although this theory offers a more realistic view of audiences, its focus is entirely on how individuals use media. That tells us little about how media affect society.

TECHNOLOGY

READING, BUT ON YOUR CELL PHONE

Talk about converging technologies! If you are a fan of romance novels, you no longer have to choose between reading books and being wired. Harlequin Books, the largest publisher of spicy romance novels, offers electronic books that can be read on cell phones. To fit today's women who often have neither long periods of time to curl up with novels nor room in briefcases to tote them around, Harlequin has divided books into daily installments that can be read in just a few minutes—usually fewer than 10. Installments are automatically downloaded to subscribers' cell phones for $2.49 a month (Flynn, 2006).

Technologies of communication maximize consumers' ability to gratify their individual tastes.

Agenda Setting

A third perspective on media asserts that media establish an agenda for us by spotlighting some issues, events, and people and downplaying others. **Agenda setting** refers to the media's ability to select and call to the public's attention ideas, events, and people (Agee, Ault, & Emery, 1996). In other words, by selecting what events and issues to cover and how to present them, mass media set the public agenda. Expressing the key idea of agenda setting, Alex Edelstein (1993) noted that media don't actually tell us what to think but rather tell us what to think *about*. In other words, media set the agenda for topics in public consciousness.

Research has offered support for the idea of agenda setting. In studies of the effects of stories covered in the news, researchers have found that viewers rate the importance of environmental issues more highly after exposure to coverage of pollution in newspapers or on televised news programs (Ader, 1995; Iyengar, & Kinder, 1987).

Mass media not only direct us to pay attention to particular topics. They also divert attention from topics. Ralph Nader (1996) criticizes media for what they do *not* cover. Nader notes that there is no national television program that highlights issues at colleges and universities outside the athletic arena. Nader also points out that we have many programs devoted to business profits and growth but no television or radio program that focuses on workers and labor issues. Nader urges us to think critically about what media do and do not offer us and how media foci affect our knowledge and sense of what's happening in the world.

Kurt Lewin coined the term *gatekeeper* in 1947 to describe the people and groups that decide which messages pass through the gates that control information flow to reach consumers. Since Lewin introduced the term, communication researchers have studied the ways in which individuals and groups control what stories and ideas are included in mass communication (Altheide, 1974; Gitlin, 1980; Shaw, 1999; Shoemaker, 1991). Gatekeepers screen messages, stories, and perspectives to create messages (programs, interviews, news clips) that shape our perceptions of events and people.

Mass communication has many gatekeepers. Editors of newspapers, books, and magazines screen the information that gets to readers; owners, executives, and producers filter information for radio and television programs; advertisers and political groups may also intervene to influence which messages reach end users of mass communication. For example, radio stations that are owned and financed by conservatives air Rush Limbaugh's comments but not those of progressives and liberals. Radio stations owned and funded by more liberal groups are likely to shut the gate on Rush Limbaugh but include Molly Ivins and Mark Shields. As a result, listeners of the two stations are likely to be aware of different issues and to have different perspectives on social life. America Online (AOL), a major Internet service provider, chooses which companies, groups, and issues to highlight on the pop-up menus that greet users each time they sign on. This gives visibility to the groups, people, and issues that AOL, not its users, decides to emphasize.

Gatekeepers screen not only information content but also sources of information. Writers, producers, and others who control programming decide which experts to feature, which people in the news to cover, and which perspectives on events to include. An example of bias in mass communication is the tendency to use members of minority groups almost exclusively as authorities on issues involving race. This can foster the misperception that members of minorities have expertise only about ethnicity.

Research on agenda setting moved media theorists back to questions of how media shapes what we think about. This set the stage for the next theory, which asks how worldviews are shaped by, in particular, television.

Cultivation Theory

A fourth view of the effects of mass communication is **cultivation theory,** which claims that television cultivates, or promotes, a worldview that is inaccurate but that viewers nonetheless may assume reflects real life. This theory is concerned exclusively with the medium of television, which it claims creates a synthetic reality that shapes heavy viewers' perspectives and beliefs about the world (Gerbner, 1990; Gerbner et al., 1986; Signorielli & Morgan, 1990).

Cultivation is the cumulative process by which television fosters beliefs about social reality. According to the theory, television fosters broad, often unrealistic understandings of the world as more violent and dangerous than statistics show it to be.

Thus, goes the reasoning, watching television promotes distorted views of life. The word *cumulative* is important to understanding cultivation. Researchers don't argue that a particular program has significant effects on viewers' beliefs or that television viewing directly determines public opinion. However, they claim that watching television over a long period of time affects viewers' basic views of the world. By extension, the more television people watch, the more distorted their ideas about life are likely to be. Simply put, the theory claims that television cumulatively cultivates a synthetic worldview that heavy viewers are likely to assume represents reality.

Cultivation theorists identify two mechanisms to explain the cultivation process: **mainstreaming** and **resonance.** Mainstreaming is the stabilizing and homogenizing of views within a society. For example, if commercial programming consistently por-

MEDIA-CREATED BODY IMAGES

Anthropologist and psychiatrist Anne Becker and her colleagues (Becker, Burwell, Gilman, Herzog, & Hamburg, 2002) reported research suggesting that media are very powerful in shaping—or distorting—body images.

For centuries, Fiji had been a food-loving society. Fijian people enjoyed eating and considered fleshy bodies attractive in women and men. In fact, when someone seemed to be losing weight, acquaintances chided her or him for "going thin." All of that changed in 1995, when television stations in Fiji began to broadcast American programs such as *Melrose Place, Seinfeld,* and *Beverly Hills 90210.* Within three years, an astonishing number of Fijian women began to diet and to develop eating disorders. When asked why they were trying to lose weight, young Fijian woman cited characters such as Amanda (Heather Locklear) on *Melrose Place* as their model.

Sally Steindorf, a cultural anthropologist working in India, reports that television has had a mainstreaming effect in India much as it has in the United States. As televisions have become common in the quiet village of Kothariya, long-standing ethnic and cultural traditions have waned. In their place, villagers have adopted Western values and seek Western products that are advertised on television. Villagers see motorcycles, color TVs, and brand-name shampoo as status symbols (Overland, 2004).

trays European Americans as upstanding citizens, and members of other races as lazy, criminal, or irresponsible, viewers may come to accept such representations as factual. If television programs, from Saturday morning cartoons to prime-time dramas, feature extensive violence, viewers may come to believe that violence is pervasive. As they interact with others, heavy viewers communicate their attitudes and thus affect the attitudes of others who watch little or no television. Thus, televised versions of life permeate the mainstream. The FYI box on this page illustrates how images on television can affect real life.

The second explanation for television's capacity to cultivate worldviews is *resonance,* the extent to which media representations are congruent with personal experience. For instance, a person who has been robbed or assaulted is likely to identify with televised violence. When media images correspond to our experiences, we are more likely to assume that they accurately represent the world in general.

People who watch a lot of television are more likely to have beliefs that reflect the worldview portrayed by television, which is not equivalent to a worldview based on empirical data. In television entertainment programming, 57% of all programs include some violence, and 77% of major characters who commit crimes perpetrate acts of violence. Compare this with the fact that roughly 10% of reported real crimes are violent. In prime-time entertainment programming on commercial networks, most criminal characters are never being brought to trial or get off at trial (National Television Violence Study, 1996). Yet of the nearly 11,000 felony arrests in California in one year, 80% went to trial, and 88% of the trials resulted in convictions. Prime-time entertainment programs portray 64% of characters as involved in violence, so heavy viewing of television is likely to cultivate the belief that becoming a victim of violence is common. In the real world, however, the average person has a 1 in 200 chance of becoming involved in a violent crime in any given week.

The world of television teems with violence. Media scholar Glenn Sparks (2006) reports that nearly 60% of all television programs include violence. This raises particular concerns about young children, for violence is common on children's TV (Ho, 2006;

Parents Television Council, 2006). By age 6, the average child in the United States has watched 5,000 hours of television; by age 18, the average person has watched fully 19,000 hours of television. The average 18-year-old in the United States has viewed 200,000 separate acts of violence on television, including 40,000 murders (Palmer & Young, 2003; Singer & Singer, 2001; Valkenburg, 2004). Given the incidence of violence on television, it's no wonder that many heavy viewers think the world is more violent than crime reports show it to be. Most young children watch television without parents present and without any rules restricting what they view (Rideout et al., 1999). Mike's commentary illustrates a concern of many parents. To read a 2006 study of violence on children's TV, go to the book's online resources and click on WebLink 14.1.

▶ Mike

Adults may be able to separate fantasy from real life, but kids aren't. What they see on the TV is real life to them. My wife and I have raised our son not to be aggressive—not a sissy, but not aggressive either. But any time he watches TV, he's picking up sticks and aiming them like they were guns or imitating karate chops he saw some TV character do.

The high incidence of violence in news programming reflects, in part, the fact that the abnormal is more newsworthy than the normal (Mander, 1999). It isn't news that 99.9% of couples are getting along or working out their problems in nonviolent ways; it is news when Lorena Bobbitt amputates her husband's penis or when O. J. Simpson's wife is murdered (Hunt, 1999). It isn't news that most of us grumble about big government but refrain from violent protest; it is news when someone blows up the Federal Building in Oklahoma City and cites dissatisfaction with big government as a motive. Simply put, violence is news.

In an effort to present as many stories as possible, news programs offer little analysis, depth, or reflection (Ferrante, 1995; Gitlin, 2002). Instead, the stories are encapsulated in dramatic film clips. In his 1985 book *Amusing Ourselves to Death*, cultural critic Neil Postman argued that the fast and furious format of news programming creates the overall impression that the world is unmanageable, beyond our control, and filled with danger and violence. Consequently, reports on crime and violence may do less to enhance understanding and informed response than to agitate, scare, and intimidate us.

Perhaps you are thinking that few people confuse what they see on television with real life. Research shows that this may not be the case. Watching violent media has been shown to make viewers less sensitive to actual violence (Sparks, 2006). Further, children—both male and female—who watched a great deal of television had higher measures of personal aggression as young adults than did people who watched less television (Huesmann, Moise-Titus, Podolski, & Eron, 2003)

Testing the Mean World Syndrome

The basic worldview studied by cultivation theorists is exemplified in research on the mean world syndrome (Gerbner et al., 1986). The **mean world syndrome** is the belief that the world is a dangerous place, full of mean people who cannot be trusted and who are likely to harm us. Although fewer than 1% of the U.S. population are victimized by violent crime in any year, television presents the world as a dangerous place in which everyone is at risk.

To test this theory, ask 10 people whether or not they basically agree or disagree with the following five statements, which are adapted from the mean world index used in research. After respondents have answered, ask them how much television they watch on an average day. Do your results support the claim that television cultivates the mean world syndrome?

1. Most public officials are not interested in the plight of the average person.

2. Despite what some people say, the lot of the average person is getting worse, not better.

3. Most people mostly look out for themselves rather than trying to help others.

4. Most people would try to take advantage of you if they had a chance.

5. You can't be too careful in dealing with people.

SHARPEN YOUR SKILL

▶ Kasheta

To earn money, I babysit two little boys four days a week. One day, they got into a fight, and I broke it up. When I told them that physical violence isn't a good way to solve problems, they reeled off a list of TV characters that beat up on each other. Another day, one of them referred to the little girl next door as a "ho." When I asked why he called her that, he started singing the lyrics from an MTV video he'd been watching. In that video, women were called "hos." It's scary what kids absorb.

Cultural Studies Theories

Cultural studies theories focus on relationships between mass communication and the rituals and patterns of everyday communication. Like some of the other theories we've discussed in this chapter, cultural studies theories assume that people are actively involved in creating and shaping meaning. In addition, cultural studies scholars are keenly interested in the reciprocally influential relationships between mass communication and cultural life, including history, politics, and economics. In other words, cultural studies scholars investigate the ways in which cultural factors such as economics, politics, and history shape mass communication, as well as the converse—how mass communication affects culture, including politics, economics, and history.

To understand this relationship of reciprocal influence, cultural studies scholars conduct textual analysis, audience studies, and political economy studies. Each of these approaches to research informs the overall perspective on mass communication advanced by cultural studies scholars.

Textual Analysis This approach to research involves closely reading texts, which are broadly defined to include books, television programs, films, fashion, rock music, and other discourses in cultural life. One method of conducting close readings is *frame analysis,* which is the examination of consistent patterns in the ways stories are presented by journalists, broadcasters, and so forth. When you read a newspaper article or watch a television news report, you do not get a set of unrelated facts. Instead, you get a narrative—a story that first captures your interest and then shapes the information into a coherent account that predisposes you to particular conclusions and perspectives on the people and events in the story.

A good example of narrative framing is one segment of the July 20, 1990, *McNeil-Lehrer NewsHour.* This segment, entitled "Focus–Logjam," reported on a protest by Earth First!, an environmental group, against logging redwood forests in northern California. Harold Schlechtweg (1992) engaged in textual analysis to identify visual and verbal factors that shaped the story's frame. Although the Earth First! protesters had emphasized that their protest was nonviolent and had tried to engage in dialogue with loggers, the "Focus–Logjam" story referred to them as "radical," "terrorists," "violent," "wrong people" who were engaging in "sabotage" (p. 273). On the other hand, loggers were described as "workers," "timber people," and "regular people" who were simply trying to survive in "small-town economies" that provide limited "jobs" and sources of "livelihood" (p. 273). Schlechtweg also called attention to visual cues, such as an Earth First! protester hammering a spike into a tree, that supported the frame of the story. The framing of this story clearly presented the protesters as the antagonists, the "bad guys," and the loggers as vulnerable protagonists who merit our sympathy and support. The FYI box on the following page provides further insights into how media frame stories and attempt to influence audiences' perceptions.

Audience Studies Another approach taken by cultural studies scholars is the audience study, or reader-response research. This line of inquiry focuses on the meanings that audiences (readers or viewers) assign to their consumption of media. Notice that this focus assumes that audiences are active, not passive. The classic audience study was conducted by Janice Radway in 1984. She investigated what romance novels mean to Midwestern women who read these novels, sometimes as many as 12 in a week. She found that readers gained pleasure by identifying with independent heroines and by escaping from the complexities of their own lives. Women who frequently read romance novels also explained that to read them was to have personal time, free from the demands of families.

© Ron Fehling/Masterfile

We often deliberately choose media that give us pleasure.

CONSTRUCTING THE NEWS

Many people think news programs present information and news in a factual, neutral way. However, most mass communication scholars think differently (Potter, 2001, 2004; Shanahan & McComas, 1999). They assert that media construct the news, shaping what is presented and how:

▶ Selecting what gets covered: Only a minute portion of human activity is reported in the news. Gatekeepers in the media decide which people and events are newsworthy and whose opinions about issues will be covered. By presenting stories on these events and people, the media make them newsworthy.

▶ Choosing the hook: Reporters and journalists choose how to focus a story, or how to "hook" people into a story. In so doing, they direct people's attention to certain aspects of the story. For example, in a story on a politician accused of sexual misconduct, the focus could be the charges made, the politician's denial, or the increase in sexual misconduct by public figures.

▶ Choosing how to tell the story: In the foregoing story, media might tell it in a way that fosters sympathy for the person who claims to have been the target of sexual misconduct (interviews with the victim, references to other victims of sexual misconduct), or they might tell it in a way that inclines people to be sympathetic toward the politician (shots of the politician with his or her family, interviews with colleagues who proclaim the politician's innocence).

Each way of telling the story encourages people to think and feel in distinct ways about the story.

Political Economy Studies A third approach taken by cultural studies scholars is political economy studies, which ask how ownership of media serve to control cultural life. As you may have realized, this approach has much in common with agenda-setting theory, which we discussed earlier in this chapter. Robert McChesney (1999; 2004) argues that media primarily benefit wealthy individuals and corporations. The evidence to support McChesney's claim is strong: In the early 1980s, 50 companies controlled most U.S. newspapers, magazines, television stations, and film organizations. In 2000, a mere 6 corporations controlled most of mass communication (Zuckerman, 2002). Thus, although there are hundreds of radio and television channels, there are far fewer gatekeepers for the media we consume.

Political economy studies go further than arguing that control of media is concentrated in the hands of a very few corporations. They also maintain that media are driven by capitalism, the goal of which is to maximize profits. If making a profit is the key objective, then corporations that own media may not be only, or even primarily, interested in the accuracy of media. Making money is the primary goal of multinational corporations such as General Electric, which owns NBC, and Westinghouse, which owns CBS (Grossberg et al., 1998). Sharon Beder (1998) notes that it is probably not a coincidence that NBC and CNBC have "not been particularly keen to expose GE's environmental record" (p. 224), which is less than commendable in some respects.

Can we expect unbiased programming about environmental issues from NBC and CBS when both corporations are strongly invested in generating power, including nuclear power? How seriously can *Time* magazine criticize AOL when both *Time* and AOL are owned by Time Warner? Should we be surprised that in 1995 CNN, which is owned by Time Warner (a major cable TV operation), refused to run an ad that claimed cable TV rates were likely to rise (Zuckerman, 2002)?

Because media are owned by for-profit corporations, mass communication's survival depends on attracting and keeping advertisers. This constrains media's ability to criticize advertisers' products or to cover news that is not consistent with advertisers' interests. For instance, some political economy scholars assert that media provide inadequate coverage of environmental dangers and threats because they don't want to offend advertisers whose companies would be hurt by additional environmental regulations (Shabecoff, 2000). Advertising is a primary means of increasing the growth of profits for a sliver of the American populace while depleting the resources of a large portion of it.

Media scholar W. James Potter (2001, 2004) reports that money spent on advertising has increased from $500 million in 1900 to more than $220 billion. To introduce a new product and stimulate consumer interest, an advertiser will spend about $50 million (Potter, 2001, 2004). Each year, the average child in America views more than 30,000 television commercials (Numbers, 1999). And commercials aren't the only source of advertising on television and in films. **Product placement,** which is paid for by advertisers and program sponsors, is the practice of featuring products in media so that the products are associated with particular characters, storylines, and so forth. Because product placement inserts advertising into programs, it blurs the traditional distinction between program content and ads (Jamieson & Campbell, 2006). For instance, Sears is the primary sponsor of the popular show *Extreme Makeover: Home Edition.* Each episode of the show features Sears' Craftsman tools and Kenmore appliances. Viewers of the program are 25% more likely to shop at Sears after an episode is aired than before it (Roberts, 2004).

In combination, textual analyses, audience studies, and political economy studies support cultural studies scholars' broad claim that mass communication functions to support prevailing power relations and dominant cultural perspectives. Because individuals and groups that have benefited from the existing social structure control mass communication, they tend to approve of and support the system that has privileged them. Support of the status quo is evident in the content of mass communication, which is more likely to portray White men as good, powerful, and successful than it is to describe women or minority men in those ways. Capitalism generally is presented positively, and consumers are encouraged to want more and to buy more.

Mass media are particularly powerful in representing the ideology of privileged groups as normal, right, and natural (Hall, 1986a, 1986b, 1988, 1989a, 1989b). Television programs, from children's shows to prime-time news, represent White, heterosexual, able-bodied males as the norm in the United States, although they are actually not the majority. Magazine covers and ads as well as billboards portray young, able-bodied, attractive White people as the norm. Despite critiques of bias in media, minorities continue to be portrayed most often as criminals, victims, subordinates, or otherwise less-than-respectable people (Braxton, 1999; Entman, 1994). Even scarcer in the world of television are Latinos and Latinas, the fastest growing ethnic–racial group in the United States (Haubegger, 1999). The FYI box on page 319 offers more information on media representation of races.

In this section, we have considered five theories of mass communication. Probably each has some validity. Surely, we make some fairly conscious choices about how to use and interpret media, as uses and gratification theory and active audience theories claim. At the same time, mass communication probably influences us in ways that we don't notice, as agenda setting and cultivation theories assert. And cultural studies scholars are probably correct in noting that mass communication tends to support prevailing social systems and privileged interests. Keep each of these theories in mind as we consider how we can improve our ability to interact with mass communication.

fyi

RACE ON TELEVISION AND IN REAL LIFE

Are 92% of Americans White? Are 85% of Americans male? No, but you wouldn't know that from watching television news on the three major national networks (View, 2001):

▶ Total number of U.S. sources interviewed by the three major networks on evening news broadcasts in 2001 (the latest year for which data are available): 14,632

▶ Percentage of U.S. sources interviewed who were White: 92%

▶ Percentage of U.S. sources interviewed who were male: 85%

▶ Percentage of U.S. sources interviewed who were Republican when party affiliations were revealed: 75%

▶ Number (not percentage) of Native Americans interviewed: 1

But some of television's gatekeepers are willing to criticize racism. In 2006, FX aired a six-part documentary series titled *Black. White.* Professional makeup artists made a White mother, father, and son, the Wurgels, appear Black and made a Black mother, father, and daughter, the Sparks, appear White. For six weeks, the two families lived as members of the other race and learned, along with viewers, how much difference race still makes in America (Peyser, 2006).

▶GUIDELINES FOR INTERACTING WITH MASS COMMUNICATION

Because mass communication surrounds and influences us, we have an ethical obligation to be responsible and thoughtful consumers. Two critical guidelines for interacting with mass communication are to develop media literacy and to respond actively.

Develop Media Literacy

The first challenge is to develop media literacy. Just as it takes work to become literate in reading, in communicating orally, and in using technologies, we need to invest effort to develop literacy in interacting with media. Instead of passively absorbing media, cultivate your ability to analyze, understand, and respond thoughtfully to media. Figure 14.2 describes key stages in developing media literacy. How literate we become, however, depends on the extent to which we commit to developing sophisticated skills in interpreting media.

Realistically Assess Media's Influence Media literacy begins with understanding how much influence you believe mass communication has on people. One view—a rather extreme one—claims that mass communication determines individual attitudes and social perspectives. Another view—also extreme—is that mass communication doesn't affect us at all. In between those two radical views

6 Months	3 Years	4 Years	7–8 Years	Throughout Life
Children pay attention to television.	Children engage in exploratory viewing.	Children search for preferred viewing.	Children make clear distinctions between ads and programs.	People who commit to media literacy learn to recognize puffery, hooks, and other devices for directing their attention and behavior.
	Children establish preferred patterns of viewing.	Children develop a viewing agenda.		
	Children do not distinguish between programs and ads.	Children's attention is held by a story line.	Children become skeptical of ads for products with which they are familiar; they are less skeptical of ads for products they haven't tried or don't own.	People who commit to media literacy learn to use media in sophisticated ways to meet their needs and to compensate for media bias and techniques.
		Children begin to distinguish between ads and programs.		
		Children do not realize that ads seek profits.		

Figure 14.2 STAGES IN THE DEVELOPMENT OF MEDIA LITERACY

is the more reasonable belief that mass communication is one of many influences on individual attitudes and social perspectives.

This last claim represents a thoughtful assessment of the qualified influence of mass communication and our ability to exercise control over its effects. Television, individual viewers, and society interact in complex ways. The same argument can be made for the influence of other mass media, such as radio, film, billboards, magazines, and newspapers. If this is so, it's inaccurate to presume that a linear relationship exists between media and individuals' attitudes.

Become Aware of Patterns in Media If you aren't aware of the patterns that make up basketball, you will not be able to understand what happens in a game. If you don't understand how church or synagogue services are organized, you won't appreciate the meaning of those services. In the same way, if you don't understand patterns in media, you can't understand fully the workings of music, advertising, programming, and so forth. Learning to recognize patterns in media empowers you to engage media in critical and sophisticated ways.

As W. James Potter (2001, 2004) points out, media use a few standard patterns repeatedly. For example, despite the variety in music, there is a small number of basic chords, melody progressions, and rhythms. Even the content of songs tends to follow stock patterns, most often love and sex (Christianson & Roberts, 1998). Most stories, whether in print, film, or television, open with some problem or conflict that progresses until it climaxes in final dramatic scenes. Romance stories typically follow a pattern in which we meet a main character who has suffered a bad relationship or has not had a relationship. The romance pattern progresses through meeting Mr. or Ms. Right, encountering complications or problems, resolving the problems, and living happily ever after (Riggs, 1999).

Actively Interrogate Media Messages

When interacting with mass communication, you should use critical thought to assess what is presented. Rather than accepting news accounts unquestioningly, you should be thoughtful and skeptical. It's important to ask questions such as these:

▶ Why is this story getting so much attention? Whose interests are served, and whose are muted?

▶ What are the sources of statistics and other forms of evidence? Are the sources current? Do the sources have any interest in taking a specific position? (For example, tobacco companies have vested interest in denying or minimizing the harms of smoking.)

▶ What's the hook for the story, and what alternative hooks might have been used?

▶ Are stories balanced so that a range of viewpoints are given voice (for example, in a report on environmental bills pending in Congress, do news reports include statements from the Sierra Club, industry leaders, environmental scientists, and so forth)?

▶ How are different people and viewpoints framed by gatekeepers (e.g., reporters, photographers, experts)?

It's equally important to be critical in interpreting mass entertainment communication, such as music, magazines, and websites. When listening to popular music, ask whose views of society it portrays and who and what it represents as normal or good, and abnormal or bad. Raise the same questions about the images in magazines and on billboards. When considering an ad, ask whether it offers meaningful evidence or merely puffery (see the FYI box on this page). Asking questions such as these allows you to be critical and careful in assessing what mass communication presents to you.

Expose Yourself to a Range of Media Sources

Many people limit their exposure to media, choosing to view and listen only to what they particularly like. For instance, if you are conservative politically, you might

---

Detecting Dominant Values in Media

Watch two hours of prime-time commercial television. Pay attention to the dominant ideology that is represented and normalized in the programming. Who are the good and bad characters? Which personal qualities are represented as admirable, and which are represented as objectionable? Who are the victims and victors, the heroes and villains? What goals and values are endorsed?

SHARPEN YOUR SKILL

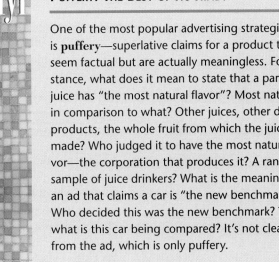

PUFFERY: THE BEST OF ITS KIND!

One of the most popular advertising strategies is **puffery**—superlative claims for a product that seem factual but are actually meaningless. For instance, what does it mean to state that a particular juice has "the most natural flavor"? Most natural in comparison to what? Other juices, other drink products, the whole fruit from which the juice is made? Who judged it to have the most natural flavor—the corporation that produces it? A random sample of juice drinkers? What is the meaning of an ad that claims a car is "the new benchmark"? Who decided this was the new benchmark? To what is this car being compared? It's not clear from the ad, which is only puffery.

read a conservative daily paper and listen to a conservative radio station. The problem with that is that you don't expose yourself to criticisms of conservative policies and stances, and you don't give yourself the opportunity to learn about more liberal alternatives. If you listen only to popular music, you'll never learn to understand, much less appreciate, classical music, jazz, or reggae. You cannot be informed about any issue or type of media unless you deliberately expose yourself to multiple sources of information and perspectives.

Exposing yourself to multiple media also means attending to more than entertainment. Television focuses primarily on entertainment and popular culture. One study of children ages 9 to 12 found that 98% of respondents knew who Michael Jordan and Michael Jackson were, but only 21% knew who Boris Yeltsin was, and only 20% recognized the name Nelson Mandela ("Names & Faces," 1997). Tuning into celebrity culture is not sufficient if you want to be media literate.

Focus on Your Motivations for Engaging Media Do you ever just turn on the TV and watch whatever is on? If so, you're not making deliberate choices that allow you to select media to suit your needs and goals. Sophisticated media users realize that media serve many purposes, and they make deliberate choices that serve their goals and needs at particular times. For example, if you feel depressed and want to watch television, it might be better to watch a comedy or action drama than to watch a television movie about personal trauma and pain.

Respond Actively

People may respond critically or uncritically to mass communication and the worldviews that it portrays, depending on how media literate they are (Fiske, 1987; S. Hall, 1982, 1989b). If we respond uncritically, we mindlessly consume messages and their ideological underpinnings. On the other hand, if we interact critically with media, we recognize that the worldviews presented in mass communication are not unvarnished truth but partial, subjective perspectives that serve the interests of some individuals and groups while disregarding the interests of others.

To assume an active role in interacting with media, you must recognize that you are an agent who can affect what happens around you. You begin to take action by noticing what media ask you to think about, believe, and do. Once you become aware of mass communication's efforts to shape perceptions and attitudes, you may then question or challenge the views of reality they advance.

▶ **Manuel**

I was really angry about a story in the local paper. It was about Mexicans who come to the U.S. The story only mentioned Mexican Americans who get in trouble with the law, are on welfare, or are illegal residents. So I wrote a letter to the editor and said the story was biased and inaccurate. The editor invited me to write an article for the opinion page, and I did. In my article, I described many Mexican Americans who are hardworking, honest citizens who are making this country better. There were a lot of responses to my article, so I know I made a difference.

Manuel's experience demonstrates that speaking out is not just personally empowering; it also enriches cultural life. People have an ethical responsibility to resist and redefine those messages of mass communication that they consider inaccurate or harmful. The Sharpen Your Skill box on this page lists websites for people who are interested in taking a voice in regard to mass communication.

Speaking out can make a difference. In 1995, Calvin Klein discontinued an ad campaign because so many individuals and groups objected to the ads. Other companies have withdrawn ads and even products in response to voices of resistance. Power relationships and social perspectives are never fixed in cultural life. They are always open to change and negotiation between voices that offer rival views of reality.

Responding Actively

If you want to learn more about gender and media, or if you want to become active in working against media that foster views of violence as normal, girls and women as subordinate, and buying as the route to happiness, visit these websites by clicking the appropriate WebLinks, all available among the book's online resources:

▸ Media Education Foundation: WebLink 14.2

▸ Children Now: WebLink 14.3

▸ Media Watch: WebLink 14.4

▸ National Association for Family and Community Education: WebLink 14.5

▸ TV Parental Guidelines Monitoring Board: WebLink 14.6

▸ Center for Media Literacy: WebLink 14.7

SHARPEN YOUR SKILL

▶SUMMARY

In this chapter, we examined mass communication. We began by discussing how the different media epochs have affected individual lives and social organization. Next, we considered five views of the functions and effects of mass communication. The earliest theory, which has been discredited, claimed that mass media directly "injects" its views into consumers. A second view is that people use mass communication to gratify their interests.

Two other theories, agenda setting and cultivation, give greater emphasis to the ways in which mass communication influences what we think about (the agenda for public discussion) and how we perceive social life (the worldview that is cultivated by media). The fifth theory, cultural studies, is particularly interested in the reciprocal influences of mass communication and the politics, history, and economics of cultural life. Cultural studies theory regards consumers of media as actively involved in shaping media's meanings and using media to affect emotions, moods, and pleasures. But the influence is not just one way. Cultural studies theory also claims that mass communication supports dominant social relations, roles, and perspectives by portraying them as normal and right. If you think about mass communication in your life, you'll probably realize that each of these views has some merit.

The second section of the chapter focused on two related guidelines for us as we interact with mass communication. The first is to develop media literacy. This requires, first, that we develop a realistic, balanced perspective on the power of mass communication. Media do not exist in isolation, nor do we as consumers of mass communication. Each of us participates in multiple and diverse social systems that shape our responses to mass communication and the worldviews it presents. To be responsible participants in social life, we need to question what is included—and what is made invisible—in mass communication.

A second guideline is to assume an active voice by responding to mass communication. We have an ethical responsibility to speak out against communication that we think is inaccurate, hurtful, or wrong. One means of negotiating social meanings is to respond to mass communication. Without our consent and support, mass communication cannot exist.

Review, Reflect, Extend

The Key Concepts, For Further Reflection and Discussion questions, Recommended Resources, and Experience Communication Case Study that follow will help you review, reflect on, and extend the information and ideas presented in this chapter. A diverse selection of online resources is also available through ThomsonNOW. These resources include Speech Builder Express, InfoTrac College Edition, interactive videos, vMentor, and Thomson Audio Study Products.

Thomson NOW! is an online study system designed to help you put your time to the best use. After reading a chapter, take the NOW pre-test to identify concepts discussed in the chapter that you may not fully understand. Based on the results of this diagnostic test, the system will create a personalized study plan that directs you to specific learning resources and activities. To see if you're ready for an exam, take the NOW post-test to check your understanding.

For more information or to access this book's online resources, visit **http://www.thomsonedu.com**.

▶ KEY CONCEPTS

The terms following are defined in the chapter on the page number indicated, and they appear in alphabetical order, with definitions, in the Glossary, which begins on page 369. The book's online resources also include flash cards and crossword puzzles to help you learn these terms and the concepts they represent.

agenda setting, 311	global village, 308	print epoch, 307
cultivation, 312	hypodermic needle model, 309	product placement, 318
cultivation theory, 312	literate epoch, 307	puffery, 321
cultural studies theories, 315	mainstreaming, 312	resonance, 312
electronic epoch, 308	mass communication, 304	tribal epoch, 306
gatekeeper, 311	mean world syndrome, 315	uses and gratification theory, 309

▶ FOR FURTHER REFLECTION AND DISCUSSION

The questions below can also be found among the book's online resources for this chapter, where you have the option of e-mailing your responses to your instructor, if required.

1. To what extent, if any, should there be control over the violence presented in media? Do you think viewers, especially children, are harmed by the prevalence of violence in media? Are you concerned about the lack of correspondence between the synthetic world of television violence and the actual incidence of violence in social life? If you think there should be some controls, what groups or individuals would you trust to establish and implement them?

2. Make a list of the forms of mass communication you use most often. Include newspapers, magazines, television programs, types of films, radio stations, and so forth. Describe your media environment. How do your choices of mass communication reflect and shape your identity and your social perspectives?

▶ RECOMMENDED RESOURCES

1. Embrace the challenge advanced in this chapter by taking an active role in responding to mass communication. Write a letter to the editor of a local paper, or write to a manufacturer to support or criticize its product or the way it advertises its product. Visit the websites mentioned in the Sharpen Your Skill box on page 323 to learn about opportunities to become a more involved consumer and controller of mass media.

2. Robert McChesney. (1999). *Rich media, poor democracy: Communication politics in dubious times.* Urbana: University of Illinois Press. This book makes a convincing argument that the concentration of media ownership in the hands of a few corporations has undercut the democratic potential of mass communication.

Experience Communication Case Study

THE POWER ZAPPER

The book's online resources include an interactive video of the communication situation featured in the case study scripted below. Apply what you've learned in this chapter by analyzing the case study, using the questions that follow the script as a guide. These questions are also available online with the video.

Charles and Tina Washington are in the kitchen area of their great room working on dinner. At the other end of the room, their six-year-old son, Derek, is watching television. Tina is tearing lettuce for a salad while Charles stirs a pot on the stove.

Tina: One of us is going to have to run by the store tomorrow. This is the last of the lettuce.

Charles: While we're at it, we'd better get more milk and cereal. We're low on those too.

Tina: I'll flip you for who has to make the store run.

Charles pulls a quarter out of his pocket, flips it in the air, and covers it with one hand when it lands on his other hand. "Call it."

Tina: Heads, you have to go by the store.

Jason Harris/© Wadsworth

Charles removes the hand covering the quarter and grins. "Tails—it's your job." She rolls her eyes and says, "Just can't win, some days."

Derek suddenly jumps up from his chair, points his finger at the chair in which he had been sitting, and shouts "Zap! You're dead! You're dead! I win!" Charles goes to Derek. An advertisement for Power Zapper is just ending on the television, and Charles turns down the volume.

Charles: What's going on, Derek? Who's dead?

Derek The chair is. I zapped it with the Power Zapper, Mom. It's the coolest weapon.
Tina walks over to join Charles and Derek.

Tina: Power Zapper? What's a Power Zapper?

Derek: It's the most popular toy in America, Mom! It's really cool!

Tina: Oh really? Who says so?

Derek: They just said it on TV.

Tina: Does that mean it's true?

Derek points a finger at his mother and shouts, "Pow! I zapped you! You're dead!" At this point, Charles walks over and takes Derek's hand.

Charles: Hold on there, son. Don't go pointing at your mother.

Derek: I was zapping her, Dad.

Charles: I see you were, but we don't hurt people, do we?

Derek: I could if I had a Power Zapper. Can I have one for my birthday? Everybody else has one.

Charles: If everybody jumped off the roof, would you do that?

Derek: I wouldn't need to if I had a Power Zapper because I could zap anyone who bothered me. I'd be so cool.

Charles: But zapping other people would hurt them. You wouldn't want to do that, would you?

Tina [to Charles]: You're overreacting. It's just a toy.

Charles [to Tina]: Kids learn from toys. I don't want Derek to learn that violence is cool.

Tina [to Charles]: He isn't going to learn that with us as his parents. Don't get so worked up over a toy.

▾ ▾

1. Identify an example of puffery in the advertisement for the Power Zapper.

2. Are Charles and Tina Washington teaching Derek to be a critical viewer of mass communication?

3. How does this scenario illustrate the process of mainstreaming?

4. Are you more in agreement with Charles or with Tina about whether toys teach important lessons to children?

15 *Communication Technologies*

▶ **FOCUS QUESTIONS**

1. What are communication technologies?

2. How will interconnectivity change how people live and work?

3. In what ways do computer technologies change how people think?

4. How do virtual communities differ from physical communities?

5. What are the democratic and nondemocratic potentials of communication technologies?

6. How, if at all, should communication technologies be regulated?

▶ You're walking to class, and your cell rings. It's your mom checking on how things are going.

▶ Your professor announces a change in the syllabus that moves the next test forward one week. You jot a note to yourself on your PDA in case the professor doesn't send a reminder e-mail on BlackBoard.

▶ Between classes, you go online to check the day's news, and you read a story claiming that the government is listening in on ordinary Americans' phone calls.

▶ After grabbing lunch on campus, you go to the library's Wi-Fi zone to e-mail your brother and log into your favorite chat room, where you've made some very close friends.

▶ You buy your child a GPS phone (or your parents buy you one) so you can monitor where the child is at all times.

Twenty years ago, none of these communications could have occurred. Although some people had computers and e-mail in 1987, wireless access was not possible, so checking the news online and e-mailing required a location with hard-wired connecting devices.

Technologies infuse every aspect of our lives. They have not changed what we do so much as they have changed *how* we do what we do. Whereas we used to go to stores to

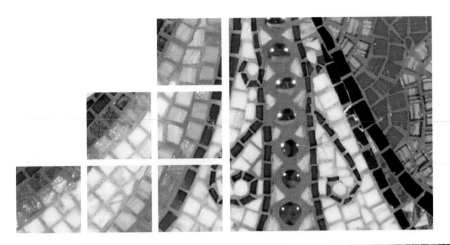

buy items, we can now go online to shop at stores or at the ever-popular eBay (Hillis & Petit with Epley, 2006a). Not many years ago, people walked to classes or talked on the phone but not both simultaneously; they drove cars or talked on the phone, but not both at the same time. Before the Internet was integrated into our lives, we had to actually engage in an experience to sense what it is like, but today virtual reality offers us another way to have experiences (Denning, 2001; Hillis, 2002). If a group of friends wanted to get together to talk, they had to be physically present in one place, but today it's as likely that they'll interact online. If managers at different companies needed to meet, they had to drive or fly to a common location; today, they can teleconference, videoconference, or webconference.

Technologies of communication are not separate from our everyday lives. Instead, they are integrated into our regular routines, goals, identities, and activities (Bakard-jieva, 2005; Haythornthwaite & Wellman, 2002; Howard & Jones, 2004). Most contemporary students are more tech savvy than their professors—they are more likely to have and know how to use the newest technological gadgets than faculty are. However, skill at using new technologies is not the same as skill in reflecting on their places in our lives. The latter is what this chapter encourages you to do.

In this chapter, we will learn about communication technologies that shape how we think, work, interact with others, define ourselves, and participate in communities. The first section of the chapter provides historical context for understanding communication technologies that are part of our lives. In the second section of the chapter, we will consider key controversies about the effects of communication technologies on people. The third section of the chapter identifies three guidelines to keep in mind as we live in a technology-saturated world. Throughout the chapter, I invite you to think critically about new technologies and the roles you choose to give them in your life.

▶A History of Communication Technologies

Many of my students think communication technologies were first developed during their lifetimes. Actually, technologies of communication have been with us since human life began. In this section of the chapter, we look at the history of communication technologies, not merely to understand specific technologies but rather to grasp the broader idea that humans continuously invent new ways to communicate and connect.

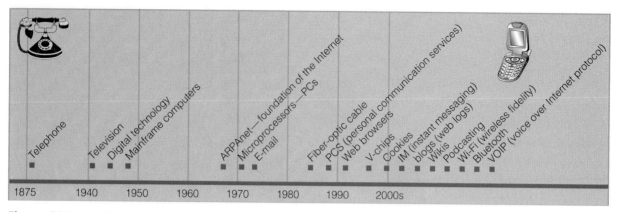

Figure 15.1 THE EVOLUTION OF COMMUNICATION TECHNOLOGIES

Communication technologies are means of recording, transferring, and working with information. Communication technologies include long-established devices, such as the telephone, and newer systems, such as wireless and Blackberry. In our discussion, we'll move from established technologies of communication to newer ones. Figure 15.1 provides a time line so you can grasp the overall history of communication technologies and notice the speedup in the past few years.

Written Communication

Although you might not think of writing as a technology, it is. Like other technologies, writing allows us to record, transfer, and work with information. People record, work with, and share information when they write letters, papers, articles, books, and so forth. They also record and transfer information in written memoranda, a word that comes from the Latin word *memorare*, which means "to be remembered." The primary advantage of written communication is that it leaves a paper trail.

Written communication has drawbacks. First, it requires time and effort to prepare thoughtfully. Second, some people have difficulty finding appropriate words and using correct grammar, syntax, punctuation, and spelling. Third, written communication may be ignored. Many people today assume that any urgent news will be sent by e-mail or fax, so hard-copy memos may not be perceived as high priority.

Telephonic Communication

When Alexander Graham Bell invented the telephone in the mid-1870s, he made it possible for people, as the marketing slogan says, to "reach out and touch someone." Telephones are an especially important communication technology for people like Rhoda, who have physical limitations.

▶ Rhoda

Telephones are a lifeline for me. I keep up with my friends with long telephone calls. Most evenings I have one- or two-hour-long conversations with members of my family or friends. I am wheelchair bound, so I don't get out as much as some people. I go to work everyday and do my shopping and go to temple each week. If I want to go out to socialize, I have to make a detailed plan. I have to get my chair ready and plan a route that is accessible. I can't just jump in my car and go like able-bodied people do. The telephone lets me stay involved with people I love without the physical stress of getting myself from here to there.

Another communication technology based on the telephone is the facsimile machine (better known as the fax), which is fast and inexpensive. Cell phones and text messaging increase the number of telephone messages we send and receive every day, and answering systems allow callers to leave messages if the person called doesn't answer. Yet, as William points out in his commentary, not everyone is a fan of answering machines—or the ways owners set them up.

▶ William

It drives me crazy when I call someone and get one of those obnoxious voice-mail greetings. When I called a classmate last week, the answering machine blared some kind of music. I couldn't even understand the words, and I had to wait through about a minute of noise before I could leave a message. It's really rude to force anyone who calls to listen to that.

Today, many people rely less on "land lines" than on cell phones and PDAs (personal digital assistants), which allow them to send and receive calls wherever they are. Cell phones were first made available in 1977, when AT&T introduced the first cellular network to serve a mere 2,000 customers in the single city of Chicago (Stone, 2004). Since 2000, the number of cell phone users in the United States has grown 29%, to more than 140 million people. Too few people, however, have learned to be considerate users of cell phones (Shostak, 2002). Last month, I was in an airport lounge waiting for my plane to begin boarding. Within twenty minutes, I learned that a woman seated two rows across from me was thinking about leaving her husband, a man pacing the lounge had "bent a few rules" on his tax returns, and a young woman seated

© Jeff Greenberg/PhotoEdit, Inc.

Cell phones have become ubiquitous in our lives.

behind me was afraid to tell her parents that she was dating a man of a race different from hers. I didn't want to know this personal information about strangers, but it was forced on me anyway.

Computer-Mediated Communication

The electronic computer was invented in 1940 (Cairncross, 2002). Soon after its invention, Thomas Watson, who founded IBM, confidently predicted that the worldwide market would probably not support more than five computers (Navasky, 1996). Clearly, Mr. Watson was a better businessman than a forecaster. By the 1970s, there were thousands of computers worldwide.

The Internet is an especially popular form. Although widespread Internet use was not widespread until the 1990s, the Internet was developed in the mid-1970s by a U.S. Defense Department network. Linking people and databases around the world, the Internet is now a major site of personal and business communication. Today, more than 75% of adults in the United States have access to the Internet (Jamieson & Campbell, 2006).

▶ Ty

I think e-mail is the greatest thing since soccer. I can send a message when it suits me and read my mail when I feel like it, unlike telephone conversations, when you have to answer when the phone rings. I also like knowing that I'm not disturbing friends when I send them messages, because they can read them when they feel like it. I think e-mail makes communication a lot easier and more relaxed.

Ty is not alone in liking e-mail. One of the most popular uses of the Internet, e-mail, including IM, allows us to have conversations without tiresome iterations of telephone tag ("I am returning the message you left on my machine by leaving this one on your machine") and the inconvenience of coordinating different time zones. Using e-mail, I advise students, stay in touch with friends and family, discuss current events, consult with attorneys, debate campus issues with colleagues, and collaborate with academics in other states and countries. Some advantages of e-mail are the speed of transmission and the convenience of using the technology when we please. However, e-mail does not automatically produce hard copy for records, and it lacks the advantage of privacy that accompanies conventional written messages. Also, as Kay, a student from a university in New York noted in a letter she wrote to me, not everyone appreciates e-mail as a means of staying in touch.

▶ Kay

Technology is turning human communication into something impersonal. Now people log on and send e-mail about what they are doing—apparently they are too busy doing all of that to pick up the telephone or write a letter. Newer technology has made us lazy. Instead of spelling out words, people write LOL and BRB. Can't we talk to each other anymore?

Wi-Fi greatly increases our ability to connect with the Internet. Wi-Fi, a wireless means of connecting devices to the Internet and to each other, uses an unlicensed part of the spectrum previously used only to power appliances such as microwave ovens and cordless phones. Originally called 802.11, marketers later gave it the cooler name Wi-Fi (Levy, 2004b). Once wireless technology was developed, it rapidly expanded beyond Internet connections. Today, GPS (Global Positioning Satellite) systems, digital voice recorders, 3G (for "third generation") cell networks, Bluetooth, cellular cards, and satellite radio are common uses of wireless connectivity (Fitzgerald, 2006; Pogue, 2006).

Electronic Conferencing

For decades, conferences took place among people who were in the same physical space. Today, many people engage in **teleconferencing,** a term incorporating the Greek prefix *tele,* which means "at a distance." Teleconferencing is discussion among people who are geographically separated. Teleconferencing can take several forms, which differ in the extent to which they emulate face-to-face meetings. Audioconferencing allows people at different locations to participate in a discussion over the telephone. The cost of a telephone conference is far less than the cost of travel, accommodations, meals, and incidentals for several people.

Computer conferencing allows multiple participants to send and receive e-mail in sequential exchanges. Chat mode and threaded discussions allow co-workers, teachers, students, and hobbyists to discuss ideas. Notable benefits of computer conferencing are its low cost and the ability of participants to stay in their regular work environments. Because most computer conferencing relies on typed messages, however, it is linear and requires each participant to wait for others to type and transmit their messages. In addition, computer conferencing without video means that communicators cannot express or interpret non-verbal messages (Rogers, 1986).

TECHNOLOGY

fyi

BIG PARENT IS WATCHING

First, parents were offered V-chips so they could control their children's television viewing. Now, parents can use cell phones to monitor their children—did they get to school, are they really at the library as they said? The newest phones have built-in technology that can tell not only our location but our speed and direction as well (Richtel, 2006). Of course, children have ways of avoiding parents' surveillance. One 16-year-old points out, "If I was going somewhere I wasn't supposed to, I'd just turn it off and say my phone died" (Richtel, 2006, p. E6).

Videoconferencing is rapidly expanding in popularity, largely because it combines the advantages of other kinds of teleconferencing while avoiding many of their disadvantages. You probably have witnessed examples of videoconferencing on news programs. Using satellites to transmit visual images, people in distant locations appear on-screen with newscasters in a studio. A number of regular computer users buy devices that allow them to see a person with whom they are communicating over the Internet. The outstanding advantage of videoconferencing is that it most closely emulates in-person communication. Because participants can see and hear one another, they can communicate verbally and nonverbally. In addition, videoconferencing allows participants to share visual materials such as charts, film clips, models, and pictures. Videoconferencing costs more than other forms of teleconferencing, although the cost is likely to decrease as technology improves and the market becomes more competitive.

Interconnected Communication Technologies

What many people call "new" technologies of communication are actually extensions and convergences of communication technologies that have been around for some time. Convergence of technologies radically alters how we conduct business, engage in research, share information and ideas, and sustain personal relationships.

Interconnectivity is the key word for the future of communication technologies. And interconnectivity promises to be good news for people who are not tech savvy. Interconnectivity is the connecting of various devices to each other and to the Internet so users don't have to independently configure each new system. For instance, yesterday's separate technologies of telephone and PC are combined today in mobile phones that allow people to send e-mail, take photos, and visit the web. Or consider the Nike+iPod, which is a shoe that has a sensor in the insole. The sensor connects to the wearer's iPod, which then links to the Nike website, and the wearer is informed of time, distance, and calories burned through walking or running ("Shoes Are Made," 2006).

One of the key people firing the interconnectivity revolution is Bill Joy, who worked as Sun Microsystems' chief scientist. Joy believes that computers should and will work

T E C H N O L O G Y

fyi

THE PC-PLUS ERA

Interconnectivity means that your home, office, car, and other locations will be filled with devices that "talk" to each other and to the Internet, and you shouldn't have to even think about how they work, much less deal with the hassles of configuring new systems. Here are a few of the innovations we can expect in the next 10 to 15 years (Gates, 1999; Hempel, 1999; Levy, 1999):

▶ *Smart homes:* Your coffeemaker will talk to your calendar to start your morning coffee later on weekends when you sleep in. Your refrigerator will notice when a product has reached its expiration date and e-mail the supermarket to send more. Your dishwasher will notice if you buy a new dishwashing detergent, will e-mail the manufacturer, and then will remotely adjust your machine for the new detergent. Your TV will be connected to the web and will know your viewing preferences. The mirror over the bathroom sink will show you the news headlines while you wash and shave in the morning. Your security system will recognize Fido and Tigger as your dog and cat so the alarm won't go off as they enter rooms or leap about.

▶ *Smart cars:* Some cars already are available with optional systems that provide everything from directions to medical assistance. Before long, such systems are likely to be a standard feature of personal vehicles. If you're lost, your car will be able to connect to the Internet and get directions. It will also notice if your battery is getting weak or your alternator is about to die, and it will give you directions to the closest garage that can repair your car. Your car will also be able to warn you of traffic jams and suggest alternative routes.

▶ *Smart offices:* You'll use smart staples that link files in your PC to those in your digital tablet. When you change an appointment in your personal digital assistant (PDA), that change will be noted automatically by a minicomputer woven into your jacket. Voice recognition will be readily available, so you won't even have to type to get and send information.

▶ *Smart toys:* Toy manufacturers aren't about to be left out of the smart revolution. On the drawing board are dolls that have "social chips" that allow them to chat with one another and have social events such as tea parties. Sensor chips in dolls will also allow them to sense and respond to a child's emotions—if the child is upset, the doll may give a hug; if the child is angry, the doll will know to talk softly to calm the child down (Sennott, 2003).

more like such simple appliances as toasters, dishwashers, alarm clocks, and electric drills (Jamieson & Campbell, 2006; Sandberg, 1999). Soon, he says, we will buy computerized products, plug them in, and they will work automatically. Central to making interconnectivity a reality is getting away from the idea of a single PC in your home or office. Instead, each appliance or device would have its own computer that could be easily connected to other devices, and all the devices would be wired to the Internet. With interconnectivity, many changes in how we live and work are possible, as the FYI box on page 334 shows.

▶Controversies about Communication Technologies

- ▶ "Computers make life more efficient."

- ▶ "E-mail devours time."

- ▶ "Computers are the bane of civilization."

- ▶ "The Internet enhances children's educational opportunities."

- ▶ "The Internet is making children antisocial."

You've probably heard statements much like these. What do you think? Are computer technologies basically good, helpful, and enhancing, or are they basically bad, dangerous, and huge time wasters? That's not a very useful question, as they do have or can have all and none of these effects. It's more useful to ask how technologies of communication shape our lives and—perhaps more important—how we want them to shape our lives.

In this section, we will discuss four controversies about the impact of communication technologies on how we think, communicate, and relate to one another. These are current debates that do not yet have clear answers. Instead, they raise important questions that each of us must consider if we are to be active, informed participants in the present era.

How Do Computer Technologies Affect Thinking?

Sherry Turkle (2004) states that "the tools we use to think change the ways in which we think" (p. B6). If this statement reminds you of McLuhan's ideas, which we covered in Chapter 14, you're making an insightful connection. Like McLuhan, Turkle believes that the communication technologies of an era shape how people think.

Scholars identify three ways in which computers and online interaction affect human thinking. First, they allow and perhaps encourage us to attempt to do multiple tasks simultaneously. Second, they prime us to react to external, visual stimuli. Third, they train us to rely on programs to direct our actions and judgments. Whether these changes serve us well or not is a matter of great debate.

They Encourage Multitasking   A primary way computers affect thinking is by encouraging **multitasking,** which is engaging in multiple tasks simultaneously or in rapid sequence in overlapping and interactive ways. As I am writing this chapter, the e-mail program running behind my word-processing program alerts me when new messages arrive. I'm not alone—the average Windows user has more than three programs running at a single time. That's not surprising, as the Windows system was designed to make it possible for a user to do multiple tasks at once.

Multitasking may not be limited to computer work. People who use computers a significant amount of the time learn to think about multiple tasks at once, and that habit of mind carries over to other contexts of communication. It's become common for people to interrupt conversations to answer cell phones, make notes on PDAs, and check pagers. Drivers talk on cell phones while navigating traffic. Students bring laptop computers to class and, when not taking notes, they check e-mail, play games, surf the Internet, or work on other tasks. Families watch television and take phone calls while eating dinner. The buzz of call waiting prompts a person to suspend the present telephone conversation and answer the new caller. Multitasking and interruptibility seem to be emblematic of our era.

Many people think they are more efficient and productive when they multitask. As one of my friends said, "I get a lot more done by multitasking." The flaw in that reasoning is that computers actually don't multitask. They do one thing at a time—just very, very quickly. A slow computer running with a 100-megahertz processor can implement a million instructions in less than a second (Harmon, 2002). But it executes each operation individually in sequence. Because a computer gives its full attention to a single task at a time, it does the task with great accuracy. When we try to do several tasks at once, we're likely to do each one less well than if we concentrated on one thing at a time (Brooks, 2001). Adults who shift between two tasks take longer to do both tasks, and they make more mistakes (Guterl, 2003). Children are no better at multitasking. Patricia Greenfield, who directs the Children's Media Center at UCLA, says, "Kids are getting better at paying attention to several things at once, but there is a cost in that you don't go into any one thing in as much depth" (Guterl, p. E8). Multitasking can also make us feel rushed, hurried, always needing to check our e-mail or voice mail, get the latest information, respond to instant messages (IMs), and visit our favorite

D I V E R S I T Y

fyi

GENDERED MULTITASKING

Is one sex better than the other at multitasking? Those who have studied the question aren't sure whether one sex is actually better or the two sexes just multitask differently. Anthropologist Helen Fisher (2000) notes that from prehistoric times women have carried on multiple tasks simultaneously— nursing babies while building fires and cooking. In contrast, says Fisher, men's roles in prehistoric times required more singular focus—stalking prey, for instance. Psychiatrist Edward Hallowell (2006) reports that men's instrumental inclination—he calls this the "just something" response— makes them vulnerable to being

© Photoodisc/Getty Images

In the 1970s, Alvin Toffler predicted that the United States would become a nation of "electronic cottages"—what we know today as home offices.

overloaded when multitasking. Men, he says, are better at focusing on one task at a time. One way to sum up the difference is to say that men have "spotlight minds" that zero in on a single thing, and women have "floodlight minds" that take in a lot of territory (Healy, 2006).

blogs and chat rooms. The habit of shifting attention moment to moment is so pervasive that Linda Stone, former Microsoft and Apple executive, defines it as a medical condition: Continuous Partial Attention (Levy, 2006).

They Encourage Response to Visual Stimuli   Computers foster skill at processing visual stimuli. We respond to what is on-screen, whether it's words, flashy game players, vibrant and shifting images, or clever avatars (Lester, 2006). The continuously shifting images and messages in computer games and other programs shape neural maps so that we expect new stimulation frequently. As a result, heavy use of computers may teach us to hold attention for only short spans of time and to be easily distracted by the next stimulus that appears on-screen (Guterl, 2003; Healy, 1990).

Because Internet sites, computer games, and so forth are visually vibrant and graphically interesting, we learn to respond to dazzling images more than to other stimuli such as verbal content or dull images. A good example of how visual emphasis affects thinking is PowerPoint, a widely used presentation software program. PowerPoint slides present ideas, often as bulleted points. According to Edward Tenner (1997), an expert in presentation design, PowerPoint gives the impression that bullets are equivalent to clear thinking. But before we have time to analyze the relationship (or lack of relationship) between the bulleted points and the main points, the next PowerPoint slide pops up, and we're busy checking its bullets (Tufte, 2003). Sherry Turkle (2004) adds that PowerPoint's emphasis on quick, visually striking presentation of information doesn't encourage analytical or integrative thinking about the content of slides.

A second way in which visual stimulation affects thinking is that it unequally stimulates the two brain lobes. The right lobe of the brain is specialized in artistic activity, parallel processing, and visual and spatial tasks. The left lobe is specialized in sequential thought, abstraction, and analytic thinking. The highly visual nature of computer technology stimulates the right side of the brain (as does television) and cultivates its development. Conversely, because computers stimulate the left side of the brain far less, computer use doesn't foster development of the skills essential for sequential activities such as reading and math. Given this, it's not surprising that children who use computers heavily may have difficulty with academic subjects that require analytic, reflective thinking (Gross, 1996; Guterl, 2003; Healy, 1990).

They Encourage Reliance on External Guides for Thinking   When we go on the Internet, we're inevitably bombarded by pop-up advertisements, some of which we must respond to or close to see the site we are trying to visit. Last week, I went to Amazon.com to order a book. When I typed in the name of the book, information on that book appeared, and so did the titles of six other books that were "bought by others who bought this book." Because I was interested in the general topic, I checked out the descriptions and reviews on the other six books. What I intended to be a 2-minute transaction wound up taking 30 minutes. Once I got on the site, I let it influence what I did and how long I spent online. You may be thinking that spending extra time online is harmless and hardly cause for worry about one's personal autonomy. However, the question is not whether on-screen prompts change our schedules, but whether computer use develops a *habit of mind* that favors responding to external stimuli instead of internal ones.

Consider another way in which we may let computers think for us. Do you use a program to check and correct grammar and spelling on papers you write? Most people do. Such programs are useful to skilled writers because they allow writers to catch typing errors or occasional errors in grammar, syntax, and punctuation. However, such programs are not as useful to people who do not know the rules of grammar, spelling, syntax, and punctuation. Most programs designed to check spelling note only combinations of letters that are not recognizable words—*kytump*, for instance. But a spell-check program won't catch the six spelling errors in the following sentence: *Wee should watch hour wait because its important four us too stay healthy.* Each misspelling in the sentence is an actual word, so most spell-checking programs will not flag it. Likewise, most programs for checking grammar will flag this phrase: *A set of rules is helpful,* and the program will suggest that the phrase be changed to this: *A set of rules are helpful.* The subject of the phrase is *set,* which is a singular noun that requires a singular verb—*is. Rules,* a plural noun, is not the subject of the phrase, so the plural verb *are* is incorrect. Users who don't know grammar are likely to rely on the program and wind up with an ungrammatical sentence.

A broader concern is that reliance on external guides for our thinking can lead to more serious consequences, such as undermining the development of imagination, independent thought, and sustained mental focus (Calvert, Jordan, & Cocking, 2002; Singer & Singer, 2001, 2002; Spitzer, 2000; Turkle, 2004; Urgo, 2000). Cognitive specialists think that imagination is ripe to develop at about the age children learn to talk (Spitzer, 2000). As children use words to create make-believe situations and invisible playmates, they enhance their imaginations. At the same time, as imaginations develop, children need more words to name things, so they ask adults how to describe and label actions and ideas, thereby increasing their vocabularies.

T E C H N O L O G Y

fyi

WHY THINGS BITE BACK

That's the short title of a book by Edward Tenner, a senior research associate at the National Museum of American History. The full title is *Why Things Bite Back: Technology and the Revenge of Unintended Consequences* (1997). In this book, Tenner argues that all our technological gadgets have made us mentally lazy—completely reliant on the gadgets instead of our own memories and cognitive skills. For instance,

▶ Do you know all the phone numbers of people you regularly call, or are they stored on your cell?

▶ When's the last time you saw a cashier compute change due to you without relying on the register?

▶ Is your schedule for the next two days in your memory or on your PDA calendar?

These are examples of how mentally lazy technology allows us to be, says Tenner. Others, however, point out that delegating rote memory tasks to gadgets frees up our minds for more important things. Visit Tenner's website by going to the book's online resources and clicking on WebLink 15.2.

▶ Dianna

When I was a kid, I played all the time without any fancy toys, much less high-tech ones. Once, when we got a new refrigerator, my sister and I took the box it came in. We thought that box was the greatest thing ever! One day it was a house, another day it was a space ship, another day a pirate ship. Last summer, we got a new stove, and I offered the box to my 5-year-old son. He said, "What do you want me to do with this?" That made me worry that he's not learning to create fantasy worlds. But I see him doing things on his Game Boy that are more sophisticated than anything I did at his age. Some of my friends are huge fans of technology for kids; some are absolutely against it. I'm more of a middle-way person. My son benefits from technology, but he also needs to learn that a big box can be anything in the world.

But what happens if children don't spend much time in play that develops their imaginations? On average, children in the United States spend 40-plus hours a week watching television, playing videogames, and on the Internet (Kalb, 2003). Today, the average teen in the United States spends 16.7 hours on the Internet alone each week (The New Media, 2003). Virtually all of that time is structured for children by plots on television programs and by the rules built into videogames. Characters on TV and in videogames are ready-made, and the possibilities for action are prestructured. Children don't have to invent characters' personalities or create the rules for what characters can and cannot do. In short, children are required to use less imagination to participate in high-tech play than in old-fashioned, make-believe activities. Research indicates that engaging in imaginative play such as make-believe games is linked to higher scores on tests of creativity and problem-solving (Kalb, 2003).

Does this mean that parents should take away videogames, TV, and the Internet and tell their children to go outside and play? Not necessarily. Research also shows that technological play promotes development of skills in visual processing and role playing. The wisest conclusion at this time is probably what Dianna advises in her commentary—to encourage activities that allow children to derive the benefits of both technology and old-fashioned play, so that they learn to operate within preset virtual worlds and to think outside the lines and ask, "What if . . . ?"

How Do Online Communities Affect Social Relations?

What does the term *community* mean to you? Conventionally, it refers to a group of people who live close enough to one another to interact on a regular basis. More and more people in our era also belong to virtual communities. Are these fundamentally new kinds of communities or merely new ways of participating in familiar communities?

In traditional communities, people lived together and had to make compromises and accommodations to get along. In contrast, we can visit our virtual communities no matter where we are. We can also tap out of those communities with a few clicks. We are free to join communities when we want and to leave when it suits us. We need not accommodate people and topics that don't interest us. Virtual communities may offer many of the benefits of community without most of the responsibilities that go along with belonging to a physical community—responsibility to adapt to and accommodate others and, most of all, to remain part of the community. Does the ease of joining and leaving electronic communities lessen ties and diminish the collectivity and continuity that historically have been associated with community?

Cyberspace is a unique environment that affects how and what we communicate. According to psychology professor John Suler (1999), many people feel they have more freedom to express themselves on the Internet. Screen names, avatars, and aliases allow people to say what they want without being easily identifiable. In a recent interview ("Bookmark," 1999, p. A29), Suler said, "On line, people are free to express aspects of themselves that they wouldn't in other kinds of encounters." Is it desirable for people to make comments online that they would not express in face-to-face conversation?

Some scholars worry that electronic communities have the potential to promote narrow-mindedness, because people may join communities that share their values and views (Kelly, 1997; Swiss, 2001; Walther, 1996). People who visit only sites, blogs, and chat rooms that support the perspectives they already have risk never learning about other perspectives and encountering useful questioning about their own views. Members of many virtual communities maintain and police community norms and ignore or oust anyone whose ideas or style transgress those norms (Jarrett, 2006).

Do Online Identities Foster Deception?

When people interact in person, they usually know certain things about one another's identities, such as sex, race, approximate age, and physical appearance. In online communication, such basic aspects of personal identity may be unclear or even deliberately misrepresented. Some people invent online identities to fit different moods and goals and even the norms of particular communities—for instance, buyers and sellers on eBay announce their identities by proclaiming their fandom and expertise regarding objects associated with their fandom (Desjardins, 2006). Some have extensive collections of avatars that represent different aspects of themselves or who they would like to be (Bookmark, 1999).

People also create on-screen identities to become comfortable with different sides of themselves, some of which may be contradictory or even threatening. An undergraduate named Arlie, who was quoted in an article by Sherry Turkle (2002, p. 156), said, "I am always very self-conscious when I create a new character. Usually, I end up creating someone I wouldn't want my parents to know about. . . . But that someone is part of me." In creating an on-screen character that would trouble her parents but is part of who she thinks she is, Arlie may be integrating this part into her overall sense of identity. As Arlie expresses this aspect of herself online, feedback from other online characters may give her insight into whether she really wants this to be part of her. This can be a healthy process because it enhances self-knowledge and self-acceptance by reducing the blind and hidden areas of the Johari Window, which we discussed in Chapter 9.

Another healthy use of on-screen personalities is to accept limitations or changes in ourselves. One woman lost her leg as a result of an automobile accident. After the amputation, she had difficulty accepting her disability. One way she coped was by logging onto a MUD (Multi-User Dungeon) and creating a one-legged character to represent her. On the MUD, she made friends who accepted her disability, and she became romantically involved with another character on the MUD. For this woman, the virtual character she created helped her accept her real self (Turkle, 2002).

The desirable impact of creating virtual selves is balanced by concerns about not-so-desirable consequences. One question is whether young people who become skilled at adopting online personas have difficulty developing authentic selves and sharing real feelings and fears with others (Turkle, 2002, 2004). In many ways, it's easier to stay within created selves than to get to know and expose our real selves. A related concern is that fabricated characters and the lives they live can be more interesting, more compelling than real people living real, but not always absorbing, lives. Virtual selves and worlds may be more seductive than the ordinariness of much of everyday life and the fact that real people are sometimes boring and uninteresting. Ned offers this reflection on his life online and offline.

▶ Ned

When I was 16, I was really into MUDs and avatars. I probably had 20 different personalities at one point. I got so charged by going online and interacting with other personalities. My online relationships were a lot more interesting than any real relationships, and I sometimes spent 10 or more hours a day in my MUDs. My parents finally cracked down on me because they said I was becoming anti-social. They restricted me to 2 hours a day online. I really hated that at the time, but, looking back, it was a good thing for me. I needed to get back into real life, where I have a real personality that isn't as cool as my online selves were.

Another concern is that fabricated online characters can mislead others, sometimes in dangerous ways (Lewis, 2002). Some people represent themselves falsely on-screen for reasons that have nothing to do with understanding themselves. Child molesters represent themselves as children's and teens' friends and sometimes seduce children and teens into meeting them in person, which can lead to awful abuses. Steven Levy (2003) points out that "No one can physically snatch a kid online, but it's all too common for very nasty adult strangers to make contact with kids, often winning trust with deception" (p. E30). Does electronic communication allow, or even promote, deception? Or, as some claim, does it enhance communication by reducing attention to such aspects of identity as physical appearance and sex? Ethical questions such as this one will become increasingly prominent as more and more people engage others in cyberspace.

Do Newer Technologies Increase Productivity?

People frequently comment that technology makes us more efficient and productive. Because computers manage information so quickly, it seems obvious that they have greatly boosted both individual productivity and our collective, economic productivity. But does technology really make us more efficient or productive? Let's consider the question more carefully. Thomas Landauer (2002) analyzed data on productivity before and after major investments in technology. Here are two of his surprising findings:

▶ The IRS spent more than $50 million to provide agents with computer systems that were expected to find information and make calculations quickly. After the systems were installed, agents' productivity declined—and not just slightly: It went down 40%.

► An insurance company invested $30 million on a computer system to increase efficiency. Sure enough, a year later employees were processing 30% more claims than before the system was installed. The only drawback was that the cost for processing each claim also increased even more—it jumped 70%, from $3.50 to $5.00 per claim.

If technologies increase productivity, then we should see a noticeable spike in productivity after companies and corporations started using computers to automate record keeping and erase the need for human workers to spend hours calculating. But between the 1990s and the 1970s, when computers began to be used by both individuals and companies, the productivity of nonfarm and nonmanufacturing sectors of the economy was basically flat for industrialized countries (Landauer, 2002). There have been increases in specific segments, such as telecommunications, during particular times since the 1970s, but the overall rate of productivity did not rise as we would expect following the widespread use of computers. Erik Bucy (2005) notes that many industries have reaped small gains from large investments in technology.

Not so fast, says Steve Lohr (2002), another person who has looked closely at data on the relationship between technology and productivity. According to Lohr, although it's true that productivity did not rise significantly during the first phase of technology (roughly from the 1970s to the mid-1990s), something very different is happening now, during the present stage of the technology revolution. Since 1996, productivity has grown at a healthy rate. In 1999, Alan Greenspan, then the chair of the Federal Reserve System, told Congress that the growth in the economy was being driven by technology-based increases in productivity. The reason is that the latest advances have greatly increased the speed and efficiency of technologies.

Technologies also have benefits that cannot be measured by sheer productivity. Although banks today may be less productive than they were in the 1970s (Lohr, 2002), 24-hour automated teller machines (ATMs) make it easier for people to withdraw money when they want to, regardless of whether a bank is open. People who buy clothes and other items online may not spend more than they did in the 1970s, but online shopping saves them a lot of time.

What about the impact of technologies on individual efficiency? When I wrote my first book in the mid-1970s, I typed every page on a typewriter. When I moved a paragraph, I had to retype the whole page plus any other pages that were affected by the change. Today, I block and move text with a few keystrokes. In the 1970s, I mailed manuscripts to reviewers, which involved driving to a post office and paying for postage, and then waiting for the package to be delivered to the recipient and the response to be mailed back to me. Today, I send drafts out as attachments—again, a few keystrokes on my keyboard and a few on the receiver's keyboard.

Yet there are also drawbacks, or costs, of my reliance on technology. Every few years, I buy a new computer, and I have to pay for my ISP. Like most people, I've also had viruses, worms, and hard drive crashes. Recovering from those can take days, and much data may not be recoverable. And then there is the time I spend refining my writing. Because it is so easy to try out new placements for sections of a chapter and to revise sentences to make them clearer, I wind up spending that time. I may write better today than in the 1970s, but I don't produce more written material than I did 30 years ago.

We also want to reflect on the assumption that more information makes us more knowledgeable. There's no doubt that we now have access to more information than ever in human history. But what is the value of having so much information? Philosopher David Rothenberg (1999) worries that we are confusing information with knowledge. The web allows us to get more information than ever before, but do we know what to do with all the information we can gather so easily? Rothenberg (1999, p. B8) points out, "Information is the details, all those data that are not so easy to locate. Knowledge is being able to put the details together and draw a clear conclusion." Knowledge requires more than information. It requires evaluating the credibility of sources of information, thinking about how bits of information fit together, and connecting information to understand the big picture and draw reasoned conclusions.

In this section, we discussed four important controversies about the relationship between communication technologies and human life. At this moment, there are no clear answers to questions such as these. We need to be mindful of how technologies influence us personally and how they shape society. In addition, we have a responsibility to make conscious, reflective choices about when and how we want to use communication technologies so that *we* decide their roles in our lives.

▶GUIDELINES FOR LIVING WITH COMMUNICATION TECHNOLOGIES

Despite some of the controversies about technologies, we're not likely to return to land lines, typewriters, and calculators. Communication technologies are here to stay. How they affect us individually and our society as a whole, however, is up to us. We need to think about how to manage the challenges that accompany living in an era of communication technologies. In this section, we consider three guidelines for doing that.

Consciously Manage Information Flow

More information has been produced in the last three decades than in the previous 5,000 years (Potter, 2001), and the amount of information is now doubling every year (Shenk, 1997). The sheer amount of information many people receive causes stress and confusion. It is ironic that technologies that were designed to save time and increase efficiency often make our lives more frenetic and busier (Nie, 2004; Urgo, 2000; Young, 2005). Cell phones make us available all the time to everyone, but what if we don't want to be available all the time? In his commentary, Mark points out another impact of phone technology.

> ▶ **Mark**
> Sometimes, I wish I hadn't bought an answering machine. When I get back to my apartment after a day on campus and at work, the red message light is always blinking. I feel like I have to listen to the messages and return calls. Instead of my apartment being a place where I can get away from the pressure, it's a source of more pressure.

Amy, on the other hand, loves having voice mail:

► Amy

I love voice mail. Before I had it, I used to worry when I wasn't home that I might miss important calls from friends. Now, I can stay out as long as I want, and I don't miss anything. If someone calls, they leave a message, and I call back. If someone sends me an e-mail note, it's there when I open my mailbox. New technologies definitely increase my personal freedom.

The difference between Mark and Amy suggests one way that we can exercise choice over how communication technologies affect our lives. For Amy, an answering machine reduces stress, but for Mark it increases stress. Personally, I would hate to live without e-mail, but I refuse to have an answering machine on my home phone, and I leave my cell in the car and don't carry it with me because I don't want to be distracted from my other activities by a phone call. Each of us can make deliberate choices about which technologies might enhance our lives. If certain technologies better our lives and we can afford them, we may choose to have them. But if they don't fit the lives and selves we want, we don't have to join the crowd.

We can choose to control information rather than be controlled by it. Some people limit their online communication to a set amount of time each day or week, some refuse to have voice mail or cell phones, and some have separate e-mail accounts for business and personal contacts. A number of faculty members inform students that they will be available online ("virtual office hours") only at specified times. These options show that there are ways for us to control the amount of information that communication technologies deliver to us.

Learn to Log Off

Take a lesson from David Levy, a professor of information and the man in charge of planning the Center for Information and the Quality of Life (Young, 2005). Levy knows tech. He's tech savvy. And he knows when to log off. Each week, he takes a full day off from technology.

To break the habit of being wired all the time, try taking a day off each week from much of the technology you normally use: computer (yep, including wireless!), cell, PDA, and so forth. Keep a record of your feelings and what you are able to do with the time you're not high-wired.

SHARPEN YOUR SKILL

Work to Ensure Democratic Access

Some scholars and social critics believe communication technologies are ushering in a global community in which everyone can participate (Gergen, 1991; Samuelson, 2002). Clearly, communication technologies have the *potential* to connect everyone and to give everyone access to tools and information. But will that potential be realized?

A number of scholars (Carvin, 2002; Cooper & Weaver, 2003) claim that the democratic potential of technologies has not been realized. These scholars are concerned about the **digital divide,** a term for the gap between the people and communities with access to communication technologies and the people and communities without access or with significantly less access. An information elite could easily develop because access to new technologies requires both knowledge and resources that not everyone has. For example, families with high incomes are more likely to have home computers and Internet access, and students who have home computers and Internet connections have an advantage over students who do not (Nussbaum, 2002). Thus, children in advantaged families are likely to reap the advantage of access to technologies, while children in disadvantaged families are likely to bear the disadvantage of lack of easy access to technology.

Consider a second example of how unequal access to communication technologies may magnify existing socioeconomic divisions. Fiber-optic networks are so costly that they might be laid between two prosperous urban areas but not routed into poorer rural communities. Thus, people living in the advantaged urban areas would have better access to video, audio, and computer technologies, whereas members of rural communities would be relegated to the margins of the information revolution and its personal and professional enrichment.

Concerns about the digital divide are based on evidence that not everyone has equal access to communication technologies. In 1999, the U.S. Department of Commerce released a report entitled "Falling Through the Net." The report detailed disturbing trends in use of the Internet. Age, rural or urban setting, and education are all factors that affect access to telecommunication. Among the many factors, two stand out: income and race. In 1999, only 12.1% of people with annual incomes under $10,000 used the Internet, whereas 58.9% of people with incomes of $75,000 or more used the Internet. Just two years later, in 2001, the census bureau reported that the gap in computer use is narrowing between different ethnic and socioeconomic groups, leading some people to think the digital divide is being overcome (Samuelson, 2002). In 2004, the U.S. Department of Commerce released the most recent report available. The report highlighted the continuing divide between urban and rural access, particularly broadband access. Although 40.4% of households in urban areas have broadband connections, only 24.7% of homes in rural areas do. The reasons rural citizens most frequently gave for not having broadband were that it is "too expensive" (it costs more to route DSL and cable in rural areas) and "not available" (the costs would be so high that companies don't even consider laying cable or DSL) (Department of Commerce, 2004). Go to the book's online resources and click on WebLink 15.3 to read the full report on broadband access.

However, just giving everyone a computer with an Internet connection won't erase the digital divide, because access is not the only reason for the gap. Contributing to the digital divide are many factors beyond access itself (Carvin, 2002). One factor is content. Currently, the Internet doesn't provide content (and in multiple languages) that appeals to the full range of people. Until it does, it won't meet everyone's needs and interests. Also, girls and women are less attracted than boys and men to many computer games and Internet content, leading some to worry that there is a gendered digital divide (Cooper & Weaver, 2003). Also contributing to the digital divide is illiteracy (Carvin, 2002). Nearly 100 million Americans are illiterate or have limited literacy. People who cannot read have little use for or ability to use the Internet.

We have an ethical responsibility to identify and work to realize the potential of communication technologies to enrich us as individuals and as members of a common world. This cannot happen if we limit access to new and converging technologies to individuals and groups who are already privileged by their social, professional, and economic status. Providing access and training to everyone would be expensive in the short run. In the long run, however, it would be far less costly than the problems of a society in which a small, technologically advanced elite is privileged and the majority of citizens are excluded from full participation.

Participate in Deciding How to Regulate Communication Technologies

A third guideline is to participate in decision making about how, if at all, we should regulate communication technologies. What guidelines are reasonable? What guidelines infringe on freedom of speech and freedom of the press? We have regulations for written and oral communication. Yet technologies of communication have outpaced our ability to develop rules to safeguard people's comfort, health, privacy, and dignity. We need to think carefully about what kinds of regulations we want and how to implement them.

There is also a question of *who* should control the Internet and the web (Dennis & Merrill, 2006; McGrath, 2002). In his book *Silent Theft: The Private Plunder of Our Common Wealth*, David Bollier (2002) claims that the Internet belongs to the public and should not be controlled by wealthy, monopolistic companies. Bollier claims that Microsoft tries to impose its platform and proprietary standards on PC users. In Bollier's judgment, this is wrong because those private companies had nothing to do with developing the Internet that they now seek to control.

T E C H N O L O G Y

INTERNET HUNTING

What would you do if you thought your partner was having an affair? A Chinese man whose web name is Freezing Blade decided to get others to help him punish the man. Freezing Blade went online and posted a message accusing Bronze Moustache (the alleged lover of Freezing Blade's wife) and identifying Bronze Moustache by his real name. Another user, Spring Azalea, wrote this response: "We call on every company, school, hospital, shopping mall and public street to reject him" (French, 2006, p. A1). In response, people teamed up to find Bronze Moustache's address and telephone number. Others went to Bronze Moustache's university and even to his parents' home. Finally, Bronze Moustache left the university and barricaded himself in a private home. Bronze Moustache was tried and convicted on the web.

This isn't the only case of what the Chinese call "Internet hunting," in which moral judgments are made by online communities and then members of those communities step out of virtual reality. spy on subjects of moral judgments, and sometimes administer whatever punishments the online communities have decided are fair.

Disturbed by the growing number of Internet hunting incidents, the Chinese government has considered imposing greater security, including forcing all Internet users to register. But that conflicts with valuing freedom of expression.

Partnerships between the federal government and universities invested taxpayers' money to fund scientists who developed the Internet. Should technologies that were supported by citizens and developed by government and universities be regulated by private companies whose primary goal is profit?

One form of communication on the Internet that irritates many people is advertising that they don't want and can't escape. If you go to a site to read a review of a movie, you may also get—without asking for them—offers to sell you the soundtrack, video version, and other items connected with the movie (Rafter, 1999). Should ads be regulated on individuals' private computers? Should users be able to opt not to have ads precede or accompany web pages they access? If so, should users have to accept the expense of buying programs to avoid the ads (Tanaka, 1999)? Does the pervasiveness of advertising on the Internet blur the boundary between content and advertising?

Privacy is a key issue that regulations must address (Tung, 1999; Shapiro, 1999). Many online advertisers collect **cookies,** bits of data that websites collect and store in users' personal browsers. This gives advertisers information about you that you might not choose to release. In 1999, the FTC reprimanded two companies for online privacy invasions, but neither company was actually penalized (Lash, 1999). Software manufacturers have developed programs to disable cookies, but this will help only people who buy and install the programs (Tanaka, 1999).

And then there is **spyware,** which allows a third party to track individuals' online activity, gain personal information, and send pop-up ads tailored to users' profiles. Spyware is often bundled without users' knowledge into software that can be downloaded for free (Himowitz, 2002). For instance, free software that people use to swap MP3 music files often contains spyware that monitors what users do on the web. Because spyware implants itself in the user's computer, the monitoring can take place even when the free software isn't being used. Many people mistakenly assume that their online communication is private and cannot be released without their permission. One threat to privacy is hackers, who break into computers and collect whatever they want. An increasing number of people are having problems with theft of credit card numbers they provide to online retailers.

Hackers aren't the only ones who can gain access to your personal electronic communication. After the shootings at Columbine High School in Colorado, FBI agents went to AOL for information that showed that suspect Eric Harris had been engaged in online communication about making bombs. David Smith, who created and unleashed the Melissa virus in 1998, was caught by tracking his online communication. Hitting the "Delete" key doesn't erase a message from storage in the computer on which it

T E C H N O L O G Y

fyi

CYBERHATE

Some online communities that specialize in hate speech are particularly adept at attracting young children. There are numerous websites where people can engage in hate speech, or hate mongering, and there is little regulation of these sites, which may provide instructions on how to make a bomb or engage in hate speech against particular groups. Should anyone be allowed to create a site that proclaims hate of particular groups and exhorts others to hate the groups and act against them? Should anyone be allowed to visit sites that exist to promote hate? Is this kind of communication protected by the constitutional right to freedom of speech? To learn more about this issue, go to the book's online resources and click on WebLink 15.4, which will give you access to the First Amendment website and an article that summarizes issues involved in the regulation of cyberhate.

was composed, the computer on which it was received, and, often, other computers between the source and intended destination. By the way, IMs can be stored in the same way.

From the annoyance of unwelcome advertising to the dangers of online predators, technologies of communication remain largely unregulated, and the idea of regulation remains highly controversial. A key challenge in the coming years will be to develop regulations that provide some protection without infringing too seriously on personal freedom.

▶SUMMARY

In this chapter, we've considered what it means to live in an era that is saturated with communication technologies. After reviewing the evolution of communication technologies, we focused on four important controversies about the impact of these technologies on individuals and societies. We considered different views of the effect of communication technologies on how we think, build and participate in communities, on how we define and express our identities, and on our efficiency and productivity.

The final section of this chapter discussed three guidelines for interacting with communication technologies. One is to make deliberate choices about how to manage the deluge of information that sometimes threatens to overwhelm us. Learning to control the steady stream of information that flows in daily is a priority for people today. Another guideline is to work for democratic access to communication technologies. If we are to realize the democratic potential of new technologies, we must find ways to make them accessible to all segments of society. Finally, we need to be informed and to participate in making decisions about how, if at all, to regulate communication technologies: How do we provide reasonable safeguards for individual and collective well-being while preserving our rights to freedom of speech and the press?

Review, Reflect, Extend

The Key Concepts, For Further Reflection and Discussion questions, Recommended Resources, and Experience Communication Case Study that follow will help you review, reflect on, and extend the information and ideas presented in this chapter. A diverse selection of online resources is also available through ThomsonNOW. These resources include Speech Builder Express, InfoTrac College Edition, interactive videos, vMentor, and Thomson Audio Study Products.

Thomson™ NOW! is an online study system designed to help you put your time to the best use. After reading a chapter, take the NOW pre-test to identify concepts discussed in the chapter that you may not fully understand. Based on the results of this diagnostic test, the system will create a personalized study plan that directs you to specific learning resources and activities. To see if you're ready for an exam, take the NOW post-test to check your understanding.

For more information or to access this book's online resources, visit **http://www.thomsonedu.com**.

▶KEY CONCEPTS

The terms following are defined in the chapter on the page number indicated, and they appear in alphabetical order, with definitions, in the Glossary, which begins on page 369. The book's online resources also include flash cards and crossword puzzles to help you learn these terms and the concepts they represent.

communication technologies, 330
cookies, 347
digital divide, 344

interconnectivity, 334
multitasking, 335
spyware, 347

teleconferencing, 333
Wi-Fi, 333

▶FOR FURTHER REFLECTION AND DISCUSSION

The questions below can also be found among the book's online resources for this chapter, where you have the option of e-mailing your responses to your instructor, if required.

1. Can you suggest ways in which we might avail ourselves of the advantages for personal and professional growth that new technologies offer, without experiencing some of the real and potential disadvantages discussed in this chapter?

2. How do relationships between people who never meet face to face differ from relationships between people who can see each other? What are the advantages and limitations of forming and sustaining relationships electronically?

3. Write out your scenario of communication technologies five years from now in the profession you intend to join. Describe how you think existing technologies will figure in that environment and what new kinds of communication systems may be invented that will affect that context.

▶RECOMMENDED RESOURCES

1. Lewis, Michael. (2002). *Next: The Future Just Happened.* New York: W. W. Norton. This is a well-written book that offers good examples and evidence about online identities and the impact of heavy online usage on the ability to interact with people offline.

2. Read the most current issue of *Wired* or a similar magazine that focuses on technologies. Identify technological products and services that are not mentioned in this book, which went to press in the fall of 2006.

Experience Communication Case Study

ONLINE DATING

The book's online resources include an interactive video of the communication situation featured in the case study scripted on the next page. Apply what you've learned in this chapter by analyzing the case study, using the questions that follow the script as a guide. These questions are also available online with the video.

Christina is visiting her family for the holidays. One evening after dinner, her mother comes into her room where Christina is typing at her computer. Her mother sits down, and the following conversation takes place.

Jason Harris/© Wadsworth

Mom: Am I disturbing you?

Chris: No, I'm just signing off on e-mail. [She finishes at the keyboard and turns to face her mom.]

Mom: E-mailing someone?

Chris: Just a guy.

Mom: Someone you've been seeing at school?

Chris: Not exactly.

Mom: [laughs] Well, either you are seeing him or you're not, honey. Are you two dating?

Chris: Sort of. Yeah, you could say we're dating.

Mom: [laughs] What's the mystery? What's he like?

Chris: He's funny and smart and so easy to talk to. We can talk for hours and it never gets dull. I've never met anyone who's so easy to be with. We're interested in the same things and we share so many values. Brandon's just super. I've never met anyone like him.

Mom: Sounds great. When do I get to meet this fellow?

Chris: Well, not until I do. [laughs] We met online and we're just starting to talk about getting together in person.

Mom: Online? You met this man online? And you act as if you know him!

Chris: I do know him, Mom. We've talked a lot—we've told each other lots of stuff, and . . .

Mom: How do you know what he's told you is true? For all you know, he's a 50-year-old mass murderer!

Chris: You've been watching too many movies on Lifetime, Mom. Brandon's 23, he's in college, and he comes from a family a lot like ours.

Mom: How do you know that? He could be lying about every part of what he's told you.

Chris: So? A guy I meet at school could lie too. Meeting someone in person is no guarantee of honesty.

Mom: Haven't you read about all of the weirdos that go to these online matching sites?

Chris: Mom, Brandon's not a weirdo, and we didn't meet in a matching site. We met in a chat room where people talk about politics. He's as normal as I am. After all, I was in that chat room too!

Mom: But, Chris, you can't be serious about someone you haven't met.

Chris: I have met him, Mom, just not face to face. Actually, I know him better than lots of guys I've dated for months. You can get to know a lot about a person from talking.

Mom: This makes me really nervous, honey. Please don't meet him by yourself.

Chris: Mom, you're making me feel sorry I told you how we met. This is exactly why I didn't tell you about him before. Nothing I say is going to change your mind about dating online.

Mom: [pauses, looks away, then looks back at Chris] You're right. I'm not giving him—or you— a chance. Let's start over. [smiles] Tell me what you like about him.

Chris: [tentatively] Well, he's thoughtful.

Mom: Thoughtful? How so?

Chris: Like, if I say something one day, he'll come back to it a day or so later and I can tell he's thought about it, like he's really interested in what I say.

Mom: So he really pays attention to what you say, huh?

Chris: Exactly. So many guys I've dated don't. They never return to things I've said. Brandon does. And another thing, when I come back to things he's said with ideas I've thought about, he really listens.

Mom: Like he values what you think and say?

Chris: Exactly! That's what's so special about him.

▾ ▾

1. Review Chapter 6, which focuses on listening and responding. Identify examples of ineffective and effective listening and responding on the part of Chris's mother.

2. Chapter 10 stated that proximity and similarities are the two most significant influences on initial romantic attraction. Does this statement hold true for the online relationship between Chris and Brandon?

3. If Chris and Brandon meet face to face, how will communication on their initial date be different from communication on first dates between people who have not met online?

4. If you were romantically attracted to a person you met online and wanted to have a face-to-face date with her or him, what would you do to maximize your safety?

Epilogue

Although this is the final page of this book, what you have learned from it and from the class you are taking will continue to serve you well throughout your life. Because communication is central to everything you do, the understandings and skills you have gained will enhance the quality of your personal life, enrich your social and community involvements, help you succeed in the world of work, and prepare you to be an informed, active user of mass communication and communication technologies.

In the years ahead, you will find that what we've discussed in this book will help you understand a range of people and communication situations. Moreover, what you have learned will allow you to interact effectively in varied contexts. Whether you are watching television, listening to a friend, participating on a work team, working through conflict with a romantic partner, or communicating online, the ideas and skills we have explored in *Communication Mosaics* will enlarge your insight into yourself, others, and the ways in which communication operates.

I hope that you have found this book worthy of the time you've invested in reading it. And I hope the theories, concepts, processes, and skills we've discussed will increase your effectiveness and pleasure as you communicate with others in all the spheres of your life.

Julia T. Wood

Appendix:
Communication in Interviews

▶ **FOCUS QUESTIONS**

1. What are the purposes of interviewing?

2. What is the basic structure that most interviews follow?

3. How do different types of questions shape answers?

4. What should you do if an interviewer asks you an illegal question?

You've probably been an interviewee many times. Perhaps you were interviewed by members of groups you sought to join. Few of us have escaped telephone interviews about our opinions of political candidates, products, and social policies. It's likely that you've interviewed more than once for part-time or full-time jobs. You've probably also been on the other side of the interviewing process; you may have interviewed people who were applying to join organizations to which you belong. Perhaps you've had jobs that required you to conduct telephone or in-person interviews. You may have interviewed experts to gain information about a topic on which you were writing a paper or preparing a speech.

In this appendix, we will discuss interviewing and identify ways you can enhance your effectiveness as both an interviewer and an interviewee. The opening section describes communication during interviews. First, we will identify a range of purposes or types of interviews in which you may participate during your life. Second, we will discuss the structure and style of interviews. Third, we will describe different kinds of questions interviewers use. The second section identifies challenges that are part of interviewing. We will focus on hiring interviews because those are particularly important to many college students. Our discussion will provide tips for preparing to interview and for dealing with inappropriate or illegal questions.

▶UNDERSTANDING COMMUNICATION IN INTERVIEWS

An **interview** is a communication transaction that emphasizes questions and answers (Lumsden & Lumsden, 2004). Rob Anderson and George Killenberg (1999, p. 2) elaborate on this definition by noting that the word *interview* suggests "a sharing of

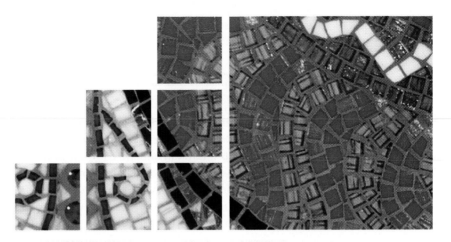

views" in which the interviewer and interviewee are involved and in which listening and speaking are equally important (Purdy & Borisoff, 1997).

Purposes of Interviews

Communication scholars (Anderson & Killenberg, 1999; Stewart & Cash, 1991) have identified distinct types of interviews. Each interview is defined by its primary purpose, although interviews often have multiple and sometimes conflicting purposes. For example, a job candidate may want to be honest and get a job offer, and the two goals may be at odds.

Perhaps the most common purposes of interviews are to give information and to get information. Doctors engage in **information-giving interviews** when they explain to patients how to take medicines. Academic advisers give students information about curricular requirements, specific courses, and administrative processes. Team leaders often inform new members of a work unit about expectations and operating procedures. Public opinion polls, census taking, and research surveys are common examples of **information-getting interviews.** Physicians also use such interviews to gain insight into patients' medical histories and current conditions. Journalists devote a great deal of time to information-getting interviews to obtain background material for stories they are writing and to learn about experts' opinions on newsworthy topics. Information-getting interviews are useful in preparing us to write reports, to give speeches, and to learn about new things.

Persuasive interviews aim to influence attitudes or actions (Anderson, 1995). In a sales interview, a salesperson attempts to persuade a customer to buy a product or service. Persuasive interviews can sell more than products. They may also promote people (a door-to-door campaign to persuade residents to support a particular political candidate) and ideas (persuading an administrator to act on your team's report; convincing a company to implement regulations to protect the environment).

When people need to solve some problem, they may engage in **problem-solving interviews.** Perhaps you have met with a professor to discuss difficulties in a course. The two of you may have collaborated to identify ways to improve your note taking, study habits, and writing. Supervisors sometimes hold problem-solving interviews with employees to discover and resolve impediments to effective work. Colleagues often talk to each other to resolve problems of morale, productivity, or other work-related issues. By seeking each other's perspectives, we can broaden our understanding of problems and our insight into potential solutions.

▶ Leroy

Mark and I have worked together for 10 years in the same department. Whenever there is a problem at the factory, one of us finds the other, and we sit down and talk it through until we come up with a solution. Sometimes, I lead with the questions, and sometimes Mark does; sometimes the hang-up is in his area, sometimes it's in mine. He understands the production end of the business better than I do, and I have more knowledge of personnel. Between the two of us, we can fix almost any problem.

Like problem-solving interviews, **counseling interviews** focus on understanding and resolving a problem. In a counseling interview, however, the problem is not mutual. A client has a problem, such as stress, depression, or compulsiveness, that she or he wants to address. The counselor attempts to help the client understand the problem more fully and collaborates with the client to develop strategies for coping with or overcoming the difficulty (Anderson, 1997; Smith, 1996). Counseling interviews also occur outside the therapeutic setting: We may seek counseling from attorneys about legal matters, from accountants about financial matters, from religious leaders about spiritual issues, and from architects about home design.

Employment interviews allow employers and job candidates to assess each other and determine whether there is a good fit between them. Typically, employment interviews include periods of information giving and information getting as well as persuasive efforts on the part of both participants. The prospective employer wants to convince the job candidate of the high quality of the company, and the candidate wants to convince the prospective employer of the high quality of his or her qualifications. Ideally, both participants gain enough information to make a sound judgment of the fit between the candidate and the job. Later in this appendix, we'll look at the employment interview in greater detail.

Complaint interviews allow people to register complaints about a product, service, or person. Many firms have departments whose sole purpose is to accept and respond to complaints. Of primary importance is letting the people who complain know that their feelings matter (see Lenny's commentary). The interviewer (company representative) attempts to gain information about the customer's dissatisfaction: What was defective or disappointing about the product? Was service inadequate? What would it take to satisfy the customer now? The person conducting complaint interviews should call recurring complaints to the attention of others who can diagnose and resolve the underlying problems.

▶ Lenny

I worked in the complaint department of a department store. The person who trained me for that position told me the number one way to satisfy customers was to let them complain without trying to argue, correct them, or tell them they misused the product. He told me that mainly people just need to be heard and have what they say accepted. I found that was true. When I let them talk and didn't defend the company or correct them, they were usually satisfied even if I didn't authorize reimbursement or replacement. It's amazing how much it matters to people to feel somebody really listens to them.

Most organizations require **performance reviews,** or performance appraisals, at regular intervals. By building performance appraisals into work life, organizations continuously monitor employees' performance and foster their professional growth. The performance review is an occasion on which a supervisor comments on a subordinate's achievements and professional development, identifies any weaknesses or problems, and collaborates with the subordinate to develop goals for future performance. During the interview, subordinates should offer their perceptions of their strengths and weaknesses and participate actively in developing goals for professional development. Supervisors should comment on strengths as well as areas for improvement and may act as coaches to encourage professional development (Waldroop & Butler, 1996).

When a person's work is unsatisfactory or when the person is creating tensions with co-workers, a supervisor may conduct a **reprimand interview.** The goals are to identify lapses in professional conduct, determine sources of problems, and establish a plan for improving future performance. Because reprimands tend to evoke defensiveness, developing a constructive, supportive communication climate for these interviews is especially important. Supervisors may foster a good climate by opening the interview with assurances that the goal is to develop a plan for improvement, not to punish the subordinate. Supervisors should also invite subordinates to express their perceptions and feelings fully.

Stress interviews are designed to create anxiety in respondents or interviewees. Although they may involve gaining or giving information, persuading, or other interview purposes, stress interviews are unique in their deliberate intent to apply pressure. Typical communication techniques for inducing stress are rapid-fire questions, intentional misinterpretations and distortions of the interviewee's responses, and hostile or skeptical nonverbal expressions. Why, you might ask, would anyone deliberately pressure another person? Actually, stress interviews may be useful in several situations.

Attorneys may intentionally intimidate reluctant or hostile witnesses or people whose honesty is suspect. Similarly, prison administrators and police officers may communicate aggressively with people they think are withholding important information. This kind of interview also may be part of hiring interviews for jobs that involve high stress. By deliberately trying to rattle the job candidate, the interviewer can assess how well the candidate manages stress.

In academic and professional life, **exit interviews** are increasingly popular. The goal of this type of interview is to gain information, insights, and perceptions about a place of work or education from a person who is leaving. While people are in a job or learning environment, they may be reluctant to mention dissatisfactions or to speak against those who have power over them. When people leave an organization, however, they can offer honest insights and perceptions with little fear of reprisal. Thus, exit interviews can be especially valuable to the organization in providing information about policies, personnel, and organizational culture. I routinely have exit interviews with graduate students when they complete their degrees. From these conferences, I gain important information that allows us to refine our curriculum, program requirements, and opportunities for graduate students. Interviewees may honestly discuss problems and suggest improvements; yet they should be polite and professional so that their employers or schools retain positive perceptions of them. Former teachers and employers are often contacted for references.

The Basic Structure of Interviews

To be effective, interviews should follow a structure that builds a good communication climate, allows both the interviewer and interviewee to deal with substantive matters, and involves listening by all parties. Experienced interviewers, even ones without professional training, tend to organize interview communication into a three-stage sequence. Interviewees who understand the purpose of each stage in the sequence increase their ability to participate effectively.

The Opening Stage The initial stage of an interview tends to be brief and aims to create an effective climate for interaction, to clarify the purpose, and to preview issues to be discussed (Wilson & Goodall, 1991). Typically, opening small talk encourages a friendly climate: "I see you're from Buffalo. Are the winters there still as harsh as they used to be?" "It's been six months since our last performance review. Any new developments in your life?" "I noticed you got your B.A. from State University. I graduated from there too. Did you ever take any courses with Doctor Mayberry in anthropology?"

After opening small talk, effective interviewers state the purpose of the interview and how they plan to accomplish that purpose: "As you know, I'm on campus today to talk with liberal arts majors who are interested in joining Hodgeson Marketing. I'd like to ask some questions about you and your background, and then I want to give you an opportunity to ask me anything you want about Hodgeson." "Pat, the reason I asked you to meet with me today is that there have been some complaints about your attitude from others on your work team. I know you are good at your job and have a fine history with the firm, so I want us to put our heads together to resolve this matter. Let's begin with me telling you what I've heard, and then I'd like to hear your perceptions of what's happening." These examples show how the opening stage of an interview establishes a comfortable climate for communication and defines the purpose of the interview.

The Substantive Stage The second stage of an interview, which generally consumes the bulk of time, focuses on the purpose of the interview. For example, in reprimand interviews the substantive stage would be devoted to identifying problem behaviors and devising solutions. In a hiring interview, the substantive stage might concentrate on the job candidate's background, experience, and qualifications.

The substantive stage requires careful planning and thought. Most interviewers prepare lists of topics or questions and use their notes to make sure they cover all important topics during an interview. They may also take notes during the interview. Communication during this phase tends to progress from broad topics to increasingly narrow, detailed, and demanding questions within each topic. After introducing a topic, the interviewer may ask general questions and then follow up with more detailed probes. Because communication moves from broad to narrow, it is called the **funnel sequence** (Cannell & Kahn, 1968; Moffatt, 1979). The interviewer may repeat the funnel sequence for each topic in an interview.

During the substantive stage, an interviewer may invite the interviewee to take the lead in communication by posing questions or volunteering perceptions and ideas in response to what has been covered thus far. To be an effective interviewee, you should be prepared with questions and topics you want to introduce. This shows the interviewer that you are self-initiating and responsible.

Figure A.1 Effective and Ineffective Closings

Effective

I've learned a good deal about your background and interests in our conversation today. Your academic training in teamwork and leadership certainly prepares you for a management trainee position with our firm, and your work experience further qualifies you. When I get back to the main office, I'm going to suggest that the company fly you out for an on-site interview. You should hear from me or someone else with the company within a week to ten days. Meanwhile, good luck with those exams—I remember how stressful exam week can be.

Ineffective

I really enjoyed talking with you. Thanks for your time. I'll be in touch.

The Closing Stage Like the opening stage, the closing stage tends to be brief. Its purposes are to summarize what has been discussed, to state what follow-up, if any, will occur, and to create goodwill in parting (Figure A.1). Summarizing the content of the interview increases the likelihood that an accurate and complete record of the interview (written or in memory) will survive. If the interviewer overlooks any topics, the interviewee may appropriately offer a reminder. Interviewees also may ask about follow-up if interviewers fail to mention this.

Most interviews follow the three-step sequence we've discussed. Occasionally, they do not. Some interviewers are ineffective because they are disorganized, unprepared, and inadequately trained in effective interviewing. They may ramble for 15 minutes or more and fail to provide any closing other than "Gee, our time is up." In other instances, interviewers may deliberately violate the standard pattern to achieve their goals. For example, in stress interviews designed to test how well a person responds to pressure, the interviewer may skip opening comments and jump immediately into tough, substantive questions. This allows the interviewer to assess how well the respondent copes with unexpected stress. Understanding the communication characteristic of each stage allows you to determine which stage you are in at any point in an interview. You can then adapt your communication appropriately.

Styles of Interviewing

As in other forms of communication, the climate of an interview shapes the interaction. The climate between participants in interviews is influenced by the degree of confirmation provided and by the openness, equality, problem orientation, empathy, spontaneity, and descriptiveness embodied in communication (as we discussed in Chapter 7). Formality and balance of power also affect the climate of an interview.

Formality Interviews may be more or less formal. In highly formal interviews, participants tend to stay within social and professional roles. They do little to acknowledge each other as unique individuals. Instead, the interviewer acts as the potential employer, the corrective supervisor, or whatever role is pertinent to the type of interview. The interviewee also acts from a defined role: prospective employee, repentant subordinate, and so forth. The content of highly formal interviews tends to follow a standard format, often one stipulated by the organization, that all interviewers follow to ensure consistency. Nonverbal communication provides further clues to formality: Business dress, formal meeting rooms, and stiff handshakes are signs of formality.

In contrast, informal interviews are more relaxed, personal, and flexible. The interviewer attempts to engage the interviewee as an individual, not just a person in a general role. In turn, the interviewee tends to communicate with the interviewer in more individualistic ways. Typically, informal interviews aren't as rigidly structured as formal interviews. The interviewer may have a list of standard topics (either mental or written down), but these are only guidelines, not a straitjacket for communication. Either participant may introduce other topics, and they may devote more time than planned to issues that arise. Informal interviews often include nonverbal cues such as smiling, relaxed postures, casual surroundings, and informal dress.

Most interviews fall between the extremes of formality and informality. Also, interviews may become more or less formal as a result of communication between participants. A person who communicates in a stilted manner is likely to encourage formality in the other person. Conversely, a person who communicates casually promotes a relaxed style of response. Although both participants affect the formality of an interview, the interviewer usually has primary control, and the interviewee adapts accordingly.

Balance of Power Another aspect of interview style is the balance of power between interviewer and interviewee. Power may be evenly balanced between participants, or it may be skewed toward either the interviewer or the interviewee.

Interviewees have the greatest power in mirror interviews. A **mirror interview,** or reflective interview, is one in which the interviewer consistently reflects the interviewee's comments to the interviewee. This may be done by restating verbatim what an interviewee says, paraphrasing an interviewee's comments, or making limited inferences based on the interviewee's comments. Skillful listening is essential for effective participation in mirror interviews. Consider this example:

> **Interviewer:** Tell me about your studies.
>
> **Interviewee:** I'm a communication major.
>
> **Interviewer:** So you've studied communication?
>
> **Interviewee:** Yes, especially organizational communication and leadership.
>
> **Interviewer:** Then you're particularly interested in leadership in organizations?
>
> **Interviewee:** Yes. I think communication is the heart of effective leadership, so studying it has taught me a lot about how to lead well.
>
> **Interviewer:** Tell me what you mean that communication is the "heart of effective leadership."
>
> **Interviewee:** Well, I see leadership as motivating others and empowering them to achieve their goals. A person who knows how to communicate clearly, listen well, and establish rapport with others is most able to motivate them.

In this exchange, the interviewer lets the interviewee lead. The interviewee's statements are the basis of the interviewer's subsequent questions and probes. Astute interviewees realize that mirror interviews give them significant opportunity to highlight their strengths and to introduce topics they want to discuss.

Distributive interviews divide (or distribute) power equally between participants. Both ask and answer questions, listen and speak, and contribute to shaping the direction and content of communication. The distributive style of interviewing generally is used when participants are equal in professional or social standing. Distributive interviews may also be used between people with unequal power if the interviewer wants to create a relaxed exchange. Recruiters often use distributive styles to put job candidates at ease.

Authoritarian interviews give the interviewer primary control over interaction. The interviewer may avoid or quickly cut off discussion of any topics not on the list and may give the interviewee little or no opportunity to ask questions or initiate topics. Efficiency is the primary strength of the authoritarian style of interviewing: Many topics can be covered in a down-to-business manner. Balanced against the advantage of efficiency are significant drawbacks. The authoritarian style of interviewing can be frustrating to interviewees, and the interviewer may miss relevant information by failing to seek it specifically and by not giving the interviewee an opportunity to initiate topics.

Stress interviews, which we discussed earlier in this appendix, are those in which the interviewer has primary control, as in authoritarian interviews. Unlike authoritarian interviews, however, stress interviews are a deliberate attempt to create anxiety in the interviewee. Thus, the interviewer controls not only the pace and content of interaction but also the psychological agenda. Interviewees have even less control than in authoritarian interviews because stress interviews often rely on trick questions, surprise turns in topic, and unsettling responses to interviewees. If you find yourself in a stress interview, recognize that it is probably a deliberate attempt to test your ability to cope with pressure. Stay alert and flexible to deal with unpredictable communication from the interviewer.

Forms of Questions in Interviews

Most interviews follow a question–answer pattern in which each person speaks only briefly before the other person speaks. Consequently, skill in asking and responding to questions is central to effectiveness. Skillful interviewers understand that different kinds of questions shape responses, and effective interviewees recognize the opportunities and constraints of distinct forms of questions (Dillon, 1990; Foddy, 1993). We'll consider seven of the most common types of questions and discuss the responses invited by each.

Open Questions Open questions are broad queries that allow interviewees a wide range of appropriate responses: "What can you tell me about yourself?" "What is your work experience?" Because open questions are broad, interviewees have an opportunity to steer communication toward specific topics that interest or reflect well on them.

Closed Questions Closed questions call for specific and brief responses, often a simple yes or no. Closed questions often follow open questions: "What was college like for you?" "Did you do senior honors project?"

Mirror Questions Mirror questions paraphrase or reflect an interviewee's previous communication. If an interviewee says, "I have worked in a lot of stressful jobs," the interviewer might respond reflectively by saying, "So you can handle pressure, right?" At the content level of meaning, a mirror question merely repeats what preceded it. At the relationship level of meaning, however, mirror questions say, "Elaborate; tell me more." They represent opportunities to expand on ideas.

► **Ranier**

My counselor uses mirror questions all the time. Whatever I say, she paraphrases it back to me. At first, that frustrated me because I expected her to provide me with some answers, or at least some direction in dealing with my problems. But now I realize that what she's doing is teaching me to solve my own problems. By nudging me to reflect on my feelings, she helps me identify what I do feel.

Hypothetical Questions Hypothetical questions ask a person to respond to an imaginary situation or issue. The questioner may describe a scenario and then ask how the respondent would handle it. Recruiters often pose hypothetical questions to see how well job candidates think on their feet. A student of mine provided the following example of a hypothetical question she was asked in a job interview: "Assume you are supervising an employee who is consistently late to work and sometimes leaves early. What would you do?" My student responded that her first course of action would be to talk with the employee to determine the reason for her tardiness and early departures. Next, she said, she would work with the employee to eliminate the source or, if company policies allowed it, to rearrange the schedule to accommodate the employee's circumstances. This response revealed that the job candidate was collaborative and supportive of subordinates—precisely the qualities the recruiter was looking for. Hypothetical questions are designed to find out how you grasp and respond to complex situations.

Probing Questions Probing questions go beneath the surface of responses to gather additional information and insight. Consider this example of several probing questions that follow an open question and a broad response:

> **Interviewer:** Tell me about your work history.
>
> **Interviewee:** I've held ten jobs while I've been attending college.
>
> **Interviewer:** Why have you held so many different jobs instead of sticking with one of them?
>
> **Interviewee:** I kept switching in the hope of finding one that would be really interesting.
>
> **Interviewer:** What makes a job interesting to you?
>
> **Interviewee:** It would have to be challenging and have enough variety not to bore me.
>
> **Interviewer:** Are you easily bored?

Leading Questions Leading questions predispose one to a certain response. For example, "You believe in teamwork, don't you?" encourages an affirmative response, whereas "You don't drink on a regular basis, do you?" encourages a negative answer. Leading questions generally are not a good way to elicit candid responses, because they suggest the way you want a person to respond (Stewart & Cash, 1991). However, leading questions can be useful to test an interviewee's commitment to an idea. An acquaintance of mine who recruits employees for sales positions that require a lot of travel often poses this leading question: "After a year or two of travel, the novelty wears off. I assume you expect a permanent location, right?" Applicants who answer yes do not get job offers, because travel is an ongoing part of sales positions.

Summary Questions A final kind of question is the summary question, which covers what has been discussed. Although summary questions often are phrased as statements, they function as questions. For example, "I believe we've covered everything" should be perceived as, "Do we need to discuss anything else?" "It seems we've agreed on expectations for your performance during the next quarter" should be perceived as, "Do you feel we have a common understanding of what's expected of you?" Communication that summarizes an interview provides an opportunity for participants to check whether they agree about what they've discussed and what will follow.

Responding to Hypothetical Questions

Read the following scenario, then quickly respond aloud, as you would in an actual interview:

> You find out that two co-workers under your supervision are romantically involved. They are of equal rank, so the relationship cannot lead to promotions or demotions. Would you be concerned about the relationship? Would you do anything about it?

An effective initial response would be to ask whether the company has specific policies regarding consensual relationships between employees. If the answer is yes, your follow-up comment might demonstrate your intention to enforce existing policies. If the answer is no, your follow-up comment might suggest you would talk with both people to make sure that they understand the problems that can accompany collegial romances. This would communicate that you are concerned about the people who work for you as well as about the company.

SHARPEN YOUR SKILL

▶GUIDELINES FOR COMMUNICATING IN INTERVIEWS

We will discuss four guidelines for effective interviewing: conduct research to prepare for interviews, engage in person-centered communication, practice responding, and know how to deal with illegal questions. We will use the hiring interview to illustrate these challenges, but the ideas we'll discuss pertain to other kinds of interviews as well.

Research to Prepare for Interviews

My students often tell me that they can't prepare for interviews because they don't know what the interviewer will ask. Even without knowing exactly what questions will arise, you can do a great deal to prepare yourself for a successful interview.

Every type of interview benefits from advance research, although the appropriate research varies according to the interview's purpose. Before performance appraisals, both the supervisor and the subordinate should review any previous performance appraisals and what has happened since the last appraisal. Have previously set goals been met? Have there been notable achievements, such as development of new skills, awards, and so forth? It's also appropriate to talk with others to learn what is expected of employees at various stages in their careers.

Wall Street Journal reporter Rochelle Sharpe (1995) notes that only about 5% of job applicants research a company before interviewing for a job with it. You can put yourself ahead of 95% of job applicants by doing advance research. To learn about a hiring organization, you'll want information about its corporate image, history, benefits, organizational culture, and so forth. If you know someone who works for the company, ask that person to share perceptions and information with you. You may also go to a library, placement office, or online service. References such as *Moody's Manuals* and *Standard & Poor's Index* provide information about organizations' size, locations, salary levels, structure, employee benefits, and financial condition. If you prefer to research companies online, most have websites that provide substantial information on their history and policies as well as profiles of their workforce. Many companies accept online job applications (USA Snapshots, 1999).

Research enhances your effectiveness in two ways. First, the information you gather provides a basis for questions that show that you've done your homework. Second, when you have good information, you can adapt your communication to expectations and norms of the interviewer. For example, if you learn that a particular employer is highly committed to a team approach, during an interview you might emphasize your experience in working on teams. If you learn that the organization expects employees to operate independently, you might highlight your experience working solo during the interview. It is not ethical to misrepresent yourself; however, it is appropriate to spotlight aspects of your experience and interests that match the culture of the organization.

Engage in Person-Centered Communication

In Chapter 4, we discussed person-centered communication, in which one person recognizes and respects the perspective of another person. To prepare for an interview, ask yourself, "What would I want to know if I were interviewing me for this position?" Don't ask what *you* want to tell the interviewer about yourself or what *you* think is most important. Instead, take the position of the interviewer as you anticipate the interaction.

▶ Glenn

I'm on the selection committee for study abroad, so I interview a lot of students. You'd be amazed at how few of them have bothered to learn about the history and goals of the program. When I ask applicants why they want to study abroad, most of them talk about their personal interests and totally ignore the program's purpose of serving as an ambassador of goodwill to people in other countries. Students who have bothered to research the program and who can link their goals to those of the program have a real edge in getting accepted.

You are not likely to know the interviewer personally, so you can't realistically expect to understand him or her as a unique individual. What matters is to recognize that in the interview situation the recruiter is a representative of a particular company with distinct goals, history, expectations, and culture. If you have researched the company, you will be able to adapt your communication to the interviewer's frame of reference.

Practice Responding

One of the most common complaints of employment recruiters is that candidates are unprepared for interviews. Examples of lack of preparation include not bringing a résumé to the interview, not knowing about the company, and not providing specific information, such as names of former supervisors and dates of employment. The ability to recall specific information is particularly important because it suggests that you are prepared and knowledgeable. Yet many people fumble when asked about specifics. Why? Because they assume they know about themselves, so they don't bother to review details and practice responses. You can prepare well by taking time before an interview to review your experiences and accomplishments and to remind yourself of key names, places, and dates. It's also a good idea to rehearse actual answers by responding aloud to questions that are likely to be posed.

Know How to Manage Illegal Questions

Just a couple of years ago, a student who was completing a professional degree was asked this question by a job recruiter: "What are your plans for a family?" Fortunately, this student knew the question was discriminatory, so she refused to answer and reported the interviewer to our campus placement service.

Know the Law The Equal Employment Opportunity Commission (EEOC) is a federally created entity that monitors various kinds of discrimination in hiring decisions. In 1970, the EEOC issued initial guidelines pertinent to employment interviews, and these have been updated periodically. EEOC guidelines also apply to tests, application forms, and other devices used to screen job applicants. EEOC regulations prohibit discrimination on the basis of criteria that are legally irrelevant to job qualifications. Because the EEOC is an arm of the federal government, it protects interviewees in all states from intrusive questions about race, ethnicity, marital status, age, sex,

DIVERSITY

fyi

CULTURAL DIVERSITY IN INTERVIEWS

The U.S. Department of Labor (1992) cautions interviewers to be sensitive to cultural diversity, which affects how interviewees represent themselves. For example, Western culture encourages people to be assertive and to highlight their strengths. In contrast, some Eastern cultures teach members to be modest about personal achievements and abilities. This can result in misunderstandings and poor decisions about job candidates.

One case study highlighted in an educational pamphlet from the Labor Department features Tran, who is Vietnamese by birth. When Tran applies for a supervisory job, he is interviewed by a woman named Marie. She is impressed by his résumé, which is professionally written and shows that Tran has a great deal of experience and is well qualified for the position. When Marie asks Tran to expand on the résumé by telling her about his skills, he says only that the résumé completely states his experience and qualifications. After several efforts to get Tran to elaborate on his abilities, Marie decides he lacks the self-confidence necessary for a supervisory position, and she decides not to hire him. What Marie doesn't understand is that Tran's culture emphasizes the importance of modesty and humility. He was taught that it is unbecoming to call attention to his talents and qualifications. His reluctance to elaborate on his experience and abilities reflects his cultural learnings, not a lack of self-confidence.

disability, and arrests. Individual states and institutions may impose additional limits on information about candidates that may be used in hiring decisions. My school, for instance, has a policy against discrimination based on military service and sexual orientation.

Illegal questions may reflect either an interviewer's ignorance of the laws or willful disregard of an interviewee's rights. People who conduct interviews should review the restrictions on questions by consulting a good source, such as Arthur Bell's 1989 book, *The Complete Manager's Guide to Interviewing*. Whether or not interviewers intend to ask illegal questions, it's important for interviewees to know what questions are not legally permissible in employment interviews. Interviewees who do not understand the legal boundaries of questions cannot protect their rights.

DELIVERY MATTERS IN INTERVIEWS

Communication scholar Mary Mino (1996) wanted to know to what extent nonverbal delivery skills and substantive content influenced perceptions of interviewees. To find out, she studied mock hiring interviews.

Mino discovered that interviewers were impressed by candidates who articulated clearly and whose nonverbal communication conveyed enthusiasm, assertiveness, and an outgoing personality. However, cautions Mino, dynamic nonverbal communication alone doesn't impress interviewers. When slick speaking is combined with poor content, interviewees are perceived as insincere.

Respond Carefully Knowing which questions are illegal doesn't tell you what to do if you are asked an inappropriate question. If the question doesn't bother you, you may choose to respond. You also have the right to point out to an interviewer that a question is inappropriate. If you don't care about the job, this is a reasonable way to respond. Even if you exercise your rights diplomatically, doing so may lessen an interviewer's willingness to recommend you for employment.

Often, interviewers who ask inappropriate questions don't intend to violate EEOC guidelines, so it's unwise to assume they have bad motives (Wilson & Goodall, 1991). One effective way to respond to unlawful questions is to provide only information that may be sought legally. For instance, if an employer asks whether you are a native Chinese speaker, you might respond, "I am fluent in both English and Chinese." If you are asked whether you belong to any political organizations, you might answer, "The only organizations to which I belong that are relevant to this job are the Training and Development Association and the National Communication Association."

If a diplomatic response, such as a partial answer, doesn't satisfy the interviewer, it is appropriate for you to be more assertive. You might ask, "How does your question pertain to qualifications for this job?" This more direct response can be effective in protecting your rights without harming the climate if your nonverbal communication is open and friendly (a questioning tone, a pleasant facial expression) rather than challenging (an accusatory tone, a glare). It is possible to be both assertive and cordial, and this is generally advisable.

►SUMMARY

Interviews are common in everyday life. They occur when we respond to pollsters' questions, apply for a job or promotion, conduct research, engage in counseling, and so forth. In this appendix, we have gained insight into the structure and processes involved in interviewing. We have learned that most interviews follow a three-part sequence and that different styles and forms of questions are used to achieve different objectives in interview situations.

In the second section of the appendix, we focused on four guidelines for effective communication when interviewing, especially in the context of job seeking. The first guideline is to prepare by researching the company and the interviewer. A second guideline is to be person centered in your interviewing communication. Third, it's wise to practice responding to possible interview questions, including difficult ones. A final suggestion is to become familiar with legal issues relevant to interviewing.

▶ Key Concepts

The terms following are defined in the chapter on the page number indicated, and they appear in alphabetical order, with definitions, in the Glossary, which begins on page 369. The book's online resources also include flash cards and crossword puzzles to help you learn these terms and the concepts they represent.

authoritarian interview, 361
complaint interview, 356
counseling interview, 356
distributive interview, 360
employment interview, 356
exit interview, 357

funnel sequence, 358
information-getting interview, 355
information-giving interview, 355
interview, 354
mirror interview, 360
performance review, 357

persuasive interview, 355
problem-solving interview, 355
reprimand interview, 357
stress interview, 357

▶ For Further Reflection and Discussion

The questions below can also be found among the book's online resources for this chapter, where you have the option of e-mailing your responses to your instructor, if required.

1. Arrange an information-seeking interview with a person in the field you hope to enter. Ask the person to tell you about the job—its advantages and disadvantages and the skills it requires.

2. Visit the website of a company you might like to join. Record the information provided on the website. Based on what you find, list five questions you could ask in an interview to show that you have researched the company.

3. Schedule an interview with a peer on a topic of mutual interest. During the interview, experiment with different forms of questions: open, closed, mirror, stress, probing, and hypothetical. How do the different types of questions affect the interviewee's comfort and responses?

4. We said that interviewees may choose to respond to illegal questions if the questions are not personally offensive or bothersome. For instance, Christians might think they have nothing to lose by responding honestly to the question, "Can you work on Saturdays?" What do you regard as the pragmatic and ethical implications of responding to questions that don't harm you? If only members of minority religions refuse to answer questions about religion, how effective are the legal protections provided by EEOC guidelines? If all Protestants answer honestly questions about religion, are members of other religions jeopardized?

5. The Virtual Interviewing Assistant provides links to help you learn to participate in many types of interviews, including the appraisal, counseling, selection, and reprimand types. This site also provides information about preparing for and following up on interviews. Access this resource by going to the book's online resources and clicking on WebLink A.1.

6. Watch a television program that features interviews of newsmakers. *Face the Nation, 20/20, Meet the*

Press, and *60 Minutes* are examples of programs that feature news interviews. Also, watch one television program that features interviews with celebrities or people in the limelight. *The Oprah Winfrey Show* is an example of this genre. Identify the form of each question posed (open, closed, leading, etc.) and the response it generates. Do the different kinds of interviews rely on distinct types of questions? Why? What do you conclude about the importance of question style to the content and pace of interviews?

Glossary

abstract Removed from concrete reality. Symbols are abstract because they refer to, but are not equivalent to, reality.

acknowledgment The second of three levels of interpersonal confirmation; communicating that you hear and understand another's expressed feelings and thoughts.

agape One of the six styles of loving; it is selfless and focused on the other's happiness.

agenda setting Media's selection of issues, events, and people to highlight for attention.

ambiguous Subject to multiple meanings. Symbols are ambiguous because their meanings vary from person to person, context to context, and so forth.

ambushing Listening carefully to a speaker in order to attack her or him.

anxious/ambivalent attachment One of the four styles of attachment; a style, characterized by preoccupation with relationships, in which intimacy is both wanted and feared. It is fostered by inconsistent treatment from a caregiver.

arbitrary Random or nonnecessary. Symbols are arbitrary because there is no need for any particular symbol to stand for a particular referent.

artifact Any personal object with which one announces one's identities or personalizes one's environment.

assimilation The giving up of one's native ways to take on the ways of another culture.

attachment style The pattern of interaction between child and primary caregiver that teaches the child who he or she is, who others are, and how to approach relationships. Four attachment styles have been identified: anxious/ambivalent, dismissive, fearful, and secure.

attribution An explanation of why things happen and why people act as they do; not necessarily correct interpretations of others and their motives.

authoritarian interview An interviewing style in which the interviewer has and exerts greater power than interviewee.

autonomy/connection One of three relationship dialectics; the tension between the need for personal autonomy, or independence, and connection, or intimacy.

bracketing Identifying and setting aside for later discussion the issues peripheral to a current conflict.

brainstorming A group technique for generating potential solutions to a problem; the free flow of ideas without immediate criticism.

brute facts Objective, concrete phenomena.

chronemics Nonverbal communication involving the perception and use of time to define identities and interaction.

climate communication One of three constructive forms of participation in group decision making; the creating and sustaining of an open, engaged atmosphere for discussion.

cognitive complexity The number of mental constructs an individual uses, how abstract they are, and how elaborately they interact to create perceptions.

cognitive restructuring A method of reducing communication apprehension that involves teaching people to revise how they think about speaking situations.

cognitive schemata Mental structures people use to organize and interpret experience. Four schemata have been identified: prototypes, personal constructs, stereotypes, and scripts.

cohesion Closeness, or feeling of esprit de corps, among members of a group.

collectivist culture A culture that regards people as deeply connected to one another and to their families, groups, and communities.

commitment The decision to remain in a relationship. One of three dimensions of enduring romantic relationships, commitment has more influence on relationship continuity than does love alone. An advanced stage in the process of escalation in romantic relationships.

communication A systemic process in which people interact with and through symbols to create and interpret meanings.

communication apprehension Anxiety associated with real or anticipated communication encounters. It is common and can be constructive.

communication climate The overall feeling, or emotional mood, between people.

communication network The links among members of an organization. May be formal (e.g., as specified in an organizational chart) or informal (friendship circles).

communication rules Shared understandings of what communication means and what behaviors are appropriate in various situations.

communication technologies Means of recording, transferring, and working with information.

comparison A form of evidence associating two things that are similar or different in some important way or ways.

complaint interview An interview that allows a person to register a complaint about a product, service, person, company, etc.

conflict The expression of different views, interests, or goals and the perception of differences as incompatible or in opposition by people who depend on each other.

constitutive rules Communication rules that specify how certain communicative acts are to be counted.

constructive conflict In groups, disagreement that is characterized by respect for diverse opinions, emphasis on shared interests and goals, and a win–win orientation.

constructivism A theory that holds that we organize and interpret experience by applying cognitive structures called schemata.

content level of meaning One of two levels of meaning; the literal information in a message.

cookies Bits of data that websites collect and store in users' personal browsers.

counseling interview An interview in which one person with expertise helps another to understand a problem and develop strategies to overcome or cope more effectively with the difficulty.

covert conflict Conflict that is expressed indirectly; generally more difficult to manage constructively than overt conflict.

credibility The ability of a person to engender belief in what he or she says or does. Listeners confer or refuse to confer credibility on speakers.

critical listening Listening to analyze and evaluate the content of communication or the character of the person speaking.

critical research method A type of data analysis that aims to identify, critique, or change communication practices that oppress, marginalize, or otherwise harm people.

cultivation A cumulative process by which the media foster beliefs about social reality, including the belief that the world is more dangerous and violent than it actually is.

cultivation theory The theory that media promote an inaccurate worldview that viewers assume reflects real life.

cultural relativism The recognition that cultures vary in thought, action, and behavior as well as in beliefs and values; not the same as moral relativism.

cultural studies theories A group of theories that focus on relationships between mass communication and rituals and patterns of everyday communication by investigating the reciprocally influential relationships between mass communication and history, politics, and economics.

culture The beliefs, understandings, practices, and ways of interpreting experience that are shared by a group of people.

defensive listening The perception of personal attacks, criticisms, or hostile undertones in communication when none is intended.

derived credibility The expertise and trustworthiness attributed to a speaker by listeners as a result of how the speaker communicates during a presentation.

digital divide The gap between those with access to communication technologies and those without such access; thought by some to potentially increase social, racial, and economic inequality.

direct definition Communication that tells us who we are by explicitly labeling us and reacting to our behaviors; usually occurs first in families and later in interaction with peers and others.

dismissive attachment One of the four attachment styles; characterized by a view of others as unworthy of love and the self as adequate yet removed from intimate relationships; fostered by disinterested, rejecting, or abusive treatment by a caregiver.

disruptive conflict In groups, disagreement characterized by competitive communication, self-interested focus on the part of members, and a win–lose orientation.

distributive interview A style of interviewing in which power is roughly equal between interviewer and interviewee.

downer A person who communicates negatively about us and our worth.

dyadic processes The second stage in relationship decay, in which partners discuss problems and alternative futures for the relationship. May include conflict as well as degeneration of established patterns, understandings, and routines that make up a relationship culture and sustain intimacy on a day-to-day basis. Not all partners experience this phase.

egocentric communication An unconstructive form of group contribution that is used to block others or to call attention to oneself.

electronic epoch The fourth era in McLuhan's media history of civilization; ushered in by the invention of the telegraph, which made it possible for people to communicate personally across distance.

empathy The ability to feel with another person, to feel what he or she feels in a situation.

employment interview An interview in which employers and job candidates assess each other to determine whether there is a good fit between them.

endorsement The third of three levels of interpersonal confirmation; the communication of acceptance of another's thoughts and feelings. Not the same as agreement.

environmental distraction In communication situations, any occurrence that interferes with listening.

environmental factor Any nonverbal element of a setting that affects how we think, feel, act, and communicate.

equity theory The theory that people are happier and more satisfied with equitable relationships than inequitable ones. In equitable relationships, partners perceive the benefits and costs of the relationship as about equal for each of them.

eros One of the six styles of loving; passionate, intense, and erotic.

ethics The branch of philosophy that deals with the goodness or rightness of particular actions. Ethical issues infuse all areas of the communication field.

ethnocentrism The tendency to assume that one way of life is normal and superior to other ways of life.

ethos One of three forms of proof; proof based on the speaker's credibility (trustworthiness, expertise, and goodwill).

evidence Material used to interest, move, inform, or persuade people: statistics, examples, comparisons, and quotations.

example A form of evidence in which a single instance is used to make a point, to dramatize an idea, or to personalize information. The four types of examples are undetailed, detailed, hypothetical, and anecdotal.

exit interview An interview designed to gain information, insights, and perceptions about a place of work or an educational program from a person who is leaving.

expectancy violation theory A theory claiming that when our expectations are violated, we become more cognitively alert as we struggle to understand and cope with unexpected behaviors.

extemporaneous delivery A presentational style that includes preparation and practice but not memorization of actual words and nonverbal behaviors.

fearful attachment One of the four styles of attachment; characterized by the perception of self as unworthy of love; fostered by dismissive, rejecting, or abusive treatment by a caregiver.

feedback Verbal or nonverbal response to a message. The concept of feedback as applied to human communication appeared first in interactive models of communication.

funnel sequence In interviews, a pattern of communication that begins with broad, general questions and moves to progressively narrower, more probing questions.

gatekeeper A person, group, or institution that controls the choice and presentation of topics by media.

generalized other The perspective that represents one's perception of the rules, roles, and attitudes endorsed by one's group or community.

global village The modern-day, worldwide community made possible by electronic communication that instantaneously links people all over the world.

grace Granting forgiveness, putting aside our own needs, or helping another save face when no standard says we should or must do so.

grave dressing processes The fourth step in the deterioration of romantic relationships, in which partners put the relationship to rest and individually assign meaning to it.

group More than two people who interact over time, who are interdependent, and who follow shared rules of conduct to reach a common goal. A team is one type of group.

groupthink The absence of critical and independent thought on the part of group members about ideas generated by the group.

halo effect The attribution of expertise to someone in areas unrelated to the person's actual expertise.

haptics Nonverbal communication involving physical touch.

hearing A physiological activity that occurs when sound waves hit our eardrums. Unlike listening, hearing is a passive process.

high-context communication style An indirect and undetailed way of speaking that conveys meanings implicitly rather than explicitly; typical of collectivist cultures.

homeostasis A state of equilibrium that systems strive for but cannot sustain.

hypodermic needle model The theory that media are powerful forces that directly affect audiences, which are vulnerable, passive recipients. Also called the *magic bullet theory* and the *direct effects model* of mass media.

hypothetical thought Thinking about experiences and ideas that do not exist or are not present to the senses.

I The creative, spontaneous, impulsive aspect of the self. The *I* is complemented by the *me*.

identity script A guide to action based on rules for living and identity. Initially communicated in families, scripts define our roles, how we are to play them, and the basic elements in the plot of our lives.

***I*-language** Language that identifies the speaker's or perceiver's thoughts and feelings. (Compare with *you*-language.)

impromptu delivery A delivery style that involves little preparation; speakers think on their feet as they talk about ideas and positions with which they are familiar.

indexing A technique of noting that every statement reflects a specific time and circumstance and may not apply to other times or circumstances.

individualism A predominant Western value that regards each person as unique, important, and to be recognized for her or his individual qualities and behavior.

individualistic culture A culture in which each person is veiwed as distinct from other people, groups, and organizations.

inference An interpretation that goes beyond the facts known but is believed to logically follow from them.

informational listening Listening to understand information and ideas.

information-getting interview An interview in which one person asks questions to learn about an-other person's qualifications, background, experience, opinions, knowledge, attitudes, or behaviors.

information-giving interview An interview in which one person provides information to another.

initial credibility The expertise and trustworthiness listeners attribute to a speaker before a presentation begins. Initial credibility is based on the speaker's titles, positions, experiences, or achievements that are known to listeners before they hear the speech.

institutional facts Meanings people assign to brute facts (objective, concrete phenomena) that are based on human interpretation.

interconnectivity The capacity of multiple devices to be connected to each other and to the Internet so that the devices can "talk" to each other.

interpersonal communication Communication between people, usually in close relationships such as friendship and romance.

interpersonal confirmation The expressed valuing of another person.

interpretation The subjective process of organizing and making sense of perceptions.

interview A communication transaction that emphasizes questions and answers.

intrapersonal communication Communication with ourselves, or self-talk.

intrapsychic processes The first stage in the disintegration of a romantic relationship; involves brooding about problems in the relationship and dissatisfactions with the partner.

investment Something put into a relationship that cannot be recovered should the relationship end. Investments, more than rewards and love, increase commitment.

judgment A belief or opinion based on observations, feelings, assumptions, or other nonfactual phenomena.

kinesics Body position and body motions, including those of the face, that may be used to communicate or may be interpreted as communicating.

leadership A set of behaviors that helps a group maintain a good climate and accomplish tasks in an organized way.

listening A complex process that consists of being mindful, hearing, selecting and organizing information, interpreting communication, responding, and remembering.

literal listening Listening only to the content level of meaning and ignoring the relationship level of meaning.

literate epoch The second era in McLuhan's media history of civilization. Invention of the phonetic alphabet inaugurated the literate epoch, in which common symbols allowed people to communicate in writing.

loaded language An extreme form of evaluative language that relies on words that strongly slant perceptions and thus meanings.

logos One of three forms of proof; proof based on logic and reasoning.

lose–lose One of three orientations to conflict; assumes that everyone loses when conflict occurs.

low-context communication style Language that is very explicit, detailed, and precise; generally used in individualistic cultures.

ludus One of six styles of loving; playful and sometimes manipulative.

mainstreaming The effect of television in stabilizing and homogenizing views within a society; one of two processes used to explain television's cultivation of synthetic worldviews.

mania One of six styles of loving; an obsessive style that often reflects personal insecurity.

manuscript delivery A presentational style that involves speaking from a complete manuscript of a speech.

mass communication All media that address mass audiences.

matching hypothesis The prediction that people will seek relationships with others who closely match their values, attitudes, social background, and physical attractiveness.

me The reflective, analytical, socially conscious aspect of self. *Me* complements the *I* aspect of self.

mean world syndrome The belief that the world is dangerous and full of mean people.

meaning The significance we attribute to a phenomenon; what it signifies to us.

memorized delivery A presentational style in which the speech is delivered word for word from memory.

message complexity The amount of detailed information or intricate reasoning in a message; can interfere with effective listening.

message overload The receiving of more messages than we can interpret, evaluate, and remember; can interfere with effective listening.

mindfulness From Buddhism, the concept of being fully present in the moment; the first step of listening and the foundation of all the other steps.

mind reading The assumption that we understand what another person thinks or how another person perceives something.

minimal encourager Communication that gently invites another person to elaborate by expressing interest in hearing more.

mirror interview A style of interviewing in which the interviewer's questions reflect previous responses and comments of the interviewee. Mirror interviews give substantial power to interviewees.

monitoring The observation and regulation of one's own communication.

monopolizing Hogging the stage by continuously focusing communication on oneself instead of on the person who is talking.

multilingual Able to speak and understand more than one language or communication style used in a social group or culture.

multitasking Engaging in multiple tasks simultaneously or in overlapping and interactive ways.

neutralization One of four responses to relationship dialectics; balancing or finding a compromise between two dialectical poles.

noise Anything that interferes with the intended meaning of communication; includes sounds (e.g., traffic) as well as psychological interferences (e.g., preoccupation).

nonverbal communication All forms of communication other than words themselves; includes inflection and other vocal qualities as well as several other behaviors such as shrugs, blushing, and eye movements.

norm An informal rule that guides how members of a culture or group think, feel, and act. Norms define what is normal or appropriate in various situations.

novelty/predictability One of three relationship dialectics; the tension between the desire for spontaneous, new experiences, and the desire for routines and familiar experiences.

olfactics The perception of scents and odors; one form of nonverbal communication.

openness The extent to which a system interacts with its surrounding environment.

openness/closedness One of three relationship dialectics; the tension between the desire to share private thoughts, feelings, and experiences with intimates and the desire to preserve personal privacy.

oral footnote Phrases or sentences in a speech that acknowledge a source of evidence and sometimes explain the source's qualifications.

oral style Visual, vocal, and verbal aspects of the delivery of a public speech or other communication.

organizational culture Understandings about identity and codes of thought and action that are shared by the members of an organization.

overt conflict Conflict expressed directly and in a straightforward manner.

paralanguage Communication that is vocal but not verbal. Paralanguage includes accent, inflection, volume, pitch, and sounds such as murmurs and gasps.

paraphrasing A method of clarifying another's meaning by reflecting one's interpretation of the other's communication back to that person.

participation A response to cultural diversity in which one incorporates some practices, customs, and traditions of other groups into one's life.

particular others Specific people who are significant to the self and who influence the self's values, perspectives, and esteem.

passion Intensely positive feelings and desires for another person. Passion is based on the rewards of involvement and is not equivalent to commitment.

pathos One of three forms of proof; proof based on appealing to listeners' emotions.

perception An active process of selecting, organizing, and interpreting people, objects, events, situations, and activities.

performance review A type of interview in which a supervisor comments on a subordinate's achievements and professional development, identifies weaknesses or problems, and collaborates to develop goals for future performance; also known as a *performance appraisal.*

personal construct A bipolar mental yardstick that allows us to measure people and situations along specific dimensions of judgment, such as "honest–dishonest."

personal relationship A relationship defined by uniqueness, rules, relationship dialectics, commitment, and embeddedness in contexts. Personal relationships, unlike social ones, are irreplaceable.

person-centeredness The ability to perceive another as a unique and distinct individual apart from social roles and generalizations.

persuasive interview An interview in which the interviewer aims to influence the attitudes, beliefs, values, or actions of the interviewee.

physical appearance A form of nonverbal communication; how we look, including the cultural meanings, values, and expectations associated with looks.

policy A formal statement of practice that reflects and upholds an organization's culture.

positive visualization A technique for reducing speaking anxiety, in which one visualizes oneself communicating effectively in progressively challenging speaking situations.

power The ability to influence others; a feature of small groups that affects participation.

power over The ability to help or harm others. Power over others usually is communicated in ways that highlight the status and influence of the person exerting the power.

power to The ability to empower others to reach their goals. People who use power to help others generally do not highlight their own status and influence.

pragma One of six styles of loving; based on practical considerations and criteria for attachment.

prejudgment Judging others or their ideas before one has heard them.

preoccupation Absorption in our own thoughts or concerns.

print epoch The third era in McLuhan's media history of civilization. Invention of the printing press made it possible to mass-produce written materials, so reading was no longer limited to elite members of society.

problem-solving interview An interview in which people collaborate to identify sources of a mutual problem and to develop means of addressing or resolving it.

procedural communication One of three constructive ways of participating in group decision making; orders ideas and coordinates contributions of members.

process An ongoing continuity, the beginning and end of which are difficult to identify; for example, communication.

product placement A practice, paid for by advertisers and program sponsors, of featuring products in media so that the products are associated with particular characters, storylines, and so forth.

prototype A knowledge structure that defines the clearest or most representative example of some category.

proxemics A form of nonverbal communication that involves space and how we use it.

pseudolistening Pretending to listen.

psychological responsibility The obligation to remember, plan, and coordinate domestic work and child care. In general, women assume psychological responsibility for child care and housework even when both partners share in the actual doing of tasks.

puffery Exaggerated, superlative claims about a product that appear to be factually based but are actually meaningless and unverifiable.

punctuation Defining the beginning and ending of interaction or interaction episodes. Punctuation is subjective and not always agreed on by those involved in the interaction.

qualitative research methods Interpretive techniques, including textual analysis and ethnography, used to understand the character of experience, particularly how people perceive and make sense of communication.

quality improvement team A group in which people from different departments or areas in an organization collaborate to solve problems, meet needs, or increase the quality of work life. Also called *continuous quality improvement team*.

quantitative research methods Techniques such as descriptive statistics, surveys, and experiments, used to gather quantifiable data.

quotation A form of evidence that uses exact citations of others' statements. Also called *testimony*.

reappropriation A group's reclamation of a term used by others to degrade the group's members; the treatment of those terms as positive self-descriptions. Aims to remove the stigma from terms that others use pejoratively.

recognition The most basic level of interpersonal confirmation; the communication of awareness that another person exists and is present.

reflected appraisal The image and estimate of ourselves that others communicate to us.

reframing One of four responses to relationship dialectics; transcends the apparent contradiction between two dialectical poles and reinterprets them as not in tension.

regulative rules Communication rules that regulate interaction by specifying when, how, where, and with whom to talk about certain things.

relationship culture A private world of rules, understandings, and patterns of acting and interpreting that partners create to give meaning to their relationship; the nucleus of intimacy.

relationship dialectics The tensions between opposing forces or tendencies that are normal parts of all relationships: autonomy/connection, novelty/predictability, and openness/closedness.

relationship level of meaning One of two levels of meaning in communication; expresses the relationship between communicators.

relationship listening Listening to support another person or to understand how another person thinks, feels, or perceives some situation, event, or other phenomenon.

remembering The process of recalling what one has heard; the sixth element of listening.

reprimand interview An interview conducted by a supervisor to identify lapses in a subordinate's professional conduct, to determine sources of problems, and to establish a plan for improving future performance.

resistance A response to cultural diversity; attacking the cultural practices of others or proclaiming that one's own cultural traditions are superior.

resonance The extent to which something (specifically phenomena on television) is congruent with personal experience; one of two mechanisms used to explain television's ability to cultivate synthetic worldviews.

respect A response to cultural diversity in which one values others' customs, traditions, and values even if one does not actively incorporate them into one's life.

responding Symbolizing interest in what is being said with observable feedback to speakers during interaction; the fifth of six elements of listening.

resurrection processes The final part of the dissolution of romantic relationships, in which individuals redefine themselves and their futures without the former partner.

rite A dramatic, planned set of activities that brings together aspects of cultural ideology in a single event.

ritual A form of regularly occurring communication that members of an organization perceive as a familiar, routine part of organizational life and that communicates a particular value or role definition.

role The responsibilities and behaviors expected of a person by virtue of his or her position.

rules Patterned ways of behaving and interpreting behavior. All relationships develop rules.

schemata Cognitive structures we use to organize and interpret experiences. The four types of schemata are prototypes, personal constructs, stereotypes, and scripts. (Singular: *schema*)

script One of four cognitive schemata; scripts define expected or appropriate sequences of action in particular settings.

secure attachment One of the four styles of attachment; a style fostered by a caregiver who communicates with an infant in consistently loving and attentive ways and which inclines people to view themselves and others as worthy and to be comfortable both alone and in intimate relationships.

segmentation One of four responses to relationship dialectics; segmentation responses meet one dialectical need while ignoring or not satisfying the contradictory dialectical need.

selective listening Focusing only on selected parts of communication; e.g., screening out parts of a message that don't interest us or with which we disagree, or riveting our attention on parts of communication that interest us or with which we agree.

self A multidimensional process that involves forming and acting from social perspectives that arise and evolve in communication with others and ourselves.

self-disclosure The revelation of personal information about ourselves that others are unlikely to discover in other ways.

self-fulfilling prophecy Acting in ways that bring about others' or our own expectations or judgments of ourselves.

self-sabotage Self-talk that communicates that we are no good, that we can't do something, that we can't change, and so forth; undermines belief in ourselves and motivation to change and grow.

self-serving bias The tendency to attribute our positive actions and successes to stable, global, internal influences that we control and to attribute negative actions and failures to unstable, specific, external influences beyond our control.

separation One of four responses to relationship dialectics, in which friends or romantic partners assign one pole of a dialectic to certain spheres of activities or topics and assign the contradictory dialectical pole to distinct spheres of activities or topics.

silence Lack of sound. Silence can be a powerful form of nonverbal communication.

skills training A method of reducing communication apprehension that assumes that anxiety results from lack of speaking skills and thus can be reduced by learning skills.

social climbing The attempt to increase personal status in a group by winning the approval of high-status members.

social community A group of people who live within a dominant culture yet also belong to another social group or groups that share values, understandings, and practices distinct from those of the dominant culture.

social comparison Comparing ourselves with others to form judgments of our talents, abilities, qualities, and so forth.

social relationship Replaceable relationships that tend to follow broad social scripts and rules and in which participants tend to assume conventional social roles in relation to one another. Contrast with *personal relationship.*

social support processes The fourth step in the disintegration of romantic relationships, during which partners talk with others to gain emotional support and practical assistance.

specific purpose What a speaker aims to accomplish by presenting a speech; often called *behavioral objectives.*

speech to entertain A speech the primary goal of which is to amuse, interest, and engage listeners.

speech to inform A speech the primary goal of which is to increase listeners' understanding, awareness, or knowledge of some topic.

speech to persuade A speech the primary goal of which is to change listeners' attitudes, beliefs, or behaviors or to motivate listeners to action.

spyware Software that allows a third party to track computer users' web activity, to collect personal information about users, and to send pop-up ads tailored to users' profiles. Spyware is often bundled without users' knowledge into software that can be downloaded for free.

standpoint The social, symbolic, and material conditions common to a group of people that influence how they understand themselves, others, and society.

standpoint theory A theory that holds that a culture includes a number of social groups that differently shape the perceptions, identities, and opportunities of members of those groups.

static evaluation An assessment that suggests that something is unchanging or static; e.g., "Bob is impatient."

statistics A form of evidence that uses numbers to summarize a great many individual cases or to demonstrate relationships between phenomena.

stereotype A predictive generalization about people or situations.

storge One of six styles of loving; based on friendship; even-keeled.

stress interview A style of interviewing in which the interviewer deliberately attempts to create anxiety in the interviewee.

structure An organized relationship and interaction between members of an organization. Structures include roles, rules, policies, and communication networks.

symbol An arbitrary, ambiguous, and abstract representation of a phenomenon. Symbols are the basis of language, much nonverbal behavior, and human thought.

synergy A special kind of collaborative vitality that enhances the energies, talents, and strengths of individual members.

system A group of interrelated elements that affect one another. Communication is systemic.

systematic desensitization A method of reducing communication apprehension that first teaches people how to relax physiologically and then helps them practice feeling relaxed as they imagine themselves in progressively more difficult communication situations.

task communication One of three constructive forms of participation in group decision making; focuses on giving and analyzing information and ideas.

team A special kind of group characterized by different and complementary resources of members and by a strong sense of collective identity. All teams are groups, but not all groups are teams.

teleconferencing Meetings, formal or informal, conducted among people who are geographically separated; can take several forms that differ in the extent to which they emulate face-to-face meetings.

terminal credibility The cumulative expertise and trustworthiness listeners attribute to a speaker as a result of initial and derived credibility; may be greater or less than initial credibility, depending on how effectively a speaker has communicated.

thesis statement The main idea of an entire speech; should capture the key message in a concise sentence that listeners can remember easily.

tolerance A response to diversity in which one accepts differences, although one may not approve of or even understand them.

totalizing Responding to a person as if one aspect of that person were the total of who the person is.

transition A word, phrase, or sentence that connects ideas and main points in a speech so that listeners can follow a speaker.

triangulation Studying phenomena from multiple points of view by relying on multiple sources of data, theories, researchers, and/or methodological approaches.

tribal epoch The first era in McLuhan's media history of civilization, during which the oral tradition reigned and face-to-face talking and listening were primary forms of communication.

uncertainty reduction theory The theory that people find uncertainty uncomfortable and so are motivated to use communication to reduce uncertainty.

understanding A response to cultural diversity that assumes that differences are rooted in cultural teachings and that no traditions, customs, or behaviors are intrinsically better than others.

upper A person who communicates positive messages about us and our worth.

uses and gratification theory The theory that people use media to gratify their needs, interests, and desires.

verbal communication Words and only words; does not include inflection, accent, volume, pitch, or other paralinguistic features of speech.

visual aid A visual image, such as a chart, graph, photograph, or physical object, that reinforces ideas presented verbally or provides information.

vulture A person who attacks a person's self-esteem; may attack others or himself or herself.

Wi-Fi A wireless means of connecting devices to the Internet and to each other.

win–lose One of three orientations toward conflict; assumes that in any conflict one person wins and the others lose.

win–win One of three orientations to conflict; assumes that everyone involved in a conflict can win and attempts to bring about a mutually satisfying solution.

***you*-language** Language that attributes intentions and motives to another person, usually the person to whom one is speaking. (Compare with *I*-language.)

References

Abbate, J. (1999). *Inventing the Internet.* Reading, MA: Addison-Wesley-Longman.

Abdullah, H. (1999, January 22). Gender roles, new rules. *Raleigh News & Observer,* p. 8A.

Abe, J. (2004). Self-esteem, perception of relationships, and emotional distress: A cross-cultural study. *Personal Relationships, 11,* 231–247.

Acitelli, L. (1988). When spouses talk to each other about their relationship. *Journal of Social and Personal Relationships, 5,* 185–199.

Acitelli, L. (1993). You, me, and us: Perspectives on relationship awareness. In S. W. Duck (Ed.), *Understanding relationship processes, 1: Individuals in relationships* (pp. 144–174). Thousand Oaks, CA: Sage.

Acker, J. (2005). *Class questions: Feminist answers.* Lanham, MD: Rowman & Littlefield.

Ackerman, D. (1990). *A natural history of the senses.* New York: Random House.

Ader, C. (1995). A longitudinal study of agenda setting for the issue of environmental pollution. *Journalism and Mass Communication Quarterly, 72,* 300–311.

Afifi, W., & Metts, S. (1998). Characteristics and consequences of expectation violations in three close relationships. *Journal of Social and Personal Relationships, 15,* 365–392.

Agee, W., Ault, P., & Emery, E. (1996). *Introduction to mass communications* (12th ed.). Reading, MA: Addison-Wesley.

Alcoff, L. (1991, Winter). The problem of speaking for others. *Cultural Critique,* 5–32.

Allan, G. (1993). Social structure and relationships. In S. W. Duck (Ed.), *Understanding relationship processes, 3: Social context and relationships* (pp. 1–25). Thousand Oaks, CA: Sage.

Allen, B. (2006). Communicating race at WeighCo. In J. T. Wood & S. W. Duck (Eds.), *Composing relationships: Communication in everyday life* (pp. 146–155). Belmont, CA: Thomson Wadsworth.

Allen, M., Hunter, J., & Donahue, W. (1989). Meta-analysis of self-report data on the effectiveness of public speaking anxiety treatment techniques. *Communication Education, 38,* 54–76.

Altheide, D. (1974). *Creating reality.* Thousand Oaks, CA: Sage.

American Social Health Association. (2005). *State of the nation 2005: Challenges facing STD prevention in youth.* Retrieved September 1, 2006, from http://www.ashastd.org/learn/learn_overview.cfm

Andersen, P. (1993). Cognitive schemata in personal relationships. In S. W. Duck (Ed.), *Understanding relationship processes, 1: Individuals in relationships* (pp. 1–29). Thousand Oaks, CA: Sage.

Andersen, P. (1999). *Nonverbal communication: Forms and functions.* Mountain View, CA: Mayfield.

Andersen, P. H., & Collins, P. H. (Eds.). (1998). *Race, class, and gender: An anthology* (3rd ed.). Belmont, CA: Wadsworth.

Anderson, H. (1997). *Conversation, language, and possibilities: A postmodern approach to therapy.* New York: Basic Books.

Anderson, P., & Guerrero, L. (Eds.). (1998). *Handbook of communication and emotion.* San Diego, CA: Academic Press.

Anderson, R. (1995). *Essentials of personal selling: The new professionalism.* Englewood Cliffs, NJ: Prentice Hall.

Anderson, R. (2003). Literature and the particularities of dialogue. *Quarterly Journal of Speech, 89,* 78–82.

Anderson, R., Baxter, L., & Cissna, K. (Eds.). (2004). *Dialogue: Theorizing difference in communication studies.* Thousand Oaks, CA: Sage.

Anderson, R., & Killenberg, G. (1999). *Interviewing: Speaking, listening, and learning for professional life.* Mountain View, CA: Mayfield.

Angelou, M. (1991). *I shall not be moved.* New York: Random House.

Anzaldúa, G. (1999). *Borderlands/la frontera: The new mestiza.* San Francisco: Spinsters/Aunt Lute.

Argyle, M., & Henderson, M. (1984). The rules of

friendship. *Journal of Social and Personal Relationships, 1,* 211–237.

Argyle, M., & Henderson, M. (1985). The rules of relationships. In S. W. Duck & D. Perlman (Eds.), *Understanding personal relationships: An interdisciplinary approach* (pp. 63–84). Thousand Oaks, CA: Sage.

Arnett, R. (2004). A dialogic ethic "between" Buber and Levinas: A responsive ethical "I." In Anderson, R., Baxter, L., & Cissna, K. (Eds.). (2004). *Dialogue: Theorizing difference in communication studies* (pp. 75–90). Thousand Oaks, CA: Sage.

Arnold, H., & Feldman, D. (1986). *Organizational behavior.* New York: McGraw-Hill.

Ashcraft, K., & Mumby, D. (2004). *Reworking gender: A feminist communicology of organization.* Thousand Oaks, CA: Sage.

Assmann, A. (2006). The printing press and the Internet: From a culture of memory to a culture of attention. In N. Gentz & S. Kramer (Eds.), *Globalization, cultural identities, and media representations* (pp. 11–24). Albany, NY: State University of New York Press.

Atkinson, P., & Housley, W. (2003). *Interactionism: An essay in sociological amnesia.* Thousand Oaks, CA: Sage.

Atsuko, A. (2003). Gender differences in interpersonal distance: From the viewpoint of oppression hypothesis. *Japanese Journal of Experimental Social Psychology, 42,* 201–218.

AXIS Center for Public Awareness of People with Disabilities. *Guidelines for communicating with people with disabilities.* [Pamphlet]. Columbus, OH: Author.

Axtell, R. (1990a). *Dos and taboos around the world* (2nd ed.). New York: Wiley.

Axtell, R. (1990b). *Dos and taboos of hosting international visitors.* New York: Wiley.

Axtell, R. (1998). *Gestures: The dos and taboos of body language around the world.* New York: Wiley.

Ayres, J., & Hopf, T. S. (1990). The long-term effect of visualization in the classroom: A brief research report. *Communication Education, 39,* 75–78.

Bailey, A. (1998, February 29). Daily bread. *The Durham Herald–Sun,* p. C5.

Bakalar, N. (2006, May 16). Link is cited between smell and sexuality. *New York Times,* p. D5.

Bakardjieva, M. (2005). *Internet society: The Internet in everyday life.* Thousand Oaks, CA: Sage.

Banse, R. (2004). Adult attachment and marital satisfaction: Evidence for dyadic configuration effects. *Journal of Social and Personal Relationships, 21,* 273–282.

Barge, K., & Keyton, J. (1994). Contextualizing power and social influence in groups. In L. Frey (Ed.), *Group communication in context: Studies of natural groups* (pp. 85–105). Mahwah, NJ: Erlbaum.

Bargh, J. (1997). *The automaticity of everyday life.* Mahwah, NJ: Erlbaum.

Bargh, J. (1999, January 29). The most powerful manipulative messages are hiding in plain sight. *Chronicle of Higher Education,* p. B6.

Barker, J. (1999). *The discipline of teamwork: Participation and concertive control.* Thousand Oaks, CA: Sage.

Barker, L., & Watson, K. (2000). *Listen up: How to improve relationships, reduce stress, and be more productive by using the power of listening.* New York: St. Martin's Press.

Barlow, J. (1996, October 31). Ethics can boost the bottom line. *Houston Chronicle,* p. C1.

Barnes, M. K., & Duck, S. (1994). Everyday communicative contexts for social support. In B. Burleson, T. Albrecht, & I. Sarason (Eds.), *The communication of social support* (pp. 175–194). Thousand Oaks, CA: Sage.

Bartholomew, K., & Horowitz, L. M. (1991). Attachment styles among young adults: A test of a four-category model. *Journal of Personality and Social Psychology, 61,* 226–244.

Bartkus, K., Howell, R., Parent, C., & Hartman, C. (1997). Managerial antecedents and individual consequences of group cohesiveness in travel service selling. *Journal of Travel Research, 35,* 56–64.

Bass, A. (1999, June 30). Web of isolation: When cybersex subs for a social life. *Raleigh News & Observer,* p. 4E.

Bateson, M. C. (1990). *Composing a life.* New York: Penguin/Plume.

Battaglia, D., Richard, F., Datter, D., & Lord, C. (1998). Breaking up is (relatively) easy to do: A script for the dissolution of close relationships. *Journal of Social and Personal Relationships, 15,* 829–845.

Baxter, L. A. (1984). Trajectories of relationship disengagement. *Journal of Social and Personal Relationships, 7,* 141–178.

Baxter, L. A. (1985). Accomplishing relational disengagement. In S. Duck & D. Perlman (Eds.),

Understanding personal relationships: An inter-disciplinary approach (pp. 243–265). Thousand Oaks, CA: Sage.

Baxter, L. A. (1987). Symbols of relationship identity in relationship cultures. *Journal of Social and Personal Relationships, 4,* 261–279.

Baxter, L. A. (1990). Dialectical contradictions in relational development. *Journal of Social and Personal Relationships, 7,* 69–88.

Baxter, L. A. (1993). The social side of personal relationships: A dialectical perspective. In S. Duck (Ed.), *Understanding relationship processes, 3: Social context and relationships* (pp. 139–165). Thousand Oaks, CA: Sage.

Baxter, L. A. (2006). Relational dialectics theory: Multivocal dialogues of family communication. In D. O. Braithwaite & L. A. Baxter (Eds.), *Engaging theories in family communication: Multiple perspectives* (pp. 130–145). Thousand Oaks, CA: Sage.

Baxter, L. A., & Beebe, E. (2004). *The basics of communication research.* Belmont, CA: Wadsworth.

Baxter, L. A., & Montgomery, B. (1996). *Relating: Dialogues and dialectics.* New York: Guilford.

Baxter, L. A., & Simon, E. P. (1993). Relationship maintenance strategies and dialectical contradictions in personal relationships. *Journal of Social and Personal Relationships, 10,* 225–242.

Beatty, M. J., & Behnke, R. R. (1991). Effects of public speaking trait anxiety and intensity of speaking task on heart rate during performance. *Human Communication Research, 18,* 147–176.

Be civil. (1994, July 5). *The Wall Street Journal,* p. A1.

Beck, A. (1988). *Love is never enough.* New York: Harper & Row.

Becker, A., Burwell, R., Gilman, S., Herzog, D., & Hamburg, P. (2002). Eating behaviours and attitudes following prolonged exposure to television among ethnic Fijian adolescent girls. *British Journal of Psychiatry, 180,* 509–514.

Beckman, H. (2003). Difficult patients. In M. Feldman & J. Christensen (Eds.), *Behavioral medicine in primary care* (pp. 23–32). New York: McGraw-Hill.

Beder, S. (1998). *Global spin: The corporate assault on environmentalism.* White River Junction, VT: Chelsea Green.

Behnke, R., & Sawyer, C. (1999). Milestones of anticipatory public speaking anxiety. *Communication Education, 48,* 164–172.

Bell, A. (1989). *The complete manager's guide to interviewing.* Homewood, IL: Dow Jones–Irwin.

Belsky, J., & Pensky, E. (1988). Developmental history, personality, and family relationships: Toward an emergent family system. In R. A. Hinde & J. Stevenson-Hinde (Eds.), *Relationships within families: Mutual influences* (pp. 193–217). Oxford, UK: Clarendon.

Benenson, J., Gordon, A., & Roy, R. (2000). Children's evaluative appraisals of competition in tetrads versus dyads. *Small Group Research, 31,* 635–652.

Berg, J. H. (1987). Responsiveness and self-disclosure. In V. J. Derlega & J. H. Berg (Eds.), *Self-disclosure: Theory, research, and therapy.* New York: Plenum.

Berger, C. (1988). Communicating under uncertainty. In M. Roloff & G. Miller (Eds.), *Interpersonal processes: New directions in communication research* (pp. 39–62). Newbury Park, CA: Sage.

Berger, C. K. (1977). The covering law perspective as a theoretical basis for the study of human communication. *Communication Quarterly, 25,* 7–18.

Berger, P. (1969). *A rumor of angels: Modern society and the rediscovery of the supernatural.* Garden City, NY: Doubleday.

Bergner, R. M., & Bergner, L. L. (1990). Sexual misunderstanding: A descriptive and pragmatic formulation. *Psychotherapy, 27,* 464–467.

Berko, R., Wolvin, A., & Wolvin, D. (1992). *Communicating: A social and career focus* (5th ed.). Boston: Houghton Mifflin.

Berne, E. (1964). *Games people play.* New York: Grove Press.

Bertman, S. (1998). *Hyperculture: The human cost of speed.* Westport, CT: Praeger.

Bevan, J. (2003). Expectancy violation theory and sexual resistance in close, cross-sex relationships. *Communication Monographs, 70,* 68–82.

Bikini Kill. (1991). *Bikini Kill, 1,* n.p.

Bingham, S. (Ed.). (1994). *Conceptualizing sexual harassment as discursive practice.* Westport, CT: Praeger.

Bingham, S. (1996). Sexual harassment: On the job, on the campus. In J. T. Wood (Ed.), *Gendered relationships* (pp. 233–252). Mountain View, CA: Mayfield.

Bippus, A., & Daly, J. (1999). What do people think causes stage fright? Naïve attributions about the reasons for public speaking anxiety. *Communication Education, 48,* 63–72.

Birdwhistell, R. (1970). *Kinesics and context*. Philadelphia: University of Pennsylvania Press.

Blair, C., Brown, J., & Baxter, L. (1994). Disciplining the feminine. *Quarterly Journal of Speech, 80,* 383–409.

Bocella, K. (2001, January 31). Eating disorders spread among minority girls, women. *Raleigh News & Observer,* p. 5E.

Bollier, D. (2002). *Silent theft: The private plunder of our common wealth.* New York: Routledge.

Bolton, R. (1986). Listening is more than merely hearing. In J. Stewart (Ed.), *Bridges, not walls* (4th ed., pp. 159–179). New York: Random House.

Bookmark. (1999, July 9). *Chronicle of Higher Education,* p. A29.

Borchers, T. (2006). *Rhetorical theory: An introduction.* Belmont, CA: Thomson Wadsworth.

Bordo, S. (1999). *The male body: A new look at men in public and in private.* New York: Farrar, Straus, & Giroux.

Bornstein, M., & Bradley, R. (Eds.). (2003). *Socioeconomic status, parenting, and child development.* Mahwah, NJ: Erlbaum.

Boulding, K. (1990). *Three faces of power.* Thousand Oaks, CA: Sage.

Bourhis, J., & Allen, M. (1992). Meta-analysis of the relationship between communication apprehension and cognitive performance. *Communication Education, 41,* 68–76.

Bowen, S. P., & Michal-Johnson, P. (1995). HIV/AIDS: A crucible for understanding the dark side of sexual interactions. In S. W. Duck & J. T. Wood (Eds.), *Understanding relationship processes, 5: Confronting relationship challenges* (pp. 150–180). Thousand Oaks, CA: Sage.

Bowen, S. P., & Michal-Johnson, P. (1996). Being sexual in the shadow of AIDS. In J. T. Wood (Ed.), *Gendered relationships* (pp. 177–196). Mountain View, CA: Mayfield.

Bowlby, J. (1973). *Separation: Attachment and loss* (Vol. 2). New York: Basic Books.

Bowlby, J. (1988). *A secure base: Parent–child attachment and healthy human development.* New York: Basic Books.

Bowles, J. G. (1990, September 24). The human side of quality. *Fortune,* pp. 47–49, 65.

Bowman, L. (2006, May 19). Teens say dates often are violent. *Raleigh News & Observer,* p. 4A.

Bradbury, T. N., & Fincham, F. D. (1990). Attributions in marriage: Review and critique. *Psychological Bulletin, 107,* 3–33.

Braithwaite, C. (1990). Communicative silence: A crosscultural study of Basso's hypothesis. In D. Carbaugh (Ed.), *Cultural communication and intercultural contact* (pp. 321–327). Hillsdale, NJ: Erlbaum.

Braxton, G. (1999, June 5). Minorities glaringly absent from fall television lineup. *Richmond Times–Dispatch,* pp. F8–F9.

Brehm, S., Miller, R., Perlman, D., & Campbell, S. (2001). *Intimate relations* (3rd ed.). New York: McGraw-Hill.

Brilhart, J., & Galanes, G. (1995). *Effective group discussion* (8th ed.). Dubuque, IA: WCB Brown & Benchmark.

Brooks, D. (2001, April 30). Time to do everything except think. *Newsweek,* p. 71.

Brooks, R., & Goldstein, S. (2001). *Raising resilient children.* New York: Contemporary Books.

Brown, J., & Cantor, J. (2000). An agenda for research on youth and the media. *Journal of Adolescent Health, 27,* 2–7.

Brownell, J. (2002). *Listening: Attitudes, principles, and skills* (2nd ed.). Boston: Allyn & Bacon.

Bruess, C., & Hoefs, A. (2006). The cat puzzle recovered: Composing relationships through family ritual. In J. T. Wood & S. W. Duck (Eds.), *Composing relationships: Communication in everyday life* (pp. 65–75). Belmont, CA: Thomson Wadsworth.

Buber, M. (1957). Distance and relation. *Psychiatry, 20,* 97–104.

Buber, M. (1970). *I and thou* (Walter Kaufmann, Trans.). New York: Scribner's.

Buck, R. (1988). Nonverbal communication: Spontaneous and symbolic aspects. *American Behavioral Scientist, 31,* 341–354.

Buckley, M. F. (1992). Focus on research: We listen a book a day; we speak a book a week: Learning from Walter Loban. *Language Arts, 69,* 622–626.

Bucy, E. (Ed.). (2005). *Living in the information age* (2nd ed.). Belmont, CA: Wadsworth.

Burgoon, J. (1993). Interpersonal expectations, expectation violations, and emotional communication. *Journal of Language and Social Psychology, 12,* 30–48.

Burgoon, J., Buller, D., & Woodhall, G. (1989). *Nonverbal communication: The unspoken dialogue.* New York: Harper & Row.

Buss, A. H. (2001). *Psychological dimensions of the self.* Thousand Oaks, CA: Sage.

Butler, J. (1990). Performative acts and gender constitution: An essay in phenomenology and feminist theory. In S. Case (Ed.), *Performing feminisms: Feminist critical theory and theatre* (pp. 270–282). Baltimore: Johns Hopkins University Press.

Butler, J. (1993). *Bodies that matter: On the discursive limits of "sex."* New York: Routledge.

Buunk, B., & Mutsaers, W. (1999). Equity perceptions and marital satisfaction in former and current marriage: A study among the remarried. *Journal of Social and Personal Relationships, 16,* 123–132.

Cairncross, F. (2002). The roots of revolution and the trendspotter's guide to new communication. In E. Bucy (Ed.), *Living in the information age* (pp. 3–10). Belmont, CA: Wadsworth.

Calvert, S., Jordan, A., & Cocking, R. (2002). *Children in the digital age: The role of entertainment technologies in children's development.* Westport, CT: Praeger.

Campbell, K. (1989). *Man cannot speak for her: II. Key texts of the early feminists.* New York: Greenwood.

Campbell, R. (2004). *Media and culture: An introduction to mass communication* (4th ed.). New York: St. Martin's Press.

Campbell, R., Martin, C., & Fabos, B. (2004). *Media and culture: An introduction to mass communication.* Boston: Bedford/St. Martin's.

Canary, D., & Stafford, L. (Eds.). (1994). *Communication and relational maintenance.* New York: Academic Press.

Cancian, F. (1989). Love and the rise of capitalism. In B. Risman & P. Schwartz (Eds.), *Gender in intimate relationships* (pp. 12–25). Belmont, CA: Wadsworth.

Cannell, C., & Kahn, R. (1968). Interviewing. In G. Lindzey & E. Aronson (Eds.), *The handbook of social psychology* (Vol. 2, 2nd ed., pp. 569–584). Reading, MA: Addison-Wesley.

Capella, J. N. (1991). The biological origins of automated patterns of human interaction. *Communication Theory, 1,* 4–35.

Carbaugh, D. (1998). "I can't do that! But I can actually see around the corners": American Indian students and the study of public communication. In J. Martin, T. Nakayama, & L. Flores (Eds.), *Readings in cultural context* (pp. 160–171). Mountain View, CA: Mayfield.

Carl, W. (1998). A sign of the times. In J. T. Wood, *But I thought you meant . . . : Misunderstandings in human communication* (pp. 195–208). Mountain View, CA: Mayfield.

Carl, W. (2006). <where r u? here u?>: Everyday communication with relational technologies. In J. T. Wood & S. W. Duck (Eds.), *Composing relationships: Communication in everyday life* (pp. 96–109). Belmont, CA: Thomson Wadsworth.

Carnes, J. (1994, Spring). An uncommon language. *Teaching Tolerance,* pp. 56–63.

Carvin, A. (2002). Mind the gap: The digital divide as the civil rights issue of the new millennium. In E. Bucy (Ed.), *Living in the information age* (pp. 251–254). Belmont, CA: Wadsworth.

Caspi, A., & Harbener, E. S. (1990). Continuity and change: Assortive marriage and the consistency of personality in adulthood. *Journal of Personality and Social Psychology, 58,* 250–258.

Cassirer, E. (1944). *An essay on man.* New Haven, CT: Yale University Press.

Cates, J. R., Herndon, N. L., Schultz, S. L., & Darroch, J. E. (2004). *Our voices, our lives, our futures: Youth and sexually transmitted diseases.* Chapel Hill: University of North Carolina at Chapel Hill.

Caughlin, J., & Ramey, M. (2005). The demand/withdraw pattern of communication in parent-adolescent dyads. *Personal Relationships, 12,* 337–355.

Caughlin, J., & Vangelisti, A. (2000). An individual differences explanation of why married couples engage in the demand/withdraw pattern of conflict. *Journal of Social and Personal Relationships, 17,* 523–551.

Centers for Disease Control. (1998). *Trends in the HIV and AIDS epidemic, 1998.* Atlanta, GA: Author.

Chan, Y. (1999). Density, crowding, and factors intervening in their relationship: Evidence from a hyperdense metropolis. *Social Indicators Research, 48,* 103–134.

Chen, V., & Starosta, W. (1998). *Foundations of intercultural communication.* Boston: Allyn & Bacon.

Chesebro, J. W. (1995). Communication technologies as cognitive systems. In J. T. Wood & R. B. Gregg (Eds.), *The future of the field* (pp. 15–46). Cresskill, NJ: Hampton.

Christensen, A., & Heavey, C. (1990). Gender and social structure in the demand/withdraw pattern in marital conflict. *Journal of Personality and Social Psychology, 59,* 73–81.

Christianson, P., & Roberts, D. (1998). *It's not only rock & roll: Popular music in the lives of adolescents.* Cresskill, NJ: Hampton Press.

Cissna, K. N. L., & Sieburg, E. (1986). Patterns of interactional confirmation and disconfirmation.

In J. Stewart (Ed.), *Bridges, not walls* (4th ed., pp. 230–239). New York: Random House.

Clair, R. P. (1993). The use of framing devices to sequester organizational narratives: Hegemony and harassment. *Communication Monographs, 60,* 113–136.

Clair, R. P. (1998). *Organizing silence: A world of possibilities.* Albany: State University of New York Press.

Clark, R. A. (1998). A comparison of topics and objectives in a cross-section of young men's and women's everyday conversations. In D. Canary & K. Dindia (Eds.), *Sex differences and similarities in communication* (pp. 303–319). Mahwah, NJ: Erlbaum.

Cloven, D. H., & Roloff, M. E. (1991). Sense-making activities and interpersonal conflict: Communicative cures for the mulling blues. *Western Journal of Speech Communication, 55,* 134–158.

Cockburn-Wootten, C., & Zorn, T. (2006). Cabbages and headache cures: Work stories within the family. In J. T. Wood & S. W. Duck (Eds.), *Composing relationships: Communication in everyday life* (pp. 137–145). Belmont, CA: Thomson Wadsworth.

Cohen, J. (2001, January 18). On the Internet, love *really* is blind. *New York Times,* pp. 1, 9.

Collins, P. H. (1998). *Fighting words: Black women and the search for justice.* Minneapolis: University of Minnesota Press.

Communication Research, 6. (1979, January). [Special issue devoted to uses and gratification theory.]

Condry, S. M., Condry, J. C., & Pogatshnik, L. W. (1983). Sex differences: A study of the ear of the beholder. *Sex Roles, 9,* 697–704.

Conley, T. (1990). *Rhetoric in the European tradition.* New York: Longman.

Conquergood, D. (1986). Is it real? Watching television with Laotian refugees. *Directions, 2,* 71–74.

Conquergood, D., Friesema, P., Hunter, A., & Mansbridge, J. (1990). *Dispersed ethnicity and community integration: Newcomers and established residents in the Albany Park area of Chicago.* Evanston, IL: Center for Urban Affairs and Policy Research, Northwestern University.

Conrad, C. (1995). Was Pogo right? In J. T. Wood & R. B. Gregg (Eds.), *The future of the field* (pp. 183–208). Cresskill, NJ: Hampton.

Conrad, C., & Poole, M. (2004). *Strategic organizational communication in a global economy* (7th ed.). New York: Harcourt.

Cooley, C. H. (1912). *Human nature and the social order.* New York: Scribner's.

Cooper, J., & Weaver, K. (2003). *Gender and computers: Understanding the digital divide.* Mahwah, NJ: Erlbaum.

Cooper, L. (1999). Listening competency in the workplace: A model for training. *Business Communication Quarterly, 60,* 75–84.

Cooper, L., Seibold, D., & Suchner, R. (1997). Listening in organizations: An analysis of error structures in models of listening competency. *Communication Research Reports, 14,* 3.

Cornwell, B., & Lundgren, D. (2001). Love on the Internet: Involvement and misrepresentation in romantic relationships in cyberspace vs. realspace. *Computers in Human Behavior, 17,* 197–211.

Cose, E. (2002). *The envy of the world.* New York: Simon & Schuster/Atria.

Cose, E. (2004). *Beyond Brown v. Board: The final battle for excellence in American education.* Mahwah, NJ: Rockefeller Foundation.

Cox, J. R. (1989). The fulfillment of time: King's "I have a dream" speech (August 28, 1963). In M. C. Leff & F. J. Kaufeld (Eds.), *Texts in context: Critical dialogues on significant episodes in American rhetoric* (pp. 181–204). Davis, CA: Hermagoras.

Cox, J. R. (2006a). *Environmental communication and the public sphere.* Thousand Oaks, CA: Sage.

Cox, J. R. (2006b). Personal communication.

Cox, J. R., & McCloskey, M. (1996). Advocacy and the Istook amendment: Efforts to restrict the civic speech of nonprofit organizations in the 104th U.S. Congress, *Journal of Applied Communication Research, 24,* 273–291.

Crandall, F., & Wallace, M. (1998). *Work and rewards in the virtual workplace: A "new deal" for organizations and employees.* Wooster, OH: AMACOM.

Crockett, W. H. (1965). Cognitive complexity and impression formation. In B. A. Maher (Ed.), *Progress in experimental personality research* (Vol. 2, pp. 47–90). New York: Academic Press.

Cronen, V., Pearce, W. B., & Snavely, L. (1979). A theory of rule-structure and types of episodes and a study of perceived enmeshment in undesired repetitive patterns ("URPs"). In D. Nimmo (Ed.), *Communication yearbook* (Vol. 3). New Brunswick, NJ: Transaction Books.

Crowley, G. (1995, March 6). Dialing the stress-meter down. *Newsweek,* p. 62.

Cunningham, J. A., Strassberg, D. S., & Haan, B. (1986). Effects of intimacy and sex-role congruency on self-disclosure. *Journal of Social and Clinical Psychology, 4,* 393–401.

Dainton, M. (2006). Cat walk conversations: Everyday communication in dating relationships. In J. T. Wood & S. W. Duck (Eds.), *Composing relationships: Communication in everyday life.* Belmont, CA: Thomson Wadsworth.

Dainton, M., & Zelley, E. (2006). Social exchange theories: Interdependence and equity. In D. O. Braithwaite & L. A. Baxter (Eds.), *Engaging theories in family communication: Multiple perspectives* (pp. 243–259). Thousand Oaks, CA: Sage.

Darling, A., & Dannels, D. (2003). Practicing engineers talk about the importance of talk: A report on the role of oral communication in the workplace. *Communication Education, 52,* 1–16.

Davis, F. (1991). *Moving the mountain: The women's movement in America since 1960.* New York: Simon & Schuster.

Davis, K. (1977). The care and cultivation of the corporate grapevine. In R. Huseman, C. Logue, & D. Freshley (Eds.), *Readings in interpersonal and organizational communication* (3rd ed., pp. 131–136). Boston: Holbrook.

Davis, K. (1980). Management communication and the grapevine. In S. Ferguson & S. Ferguson (Eds.), *Intercom: Readings in organizational communication* (pp. 55–66). Rochelle Park, NJ: Hayden.

Davis, R. (1997). *The myth of black ethnicity: Monophylety, diversity, and the dilemma of identity.* Greenwich, CT: Ablex.

Davis, S., & Kieffer, J. (1998). Restaurant servers influence tipping behaviors. *Psychological Reports, 83,* 223–236.

Davison, K., & Birch, L. (2001). Weight, status, parent reaction, and self-concept in five-year-old girls. *Pediatrics, 107,* 42–53.

Deal, T., & Kennedy, A. (1999). *The new corporate cultures: Revitalizing the workplace after downsizing, mergers, and reengineering.* Reading, MA: Perseus Books.

DeCremer, D., & Leonardelli, G. J. (2003). Group dynamics. *Theory, Research, and Practice, 7,* 168–174.

DeFrancisco, V. (1991). The sounds of silence: How men silence women in marital relations. *Discourse & Society, 2,* 413–423.

Delgado, F. (1998). Moving beyond the screen: Hollywood and Mexican American stereotypes. In Y. Kamalipour & T. Carilli (Eds.), *Cultural diversity in the U.S. media* (pp. 169–182). Albany: State University of New York Press.

Delia, J., Clark, R. A., & Switzer, D. (1974). Cognitive complexity and impression formation in informal social interaction. *Speech Monographs, 41,* 299–308.

Denning, P. (1998). *Talking back to the machine: Computers and human aspiration.* New York: Copernicus Press.

Denning, P. (2001). *The invisible future: The seamless integration of technology into everyday life.* New York: McGraw-Hill Professional.

Dennis, E., & Merrill, J. (2006). *Media debates: Great issues for the digital age* (4th ed.). Belmont, CA: Thomson Wadsworth.

Derlega, V. J., & Berg, J. H. (1987). *Self-disclosure: Research, theory, and therapy.* New York: Plenum.

Derlega, V. J., Metts, S., Petronio, S., & Margulis, S. (1993). *Self-disclosure.* Thousand Oaks, CA: Sage.

Desjardins, M. (2006). Ephemeral culture/eBay culture: Film collectibles and fan investments. In K. Hillis & M. Petit, with N. Epley (Eds.), *Everyday eBay: Culture, collecting, and desire* (pp. 31–43). New York: Routledge.

Dewey, J. (1910). *How we think.* Boston: Heath.

Dickson, F. (1995). The best is yet to be: Research on long-lasting marriages. In J. T. Wood & S. W. Duck (Eds.), *Understanding relationship processes: 6: Understudied relationships* (pp. 22–50). Thousand Oaks, CA: Sage.

Did you know? (1998, September 30). *Raleigh News & Observer,* p. F1.

Dillard, J. P., & Pfau, M. (2002). *The persuasion handbook: Developments in theory and practice.* Thousand Oaks, CA: Sage.

Dillon, J. (1990). *The practice of questioning.* New York: Routledge.

Dindia, K. (1994). A multiphasic view of relationship maintenance strategies. In D. Canary & L. Stafford (Eds.), *Communication and relational maintenance* (pp. 91–112). New York: Academic Press.

Dindia, K. (2000). Self-disclosure, identity, and relationship development. In K. Dindia & S. W. Duck (Eds.), *Communication and personal relationships* (pp. 147–162). Chichester: Wiley.

Dixson, M., & Duck, S. W. (1993). Understanding relationship processes: Uncovering the human search for meaning. In S. W. Duck (Ed.), *Understanding relationship processes, 1: Individuals in relationships* (pp. 175–206). Thousand Oaks, CA: Sage.

Donahue, H., Leonard, J., & Wiliams, M. (Writers/Directors/Producers). (1999). *The Blair Witch Project* [Motion picture]. United States: Artisan Entertainment.

Douglas, S. (2004, May 10). Confronting the mommy myth. *In These Times*, pp. 28–29.

Dow, B. (2004). Fixing feminism: Women's liberation and the rhetoric of television documentary. *Quarterly Journal of Speech, 90*, 53–80.

Drummond, K., & Hopper, R. (1993). Acknowledgment tokens in series. *Communication Reports, 6*, 47–53.

Duck, S. W. (1982). A topography of relationship disengagement and dissolution. In S. W. Duck (Ed.), *Personal relationships, 4: Dissolving personal relationships* (pp. 1–30). New York: Academic Press.

Duck, S. W. (1990). Relationships as unfinished business: Out of the frying pan and into the 1990s. *Journal of Social and Personal Relationships, 7*, 5–24.

Duck, S. W. (1992). *Human relationships* (2nd ed.). Thousand Oaks, CA: Sage.

Duck, S. W. (1994a). *Meaningful relationships*. Thousand Oaks, CA: Sage.

Duck, S. W. (1994b). Steady as (s)he goes: Relational maintenance as a shared meaning system. In D. Canary & L. Stafford (Eds.), *Communication and relational maintenance* (pp. 45–60). New York: Academic Press.

Duck, S. W. (2006). The play, playfulness and the players: Everyday interaction as improvised rehearsal of relationships. In J. T. Wood & S. W. Duck (Eds.), *Composing relationships: Communication in everyday life* (pp. 15–23). Belmont, CA: Wadsworth.

Duck, S. W., & Wood, J. T. (Eds.). (1995). *Understanding relationship processes, 5: Confronting relationship challenges*. Thousand Oaks, CA: Sage.

Duck, S. W., & Wood, J. T. (2006). What goes up may come down: Sex and gendered patterns in relational dissolution. In M. A. Fine & J. H. Harvey (Eds.), *The handbook of divorce and relationship dissolution* (pp. 169–187). Mahwah, NJ: Erlbaum.

Earley, P., & Gibson, C. (2002). *Multinational work teams*. Mahwah, NJ: Erlbaum.

Eastman, S., & Billings, A. (2000). Sportscasting and news reporting: The power of gender bias. *Journal of Sport and Social Issues, 24*, 192–213.

Edelstein, A. (1993). Thinking about the criterion variable in agenda-setting research. *Journal of Communication, 48*, 85–99.

Egan, G. (1973). Listening as empathic support. In J. Stewart (Ed.), *Bridges, not walls*. Reading, MA: Addison-Wesley.

Einhorn, L. (2000). *The Native American oral tradition: Voices of the spirit and soul*. Westport, CT: Praeger.

Ellis, A., & Harper, R. (1977). *A new guide to rational living*. North Hollywood, CA: Wilshire.

Emmons, S. (1998, February 3). The look on his face: Yes, it's culture shock. *Raleigh News & Observer*, p. 5E.

Entman, R. (1994). African Americans according to TV news. Special issue: Race: America's rawest nerve. *Media Studies Journal, 8*, 29–38.

Entman, R., & Rojecki, A. (2000). *The Black image in the White mind: Media and race in America*. Chicago: University of Chicago Press.

Erbert, L. (2000). Conflict and dialectics: Perceptions of dialectical contradictions in marital conflict. *Journal of Social and Personal Relationships, 17*, 638–659.

Estes, W. K. (1989). Learning theory. In A. Lessold & R. Glaser (Eds.), *Foundations for a psychology of education*. Mahwah, NJ: Erlbaum.

Estioko-Griffin, A., & Griffin, P. (1997). Woman the hunter: The Agta. In C. Brettell & C. Sargent (Eds.), *Gender in cross cultural perspectives* (pp. 123–149). Englewood Cliffs, NJ: Prentice Hall.

Evans, D. (1993, March 1). The wrong examples. *Newsweek*, p. 10.

Fackelmann, K. (2006, March 6). Arguing hurts the heart in more ways than one. *USA Today*, p. 10D.

Farr, J. (Ed.). (2003). *Stereotype threat effects in employment settings*. [Special issue]. *Human Performance, 16*.

Fehr, B. (1993). How do I love thee? Let me consult my prototype. In S. W. Duck (Ed.), *Understanding relationship processes, 1: Individuals in relationships* (pp. 87–122). Thousand Oaks, CA: Sage.

Feldman, C., & Ridley, C. (2000). The role of conflict-based responses and outcomes in male domestic violence toward female partners. *Journal of Social and Personal Relationships, 17*, 552–573.

Felmlee, D. H. (2001). No couple is an island: A social network perspective on dyadic stability. *Social Forces, 79*, 1259–1287.

Ferrante, J. (1995). *Sociology: A global perspective* (2nd ed.). Belmont, CA: Wadsworth.

Fincham, F. D., & Bradbury, T. N. (1987). The impact of attributions in marriage: A longitudinal analysis.

Journal of Personality and Social Psychology, 53, 510–517.

Fisher, A. (1998, June 22). Don't blow your new job. *Fortune, 137,* 159–162.

Fisher, B. A. (1987). *Interpersonal communication: The pragmatics of human relationships.* New York: Random House.

Fisher, H. (2000). *The first sex: The natural talents of women and how they are changing the world.* New York: Ballantine.

Fiske, J. (1987). *Television culture.* London: Methuen.

Fitch, N. E. (Ed.). (1999). *How sweet the sound: The spirit of African American history.* New York: Harcourt College.

Fitzgerald, T. (2006, May 18). Going wireless most places you go. *New York Times,* p. C7.

Fitzpatrick, M. A. (1988). *Between husbands and wives: Communication in marriage.* Thousand Oaks, CA: Sage.

Flanigin, A., Farinola, W., & Metzger, M. (2000). The technical code of the Internet/World Wide Web. *Critical Studies in Media Communication, 17,* 409–428.

Fletcher, G. J., & Fincham, F. D. (1991). Attribution in close relationships. In G. J. Fletcher & F. D. Fincham (Eds.), *Cognition in close relationships* (pp. 7–35). Mahwah, NJ: Erlbaum.

Flynn, L. (2006, May 3). A romantic read between cell calls. *New York Times,* p. E3.

Foddy, W. (1993). *Constructing questions for interviews and questionnaires.* Cambridge, UK: Cambridge University Press.

Foeman, A., & Nance, T. (1999). From miscegenation to multiculturalism: Perceptions and stages of interracial relationship development. *Journal of Black Studies, 29,* 540–557.

Foss, S., Foss, K., & Trapp, R. (1991). *Contemporary perspectives on rhetoric* (2nd ed.). Prospect Heights, IL: Waveland.

Foucault, M. (1970). *The order of things: An archaeology of the human sciences.* New York: Pantheon.

Foucault, M. (1972a). The discourse on language. In *The archaeology of knowledge* (Sheridan Smith, Trans., pp. 215–237). New York: Pantheon.

Foucault, M. (1972b). In C. Gordon (Ed.), *Power/ knowledge: Selected interviews and other writings 1972–1977* (C. Gordon, L. Marshall, J. Mepham, & K. Soper, Trans.). New York: Pantheon.

Foucault, M. (1978). Politics and the study of discourse (C. Gordon, Trans.). *Ideology and Consciousness, 3,* 7–26.

Fox, G. (1998). *Everyday etiquette: A guide to modern manners.* New York: Berkeley Books.

Franklin, M., & Ramage, J. (1999). Til a long-distance job do us part. *Kiplinger's Personal Finance, 53,* p. 56.

French, H. (2006, June 3). Online throngs impose a stern morality in China. *New York Times,* pp. A1, A7.

Frey, L. (Ed.). (2003). *The handbook of group communication theory & research* (2nd ed.). Thousand Oaks, CA: Sage.

Friedlin. J. (2006, June). "Is it easier to get a gun or a restraining order?" *Marie Claire,* pp. 92–100.

Gaines, S., Jr. (1995). Relationships between members of cultural minorities. In J. T. Wood & S. W. Duck (Eds.), *Understanding relationship processes, 6: Understudied relationships: Off the beaten track* (pp. 51–88). Thousand Oaks, CA: Sage.

Galvin, K. (2006). Gender and family interaction: Dress rehearsal for an improvisation? In B. Dow & J. T. Wood (Eds.), *Handbook of gender and communication research* (pp. 41–55). Thousand Oaks, CA: Sage.

Galvin, K., Dickson, F., & Marrow, S. (2006). Systems theory: Patterns and (w)holes in family communication. In D. O. Braithwaite & L. A. Baxter (Eds.), *Engaging theories in family communication: Multiple perspectives* (pp. 309–324). Thousand Oaks, CA: Sage.

Gants, D. (1999, April 9). Peer review for cyberspace: Evaluating scholarly Web sites. *Chronicle of Higher Education,* p. B8.

Garner, T. (1994). Oral rhetorical practice in African American culture. In A. Gonzaléz, M. Houston, & V. Chen (Eds.), *Our voices: Essays in culture, ethnicity, and communication* (pp. 81–91). Los Angeles: Roxbury.

Gates, B. (1999, May 31). Why the PC will not die. *Newsweek,* p. 64.

Gates, H. L. (1992). *Loose canons: Notes on the culture wars.* New York: Oxford University Press.

Gerbner, G. (1990). Epilogue: Advancing on the path of righteousness (maybe). In N. Signorielli & M. Morgan (Eds.), *Cultivation analysis: New directions in media effects research* (pp. 250–261). Thousand Oaks, CA: Sage.

Gerbner, G. (1997a). *The crisis of the cultural environment: Media and democracy in the 21st century.* Northampton, MA: Media Education Foundation (http://www.mediaed.org).

Gerbner, G. (1997b). *The electronic storyteller: Televi-*

sion and the cultivation of values. Northampton, MA: Media Education Foundation (http://www .mediaed.org).

Gerbner, G., Gross, L., Morgan, M., & Signorielli, N. (1986). Living with television: The dynamics of the cultivation process. In J. Bryant & D. Zillmann (Eds.), *Perspectives on media effects* (pp. 17–40). Mahwah, NJ: Erlbaum.

Gergen, K. (1991). *The saturated self: Dilemmas of identity in contemporary life.* New York: Basic Books.

Gerson, K. (2004). Moral dilemmas, moral strategies, and the transformation of gender: Lessons from two generations of work and family change. In J. Spade & C. Valentine (Eds.), *The kaleidoscope of gender* (pp. 413–424). Belmont, CA: Wadsworth.

Gerstel, N., & Gross, H. (1985). *Commuter marriage.* New York: Guilford.

Gibb, J. R. (1961). Defensive communication. *Journal of Communication, 11,* 141–148.

Gibb, J. R. (1964). Climate for trust formation. In L. Bradford, J. Gibb, & K. Benne (Eds.), *T-group theory and laboratory method* (pp. 279–309). New York: Wiley.

Gibb, J. R. (1970). Sensitivity training as a medium for personal growth and improved interpersonal relationships. *Interpersonal Development, 1,* 6–31.

Gilman, S. (1999a). *Creating beauty to cure the soul: Race and psychology in the shaping of aesthetic surgery.* Durham, NC: Duke University Press.

Gilman, S. (1999b). *Making the body beautiful: A cultural history of aesthetic surgery.* Princeton, NJ: Princeton University Press.

Gitlin, T. (1980). *The whole world is watching: Mass media in the making and unmaking of the new left.* Berkeley: University of California Press.

Gitlin, T. (2002). *Media unlimited: How the torrent of images and sounds overwhelms us.* New York: Metropolitan.

Gitlin, T. (2005). Supersaturation, or the media torrent and disposable feeling. In. E. Bucy (Ed.), *Living in the information age: A new media reader* (2nd ed., pp. 139–146). Belmont, CA: Thomson Wadsworth.

Glazer, A. (2006, May 20). LAPD cops get personal via blog. *Raleigh News & Observer,* p. 6A.

Glenn, D. (2002, November 22). Practices, identities, and desires. *Chronicle of Higher Education,* pp. A20–A21.

Global reach. (2003, September 30). *Global Internet statistics (by language).* Retrieved December 20,

2003, from http://global-reach.biz/globstats/index .php.3

Godar, S. H., & Ferris, S. P. (2004). *Virtual and collaborative teams: Process, technologies and practice.* London: Idea Group Publishing.

Goldsmith, D., & Fulfs, P. (1999). You just don't have the evidence: An analysis of claims and evidence in Deborah Tannen's *You Just Don't Understand.* In M. Roloff (Ed.), *Communication yearbook, 22* (pp. 1–49). Thousand Oaks, CA: Sage.

Goleman, D., McKee, A., & Boyatzis, R. (2002). *Primal leadership: Realizing the power of emotional intelligence.* Cambridge, MA: Harvard Business School Press.

González, A., Houston, M., & Chen, V. (Eds.). (2004). *Our voices: Essays in culture, ethnicity, and communication* (4th ed.). Los Angeles: Roxbury.

Goode, E. (2001, August 1). 20% of girls report abuse by a date. *Raleigh News & Observer,* p. 10A.

Gottlieb, L. (2000). *Stick figure: A diary of my former self.* New York: Simon & Schuster.

Gottman, J. M. (1993). The roles of conflict engagement, escalation or avoidance in marital interaction: A longitudinal view of five types of couples. *Journal of Consulting and Clinical Psychology, 61,* 6–15.

Gottman, J. M., & Carrère, S. (1994). Why can't men and women get along? Developmental roots and marital inequities. In D. Canary & L. Stafford (Eds.), *Communication and relational maintenance* (pp. 203–229). New York: Academic Press.

Gottman, J., & DeClaire, J. (2001). *The relationship cure: A five-step guide for building better connections with family, friends, and lovers.* New York: Crown Books.

Graham, J. M., & Conoley, C. (2006). The role of marital attributions in the relationship between life stressors and marital quality. *Personal Relationships, 13,* 231–241.

Greenberg, S. (1997, Spring/Summer Special Issue). The loving ties that bind. *Newsweek,* pp. 68–72.

Greene, K., Frey, L., Derlega, V. (2002). Interpersonalizing AIDS: Attending to the personal and social relationships of individuals living with HIV and/or AIDS. *Journal of Social and Personal Relationships, 19,* 5–18.

Greenfield, L. (2002). *Girl culture.* San Francisco: Chronicle Books.

Griffin, C. (2006). *Invitation to public speaking* (2nd ed.). Belmont, CA: Thomson Wadsworth.

Gronbeck, B. (1999). *Paradigms of speech communi-*

cation studies: Looking back toward the future. Needham Heights, MA: Allyn & Bacon.

Gronbeck, B. E., McKerro, R., Ehninger, D., & Monroe, A. H. (1994). *Principles and types of speech communication* (12th ed.). Glenview, IL: Scott, Foresman.

Gross, N. (1996, December 23). Zap! Splat! Smarts? *Newsweek,* pp. 64–71.

Grossberg, L. (1997). *Bringing it all back home: Essays in cultural studies.* Durham, NC: Duke University Press.

Grossberg, L., Wartella, E., & Whitney, C. (1998). *Mediamaking: Mass media in a popular culture.* Thousand Oaks, CA: Sage.

Gudykunst, W. (1991). *Bridging differences: Effective intergroup communication.* Newbury Park, CA: Sage.

Gudykunst, W. (1995). Anxiety uncertainty management (AUM) theory: Current status. In R. Wiseman (Ed.), *Intercultural communication theory* (pp. 33–71). Newbury Park, CA: Sage.

Gueguen, N., & De Gail, M. (2003). The effect of smiling on helping behavior: Smiling and good Samaritan behavior. *Communication Reports, 16,* 133–140.

Guerrero, L. (1996). Attachment style differences in intimacy and involvement: A test of the four-category model. *Communication Monographs, 63,* 269–292.

Guerrero, L., & Floyd, K. (2006). *Nonverbal communication in close relationships.* Mahwah, NJ: Erlbaum.

Guldner, G. (2003). *Long-distance relationships.* Corona, CA: J. F. Milne Publications.

Gunns, R., Johnston, L., & Hudson, S. (2002). Victim selection and kinematics: A point-light investigation of vulnerability to attack. *Journal of Nonverbal Behavior, 26,* 129–158.

Guterl, F. (2003, September 8). Overloaded? *Newsweek,* pp. E4–E8.

Hacker, K., Gross, B., & Townley, C. (1998). Employee attitudes regarding electronic mail policies: A case study. *Management Communication Quarterly, 11,* 422–432.

Hakansson, J., & Montgomery, H. (2003). Empathy as an interpersonal phenomenon. *Journal of Social and Personal Relationships, 20,* 267–284.

Hall, D. (1995). *Revolution grrrl style now! The rhetoric and subcultural practices of Riot Grrrls.* Unpublished master's thesis, Department of Communication Studies, University of North Carolina, Chapel Hill.

Hall, E. T. (1968). Proxemics. *Current Anthropology, 9,* 83–108.

Hall, E. T. (1969). *The hidden dimension.* New York: Anchor.

Hall, E. T. (1981). *Beyond culture.* New York: Doubleday.

Hall, J. A. (1987). On explaining gender differences: The case of nonverbal communication. In P. Shaver & C. Hendricks (Eds.), *Sex and gender* (pp. 177–200). Thousand Oaks, CA: Sage.

Hall, J. A., Coats, E., & Smith-LeBeau, L. (2004). Nonverbal behavior and the vertical dimension of social relations: A meta-analysis. Cited in M. L. Knapp & J. A. Hall (2006).

Hall, K. (2006, May 19). Dad will see grad via Web in Iraq. *Raleigh News & Observer,* p. 9A.

Hall, S. (1982). The rediscovery of "ideology": Return of the repressed in media studies. In M. Gurevitch, T. Bennett, J. Curran, & J. Woollacott (Eds.), *Culture, society, and the media* (pp. 56–90). London: Methuen.

Hall, S. (1986a). Cultural studies: Two paradigms. In R. Collins (Ed.), *Media, culture, and society: A critical reader.* London: Sage.

Hall, S. (1986b). The problem of ideology: Marxism without guarantees. *Journal of Communication Inquiry, 10,* 28–44.

Hall, S. (1988). *The hard road to renewal: Thatcherism and the crisis on the left.* London: Verso.

Hall, S. (1989a). Ideology. In E. Barnouw et al. (Eds.), *International encyclopedia of communication* (Vol. 2, pp. 307–311). New York: Oxford University Press.

Hall, S. (1989b). Ideology and communication theory. In B. Dervin, L. Grossberg, B. O'Keefe, & E. Wartella (Eds.), *Rethinking communication theory* (Vol. 1, pp. 40–52). Thousand Oaks, CA: Sage.

Hallowell, E. (2006). *Crazy busy: Strategies for coping in a world gone ADD.* New York: Ballantine.

Hamachek, D. (1992). *Encounters with the self* (3rd ed.). New York: Harcourt, Brace, Jovanovich.

Hamilton, C. (1996). *Successful public speaking.* Belmont, CA: Wadsworth.

Hamilton, C., & Parker, C. (2001). *Communicating for results* (6th ed.). Belmont, CA: Wadsworth.

Hansen, J. E., & Schuldt, W. J. (1984). Marital self-disclosure and marital satisfaction. *Journal of Marriage and the Family, 46,* 923–926.

Harding, S. (Ed.). (2004). *The feminist standpoint theory reader.* New York: Routledge.

Harlos, K., & Pinder, C. (1999). Patterns of organizational injustice: A taxonomy of what employees regard as unjust. In J. Wagner (Ed.), *Advances in qualitative organizational research, Volume 2* (pp. 97–125). Stamford, CT: JAI Press.

Harmon, A. (2002). Talk, type, read e-mail: The trials of multitasking. In E. Bucy (Ed.), *Living in the information age* (pp. 79–181). Belmont, CA: Wadsworth.

Harris, T. (2002). *Applied organizational communication.* Mahwah, NJ: Erlbaum.

Harris, T. J. (1969). *I'm OK, you're OK.* New York: Harper & Row.

Hartzler, M., & Henry, J. (1998). *Tolls for virtual teams.* New York: McGraw-Hill.

Haubegger, C. (1999, July 12). The legacy of generation —. *Newsweek,* p. 61.

Hayakawa, S. I. (1962). *The use and misuse of language.* New York: Fawcett.

Hayakawa, S. I. (1964). *Language in thought and action* (2nd ed.). New York: Harcourt, Brace & World.

Haythornthwaite, C., & Wellman, B. (Eds.). (2002). *The Internet in everyday life.* Oxford, UK: Blackwell.

Healey, J., & O'Brien, E. (Eds.). (2004). *Race, ethnicity, and gender: Selected readings.* Thousand Oaks, CA: Sage.

Healy, J. (1990). *Endangered minds: Why children don't think and what we can do about it.* New York: Simon & Schuster.

Healy, M. (2006, May 19). In multitasking, women take lead but men can do it too. *Raleigh News & Observer,* p. 12E.

Hecht, M. L., Collier, M. J., & Ribeau, S. A. (1993). *African American communication: Ethnic identity and cultural interpretation.* Thousand Oaks, CA: Sage.

Hecht, M. L., Marston, P. J., & Larkey, L. K. (1994). Love ways and relationship quality in heterosexual relationships. *Journal of Social and Personal Relationships, 11,* 25–44.

Hegel, G. W. F. (1807). *Phenomenology of mind* (J. B. Baillie, Trans.). Germany: Wurzburg & Bamburg.

Heider, F. (1958). *The psychology of interpersonal relations.* New York: Wiley.

Helgeson, S. (1990). *The female advantage: Women's ways of leadership.* New York: Doubleday/Currency.

Hellweg, S. (1992). Organizational grapevines. In K. L. Hutchinson (Ed.), *Readings in organizational communication* (pp. 159–172). Dubuque, IA: Wm. C. Brown.

Hempel, C. (1999, July 9). The brains in the family may be your wired home. *Raleigh News & Observer,* pp. 1D, 6D.

Hendrick, C., & Hendrick, S. (1988). Lovers wear rosecolored glasses. *Journal of Social and Personal Relationships, 5,* 161–184.

Hendrick, C., & Hendrick, S. (1996). Gender and the experience of heterosexual love. In J. T. Wood (Ed.), *Gendered relationships* (pp. 131–148). Mountain View, CA: Mayfield.

Hendrick, C., & Hendrick, S. (Eds.). 2000. *Close relationships: A sourcebook.* Thousand Oaks, CA: Sage.

Hendrick, C., Hendrick, S., Foote, F. H., & Slapion-Foote, M. J. (1984). Do men and women love differently? *Journal of Social and Personal Relationships, 2,* 177–196.

Hernández, D., & Rheman, B. (Eds.). (2002). *Colonize this! Young women of color on today's feminism.* Seattle, WA: Seal Press.

Herzog, H. (1944). What do we really know about daytime serial listeners? In P. Lazarsfeld & F. Stanton (Eds.), *Radio research 1942–1943.* New York: Duell, Sloan & Pearce.

Higginbotham, E. (1992). We were never on a pedestal: Women of color continue to struggle with poverty, racism, and sexism. In M. L. Andersen & P. H. Collins (Eds.), *Race, class, and gender: An anthology* (pp. 183–190). Belmont, CA: Wadsworth.

Hillis, K. (2002). *Digital sensations: Space, identity, and embodiment in virtual reality.* Research presentation at the University of North Carolina, Chapel Hill.

Hillis, K., & Petit, M., with Epley, N. (2006a). *Everyday eBay: Culture, collecting and desire.* New York: Routledge.

Hillis, K., & Petit, M., with Epley, N. (2006b). Introducing Everyday eBay. *Everyday eBay: Culture, collecting and desire* (pp. 1–17). New York: Routledge.

Himowitz, M. (2002, April 11). Beware of freeware set to bug your PC and you. *Baltimore Sun,* p. 1C. (Quoted in Campbell, Martin, & Fabos, 2004).

Ho, D. (2006, March 3, 2006). Study criticizes kids' TV violence. *Raleigh News & Observer,* p. 5A.

Hochschild, A., & Machung, A. (1989). *The second shift.* New York: Viking.

Hochschild, A., with Machung, A. (2003). *The second shift: Working parents and the revolution at home* (Rev. ed.). New York: Viking/Penguin Press.

Hofstede, G. (1991). *Culture and organizations: Software of the mind.* New York: McGraw-Hill.

Holmberg, D., & MacKenzie, S. (2002). So far, so good: Scripts for romantic relationship development as predictors of relational well-being. *Journal of Social and Personal Relationships, 19,* 777–796.

Holtzman, L. (2000). *Media messages: What film, television, and popular music teach us about race, class, gender, and sexual orientation.* New York: M. E. Sharpe.

Honeycutt, J. M., Woods, B., & Fontenot, K. (1993). The endorsement of communication conflict rules as a function of engagement, marriage, and marital ideology. *Journal of Social and Personal Relationships, 10,* 285–304.

Hoover, J. (2002). *Effective small group and team communication.* New York: Harcourt.

Houston, M. (2004). When Black women talk with White women: Why dialogues are difficult. In A. Gonzaléz, M. Houston, & V. Chen (Eds.), *Our voices: Essays in culture, ethnicity, and communication* (4th ed., pp. 119–125). Los Angeles: Roxbury.

Houston, M., & Wood, J. T. (1996). Difficult dialogues, expanded horizons: Communicating across race and class. In J. T. Wood (Ed.), *Gendered relationships* (pp. 39–56). Mountain View, CA: Mayfield.

Howard, P., & Jones, S. (Eds.). (2004). *Society online: The Internet in context.* Thousand Oaks, CA: Sage.

Hower, W. (1999, June 29). Cybermemorials. *Raleigh News & Observer,* p. 1E.

Howey, N. (2002). *Dress codes: Of three girlhoods: My mother's, my father's and mine.* New York: Picador USA.

Huesmann, L. R., Moise-Titus, J., Podolski, C., & Eron, L. D. (2003). Longitudinal relations between children's exposure to TV violence and their aggressive and violent behavior in young adulthood: 1977–1992. *Developmental Psychology, 39,* 201–221.

Hunt, D. (1999). *O. J. Simpson facts and fictions: News rituals in the construction of reality.* Cambridge, UK: Cambridge University Press.

Huston, M., & Schwartz, P. (1995). Relationships of lesbians and gay men. In J. T. Wood & S. W. Duck (Eds.), *Understanding relationship processes, 6:*

Understudied relationships: Off the beaten track (pp. 89–121). Thousand Oaks, CA: Sage.

Hyde, M. J. (1995). Human being and the call of technology. In J. T. Wood & R. B. Gregg (Eds.), *The future of the field* (pp. 47–79). Cresskill, NJ: Hampton.

Hymowitz, C. (2000, February 8). Racing onto the Web, one manager's secret is simple: Listening. *Wall Street Journal,* p. B1.

Inman, C. C. (1996). Men's friendships: Closeness in the doing. In J. T. Wood (Ed.), *Gendered Relationships* (pp. 95–110). Mountain View, CA: Mayfield.

Isaacs, W. (1999). *Dialogue and the art of thinking together.* New York: Doubleday.

Isikoff, M. (2004, July 19). The dots never existed. *Newsweek,* pp. 36–38.

Iyengar, S., & Kinder, D. (1987). *News that matters: Television and American opinion.* Chicago: University of Chicago Press.

Jaffe, C. (2007). *Public speaking: Concepts and skills for a diverse society* (5th ed.). Belmont, CA: Thomson Wadsworth.

Jamieson, K., & Campbell, K. K. (2006). *The interplay of influence* (6th ed.). Belmont, CA: Thomson Wadsworth.

Janis, I. L. (1977). *Victims of groupthink.* Boston: Houghton Mifflin.

Jarrett, K. (2006). The perfect community: Disciplining the eBay user. In K. Hillis & M. Petit with N. Epley (Eds.), *Everyday eBay: Culture, collecting and desire* (pp. 107–121). New York: Routledge.

Jhally, S., & Katz, J. (2001, Winter). Big trouble, little pond. *Umass,* pp. 26–31.

Johnson, C. B., Stockdale, M. S., & Saal, F. E. (1991). Persistence of men's misperceptions of friendly cues across a variety of interpersonal encounters. *Psychology of Women Quarterly, 15,* 463–465.

Johnson, F. L. (1996). Women's friendships: Closeness in dialogue. In J. T. Wood (Ed.), *Gendered relationships* (pp. 79–94). Mountain View, CA: Mayfield.

Johnson, F. L. (2000). *Speaking culturally: Language diversity in the United States.* Thousand Oaks, CA: Sage.

Johnson, M. (2006). Gendered Communication and Intimate Partner Violence. In B. Dow & J. T. Wood (Eds.), *Handbook of gender and communication research* (pp .71–87). Thousand Oaks, CA: Sage.

Johnson, M. P., & Ferraro, K. J. (2000). Research on domestic violence in the 1990s: Making distinctions. *Journal of Marriage and the Family, 62,* 948–963.

Johnson, N., Roberts, M., & Warell, J. (Eds.). (2002). *Beyond appearance: A new look at adolescent girls.* Washington, DC: American Psychological Association.

Johnson, P. (1999). Reflections on critical White(ness) studies. In T. Nakayama & J. Martin (Eds.), *Whiteness: The communication of social identity* (pp. 1–12). Thousand Oaks, CA: Sage.

Jones, E., & Gallois, C. (1989). Spouses' impressions of rules for communication in public and private marital conflicts. *Journal of Marriage and the Family, 51,* 957–967.

Jones, S. (1999, July 24). Some don't get the message. *Raleigh News & Observer,* pp. 1D, 6D.

Jones, W. H., & Moore, T. L. (1989). Loneliness and social support. In M. Hojat & R. Crandall (Eds.), *Loneliness: Theory, research, and applications* (pp. 145–156). Thousand Oaks, CA: Sage.

Justice, R. (1999). We're happily married and living apart. *Newsweek, 134,* p. 12.

Kalb, C. (2003, September 8). Playing ye olde way. *Newsweek,* pp. E-26–E-28.

Kanno, Y. (2003). *Negotiating bilingual and bicultural identities.* Mahwah, NJ: Erlbaum.

Katriel, T. (1990). "Griping" as a verbal ritual in some Israeli discourse. In D. Carbaugh (Ed.), *Cultural communication and intercultural contact* (pp. 99–114). Mahwah, NJ: Erlbaum.

Katz, J. (1999). *Connections: Social and cultural studies of the telephone in American life.* New Brunswick, NJ: Transaction Press.

Kaufman, J. (1996, January 18). Feng shui puts your furniture and your life in order. *Wall Street Journal,* p. A12.

Keeley, M. P., & Hart, A. J. (1994). Nonverbal behavior in dyadic interaction. In S. W. Duck (Ed.), *Understanding relationship processes, 4: Dynamics of relationships* (pp. 135–162). Thousand Oaks, CA: Sage.

Kelley, H. H. (1967). Attribution theory in social psychology. In D. Levine (Ed.), *Nebraska symposium on motivation* (Vol. 15, pp. 192–238). Lincoln: University of Nebraska Press.

Kelly, G. A. (1955). *The psychology of personal constructs.* New York: Norton.

Kelly, T. (1997). *Conversational narcissism in hyperpersonal interaction.* Retrieved April 19, 1999, from http://odin.cc.pdx.edu/~psu17799/sp511.htm

Kennedy, R. (2002). *Nigger: The strange career of a troublesome word.* New York: Pantheon.

Kerem, E., Fishman, N., & Josselson, R. (2002). The experience of empathy in everyday relationships: Cognitive and affective elements. *Journal of Social and Personal Relationships, 18,* 609–729.

Keyes, R. (1992, February 22). Do you have the time? *Parade,* pp. 22–25.

Keyton, J. (1999a). *Group communication: Process and analysis.* Mountain View, CA: Mayfield.

Keyton, J. (1999b). Relational communication in groups. In L. Frey, D. Gouran, & S. Poole (Eds.), *Handbook of group communication theory and research* (pp. 192–222). Thousand Oaks, CA: Sage.

Kiernan, V. (2006, May 12). Sign of the times. *Chronicle of Higher Education,* pp. A37–A38.

Kilbourne, J. (2004). The more you subtract, the more you add: Cutting girls down to size. In J. Spade & C. Valentine (Eds.), *The kaleidoscope of gender* (pp. 234–244). Belmont, CA: Wadsworth.

Kim, Y. (1995). Cross cultural adaptation: An integrated theory. In R. Wiseman (Ed.), *Intercultural communication theory* (pp. 170–193). Newbury Park, CA: Sage.

Klein, R. (2001). *Jewelry talks: A novel thesis.* New York: Pantheon.

Klein, R., & Milardo, R. (2000). The social context of couple conflict: Support and criticism from informal third parties. *Journal of Social and Personal Relationships, 17,* 618–637.

Klopf, D. (1991). *Intercultural encounters: The fundamentals of intercultural communication* (2nd ed.). Englewood Cliffs, NJ: Morgan.

Knapp, M. L., & Hall, J. A. (2006). *Nonverbal communication in human interaction* (6th ed.). Belmont, CA: Thomson Wadsworth.

Korzybski, A. (1933). *Science and sanity.* Lakeville, CT: Institute of General Semantics.

Korzybski, A. (1948). *Science and sanity* (3rd ed.). Lakeville, CT: International Non-Aristotelian Library.

Kruger, P. (1999, June). A leader's journey. *Fast Company,* pp. 116–138.

Krzyzewski, M., & Phillips, D. (2001). *Leading with the heart: Coach K's successful strategies for basketball, business, and life.* New York: Warner Books.

Kurdek, L. A. (1993). The allocation of household labor in gay, lesbian, and heterosexual married couples. *Journal of Social Issues, 49,* 127–139.

LaFasto, F., & Larson, C. (2001). *When teams work best: 6,000 team members and leaders tell what it takes to succeed.* Thousand Oaks, CA: Sage.

La Gaipa, J. J. (1982). Rituals of disengagement. In S. W. Duck (Ed.), *Personal relationships, 4: Dissolving personal relationships.* London: Academic Press.

Lakoff, G., & Johnson, M. (1980). *Metaphors we live by.* Chicago: University of Chicago Press.

Landauer, T. (2002). The productivity puzzle. In E. Bucy (Ed.), *Living in the information age* (pp. 194–199). Belmont, CA: Wadsworth.

Lane, R., & Shelton, M. (2001). The centrality of communication education in classroom computer-mediated communication: Toward a practical and evaluative pedagogy. *Communication Education, 50,* 224–255.

Langer, S. (1953). *Feeling and form: A theory of art.* New York: Scribner's.

Langer, S. (1979*). Philosophy in a new key: A study in the symbolism of reason, rite, and art* (3rd ed.). Cambridge, MA: Harvard University Press.

Langston, D. (1998). Tired of playing monopoly? In M. L. Andersen & P. H. Collins (Eds.), *Race, class, and gender: An anthology* (3rd ed., pp. 126–135). Belmont, CA: Wadsworth.

Lareau, A. (2003). *Unequal childhoods: Class, race, and family life.* Berkeley, CA: University of California Press.

Larson, J. R. (1984). The performance feedback process: A preliminary model. *Organizational Behavior and Human Performance, 33,* 42–76.

Lash, A. (1999, August 2–9). Privacy, practically speaking. *Industry Standard,* pp. 121–124.

Laswell, H. D. (1948). The structure and function of communication in society. In L. Bryson (Ed.), *The communication of ideas.* New York: Harper & Row.

Lau, B. (1989). Imagining your path to success. *Management Quarterly, 30,* 30–41.

Le, B., & Agnew, C. (2003). Commitment and its theorized determinants: A meta-analysis of the investment model. *Personal Relationships, 10,* 37–57.

Lea, M., & Spears, R. (1995). Relationships conducted over electronic systems. In J. T. Wood & S. W. Duck (Eds.), *Understanding relationship processes, 6: Understudied relationships: Off the beaten track* (pp. 197–233). Thousand Oaks, CA: Sage.

Lederman, L. (1990). Assessing educational effectiveness: The focus group interview as a technique for data collection. *Communication Education, 39,* 117–127.

Lee, J. A. (1973). *The colors of love: An exploration of the ways of loving.* Don Mills, Ontario, Canada: New Press.

Lee, J. A. (1988). Love-styles. In R. J. Sternberg & M. L. Barnes (Eds.), *The psychology of love* (pp. 38–67). New Haven, CT: Yale University Press.

Lee, W. S. (1994). On not missing the boat: A processual method for intercultural understandings of idioms and lifeworld. *Journal of Applied Communication Research, 22,* 141–161.

Lee, W. S. (2000). That's Greek to me: Between a rock and a hard place in intercultural encounters. In L. Samovar & R. Porter (Eds.), *Intercultural communication: A reader* (9th ed., pp. 217–224). Belmont, CA: Wadsworth.

Leeds-Hurwitz, W. (2006). Social theories: Social constructionism and symbolic interactionism. In D. O. Braithwaite & L. A. Baxter (Eds.), *Engaging theories in family communication: Multiple perspectives* (pp. 229–242). Thousand Oaks, CA: Sage.

Lefkowitz, J. (2003). *Ethics and values in industrial–organizational psychology.* Mahwah, NJ: Erlbaum.

LePoire, B. A., Burgoon, J. K., & Parrott, R. (1992). Status and privacy restoring communication in the workplace. *Journal of Applied Communication Research, 4,* 419–436.

Lester, P. M. (2006). *Visual communication: Images with messages* (4th ed.). Belmont, CA: Thomson Wadsworth.

Levine, M. (2004, June 1). Tell the doc all your problems, but keep it to less than a minute. *New York Times,* p. D6.

Levine, R., & Norenzayan, A. (1999). The pace of life in 31 countries. *Journal of Cross-Cultural Psychology, 30,* 178–205.

Levinson, P. (1999). *Digital McLuhan: A guide to the information millennium.* New York: Routledge.

Levy, S. (1999, May 31). The new digital galaxy. *Newsweek,* pp. 57–62.

Levy, S. (2003, September 8). A geek bill of rights. *Newsweek,* p. E30.

Levy, S. (2004a, June 7). A future with nowhere to hide? *Newsweek,* p. 76.

Levy, S. (2004b, June 7). Something in the air. *Newsweek,* pp. 46–49.

Levy, S. (2006, March 27). (Some) attention must be paid! *Newsweek*, p. 16

Lewin, K. (1947). *Human relations.* New York: Harper & Row.

Lewis, M. (2002). *Next: The future just happened.* New York: Norton.

Lewis, R. D. (1996). *When cultures collide: Managing successfully across cultures.* London: Nicholas Brealey.

Lightner, C. (1990). *Giving sorrow words: How to cope with grief and get on with your life.* New York: Warner.

Lloyd, S., & Emery, B. (2000). The context and dynamics of intimate aggression against women. *Journal of Social and Personal Relationships, 17,* 503–521.

Lohr, S. (2002). Computer age gains respect of economics. In E. Bucy (Ed.), *Living in the information age* (pp. 181–203). Belmont, CA: Wadsworth.

Lorde, A. (1992). Age, race, class, and sex: Women redefining difference. In M. L. Andersen & P. H. Collins (Eds.), *Race, class, and gender: An anthology* (pp. 495–502). Belmont, CA: Wadsworth.

Ludington-Hoe, S. (1993). *Kangaroo care: The best you can do to help your preterm infant.* New York: Bantam.

Luft, J. (1969). *Of human interaction.* Palo Alto, CA: Natural Press.

Lumsden, G., & Lumsden, D. (2004). *Communicating in groups and teams* (2nd ed.). Belmont, CA: Wadsworth.

Lund, M. (1985). The development of investment and commitment scales for predicting continuity of personal relationships. *Journal of Social and Personal Relationships, 2,* 3–23.

Major, B., Schmidlin, A. M., & Williams, L. (1990). Gender patterns in social touch: The impact of setting and age. In C. Mayo & N. M. Henley (Eds.), *Gender and nonverbal behavior* (pp. 3–37). New York: Springer-Verlag.

Maltz, D. N., & Borker, R. (1982). A cultural approach to male–female miscommunication. In J. J. Gumperz (Ed.), *Language and social identity* (pp. 196–216). Cambridge, UK: Cambridge University Press.

Mander, M. (Ed.). (1999). *Framing friction: Media and social conflict.* Urbana: University of Illinois Press.

Manusov, V. (Ed.). (2004). *The sourcebook of nonverbal measures.* Mahwah, NJ: Erlbaum.

Manusov, V. (2006). Attribution theories: Assessing causal and responsibility judgments in families. In D. O. Braithwaite & L. A. Baxter (Eds.), *Engaging theories in family communication: Multiple perspectives* (pp. 181–196). Thousand Oaks, CA: Sage.

Marling, K. (2002, May 26). They want their mean TV. *New York Times*, Section 2, pp. 1, 32, 33.

Martin, C., Fabes, R., Evans, S., & Wyman, H. (2000). Social cognition on the playground: Children's beliefs about playing with girls and boys and their relations to sex-segregated play. *Journal of Social and Personal Relationships, 17,* 751–771.

Martin, J., Krizek, R., Nakayama, T., & Bradford, L. (1996). Exploring Whiteness: A study of self labels for White Americans. *Communication Quarterly, 44,* 125–144.

Mastro, D. (2003). A social identity approach to understanding the impact of television messages. *Communication Monographs, 70,* 98–113.

Maugh, T. H., II (2002, February 26). Center says AIDS virus is nearly 1 million in U.S. *Raleigh News & Observer*, p. 8B.

McChesney, R. (1999). *Rich media, poor democracy: Communication politics in dubious times.* Urbana: University of Illinois Press.

McChesney, R. (2004). *The problem of the media: U.S. communication politics in the twenty-first century.* New York: Monthly Review Press.

McClure, B. (2005). *Putting a new spin on groups: The science of chaos* (2nd ed.). Mahwah, NJ: Erlbaum.

McClure, M. (1997). Mind/body medicine: Evidence of efficacy. *Health and Healing, 1,* 3.

McCollum, K. (1999, May 14). Students find sex, drugs, and more than a little education on line, survey finds. *Chronicle of Higher Education*, p. A31.

McCroskey, J., & Teven, J. (1999). Goodwill: A reexamination of the construct and its measurement. *Communication Monographs, 66,* 90–103.

McCroskey, J. C. (1977). Oral communication apprehension: A summary of recent theory and research. *Human Communication Research, 4,* 78–96.

McGee-Cooper, A., Trammel, D., & Lau, B. (1992). *You don't have to go home from work exhausted.* New York: Bantam.

McGrath, P. (2002, June 10). Public or private? *Newsweek*, p. 32R.

McGuire, W. J. (1989). Theoretical foundations of campaigns. In R. E. Rice & C. K. Atkin (Eds.),

Public communication campaigns (2nd ed., pp. 43–65). Thousand Oaks, CA: Sage.

McKinney, B., Kelly, L., & Duran, R. (1997). The relationship between conflict message style and dimensions of communication competence. *Communication Reports, 10,* 185–196.

McLuhan, M. (1962). *The Gutenberg galaxy.* Toronto: University of Toronto Press.

McLuhan, M. (1964). *Understanding media.* New York: McGraw-Hill.

McLuhan, M. (1969, March). Interview. *Playboy,* pp. 53–54, 56, 59–62, 64–66, 68, 70.

McLuhan, M., & Fiore, Q. (1967). *The medium is the message.* New York: Random House.

McNulty, J. K., & Karney, B. R. (2001). Attributions in marriage: Integrating specific and global evaluations of a relationship. *Personality and Social Psychology Bulletin, 27,* 943–955.

McNutt, P. (1997, October/November). When strategic decisions are ignored. *Fast Company,* p. 12.

McQuillen, J. (2003). The influence of technology on the initiation of interpersonal relationships. *Education, 123,* 616–624.

Mead, G. H. (1934). *Mind, self, and society.* Chicago: University of Chicago Press.

Meares, M., Oetzel, J., Torres, A., Derkacs, D., & Ginossar, T. (2004). Employee mistreatment and muted voices in the culturally diverse workplace. *Journal of Applied Communication Research, 32,* 4–27.

Meeks, B., Hendrick, S., & Hendrick, C. (1998). Communication, love, and satisfaction. *Journal of Social and Personal Relationships, 15,* 755–773.

Mehrabian, A. (1981). *Silent messages: Implicit communication of emotion and attitudes* (2nd ed.). Belmont, CA: Wadsworth.

Men use half a brain to listen, study finds. (2000, November 29). *Raleigh News & Observer,* p. 8A.

Merritt, B. (2000). Illusive reflections: African American women on primetime television. In A. González, M. Houston, & V. Chen (Eds.), *Our voices: Essays in culture, ethnicity, and communication* (3rd ed., pp. 47–53). Los Angeles: Roxbury.

Metts, S. (2006). Gendered communication in dating relationships. In B. Dow & J. T. Wood (Eds.), *Handbook of gender and communication research* (pp. 25–40). Thousand Oaks, CA: Sage.

Metts, S., Cupach, W. R., & Bejlovec, R. A. (1989). "I love you too much to ever start liking you": Redefining romantic relationships. *Journal of Social and Personal Relationships, 6,* 259–274.

Meyers, M. (1994). News of battering. *Journal of Communication, 44,* 47–62.

Meyers, M. (1997). *News coverage of violence against women: Engendering violence.* Thousand Oaks, CA: Sage.

Meyrowitz, J. (1985). *No sense of place: The impact of electronic media on social behavior.* New York: Oxford University Press.

Milia, T. (2003). *Doctor, you're not listening.* Philadelphia: Xlibris.

Miller, E. (1974). Speech introductions and conclusions. *Quarterly Journal of Speech, 32,* 118–127.

Miller, J. (2006, May 9). Touch. *Raleigh News & Observer,* pp. 1E, 3E.

Miller, J. B. (1993). Learning from early relationship experience. In S. W. Duck (Ed.), *Understanding relationship processes, 2: Learning about relationships* (pp. 1–29). Thousand Oaks, CA: Sage.

Mino, M. (1996). The relative effects of content and vocal delivery during a simulated employment interview. *Communication Research Reports, 13,* 225–238.

Mirzoeff, N. (Ed.). (1998). *The visual culture reader.* New York: Routledge.

Moffatt, T. (1979). *Selection interviewing for managers.* New York: Harper & Row.

Mokros, H. (2006). Composing relationships at work. In J. T. Wood & S. W. Duck (Eds.), *Composing relationships: Communication in everyday life* (pp. 175–185). Belmont, CA: Thomson Wadsworth.

Monastersky, R. (2001, July 6). Look who's listening. *Chronicle of Higher Education,* pp. A14–A16.

Monastersky, R. (2002, March 29). Speak before you think. *Chronicle of Higher Education,* pp. A17–A18.

Monmonier, M. (2002). *Spying with maps.* Chicago: University of Chicago Press.

Monroe, A. H. (1935). *Principles and types of speech.* Glenview, IL: Scott, Foresman.

Monsour, M. (2002). *Women and men as friends.* Mahwah, NJ: Erlbaum.

Monsour, M. (2006). Communication and gender among adult friends. In B. Dow & J. T. Wood (Eds.), *Handbook of gender and communication research* (pp. 57–69). Thousand Oaks, CA: Sage.

Montgomery, B. (1988). Quality communication in personal relationships. In S. W. Duck (Ed.), *Handbook of personal relationships* (pp. 343–366). New York: Wiley.

Morreale, S. (2001, May). Communication important to employers. *Spectra,* p. 8.

Morreale, S. P., & Vogl, M. (Eds.). (1998). *Pathways to careers in communication* (5th ed.). Annandale, VA: National Communication Association.

Motley, M., & Molloy, J. (1994). An efficacy test of a new therapy ("communication-orientation motivation") for public speaking anxiety. *Journal of Applied Communication Research, 22,* 48–58.

Muehlhoff, T. (2006). "He started it": Everyday communication in parenting. In J. T. Wood & S. W. Duck (Eds.), *Composing relationships: Communication in everyday life* (pp. 46–54). Belmont, CA: Wadsworth.

Mumby, D. (Ed.). (1993). *Narratives and social control: Critical perspectives.* Newbury Park, CA: Sage.

Mumby, D. (2006). Constructing working-class masculinity in the workplace. In J. T. Wood & S. W. Duck (Eds.), *Composing relationships: Communication in everyday life* (pp. 166–174). Belmont, CA: Thomson Wadsworth.

Mumby, D. (2007). Introduction: Gendering organization. In B. Dow & J. T. Wood (Eds.), *Handbook of gender and communication research.* Thousand Oaks, CA: Sage.

Mumby, D., & Stohl, C. (1992). Power and discourse in organization studies: Absence and the dialectic of control. *Discourse & Society, 2,* 313–332.

Munter, M. (1993). Cross-cultural communication for managers. *Business Horizons, 36,* 68–77.

Murphy, B. O., & Zorn, T. (1996). Gendered interaction in professional relationships. In J. T. Wood (Ed.), *Gendered relationships* (pp. 213–231). Mountain View, CA: Mayfield.

Mwakalye, N., & DeAngelis, T. (1995, October). The power of touch helps babies survive. *APA Monitor,* p. 25.

Nader, R. (1996, January 1). Imagine that! *The Nation,* p. 10.

Nagourney, E. (2006, May 9). Surgical teams found lacking, in teamwork. *New York Times,* p. D6.

Nakayama, T., & Martin, J. (Eds.). (1999). *Whiteness: The communication of social identity.* Thousand Oaks, CA: Sage.

Names & faces. (1997, September 11). *The Santa Barbara News–Press,* p. B8.

Namie, G. (2000, September). U.S. hostile workplace survey. Retrieved September 17, 2003, from http://bullyinginstitute.org/home/twd/bb/res/bullyinst.pdf

Nanda, S. (2004). Multiple genders among North American Indians. In J. Spade & C. Valentine (Eds.), *The kaleidoscope of gender* (pp. 64–70). Belmont, CA: Wadsworth.

Natalle, E. (1996). Gendered issues in the workplace. In J. T. Wood (Ed.), *Gendered relationships* (pp. 253–274). Mountain View, CA: Mayfield.

National Coalition Against Domestic Violence. (1999). [Website]. Accessed July 10, 1999. http://www.ncadv.org

National Telecommunications and Information Agency. *Falling through the net.* (1999). Retrieved September 25, 2004, from http:// www.ntia.doc.gov/ntiahome/fftn99/contents.html

National Television Violence Study. (1996). *Scientific report.* Thousand Oaks, CA: Sage.

Navasky, V. (1996, September 29). Tomorrow never knows. *New York Times Magazine,* p. 216.

Nelson, M. (1998). *Embracing victory: Life lessons in competition and compassion.* New York: William Morrow.

The new media. (2003, September 8). *Newsweek,* p. E8.

Neyer, F. (2002). The dyadic interdependence of attachment security and dependency: A conceptual replication across older twin pairs and young couples. *Journal of Social and Personal Relationships, 19,* 483–503.

Nichols, M. (1996). *The lost art of listening.* New York: Guilford.

Nicholson, J. (2006). "Them's fightin' words": Naming in everyday talk between siblings. In J. T. Wood & S. W. Duck (Eds.), *Composing relationships: Communication in everyday life* (pp. 55–63). Belmont, CA: Thomson Wadsworth.

Nichter, M. (2000). *Fat talk: What girls and their parents say about dieting.* New Haven, CT: Harvard University Press.

Nie, N. (2004). *Better off: Flipping the switch on technology.* New York: HarperCollins

Noller, P. (1986). Sex differences in nonverbal communication: Advantage lost or supremacy regained? *Australian Journal of Psychology, 38,* 23–32.

Noller, P. (1987). Nonverbal communication in marriage. In D. Perlman & S. Duck (Eds.), *Intimate relationships: Development, dynamics, and deterioration* (pp. 149–176). Thousand Oaks, CA: Sage.

Nua Internet Surveys. (2002). How many online? Retrieved June 11, 2002, from http//www.nua.ie/surveys/how_manyonline/index.html

Numbers. (1999, August 16). *Time,* pp. 21, 76.

Nussbaum, D. (2002). Computer haves and have-nots in the schools. In E. Bucy (Ed.), *Living in the information age* (pp. 254–257). Belmont, CA: Wadsworth.

Oetzel, J. (1998). Explaining individual communication processes in homogeneous and heterogeneous groups through individualism-collectivism and self construal. *Human Communication Research, 25,* 202–224.

O'Keefe, D. (2002). *Persuasion: Theory and research* (2nd ed.). Thousand Oaks, CA: Sage.

Olien, M. (1978). *The human myth.* New York: Harper & Row.

Olson, J. M., & Cal, A. V. (1984). Source credibility, attitudes, and the recall of past behaviors. *European Journal of Social Psychology, 14,* 203–210.

O'Meara, J. D. (1989). Cross-sex friendship: Four basic challenges of an ignored relationship. *Sex Roles, 21,* 525–543.

One in three U.S. residents is a minority. (2006, May 10). *Raleigh News & Observer,* p. 1A.

Ong, W. J. (2002). Orality and literacy. London: Routledge.

Orbe, M. P. (1994). "Remember, it's always the Whites' ball": Descriptions of African American male communication. *Communication Quarterly, 42,* 287–300.

Orbe, M. P., & Harris, T. M. (2001). *Interracial communication: Theory into practice.* Belmont, CA: Wadsworth.

Ornish, D. (1998). *Love and survival: The scientific basis for the healing power of intimacy.* New York: HarperCollins.

Overland, M. (2004, January 9). Tea, TV, and sympathy. *Chronicle of Higher Education,* p. A48.

Pacanowsky, M. (1989). Creating and narrating organizational realities. In B. Dervin, L. Grossberg, B. O'Keefe, & E. Wartella (Eds.), *Rethinking communication: Paradigm exemplars* (pp. 250–257). Thousand Oaks, CA: Sage.

Pacanowsky, M., & O'Donnell-Trujillo, N. (1982). Communication and organizational cultures. *Western Journal of Speech Communication, 46,* 115–130.

Pacanowsky, M., & O'Donnell-Trujillo, N. (1983). Organizational communication as cultural performance. *Communication Monographs, 30,* 126–147.

Padavic, I., & Reskin, B. (2002). *Women and men at work.* Thousand Oaks, CA: Sage.

Palmer, E., & Young, B. (Eds.). (2003). *The faces of televisual media.* Mahwah, NJ: Erlbaum.

Parents Television Council (2006). [Website]. Accessed May 20, 2006. http://www.parentstv.org/PTC/publications/reports/childrensstudy/main.asp

Parks, M., & Floyd, K. (1996). Making friends in cyberspace. *Journal of Communication, 46,* 80–97.

Parks, M., & Roberts, L. (1998). "Making MOOsic": The development of personal relationships on line and a comparison to their off-line counterparts. *Journal of Social and Personal Relationships, 15,* 517–537.

Patterson, M. L. (1992). A functional approach to nonverbal exchange. In R. S. Feldman & B. Rime (Eds.), *Fundamentals of nonverbal behavior* (pp. 458–495). New York: Cambridge University Press.

Pearce, W. B., Cronen, V. E., & Conklin, F. (1979). On what to look at when analyzing communication: A hierarchical model of actors' meanings. *Communication, 4,* 195–220.

Petronio, S. (1991). Communication boundary management: A theoretical model of managing disclosure of private information between married couples. *Communication Theory, 1,* 311–335.

Petronio, S., & Caughlin, J. (2006). Communication privacy management theory: Understanding families. In D. O. Braithwaite & L. A. Baxter (Eds.), *Engaging theories in family communication: Multiple perspectives* (pp. 35–49). Thousand Oaks, CA: Sage.

Peyser, M. (2006, March 6). Color us impressed. *Newsweek,* p. 59.

Pezzullo, P. (2001). Performing critical interruptions: Stories, rhetorical invention, and the environmental justice movement. *Western Journal of Communication, 65,* 1–25.

Phillips, G. M. (1991). *Communication incompetencies.* Carbondale: Southern Illinois University Press.

Pinsonneault, A., & Barki, H. (1999). Electronic brainstorming: The illusion of productivity. *Information Systems Research, 10,* 110–133.

Pogue, D. (2006, May 3). Going online on the go: Options. *New York Times,* pp. E1, E5.

Pollock, W. (2000). *Real boys: Rescuing ourselves from the myths of boyhood.* New York: Owl Books.

Porter, K., & Foster, J. (1986). *The mental athlete: Inner training for peak performance.* New York: Ballantine.

Postman, N. (1985). *Amusing ourselves to death.* New York: Penguin.

Potter, W. J. (2001). *Media literacy* (2nd ed.). Thousand Oaks, CA: Sage.

Potter, W. J. (2002). *The 11 myths of media violence.* Thousand Oaks, CA: Sage.

Potter, W. J. (2004). *Theory of media literacy: A cognitive approach.* Thousand Oaks, CA: Sage.

Public pillow talk. (1987, October). *Psychology Today,* p. 18.

Purdy, M., & Borisoff, D. (Eds.). (1997). *Listening in everyday life: A personal and professional approach* (2nd ed.). Lanham, MD: University of America Press.

Quality circles help sharpen competitive edge. (1991, Winter). *The Scorpion: The Official All-State Legal Supply Employee Publication,* p. 12.

Radway, J. (1984). *Reading the romance.* Chapel Hill: University of North Carolina Press.

Rafter, M. (1999, August 2–9). Check it out. *The Industry Standard,* pp. 87–90.

Ragan, P. (2003). *The mating game: A primer on love, sex and marriage.* Thousand Oaks, CA: Sage.

Rakow, L. (1992). "Don't hate me because I'm beautiful": Feminist resistance to advertising's irresistible meanings. *Southern Journal of Speech Communication, 36,* 11–26.

Rantanen, T. (2004). *The media and globalization.* Thousand Oaks, CA: Sage.

Raspberry, W. (1994, July 5). Major gains in minorities' grades at Tech. *Raleigh News & Observer,* p. 9A.

Rawlins, W. K. (1981). *Friendship as a communicative achievement: A theory and an interpretive analysis of verbal reports.* Doctoral dissertation, Temple University, Philadelphia.

Rawlins, W. K. (1994). Being there and growing apart: Sustaining friendships during adulthood. In D. Canary & Laura Stafford (Eds.), *Communication and relational maintenance* (pp. 275–294). New York: Academic Press.

Reeder, H. (2000). "I like you . . . as a friend": The role of attraction in cross-sex friendship. *Journal of Social and Personal Relationships, 17,* 329–348.

Reel, B. W., & Thompson, T. L. (1994). A test of the effectiveness of strategies for talking about AIDS and condom use. *Journal of Applied Communication Research, 22,* 127–141.

Reich, N., & Wood, J. T. (2003). Sex, gender and communication in small groups. In R. Cathcart, L. Samovar, & R. Hirokawa (Eds.). *Communication in small groups.* Los Angeles: Roxbury.

Remland, M. (2000). *Nonverbal communication in everyday life.* Boston: Houghton Mifflin.

Ribeau, S. A., Baldwin, J. R., & Hecht, M. L. (1994). An African-American communication perspective. In L. Samovar and R. Porter (Eds.), *International communication: A reader* (7th ed., pp. 140–147). Belmont, CA: Wadsworth.

Richmond, V. P., & McCroskey, J. C. (1992). *Communication: Apprehension, avoidance, and effectiveness* (3rd ed.). Scottsdale, AZ: Gorsuch Scarisbrick.

Richmond, V. P., & McCroskey, J. C. (1995). *Nonverbal communication in interpersonal relations* (3rd ed.). Boston: Allyn & Bacon.

Richtel, M. (2006, May 3). Selling surveillance to anxious parents. *New York Times,* p. E6.

Rideout, V., Foehr, U., Roberts, D., & Brodie, M. (1999). *Kids & media @ the new millennium.* Menlo Park, CA: Kaiser Foundation.

Riessman, C. (1990). *Divorce talk: Women and men make sense of personal relationships.* New Brunswick, NJ: Rutgers University Press.

Riggs, D. (1999, February 28). True love is alive and well, say romance book writers. *Tallahassee Democrat,* p. 3D.

Riley, P. (1983). A structurationist account of political culture. *Administrative Science Quarterly, 28,* 414–437.

Rios, D. (1997). Mexican American cultural experiences with mass-mediated communication. In A. González, M. Houston, & V. Chen (Eds.), *Our voices: Essays in culture, ethnicity, and communication* (pp. 105–112). Los Angeles: Roxbury.

Risman, B., & Godwin, S. (2001). Twentieth-century changes in economic work and family. In D. Vannoy (Ed.), *Gender mosaics* (pp. 134–144). Los Angeles: Roxbury.

Roberts, J. (2004, November 22). TV's new brand of stars. *Newsweek,* pp. 62–64.

Rogers, E. M. (1986). *Communication technology: The new media in society.* New York: Free Press.

Rohlfing, M. (1995). "Doesn't anybody stay in one place anymore?": An exploration of the understudied phenomenon of long-distance relationships. In J. T. Wood & S. W. Duck (Eds.), *Understanding relationship processes, 6: Understudied relationships: Off the beaten track* (pp. 173–196). Thousand Oaks, CA: Sage.

Rollie, S. S., & Duck, S. W. (in press). Divorce and dissolution of romantic relationships: Stage models and their imitations. In M. Fine & J. Harvey

(Eds.), *Handbook of divorce and dissolution of romantic relationships*. Mahwah, NJ: Erlbaum.

Root, M. P. (1990). Disordered eating habits in women of color. *Sex Roles, 22*, 525–536.

Roper Starch. *How Americans communicate*. Retrieved September 1, 2006, from http://www.natcom.org/research/Roper/how_americans_communicate.htm

Rothenberg, D. (1999, July 16). Use the Web to connect with "ideas in motion." *Chronicle of Higher Education*, p. B8.

Rothwell, J. D. (2004). *In the company of others*. New York: McGraw-Hill.

Rothwell, J. D. (2007). *In mixed company: Small group communication* (6th ed.). Belmont, CA: Thomson Wadsworth.

Ruberman, T. R. (1992, January). Psychosocial influences on mortality of patients with coronary heart disease. *Journal of the American Medical Association, 267*, 559–560.

Rubin, L. (1985*). Just friends: The role of friendship in our lives*. New York: Harper & Row.

Rusbult, C. E. (1987). Responses to dissatisfaction in close relationships: The exit–voice–loyalty–neglect model. In D. Perlman & S. W. Duck (Eds.), *Intimate relationships: Development, dynamics, and deterioration* (pp. 109–238). London: Sage.

Rusbult, C. E., Drigotas, S. M., & Verette, J. (1994). The investment model: An interdependence analysis of commitment processes and relationship maintenance phenomena. In D. J. Canary and L. Stafford (Eds.), *Communication and relational maintenance* (pp. 115–140). New York: Academic Press.

Rusbult, C. E., Johnson, D. J., & Morrow, G. D. (1986). Impact of couple patterns of problem solving on distress and nondistress in dating relationships. *Journal of Personality and Social Psychology, 50*, 744–753.

Rusbult, C. E., & Zembrodt, I. M. (1983). Responses to dissatisfaction in romantic involvement: A multidimensional scaling analysis. *Journal of Experimental Social Psychology, 19*, 274–293.

Rusbult, C. E., Zembrodt, I. M., & Iwaniszek, J. (1986). The impact of gender and sex-role orientation on responses to dissatisfaction in close relationships. *Sex Roles, 15*, 1–20.

Rusk, T., & Rusk, N. (1988). *Mind traps: Change your mind, change your life*. Los Angeles: Price Stern Sloan.

Sabourin, T., & Stamp, G. (1995). Communication and the experience of dialectical tensions in family life: An examination of abusive and nonabusive families. *Communication Monographs, 62*, 213–242.

Sahlstein, E. (2006a). Relational life in the 21st century: Managing people, time, and distance. In J. T. Wood & S. W. Duck (Eds.), *Composing relationships: Communication in everyday life* (pp. 110–118). Belmont, CA: Thomson Wadsworth.

Sahlstein, E. (2006b). The trouble with distance. In C. Kirpatrick, S. W. Duck, & M. Foley (Eds.), *Relating difficulty* (pp.118–140). Mahwah, NJ: Erlbaum.

Sallinen-Kuparinen, A. (1992). Teacher communicator style. *Communication Education, 41*, 153–166.

Samovar, L., & Porter, R. (Eds.). (2001). *Intercultural communication: A reader* (9th ed.). Belmont, CA: Wadsworth.

Samuelson, R. (2002, March 25). Debunking the digital divide. *Newsweek*, p. 37.

Sandberg, J. (1995, October 30). Online population reaches 24 million in North America. *Wall Street Journal*, p. B3.

Sandberg, J. (1999, May 31). The quiet genius who brings it all together. *Newsweek*, p. 63.

Sandstrom, K. L., Martin, D. D., & Fine, G. A. (2001). Symbolic interactionism and the end of the century. In G. Ritzer & B. Smart (Eds.), *Handbook of social theory* (pp. 217–231). Thousand Oaks, CA: Sage.

Schaller, M., & Crandall, C. (2004). *The psychological foundations of culture*. Mahwah, NJ: Erlbaum.

Schiesel, S. (2006, May 9). The Sims' stimulate kids who play. *Raleigh News & Observer*, p. 8E.

Schlechtweg, H. (1992). Framing Earth First!: *The McNeil-Lehrer NewsHour* and redwood summer. In C. Oravec & J. Cantrill (Eds.), *The conference on the discourse of environmental advocacy* (pp. 262–287). Salt Lake City, UT: University of Utah Humanities Center.

Schnarch, D. (1997). Sex, intimacy, and the Internet. *Journal of Sex Education and Therapy, 22*, 15–20.

Schneider, A. (1999, March 26). Taking aim at student incoherence. *Chronicle of Higher Education*, pp. A16–A18.

Schneider, C., & Kenny, D. (2000). Cross-sex friends who were once romantic partners: Are they platonic friends now? *Journal of Social and Personal Relationships, 17*, 451–466.

Schramm, W. (1955). *The process and effects of mass communication*. Urbana: University of Illinois Press.

Schutz, A. (1999). It was your fault! Self-serving bias in autobiographical accounts of conflicts in married couples. *Journal of Social and Personal Relationships, 16,* 193–208.

Schwartz, T. (1989, January–February). Acceleration syndrome: Does everyone live in the fast lane nowadays? *Utne Reader,* pp. 36–43.

Scott, C., & Myers, K. (2005). The socialization of emotion: Learning emotion management at the fire station. *Journal of Applied Communication Research, 33,* 67–92.

Searle, J. (1976). *Speech acts: An essay in the philosophy of language.* London: Cambridge University Press.

Searle, J. (1995). *The construction of social reality.* New York: Free Press.

Sedikides, C., Campbell, W., Reeder, G., & Elliot, A. (1998). The self-serving bias in relational context. *Journal of Personality and Social Psychology, 74,* 3763–3864.

Setoodeh, R. (2006, May 22). The long goodbye. *Newsweek,* pp. 60–61.

Seligman, M. E. P. (1990). *Learned optimism.* New York: Simon & Schuster/Pocket Books.

Seligman, M. E. P. (2002). *Authentic happiness: Using the new positive psychology to realize your potential for lasting fulfillment.* New York: Free Press.

Sellinger, M. B. (1994, July 9). Candy Lightner prods Congress. *People,* pp. 102, 105.

Sennott, S. (2003, September 8). Next in toyland. *Newsweek,* p. E29.

Severin, W., & Tankard, J., Jr. (2002). Uses of the mass media. In E. Bucy (Ed.), *Living in the information age* (pp. 35–41). Belmont, CA: Wadsworth.

Sewell, G. (1998). The discipline of teams: The control of team-based industrial work through electronic and peer surveillance. *Administrative Science Quarterly, 43,* 397–428.

Shabecoff, P. (2000). *Earth rising: American environmentalism in the 21st century.* Washington, DC: Island Press.

Shanahan, J., & McComas, K. (1999). *Nature stories: Depictions of the environment and their effects.* Cresskill, NJ: Hampton Press.

Shannon, C., & Weaver, W. (1949). *The mathematical theory of communication.* Urbana: University of Illinois Press.

Shapiro, A. (1999). *The control revolution.* New York: HarperCollins.

Sharpe, R. (1995, October 31). The checkoff. *Wall Street Journal,* p. A1.

Shattuck, T. R. (1980). *The forbidden experiment: The story of the wild boy of Aveyron.* New York: Farrar, Straus & Giroux.

Shaw, C. (1999). *Deciding what we watch: Taste, decency, and media ethics in the UK and the USA.* Oxford, UK: Oxford University Press.

Shenk, D. (1997). *Data smog: Surviving the information glut.* San Francisco: HarperEdge.

Sher, B., & Gottlieb, A. (1989). *Teamworks!* New York: Warner.

Sheridan, V. (2001). *Crossing over: Liberating the transgendered Christian.* Cleveland, OH: Pilgrim.

Shim, J. (1997). The importance of ethnic newspapers to U.S. newcomers. In S. Biagi & M. Kem-Foxworth (Eds.), *Facing difference: Race, gender, and mass media* (pp. 250–255). Thousand Oaks, CA: Pine Forge Press.

Shimanoff, S. B. (1980). *Communication rules: Theory and research.* Thousand Oaks, CA: Sage.

Shoemaker, P. (1991). *Gatekeeping.* Thousand Oaks, CA: Sage.

Shoes are made for talking: Telling Your iPod about you. (2006, May 25). *New York Times,* p. C4.

Shostak, S. (2002). You call this progress? E-mail has become a steady drip of dubious prose, bad jokes, and impatient requests. In E. Bucy (Ed.), *Living in the information age* (pp. 182–184). Belmont, CA: Wadsworth.

Shotter, J. (1993). *Conversational realities: The construction of life through language.* Thousand Oaks, CA: Sage.

Sias, P., Heath, R., Perry, T., Silva, D., & Fix, B. (2004). Narratives of workplace friendship deterioration. *Journal of Social and Personal Relationships, 21,* 321–340.

Signorielli, N. (1990). Television's mean and dangerous world: A continuation of the cultural indicators perspective. In N. Signorielli & M. Morgan (Eds.), *Cultivation analysis: New directions in media effects research* (pp. 85–106). Thousand Oaks, CA: Sage.

Signorielli, N., & Morgan, M. (Eds.). (1990). *Cultivation analysis: New directions in media research.* Thousand Oaks, CA: Sage.

Silverstone, D., Greenbaum, M., & MacGregor, S., III. (1987). *The preferred college graduate as seen by the N.Y. business community.* Unpublished manuscript.

Simmons, R. (2002). *Odd girl out: The hidden culture of aggression in girls.* Orlando, FL: Harvest Books.

Simon, S. B. (1977). *Vulture: A modern allegory on the art of putting oneself down.* Niles, IL: Argus Communications.

Simons, G. F., Vázquez, C., & Harris, P. R. (1993). *Transcultural leadership: Empowering the diverse workforce.* Houston: Gulf.

Simons, H., Morreale, J., Gronbeck, B. (2001). *Persuasion in society.* Thousand Oaks, CA: Sage.

Simons, L. I., & Zielenziger, M. (1996, March 3). Culture clash dims U.S. future in Asia. *San Jose Mercury News,* pp. A1, A22. Cited in J. D. Rothwell (2004).

Singer, D. & Singer, J. (Eds.). (2001). *Handbook of children and the media.* Thousand Oaks, CA: Sage.

Singer, D. & Singer, J. (2002). *Make-believe: Games and activities for imaginative play.* Washington, DC: Magination.

Smart Money. (2006). Retrieved May 22, 2006 from http://www.smartmoney.com/consumer/index.cfm?story=tenthings-july03

Smircich, L. (1983). Concepts of culture and organizational analysis. *Administrative Quarterly, 28,* 339–358.

Smith, R. (1996). *The patient's story: Integrated patient–doctor interviewing.* Boston: Little, Brown.

Smith, S. (1999, February 11). Test a bevy of new words. *Raleigh News & Observer,* p. 3F.

Spano, S. (2003, June 1). Rude encounters versus cultural differences. *Raleigh News & Observer,* pp. 1H, 5H.

Sparks, G. (2006). *Media effects research: A basic overview* (2nd ed). Belmont, CA: Thomson Wadsworth.

Spear, W. (1996). *Feng shui made easy: Designing your life with the ancient art of placement.* New York: HarperCollins.

Spencer, M. (1982). *Foundations of modern sociology.* Englewood Cliffs, NJ: Prentice Hall.

Spencer, T. (1994). Transforming personal relationships through ordinary talk. In S. W. Duck (Ed.), *Understanding relationship processes, 4: Dynamics of relationships* (pp. 58–85). Thousand Oaks, CA: Sage.

Spitzer, M. (2000). *The mind within the net: Models of learning, thinking, and acting.* Boston, MA: MIT Press.

Stafford, L. (2005). *Maintaining long-distance and cross-residential relationships.* Mahwah, NJ: Erlbaum.

Stamp, G., & Sabourin, T. (1995). Accounting for violence: An analysis of male spousal abuse narratives. *Journal of Applied Communication Research, 23,* 284–307.

Steil, J. (2000). Contemporary marriage: Still an unequal partnership. In C. Hendrick & S. Hendrick (Eds.), *Close relationships: A sourcebook* (pp. 124–136). Thousand Oaks, CA: Sage.

Stewart, C., & Cash, W. (1991). *Interviewing: Principles and practices* (6th ed.). Dubuque, IA: Wm. C. Brown.

Stewart, J., Zediker, K., & Black, L. (2004). Relationships among philosophies of dialogue. In R. Anderson, L. Baxter, & K. Cissna (Eds.), *Dialogue: Theorizing difference in communication studies* (pp. 21–38). Thousand Oaks, CA: Sage.

Stone, B. (2004, June 7). Your next computer. *Newsweek,* pp. 51–54.

Stone, D., Patton, B., & Heen, S. (1999). *Difficult conversations: How to discuss what matters most.* New York: Viking Press.

Strasser, M. (1997). *Legally wed: Same-sex marriage and the constitution.* Ithaca, New York: Cornell University Press.

Strine, M. S. (1992). Understanding "how things work": Sexual harassment and academic culture. *Journal of Applied Communication Research, 20,* 391–400.

Stroup, K. (2001, April 30). Business connections: The wired way we work. *Newsweek,* pp. 59–61.

Subrahmanyam, K., Kraut, R., Greenfield, P., & Gross, E. (2001). New forms of electronic media. In D. Singer & J. Singer (Eds.), *Handbook of children and the media* (pp. 73–99). Thousand Oaks, CA: Sage.

Suler, J. (1999). *The psychology of cyberspace.* Retrieved September 10, 2006, from http://www.rider.edu/~suler/psycyber/

Surfing Web at work is no big deal, judge says. (2006, April 25). *Raleigh News & Observer,* p. 3A.

Surra, C., Arizzi, P., & Rasmussen, L. (1988). The association between reasons for commitment and the development and outcome of marital relationships. *Journal of Social and Personal Relationships, 5,* 47–64.

Swain, S. (1989). Covert intimacy: Closeness in men's friendships. In B. Risman & P. Schwartz (Ed.), *Gender and intimate relationships* (pp. 71–86). Belmont, CA: Wadsworth.

Swiss, T. (2001). *Unspun: Key concepts for understanding the World Wide Web.* New York: New York University Press.

Sypher, B. (1984). Seeing ourselves as others see us. *Communication Research, 11,* 97–115.

Tanaka, J. (1999, July 5). Mad about online ads. *Newsweek,* p. 66.

Tannen, D. (1990). *You just don't understand: Women and men in conversation.* New York: Morrow.

Tanno, D. (1997). Names, narratives, and the evolution of ethnic identity. In A. González, M. Houston, & V. Chen (Eds.), *Our voices: Essays in culture, ethnicity, and communication* (pp. 28–34). Los Angeles: Roxbury.

Tashiro, T., & Frazier, P. (2003). "I'll never be in a relationship like that again": Personal growth following romantic relationship breakup. *Personal Relationships, 10,* 113–128.

Tavris, C. (1992). *The mismeasure of woman.* New York: Simon & Schuster.

Taylor, B., & Conrad, C. (1992). Narratives of sexual harassment: Organizational dimensions. *Journal of Applied Communication Research, 20,* 401–418.

Taylor, M. (1999). *Imaginary companions and the children who create them.* New York: Oxford University Press.

Taylor, S. (2002). *The tending instinct: Women, men, and the biology of relationships.* New York: Times Books.

Tenner, E. (1997). *Why things bite back: Technology and the revenge of unintended consequences.* New York: Knopf.

Thomas, J. (1999). So you hear what I hear? *Women in Business, 51,* 1–14.

Thomas, V. G. (1989). Body-image satisfaction among Black women. *Journal of Social Psychology, 129,* 107–112.

Thompson, F., & Grundgenett, D. (1999). Helping disadvantaged learners build effective learning skills. *Education, 120,* 130–135.

Timmerman, C., & Scott, C. (2006). Virtually working: Communicative and structural predictors of media use and key outcomes in virtual work teams. *Communication Monographs, 73,* 108–136.

Tolhuizen, J. H. (1989). Communication strategies for intensifying dating relationships: Identification, use, and structure. *Journal of Social and Personal Relationships, 6,* 413–434.

Trees, A. (2006). Attachment theory: The reciprocal relationship between family communication and attachment patterns. In D. O. Braithwaite & L. A. Baxter (Eds.), *Engaging theories in family communication: Multiple perspectives* (pp. 165–180). Thousand Oaks, CA: Sage.

Trees, A. R. (2000). Nonverbal communication and the support process: International sensitivity in interactions between mothers and young adult children. *Communication Monographs, 67,* 239–261.

Triandis, H. C. (1990). Cross-cultural studies of individualism and collectivism. In J. J. Berman (Ed.), *Cross-cultural perspectives* (pp. 41–133). Lincoln: University of Nebraska Press.

Triandis, H. C. (1995). *Individualism and collectivism.* Boulder, CO: Westview Press.

Trice, H., & Beyer, J. (1984). Studying organizational cultures through rites and ceremonials. *Academy of Management Review, 9,* 653–669.

Troy, A., & Laurenceau, J. (2006). Interracial and intraracial romantic relationships: The search for differences in satisfaction, conflict, and attachment style. *Journal of Social and Personal Relationships, 23,* 65–80.

Tufte, E. (2003). *The cognitive style of PowerPoint.* Cheshire, CT: Graphics Press.

Tung, B. (1999). *Kerberas: A network authentication system.* Reading, MA: Addison-Wesley.

Turkle, S. (1997). *Life on the screen.* New York: Touchstone.

Turkle, S. (2002). Identity crisis. In E. Bucy (Ed.), *Living in the information age* (pp. 155–161). Belmont, CA: Wadsworth.

Turkle, S. (2004, January 30). How computers change the way we think. *Chronicle of Higher Education,* pp. B26–B28.

Tusing, K., & Dillard, J. (2000). The sounds of dominance: Vocal precursors of perceived dominance during interpersonal influence. *Human Communication Research, 26,* 148–171.

Ueland, B. (1992, November–December). Tell me more: On the fine art of listening. *Utne Reader,* pp. 104–109.

Upton, H. (1995, May 8). Peerless advice from small-business peers. *Wall Street Journal,* p. A14.

Urgo, J. (2000). *The age of distraction.* Jackson: Mississippi University Press.

USA Snapshots. (1999, May 10). *USA Today,* p. 1B.

U.S. Bureau of the Census. (2001). *The census report.* Washington, DC: Author.

U.S. Bureau of the Census. (2003). *The census report.* Washington, DC: Author.

U.S. Bureau of the Census. (2004). *The census report.* Washington, DC: Author.

U.S. Department of Commerce. (2004). *A nation online: Entering the broadband age.* Washington, DC: Author.

U.S. Department of Labor. (1992). *Cultural diversity in the workplace.* Washington, DC: Government Printing Office.

Vachss, A. (1994, August 28). You carry the cure in your own heart. *Parade*, pp. 4–6.

Valkenburg, P. (2004). *Children's responses to the screen.* Mahwah, NJ: Erlbaum.

Value of children's shows is questionable, study finds. (1999, June 28). *Raleigh News & Observer*, p. 5A.

Van Maanen, J., & Barley, S. (1985). Cultural organization: Fragments of a theory. In P. J. Frost et al. (Eds.), *Organizational culture* (pp. 31–54). Thousand Oaks, CA: Sage.

Vannoy, D. (Ed.). (2001). *Gender mosaics.* Los Angeles: Roxbury.

Van Styke, E. (1999). *Listening to conflict: Finding constructive solutions to workplace disputes.* New York: AMA Communications.

Vardi, Y., & Weitz, E. (2004). *Misbehavior in organizations.* Thousand Oaks, CA: Sage.

View. (2001, November–December). *Utne Reader*, p. 24.

Vocate, D. (Ed.). (1994). *Intrapersonal communication: Different voices, different minds.* Mahwah, NJ: Erlbaum.

Waldroop, J., & Butler, T. (1996, November/December). The executive as coach. *Harvard Business Review*, pp. 111–117.

Walker, M. B., & Trimboli, A. (1989). Communicating affect: The role of verbal and nonverbal content. *Journal of Language and Social Psychology, 8,* 229–248.

Walther, J. (1996). Computer-mediated communication: Impersonal, interpersonal, and hyperpersonal interaction. Special issue of *Communication Research, 23,* 3–43.

Walther, J. (1997, November). *Selective self-presentation in computer-mediated communication.* Paper presented at the annual conference of the National Communication Association. Chicago, IL.

Warschauer, M. (2003). *Technology and social inclusion: Rethinking the digital divide.* Cambridge: MIT Press.

Watzlawick, P., Beavin, J., & Jackson, D. D. (1967). *Pragmatics of human communication.* New York: Norton.

Weaver, C. (1972). *Human listening: Processes and behavior.* Indianapolis: Bobbs-Merrill.

Weber, S. N. (1994). The need to be: The sociocultural significance of Black language. In L. Samovar & R. Porter (Eds.), *Intercultural communication: A reader* (7th ed., pp. 221–226). Belmont, CA: Wadsworth.

Weinstock, H., Berman, S., & Cates, W., Jr. (2004). Sexually transmitted diseases among American youth: Incidence and prevalence estimates, 2000. *Perspectives on Sexual and Reproductive Health, 36,* 6–10.

Weinstock, J., & Bond, L. (2000). Conceptions of conflict in close friendships and ways of knowing among young college women: A developmental framework. *Journal of Social and Personal Relationships, 17,* 687–696.

Weisinger, H. (1996). *Anger at work.* New York: William Morrow.

Weiss, K. (1999, January 25). *Los Angeles Times* [Online]. Retrieved from http://www.latimes.com/home/news/asection/t000007602.html

Weiss, S. E. (1987). The changing logic of a former minor power. In H. Binnendijk (Ed.), *National negotiating styles* (pp. 44–74). Washington, DC: Department of State.

Weitz, P., and Weitz, C. (Directors). 2002. *About a boy* [Motion picture]. USA: Universal Studios.

Werner, C., Altman, I., & Oxley, D. (1985). Temporal aspects of homes: A transactional perspective. In I. Altman & C. M. Werner (Eds.), *Home environments: Vol. 8: Human behavior and environment: Advances in theory and research* (pp. 1–32). Thousand Oaks, CA: Sage.

West, C., & Zimmerman, D. H. (1987). Doing gender. *Gender and Society, 1,* 125–151.

West, J. (1995). Understanding how the dynamics of ideology influence violence between intimates. In S. W. Duck & J. T. Wood (Eds.), *Understanding relationship processes, 5: Confronting relationship challenges* (pp. 129–149). Thousand Oaks, CA: Sage.

Whitbeck, L. B., & Hoyt, D. R. (1994). Social prestige and assortive mating: A comparison of students from 1956 and 1988. *Journal of Social and Personal Relationships, 11,* 137–145.

Whitman, T., White, R., O'Mara, K., & Goeke-Morey, M. (1999). Environmental aspects of infant health and illness. In T. Whitman & T. Merluzzi (Eds.), *Life-span perspectives on health and illness* (pp. 105–124). Mahwah, NJ: Erlbaum.

Whorf, B. (1956). *Language, thought, and reality.* New York: MIT Press/Wiley.

Wildemuth, S. (2001). Love on the line: Participants' descriptions of computer-mediated close relationships. *Qualitative Research Reports in Communication, 2,* 89–95.

Williams, K. D. (2001). *Ostracism: The power of silence.* New York: Guilford.

Wilson, C., Gutiérrez, F., & Chao, L. (2003). Racism, sexism, and the media: *The rise of class communication in multicultural America* (3rd ed.). Thousand Oaks, CA: Sage.

Wilson, G., & Goodall, H., Jr. (1991). *Interviewing in context.* New York: McGraw-Hill.

Wilson, J. F., & Arnold, C. C. (1974). *Public speaking as a liberal art* (4th ed.). Boston: Allyn & Bacon.

Winans, J. A. (1938). *Speechmaking.* New York: Appleton-Century-Crofts.

Windsor, J., Curtis, D., & Stephens, R. (1997). National preferences in business and communication education: An update. *Journal of the Association for Communication Administration, 3,* 170–179.

Winters, L., & DeBose, H. (Eds.). (2004). *New faces in a changing America.* Thousand Oaks, CA: Sage.

Wiseman, R. (2003). LaughLab. Retrieved February 13, 2004, from http:// www.laughlab.co.uk/home.html

Wood, J. T. (1982). Communication and relational culture: Bases for the study of human relationships. *Communication Quarterly, 30,* 75–84.

Wood, J. T. (1992a). *Spinning the symbolic web: Human communication as symbolic interaction.* Norwood, NJ: Ablex.

Wood, J. T. (1992b). Telling our stories: Narratives as a basis for theorizing sexual harassment. *Journal of Applied Communication Research, 4,* 349–363.

Wood, J. T. (1993a). Diversity and commonality: Sustaining their tension in communication courses. *Western Journal of Communication, 57,* 367–380.

Wood, J. T. (1993b). Engendered relations: Interaction, caring, power, and responsibility in intimacy. In S. W. Duck (Ed.), *Understanding relationship processes, 3: Social context and relationships* (pp. 26–54). Thousand Oaks, CA: Sage.

Wood, J. T. (1993c). Enlarging conceptual boundaries: A critique of research on interpersonal communication. In S. P. Bowen & N. J. Wyatt (Eds.), *Transforming visions: Feminist critiques in communication studies* (pp. 19–49). Cresskill, NJ: Hampton.

Wood, J. T. (1993d). Gender and moral voice: From woman's nature to standpoint theory. *Women's Studies in Communication, 15,* 1–24.

Wood, J. T. (1994a). Engendered identities: Shaping voice and mind through gender. In D. Vocate (Ed.), *Intrapersonal communication: Different voices, different minds* (pp. 145–167). Mahwah, NJ: Erlbaum.

Wood, J. T. (1994b). Gender and relationship crises: Contrasting reasons, responses, and relational orientations. In J. Ringer (Ed.), *Queer words, queer images: The construction of homosexuality* (pp. 238–264). New York: New York University Press.

Wood, J. T. (1994c). Saying it makes it so: The discursive construction of sexual harassment. In S. Bingham (Ed.), *Conceptualizing sexual harassment as discursive practice* (pp. 17–30). Westport, CT: Praeger.

Wood, J. T. (1994d). *Who cares? Women, care, and culture.* Carbondale: Southern Illinois University Press.

Wood, J. T. (1997). Diversity in dialogue: Communication between friends. In J. Makau and R. Arnett (Eds.), *Ethics of communication in an age of diversity* (pp. 5–26). Urbana: University of Illinois Press.

Wood, J. T. (1998). *But I thought you meant . . . : Misunderstandings in human communication.* Mountain View, CA: Mayfield.

Wood, J. T. (2000). *Relational communication* (2nd ed.). Belmont, CA: Wadsworth.

Wood, J. T. (2001a). *Communication theories in action* (2nd ed.). Belmont, CA: Wadsworth.

Wood, J. T. (2001b). The normalization of violence in heterosexual relationships: Women's narratives of love and violence. *Journal of Social and Personal Relationships, 18,* 239–261.

Wood, J. T. (2001c). He says/she says: Misunderstandings between men and women. In D. Braithwaite & J. T. Wood (Eds.), *Case studies in interpersonal communication: Processes and problems* (pp. 93–100). Belmont, CA: Wadsworth.

Wood, J. T. (2004a). Buddhist influences on scholarship and teaching. *Journal of Communication and Religion,* pp. 32–39.

Wood, J. T. (2004b). Monsters and victims: Male felons' accounts of intimate partner violence. *Journal of Social and Personal Relationships, 21,* 555–576.

Wood, J. T. (2006). Critical feminist theories of interpersonal communication: Voice and visibility in cultural life. In D. O. Braithwaite & L. A. Baxter

(Eds.), *Engaging theories of interpersonal communication: Multiple perspectives* (pp. 197–212). Thousand Oaks, CA: Sage.

Wood, J. T. (2006a). Chopping the carrots: Creating intimacy, moment by moment. In J. T. Wood & S. Duck (Eds.), *Composing Relationships: Communication in everyday life* (pp. 24–35). Belmont, CA: Thomson Wadsworth.

Wood, J. T. (2006b). Critical feminist theories: A provocative perspective on families. In D. O. Braithwaite & L. A. Baxter (Eds.), *Engaging theories in family communication: Multiple perspectives* (pp. 197–242). Thousand Oaks, CA: Sage.

Wood, J. T. (2006c). Gender, power and violence in heterosexual relationships. In K. Dindia & D. Canary (Eds.), *Sex differences and similarities in communication* (2nd ed., pp. 397–411). Mahwah, NJ: Erlbaum.

Wood, J. T. (2007). *Gendered lives: Communication, gender and culture* (7th ed.). Belmont, CA: Wadsworth.

Wood, J. T., Dendy, L., Dordek, E., Germany, M., & Varallo, S. (1994). Dialectic of difference: A thematic analysis of intimates' meanings for differences. In K. Carter & M. Presnell (Eds.), *Interpretive approaches to interpersonal communication* (pp. 115–136). New York: State University of New York Press.

Wood, J. T., & Duck, S. W. (1995a). Off the beaten track: New shores for relationship research. In J. T. Wood, & S. W. Duck (Eds.), *Understanding relationship processes, 6: Understudied relationships: Off the beaten track* (pp. 1–21). Thousand Oaks, CA: Sage.

Wood, J. T., & Duck, S. W. (Eds.). (1995b). *Understanding relationship processes, 6: Understudied relationships: Off the beaten track*. Thousand Oaks, CA: Sage.

Wood, J. T., & Duck, S. W. (Eds.) (2006a). *Composing relationships: Communication in everyday life.* Belmont, CA: Thomson Wadsworth.

Wood, J. T., & Duck, S. W. (2006b). Composing relationships: Communication in everyday life. In J. T. Wood & S. W. Duck (Eds.), *Composing relationships: Communication in everyday life* (pp. 1–13). Belmont, CA: Thomson Wadsworth.

Wood, J. T., & Inman, C. C. (1993). In a different mode: Masculine styles of communicating closeness. *Journal of Applied Communication Research, 21,* 279–295.

Woolfolk, A. E. (1987). *Educational psychology.* Englewood Cliffs, NJ: Prentice Hall.

Wurman, R. (1989). *Information anxiety.* Garden City, NY: Doubleday.

Wydra, N. (1998). *Look before you love: Feng shui techniques for revealing anyone's true nature.* Lincolnwood, IL: Contemporary Books.

Yakin, B. (Director). 2000. *Remember the titans* [Motion picture]. USA: Buena Vista Pictures.

Yankelovich, D. (2005, November 25). Ferment and change: Higher education in 2015. *Chronicle of Higher Education,* pp. B6–B9.

Yerby, J., Buerkel-Rothfuss, N., & Bochner, A. (1990). *Understanding family communication.* Scottsdale, AZ: Gorsuch Scarisbrick.

Yost, B. (2004). We all need someone to lean on. Online edition of *IndyStar.* Retrieved May 21, 2004, from http:// www.indystar.com/articles/2/148176-9362-052.html

Young, J. (2005, April 22). Knowing when to log off. *Chronicle of Higher Education,* pp. A34–A35.

Young, J. (2006, June 2). The fight for classroom attention: Professor vs. laptop. *Chronicle of Higher Education,* pp. A27–A29.

Young, S., Wood, J. T., Phillips, G. M., & Pedersen, D. (2001). *Group discussion: A practical guide to participation and leadership* (3rd ed.). Prospect Heights, IL: Waveland.

Zinn, M., & Dill, B. (1996). Theorizing difference from multicultural feminism. *Feminist Studies, 22,* 321–331.

Zormeier, S., & Samovar, L. (2000). Language as a mirror of reality: Mexican proverbs. In L. Samovar & R. Porter (Eds.), *Intercultural communication: A reader* (9th ed., pp. 225–230). Belmont, CA: Wadsworth.

Zorn, T. (1991). Construct system development, transformational leadership, and leadership messages. *Southern Communication Journal, 56,* 178–193.

Zorn, T. (1995). Bosses and buddies: Constructing and performing simultaneously hierarchical and close friendship relationships. In J. T. Wood & S. W. Duck (Eds.), *Understanding relationship processes, 6: Understudied relationships: Off the beaten track* (pp. 122–147). Thousand Oaks, CA: Sage.

Zuckerman, L. (2002). Questions abound as media influence grows for a handful. In E. Bucy (Ed.), *Living in the information age* (pp. 139–142). Belmont, CA: Wadsworth.

Credits

Chapter 1
3: © Julia T. Wood 6: Hulton Archive/ Getty Images 8: © Fisher/Thatcher/Stone/ Getty Images 17: © Tom & Dee Ann McCarthy/Corbis 21: Jason Harris/ © Wadsworth

Chapter 2
27: © Keith Dannemiller/Corbis 38: © Michael Keller/Corbis 42: Jason Harris/© Wadsworth

Chapter 3
47: © Amy Etra/PhotoEdit 50: © Michael Keller/Corbis 56: © Jeff Greenberg/ PhotoEdit 62: © Rob Lewine/Corbis 65: Jason Harris/© Wadsworth

Chapter 4
69: © Photodisc Green/Getty Images 81: © Julia T. Wood 82: © Carolyn C. Wood 90: Jason Harris/© Wadsworth

Chapter 5
97: © Goodshoot/Jupiter Images 99: AP/ Wide World Photos 105: left, © Charles Jean Marc/Corbis; right, © Warren Morgan/Corbis 113: Jason Harris/ © Wadsworth

Chapter 6
122: © image 100/Alamy 130: © Tom Bean/Corbis 136: Jason Harris/ © Wadsworth

Chapter 7
141: © Image Source Limited/Index Stock Imagery 145: © Jon Feingersh/Corbis 148: © Steve Chenn/Corbis 159: Jason Harris/ © Wadsworth

Chapter 8
163: © Ron Chapple/Taxi/Getty Images 164: © Liu Liqun/Corbis 171: © Bill Aron/PhotoEdit 182: Jason Harris/ © Wadsworth

Chapter 9
187: © Leigh M. Wilco 188: © Steve Chenn/Corbis 192: © Dennis MacDonald/ PhotoEdit 203: © Jeffry W. Myers/Corbis 207: Jason Harris/© Wadsworth

Chapter 10
210: © Royalty-Free/Corbis 219: © Steve Prezant/Corbis 222: © Stockbyte/Getty Images 233: Jason Harris/© Wadsworth

Chapter 11
236: © AFP/Getty Images 248: © Mark Richards/PhotoEdit 256: Jason Harris/ © Wadsworth

Chapter 12
262: left, © Dennis Degnan/Corbis; right, © Photodisc Red/Getty Images 264: © Real Life/The Image Bank/Getty Images 265: © Flying Colours Ltd/Digital Vision/Getty Images 277: Jason Harris/ © Wadsworth

Chapter 13
282: © Lawrence Migdale/Photo Researchers, Inc. 284: © AP Wide World Photos 292: © Chuck Savage/Corbis 300: Jason Harris/© Wadsworth

Chapter 14
305: © Najlah Feanny/Corbis 308: © Rick Gomez/Masterfile 311: © Anthony Redpath/Corbis 316: © Ron Fehling/Masterfile 326: Jason Harris/© Wadsworth

Chapter 15
331: © Jeff Greenberg/PhotoEdit 336: © Photodisc/Getty Images 350: Jason Harris/© Wadsworth

Epilogue
353: © Digital Vision/Getty Images

Index